Second Edit

Philosophical, Ideological, and Theoretical Perspectives on Education

Gerald L. Gutek

Loyola University Chicago

PEARSON

Boston Columbus Indianapolis New York San Francisco Upper Saddle River
Amsterdam Cape Town Dubai London Madrid Milan Munich Paris Montréal Toronto
Delhi Mexico City São Paulo Sydney Hong Kong Seoul Singapore Taipei Tokyo

Vice President and Editorial Director: Jeffery W. Johnston
Executive Editor: Ann Castel Davis
Editorial Assistant: Krista Slavicek
Vice President, Director of Marketing: Margaret Waples
Marketing Manager: Darcy Betts
Senior Managing Editor: Pamela D. Bennett
Project Manager: Sheryl Glicker Langner
Production Manager: Laura Messerly
Senior Art Director: Jayne Conte
Cover Designer: Suzanne Behnke
Cover Image: Fotolia/© jannoon028
Media Producer: Autumn Benson
Media Project Manager: Noelle Chun
Full-Service Project Management: Shylaja Gattupalli, Jouve India
Composition: Jouve India Private Limited
Printer/Binder: LSC Communications
Cover Printer: LSC Communications
Text Font: ITC Garamond Std

Credits and acknowledgments for materials borrowed from other sources and reproduced, with permission, in this text appear on the appropriate pages within the text.

Photo Credits: © Gabriela, p. 2; Library of Congress, pp. 18, 74, 216, 272; © Argus/Fotolia, p. 46; Pantheon / SuperStock, p. 104; © INTERFOTO / Alamy, p. 138; Globo/Getty Images, p. 166; © H. Mark Weidman Photography / Alamy, p. 194; H. Robinson/ Shutterstock, p. 250; © AF archive / Alamy, p. 298; Wisconsin Historical Society, p. 310; Getty Images, p. 340; SIU Morris Library, p. 362; © Tomas Abad / Alamy, p. 388; © jannoon028/Fotolia, p. 420.

Library of Congress Cataloging-in-Publication Data

Gutek, Gerald Lee.
Philosophical, ideological and theoretical perspectives on education / Gerald L. Gutek, Loyola University, Chicago. — Second edition.
pages cm
ISBN-13: 978-0-13-285238-8
ISBN-10: 0-13-285238-1
1. Education—Philosophy. 2. Philosophy. I. Title.
LB1025.2.G92 2014
370.1—dc23

2013014672

ISBN 10: 0-13-285238-1
ISBN 13: 978-0-13-285238-8

21 2020

To the memory of my father
and mother, Albert and Irene Gutek,
and my brother, Terry Gutek

PREFACE

Philosophical, Ideological, and Theoretical Perspectives on Education, Second Edition, is a new edition of my earlier books, *Philosophical and Ideological Perspectives on Education* and *New Perspectives on Philosophy and Education.* The second edition, like the earlier one, is organized on a connected scaffolding of three major parts: One on Philosophies, Two on Ideologies, and Three on Theories. Each part leads the reader forward to the next section. It examines the following philosophies: Idealism, Realism, Pragmatism, Existentialism, and Postmodernism. It then examines the following ideologies: Nationalism, Liberalism, Conservatism, and Marxism. It examines the following theories: Essentialism, Perennialism, Progressivism, and Critical Theory. The chapters are written so that each one can stand alone or be used in a different order if the instructor so wishes.

The book provides the following pedagogical features: Questions for Reflection and Discussion, Inquiry and Research Projects, Internet Resources, and Suggestions for Further Reading. A new feature in the second edition is the extensive marginal notes that identify and clarify key concepts and terms so that students can construct a vocabulary for discussing philosophy of education. Each chapter features the theme of **Constructing Your Own Philosophy of Education** that is related to the sub-themes of "reflection" and "conceptual frameworks" that are often emphasized in institutional mission statements and accreditation standards.

NEW TO THIS EDITION

- In Chapter 1, *Philosophy and Education*, added comments on "reflection" and "conceptual frameworks."
- In Chapter 2, *Idealism and Education*, added commentaries on Plato's *Allegory of the Cave* and *Meno*.
- In Chapter 3, *Realism and Education*, added sections on Alasdair MacIntyre and contemporary Aristotelian interpretations.
- In Chapter 4, *Pragmatism and Education*, added new sections on Dewey's early work at the University of Chicago and on contemporary Pragmatism.
- In Chapter 5, *Existentialism and Education*, added a section on Maxine Greene's philosophy.
- In Chapter 6, *Postmodernism and Education*, added a discussion of the Enlightenment Project.
- The reinstatement of *Perennialism and Education* as Chapter 14 (this had been deleted from the previous edition).
- Sections on "My Reflections of Philosophy of Education" in each chapter.

MY REFLECTIONS ON PREPARING THE SECOND EDITION

I find that revising a book for a new edition is often more difficult than writing a new book. There is always the overriding issue that all authors face—what should be included and what should be excluded? There is the need to add more but to do it in fewer pages. In revising, I was aided by the helpful suggestions of users, non-users, reviewers, and editors. I relied on reading about trends in philosophy of education, on the advice of reviewers, and on what I think is important for teachers to know to construct their own philosophies of education. However, I took the author's prerogative to include topics of my own special research and interests, especially on ideology and education. I consider ideology to be an important influence in shaping educational policies and practices. The debates between conservatives and liberals in the United States over policy, both at home and abroad, cannot be understood without an examination of their ideological origins and development.

I have also added historical perspectives based on my interest in the history of education. Throughout the book, I encourage teachers to reflect on their experiences and to use their reflections in constructing their own philosophy of education. I took my own advice and am occasionally autobiographical in my own reflections on philosophy of education.

The second edition is based on my continuing interest in the cultural foundations of education, especially the interrelationships between philosophies, ideologies, and theories of education. The scaffolding of philosophies, ideologies, and theories is developed as I taught and wrote about philosophy of education.

As a teacher who began his career as an instructor in the history of Western Civilization in the Division of General Studies at the University of Illinois, I think we cannot begin to understand philosophy without returning to its origins with Plato and Aristotle. Therefore, I include Idealism and Realism. Pragmatism, especially Dewey's Experimentalism, has had such a pervasive influence on American education that it has to be included in any book on the subject. As I reread books on Existentialism, I felt once again its dramatic appeal and believe that it will touch a responsive chord with today's students. Because we live in what is called the "postmodern" era, Postmodernism, with its pervasive influence on contemporary humanities and social science, needed to be included.

I have noted a revival of interest in and research on Essentialism, especially in the books by Diane Ravitch and J. Wesley Null. My own doctoral dissertation at the University of Illinois examined the educational ideas of George S. Counts, who originated Social Reconstructionism when he asked, "Dare the school build a new social order?" The research and writing of Karen Riley and her colleagues convinced me that Social Reconstructionism is still highly relevant for teachers and educational policy-makers. As I attend conferences and read recent books in the field, I note pervasive interest in Critical Theory, and so a chapter on it is indispensable.

I understand that there are many ways to organize and to teach courses in the Foundations of Education, especially Philosophy of Education. During my career, I experimented with teaching one particular philosophy, such as Realism or Experimentalism, in depth. I also used several selected books, advocating particular philosophies, as primary source readings. Over time, I became convinced that teachers need what I call a cognitive map, a guide to the field, that is useful in placing educational ideas, innovations, and trends in perspective and in relating them to the broader philosophical and ideological contexts from which they come and of which they are a part. I have used this approach in the second as well as in its earlier edition. What makes this book unusual is the relationship that I make among philosophies, ideologies, and theories of education.

The book's organization is based on my teaching of Philosophy of Education at Loyola University Chicago and at other institutions. I also have used this method in teaching Philosophy of Education in the international courses offered by Framingham University. Each chapter moves from a general overview of the philosophy, ideology, or theory; a discussion of its leading founders or proponents; identification and discussion of its major principles about truth, knowing, and values; and its implications for education, schooling, curriculum, and instruction. Professors who use the book, of course, have their own designs and approaches to instruction. They might want to use the book as a structural framework that relates philosophies, ideologies, and theories of education. Because each chapter can stand on its own, professors might wish to use them selectively and develop their own sequence of presentation.

As I wrote the book, I had some autobiographical moments and some recollections from my past rose to the surface of my consciousness. I had particularly strong remembrances of my high school teachers. I learned much about writing from some talented teachers of English—Gwendolyn Harris, Faye Homrighous, and Grace Magierski—at Streator High School back in the early 1950s. These teachers worked persistently at getting us to express ourselves as clearly and directly as possible in our writing. We had numerous exercises in précis writing—taking large and often ambiguous statements and rewriting them so that they were succinct and clear. I later found out that Thomas Jefferson used the same method in his writing. These teachers were all proponents of gathering evidence and interpreting it in required term papers. So for me, writing a book is an extension of research and writing those required term papers.

When I was working on my master's degree in American history at the University of Illinois, my thesis director was J. Leonard Bates, a distinguished historian of the Progressive period. I wrote a thesis on the Illinois delegation at the Democratic National Convention in 1924—it was the longest convention in American political history. Professor Bates was a busy scholar but a patient one. He read several drafts of my thesis, carefully editing and correcting it with his red or blue pencils. Like my high school teachers, he wanted the narrative to be clear, succinct, and direct.

I am very grateful to the Foundations of Education professors in the College of Education at the University of Illinois who introduced me to the history and philosophy of education: Harry S. Broudy, William O. Stanley, Joe R. Burnett, and Archibald Anderson. My book, in many ways, draws on and continues what they taught me. I especially remember how Professor Anderson encouraged me to write my doctoral dissertation on George S. Counts.

As I did this revision, I missed the advice and comments of Professor Steven I. Miller, my friend and colleague at Loyola University, who died several years ago. I used to call or email Steve asking questions such as: What is a good source for Scientific Realism? Why are so many professors in the field attracted to Neo-Marxism? What is the continuing relevance of the Essentialists? Sighing to himself, but loud enough so I could hear him, Steve would answer my questions. Steve could be a critic who did not appreciate the trend in textbooks to put big ideas into small boxes. He would often gibe me with, "What are you trying to do? Put Plato in a box?"

I would like to thank the following professors who reviewed my plans for a second edition and made insightful and very useful suggestions: Patricia Walsh Coates, Kutztown University of Pennsylvania; Ruthanne Kurth-Schai, Macalester College; and Wayne Willis, Morehead State University.

I want to thank my editor at Pearson, Ann Davis, for supporting the idea of a second edition. I also appreciate the help that her assistant, Krista Slavicek, patiently provided to an often technologically challenged author.

Finally, I come to my family, especially my wife, Patricia, who is always steadying and encouraging of my work. My grandchildren—Claire, Abigail, Luke, Drew, Mills, and Anna Hope—keep giving me new insights into the mysteries of childhood and learning. I am especially awed by the question my grandson Luke asked about dinosaurs when he was four years old. Luke asked, "What happened to the dinosaurs?" His mother told him that they were gone—they were extinct. He, of course, then had another question, "What comes after people?" I end with this child's question—hoping that as a people we will find a way to sustain our lives and pass on a green and peaceful planet to future generations.

—Gerald Gutek

BRIEF CONTENTS

CONTENTS

Philosophy and Education

The National Academy of Athens in Athens, Greece. Seated on either side of the entrance are the statues of Plato and Socrates. Plato, along with his mentor, Socrates, and his student, Aristotle, helped to lay the foundations of Western philosophy.

1

CHAPTER PREVIEW

Chapter 1 introduces philosophy of education in terms of its relationships with both philosophy and education. We begin our discussion with a preliminary and tentative definition of philosophy as the most general way of reflecting on the meaning of our lives in the world and reflecting deeply on what is true or false, good or evil, right or wrong, and beautiful or ugly.[1]

Throughout the book, we will return to our initial definition, restating, expanding, and revising it. You will notice that in the first paragraph we invite the reader to reflect on the meaning of life, education, and schooling. Philosophical reflection causes us to think deeply and profoundly about meaning in the world, in our country, and in our schools. Another way of reflecting is to ask yourself, "What difference does it make that I am here and am a teacher? What difference does it make to my students and to me?"

So far we have used the term *reflection* several times. It is useful to think about how we go about reflecting on education. John Dewey, in *How We Think,* defined *reflective thinking* as the "active, persistent, and careful" examination of our beliefs in terms of the evidence that supports them and the conclusions to which they lead. Reflection, according to this definition, is not daydreaming, listening to a teacher or professor lecture, or passive contemplation. It means thinking about the consequences our ideas of education will have on our students, our colleagues, society, and ourselves when we act on them. When we think reflectively, Dewey said that our thoughts are "persistent," which means that they stay with us. They grow out of, relate to, and are connected in a chain, or continuum, to the events in our lives. Reflecting about our ideas on education takes us back to their origins and how we have continued to develop these original thoughts. The term *careful* means that we hold back from jumping to a premature conclusion and take the time to examine the evidence needed to support it. Although we will reach a conclusion, we defer a judgment for a time so that we can think about its likely consequences on students and on ourselves.[2]

Although reflection begins with us as individuals, it also has professional implications for us as teachers. Professional teacher organizations such as the National Council on the Accreditation of Teacher Education (NCATE) encourage teachers to reflect on their work. When we begin to put into practice the ideas that we have constructed during reflection, we can develop what the NCATE standards call a "**conceptual framework**," a philosophy of education that gives meaning to teaching by integrating its daily demands with long-term professional commitment and direction.[3]

A conceptual framework, essentially a philosophy of education, can provide teachers with a sense of personal integration and professional coherence that places ongoing elements and episodes in teaching and learning in relation to and in perspective with each other. It provides a strategy for

Conceptual Framework: The key principles and ideas that make an activity intelligible and transferable, as is the case with professional education.

integrating short-term objectives with long-term goals. To become reflective educators, teachers need to think philosophically about education's broad social, cultural, and ethical implications.

The chapters in this book that examine philosophies, ideologies, and theories of education are designed to provide a conceptual map to help you focus your reflections on education.

You can move from the conceptual framework to constructing your own philosophy of education. There are many ways to construct your philosophy of education. You can keep a log of classroom events and relate these events to the philosophies in this book. Or you can begin by writing an essay to yourself about what you believe is true and valuable and how your educational experiences up to this time have shaped these beliefs. As you then proceed through the book, you can add to, delete from, reaffirm, or revise your beginning ideas about philosophy of education. To begin reflecting on your own philosophy of education, you might ask yourself the following questions: What do I believe is real, and why do I believe this? What do I believe is true, and why do I believe this? What do I value, and why do I value it? Is there some system of logic that guides me? How does my conception of reality, truth, knowledge, values, and logic affect my ideas about education and my teaching?

You can determine whether the philosophies, ideologies, and theories discussed here are reflected in your own experience. You can see whether your encounters with them cause you to revise or rethink your beliefs about what is true, good, and valuable. When you have finished, you should have a statement of your own philosophy of education, a conceptual framework for your teaching.

You and your classmates in this course might wish to share your reflections on philosophy of education and compare and contrast them as you discuss the chapters in the book. These discussions can help you and your colleagues to examine and analyze your ideas about philosophy of education. Discuss the agreements and disagreements that emerge. Reflect on strategies that might be used to bring your school and teaching into more coherence with your philosophical beliefs.

To begin the process of constructing a personal philosophy of education, we need to expand our initial definition and discussion of philosophy. To do this, we examine philosophy's major subdivisions: metaphysics, epistemology, axiology (ethics and aesthetics), and logic. We then relate these philosophical areas to education. The chapter next considers education as both a formal process in the school and an informal process that takes place through agencies in society such as the home, church, and media. Schooling is discussed in terms of curriculum, methods of instruction, and teacher–student relationships. These areas of formal education are then related to the subdivisions of philosophy. The chapter examines the following major topics:

- Areas of philosophy
- Education in terms of curriculum, methodology of instruction, and teachers and learners
- Philosophies of education

AREAS OF PHILOSOPHY

During early teaching experiences, there is often little time to reflect on the deeper philosophical meaning of what it means to be a teacher. Often, teaching is a hurried series of episodes in which the teacher reacts to the immediate demands of students, parents, administrators, colleagues, and community and school organizations. In the first years of a teaching career, the teacher must meet the day-to-day demands of planning lessons, conducting classes, and attending conferences both in and out of school. Little time is available to reflect on education. For a teacher to become a genuine professional, however, exclusive attention to daily routine and detail is insufficient. Every teacher knows that education is a powerful instrument for shaping individual lives and society. When teachers begin to reflect on this role, they are moving from a preoccupation with the immediately practical to an examination of the theory that underlies and sustains practice. Teaching requires the careful blending of theory and practice. Theory without practice is insufficient; practice unguided by theory is aimless.

Blending theory and practice, teaching has both a reflective and an active dimension. It has effects that transcend the classroom's immediate instructional episodes. The way in which teachers relate to their students depends on their conception of human nature. Instruction is about something; it is about a skill or about knowledge. One's view of reality shapes one's beliefs about knowledge. When the teacher begins to reflect on the conception of reality, of human nature, and of society, he or she is philosophizing about education. In its most general terms, philosophy is the human being's attempt to think speculatively, reflectively, and systematically about the universe and the human relationship to that universe.

Metaphysics

Metaphysics: the subdivision of philosophy that examines the nature of ultimate reality.

Metaphysics, the study of the nature of ultimate reality, involves speculation about the nature of existence. It asks the question: After all the nonessentials of life have been stripped away, what is genuinely real? Our beliefs about the nature of reality determine how we perceive our relationships to both the universe and society. These beliefs raise our most important questions—what is and what is not real—and also begin to provide the answers to these questions. Is there a spiritual realm of existence or is reality material? What is the origin of the universe? Is it inherently purposeful by its own design or do we create our own purposes?

In their speculations into the nature of reality, metaphysicians have drawn varying conclusions. Whereas an Idealist defines reality in spiritual or nonmaterial terms, a Realist sees reality as an order of objects that exist independently of human beings. Conversely, a Pragmatist, rejecting metaphysics, holds that the human conception of reality is based on experience.

For their views on reality, see the chapters on Idealism, Realism, and Pragmatism.

Metaphysics relates to educational theory and practice in many ways. The subjects, experiences, and skills in the curriculum reflect the conception of reality held by the society that supports the school. Much formal schooling represents the attempt of curriculum makers, teachers, and textbook authors to describe certain aspects of reality to students. For example, subjects such as history, geography, chemistry, and so on describe certain dimensions of reality to students.

Epistemology

Epistemology: the subdivision of philosophy that examines knowledge and knowing.

Epistemology, the theory of knowing and knowledge, is of crucial importance to educators. Defining the foundations of knowledge, epistemology considers such important questions as: (1) How do we know what we know? (2) On what process of knowing do we base our knowledge of the world and society? (3) What is the authority on which we base our claims to truth? (4) Do our knowledge claims derive from divine revelation, empirical evidence, or personal and subjective experience?

Historically, much authority has rested on a belief in God or the supernatural and revelations of divine truths to inspired men and women. Civilization's great religions—Judaism, Christianity, Islam, Hinduism, and Buddhism, for example—rest on knowledge claims arising from a holy book or scriptures, such as the Bible or the Koran. Implied is the believer's faith in a transcendent, universal, spiritual authority, which, while prior to and independent of human experience, is life's true guide. These divinely revealed truths are universally valid in every time and place. While not necessarily religious, philosophies such as Idealism and Realism also claim to represent universal knowledge. Other philosophies, such as Pragmatism, base knowledge claims on human experience, especially publicly verifiable empirical evidence. Existentialism, which is highly subjective, roots knowledge in a person's intuitive perception of his or her own needs and psychological disposition.

Dealing with the most general and basic conceptions of knowing, epistemology is closely related to methods of teaching and of learning. For example, an Idealist may hold that knowing, or the cognitive process, is really the recall of ideas that are present latently in the mind. The appropriate educational method for Idealists would be the Socratic dialogue, in which the teacher attempts to bring latent ideas to the student's consciousness by asking leading questions. Realists hold that knowledge originates in the sensations we have of objects in our environment. We arrive at concepts from these sensations. Through the abstraction of sensory data, we build concepts that correspond to these objects in reality. A teacher who wishes to structure instruction based on the Realist sensation–abstraction formula might use classroom demonstrations to explain natural phenomena to students. A Pragmatist, in contrast, holds that we construct our knowledge by interacting with our environment in problem-solving episodes. Thus, problem solving is the appropriate method of instruction for those who accept the Pragmatist's view of knowledge. Existentialists contend that we create our own knowledge by choosing what we wish to believe and appropriating it as our own. Postmodernists challenge universal claims to knowledge as the historical constructions of powerful groups at particular times in history.

For their views on knowledge and knowing, see the chapters on Idealism, Realism, Pragmatism, Existentialism, and Postmodernism.

Axiology

Axiology: the subdivision of philosophy that examines ethical and aesthetic values.

Ethics: the subdivision of axiology that examines morally just behavior.

Aesthetics: the subdivision of axiology that examines questions of beauty.

Axiology is concerned with value theory and attempts to prescribe what is good and right conduct. The subdivisions of axiology are **ethics** and **aesthetics**. Ethics examines moral values and conduct. Aesthetics deals with values in art. Whereas metaphysics attempts to describe the nature of ultimate reality, axiology refers to prescriptions of moral behavior and beauty. Educators have always been concerned with both the formation of values in the young and the encouragement of certain kinds of preferred behaviors.

In a general way, each person is influenced by those who seek to shape his or her behavior along certain lines. Children are continually told that they should or should not do certain things. Statements such as "you should be kind to others," "you should wash your hands before eating," "you should not break the school's windows," or "you should love your country" are all obvious value statements. In the process of growing to maturity, an individual encounters countless attempts to mold behavior along preferred modes of action. In a very direct way, parents, teachers, and society reward or punish behavior as it conforms to or deviates from their conceptions of appropriateness, correctness, goodness, or beauty.

Cultural Ethos: the significant beliefs and values held in a culture that give identity and meaning to its members.

Cultural ethos refers to the value core that provides a sense of identity, purpose, and community to a society. In the contemporary United States, strong cultural divisions exist in defining the nation's ethos and character. James Hunter, a noted author on American values, has found these divisions to be so deep that they constitute a veritable "culture war."[4] Among the divisive value issues that impact contemporary U.S. society are the following: Is the national character religious or secular? Should there be prayer in the schools? What is the role of women in society? What is the nature of the family? These fundamental issues are intertwined with issues of national identity. Is there and should there be a national character? Or should the United States be a place of many diverse identities, cultures, and lifestyles? Further, how does this clash of values impact schooling? What is the role of schools in transmitting and cultivating values?

The classical conflict in values is that of objective versus subjective value theory. Advocates of objective value theory assert that what is good is rooted in the universe itself and is applicable everywhere for all time. In contrast, subjectivists assert that values are group or personal preferences—likes or dislikes—that depend on particular circumstances, times, and places. For them, values are not universally valid but are relative to particular situations.

The aesthetic dimension of life frequently has been neglected in U.S. education. In its broadest sense, aesthetic theory refers to the cultivation of taste and appreciation for what is beautiful. Although aesthetic theory is concerned with the human attempt to objectify insights and feelings in various art forms, it is equally concerned with the cultivation of persons whose lives are harmonious, balanced, and beautiful. Aesthetic values have an obvious place in art, literature, drama, music, and dancing classes; they are also relevant to the cultivation of the public taste and style of life.

Logic

Logic is the subdivision of philosophy that deals with correct thinking. It is concerned with how we organize and sequence our thinking and frame our arguments according to a coherent pattern, that is, how we organize our supporting evidence to make a case for or to explain something. The two major patterns of logic are deduction and induction.

Deductive Logic: reasoning that proceeds from the general principle to the specific case, example, or illustration.

In **deductive logic**, or deduction, reasoning moves from general statements or principles to specific cases or examples. We are all familiar with the classic statement of deduction: (1) All men are mortal; (2) Socrates is a mortal; (3) therefore, Socrates is a man. We can also think of how Thomas Jefferson framed his arguments in the Declaration of Independence: (1) All men are endowed with inalienable rights of life, liberty, and the pursuit of happiness; (2) the American colonists had these inalienable rights; (3) because George III was violating these rights, the colonists had the right to rebel against British rule. In the above examples of deductive logic, if the premises are true, then, if we reason correctly, the conclusions will also be true.

Inductive Logic: reasoning that proceeds from the particular instance, case, or example to a generalization.

Inductive logic, or induction, moves from specific instances, cases, or situations to a larger generalization that includes and encompasses them. For example, a particular suburban high school spends more funds on each student than a particular urban high school in a particular county in a state. Further research shows that same expenditure pattern is found at other suburban and urban high schools throughout that state. The general conclusion is that this trend occurs in high schools throughout the state.

Instructional materials—manuals, books, handouts, videos, computer programs—are organized according to some kind of logic. Some state general principles and then illustrate these principles with specific examples. Others introduce a number of specific examples and then lead the student to make a generalization.

The traditional curriculum, in its general organization, follows a pattern of logic that tends to be deductive in that it is sequential and cumulative. Experiences and courses are organized so that they follow each other in a sequence—often moving from the simple and easy to the more complicated and difficult. They are cumulative in that each skill or subject learned is a foundation for the next higher order skill or subject. Progressive or constructivist curricular strategies, in contrast, are inductive. By examining objects or issues in their environment, the students are expected to generalize from their experience.

Subdivisions of Philosophies of Education and Questions They Raise

Metaphysics	Epistemology	Axiology (Ethical Values)	Axiology (Aesthetic Values)	Logic
Examines what ultimately is real.	Examines what is knowledge and how do we know.	Examines what is right and wrong; good and evil.	Examines what is beautiful or ugly.	Examines rules of correct thinking.
Is reality mental or spiritual?	Is truth intuitive, subjective, and personal?	Are ethics, the standards of behavior, objective and universal, reflecting the nature of the universe?	Is beauty a reflection of the universal, absolute, and unchanging?	Is logic deductive, from the general principle to the specific example?
Is reality objective, existing outside of our minds?	Is truth revealed from God in a sacred or holy book?	Are ethics subjective, personal likes and dislikes?	Is beauty subjective, in the eye of the beholder?	Is logic inductive, from the specific example to the general principle or finding?
Is reality based on our experiences?	Is truth revealed from reasoning?	Are ethics culturally relative, depending on cultural norms at a given time?	Is beauty determined by cultural preferences?	
Do we construct or make our own reality?	Is truth empirical, constructed by using our senses and the scientific method?			

EDUCATION

Education: the learned social processes that contribute to participation in a society and a culture.

The word **education** refers very broadly to the total social processes that bring a person into cultural life. The human species reproduces biologically, as do all other living organisms. Biological reproduction, however, is not cultural reproduction. By living and participating in a culture, the immature human being gradually becomes a recipient of and a participant in a culture.

Many people and social agencies are involved in the process of enculturation of the young. The family, the peer group, the community, the media, the church, and the state all have formative effects on the individual. By living with other people, the immature child learns how to relate to them. He or she takes on their language, their manners, and their behavior. Educational theorists and philosophers have long recognized the educative role of interactions of human beings and society, and they have tried to indicate the kind of social order that is based on and fulfills human potentiality.

School: a formal educational agency, established and supported by a society, to educate children; it is staffed by teachers, experts in curriculum and instruction, who deliberately instruct students.

Education, in a more formal and deliberate sense, takes place in the **school**, a specialized social agency established to cultivate preferred skills, knowledge, and values in the learner. The school is staffed by teachers who are regarded as experts in the learning processes. Informal or milieu education is related to formal education, or schooling. If the school is to succeed in its program of instruction, its curriculum and methods must be viable in relation to society.

Curriculum

Curriculum: the deliberately selected experiences presented to learners in a school; or a program of skills and subjects.

As the vital center of the school's educational efforts, the **curriculum** is the locus of the sharpest controversies. Decision making in curricular matters involves considering, examining, and formulating the goals of formal education. Those concerned with curriculum planning and organization ask such questions as: What knowledge is of most worth? What knowledge should be introduced to the learner? What are the criteria for selecting knowledge? What is valuable for the learner as a person and as a member of society? The answers to these questions not only determine what is included or excluded from the school's curriculum but also rest on assumptions about the nature of the universe, of human beings, of society, and of the good life. In the philosophies examined in this book, we will find a variety of basic and general assumptions that provide alternatives to making the curriculum.

Curriculum has been defined in various ways. Throughout most of the history of education, the curriculum consisted of the basic skills of reading, writing, and mathematical computation at the primary or elementary level and the arts and sciences at the secondary and higher levels. For many educators, the curriculum remains essentially a program of studies, skills, and subjects offered to a learner in a formal sequence. Since the appearance of the activity, experience, process, or constructivist approach, some educators have moved to a more generalized conception of curriculum. For them, the curriculum includes all of the learner's experiences for which the school assumes responsibility.

In the broadest sense, the curriculum can be defined as the organized experiences that a student is provided under the guidance and control of the school. In a more precise but restricted sense, the curriculum is the systematic sequence of courses or subjects that forms the school's formal instructional program. These two major definitions of curriculum, as well as the variations that lie between them, are based on particular conceptions of knowledge and value. The philosophies of education examined in this book hold conceptions of the curriculum that range from the broad view that includes all of the learner's experiences to the more specific view that sees it as academic subject matter.

There can be no question that curriculum designers, regardless of their philosophical convictions, attempt to identify what is of the greatest worth to the learner. The problem lies in identifying and agreeing on the greatest truth, beauty, and goodness. This question has metaphysical, epistemological, axiological, and logical dimensions. Philosophers and educational theorists, however, have responded to this question with different answers, and their disagreements have resulted in a variety of curricula.

For their perspectives on curriculum, see the chapters on Idealism, Realism, Essentialism, and Perennialism.

For the Idealist, Realist, and Thomist philosophers, as well as for the Essentialist and Perennialist theorists, the curriculum consists of skills and subjects organized in a systematic and sequential fashion. They regard basic skills as necessary tools that have generative power for the later study of the more sophisticated subjects based on such learned disciplines as mathematics, science, and history. For these more traditional philosophies, the preferred curricular design focuses on subject matter. Their major goal is the transmission and preservation of the cultural heritage. Scientists and scholars, through their research, have developed the learned disciplines that explain the various dimensions of reality. The curriculum, then, is the means of transmitting this heritage in learnable units to the immature so that they can participate in the culture. Civilization's survival is believed to depend on schools' ability to transmit tested truth and values to the young. The subject-matter curriculum is a form of the conscious and deliberate transmission of the adult view of reality to children. Although children may be initially imposed on, the acquisition of knowledge will expand their freedom by informing and increasing their choices.

For their perspectives on curriculum, see the chapters on Experimentalism, Progressivism, and Reconstructionism.

The subject-matter curriculum is arranged in a hierarchy with priority given to the more general and theoretical subjects.

In contrast to the subject-matter design, various other curricula have been developed as alternative ways of organizing schools' instructional programs. Experimentalists, Progressives, and Reconstructionists primarily emphasize the process of learning over the transmission of subject matter. This process-oriented curricular design is often called the activity, the experience, or the problem-solving curriculum. In contrast to the differentiated knowledge in the subject-matter curriculum, the process approach concentrates on developing methodological skills to work through and organize undifferentiated human experience. According to John Dewey's experimental mode of learning, the method of scientific inquiry can be applied to all human problems. The curriculum that evolved from Dewey's methodological premise is a series of problem-solving episodes based on the learner's needs and interests as well as on social situations and issues.

Methodology of Instruction

Method of Instruction: the strategy or process teachers use to bring about learning in students.

The **method of instruction** is closely related to the goals or ends specified in the curriculum. *Methodology* refers to the processes of teaching and learning by which the learner is brought into relationship with the skills and knowledge specified by and contained in the curriculum. In the school, methods are the procedures a teacher uses to aid students in having an experience, mastering a skill or process, or acquiring an area of knowledge. If efficient and effective, the methods of instruction will achieve the desired end.

John Colman has defined *method* as "An ordered system by which a teacher puts educative agents to work on humans to produce certain changes or results." He has identified five necessary elements in instructional methodology: (1) an aim, or the specific objective or purpose of instruction; (2) an introduction that relates the particular lesson to previous learning or experiences; (3) content, or the substance or subject of a lesson; (4) a summary to reinforce the particular learning; and (5) an evaluation that determines whether the particular aim has been achieved by the learner.[5]

Because teaching implies using a procedure to achieve a desired objective, educators are involved in methodological questions. In programs of teacher education, attention is given to courses in methods and materials of instruction. For example, there are methods courses in teaching reading, language arts, science, social studies, mathematics, music, art, and physical education. Preservice clinical experiences, especially supervised student or practice teaching, are designed to provide the prospective teacher with experience in integrating content and methodology in a classroom situation. Experienced teachers frequently participate in inservice training programs designed to familiarize them with innovations in curriculum and instruction, including using educational technology. School superintendents and principals allocate time and resources to introducing and experimenting with methodological innovations. Even a cursory examination of the literature of professional education gives evidence of a keen interest in methodology. One will find articles on the Socratic method, the project method, the discovery method, the inquiry method, collaborative learning, authentic assessment, critical thinking, constructivism, the integration of technology, and other approaches to instruction.

The methods of teaching and of learning are most closely related to epistemology, or knowing, and to logic, the correct patterns of thinking. Philosophy of education provides important insights into the epistemologies that underlie various methods of instruction. If knowledge, or ideas, is innately present in the mind as Plato asserts, then the most appropriate and effective instructional strategy is the Socratic method in which the teacher asks probing and directed questions to bring these ideas to learners' consciousness. If, however, learning is a transaction between the person and the environment, as Dewey asserts, then the most effective method is problem solving.

Teachers and Learners

Formal education involves a teacher and a learner. One's conception of the roles and functions of the teacher and the learner depends on one's view of human nature and society. The Thomist view of a human being as an "incarnate spirit-in-the-world" is very different from the Pragmatist conception of the human being as a biological-sociological-vocal phenomenon. The Existentialist belief that the person creates his or her own essence differs from the philosophies that position the human being as a category in a metaphysical system. From each of these perspectives, the roles of the teacher and the learner would be seen quite differently.

For their views on human nature, see the chapters on Realism, Pragmatism, and Existentialism.

In the subject-matter curriculum, the teacher is an authority figure who is expert in the content and teaching of a body of organized knowledge. In this situation, the learner, often a child or adolescent, is an immature person who attends school to acquire and master that knowledge. In such a curricular framework, the teacher–learner relationship involves a great deal of transmission of information from the teacher to the student. How the teacher organizes instruction depends on the structure and logic of the subject matter.

In contrast to the subject-matter approach, the process-oriented educator looks to the child's interests to set the stage for initiating the teacher–learner relationship. The child, rather than subject, is the center of the relationship. The teacher guides but does not dominate the learning process. The teacher's assumptions about reality, knowledge and knowing, and human nature and behavior influence his or her attitudes about students, what they should know, and how they are to learn. Assumptions about human nature influence the type of curriculum, the particular method of instruction, and the school's climate.

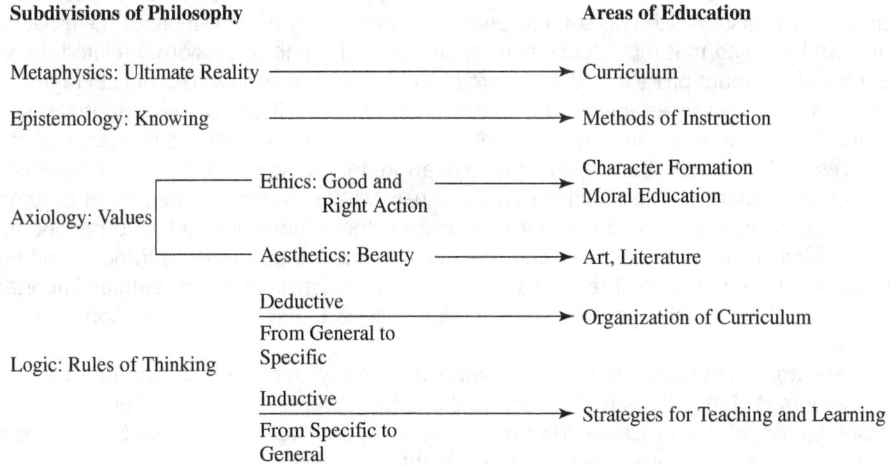

Relationships of Philosophy and Education

My Reflections on Philosophy of Education: Students' Autobiographies

I once spent a summer as a visiting professor at the University of Northern Michigan in Marquette, in the Upper Peninsula. It was a change from my home university, Loyola in Chicago. Loyola is an independent, Jesuit, Catholic institution whereas Northern Michigan is a state-supported public institution. Loyola, an urban university, serves a large metropolitan area. Loyola's downtown campus is on Michigan Avenue, called Chicago's magnificent mile. Northern Michigan, in sharp contrast, is located on a very scenic but remote peninsula that juts out from Wisconsin into Lake Superior. Heavily forested with abundant wildlife, the Upper Peninsula is a region of small towns with a sparse population.

As a beginning exercise in a course in philosophy of education that I was teaching, I asked my students to write short educational autobiographies. A starting point for examining their philosophies of education, the assignment was designed to stimulate the students to reflect on how they had constructed their ideas about education in general, the purposes of schools, and why they were teachers. Also, it would help me get to know them.

After I had read and commented on their autobiographies, I planned to return them to the students, who were then to revise them in terms of their reactions to lectures, readings, and discussions in the course. While reading the initial autobiographies, I discovered some things about my students and gained new insights into their thinking about education. Although there were variations among the autobiographies, some general common themes emerged.

My students saw their lives and interpreted their education in terms of their place—the Upper Peninsula. They were shaped by having grown up in an environment where the winters were long, cold, and snowy. They delighted in the region's recreational activities—hiking, fishing, hunting, and snowmobiling. They had come to adulthood in the Upper Peninsula and wanted to spend the rest of their lives there. I was impressed with the importance of place in their lives. I came to appreciate the genuineness of their commitment to their home area. I knew that in teaching the course I would need to draw insights on the importance of a place in a person's life. The desire to be rooted in a place was very different from the openness to urban mobility that I found in many of my students at Loyola. I also thought about how place, while creating identity, also can be a cause of looking inward rather than outward. Perhaps there was a need to extend horizons and broaden the students' worldviews.

My students were inservice teachers who saw education largely in terms of processes—how to teach in ways that engaged students. Their essays emphasized *process-based education.* They appeared to be more directed to methods of teaching than to content. This awareness of my students' orientation caused me to reconstruct my approach to the course. I felt that I needed to connect my course, which was content-oriented in philosophy of education, to the aspects of teaching and learning that most concerned my students. Through discussions, I related the students' comments about process to the content of the course. It was easy to connect Pragmatism and Progressivism to process-oriented education. For Idealism, Realism, and Essentialism, our discussion focused on how these more traditional approaches to education emphasized content over process. I also learned that my students were aware that they were living in an economically challenged area. Many of their grandparents and parents had worked in the fishing or lumber industries, or in the copper and iron mines. However, these industries had seriously declined. There was significant unemployment and the students knew that earning a living would be a challenge. As I reflected on their reactions, I saw that the students were living with an important, maybe a life-defining challenge—the commitment to a place and the need to support oneself and family.

There were many more things that I learned from my students that summer. I saw the movie *Freedom Writers,* in which a teacher used autobiographical writing with her students in a depressed Los Angeles high school. Maybe, I thought, my idea about autobiography as an entry into constructing a philosophy of education had merit.[6]

PHILOSOPHIES OF EDUCATION

Over time, a number of systematic philosophies have been developed. Idealism and Realism represent major philosophies that have had a long history in Western civilization. They remain philosophies that guide educational processes and support various curricular designs. Closely related to these more traditional philosophies are the educational theories of Perennialism, which emphasizes the human being's rationality, and Essentialism, which stresses basic skills and subjects.

For these traditional philosophies and theories, see the chapters on Idealism, Realism, Perennialism, and Essentialism.

In contrast to the more traditional philosophies, John Dewey's Pragmatism emphasizes the educational process as a transaction between the person and the environment. Among the educational theories that are related to Pragmatism are Progressivism and Reconstructionism. Progressivism, a reaction against traditionalism in schooling, stresses the liberation of the child's needs and interests. Reconstructionism urges that schools play a significant role in cultural criticism and change.

Existentialism and Postmodernism are two contemporary philosophies that have significant educational implications. The Existentialist is concerned about the conformity found in mass society and bureaucratic schools that dehumanizes students by reducing them to objects or functions. The Postmodernist critiques rationales, or canons, that legitimize existing knowledge and values. Challenging universalizing philosophies, Postmodernism deconstructs the rationales that support them.

For their educational implications, see the chapters on Pragmatism, Progressivism, Reconstructionism, Existentialism, and Postmodernism.

In addition to examining significant philosophies of education, later chapters examine leading ideologies that have shaped the Western political, social, and educational perspective. Based on political and social contexts, ideologies such as Nationalism, Liberalism, Conservatism, and Marxism have shaped schools, curricula, and styles of teaching and learning. At times, elements of philosophical systems have been fused with particular ideologies. The text concludes with a discussion of theories of education and then examines Essentialism, Perennialism, Progressivism, Social Reconstructionism, and Critical Theory.

For these ideologies, see the chapters on Nationalism, Liberalism, Conservatism, and Marxism.

Constructing Your Philosophy of Education

Using the definitions and discussion of philosophy and education in Chapter 1, you can begin to construct your own philosophy of education. First, reflect on and record your beliefs about reality, knowledge and knowing, values, and logic. Then reflect on how you came to have these beliefs, especially on how your own education helped to form them. Your initial statement is a "formative" and tentative expression of philosophy of education; it is a point of departure that can be re-formed, reshaped, and revised until it becomes more complete. Expressing your beginning thoughts about philosophy of education, your formative statement is likely to be based on your experiences with education up to this point. You may wish to reflect on your own formal education, your schooling, and how it contributed to shaping your ideas. You may wish also to reflect on how informal agents shaped your ideas about education. Consider how parents, family members, friends, teachers, and classmates shaped your ideas about education—its purposes, processes, and outcomes. You may also wish to consider how books, movies, television, social media, and the Internet have influenced your view of education.

Then, as you read the book, analyze each philosophy, ideology, and theory that is presented and discussed in class. Reflect on how the ideas and themes developed in each chapter either reinforce or challenge your initial ideas and first reflections about philosophy of education. They may confirm them or cause you to change your mind.

(continued)

You can begin to construct your own philosophy of education by reflecting on and answering such questions as:

1. Do you believe that knowledge is based on universal and eternal truths or do you think that it is relative to different times, places, and situations?
2. What is the purpose or the purposes of education? Is it to transmit the cultural heritage; to train people in economic, social, and technological skills; to develop reasoning and critical thinking; to advance political socialization in a democratic society; to promote understanding and appreciation of people from other cultures; or to criticize and reform society?
3. What are schools for? Do they have a primary purpose or are they multifunctional institutions? Why does society support schools as institutions? Are schools intended to teach academic skills and subjects, encourage personal self-definition, develop human intelligence, or create patriotic and economically productive citizens?
4. What should be the content of the curriculum: basic skills and subjects, experiences and projects, the great books and classics, inquiry processes or critical thinking, or activities for personal, physical, and social development?
5. What should be the relationship between teachers and students? Transmitting the heritage, teaching and learning skills and subjects, examining great ideas, encouraging self-expression and self-definition, constructing knowledge, or solving problems? Should it be formal or informal? Should it involve mentoring?

As you think about and answer these questions you will be constructing your own philosophy of education. After you read the following chapters, you can revisit your philosophy and revise or enlarge it.

Conclusion

Chapter 1 provided an introductory entry into philosophy of education. It examined the key areas of philosophy—metaphysics, epistemology, axiology, and logic. It then related these philosophical areas to education, especially to informal and formal learning, schooling, curriculum, methods of instruction, and the relationships between teachers and students. By defining and relating the areas, or subdivisions, of philosophy to education, the chapter develops a structure and process for thinking, reflecting, and philosophizing about meanings and issues in education. An assumption, followed in the chapters throughout the book, is that it is valuable for teachers to recognize various philosophies of education and to examine educational policies, curricula, and methods in terms of their particular philosophical underpinnings. This competency aids teachers in developing their own conceptual frameworks that can be used to examine, reflect on, and critique educational policies and programs. For example, many of the proposals made in educational reports such as *A Nation at Risk,* legislation such as the No Child Left Behind Act, and the Common Core State Standards rest on philosophical and ideological assumptions. Some of these represent a revival of Neo-Conservatism and Essentialism.

Philosophies of education also can be derived from more general philosophies. For example, as we shall see in later chapters, educational policies, goals, curricula, methods, and ends can be extrapolated from philosophical systems such as Idealism, Realism, and Thomism. In turn, philosophies of education can arise from generalizations based on observations, research, experiences, and practices of teachers and students in actual learning situations, as is the case with the Essentialists and Progressives. Still others, such as Postmodernists, offer a critique of political, social, and educational situations and conditions. Throughout history, education has been the subject of debate and controversy. These divergent viewpoints are a sign that discussions about educational philosophy comprise an ongoing process in human experience. As a social institution, the school is the focal point of controversies about the purpose, meaning, goals, and outcomes of formal education. Philosophers such as Ivan Illich have proposed the deschooling of society and abandoning the school as society's primary educational institution. Others such as Thomists and, Conservatives want schools to deliberately instill religious and spiritual values in the young; still others plead for an emphasis on law and order. Some views like those of the Perennialists and Essentialists proclaim that schools must return to the intellectual virtues, to the liberal arts and sciences, or to basic education. Others such as Social Reconstructionists and Critical Theorists see schools as agencies of social criticism and as agencies for initiating social, political, and economic reforms.

There have been and continue to be many proposals for reforming American education. Among them are higher academic standards, more charter schools, the yearlong school calendar, more homework, less homework, establishing a cultural core in Western and American values, a multicultural curriculum, assessment by standardized tests, and assessment by portfolios. Behind these proposals are philosophical assumptions about reality, knowledge, human nature, and society. By examining these assumptions in their philosophical matrix, these proposals can be explored, analyzed, and critiqued.

Questions for Reflection and Discussion

1. Reflect on your ideas about knowledge, education and schooling, and teaching and learning. What would you say is your philosophy of education? If you have the opportunity, share your thoughts with your classmates and listen to their philosophies. Discuss the agreements and disagreements that emerge in the discussion.
2. Reflect on how your philosophy of education has been influenced by significant teachers in your school experience or by books, movies, or television programs about teachers and teaching. Share and discuss such influences with your classmates.
3. What underlying philosophical orientations can you identify in your teacher-education program? For example, what are the views on knowledge, values, curriculum, instruction, teachers, and students?
4. Reflect on your educational experience. What value conflicts have you observed in schools, between teachers and teachers, between teachers and students, and between students and students?
5. How is teaching both reflective and active?
6. Reflect on values in contemporary American society and culture. Do you find evidence of conflict between those who subscribe to universal and objective values and those who take a relativist or subjective view?

Inquiry and Research Projects

1. Maintain a journal that identifies the philosophies or theories that you find in the schools and classrooms in your clinical experience.
2. Create and maintain a clippings file of articles about education that appear in the popular press—newspapers and magazines—either critiquing schools or proposing educational reforms. Analyze the philosophical and theoretical positions underlying these critiques and proposed reforms.
3. Analyze the philosophy of education approved by the board of education for your school. What does it state about the school's mission and purpose?
4. Visit several elementary and secondary school classes. Observe the curriculum and teaching methods being used. In a report to the class, reflect on your observations in terms of the underlying philosophical assumptions that you found.
5. Read and review a book that is used in teacher education in terms of the author's view of knowledge and teaching and learning. What are the author's philosophical assumptions?
6. Read a novel or see a movie about teaching and analyze the author's or the film's representation of the teacher–learner relationship.
7. Analyze several academic majors described in the catalogue of your college or university. What conceptions of knowledge are implied in the course requirements for these majors?

As you read the next chapters on Idealism, Realism, Pragmatism, Existentialism, and Postmodernism, you might find it useful to refer to the following Overview table.

Overview of Philosophies of Education

Philosophy	Metaphysics	Epistemology	Axiology	Educational Implications	Proponents
Idealism	Reality is spiritual or intellectual and unchanging, eternal, and universal.	Knowing is reminiscence, the recollection of latent ideas through introspection and intuition.	Values are universal, absolute, and eternal and are based on the goodness and beauty of the World Mind.	A subject-matter curriculum that includes the culture's most noble and enduring ideas. Socratic method. Teachers as exemplars.	Plato Hegel Emerson
Realism	Reality is objective and is composed of matter and form; it follows the patterns in the laws of nature.	Knowing consists of conceptualization based on sensation and abstraction.	Values are absolute and eternal, based on universal laws.	A subject-matter curriculum emphasizes humanistic and scientific disciplines. The great books of Western civilization. Methods that demonstrate reality.	Aquinas Aristotle Hutchins Adler Maritain Broudy
Pragmatism (experimentalism)	Rejects metaphysics as unverifiable speculations. Humans construct their concepts of reality on experience, the interaction with environment; it is always changing.	What we know comes from experiencing and using the scientific method.	Values are situational and relative to cultures and societies.	Instruction is organized around problem solving according to the scientific method.	Dewey James Peirce
Existentialism	To be metaphysical or not is a personal choice. Reality is subjective, with existence preceding essence. Existence creates essence.	Knowing is to make personal choices. To choose or appropriate what I want to know.	Values should be freely chosen.	Classroom dialogues stimulate awareness that each person creates a self-concept through significant choices.	Sartre Marcel Morris Kierkegaard Greene
Postmodernism	Rejects metaphysics as historical constructions used for socio-economic domination.	Deconstructs texts (canons) to find their origin and use by dominant groups and classes.	Emphasizes the values of marginalized persons and groups.	Schools are sites of democratic criticism and social change to empower dominated groups.	Derrida Foucault

Internet Resources

For an introduction to philosophy of education, access http://www.everythingphilosophy.com/philosophy-of-education.

For a thorough introduction and a useful bibliography from the *Stanford Encyclopedia of Philosophy,* access http://plato.stanford.edu/entries/education-philosophy.

For publications and resources, access the Philosophy of Education Society home page at http://philosophyofeducation.org. For suggestions on writing your philosophy of education, access Dr. Jurgen Combs' "Writing Your Own Educational Philosophy" at http://www.edulink.org/portfolio/philosophies.htm.

Further Readings

Bailey, Richard. *Philosophy of Education: An Introduction* New York: Continuum, 2011.

Barrow, Robin, and Ronald G. Woods. *An Introduction to Philosophy of Education.* New York: Routledge, 2006.

Cahn, Steven M. *Classic and Contemporary Readings in the Philosophy of Education.* New York: Oxford University Press, 2011.

___, ed. *Philosophy of Education: The Essential Texts.* New York: Routledge, 2009.

Carr, David. *Making Sense of Education: An Introduction to the Philosophy and Theory of Education and Teaching.* New York: Routledge Falmer, 2003.

Curren, Randall. *Philosophy of Education: An Anthology.* Malden, MA, and Oxford, UK: Blackwell, 2007.

___, ed. *A Companion to the Philosophy of Education.* Malden, MA, and Oxford, UK: Blackwell, 2006.

Erneling, Christina E. *Towards Discursive Education: Philosophy, Technology, and Modern Education.* New York: Cambridge University Press, 2010.

The Freedom Writers, with Erin Gruwell. *The Freedom Writers Diary: How a Teacher and 150 Teens Used Writing to Change Themselves and the World Around Them.* New York: Doubleday/Random House, 1999.

Gingell, John, and Christopher Winch. *Philosophy of Education: The Key Concepts.* New York: Routledge, 2008.

Gutek, Gerald L. *Philosophical and Ideological Voices in Education.* Boston: Allyn & Bacon, 2004.

Johnson, Tony W., and Robert F. Reed. *Philosophical Documents in Education.* Upper Saddle River, NJ: Prentice Hall, 2011.

Lone, Jane Mohr, and Roberta Israeloff. *Philosophy of Education.* Newcastle, UK: Cambridge Scholars Publishing, 2012.

Noddings, Nel. *Educating Moral People: A Caring Alternative to Character Education.* New York: Teachers College Press, 2002.

___. *Philosophy of Education.* Boulder, CO: Westview Press, 2011.

Ozman, Howard A. *Philosophical Foundations of Education.* Upper Saddle River, NJ: Prentice Hall, 2011.

Titone, Connie, and Karen Maloney. *Women's Philosophies of Education: Thinking Through Our Mothers.* Upper Saddle River, NJ: Merrill/Prentice Hall, 1999.

Watras, Joseph. *Philosophical Conflicts in American Education, 1893–2000.* Boston: Allyn & Bacon, 2004.

Watts, Leonard J., ed. *Leaders in Philosophy of Education: Intellectual Self Portraits.* Boston: Sense Publishers, 2008.

Notes

1. For further reading on philosophy of education, see Robin Barrow and Ronald Woods, *An Introduction to the Philosophy of Education* (New York: Routledge, 2006); Sheila G. Dunn, *Philosophical Foundations of Education: Connecting Philosophy to Theory and Practice* (Upper Saddle River, NJ: Pearson, 2005); and David Carr, *Making Sense of Education: An Introduction to the Philosophy and Theory of Education and Teaching* (New York: Routledge Falmer, 2003).
2. John Dewey, *How We Think,* introduction by Gerald Gutek (New York: Barnes and Noble, 2005), 6.
3. Available at www.ncate.org/public/standards.asp (2006).
4. James D. Hunter, *Culture Wars: The Struggle to Define America* (New York: Basic Books, 1991), 3–29, 44.
5. John E. Colman, *The Master Teachers and the Art of Teaching* (New York: Pitman, 1967), 5–11.
6. The Freedom Writers, with Erin Gruwell, *The Freedom Writers Diary: How a Teacher and 150 Teens Used Writing to Change Themselves and the World Around Them* (New York: Doubleday/Random House, 1999).

Idealism and Education

Ralph Waldo Emerson (1803–1882), an American philosopher, who developed Transcendentalism, a version of Idealism.

2

CHAPTER PREVIEW

Idealism, which asserts that reality is essentially spiritual or ideational, is one of humankind's oldest and most enduring philosophies. The belief that the world and human beings within it are part of an unfolding universal spirit has long been a cosmic principle in Asian religions such as Hinduism and Buddhism. It was probably through cultural interactions between East and West that Idealist concepts entered Western thought. Buddhism often is found in the contemporary movement in which individuals seek a spiritual center for their lives. Spirituality, highly compatible with Idealism, offers an alternative to the materialism and consumerism of contemporary society.

In Western philosophy, Idealism's origins are usually traced to the ancient Greek philosopher Plato. Idealism has often dominated philosophical discourse in the past. In eighteenth- and nineteenth-century Germany, Idealists such as Johann Gottlieb Fichte (1762–1814), Friedrich Schelling (1775–1854), and Georg Wilhelm Friedrich Hegel (1770–1831) were dominant figures in continental European philosophy. Hegel's monumental work, *The Philosophy of History*, influenced philosophical thought both in Germany and elsewhere, including the United States. Both Karl Marx (1818–1883) and John Dewey (1859–1952) were influenced by Idealism in their studies and early careers as philosophers. Friedrich Froebel (1782–1852), the founder of the concept of the kindergarten, grounded his approach to early childhood education on Idealism.

In the United States, the New England Transcendentalists Ralph Waldo Emerson (1803–1882) and Henry David Thoreau (1817–1862) used some aspects of German Idealism to construct their concepts of the Oversoul, or Macrocosm, and Nature. William Torrey Harris (1835–1909) used Hegelian Idealism as a philosophical rationale for school organization and curriculum.

While Idealism is historically significant, some contemporary ideas in education continue to reflect their Idealist origins. Among them are:

- Education is a process of developing, or externalizing, the potentialities in the individual child.
- The teacher should be a model of the best that is in the culture and society.
- The Socratic dialogue, in which the teacher asks leading questions, is an excellent method to get students to reflect on their ideas.
- Individuals possess universal human rights that are intrinsic to their human nature and not dependent on social or cultural norms.
- The teacher, especially the teacher educator, should be a mentor to those seeking to become teachers.

Idealism: a philosophy that asserts that reality is essentially spiritual, ideational, and nonmaterial.

This chapter examines the following topics:

- Plato, Hegel, and Emerson as founders of Idealism
- Idealism as a systematic philosophy and its view of metaphysics, epistemology, axiology, and logic
- Idealism's implications for education, schooling, curriculum and instruction, character formation, and teacher–student relationships

As you read the chapter, think about Idealism and how it relates to the construction of your own philosophy of education. Is Idealism or some aspects of this philosophy meaningful to you? As you reflect on constructing your own philosophy of education, what elements of Idealism do you especially like or dislike? Are there aspects of Idealism that you plan to incorporate into your philosophy of education?

PLATO: FOUNDER OF WESTERN IDEALISM

This section examines how Plato established the foundations of philosophy, especially Idealism. Some philosophers believe that Plato was the originator of the questions they still seek to answer. To understand Plato, we need to examine his relationship to his teacher, Socrates. The story of Socrates and Plato takes us back to Athens, a city-state, or *polis* in ancient Greece. Styling himself as a midwife of ideas who brings them out of the minds of people, Socrates (469–399 BCE), frequented the agora, Athens' central square, attracting a following of young men, like Plato, as his students. To examine philosophical issues, Socrates used a dialogue method in which he asked probing questions to antagonists who claimed that they knew what was true and good and what it meant to be wise and virtuous. Because Socrates asked uncomfortable and unconventional questions that challenged conformity to traditional ideas and institutions, the Athenian political establishment viewed him as a threat to the security of the state. He was tried and convicted of undermining the morals of Athenian youth and blasphemy against the traditional gods of Athens. An early martyr for academic freedom, Socrates, sentenced to death, accepted his fate and refused to flee Athens.

What we know about Socrates is based on Plato's portrayal of him as the central figure in his writings, the dialogues. Therefore, it is not always possible to distinguish between the ideas of Socrates, the teacher, and Plato, the student. The important point, however, is that while Socrates raised fundamental questions about reality, knowledge, and human nature, Plato went beyond his teacher to construct a philosophy that sought to answer the metaphysical question: What is the nature of reality? and the epistemological question: What is the nature of knowledge and how do we know?

The educational bond between Socrates, as teacher, and Plato, as student, provides enduring insights into the teacher–learner relationship that still have meaning for contemporary teachers. Insights that resonated well in Idealism include the concepts of discipleship, **mentoring**, and modeling. Although the word *disciple* is not much used in education today, there are still many instances of it. Most evident is when the students of a professor embrace his or her ideas and promulgate them in their own teaching. Just as Plato was a disciple of Socrates, we shall see in later chapters that John Dewey and Paulo Freire had students who became committed disciples of their philosophies.

Mentoring: the relationship in which a mentor, an experienced teacher, guides a beginning teacher.

The relationship between Socrates, the master, and Plato, his most famous student, exemplified the Idealist concept of mentorship. While discipleship is usually long lasting, mentoring is a stage in a student's development in which he or she is tutored by a master teacher. Mentoring is frequently used in education today. Typically, a mentor is an experienced teacher, often a senior cooperating teacher who provides guidance and advice to the beginning teacher. Just as Socrates shared his insights into reality and his dialogue method of teaching with Plato, the mentor shares insights, methods, and experiences in teaching so that the beginner can incorporate them into her or his emerging teaching strategy.

From Socrates and Plato onward, Idealists have emphasized that the teacher should embody the finest and highest qualities of the culture. The teacher as a model knows and values these finest qualities so students can come into contact with them. The teacher as a wise person should be worthy of emulation by the student. Plato, who established the Academy, a school of philosophic studies in Athens, in 387 BCE, became a model for later generations of professors. To see how Plato reconceptualized Socrates' ideas and method, we turn to two of Plato's dialogues, *Phaedo* and *Meno*.

Plato's *Phaedo*

Plato's dialogue *Phaedo* is an account of Socrates on the eve of his death. Engaged in a dialogue with Phaedo, Socrates tells him that he is prepared to die because he has fulfilled his mission to search for truth. This quest has brought him to understand that every individual possesses an immortal soul that will continue to exist after the body perishes. After the body's death, the soul enjoys the vision and presence of universal absolute and eternal truth and goodness that are found in the Form of the Good. The dialogue points out: (1) there is a universal Presence, the Form of the Good; (2) the human being has a soul; (3) truth and goodness are universals that transcend particulars of time, place, and circumstances.

As a backdrop to the *Phaedo,* it is important to understand the educational rivalry between Socrates and the **Sophists.** (Phaedo was a student of the Sophists.) In his search to discover the universal principles of truth, justice, and beauty that governed all humankind, Socrates ran into conflict with the Sophists, a group of traveling for-profit teachers who, for a fee, promised to teach any skill or subject, even wisdom, to anyone who studied with them. The Sophists specialized in teaching the technique of effective public speaking, or oratory, which was the key to political power in Athens. Denying that there were universal truths or justice, the Sophists argued that what mattered most in life and society was power since the powerful made the laws that determined what was right and wrong. In *Theaetetus,* a companion dialogue to *Phaedo,* Plato uses Socrates' voice to attack the Sophists with the following arguments: (1) the Sophists rely on persuasion to convince their students that they know and can teach the truth; and (2) although persuasion may convince people to believe what you want them to believe, these beliefs are merely the opinions of others and not the truth.[1]

Sophists: itinerant teachers in ancient Greece who taught public speaking, oratory, and other skills and subjects; Socrates and Plato opposed their relativism. The term *sophistry* refers to arguments based on false reasoning.

The argument between Socrates and the Sophists points to a recurrent issue in education. Claiming that ethical decisions and actions are really how an individual responds to changing situations at particular times and places, the Sophists dismissed Socrates' search for universal truths and values as idle speculation. Disputing their **ethical relativism,** Socrates argued that what is true, good, and beautiful is the same throughout the world, regardless of time or place.

Ethical Relativism: the belief that what is held to be morally good or bad or right and wrong depends on particular social or cultural situations or personal preferences.

Plato's critique of the Sophists has important implications for an Idealist version of education. First, education has an overall very general purpose: It is to lead individuals to the truth so that they can enjoy intellectually and morally excellent lives. To fulfill its general purpose, education, too, must be general rather than specific training, in public speaking as the Sophists were doing, or in marketable skills and technologies as some contemporary educators recommend. Second, education is foremost intellectual in that it develops the mind's power to search for the truth; the most general and intellectual education is provided in the liberal arts and sciences.

Plato's *Meno*

Plato developed his theory of knowledge in *Meno,* a dialogue between Socrates and Meno, a student of Gorgias and a leading Sophist. The dialogue begins when Meno asks Socrates if virtue can be taught. Socrates does not give a quick yes or no answer, but poses a series of leading and probing questions. Meno complains that Socrates is leading him into confusion without giving him a clear answer. Meno's confusion is a necessary step in the Socratic method; it signals that the student is beginning to realize that his opinion is either false or incomplete. Now, Meno understands that his question needs further definition and clarification. Guided by Socrates' questioning, Meno identifies instances of particular kinds of virtue such as that displayed by the prudent lawmaker, the caring mother, and the courageous soldier. Through further questioning, Socrates leads Meno to recognize that these instances of virtue are really manifestations of a more general and unifying idea of the form or general concept of virtue that is universal to all of the particulars. The dialogue discloses three major features of Socratic–Platonic epistemology: (1) it uses the Socratic method of focused conversations, or dialogues, that involve questions and answers; (2) it asserts that truth can be discovered as innate but latent ideas in the mind; (3) it asserts that learning is the recollection of ideas present in the person's mind.

DIALOGUE, THE SOCRATIC METHOD. Although teachers generally include the development of critical thinking skills as an important goal of education, it is necessary to ask what it means to be a critical thinker. The various philosophies, ideologies, and theories discussed in the book suggest different definitions of critical thinking. For Plato, critical thinking is best done through question-and-answer conversation, or dialogue, between individuals. This method is different from transmitting information, exhortation, or preaching. Socrates is proposing ongoing rational inquiry—critical examination and introspection—about the nature of truth.

Innate Ideas: concepts that are already present in our minds without resulting from sensation.

KNOWLEDGE AS IDEAS IN THE MIND. In *Meno,* Plato uses Socrates to advance the epistemology that the individual possesses **innate ideas**, or conceptual forms, that are true knowledge. The idea of virtue exists within our minds; through introspection, we recollect and bring the concept of virtue into our consciousness. The mind has the inherent power to reason but also possesses innate concepts or universals.[2]

Socratic Method: Socrates' method of asking probing questions about truth, beauty, and justice.

Unlike the Sophists, Socrates denied that true wisdom would result from merely telling students about some body of information or training them in particular techniques. He asserted that concepts, the structures of true knowledge, exist within the mind and can be brought to consciousness. In the **Socratic Method**, probing questions stimulate the learner to discover the truth in his or her mind by bringing latent concepts to consciousness.

LEARNING AS RECOLLECTION. For Plato, learning is a process of self-examination, or rediscovery. To learn is to recognize something again—to "re" "cognize" it. In the *Meno,* Socrates illustrates recollection by leading an untutored slave boy to recognize the geometrical principle of the Pythagorean Theorem. Meno's slave "recalled" the knowledge that the square on the diagonal of a square is equivalent to the squares on the other two sides.[3]

Socrates' guiding educational aim, as Plato tells us, was to stimulate individuals, even if he had to provoke them to engage in a lifelong quest for the truth, the real truth that made life worth living. Through rigorous self-reflection, each person should seek the truth that is universally present in all members of the human race. As a teacher, Socrates asked probing questions that stimulated his students to investigate the perennial human concerns about the meaning of life, truth, and justice.[4] Through dialogue, Socrates and his students dealt with basic questions by defining them, criticizing them, and developing more adequate and comprehensive definitions.

Plato's Allegory of the Cave

In the "Allegory of the Cave," in *The Republic,* Plato depicted people chained as prisoners in such a way that they can see only in one direction. With a fire behind them, they can only see shadows of objects that are carried by others before the flames. When one prisoner is freed, he makes his way to the mouth of the cave and experiences the very difficult process of moving from the dark world of shadows to the bright light of reality. At first, his vision is dim; then, as his eyes adjust to the light, he begins to see more clearly. Looking upward, he sees the moon, and the stars, and then the sun. Having glimpsed the sun, he eagerly returns to tell the prisoners the good news that he has seen the source of light, the sun. However, the prisoners are so used to living in a world of shadows that they refuse to believe him.

In the Allegory, the sun represents the **Form of the Good**, the source of all that is bright and beautiful and good and true. This is in contrast to the world of shadows, which the prisoners mistakenly believe is the world of truth. In the Allegory, there are those who hold the objects before the flame that casts the deceiving shadows. These are the false teachers, like the Sophists, who substitute opinion for truth.

Form of the Good: Plato's highest and all-encompassing universal metaphysical construct that contains all truth, goodness, and value.

The difficult process of turning away from shadows to truth represents the process of self-examination and reflection found in the Socratic method. Plato's dialogues tell of education by conversion, sparked by Socrates' questions, from the shadows of opinion to truth. True knowledge comes as we escape the cave of sensation and opinion and go into the light where the sun, the light of reason, shows things as they truly are.

Plato's Idealism

While Plato retained many of Socrates' ideas, he moved beyond his mentor to construct his own philosophy, The student, Plato, honored his teacher by organizing Socrates' ideas into the systematic philosophy of Idealism.

Plato's Metaphysics

Plato's metaphysics asserts the existence of an ideal, hence unchanging, world of perfect ideas, the universal and timeless concepts of truth, goodness, justice, and beauty.[5] The particular examples or cases of these general concepts are specific but imperfect reflections or shadows of the perfect forms from which they are derived. These perfect forms are contained in a great all-inclusive and most general and abstract form that Plato called the Form of the Good. Plato's philosophy of a universal, unchanging, and eternal reality was designed to counter the Sophists' relativism. In contrast, he asserted that human beings are wise and virtuous when their knowledge and behavior conform to reflect the ideal and universal concepts of truth, goodness, and beauty.

Plato's Epistemology

Plato's epistemology, or theory of knowledge, focuses on the concept of **reminiscence** or recollection by which human beings recall the truths that are unconsciously present but latent in their minds. Reminiscence implies that every human being possesses a soul, which prior to birth, dwelt in the spiritual world of perfect forms or ideas. With the shock of birth—actually, an imprisoning of the psyche in a material flesh-and-blood body—this knowledge of the perfect ideas is repressed within the mind's

Reminiscence: Plato's epistemology in which knowing is the recalling or remembering of ideas or concepts that are present but latent in the mind.

unconscious part. However, the ideas of the perfect forms are still there and, with effort, can be brought to consciousness. When Plato's epistemology of Reminiscence is applied to reflective learning, it means that students are (1) motivated and ready to learn; (2) willing to detect and discard false opinions; and (3) seeking to discover the truth.

True knowledge, according to Plato, is intellectual and eternal, as are the perfect forms from which it is derived. There is but one idea of perfection common to all human beings regardless of where and when they live or the circumstances under which they live. Like truth itself, a genuine education is also universal and timeless. Because reality can only be discovered intellectually, the best kind of education is also intellectual. Although Plato developed his educational philosophy in ancient Greece, his ideas have been reiterated many times since then. Defenders of liberal education often rely on Plato's ideas. For example, Allan Bloom, in his attack on relativism in *The Closing of the American Mind,* calls Plato's *Republic* "the book on education" that really explains genuine teaching and learning.[6]

Plato's *Republic*

In addition to their considerations about metaphysics, epistemology, and axiology, philosophies of education are concerned about the relationships between the individual and the social and political order. Just as contemporary teachers are concerned with issues of social justice and fairness, philosophers ask: What is the nature of the good and just society? In his monumental work, ***The Republic,*** Plato presents his ideas about the good and just social and political order.

The Republic: Plato's book about a perfect organic society in which each class performs the functions for which it is suited by its nature.

Plato compared the well-ordered social and political state (the Greek polis) to the healthy well-functioning human organism. The perfectly functioning state and the perfectly functioning person both exemplify the form of justice. For Plato, the just state exists to cultivate truth and virtue in its citizens.

Plato organized the inhabitants of his Republic into three basic classes: the philosopher-kings, the state's intellectual rulers; the auxiliaries, the state's military defenders; and the workers, who performed the services and produced the economic goods needed in the society. By way of analogy, the philosopher-kings could be compared to the state's mind, the auxiliaries to its limbs, and workers to its stomach. Assignment to one of these three basic classes depended on an assessment of each individual's potentials or aptitude, especially intellectual ability. Educators played an important role in assessing a child's intellectual potentiality. Once the child's intellectual capability had been assessed, he or she received the education appropriate to this ability and ultimately to her or his role in the state.

The philosopher-kings, the republic's supreme rulers, were highly educated intellectuals who, after a long period of studying philosophy, had a clear vision of the truth. The philosopher-kings were virtuous, intelligent, and talented persons who had the capacity for leadership. They were the Republic's supreme educators in that they supervised the assessment process and determined the kind of education a person needed to perform his or her future role in the state.

The auxiliaries, or warriors, who comprised the second class were subordinate to the philosopher-kings. More willful than intellectual, the auxiliaries—because of their courage—were to defend the republic. Based on their capacities, the education of the auxiliaries was primarily military. The third class of people, the workers, who produced the state's goods and services, had a limited capacity for intellectual abstraction but enjoyed farming, fishing, and making things. Their education consisted primarily of vocational training based on the particular service or productive work they would do. The citizens of the Republic—philosopher-kings, auxiliaries, and workers—were happy because they were doing what their nature intended them to do.

Plato's Idealist philosophy originated in ancient Greece's classical period; centuries later, Idealism had a strong resurgence in the nineteenth century in the works of Hegel, a German philosopher, and Emerson, an American philosopher.

HEGEL'S IDEALIST PHILOSOPHY OF HISTORY

Georg Wilhelm Friedrich Hegel (1770–1831) developed an Idealist philosophy of history that influenced Western thought throughout the nineteenth and early twentieth centuries. A professor of philosophy at the University of Heidelberg and then at the prestigious University of Berlin, Hegel attracted numerous students to his lectures on Idealism.[7] Among his works were *The Science of Logic, The Encyclopedia of Philosophical Sciences,* and *The Philosophy of History.*[8] In this section, we examine how Hegel's views on history and change shaped Western education.

Hegel's Philosophy of History

Similar to Plato's Form of the Good, Hegel believed all ideas originated in and flowed outward from the Divine Mind, which Hegel designated the **Absolute Mind**. With its consummate and perfect intelligence, the Absolute Mind gives order to a purposeful world.

Absolute Mind: Hegel's concept of the most general, most abstract, complete, and perfect idea in the universe from which all other ideas are derived.

Human life is not a purposeless accident, somehow born in chaos, but is an intrinsic part of a universal plan. Not aimless, nor a series of random happenings, history, governed by the Absolute Mind, is purposeful and is moving ever forward toward the goal established in the Absolute Mind. People, living through the **stages of history** (prehistory, ancient, medieval, and modern), are marching forward along the path that leads to one harmonious destination.

Stages of History: in Hegel's philosophy of history, the stages of history reveal the evolution of culture and institutions as the ideas in the mind of the Absolute are unfolded and revealed over time.

While Plato conceived of his Republic as the perfect but not yet realized state, Hegel, living in the early nineteenth century, saw the modern, rationally organized nation-state as the embodiment of the concept of the ideal polity in the Absolute Mind. Further, the ideal was being realized in Prussia, the tightly organized leading German nation-state.[9] The individual's identity and self-realization came from joining with others who were like him in fully participating in the nation-state.[10] The implications of the nation-state as the embodiment of the Absolute Mind were great for educational policy. Drawing on Martin Luther's injunction that the state should establish and supervise schools, Hegel moved schooling beyond the religious sector and into the universal sphere. Schools should reflect what the Absolute Mind had wrought and become cooperating agencies in bringing children into cultural, social, and political participation.

The Dialectic

The movement from one historical period to another, for Hegel, is caused by the dialectical process, in which a regnant idea (a thesis) is challenged by its opposite (an antithesis). The clash of these two ideas results in a higher level and more complex idea, a synthesis, which combines elements of both ideas. The synthesis is then a thesis that contains its antithesis, and the dialectical process continues in increasing comprehensiveness and complexity. This process resembles the way in which the Absolute Mind works in history, moving it forward, until it reaches its conclusion.[11]

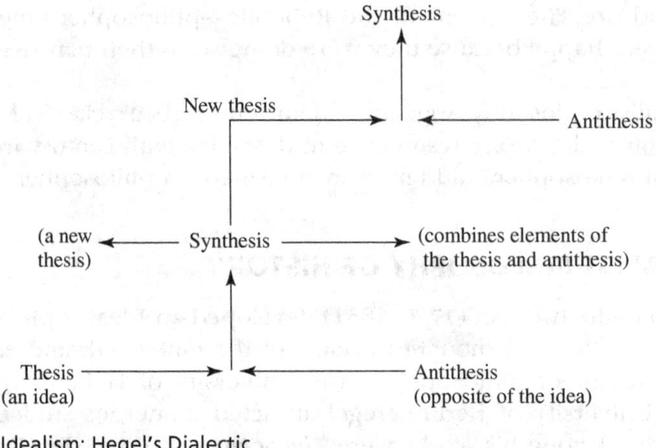

Idealism: Hegel's Dialectic

Development as Unfolding

With Hegel's dialectical process comes the concept of change as gradual development, an unfolding of what is contained in the Absolute Mind through history. The concept of development as unfolding is significant in education. It means that human growth is the unfolding of what is already present in the child, who possesses a spirit that is manifesting itself outward. Hegel is reiterating Plato's contention that the human mind possesses latent powers or potentialities that can be activated by the right kind of education. The stages of human development, when seen as a spiritual progression, give a dignity to children's play and activities by which they begin to externalize their innermost but largely latent ideas. The development is from within outward.

In terms of the social and political order, Hegel emphasized the course of events as a gradual, slow, steady, serial unfolding of events. He rejected violent revolutions such as the French Revolution. Futile attempts by misguided activists to interfere with the dialectical process of unfolding, revolutions caused discord, disorder, and a tyranny that violated human freedom. Hegel's concept of development as the unhurried and inevitable unfolding of the Absolute Mind opposes Marx's use of the dialectical as class conflict that leads to revolution. He would also reject the Social Reconstructionist use of education to create a new social order as an unwarranted utopianism that leads to indoctrination.

For their views on revolution and directed social change, see the chapters on Marxism and Social Reconstruction.

Hegel aligned his philosophy with a spiritual and religious dimension that is common to Idealism. He saw the emergence of Christianity as a profound development in history in which human beings were enlightened to recognize that they are endowed with a spiritual soul and have an eternal destiny. Christianity was revitalized when Martin Luther inaugurated the Protestant Reformation.[12]

With the Reformation, the human person came to understand that he or she has a direct spiritual relationship with God. With each person as a free spiritual agent, history has unfolded to reveal that individuals can experience their true freedom by giving their assent to a culture and society that conforms to rational standards. Notice that the person reaches true freedom not by rejecting culture and society but by conforming to it. In the modern state, exemplified by Prussia, all social institutions now conform to the general principles of reason. Plato's Republic is now realized on earth. In this rationally organized state, citizens, following their inner consciences, will freely choose to act in accord with law and morality of the objective state order and perfect harmony will be achieved between the individual and society.

The perfect state for Hegel, as for Plato, is an organic community that integrates individuals with the society, the state. In the organic community, discord yields to harmony between private interests and community welfare. Personal identity comes from membership in the community.[13]

EDUCATIONAL IMPLICATIONS. Just as Plato cast a long shadow over Western philosophy, Hegel's Idealism had a pronounced impact on education. He advised educational policy makers that they could not and should not attempt to use schools to promote social change. Rather, educational policy should correspond to and reflect the larger developments, the unfolding of the Absolute Mind, in history. Schools and the curriculum should reflect the dominant customs and traditions, which, in turn, reflected the rational principles revealed by the Absolute Mind. Hegel saw the modern nation-state as the highest embodiment of the Absolute Mind on earth. National school systems were an important, legitimate, and necessary part of the state system. Reformed Protestant Christianity could and should provide the values that would lead to a stable and law-abiding society.

INFLUENCE ON LATER PHILOSOPHERS. Before leaving Hegel, we need to consider his influence on the ideas of later philosophers. Many philosophers of the nineteenth and early twentieth centuries studied Hegelian Idealism, which was dominant in the universities. As a student in Germany, Karl Marx studied Hegel, and he incorporated the dialectic into his philosophy of dialectical materialism. Marx transferred the concept of the dialectic from the realm of ideas into the material world. He retained the idea that history was preordained and would reach a perfect state, which for him was not the Platonic or Hegelian organic society but the classless society in which the state would wither away.

For Marx's study of Hegel, see the chapter on Marxism and Education.

John Dewey also studied Hegelian Idealism as a doctoral student at Johns Hopkins University. Like Marx, he would abandon Idealism to create his own Experimentalist version of Pragmatism. However, his great society, much like Hegel's rational state, was one in which private interests would be absorbed in the good of the community based on mutual and reciprocal shared interests.

For Hegel's influence on Dewey, see the chapter on Pragmatism and Education.

Friedrich Froebel's Kindergarten

This section examines how Friedrich Froebel (1782–1852), a nineteenth-century German educator, institutionalized Idealism in the Kindergarten. Froebel's *The Education of Man* (1826) revealed how Idealism shaped his ideas of early childhood education.[14] He saw God both as a personal Creator, in the Lutheran religious sense, and as an all-encompassing Absolute Idea in the Hegelian sense. Human beings, he reasoned, are endowed by their creator with a divine or spiritual essence and with a body that makes them part of the natural physical order. It is the spiritual essence, like the Platonic psyche or soul, that vitalizes humans and leads then to develop their inherent potentiality. Froebel asserted that every child is born with an innate spiritual essence, an interior life force that seeks to be externalized. Through their own self-activity, children externalize their inner spiritual essence.

Froebel emphasized the Idealist metaphysical principle that all ideas were related to and interconnected with each other and both originated and culminated in the great, all-encompassing supreme Idea of God. All existence was united and related in a great chain of being, a universal unity. In educating young children, it was highly important to emphasize the principle of interconnectedness so that children learned they were participants in a great, universal, spiritual community.

Froebel believed that children's growth and development followed the doctrine of preformation, the unfolding of what is present but latent. What the child would be as an adult man or woman was already there but needed to be acted upon. Idealists, like Froebel, often used analogy to explain their highly abstract concepts. Their use of analogy, like Plato's Allegory of the Cave, was a device to help the student move from the known to that which was beyond the known. The child's spiritual essence could be compared to the seed of a plant. Just as the roots, stalk, leaves, and blossoms of a daisy are all present in the seed, the child's spirit contains, in embryo, all that she or he will become as a woman or man. The analogy continued: Just as the seed requires a garden with fertile soil, rainfall, and sunlight to sprout and grow, children, too, need a specially prepared garden, the kindergarten, to grow and develop. Just as the tender sprouts of flowers need a gardener to tend them, children, too, need a kindly, gentle, and caring human gardener, the kindergarten teacher.

Froebel developed his concept of the child, the kindergarten, and the teacher from his early childhood experiences in the Lutheran Church, his introspective reflections on his own unhappy childhood, and his observations of children's activities, especially their play and games. Then, he encased his insights into a philosophy of Idealism. He advised kindergarten teachers to reflect on their own childhood experiences so that they could release the hidden clues about childhood that were locked in their memories. By observing children at play, Froebel and the teachers who followed him could discover the activities and movements that interested and activated children. Then, they could structure these random activities into more systematic learning experiences.[15]

PLAY'S SYMBOLIC MEANING. For Idealists like Froebel, there was always something more to an object, an activity, or an idea than appeared on the surface. Froebel designed a series of objects for use in the kindergarten that he called *gifts*. Among the gifts were balls, spheres, cubes, and cylinders, as well as blocks of various sizes and colors. These gifts, representing fundamental forms, carried two meanings: their actual obvious physical appearance and their important but hidden symbolic meaning. Symbolically, they were intended to stimulate children to bring the fundamental form their physical presence suggested into mental consciousness.[16]

Play was the key to understanding children's development. It was the medium through which children imitated adult occupations and most importantly recapitulated the great epochs in human history. Through play, children imitate adult social and work activities such as cleaning rooms, sweeping floors, serving food, planting gardens, and caring or animals. Like Hegel, Froebel believed the human race, in its collective history, had moved progressively through unfolding stages of cultural development. For example, humans at the earliest stage of their history were cave dwellers; then, they advanced as nomadic hunters and food gatherers living in tents or reed huts; later, as farmers in the agricultural stage, they lived in permanent houses.

Children, in their play, relive the major epochs of history through the process of cultural recapitulation. When they draw pictures on walls, their simple and primitive art is like that of the ancient cave dwellers. As they play at hunting and gathering, they are reliving the human race's nomadic stage.

AMERICAN TRANSCENDENTALISM

In the first half of the nineteenth century, Transcendentalism, an American version of Idealism, significantly influenced society and education in the United States. A revival of Plato's Idealism in England and Kant's transcendental philosophy in Germany entered the thinking of American philosophers, especially Ralph Waldo Emerson and his circle of Transcendentalists at Concord, Massachusetts.

Transcendentalism was named after the philosophy of Emmanuel Kant, a German philosopher, who argued in the *Critique of Pure Reason* (1781) that ideas, or transcendent imperative forms, exist in the mind prior to experience. These preexisting transcendental intellectual structures, similar to Plato's forms or latent ideas, are the mental structures on which people locate their experience and construct concepts. Knowledge is possible because our minds organize and systematize what we experience within a framework of space, time, and substances. Our intuition of space, time, and substance make it possible to comprehend the world.[17]

Transcendentalism: American variety of Idealism developed by Ralph Waldo Emerson in the nineteenth century.

The Transcendentalists believed that even though individuals lived in an imperfect society, they could improve themselves and their society through their relationship to the larger moral universe. Human improvement could be brought about as individual knowledge and deeds corresponded with the universe's higher spiritual and moral principles. A Transcendentalist life and education is directed to take persons to a higher plane of understanding that transcends materialist ambition.

Ralph Waldo Emerson

Foremost among the Transcendentalists, Ralph Waldo Emerson (1803–1882) was the nineteenth century's most prominent American intellectual. He was an unusual blending of essayist, poet, mystic, orator, and philosopher. Emerson's ideas about individualism and self-reliance were so influential in shaping American character that his essays were required reading in high school courses in American literature throughout the nineteenth and twentieth centuries. Emerson's Idealist individualism appealed to Americans who wanted to freely shape their own lives and not be forced to conform to external pressures and authorities. There was no place for external doctrines or dogmas in Emerson's philosophy. The truth came from within the person.

Emerson's Harvard Divinity School Address

Trained as a Unitarian minister, Emerson abandoned denominational Christianity, which he believed had become mired in theology and ritual. Rejecting denominational creeds, he believed that all religions originated in Nature, the universal world religion. In his 1838 address at the Harvard University Divinity School, his alma mater, Emerson argued that philosophy's overriding challenge was to extricate the great doctrines of the higher law, individual freedom, and human progress from traditional dogmas.[18] True religion, he said, comes not from revelation but from intuition from a person's heart and mind. Through the soul, every person can reach the great Mind and Heart of the universe.

Morality, for Emerson, is above and beyond the contingencies of time and the relativism of place and culture. Universal moral laws are in the nature of reality. People intuitively know these laws in their conscience, and personal virtue comes from the reverence and awe of being in the presence of these divine laws. The operations of the interior principle of justice are instant and entire. The person who performs a good action is instantly ennobled, whereas the one who does a mean deed is instantly contracted.

With philosophy as his primary undertaking, Emerson developed the following overriding Transcendentalist principles: (1) Reality originates in, emanates from, and is unified in the **Oversoul**, the Macrocosm, similar to Plato's Form of the Good; (2) each individual possesses a microcosm, an individual spiritual essence, that is vitalized by the spiritual energy that flows into them from the Universal Spirit, the Oversoul; (3) Nature, a universal reality, is the way by which the Oversoul is manifested to human beings, and through Nature we discover the truth that is in us; and (4) we find our truth by our own introspection, contemplation, and intuition of the ideas within our minds.[19] For Emerson, a great spiritual force, the Oversoul, sustains

Oversoul: Emerson's name for the great idea of the universe, the Macrocosm.

and permeates the universe, which emanates and radiates from this divine and benevolent spiritual force.

The individual human being possesses a spiritual soul that is a more limited microcosmic part of the Oversoul, but is made of the same spiritual substance. The Oversoul is too great, abstract, and powerful to be grasped empirically by the senses, which can give us only a partial, limited, and incomplete view of reality. Grasping only what is material, the senses cannot penetrate to reality's deeper spiritual essence and meaning. The human mind, a microcosm, can only begin to approach this spiritual reality by intuition, introspection, and contemplation. The way to grasp this spiritual reality is for individuals to transcend the ordinary world of sensation and find the truth in Nature, the means by which the World Spirit manifested itself. The individual human mind is a conduit through which flows the spiritual, intellectual, and moral energy radiating outward from the Oversoul.[20]

In searching for the truth, Emerson advises us to go beyond, indeed to see through, the everyday world of sensation and consumerism and to look to Nature to find the truth present in our minds.[21] The world of Nature corresponds to the World Mind and to our individual minds. It connects us to the World Mind. If we work at it, we can discover the truth through contemplation and meditation, but we need to overcome the external pressures of materialism and consumerism that distract our quest for the truth.

TRANSCENDENTALISM AS A GREEN PHILOSOPHY. The Transcendentalists were naturalists and environmentalists who anticipated the contemporary "green" movement. Philosophically, Nature, emanating from a benevolent source, the Oversoul, reflects a moral conscience and reveals moral laws. Moral law lies at the heart of Nature and radiates to its circumference. The Transcendentalist idea of Nature seeks to correct the misguided materialist view that Nature is something to be exploited by those who seek profits from tapping into and selling its resources. In many ways, the Transcendentalists were among the country's early environmentalists and conservationists. They regarded America's natural landscape—plains, mountains, forests, rivers, deserts—not only as a rich source of natural resources but also as the means by which people could transcend their own experiences and feel, or intuit, something greater than themselves but of which they were an intricate and unique part. Nature was much more than trees to be cut into lumber or oil and coal to be drawn to the earth's surface for fuel; it was an intricate totality that touched the human spirit.[22] For them, education needs to impress on people that they and the animals and plants, the air and water, are related and connected to each other in a great chain of being. Nature needs to be seen in terms that transcend the material and enter into the poetical—seeing the reflection of trees on the surface of a quiet and glassy lake, for example.

EDUCATION AND "THE AMERICAN SCHOLAR." In "The American Scholar," Emerson directly addressed education. An educated person who enjoys literature and philosophy, the scholar is not bound to his or her desk but also leaves the library to learn from Nature.[23] An Emersonian teacher would use books as intellectual sources and Nature, the natural environment, to stimulate students' search for the truth. Through intuition, the person can grasp the truth, as it is: a unified and integrated whole. As a universalist, Emerson, discounting relativism, saw the truth as one in all places and at all times. When we empirically dissect or deconstruct the truth, its unity, too, is ripped apart. Because it is directed to dissection of physical and natural aspects of reality rather than its totality, science cannot capture the aesthetic beauty of truth. When we transcend the immediate and the partial, we can unite our cognitive knowing and our aesthetic feeling into a unified experience of reality.

Though much of the teacher's language is descriptive and narrative, Emerson advises teachers to also use metaphors, allegories, and poetry to inspire and provoke students' self-reflection. Emerson wrote, "Life is good only when it is magical and musical, a perfect timing and consent, and when we do not anatomize it. . . . You must hear the bird's song without attempting to render it into nouns and verbs."[24]

Applying Emerson's concept of transcendental knowing to education requires us to resist trends that confuse the instantaneous electronic flow of information on the Internet and social media with knowledge. It calls for teachers to expand rather than contract the attention span and to provide the quiet times and the uncluttered spaces that stimulate students to contemplate, meditate, and reflect on their lives, beliefs, and values. Though not in tune with today's flood of instantaneous information and scattered bits of information called factoids, Emersonian teaching involves leading students, through probing questions, to examine themselves and the world in which they live.

Henry David Thoreau

Henry David Thoreau (1817–1862), a member of the Transcendentalist circle in Concord, is known for his memorable account of his search for truth at Walden Pond. The incident that provoked Thoreau's most famous essay, *Civil Disobedience* (1849), was his arrest for refusing to pay the annual Massachusetts state poll tax. He did not want his tax payment to be used to fund the war with Mexico, which he opposed as being an unjust act of aggression by the United States on its southern neighbor. He spent a night in jail rather than pay the tax. For Thoreau, it is an individual's personal ethical obligation to live according to the dictates of her or his conscience, regardless of public opinion or social pressure. To live according to conscience meant that the individual, when necessary, had to dissent from popular opinion, regardless of the consequences. Thoreau affirmed the higher law principle, the right to dissent, and the need to protest against injustice, especially when made official by law. He argued that the individual, as a unique and independent personality, has a conscience that enables him or her to know and to obey the higher law of his nature. Even if a minority of one, the individual, in conscience, is to follow the higher law and cannot abandon it to the state or to majorities. His belief in a higher law and the practice of civil disobedience inspired Mohandas Gandhi, Martin Luther King, Jr., and other later nonviolent protestors against injustice.

Bronson Alcott

Bronson Alcott (1799–1888), the father of Louisa May Alcott, was the foremost Transcendentalist schoolman and teacher. Like Froebel, he believed that children possessed interior spiritual potentialities to know intellectually, to develop physically, and to behave morally. Reflecting the spiritual life force of the universe, education was a process of unfolding what was already present, or enfolded, in children, both as ideas and as moral and physical potentialities. He emphasized the poetical aspects of teaching that he related to the development of children's imagination. One of the earliest powers to develop in children, imagination, much more than mere fantasy or make believe, was stimulated by the child's inner spiritual nature. To stimulate the imagination, Alcott used parables, allegories, fables, fiction, and poetry.[25] Describing his teaching, Alcott said, "I ask and ask till I get something fit and worthy. I am not thinking, generally, of any particular answers. Sometimes I ask because I do not think myself. . . . I seek to assist . . . in finding the answer. . . . All truth is within. My business is to lead you to find it in your own Souls."[26] Louisa May Alcott, the author of *Little Women,* wrote, "My father taught in the wise ways which unfold what lies in the child's nature, as a flower blooms, rather than crammed it . . . with more than it could digest."[27]

IDEALISM AS A SYSTEMATIC PHILOSOPHY

The next section of the chapter examines the following major components of Idealism as a systematic philosophy: (1) metaphysics, (2) epistemology, and (3) axiology.

Idealist Metaphysics

Idealism asserts the primacy of the mental, spiritual, and ideal as the basis of reality. It affirms that reality is essentially spiritual or mental and that our knowledge is about ideas. It also argues that the universe is a manifestation of a highly generalized intelligence and will.[28]

Idealists affirm that individual human beings share and participate in a universal human nature. A person's spiritual essence is her or his essential and permanent characteristic. The spirit (the soul or mind) generates the necessary life force that gives the person vitality and dynamism. Mind is evidenced by doubting; doubting is thinking; thinking gives evidence of the presence of intellect or of mind.

The person's true self is nonmaterial, spiritual, or mental. Selfhood, an integrating core of personal beliefs and values, provides identity for the person because it separates that which *is* from that which *is not* the self.

Reality is spiritual in substance rather than material. Although it may exhibit nonmental entities, the irreducible realities of the universe are spiritual or mental and hence really existent. Spirit is more inclusive than matter and encompasses it. Matter is dependent on spirit, for spirit both energizes and vitalizes it.

Although the spiritual is ultimately real, it is possible to speak of the "real" world and the world of "appearance" in the language of Idealism. The real world of mind and ideas is eternal, permanent, regular, and orderly. Representing a perfect order of reality, the eternal ideas are unalterable because change is inconsistent and unnecessary in a perfect world. It is possible, then, to assert the existence of absolute, universal, and eternal truth and value in contrast to changing sensations or opinion.

In contrast to eternal truth, which is above sensation, the "world of appearance" or of opinion is characterized by change, imperfection, irregularity, and disorder. In terms of the real and the apparent, the educational task is to redirect students from sensation and opinion to the reality of ideas. Just as Socrates and Plato argued against the Sophists' relativism and Emerson opposed crass materialism, today's educators need to encourage their students to undertake the continuous and arduous search for the truth. Today's students need to free themselves from the relativism that says "anything goes." They need to embark on a Socratic journey to find the universal truths that will shape their beliefs and values.

Idealist metaphysics involves a leap from the belief in an individual mind to the assumption that the entire universe is powered by a larger, more comprehensive, universal, and timeless spiritual mind. Through the principle of relationship, the individual mind is related to the minds of other individuals and to the Universal Mind. This spiritual or intellectual relationship makes it possible for the subjective individual mind to know and understand other minds.

Idealists explain the principle of the relationships between minds by using the concepts of the Macrocosm and the Microcosm. Idealists have given various names to the concept of the World or Macrocosmic Mind such as the Ground-of-Being, the Absolute Self, the World Mind, the First Cause, or the Universal. For religious Idealists, the Macrocosm is God or the Creator. Regardless of the name, the Macrocosmic or Absolute Mind, transcending all limiting qualifications, signifies the principle of intelligence that pervades reality. Because the Absolute Mind is underived, complete, perfect, and unconditioned, it does not need to change. The universe is one all-inclusive and complete mind of which the lesser minds are limited parts. The Universal, or

Macrocosmic, Mind can be thought of as an absolute person, which is continually thinking, valuing, perceiving, and willing. The Macrocosmic Mind or Self is both a substance and a process. Although the language may seem vague or poetical, the Macrocosm can be said to be thought thinking, contemplation contemplating, and will willing.

Although the essence of the individual person, the Microcosmic mind or soul is spiritual like the Macrocosm; it is a limited lesser self. A qualitative relationship exists between the Absolute Mind and the individual Microcosmic Self. The individual self, or mind, is a complete entity insofar as it is a self. However, in relationship to the universe, it is part of the whole.

Although subtle metaphysical distinctions run through Idealism in its various forms, the following common principles are the philosophy's underlying basis: (1) The universe is intelligent and spiritual and contains distinctively mental, or nonmaterial, realities; (2) these mental realities are both universal and personal; and (3) the universe is one all-inclusive and complete whole in which the lesser selves are genuinely spiritual and in relationship to the whole.

Idealist Epistemology

In considering Idealist epistemology, it is important to note that the Absolute Mind, the guiding source and principle of intelligence, is eternally thinking. The Microcosmic human mind, though spiritual like the Absolute Mind, is capable of being intelligent, but it is limited in its scope of thinking and valuing. Nevertheless, the individual mind can communicate with and share the ideas of the Absolute Self or the Macrocosmic Mind, whose knowledge is complete. The human mind, present in the individual at birth, has the potential to be intelligent. If properly nurtured and educated, this emerging potentiality grows and develops.

For Idealists such as Plato, knowing is recognition, reminiscence, or recalling of latent ideas that are already present in the mind. By reminiscence, the human mind in its ideas can discover the ideas of the Macrocosmic Mind. For Emerson, a Transcendentalist, the individual through intuition, introspection, and insight looks within his or her own mind and therein finds a copy of the Absolute. Since what is to be known is already present but locked in the mind's subconscious region, the challenge of teaching and learning is to bring this latent knowledge to consciousness.

Idealist Axiology

Since Idealists see the paramount guiding force in the universe as spiritual and intellectual and view human nature as essentially spiritual and intellectual, values, too, are spiritual and intellectual. Because the origin of this spirituality and intellectuality is in a Supreme Supernatural Being or an Absolute Principle, values, like truth, are universal, eternal, and unchanging. What is right, good, just, and beautiful has been so at every time and in every place. For Idealists, values are more than mere emotional likes and dislikes; they are more than cultural preferences; they really exist and are inherent intrinsically in the universe. The truthfulness, goodness, and beauty that make the highest human character are essentially an imitation of the Good, which is present in the Absolute. People make bad choices because they lack perspective and make mistakes, erroneous judgments, in their decisions. Mistakes in choosing what is truly good and beautiful are caused by sensation, opinion, materialism, and confusion.

For Idealists, what is important in making correct value choices are the principles of generality, hierarchy, and perspective. The most general kinds of values are those that are comprehensive, broad, and because of their breadth and depth, cover a wide range of more specific situations. Specific value decisions need to conform to the more general values. Values are not equal to each other—some values are more important than others. There is a hierarchy of values, with the more general ranked higher than the more specific ones. In making value choices, it is important to see the "big picture" rather than be driven by the moment. The big picture comes from a perspective that gives order to time and space. In our search for values, Idealists, especially those informed by Hegel, advise that we should look to the ethical core found in the wisdom of the human race that has persisted over time. Ethical conduct grows out of the permanent aspects of a social and cultural tradition that in reality is the wisdom of the past functioning in the present. Rich sources of value education can be found in history, literature, religion, and philosophy.

For the Idealist, our aesthetic experience comes from the idealization of the world around us. For example, Thoreau found great beauty and meaning in Nature. Great art captures our ideas about what is good and beautiful. Art succeeds when it portrays the idealized representations of what appears commonplace in our life. Good art—literature, drama, painting, sculpture, and music—succeeds when it creates perspective and harmony. Like a work of art, an aesthetic personality is one of harmony and balance. In aesthetic education, the student should be exposed to the great works of art, literature, and music and should try to find the essence that makes them timeless.

Idealist Logic

For the Idealist, logic requires that the part, the individual, or specific element be properly related to or ordered to the whole, the Universal. Truth exists within the Macrocosm, or the Absolute, in an order or pattern that is logical, systematic, and related. Each proposition is derived from and related to a larger and more comprehensive general higher proposition. While the whole includes the parts, the parts must be consistent with the whole.

According to the Idealists, to be, or to exist, means to be involved systematically in the whole–part, or Macrocosmic–Microcosmic, relationship. As an assimilator and arranger, mind locates consistency and exposes inconsistency. The properly functioning intellect seeks to establish a perspective based on relating the parts to the whole. Since it is eternal or timeless, the Whole Mind, or the Macrocosmic Mind is contemplating the universe according to a total perspective that orders time and space. The properly functioning individual mind, striving to imitate the Universal Mind, seeks to fashion a coherent perspective into the universe. The consistent mind, because of its intellectual structures, is able to relate the parts—time, space, circumstance, and event—into a coherent pattern or whole. Inconsistency occurs when the individual is unable to relate time, place, circumstance, and condition into a perspective.

IDEALISM'S EDUCATIONAL IMPLICATIONS

In the following section, we examine (1) the educational goals of Idealism, (2) the school, (3) the Idealist curriculum, (4) the value dimension, (5) Idealist methodology, and (6) the teacher–learner relationship.

Idealism's Educational Goals

The most general goal of an Idealist education is to search for the truth and to use our knowledge of that truth to guide our lives. All other aims come from, are derived from, and are subordinate to that overarching goal. Note that the Truth is singular and not plural. There is one truth, not many claims to or variations of truth. Truth is universal and not dependent on different cultures in different places. Truth is absolute and does not need to be constantly tested and revised. Neither do we make the truth, as Constructivism asserts; rather, it is there, waiting to be discovered. Idealism's absolute, eternal, and universal truth runs against many of the trends in education in the twenty-first century.

To seek the truth and to live according to it means that people must first want to find the truth and then be willing to work to attain it through profound thought, rigorous study, and reflection. To be a truth-seeker means that the student needs to be motivated to begin the journey and is set on the right path to achieve that goal. This path to truth is guided by the following principles: Their spiritual human nature endows all persons, including students and teachers, with an intrinsic dignity. Idealism holds the following implications for education and schooling:

1. Education should assist students to realize fully the potentialities inherent in their human nature.
2. The school, as a social institution, should expose students to the wisdom contained in their cultural heritage so that they can know, share in, and extend it through their own personal contributions.

Critics might argue that the goals of an Idealist education are too abstract and altruistic for today's social and economic realities. It does not train people for jobs, contribute to personal and social adjustment, or equip individuals to succeed in a global technological world. Just as Socrates and Plato combated the Sophists' relativism in ancient Greece and Emerson and Thoreau fought materialism and acquisitiveness in nineteenth-century America, contemporary Idealists contend with materialism, greed, and the trivial pursuit of celebrity today.

Idealists see a genuine education as general rather than as training for a specific occupation or profession. The goal of vocationalism is expertise in job performance and is subordinate to the more general pursuit of wholeness, integrity, and excellence as a human being. While Idealists want people prepared to earn their livelihood and contribute to society's economic well-being, they oppose—as a matter of educational policy—giving vocational training priority over general education. The good lawyer, nurse, and teacher must first be a good human being. If the character of the lawyer is flawed, so will be her or his practice of the law. Acquisitiveness and a crude consumerism are results of what Idealists would diagnose as a major ill of modern times—namely, a lack of wholeness caused by a myopic vision and a limited and blurred perspective. From Plato onward, Idealists have condemned materialism as an obstacle to a true vision of reality. A clear and true vision comes from having a proper distance from the sensory world of things so that one can see ideas, values, motives, and ambition from a broad and long-range perspective. For example, to really see a great painting, the perceiver needs to stand back from the work of art. Standing back enables one to gain a greater perspective. When we are too close to the work of art, we may see color and shape but miss the entirety, the wholeness, of the experience. The Idealist educator, like Plato and Thoreau, is swimming against the tide of immediacy, materialism, and consumerism. The quick immediacy of the sound bite, the email, and the infomercial all work against taking the time and creating the distance needed to establish a perspective on meaning, life, and education. Like Socrates, the Idealist educator does not abandon the mission and float with the current. The teacher does everything he or she can do to provide quiet times to think and settings for probing, but calm, discussion. The teacher works to help students resist the noisy and the immediate so that they can increase their attention span. Regardless of whether we agree with the metaphysical and epistemological underpinnings of Idealism, the sense of perspective and relationship that it seeks to develop is a worthy educational goal.

The Role of the School

Principle of Generality: the principle that more general, abstract, and theoretical ideas and concepts transfer to more situations than specific ones and that specific ideas and concepts should conform to more general ones.

For Idealists, the school's purpose is determined by the universal **principle of generality**, according to which more specific, immediate, and particular goals are derived from those that are higher, more abstract, general, and inclusive. If the primary goal of education is the student's spiritual or intellectual development, then the school's primary function is very clear. Schools are institutions, established by society, for the primary purpose of developing a student's spirituality or intellectuality. Just as God or the Absolute is eternal and universal, the purpose of education, too, is universal and unchanging from generation to generation. All other educational aims are subordinate to the general goal of spiritual and intellectual development. Nothing should be permitted to interfere with or obscure that primary goal.

Idealists like Hegel and Froebel saw human development as the historical evolution of culture from its primitive origins to successive and cumulative stages of higher and more advanced levels of civilization. Throughout the centuries of human history, the core ideas and values remain the same and are conveyed through a growing body of knowledge. Artists, musicians, poets, writers, scholars, and scientists discover the Ideal; their creative insights into reality advance civilization to higher stages of development. The flow of time itself selects those contributions to art, literature, philosophy, music, and science; those contributions that endure over the centuries become classics that speak meaningfully to each oncoming generation. Some books, works of art and music, and philosophical and historical interpretations that seemed so important and enjoyed great popularity for a time, however, do not meet the test of time and become neglected period pieces. They fail to capture the insights into the universal reality.

For Idealist educators, the terms *successive* and *cumulative* have a special meaning for the school and the curriculum. Administrators and teachers are to arrange knowledge into a structured curriculum in which subjects—that is, organized bodies of knowledge—succeed each other in increasingly complex and sophisticated content. As students progress through schooling, their learning is cumulative in that the knowledge attained at one level or grade is added to in the next higher level.

Civilization preserves truth and knowledge by institutionalizing them. In this way, the achievements of each generation are transmitted to the succeeding generation. In particular, it is the task of the school to preserve knowledge by transmitting the cultural heritage in a deliberate fashion by way of systematically ordered, sequential, and cumulative curricula.

Curriculum

Because metaphysics deals with questions of what is ultimately real, it can have a strong influence on curriculum, or the "whatness" of education. What do we hold to be most real and important? How does our belief about reality determine which skills and subjects are taught in the school curriculum? The answers to these questions are based on the major Idealist principles discussed earlier: (1) that which is ultimately real is spiritual or ideational; (2) that which is immediate and particular agrees with that which is more abstract and general; and (3) schools are to cultivate spirituality or intellectuality.

Universal: the assertion that truth and values are unchanging in every place and at every time, in contrast to cultural relativism, which claims that they depend on particular times and places and their cultures.

To these principles that influence curriculum, we re-emphasize Hegel's assumption about human history and culture. For Idealists, inspired by Hegel, human history represents the unfolding or revealing of ideas that are present in the mind of God or the totality of concepts found in the great unifying idea of the Absolute. These ideas, like their source, are eternal, **universal**, and unchanging and not dependent on or relative to changing times, situations, or circumstances. What is good, true, and beautiful now has always been good, true, and beautiful.

These enduring truths and values have been encased in great works of literature, art, and music that have existed and been enjoyed and used by people across the generations. These **classics** are permanent sources of God's or the Absolute's unfolding or revelation to human beings over time. They constitute the knowledge that is of most worth and should form the core of the curriculum. A book's or a song's current popularity is not a criterion for including it in the curriculum. The real test is that of time: Has it captured something that touches people across the ages?

Classics: great and enduring works of art, music, literature, and philosophy that are permanent sources of God's or the Absolute's unfolding or revelation to human beings over time; should form the core of the curriculum.

Throughout history, human beings have organized their knowledge of the Absolute into bodies of knowledge, subject matter disciplines such as theology, philosophy, mathematics, languages, and science. These subjects consist of related concepts, or conceptual systems, that explain reality in an organized and systematic way. The various subject matters represent the varying dimensions of the Absolute that have unfolded and been discovered over time by human beings. However, their cause, origin, and culmination are in the underlying unity. For example, the liberal arts are arranged into many conceptual systems, or learned disciplines, such as history, language, philosophy, mathematics, chemistry, and so forth. However, the highest degree of knowledge is that which sees the relationships of these various subject matters as an integrated unity.

Conceptual systems derived from the Universal Absolute constitute the cultural inheritance, a legacy to which each generation can make a cultural contribution. According to the Idealist principle of a hierarchy of generality, the curriculum is organized in a ladder-like pattern that a student climbs upward, going from the more specific to the higher general level. The more general subject matters rank higher on the ladder of knowledge in that they are abstract and transcend the limitations of a particular time, place, and circumstance. Because they are general and abstract, they can transfer to a wide variety of situations. The more particular and specialized subjects are located downward in a priority based on their derivation and relationship to the more general subjects. For example, the most general and abstract disciplines such as theology and philosophy, which explain humankind's relationships to God and the Cosmos, are elevated to the summit of the hierarchy. Mathematics also ranks at the top of the hierarchy because it is abstract, free of particular content, and universally valid. History and literature, though prominent subjects, are ranked somewhat lower on the curriculum hierarchy. Rather than being free of context like mathematics, they are more contextual in that they deal with persons, either historically situated or fictional, who live in a particular time and place. However, history and literature are value-laden subjects. History, biography, and autobiography can be examined as sources of moral and cultural models, exemplars, and heroines and heroes. History can be viewed as the record of the Absolute unfolding over time and in the lives of persons, especially those men and women of heroic dimension.

Idealists subscribe to the **doctrine of preparation**. The school curriculum is designed to prepare students for adult life. It helps students to develop the skills and knowledge to recognize and, indeed, to want to learn what it is important to learn. Preparation supposes that the adults—the administrators and teachers—who organize the curriculum are knowledgeable experts in their field. Students are immature but eager to learn. The doctrine of preparation implies that teachers, as knowledgeable adults, know what is in the best interests of students to learn, regardless of whether they are interested in learning at that time.

Doctrine of Preparation: the belief that the lower level or stage of education provides students with the skills and knowledge needed for the next higher stage.

For Idealists, the elementary school curriculum cultivates the basic skills of literacy, numeracy, and civility that prepare a person for more advanced learning, especially the study of the classics. In this respect, the Idealists can be considered supporters of basic education (i.e., learning to read, write, and calculate), as these are tool skills that enable one to study the important philosophical, historical, and literary works of the cultural heritage. The Idealists would also accept the use of computer skills as another tool in acquiring knowledge. In art, they would encourage the study of the great paintings and musical compositions for both appreciation and creative inspiration. Civility, defined as a respect for spirituality, learning, and art, also is an important behavior.

Generality: An Idealist principle that more specific, immediate, and particular subjects are derived from those that are higher, more abstract, general, and inclusive.

The principle of a hierarchy of **generality** operates most evidently when organizing the curriculum—the most general and abstract subjects are higher in the curriculum, deserving of the most time and effort. The tool skills learned in elementary school prepare the student to read, study, and discuss the great works of literature, philosophy, politics, and history at the secondary and higher levels. Mathematics, especially algebra, geometry, and calculus, with their high abstract power, also would rank high in the curriculum. Idealists would also include the sciences but with an emphasis on theory. If the Idealist operates from a religious orientation, then the holy and sacred books of the particular religion (e.g., the Hebrew scriptures, the Christian Bible, the Hindu Gita, and the Islamic Koran) would be placed at the summit of the curricular hierarchy.

Idealists can be identified with those who see the curriculum as a body of subjects organized around basic principles. Although subjects are taught as separate disciplines, students are encouraged to develop integrative and interdisciplinary insights into the unity of knowledge. It is thorough knowledge of individual disciplines, however, that makes true interdisciplinary knowledge a possibility.

Idealist Methodology

Idealist instruction is derived from its epistemology in that how we teach and learn should be based on how we know. The thought process is essentially that of recognition, an introspective self-examination in which learners examine their ideas and therein find the truth shared by all others because it reflects the universal truth present in the World Mind. Idealist educators such as Friedrich Froebel, the founder of the kindergarten, have emphasized the principle of the learner's own self-activity. The learning process is made more efficient by the stimulation offered by a teacher and school environment committed to intellectual activity. Immersion in the cultural heritage, via the curriculum, is part of formal schooling, according to Idealists.

The learner's own self-activity is related to his or her interests and willingness to expend effort. Students have their own intuitive self-interests, which attract them to certain acts, events, and objects. With such intrinsic interests, no external prodding is needed. When interest is intrinsic, or internal to the learner, the positive attraction of the task is such that no conscious exertion is needed.

Although learners have their own interests, these are not always important in the long run. Since some learning is difficult, students may quickly abandon their initial enthusiasm. For example, some children begin violin, piano, or ballet lessons with great enthusiasm but drop them when the lessons require more diligent and sustained practice. In the modern world, students may be easily distracted by what appears to be more fun, more colorful, and more dynamic than pursuing a difficult subject or a challenging idea. Playing video games, watching television sit-coms, and texting on social media require less effort and provide immediate gratification, but they only lead to more of the same thing. While some educators advise teachers to mimic what excites students' immediate interests, Idealist teachers, remembering Plato's Allegory of the Cave, would resist the temptation to substitute the trivial for the important. The more the outside world succumbs to the trivial, the more important it is for the teacher to create an alternative environment in the classroom.

Students may be distracted by the world of appearance and may seek ends not genuinely related to their own intellectual and moral self-development. At these times, effort is required when the task does not elicit sufficient interest on the part of students. At such a time, the teacher, a mature model of cultural values, should encourage every student's redirection to truth. After an expenditure of interest and the application of self-discipline, the student may become interested in the learning task. Again, the cultural heritage comes into play to generate the student's interests. The broader the exposure to the cultural heritage, the more likely it is that the student will have many interests. The more interests that are present, the greater will be the possibilities for further self-development.

Although no one particular teaching method can be specified, the Socratic dialogue is highly appropriate in Idealist instruction. The Socratic dialogue is a process in which the mature person, the teacher, acts to stimulate the learner's awareness of ideas. The teacher must be prepared to ask leading questions about crucial human concerns. When using the Socratic dialogue in a classroom situation, the teacher needs to use the group process so that a community of shared interest is created in which all students want to participate. The Socratic method requires skillful questioning on the part of the teacher and thus is not a simple recall of facts that have been memorized in advance. However, this may be a necessary first step so that the dialogue does not degenerate into a pooling of ignorant and uninformed opinions.

Idealist Value Education

Because the ethical core is contained within and is transmitted by the cultural heritage, subjects such as philosophy, theology, history, literature, and art and music appreciation provide rich sources of value. These subjects, which integrate thought and value, are the bearers of the human moral tradition and represent civilization's generalized ethical and cultural conscience. The humanities can be used as sources of cognitive stimulation and also absorbed emotionally to construct models of value. Value, or character, education requires students to learn about worthy models and exemplars so that their styles might be imitated and extended in the students' emerging moral character. Therefore, the student should be exposed to and should examine critically the great works of art and literature that have endured through time.

Idealist character education accentuates the importance of having a sense of **perspective** that comes from studying the great works of civilization. The Idealist sense of perspective can be compared to perspective in art. In a painting, for example, the artist portrays the subject on a flat surface but is able to use her or his brush and oils to convey a sense relationship not only of color and stroke but also of depth, dimension, and distance. In viewing the painting, it is necessary that we stand back a bit so that we can capture the artist's perspective and see the painting as a whole and unified work of art. In addition and more importantly, the artist needs to capture something in the painting that conveys her or his aesthetic insights in a way that is meaningful to the viewer and elicits a response in people across time and place (e.g., the timelessness of the *Mona Lisa*).

Perspective: the process of studying the classics of art, literature, and history to gain a long-range view and understanding of the cultural heritage.

In education, perspective means that the student has learned how to take a long-range view of ethical and aesthetic values rather than acting on fleeting short-term popular images. The sense of perspective is not developed quickly but instead comes from gradual and steady exposure to enduring works of literature, music, and art. It means that the person has developed a sufficient psychic distance to appreciate the wholeness and relationships of ethical and aesthetic choices. By studying the great works of art, literature, and history, students can acquire a sense of perspective that unites them and places them within the cultural heritage.

Developing the Idealist sense of perspective is obviously difficult in the contemporary world of rapid and vivid images and loud sounds that bombard us constantly. Think about how a commercial on television is often more vividly conveyed at higher sound decibels than the rest of the program. The sensual bombardment is instantaneous and works in a way that is contrary to building perspective. It shortens our attention span and gets us to act impulsively rather than taking our time and creating a distance that places things in a relationship of perspective—from the most general and important to the most immediate and least important. Although the contemporary situation is very challenging to the building of perspective through education, the Idealist would seek to inspire us to accept the challenge and run against the tide, as Emerson urged. The more the external society works against building perspective, the more important it is that schools and teachers be agents of helping students to gain it.

Imitation of the model or exemplar is important in Idealist character formation. Students are exposed to valuable lessons based on worthy models or exemplars from history, literature, religion, biography, and philosophy. They are encouraged to study and to analyze the model so that the particular person being studied serves as a source of value. The teacher is also a constant model in that he or she is a mature embodiment of the culture's highest values. Although the teacher should be selected for competency in both subject matter and pedagogy, he or she should be an ethical and aesthetic person who is worthy of imitation by students. Students imitate the model by incorporating the exemplar's value schema into their own lives. Emulation is not mimicry; rather, it is an extension of the good into one's own life.

The Teacher–Learner Relationship

In *Idealism in Education,* J. Donald Butler states that the good teacher should (1) personify culture and reality for the student; (2) be a specialist in human personality; (3) as an expert in the learning process, be capable of uniting expertise with enthusiasm; (4) merit students' friendship; (5) awaken students' desire to learn; (6) realize that teaching's moral significance lies in its goal of perfecting human beings; and (7) aid in the cultural rebirth of each generation.[29]

Building on Butler's list of desirable characteristics, we can say that in the Idealist teacher–student relationship, the teacher has a central and crucial role. The teacher is expected to be a culturally and emotionally mature person who has established a cultural perspective and has integrated various roles into a harmonious value orientation. Although the learner is immature and is in the process of developing a cultural perspective, the teacher is to respect each student's personal dignity. Thus, the teacher should respect the learner and help him or her to realize the fullness of his or her own personality. Because the teacher is a mature model and representative of the culture, the teacher should embody values, love students, and be enthusiastic about the learning process.

Since the school's primary goal is the students' spiritual and intellectual development, the teacher's role is very clear. Teachers are to help students realize their spiritual and intellectual potentiality. More than instructional managers or guides to educational resources, teachers are spiritual and intellectual agents who are engaged in the great moral calling of assisting students in their spiritual and intellectual self-development.

Students, too, are spiritual and intellectual persons who, though they may be immature physically and socially, have the internal power to exercise, activate, and fulfill their potentiality. Like Socrates, expert teachers are dedicated to stimulating students to search within themselves to find the truth that is present in all persons. The true student, aided by the teacher, then is on a spiritual and intellectual journey to discover what is true, and good, and beautiful—first by looking inward and then moving with all the inner resources possible to achieve the fullness of her or his human nature.

MENTORING IN TEACHER EDUCATION. Contemporary teacher education emphasizes the concept of mentoring in which the more experienced, often older, teacher acts as a guide for the inexperienced younger teacher. Some universities have mentoring programs for their faculty in which established senior scholars guide beginning instructors in teaching, research, and publication. The concept of mentoring is not new and can be traced to the Idealist educators. In the history of philosophy, one of the great mentoring situations occurred in ancient Athens when Plato became Socrates' student. Plato learned his philosophical strategy of probing for truth through dialogues—a conversation in which the participants ask and answer each other's leading questions—from Socrates. Plato, in turn, was a mentor for Aristotle. The American Transcendentalist Emerson was a mentor for the young Thoreau. All positive teacher–student relationships have an element of mentoring in them. As mentors, Idealists teachers are to be models of the culture, persons who inspire students and are worthy of their emulation.

My Reflections on Philosophy of Education: An Idealist Scenario

As I reflected on this chapter, I thought about how I might illustrate an Idealist lesson. I considered how a high school English teacher could use literature in illustrating the Transcendentalist principle of the higher law. In my scenario, the teacher is leading a discussion of Mark Twain's *Huckleberry Finn* in a course in American literature. The class is examining the moral dilemma that Huck faces when he must either follow the law of the state—that a slave is property—or the higher law of his conscience that Jim, though a slave, is a free person. Specifically, Huck must decide whether he should surrender the escaped slave Jim to the authorities for return to his slave master or help Jim escape to a free state. Huck's dilemma reveals the apparent conflict between the more general and abstract values and those that are more immediate and particular.

The teacher uses *Huckleberry Finn,* a classic work of the American experience, to represent perennial values. It is important that the teacher place the story in its historical and literary context so that the students are aware of its relationship to the American experience. The relationships of the book to the history of the Dred Scott decision and the fugitive slave law should also be made clear. It is important that the moral dilemma is not obscured by facts but rather that the historical context illustrates the ethical situation.

It is important that students have read the book before discussing it. While welcoming a free-flowing discussion, the Idealist teacher does not encourage misinformation or permit unfounded opinion to obscure the real meaning of the learning episode. Once the students are aware of Mark Twain's own life, the context of the novel, the characters, and the plot, then the serious exploratory learning can take place through the asking of stimulating questions. Avoiding those questions that can be answered with a simple yes or no, the teacher's questions should lead to still other questions—eventually to asking the students: What would you do if you were Huck? Have you faced a situation like that of Huck Finn?

Then, moving to a higher level of generality, the teacher leads the students to consider the conflict between civil law and higher law as a crucial issue that has persisted throughout human history. What should a person do when the law of the state and the dictates of his or her conscience conflict? Is there a distinction between the good person and the good citizen? Should the person follow his or her conscience and take the risks attendant to such a decision? Should he or she seek to change the law? Is the inner law of conscience part of a universal and higher law that binds all human beings?

Once the students have explored the theme of the human conflict presented by Huck's dilemma, other instances of the same conflict can be illustrated by pointing to examples of civil disobedience as practiced by Henry David Thoreau, Mohandas Gandhi, and Martin Luther King, Jr. The moral questions raised by the Holocaust during World War II and the Nuremberg trials of the Nazi leaders can be examined to illustrate the persistence of these broad moral issues. The students can be led to consider the Holocaust in World War II. If you lived in a country occupied by the Nazis and there was a knock on your door and a Jew was standing on your doorstep, would you let him or her in or would you close the door?

CONSTRUCTING YOUR OWN PHILOSOPHY OF EDUCATION

After reading, discussing, and reflecting on Idealism, you can relate Idealism to constructing your own philosophy of education. Have you encountered Idealist teachers and situations in your own education? Are there aspects of Idealism that you plan to include or exclude from your personal philosophy of education? For example, do you believe, like Plato, that universal truth and values really exist, and that good people incorporate these universal standards in their lives?

Conclusion

Idealism, proclaiming the spiritual and intellectual nature of the universe and human beings within it, asserts that the good, true, and beautiful are permanently part of the structure of a related, coherent, orderly, and unchanging reality. Idealist educators advocate for a subject-matter curriculum that emphasizes truths gained from enduring theological, philosophical, historical, literary, and artistic works. The following concepts, rooted in Idealist philosophy, have a special relevance for educational practice:

1. Education is a process of unfolding and developing that which is a potential in the human person.
2. Learning is a discovery process in which the learner is stimulated to recall the truths present within the mind
3. The curriculum, organized as subject matter disciplines, is a repository of the cultural heritage that has evolved through human history.
4. The teacher should be a moral and cultural exemplar or model of values that represent the highest and best expression of personal and humane development.

Questions for Reflection and Discussion

1. Do you believe that Idealism as a philosophy of education is too abstract and removed from the real problems of education to be relevant to today's teachers and students?
2. Why do Idealists reject the assumption that values depend on situations and circumstances? Do you agree or disagree with them?
3. Have you encountered teachers who used the Socratic method? If so, how did they use the method and what were the consequences of its use?
4. Have you had teachers who were exemplary models of the educated person? Why do you think they are models? What was their influence on you?
5. Do you think contemporary culture makes it difficult to see things in perspective and to separate what is important from what is trivial? What do you think teachers should do about this issue?
6. Have you ever had a mentor? What made this person a mentor?
7. In Plato's *Republic,* education was used to sort people by their intellectual ability. Have you seen this kind of selection function in contemporary education? What is your opinion of the selective function of education?

Inquiry and Research Projects

1. Develop an outline for a secondary school curriculum that is organized according to the Idealist principle of a hierarchy of generality.
2. Read Henry David Thoreau's *Walden*. What method and processes did he use to develop his insights about Nature?
3. Devise a lesson plan for a unit on the environment that is based on the Transcendentalist idea of Nature.
4. Develop a bibliography of ten books in American literature that you consider to be classics. Annotate each book with a short statement indicating why it is a classic.
5. In a short description, list the qualities that you would expect in a teacher–mentor.
6. Read an autobiography written by a teacher about teaching or see a movie about a teacher in a school situation. Do you find any evidence that the author acted as a model or a mentor to her or his students?

Internet Resources

For Herman Harrell Horne's classic book, *Idealism in Education,* access http://www.openlibrary.org (http://www.archive.org/stream/idealismed).

For the Development of Absolute Idealism, access http://www.philosophypages.com/hy/5k.htm.

For Hegel's social and political ideas, access http://www.iep.utm.edu/hegel/soc.

For Plato, access www.plato.stanford.edu/entries/plato.

For Emerson, access www.transcendentalists.com/emerson.html.

Suggestions for Further Readings

Ahrensdorf, Peter J. *The Death of Socrates and the Life of Philosophy: An Interpretation of Plato's* Phaedo. Albany: State University of New York Press, 1995.

Annas, Julia. *An Introduction to Plato's* Republic. Oxford, UK: Clarendon Press, 1991.

Bloom, Allan. *The Republic of Plato.* New York: Basic Books, 1968.

Blondel, Maurice. *The Idealist Illusion and Other Essays.* Translated by Fiachra Long. Dordrecht, Netherlands: Kluwer Academic, 1997.

Budner, Rudiger, ed. *German Idealist Philosophy.* New York: Penguin Books, 1997.

Copeland, Matt. *Socratic Circles Fostering Critical and Creative Thinking in Middle and High School.* Portland, ME: Stenhouse Publishers, 2005.

Graham, William. *Idealism: An Essay, Metaphysical and Critical.* Bristol, UK: Thoemmes, 1991.

Henrich, Dieter. *Between Kant and Hegel: Lectures on German Idealism.* Edited by David S. Pacini. Cambridge, MA: Harvard University Press, 2003.

Irwin, Terence. *Plato's* Ethics. New York: Oxford University Press, 1995.

Lilley, Irene M. *Friedrich Froebel: A Selection from His Writings.* New York: Cambridge University Press, 2010.

Myerson, Joel. *Transcendentalism: A Reader.* New York: Oxford University Press, 2000.

Pinkard, Terry B. *Hegel: A Biography.* Cambridge, UK: Cambridge University Press, 2000.

Richardson, Robert D. *Emerson: The Mind on Fire.* Berkeley and Los Angeles: University of California Press, 1995.

Saron, Rene, and Barbara Neisser, eds. *Enquiring Minds: Socratic Dialogue in Education.* Oakhill, Stratfordshire, UK: Trentham Books, 2004.

Schott, Gary A. *Plato's Socrates as Educator.* Albany: State University of New York Press, 2000.

Singer, Peter. *Hegel: A Very Short Introduction.* Oxford, UK: Oxford University Press, 2001.

Stauffer, Deven. *Plato's Introduction to the Question of Justice.* Albany: State University of New York Press, 2001.

Winterer, Caroline. *The Culture of Classicism: Ancient Greece and Rome in American Intellectual Life, 1780–1910.* Baltimore: Johns Hopkins Press, 2004.

Notes

1. Julia Annas, *Plato: A Very Short Introduction* (Oxford, UK: Oxford University Press, 2003), 2–6.
2. Ian Johnston, "Lecture on Plato's *Meno,*" *Liberal Studies,* Vancouver Island University, November 2000.
3. http://classics.mit.edu/Plato/meno.html.
4. John E. Colman, *The Master Teachers and the Art of Teaching* (New York: Pitman, 1967), 28–34.
5. Robert S. Brumbaugh and Nathaniel M. Lawrence, *Philosophers on Education: Six Essays on the Foundations of Western Thought* (Boston: Houghton Mifflin, 1963), 10–48.
6. Allan Bloom, *The Closing of the American Mind* (New York: Simon and Schuster, 1987), 381.
7. For Hegel's biography, see Terry P. Pinkard, *Hegel: A Biography* (Cambridge, UK: Cambridge University Press, 2000).
8. For Hegel's works, see Stephen Houlgate, ed., *The Hegel Reader* (Oxford, UK, and New York: Blackwell, 1998).
9. Peter Singer, *Hegel: A Very Short Introduction* (Oxford, UK: Oxford University Press, 2001), 15.
10. Singer, 21.
11. Singer, 104.
12. Singer, 24.
13. Singer, 45–46.
14. Friedrich Froebel, *Autobiography,* translated by Emilie Michaelis and H. Keatley Moore (Syracuse, NY: C.W. Bardeen, 1889). For a biography, see Robert B. Downs, *Friedrich Froebel* (Boston: Twayne, 1978).
15. Froebel, *Autobiography,* 20–21, 24.
16. Norman Brosterman, *Inventing Kindergarten* (New York: Harry N. Abrams, 1997), 17.

17. Roger Scranton, *Kant: A Very Short Introduction* (New York: Oxford University Press, 2001), 40–43, 129–132.
18. Frederick Mayer, *American Ideas and Education* (Columbus, OH: Charles Merrill, 1964), 165–189.
19. Ralph Waldo Emerson, *Emerson on Transcendentalism* (New York: Continuum, 1994).
20. Ibid.
21. Ralph H. Gabriel, *The Course of American Democratic Thought* (New York: Ronald Press, 1956), 41. koFrederick Mayer, *American Ideas and Education* (Columbus, OH: Charles E. Merrill, 1964), 165–189.
22. For an analysis of Transcendentalism's relationships to environmentalism, see Andrew McMurry, *Environmental Renaissance: Emerson, Thoreau & the System of Nature* (Athens: University of Georgia Press, 2003).
23. For an analysis of Emerson's "American Scholar," see Kenneth Seeks, *Understanding Emerson: "The American Scholar" and His Struggle for Self-Reliance* (Princeton, NJ: Princeton University Press, 2003).
24. Mayer, *American Ideas and Education,* 165–189.
25. Odell Shepard, *Pedlar's Progress: The Life of Bronson Alcott* (Boston: Little, Brown and Co., 1937), 174, 181.
26. Amos Bronson Alcott, *Conversations with Children on the Gospels* (New York: Arno Press, 1972).
27. Madelon Bedell, *The Alcotts: Biography of a Family* (New York: Clarks and Potter, 1980), 132.
28. For an analysis of Idealism, see John P. Strain, "Idealism: A Clarification of an Educational Philosophy," *Educational Theory 25* (Summer 1975), 263–271.
29. J. Donald Butler, *Idealism in Education* (New York: Harper and Row, 1966), 120.

Realism and Education

Aristotle (384–321 BCE), Greek philosopher-teacher who founded Realism.

3

CHAPTER PREVIEW

Realism as a philosophy of education argues that we inhabit a world, an objective order of reality, that was not constructed by us but that we have the ability to know. We can discover the truth about this reality and organize it as knowledge. This knowledge is our best guide to conduct, choice, and action. To begin our discussion, we return to Realism's origins in ancient Greece with Aristotle and then move historically to the Middle Ages to examine Thomas Aquinas's Theistic Realism as a synthesis of Aristotle's philosophy with Christian doctrines. We then explore Realism as a philosophy and consider its implications for education. The chapter is organized into the following major components:

- Aristotle as a founder of Realism
- MacIntyre's revival of Aristotelianism
- Theistic Realism (Thomism)
- Realism's philosophical and educational relationships
- Realism's educational implications

As you read the chapter, reflect on how Realism relates to constructing your own philosophy of education. Did you encounter Realism in your education? Does Realism appeal to you as a philosophy of education? Are there elements in Realism that you plan to incorporate into your own philosophy of education? Are there aspects that you would definitely not include?

ARISTOTLE: FOUNDER OF REALISM

Aristotle (384–321 BCE), a student of Plato, was also a major founder of Western philosophy and education. Plato established Idealism's foundations; Aristotle developed Realism. Aristotle was born in the northern Greek kingdom of Macedonia, where his father, Nichomachus, was court physician to King Amyntas II. Encouraged by his father, a collector of scientific and medical materials, young Aristotle followed his lifelong fascination with scientific research.[1] At age seventeen, Aristotle journeyed to Athens, where he studied for twenty years with Plato. As many students do with their mentor's teaching, Aristotle reinterpreted and revised Plato's philosophy.

Aristotle, a theory builder and philosophical synthesizer, combined his scientific curiosity about nature with Plato's more speculative Idealism. Whereas Plato based his worldview on a perfect and unchanging view of reality that could be glimpsed by philosophers who were expert in metaphysics, Aristotle began his inquiries with his senses and his observations. The young philosopher-scientist

Realism: a philosophy that asserts the existence of an objective order of reality that is independent of the knower but is knowable.

For Plato, see the chapter on Idealism and Education.

was driven by a desire to know how things developed and changed. Aristotle set out to reconcile Plato's theory of perfect forms or ideas with his own findings about natural development.[2]

Aristotle replaced Plato's belief that reality consists of pure ideas, derived from the Form of the Good, with a metaphysical dualism in which reality consists of matter and form. Plato believed that knowing means using intuition to recall innate ideas; Aristotle's epistemology begins with sensation of objects in the environment and is completed by forming, or abstracting, concepts from that experience.

In 343 BCE, Aristotle went to Macedonia as a tutor to King Philip's son, who as Alexander the Great would conquer the then known world. Aristotle returned to Athens and established a school, the Lyceum, where he taught from 336 BCE to 323 BCE.

Aristotle, like Plato, was a philosopher-teacher, whose search for truth led him to research many areas—metaphysics, ethics, rhetoric, logic, natural science, psychology, and language. An early prototype of the traditional university professor, Aristotle closely connected research and teaching. He would do his research, reflect on and digest his findings, and arrive at generalizations that he would transmit to his students in his lectures. Aristotle's teaching, however, differed from Plato's. Whereas Plato, following his own mentor, Socrates, used the dialectical process to probe large questions about reality with his students, Aristotle, who believed that there was much to know, turned to lecturing as an efficient process of transmitting knowledge to students. His treatises, based on his lectures, held important ideas for education; his most significant writings about education are *Metaphysics, Nicomachean Ethics, On Justice, On the Sciences, Political Theory,* and *Art of Rhetoric*. Aristotle died in 321 BCE in retirement on the island of Chalcis.

Aristotle and Scientific Realism

Aristotle was an early research scientist as well as a philosopher. He investigated a range of natural areas—astronomy, meteorology, zoology, botany, and biology—and collected data in all these areas. Although his method was crude in comparison to modern science's controlled experimentation in a laboratory setting, Aristotle made the whole natural world his laboratory. His method involved reviewing what was known about an area of knowledge, identifying questions to be probed, carefully observing and collecting specimens, recording his findings, and then reaching some generalizations or conclusions—all of which remain germane to modern science.[3]

Similar to the contemporary researcher's review of the literature, Aristotle examined the findings of his philosophical predecessors before beginning his own investigations of natural phenomena. His review of earlier Greek thinkers' scholarship served as his point of entry into his own scientific explorations.

From Thales of Miletus, Aristotle learned that the natural world operates according to a plan that humans can discover. From Pythagoras, who used mathematics to explain the universe's harmony, Aristotle learned the need to discover the original principles that explained reality. He became familiar with Anaximander's thesis that nature is a balance of forces. Aristotle was aware of Parmenides' atomic theory and of Heraclitus' belief in a constantly changing reality. Building on the ideas of these earlier Greek philosophers, as well as those of Socrates and Plato, Aristotle began his own lifelong search to discover the nature of reality and how it functioned.[4] He wanted to discover what an object is and how it develops.

Aristotle revised Plato's concept of reality of perfect forms that were outside of human experience. He brought Plato's idea of form into the natural world. Aristotle reconstructed the Platonic principle of a hierarchy of ideas into one in which natural phenomena are organized in a hierarchy that progresses from inanimate objects into those that are animate. At the lowest level—the bottom of the hierarchy—are lifeless things, inanimate objects, such as rocks and minerals. Upward, in the next higher rung, are plants, which, although alive in comparison to inanimate objects, lack many of the powers of the animals. In the animal realm, at the next highest rung, there is a continuous upward progression that culminates in human beings, who, because of their rationality, are positioned at the top of the **hierarchy of natural progression**.

Hierarchy of Natural Progression: Aristotle's arrangement of objects and living thing that begins with inanimate objects at the bottom and rises to living creatures in the higher levels.

Based on his hierarchy of natural progression, Aristotle devised a system to classify and categorize natural phenomena. From the crude but inclusive general categories of mineral, plant, and animal, he developed a more specialized schema of classification that could be finely tuned and calibrated into an immense array of subcategories. The information derived from the study of these subcategories could be classified into biology, zoology, anthropology, anatomy, physiology, and so on. In the Aristotelian system, everything that exists can be categorized and classified.

Running through Aristotle's science is the Realist assumption that we can understand the world objectively. Using our investigations of natural and social reality and our intelligence, guided by rationality, we can discover considerable verifiable information about the world. We can formulate theories about what the world contains and how it works. As we do more research and improve our instruments of investigation, our theories can be revised to become increasingly more accurate; our theoretical revisionism does not change the object we are researching but enables us to refine and clarify our understanding of it. Further, although there are various social uses, and often there are technological changes in how we use objects, these utilitarian factors do not change the nature and structure of objects. In fact, how we use objects depends on their composition.

Contemporary **Scientific Realists** are concerned with investigating the objects in the world to discover their constituent makeup, how they function, and how they may or may not relate to us. They discount the metaphysical aspects of Aristotle's philosophy and instead focus on the empirically observable aspects of reality—that which can be seen, examined, analyzed, and tested. For them, the aim of science is to provide the most accurate descriptions of reality that are available at a particular time. As the scientific instruments of observation are further improved, the findings about reality will become more detailed and give a more complete picture of reality. This means that our scientific knowledge will be revised, made more comprehensive and more accurate, if we continue to pursue objective scientific research. Scientific experimentation keeps filling in the details through improved observation. The more details we have, the more we know and the more accurately our concepts will conform to what is really out there. In genetics, for example, scientists have made significant discoveries about DNA in which we have acquired increasingly detailed information about human genes. Certain combinations of genes result in differences in the physical appearance and health of individuals. Genetic scientists can study these genes and make generalizations and propose principles that can be applied to specific cases. For example, certain genes in certain combinations may cause specific kinds of inherited diseases. By identifying these combinations in individuals, physicians can make accurate diagnoses and prescribe appropriate treatment plans.

Scientific Realism: emphasizes using the scientific method to develop verified assertions about reality, especially from the physical and natural sciences.

KNOWING THE WORLD

Unlike his mentor Plato, who searched for a perfect world beyond the senses, Aristotle began with the natural and social environments in which he lived but continued his search upward to discover the underlying structure of this world in the higher realm of metaphysics. His search led him to formulate the classical suppositions of Realism—we live in an objective order of reality, a world of objects that exists outside of our mind but that we can come to know. Using their senses and their power to reason, human beings can acquire knowledge about objects and develop generalizations about their structure (what they are) and their function (what they do).

Matter and Form

Matter–Form Hypothesis: Aristotle's hypothesis that an object is composed of matter in a form.

For the Pragmatist attack on dualism, see the chapter on Pragmatism and Education.

Dualism: a conception of reality that sees it in two parts.

In explaining the meaning of an objective order of reality, Aristotle developed his **matter–form hypothesis**. All the objects that we perceive through our senses are composed of matter. Matter, the stuff of every object, however, is organized into different objects—rocks, plants, trees, animals—that have different structures, which Aristotle called *forms.* Everything that exists has matter but matter needs to take a form. At this point, Aristotle began to create the dualism—the division of everything into two elements—that is basic to Realism. Recall that for the Idealists, reality possesses a unity—a singularity—a oneness with the Absolute. Now, Aristotle has departed again from his mentor, Plato, in seeing the universe as two elements. Later philosophers such as the Pragmatists would wage a continual battle against Aristotelian **dualism**.

Aristotle also devised two explanatory principles; *potentiality*, which means that matter has the possibility, the potentiality, of becoming something, and *actuality,* which means that when matter takes a form, its potential to become an object is actualized.

So far, Aristotle has given us two essential and necessary components of the objects that comprise the objective reality—their *matter,* their material component from which something is made, and their *form,* or essence, what a thing is, based on its structural component or design.

Matter can become an object by being actualized. How actualization occurs led Aristotle to consider the process of change—what caused matter to move from the potential of being something to actually being it. He explained change through his theory of the four causes: material, formal, efficient, and final. Every object has a **material cause**—the matter from which it is made.

Material Cause: according to Aristotle, the matter that is at the base of an object.

For example, the chair on which you are sitting may be made of wood—the chair's material cause. (We are simply calling the material cause in this instance wood. If we wish we can call it the hard fibrous material from the trunk of a tree made into lumber; we can push this back further into an analysis of its chemistry, if we wish.)

Formal Cause: according to Aristotle, the form that gives an object its structure or design and puts it in a class with similar objects.

The **formal cause** gives the object its structure. In our example, the wood has been structured into a chair, which gives it its definition. We now have a definition, which means we have conceptualized the structural component of the object. In this case, it belongs to the concept of chair—a seat for a person, supported by four legs, and a rest for the person's back. It is in the class of the same objects that have "chairness" about them. The formal cause, or form, constitutes the essence of an object, what it needs to be in a particular class of objects.

Efficient Cause: according to Aristotle, the agent who actualizes matter's potential to become an object.

Final Cause: for Aristotle, the purpose for which an action is done or an object is made.

Although chairs may be made of wood, metal, or plastic and come in different colors, these are accidental or incidental in that they do not constitute the essence of what is always needed to be a chair. It is the essence that is the object of our intellectual knowledge. The **efficient cause** refers to the agent who actualized the matter's potentiality. In the case of the chair, it is the woodworker who made the wood into the chair. The **final cause** is that purpose for which the action is done. For the woodworker, the final cause is making the chair.

Teleological: the philosophical assumption that everything has a design to realize its intrinsic purpose or end.

Aristotle's belief that we live in a purposeful universe rests on his conception of causation, the movement from potentiality to actuality. Aristotle's emphasis on a purposeful universe is **teleological** in that everything is moving toward its end, or built-in, goal.

What occurs in Nature—the seasons of the year, the sprouting and growing of plants from seeds, and human conception, birth, and growth—are all meaningful, not accidental or random, processes that are purposeful. They are moving toward an end during which potentiality is actualized. Aristotle's affirmation of a purposeful universe supposes that there is a First Cause, a principle of rationality that operates in a purposeful way in the universe. The reality of an orderly and purposeful universe has immense implications for education. It means that human life has a purpose and is meaningful rather than meaningless. It means that human beings, inherently defined as rational beings, can realize their potential. The meaning of human life in Aristotelian terms is the pursuit of happiness, defined as the fulfillment of all human potentiality, especially the power and quality of reason. In Aristotelian terms, the purpose of education is to cultivate, to develop, and to exercise each child's potentiality to be a fully rational human being.

EPISTEMOLOGY AS SENSATION AND ABSTRACTION. Just as he had divided reality into two parts, form and matter, Aristotle's epistemology is also dualistic and divided into two sequential phases: sensation and abstraction. **Sensation** is the process human beings use to acquire sensory information and data about the material, the matter, of an object. **Abstraction** is the process we use to sort out sensory information and extract the necessary qualities, the essence, of an object that makes it what it is. When we have discovered these necessary qualities we have formed a concept about an object.[5] We first begin our process of knowing through our senses, our bodies' physical organs that bring us into contact with objects. Our eyes give us sight of an object, our nose its smell, our ears its sound, our tongue its taste, and our fingers its tactile qualities. Our senses, perceiving the matter of the object, carry information about the object's size, color, hardness or softness, sound, and other data to our minds.

Sensation: the process by which the senses convey impressions about the external world to the mind.

Abstraction: in Aristotelian cognition, the process by which the mind forms concepts by extracting from sensory information what is necessary for them to be what they are.

Somewhat like a computer, the mind sorts out information into those qualities or conditions that are always present, or necessary to the object, as distinct from those that are sometimes or occasionally found in the object. The **necessary conditions** that give us the idea of an object's form are the basis of a concept.

Necessary Conditions: characteristics that are always present in a particular class of objects, hence necessary for them.

For Aristotle, a concept is based on the formal or essential qualities abstracted from an object. These are the qualities that it shares with other members or individuals of its class but with no other objects.

To illustrate Aristotle's process of **conceptualization**, we can return to our example of a chair. Chairs come in a variety of sizes—children's chairs and adult chairs—colors, and materials. Their styles are variations on a theme—straight back, Windsor, Hitchcock, folding, Shaker, and so on. Underlying these differences that appear to the senses, the mind is able to abstract a common set of conditions that are necessary for an object to be a chair—a seat for a person, supported by legs, and a rest for the person's back.

Conceptualization: for Realists, a twofold process of sensation and abstraction by which the human mind arrives at concepts.

Aristotle's epistemology carries educational implications for instruction. Because we know through our senses and abstraction, we should use this pattern as the basis of our teaching. Instruction—teaching and learning—should provide occasions for students to examine, observe, and deal with objects. It should provide situations in which students create categories of objects that share certain essential characteristics and also recognize those objects that are similar and different.

Dualism

Dualism, seeing reality as composed of two constituent elements, is a very important concept in Aristotle's philosophy. Dualism means that two related entities exist, neither of which can be reduced to the other. For example, mind and body are two separate entities. Metaphysical dualism asserts that the two essential components of reality, while related, remain distinct. Thus, Aristotle viewed existence as the uniting of the two elements of actuality and potentiality, of form and matter. This dualistic conception of reality profoundly affected Western thought. Human beings are viewed as composite creatures made of spirit and matter, or mind and matter. Such a dichotomous view of human nature leads to distinctions that have significant educational consequences. Knowledge can be separated into the theoretical and the practical arts; aesthetic experience can be viewed as dealing with either the fine or applied arts; education can be categorized as either liberal or vocational. In the context of these Aristotelian dualisms, that which is abstract, theoretical, fine, and liberal takes priority over that which is practical, applied, and vocational. In the chapter on Pragmatism, we will examine John Dewey's attack on dualism.

Substance: for Aristotle, that which is essential and necessary for an object.

Accident: a variable and nonessential characteristic of something; for example, people have eyes but they may be blue, brown, or gray.

The Aristotelian conception of a dualistic universe can also be seen in the categories of substance and accident. **Substance** is the ultimate "element," that which exists of and by itself, of which any object is made; it is the underlying reality to which the primary qualities of an object adhere. Substance is the continuing essence of an object that remains constant through all the alterations in the object's accidental characteristics. In contrast, **accident** refers to the variable changes that do not alter the essence of a being but individuate it.

For their view of change, see the chapter on Pragmatism and Education.

In various treatments of Pragmatism, which is examined later in the book, one encounters the statements that everything is constantly changing or that the only reality is change. The Realist offers the counterargument that to measure change, there must be some stable object that is changing. The important question is: What is changing? For the Realist, that which undergoes change is substantial, whereas the changes themselves are accidental. For example, all human beings share a common rational human nature, which is their essence. Particular persons, however, are of different races, ethnic groups, weights, and heights. These individualizing characteristics are accidents.

When Aristotelians refer to the essence of a human being, they mean those substantial elements that are unchanging, regardless of time, place, and circumstances. It is from these universals that educators should establish the curriculum. For example, Aristotelians define humans as rational beings who possess an intellect that enables them to abstract from experience, to frame generalizations, to structure alternatives, and then choose and act on them. Regardless of their race, nationality, sex, or ethnicity, all human beings have the power to reason. Nevertheless, particular persons live at different times and in different places. Varying environmental and social conditions contribute to cultural variations within the common human experience. Although a particular person may be American, Chinese, Russian, or Nigerian because of the accident of being born in a particular place, all people share a common human nature. As a result of being born in a certain location, some people will speak a particular language, such as English, Russian, Swahili, or French. But regardless of their particular languages, all people use language as a means of communication.

ARISTOTLE'S *NICOMACHEAN ETHICS*

In *Nicomachean Ethics,* Aristotle examines the relationship between knowledge and virtue and human nature and psychology. After observing particular situations involving human personal, social, and political relationships and behavior, Aristotle arrived at generalizations based on his observations. Along with other animals, humans share the functions of respiration, nutrition, locomotion, and reproduction. But as more complex and sophisticated beings, humans also have functions of sense, imagination, habit, pain, and pleasure. Following his dualistic worldview, Aristotle described the two planes of human existence: the rational and the emotional. As rational beings, humans are abstractive, symbolic, and choice-making creatures. However, a nonrational component also exists in human nature in that the same person who is rational is also emotional and volitional. The human being's reason for being is to recognize, cultivate, develop, and use his or her rationality. The greatest source of human happiness lies in the active cultivation of rationality, which contributes to self-actualization or self-cultivation and self-perfection. The person who truly acts as a human being is governed by his or her highest and defining power—reason. Although emotions are the means to experience pleasure and will is the instrument of obtaining ends, both the emotions and the will should be governed properly by reason. When governed by appetites, emotions, and will, the human being acts unintelligently, is unreasoning, and debases his or her own essential humanity. When governed by reason, human beings can realize or actualize the excellence of moral character.

We live in a purposeful and orderly universe and so our actions, too, should be purposeful. In human character formation, ethical behavior originates in predispositions, early habits learned from parents and teachers, that incline us, as children who have not yet developed our rational potentiality, to virtue. An important predisposition to virtue is coming to understand that what we do will have a consequence.

Aristotle's philosophy is permeated by a teleological perspective. Metaphysically, there is purpose and order in the universe that is directed to an end. As part of that universe, human beings, too, have a purpose. Concerning virtues and practices, ethics begins with individuals where they are in the present moment and projects what they might become, if they cooperate in actualizing their potentiality. Ethics offers the prescriptions, the guidelines, on how individuals can achieve the good life if they are willing to develop the virtues and perform the practices that achieve the fullest potential of their nature.[6] Our desires and emotions are to be ordered by cultivating those virtues and habits that lead to our true end.

Virtues are universal in that they are based on the general human purpose of seeking to realize the good that is potentiality available to all people. For Aristotle, this good is signified by the Greek term, ***eudaimonia***, which means the state of being well and doing well in all that is human.[7] While the nature of virtue is universal, virtues are exhibited locally in that their general universal purpose is shared by human beings who live in communities, or social contexts, in different times and places.[8] Although virtues are experienced and exhibited in contexts, values, because of their universal origin and purpose, are not relative. Aristotle, like Plato, believed that the good person lives in the good polis, or community.[9] The overall goal of the practice of virtue is the well-lived harmonious and integrated life. The virtuous person is educated (has the knowledge) to make good and right decisions and has the practical wisdom to take good and right actions.[10]

Eudaimonia: Greek term that means a person is doing well in all the human potentialities.

Aristotle provides the important ethical guideline of taking the middle course and acting in moderation, avoiding extremes of unbridled expression and stifling repression. For example, the admirable virtue of courage lies in the middle and avoids the excesses of being foolhardy or rash or being cowardly and overly timid.[11]

Aristotle organized values into moral and intellectual virtues. A moral virtue is a habit by which the individual makes prudent choices, those that any rational person would make. For example, the prudent person would develop a balanced diet based upon the consumption of foods that promote physical health and well-being. Gorging oneself leads to obesity, which has deleterious consequences for health such as impaired circulation, diabetes, and other illnesses. At the other extreme, starving oneself into a state of anorexia impairs health by depriving the body of proper nutrition.

Aristotle, like his mentor Plato, was motivated by an intense desire to know the truth and to acquire knowledge. He believed that his desire for the truth was not his alone but was shared by all other human beings. As reasoning beings, humans came to philosophy, the love of wisdom. Indeed, he saw the greatest human activity and the source of human happiness to be the intellectual engagement with reality.[12] The intellectual virtues contribute to the perfection of the human intellect or power of reason that makes it possible to discover the truth that is genuine knowledge. Aristotle, a consistent categorizer and classifier, subdivided knowledge into three categories: theoretical, practical, and productive. Theoretical knowledge is the highest form of knowledge in that its end is the truth. Practical knowledge guides us in our political and social affairs, advising us about moral and ethical decisions and actions. Aristotle was the least concerned with productive knowledge about how to make things.[13] Realist educators, like the founder of their philosophy, give the highest priority to theory that, for them, is the surest guide to rational choice and ethical behavior.

FORMING POSITIVE HABITS. The concepts of *habit* and *habituation* are important in Aristotle's ethical theory and in his idea of character education. A habit arises from the predisposition to want to do something or to take an action and is formed by practice. For example, we learn to be courageous by (1) having examples or models of courage; (2) wanting to, desiring, to be courageous; and (3) performing courageous actions and taking pleasure in doing them. Though it arises from a natural human capacity, courage, as a habit, is acquired. Over time, habits become habituated, or ingrained, in a person's character so that we can say that a particular person is courageous.

Polis: the Greek word for the city-state, the social, political, cultural, and educational community.

For Aristotle, cultivation of both intellectual and ethical virtues takes place in human community. In the ***polis,*** the Greek locus of the human community, shared perceptions of human life arose. The city-state, Aristotle argued, exists so that its inhabitants have a place to experience happiness or to live well. The city-state's constitution and laws should foster knowledge and virtue. As it cultivates proper virtues, education works to create a commonality of shared ideas and values that unite a city's citizens.[14]

Aristotle and the Liberal Arts and Sciences

One of ancient Greece's most significant legacies to Western education, to which Aristotle contributed, is the liberal arts and science tradition. Aristotle was familiar with the Greek curriculum of higher education, which included grammar, rhetoric, literature, poetry, mathematics, and philosophy. Intrigued by science, his curiosity led him to the natural sciences—biology, botany, physiology, and zoology—areas that he developed in his own teaching and writing. Aristotle's system of classification of objects and of creating bodies of information about them helped organize the liberal arts and sciences. It is these bodies of knowledge that make a person liberally educated or free to make rational choices. Over time, people constructed vast arrays of related concepts that became a storehouse of knowledge and provided a cognitive map of reality. The liberal arts and science tradition of education profoundly shaped Realist and Thomist philosophies of education that are discussed in a later chapter.

For the importance of the liberal arts tradition, see the chapters on Essentialism and Perennialism.

THE REVIVAL OF ARISTOTELIAN PHILOSOPHY

Alisdair MacIntyre (1929–) is a leading voice in the contemporary revival of Aristotle's philosophy. He reaffirms Aristotle's metaphysical belief in a general rational human nature in which is embedded an intrinsic purpose (a goal and end). The purpose of life is to realize excellence—being excellent in all that relates to being a human being. Human beings have an end toward which they are directed by reason of their nature; it is this end that enables traditions and practices to function.[15]

A virtue, for Aristotle as well as for MacIntyre, means that the person has a good habit that inclines her or him to excellence. Our values, or virtues, express a persisting and continuing human nature that operates in the lives of individuals and communities. This general human purpose and the virtues that exemplify it take place historically in the traditions that arise in cultural contexts over time. Philosophy does not stand apart from its history but is about the moral traditions in which humans have sought to realize their nature. This living out of their general human nature generates "practices" that take place within traditions.

MacIntyre's reassertion of Aristotle's ethics opposes trends in contemporary value theory such as **emotivism and ethical relativism**. He rejects the view that values relate only to present situations and are merely assertions of emotional preferences—likes or dislikes—based on our desires. Value conflicts, too, are more than linguistic controversies over how we express our likes or dislikes.

Emotivism and Ethical Relativism: the assertion that values are emotional preferences or responses to particular situations.

Arguing against ethical relativism, MacIntyre contends that philosophies that ignore the importance of tradition are fragmented and incoherent. Understanding a tradition provides an explanation of how ideas and values were expressed and developed in a cultural context. While reasoning is an inherent power of humankind's general universal nature, this rational potentiality is manifested in societies that create their own traditions. A tradition provides a worldview that reflects a society's history and practices.

MacIntyre's interpretation of Aristotle's philosophy is rich in its educational implications. Education, like human life, has a general purpose; it is to provide the knowledge needed for rational decisions and to cultivate the virtues and practices that enable individuals to fulfill their potentialities and to live the good life. Societies establish schools as educational institutions that provide an academic setting in which ideas and values are introduced, developed, and examined. In these settings, students learn that the good life is one that is rationally examined. Teachers, within schools, operate from a set of historically derived traditions.

Good teachers know that their own lives as well as the lives of their students should be guided by knowledge and virtues that exemplify the good life. Good teachers need to be virtuous individuals who are expert in the practices of educating students. Guided by Aristotle's principle of moderation, their relationships to students follow the mean of avoiding the excesses of being authoritarian and repressive and of being overly permissive and letting anything go on in the classroom.

Good practices are those that relate to and fulfill humankind's overriding and defining purpose. Teachers need to know where their students are in their intellectual and ethical development and to use the good practices that will enable them to fulfill their potentiality.

An outcome of good teaching practices is that students develop the sense and skill of practical wisdom—the desire and capability of applying knowledge and virtue to their decisions in life.[16] Exercising practical wisdom means that the student has acquired the knowledge needed to formulate good and right decisions and to take the appropriate actions that will achieve the end desired. As students continue to make good and right decisions, they become habituated to doing what is good or right.[17]

MacIntyre's exposition of Aristotelianism emphasizes the relationship between virtues and practices. He defines a **virtue** as the possession and exercise of "an acquired human quality" that "enables individuals and societies to achieve those goods . . . internal to practices." The absence of a virtue "effectively prevents us from

Virtue: an inclination and disposition to do that which leads a person to the good life.

Practice: a well-defined skilled human activity that realizes value and contributes to excellence.

achieving any such goods."[18] For him, a **practice** is a coherent, complex, and socially cooperative activity that realizes good results through the activity itself or in the ends that the activity achieves.[19]

The medical knowledge, skills, and ethics that doctors use in treating patients is an example of a practice. The practice of medicine seeks to heal people who are sick. It is a virtue itself (internally) to heal sick people and this internal purpose is informed and exemplified by the higher and more general human purpose of living a good life. Then the practice of medicine can be related to the community and to a public policy that provides for medical schools that train physicians in the practice of medicine and hospitals in which physicians can practice the arts and skills of healing. A medical practice that has a good and right aim to heal people becomes rational when the practice is informed by knowledge about the human body—by disciplines such as anatomy, physiology, chemistry, epidemiology, and so forth. The practice of medicine, law, or education is informed by the practices and traditions that have functioned in a given community over time.

As a practice, or a profession, teaching requires a body of knowledge, sets of skills, and standards of ethics. The ethical teacher evaluates students' performance according to standards that come from practice, that is, to teach a student to read or to calculate. The just teacher judges a student's performance on his or her mastery of the skill or body of knowledge. It would be unjust to make that judgment on a student's appearance, height, or weight or factors extraneous to these standards of practice.

THEISTIC REALISM OR THOMISM

Theistic Realism: also known as Thomism; developed by Thomas Aquinas in the thirteenth century as a synthesis of Aristotle's natural realism and Christian doctrine.

Theism: the belief in the existence of a supernatural and omnipotent God.

We now turn to **Theistic Realism**, a synthesis of Aristotle's natural Realism and Christian doctrine developed during the Middle Ages. Realism's belief in an objective order of reality and the capability of human beings to acquire knowledge of it applies to Theistic Realism. In addition, we add the term **Theism**, the belief in the existence of an omnipotent, omniscient, and personal God who created the world and all its creatures, including human beings and keeps them in existence.

Theistic Realism represents the fusion of the ideas of Greek rationality, represented by Aristotle, and Christian theology. Although Christianity had earlier entered the Western world in the Roman period, Christian intellectuals, or scholastics, such as Thomas Aquinas, worked to formulate a rational organization of religious doctrines to render them logically coherent and philosophically meaningful.

Thomism, Theistic Realism's dominant form, has been associated historically with Roman Catholicism; however, not all Theistic Realists or Thomists are Roman Catholics. Also, not all Christians are Theistic Realists. Saint Augustine and other fathers of the Christian Church subscribed to Idealism. In addition, some philosophers associated with Christianity have been Existentialists.

THOMAS AQUINAS: FOUNDER OF THEISTIC REALISM

The development of Theistic Realism by Thomas Aquinas (1225–1274) can best be understood in the context of the scholastic movement that began in CE 1100 and reached its zenith in the thirteenth century. Scholasticism, the doctrines articulated by religious scholars, developed when some of the ancient Greek classics, including Aristotle's philosophical works, were rediscovered and studied in Western European schools and universities, especially the University of Paris. Scholastic philosophers such as Anselm of Canterbury (1033–1109), Bernard of Clairvaux (1091–1153), Peter Abelard (1079–1142), Albertus Magnus (1200–1280), and Thomas Aquinas sought to create a synthesis of Greek rationalism, especially Aristotle's philosophy, and Christian doctrines.

The philosophy developed by the Scholastics should be viewed in terms of the hierarchical system of governing the Christian church and its doctrines. The Bible, the writings of the church fathers, the councils of the church, and the body of tradition were authoritative sources for Western (Roman or Latin) Christianity. From these sources, doctrines were articulated, interpreted, and enforced by church councils. As the primary medieval educational agency, the church, through its teachers and schools, transmitted the corpus of Christian doctrine to Western men and women. According to the medieval scholars, the church's divinely sanctioned teaching authority rested on sacred scripture and inspired doctrine.

From this body of theological doctrines, certain basic beliefs that characterized the Christian life can be identified. God is an omnipotent, perfect, and personal being who created all existence; human beings, possessing a spiritual soul and a corporeal body, were created to share in divine happiness. Endowed with an intellect and a will, the human being has freedom of choice. Because of Adam's sin, his descendants, who inherited the legacy of original sin, were spiritually deprived. God sent his son, Jesus Christ, to redeem humankind through his death and resurrection. To aid human beings in achieving salvation, Christ instituted the church and charged it with administering the grace-giving sacraments. These core Christian beliefs held great importance for medieval education and continue to influence contemporary Roman Catholic education.

Scholastic philosophy and education reached its high point in the writings of Saint Thomas Aquinas, a Dominican theologian. Born into an Italian noble family, Aquinas was enrolled at the age of five in the Benedictine abbey of Monte Cassino, where he received his education. Between the ages of fourteen and eighteen, he attended the University of Naples, where he studied Aristotelian philosophy. Aquinas entered the Dominican order, studied at the monastery of the Holy Cross at Cologne from 1246 to 1252, and was ordained as a priest. In 1252, he entered the University of Paris, Western Europe's major theological center, where he taught and earned his master's degree in theology. In 1256, he became a professor of theology. From 1269 until 1272, he wrote *Summa Theologiae*, his most important philosophical work, which sought to create a synthesis of Aristotelian philosophy and Christian doctrine.

In the tradition of medieval scholasticism, Aquinas was both a theologian and a philosopher. Using both faith and reason, he sought to answer questions dealing with the Christian conception of God, the nature of the universe, and the relationship between God and humans. A philosopher-theologian, Aquinas devoted his life to reconciling the claims of faith and reason.

Following Christian doctrine, Aquinas asserted that the universe and life within it had been created by God, a supreme being who, in creating human life, had endowed it with an immaterial and deathless spiritual soul, which is the basis of human self-awareness and freedom. God had also given human beings a physical body, which on earth is temporal, that is, existing at a particular time and in a particular place. Although the human being lives for a time on earth, the purpose of life is that the soul should live eternally with God in heaven.

Like Aristotle, Aquinas construed human beings to be rational creatures distinguished by their intellectual powers. Again, like Aristotle, Aquinas asserted that human knowledge begins with sensation and is completed through conceptualization or abstraction. However, the natural process of knowing is enhanced by the human being's cooperation with supernatural grace and acceptance of the truth of Christian doctrine.

Again, like Aristotle, Aquinas held a teleological conception of the universe, agreeing that the universe functioned in a purposeful way rather than by mere chance or accident. Human history—indeed, every person's life—expresses purposeful movement toward a goal. Aristotle saw the "good life of happiness" as the human being's reason for existence. While accepting the good life as the human being's purpose on earth, Aquinas believed in an even higher purpose—the beatific vision, or the experience of being in the presence of God.

Thomism's Theological and Philosophical Bases

While accepting much of Aristotle's Natural Realism, Thomists also embrace supernaturalism and find revelation, recorded in the Bible, to be an authoritative source of divinely inspired truth. Thomists assert that human beings have as their ultimate goal the beatific vision of God, which is the final, highest, and most complete happiness. However, through their own actions, human beings sinned and were alienated from God, their creator. This "estrangement" or "alienation" was overcome through the redemptive act of Jesus Christ, the son of God, who instituted grace and founded a new "people of God." As a free agent, the individual can choose either to cooperate with or to oppose the work of his or her own salvation.

Because it draws from both Aristotelian Natural Realism and from Catholic Christian theology, Thomism represents the interpenetration of the two. Thomism asserts a dualistic view of reality, which has both a spiritual and a material dimension. Possessing both a body and a soul, human beings exist on both a supernatural and a natural plane. God, the first cause and creator, the source of all existence, is a personal and caring creator, not an impersonal "ground of being."

William Cunningham, in *Pivotal Problems of Education,* referred to this synthesis of Realism and Theism as "Supernaturalism." He asserts that human beings, possessing a soul and body, are properly guided by faith and reason. For him, education has a perennial and unchanging character. For Cunningham, an educational philosophy founded on Supernaturalism can specify educational aims in terms of human origin, nature, and destiny. Humankind originated from God through the act of creation; human nature was created in God's image and likeness; the human destiny is to return to God.[20]

Thomism and Knowledge

Aquinas agreed with Aristotle that rationality is one of the human being's highest powers. Through conceptualization, we can formulate plans and structure ends. Through art, science, and technology, we can use our intelligence to humanize the material environment.

Aquinas agreed with Aristotle that humans act humanely when they reason. However, Aquinas qualified his agreement; while reason is the human being's highest and most satisfying earthly power, it nevertheless provides incomplete and imperfect happiness. Perfect happiness comes only after the death of the body when, through the gift of divine elevation, the human being experiences an immediate cognitive and affective union with God.

Thomist educators, like most Realists, emphasize the intellectual function of the school as an agency designed to cultivate and exercise human reason by the transmission of subject-matter disciplines. For Thomists, a subject-matter discipline is called **scientia**, which means that it is a body of accumulated, demonstrated, and organized knowledge that is arranged in a deductive hierarchy based on first principles.

Scientia: a form of knowledge, in Thomism, organized in a deductive hierarchy based on first principles known to be true and logically developed and illustrated by analogies, cases, and examples.

For Thomists, such subject matters are organized on the basis of major premises that are either self-evident or derived from experimentation or from a higher science. These bodies of knowledge are transmitted by teachers, who are expert in the disciplines they teach to students and are expected to use their intellectual powers in understanding, mastering, and applying the principles contained in the subject matter.

The interpenetration of Realism and Theism in Thomistic philosophy has pronounced educational implications. Education has complementary aims based on human nature: to provide the knowledge, exercises, and activities that cultivate both human spirituality and human reason.

Moral Education

Thomist education is deliberately committed to cultivating supernatural values. In its goal of forming Christlike individuals, it encompasses religious and theological studies. Value formation that takes place in religious studies is also reinforced by the school milieu and activities that involve an exposure to religious practices, habits, and rituals.

Aquinas was careful to point out, however, that knowledge does not necessarily lead to morality. Although a person may know the principles of religion and may know about religious observance, knowledge cannot be equated with goodness. However, intelligent men and women can distinguish between moral right and wrong in making choices. The exercise of freedom means that every person possesses the ability to frame, recognize, and evaluate alternative courses of action.

In the Thomist context, similar to the Aristotelian one, moral education is a process of habituating the learner to a climate of virtue. Such an environment should contain models of value worthy of imitation. The Christian school milieu should provide the exercises and conditions that help to form dispositions inclined to virtue.

Curricular Implications of the Thomist Conception of Human Nature

Aquinas defined the human being as a "spirit-in-the-world," an incarnate spirit who also possesses an animated body. Unique among creatures, human beings are composed of both corporeal and spiritual substance and live between two worlds, with their souls situated on the boundary between heaven and earth. Possessing an immortal, deathless, and immaterial soul that vitalizes each person's self-awareness and freedom, the soul's embodiment affords each person a historical time and a social and political place, or temporal and spatial contexts, in which to know, love, and choose.

In continuity with nature, all people create their own personal biographies over the course of their lives. The human being is a social creature who is born, grows, matures, and dies within families and communities. As social beings, humans have developed communication systems, such as speaking, writing, and reading. These communication systems, needed in community life, are acquired and must be learned. As social agencies, schools contribute to human development as they encourage reasoning, communicating, and participating in community life.

Thomists recognize that people live in a particular place at a particular time. Because of historical variations and social adaptations to changing conditions, various cultures, societies, and polities exist. While recognizing these variations, the Thomist, rejecting culturally relative truth and values, asserts that the commonality of human nature and culture is more important than these variations. All people possess a common human nature as a result of the underlying spiritual and material realities in which they participate. This assertion makes it possible to speak of universal human rights and responsibilities. Thomists contend that culturally or situationally relative theories of ethics evade the claims that universal moral and ethical standards should have on us.

The Thomist conception of human nature, or "spirit-in-the-world," provides a curriculum rationale in which the principle of the hierarchy of generality operates. Note that this principle is also found in Idealism and Natural Realism. Those aspects of existence that are most general, abstract, and durable are located at the summit of the hierarchy. Those aspects of life that are particular, specific, and transitory are located in a lower position. Subjects leading to spiritual growth and formation such as theology and scriptural and religious studies receive curricular emphasis. Because the person as a rational being is a free agent, knowledge that cultivates reason, such as philosophy and logic, is emphasized so that each person will be prepared to exercise freedom of choice. And because humans live in a natural and a social environment, knowledge and skills that sustain economic well-being should be included in the curriculum.

Living in society, people need knowledge of legal, political, and economic systems that contribute to personal and social well-being. Because we are social and communal beings, the language and literary skills that contribute to communication and community are also a major foundation of formal education. The skills of reading, speaking, and writing are an important part of every person's basic education.

The Thomist Teacher–Learner Relationship

Thomist educational philosophy provides useful definitions of and distinctions between education and schooling, and thinking and learning, even for those who do not share its theological premises. Although they recognize that education and schooling are related concepts and processes, Thomists carefully distinguish between education, the broader and more inclusive concept, and schooling, its more limited form. These distinctions help to define areas of competence and responsibility for teachers.

For Thomists, education—the complete formation of a person—is a lifelong process that involves many persons and agencies, such as the family, the church, and the community. Schooling, or formal education, is the responsibility of teachers who are deliberately responsible for instructing children and youth in the school, a specialized institution.

Although the Thomist distinction between education and schooling may seem obvious, it has often been ignored or neglected by educators. When it is ignored, areas of responsibility are blurred and confused. By recognizing that other agencies, such as the family, perform educational functions, Thomists argue that these agencies have responsibilities for educating children. In fact, Thomists strongly assert that parents should exercise the primary role in their children's education. This parental role is primarily informal, involving the cultivation of predispositions, habits, and values that support morality, religion, and education. These values are supportive and conducive to the school's and the teacher's more specific and formal educational mission. The Thomist distinctions between education and schooling also make clear that the school is not an all-powerful educational institution. Its effectiveness as an instructional agency depends on other agencies, such as the family, performing their educational responsibilities well.

Educatio: Aquinas's Latin term that refers to a person's general education and formation both in and out of school.

Disciplina: according to Aquinas, formal education or schooling in which a teacher deliberately teaches a skill or a subject to a learner.

For the Thomists, **educatio**, or education, is defined as a person's general formation in the broadest possible sense—spiritually, intellectually, socially, morally, politically, economically, and so forth. In the case of children, education refers to the child's total upbringing. Education, as a total process of human development, encompasses more than the formal instruction that takes place in the school's more limited environment. Because a person's total formation rests on both informal and formal educational agencies, the school's role must be considered in relationship to total human development.[21] In the school, a student is exposed to **disciplina**, or a deliberate instruction such as when a teacher teaches some knowledge or imparts some skill to the learner. The success or failure of such deliberate instruction depends at least in part on its relationship to the general formation taking place outside of the school.

In the Thomist school, the teacher, a mature person, possesses a disciplined body of knowledge or skill and through deliberate instruction seeks to impart this to a learner. Instruction is primarily a verbal process by which the teacher carefully selects the appropriate words and phrases to illustrate the principles or demonstrate the skill that the learner is to acquire. The teacher's language is a stimulus that serves to motivate and explain so that the student can exercise his or her intellect. The student must be an active participant in the teacher–learner relationship, for he or she possesses the potentiality for intellectually grasping and appropriating knowledge.

The Thomist teacher should be a skilled communicator. To communicate effectively, the teacher has to select the correct words, use the proper speaking style, and cite appropriate examples, illustrations, and analogies. The teacher should be careful that instruction does not degenerate into mere verbalism or preachment, however, in which the words used are remote from the learner's experience. Instruction should always begin with what the student already knows and should lead to an outcome that is new. As such, teaching involves a careful structuring and organizing of lessons.

Thomas Aquinas saw teaching as a vocation, a calling to serve humanity. Because of a desire to serve others, the good teacher should be motivated by a love of truth, a love of persons, and a love of God. Unlike the emotionalism of such romantic naturalist educators as Rousseau, who also preached a doctrine of love, the Thomist teacher prizes the cultivation of rationality. As true Aristotelians, Thomists emphasize that genuine love comes from knowing and is based on reason. Therefore, teaching is not allowed to degenerate into a merely emotional relationship. It is always about some knowledge, some truth, that is worthy of being known by a learner.

For Rousseau's romantic naturalism, see the chapter on Progressivism and Education.

In the Thomist conception of the teacher, the art of teaching integrates the contemplative life and the active life. As a contemplative, the teacher must spend time researching and planning instruction. Much of this research takes place in the quiet of a library. The teacher is to know the subject matter thoroughly, be it theology, mathematics, or science. The teacher is also an active person who is involved with students and who communicates knowledge to them.

REALISM'S PHILOSOPHICAL AND EDUCATIONAL RELATIONSHIPS

We have discussed Aristotle's Natural Realism and Thomas Aquinas's Theistic Realism, a synthesis of Aristotle's principles and Christian doctrines. We now discuss Realism's philosophical and educational relationships. In the following sections, we consider Realism as a philosophy, especially in terms of metaphysics, epistemology, axiology, and logic, and relate these subdivisions to education. We then consider Realism's more direct educational implications for the school, curriculum, and teaching and learning.

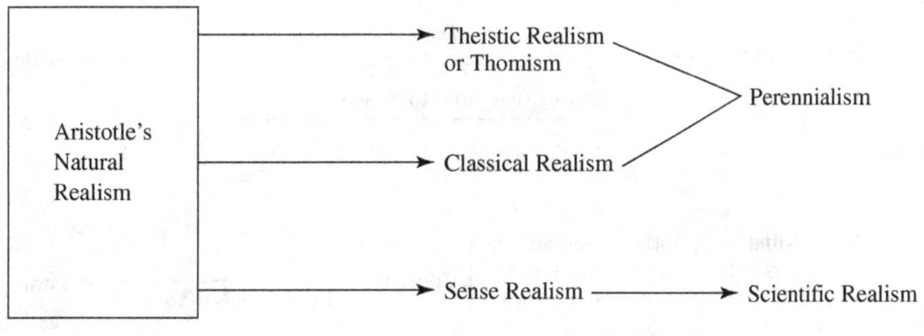

Development of Realism

Realist Metaphysics

Realism's essential metaphysical proposition is that we live in an objective order of reality that exists independent of and external to our minds. Objects, that is, material things, exist in time and in space, and we can come to know something about them. An object, then, is outside of us and consists of two dimensions—matter and form. Matter, the material substratum of an object, has the potential of becoming something. To become an object, matter has to be organized according to some form, design, or structure.

Realist Epistemology

For the Realist, knowing is a twofold process involving sensation and abstraction that corresponds to the conception of a dualistic universe composed of a material and a structural, or formal, component. Whereas sensation relates to matter, abstraction pertains to form or structure. Cognition, or knowing, involves an interaction between the human mind and the world outside of the mind.

Contingent Conditions: Features or aspects that are sometimes but not always present in an object and are not necessary to or defining of it.

Sensation concerns the material component of an object, or matter. Because the material is changing, the information from sensation varies from time to time and from place to place. It is **contingent** and circumstantial. Sensation is the beginning of knowing, but it is not the end of knowledge. Our knowledge about an object originates with sensations such as light, sound, pressure, heat, cold, vapor, or taste that come from the object. Each of our senses has a proper object of sensation. Touch apprehends pressure or physical resistance; temperature reveals whether the object is hot or cold; taste, localized in the tongue, detects flavors; smell, localized in the nasal passages, informs us of odors; hearing perceives sounds; sight, the highest and most objective sense, has color as its proper object. Sensation, then, first involves the physical action of something impinging on our sensory organs.

We first experience the immediate qualities of the object such as color, odor, taste, hardness, softness, and pitch. Needing no other senses to mediate for them, these immediate qualities are conveyed to us from the outside by the different energy patterns that activate the sensory organs. The mediate sensory qualities of size, distance, position, shape, motion, and weight are based on comparisons and contrasts of the immediate sensory data.

Concept: a general idea that represents a class of objects possessing the same necessary or essential qualities.

As a result of sensation, we acquire sensory data, which our mind sorts out and arranges in computer-like fashion. Our common sense, the intellectual power of abstraction, sorts out our sense perceptions into the necessary conditions, those qualities always present in an object, and the contingent conditions that are sometimes found in the object. The necessary qualities, which are always present in the object, are its essential constituents and form the basis of our concept of the object. A **concept**, a meaning that applies to all things of the same class, has qualities that it shares with other objects in the same class but not with other objects.

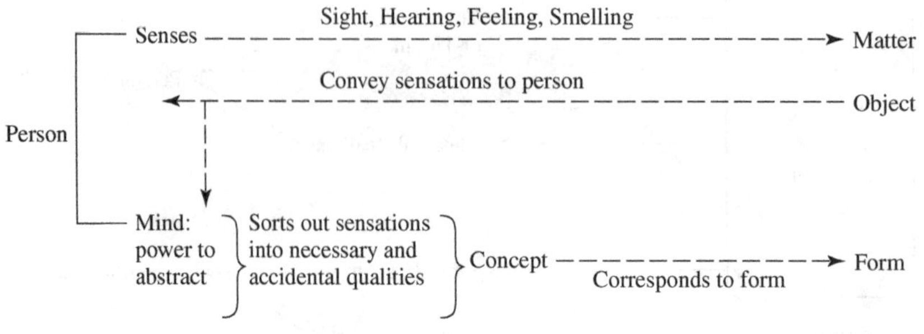

Realist Epistemology

Conceptualization, or concept formation, takes place when our mind has extracted and abstracted the form of an object and recognized it as belonging to a class. Objects are classified, or put in a category, when we recognize them as possessing qualities that they share with other members of the class but not with objects belonging to different classes.

For example, in our experiences, we encounter other human beings. Some of these people are of different heights and weights, speak different languages, and are of different ethnic or racial origins. They may be Chinese, Russian, English, Nigerian, or Mexican, to name only a few of the many nationalities of people. However, underlying the variations of size, weight, height, ethnic origin, and nationality, there is something, some "whatness" or "quidity," that is common to all human beings. A common human nature identifies them as members of the class *Homo sapiens* and not of other classes of objects. A human being is different from a horse, a tree, a house, or a rock. The varieties of human beings share something that is common to them all. This commonness is what differentiates them from other objects; it is their defining quality or essential characteristic.

Realist epistemology has been called a "spectator theory," which means that we are observers of reality. While we all commonly share the same cognitive process, our "spectating" can range from the crudely unsophisticated to highly precise data gathering. As childlike watchers of reality, we begin early to sort out objects into mineral, vegetable, and animal. Through the course of time, humankind has developed a range of sophisticated instruments—telescopes, microscopes, X-ray machines, space probes, and so on—that have enhanced our knowledge and rendered it more accurate. For example, the moon, as a physical entity, exists independently of us and was present prior to our knowing about it. The moon has figured in many religious rituals and festivals; it has been the object of poetry and song. With the coming of the space age and interplanetary exploration, astronauts have journeyed to the moon and, with sophisticated instruments, have made our knowledge of this heavenly body more accurate. Although the process of knowing remains the same, the instruments that we develop are dynamic. Our knowledge about the moon becomes accurate when it corresponds correctly to the moon as it is in reality.

The "spectator theory of knowing" may appear to be passive, but it has many dynamic educational implications. Education should provide the experience, training, and practice that will cultivate our potentiality to be accurate observers, discoverers of reality. It should assist us in using the instruments and technology that contribute to the accuracy of our knowledge of the universe and the world. While Realists would still agree with Aristotle that human beings intrinsically seek to know, they would also recognize the instrumental, or use, value of knowledge. For scientific Realists, accurate knowledge about the world helps us to structure choices—to make decisions—that contribute to our continuing liberation from ignorance, superstition, disease, famine, and other human impediments.

As a systematic spectator, the Realist is concerned with discovering the essential plan or design of the universe. The philosophical and educational problem is that of extracting or abstracting the structures that explain the workings of the universe, of human beings, and of society. The discovery of structure involves extracting it from the matter that conveys it. Such organized spectating, involving the scientific method, deals with the discovery of principles and laws that explain reality to us.

In humankind's long and continuing quest to discover the structures of reality, bodies of knowledge—scholarly academic and scientific disciplines—have been developed, added, and refined by researchers over time. For example, linguists have worked to extract the structure of speech by analyzing various languages; the natural and physical sciences—zoology, botany, chemistry, physics, astronomy—have sought to identify the structure and patterns of natural and physical phenomena;

the social sciences—sociology, economics, political science, anthropology, and psychology—have as their object of inquiry the structure of human interaction. Bodies of knowledge that are the products of this quest for structure—the liberal arts and sciences—constitute the Realist curriculum. Realists emphasize the importance of the liberal arts and sciences as the essential or perennial core of knowledge. They see the skills taught in the primary grades—reading, writing, listening, observing, and arithmetic—as leading to and necessary for studying such subjects as languages, mathematics, history, science, and social sciences that are derived from the liberal arts and sciences.

As a spectator searching to discover structure in reality, the Realist is a discoverer of reality that is preexistent, independent, and antecedent to his or her experience of it. Through careful observation, we can discover the structures of objects and determine how they interact with each other and with us. We can frame generalizations based on the patterns and regularities that occur in these interactions between objects. For instance, meteorologists have observed and recorded daily temperatures. As a result of this careful observation, variations in temperature can be detected over time, and thus it is possible to generalize about temperature variations and speak about seasons. Such generalizations form basic meteorological theory that can guide such practical activities as planting crops, wearing appropriate clothes, and constructing dwellings. It is also of use in defining and examining current issues such as climate change and global warming.

The Realist theory of knowledge is also referred to as a "correspondence theory." Our ideas are true when our concepts conform to or correspond with the object in reality. Because knowledge is to conform to reality, what is taught should also conform to reality. For example, Newton's law of universal gravitation corresponds to the way the universe actually works. It is true and should be both transmitted to the young and perpetuated.

Realist Axiology

Prizing rationality as the human being's distinguishing characteristic and defining power, Realists encourage us to shape our choices and actions on knowledge about structures of reality. By knowing the structures of physical, natural, social, and human reality, we can frame realistic and viable alternatives. Through knowledge, we can rationally frame choices about life. The ability to develop such choices is at the core of a liberal, or liberating, education.

Harry S. Broudy, a Classical Realist, illuminated the value dimension of education, especially ethical and aesthetic concerns. For Broudy, like Aristotle, education's ultimate and guiding aim is "living the good life" of cultivating human potentialities to their highest levels of actualization through the processes of self-determination, self-realization, and self-integration.[22] The role of education and of schooling is to provide individuals with the knowledge that helps them to make informed decisions based on knowledge. These informed decisions make it possible for individuals to realize the good life that fulfills their human potentiality. The source of values lies in the relationship between the structure of objects and the structure of human nature. An object's structure makes it both intrinsically and instrumentally valuable. Like Aristotle, Broudy asserted that our ethical decisions should be made on rational grounds. To be self-determined means that we have framed or defined our potentialities so that we can achieve worthy goals; to be self-integrated means that we have organized our values hierarchically and have resolved conflicts and inconsistencies.

Aesthetic judgment involves an interaction between a person, the perceiver, and an art object—a painting, drama, musical piece, dance, or sculpture, for example. Education enhances our aesthetic experience by cultivating our readiness to appreciate art, by providing and enlarging our range of experiences with art, and by offering criteria for judging and enjoying art.[23] Although art forms exhibit cultural variations, Realists hold that the human desire for artistic expression and aesthetic enjoyment is universal.

Logic

For the Realist, logic is both inductive and deductive. We use induction as part of our cognitive process as we acquire sensory information about objects in the environment. From these sensations, our minds inductively create concepts as we abstract the various data into classes and categories. Teachers can use the inductive processes by which learners study the objects they encounter in the environment and arrive at concepts and generalizations about them. Sense Realists, such as Johann Heinrich Pestalozzi, the early nineteenth-century Swiss educator, devised object lessons to facilitate concept formation based on sensation. In the process of moving from sensation to abstraction, there is a logic of going from the specific to the general and from the concrete to the abstract that is used in teaching and learning strategies. Through induction, individuals are discovering knowledge about reality but not constructing it as Constructivists assert. This kind of knowing and the logic based on it is inductive in that it moves from specific elements of sensory information to general concepts.

We also noted that, over time, scholars and scientists have arranged these concepts into conceptual systems: the theoretical framework of disciplined knowledge, or subject matters, as in the liberal arts and sciences. Deductive logic is used in Realist instruction when the teacher designs lessons that begin with generalizations and principles already established in prior research. Using deduction, the teacher can begin with these authoritative generalizations, provide examples that illustrate them, and then conclude with their current application.

REALISM'S EDUCATIONAL IMPLICATIONS

In this section, we examine Realism's educational implications in terms of educational goals, the role of the school, the curriculum, instructional methods, and the teacher–learner relationship.

Realism's Educational Goals

The ultimate educational goal of Realism remains that articulated by Aristotle—namely, to aid human beings in attaining happiness by cultivating their potentiality for excellence to its fullest. As such, education is to

1. Cultivate rationality, the human's highest power, through the study of organized bodies of knowledge; and
2. Encourage human beings to define themselves by framing their choices rationally, to realize themselves by exercising to the fullest their potentiality for excellence, and to integrate themselves by ordering the various roles and claims of life according to a rational and hierarchical order.

The Realist Conception of the School

Realists believe that each institution has a primary role and function in society. The government, the church, and the family perform definite roles. For example, the Classical Realist philosopher Harry Broudy asserts that the school has the primary purpose of forming intellectual habits in students. Broudy's emphasis on intellectual habits is similar to Alasdair MacIntyre's stress on habits and practices that was discussed earlier in the chapter. As a primarily academic institution, the school's mission is to cultivate rationality. Closely related to the person's defining purpose, the cultivation of knowledge and intellectual habits liberates him or her, in that based on knowledge, he or she is free to make informed decisions.[24] As a formal institution, the school should be staffed by competent teachers who possess knowledge of a subject or skill and know how to teach it to students who want to acquire that knowledge.

The school has the well-defined and specific intellectual function of transmitting bodies of knowledge and inquiry skills to students. Although the school may perform recreational, community, health, and social functions, these are secondary and should not interfere with the efficient performance of its primary intellectual function. In such a setting, the principal's role is to make sure that teachers in a school are not distracted from their primary task or unnecessarily burdened with noneducational duties that detract from it. The principal is charged with protecting the academic freedom of teachers to teach and of students to learn.

Residual Function: the progressive concept that schools should perform roles or functions no longer exercised by other institutions.

The Realist conception of the school clearly prescribes policies designed to protect the school from interference that detracts from its central mission. Realists reject the **residual function** of schooling that asserts that schools are responsible for providing services neglected or no longer performed by other institutions. They argue that the more schools act as health care, recreational, and social service agencies, the less time and fewer resources will be available for them to fulfill their primary function. To use schools as multipurpose social service agencies not only confuses their purpose but also is inefficient and costly.

The Realist Curriculum

The curriculum is typically organized as skills, activities, and subjects that are taught in relation to the students' readiness and stage of development. From an Aristotelian perspective, the stages of human development are integrated by the unifying purpose of realizing all that is good in being human. Each stage contributes to and fulfills that overarching purpose. Childhood, adolescence, adult maturity, and old age are all related phases, not separate parts.[25] The intrinsic purpose of life remains throughout life but finds more complex ways of being fulfilled as a person matures.

As indicated earlier, the Realist conceives of an objective order of reality. The objects that comprise reality can be classified into categories on the basis of their structural similarities. The various learned disciplines, or subjects, of history, geography, language, mathematics, biology, botany, and chemistry, for example, consist of clusters of related concepts and of generalizations that interpret and explain interactions among the objects that these concepts represent. Each discipline as a conceptual system has a structure. **Structure** refers to a framework of related conceptual meanings and their generalizations that explain physical, natural, social, and human realities. For instance, biology consists of a number of necessary concepts appropriate to the study of plants and animals.

Structure: a subject-matter discipline's framework of related concepts, their definitions and meanings, and generalizations about them that explain an aspect of reality.

The role of the expert scientist and scholar is crucial in defining curricular areas. The scholar or the scientist is an expert who studies and carefully observes certain well-defined sections of reality. For example, the historian studies the past and analyzes documents explaining past events. By using the historical method, he or she writes narratives about past events and develops generalizations or interpretations that explain and give them meaning. The historian as an expert in explaining the past has mastered a particular area of reality. He or she knows the limits of his or her expertise and is aware of what is appropriate to history and what lies in another learned discipline. The scholar or scientist is also skilled in the inquiry method, which is an efficient mode of discovery in the particular research area. Through monographs, lectures, and books, scholars make their findings available to the public and to other experts in their fields. Although scholars and scientists may disagree on interpretations, they are expected to follow the appropriate methods of investigation and conceptual framework of their disciplines.

Scientists and scholars are often, but not always, found in universities or research centers. Institutions of higher learning are expected to encourage, support, and reward research and teaching. Scholars and scientists are expected to make their findings known by publishing their research. Underlying scholarship in the Realist mode is the assumption that generalizations about reality are most accurately made by experts who have carefully investigated certain selected aspects of reality. In universities, these experts are usually organized into academic departments of history, language, chemistry, physics, English, political science, and so on. Students attend colleges and universities to study with and to obtain knowledge from these academic experts. Prospective teachers, especially secondary teachers, study academic subject matters, usually referred to as majors. They, in turn, use the descriptions, concepts, and generalizations provided by the expert to organize subject matter into instructional units for their students.

Basic to the Realist curriculum is the rationale that the most efficient and effective way to find out about reality is to study it through systematically organized subject-matter disciplines. The liberal arts and science curriculum of the undergraduate college and the departmentalized secondary school curriculum represent the subject-matter mode of curricular organization. The subject-matter curriculum consists of two basic components: (1) the body of knowledge that is the structure of a learned discipline—an organized way of viewing a certain aspect of reality, that is, historical, sociological, biological, chemical, psychological, geographical, and so on; and (2) the appropriate pedagogical ordering of the subject matter according to the readiness, maturation, and previous learning of the student. In such a curricular design, teachers are expected to be knowledgeable about their subject matters and well prepared in the methods of teaching them to students.

The Realist curriculum at the primary level involves instruction in the tools of reading, writing, computation, and computer literacy needed for subsequent successful study and inquiry into the systematic subject-matter disciplines. It is equally important that early childhood and primary schooling foster predispositions, attitudes, and habits that value learning as a positive goal. Children should also gain experience with research methods, such as using the library and the computer, which aid in later learning.

Realist Instructional Methods

Instruction in the Realist school involves a teacher teaching some skill or subject to a student. While this may appear to be a simple statement, it carefully defines and prescribes the instructional act. Notice that there are three elements in the act of instruction: the teacher, the skill or subject, and the student. Because each of these components is essential to the teaching or instructional act, we will comment on all three.

The teacher is knowledgeable in the content of the subject; he or she is a generally educated person who knows how the subject relates to other areas of knowledge. The teacher also knows the limits of his or her competence. Thus, the goal of instruction is to provide the student with the body of knowledge possessed by the teacher. Ethically, the teacher should be committed to the goal of aiding the student in fulfilling her or his fullest potentiality.

The second element in instruction is some body of knowledge, such as history, or some skill, such as reading, that is to be taught to the student. In some situations, this second element is missing in schools, for example, in therapy or sensitivity sessions, or during entertainment or unfocused talking. Situations such as these, which lack the knowledge or skill element, are not really teaching situations. Realist teachers, like any teacher, need to know their students' backgrounds and how to motivate them. They need to know where their students are in the present time and place and also seek to aid them in developing themselves as far as possible in the future. Teachers can be entertaining as well as informative. However, they also need to keep their focus on knowledge and students' rational development.

The third element in instruction is the student, the person who is present to learn the skill or knowledge. Students are expected to be ready to learn and willing to expend the effort required. While students may have many interests, they are expected to focus their attention on what is being taught.

The Realist teacher should command a variety of methods that may include lecture, discussion, dialogue, demonstration, or experimentation. The teacher should use the method appropriate to the learner's background, the subject matter, and the situation. An ideal method, which needs to be used with great skill, would structure a learning situation that replicates the research activity of the scholar or scientist. For example, students in a history course would use the historical method to analyze and interpret primary sources.

The Realist Teacher–Learner Relationship

In our discussion of Realist philosophy, curriculum, and methodology, we have already suggested the basis of the teacher–learner relationship. The overriding professional commitment of the teacher is to aid the students in forming intellectual virtues. The teacher, possessing subject-matter knowledge and instructional skill, is a professional educator, knowledgeable in the traditions of the teaching profession and skilled in its practices. Teachers should be generally educated in both the liberal arts and sciences; this general knowledge is designed to assist them in being educated persons who appreciate the relationships of bodies of knowledge to each other and to the cultivation of human rationality. In addition to being generalists, teachers should be specialists in the skills and subjects that they teach and in the methods appropriate to teaching them. The learner is regarded as an individual who has the essential human right to self-determination, self-realization, and self-integration. Seeking to grow in maturity in the areas of human knowledge, students have the right to have educated and professionally prepared experts as teachers. Learning, however, which requires commitment and application, is the student's primary responsibility.

My Reflections on Philosophy of Education: Professor Harry S. Broudy as a Mentor

Throughout this book, I have encouraged readers to construct their own philosophies of education. As part of this process, I have recommended reflecting on your own educational experiences to recall persons who influenced your thinking about education. In writing this chapter on Realism, I reflected on a professor who shaped my ideas about education, especially philosophy of education.

When working on my doctorate at the University of Illinois, I enrolled in several seminars on philosophy of education with Professor Harry S. Broudy (1905–1998), a distinguished philosopher who had a formative influence on my thinking about education. My recollection of these seminars illustrates Realist teaching and learning. The seminars focused on a topic in philosophy of education, such as value theory, with assigned primary source readings. Professor Broudy would introduce the topic, give some explanation, relate it to the field historically and to contemporary issues, and then ask questions to stimulate discussion. We were to write short papers on a particular aspect of the topic and a longer one based on our research. True to Realist teaching principles, we stayed with the subject. Professor Broudy did not let the seminar degenerate into a sharing of uninformed opinions. Although he led us to relate the topic to contemporary issues, Dr. Broudy always structured the discussion in a larger philosophical perspective. In fact, the perspective was a very large in-depth one that began with the ancient Greek philosophers Plato and, especially, Aristotle, and led to the present.

I recall Professor Broudy maintaining what I would call a "professorial distance" from the students. The subject matter was always there between us. I don't recall the entry of personal matters into the class. However, I found out that he did know his students. His knowledge was based on how we related to the subject, how we expressed ourselves, and the kinds of questions we raised.

Professor Broudy introduced the other doctoral students and me to the field of philosophy of education. He encouraged us to attend meetings of the Midwest Philosophy of Education Society and the Philosophy of Education Society. When I went to these meetings, I discovered that Professor Broudy was much more than an ordinary professor of philosophy of education. He was a prominent and respected leader in the field who was widely recognized for his work on general, teacher, and aesthetic education. I came to realize that taking his courses was a rare experience that not many graduate students had. I found out that he had earned his doctorate at Harvard University and that his own professors had been famous scholars such as William E. Hocking, C. I. Lewis, Alfred North Whitehead, and John Wild.

Although I did not realize that Professor Broudy had noticed much about me, I was very wrong. As I was finishing my doctoral dissertation and searching for my first job, Professor Broudy did take a definite interest. He wrote letters of support and recommended me for a position at Loyola University in Chicago. I got the job and began teaching philosophy of education. In looking for a textbook, I came across Professor Broudy's book *Building a Philosophy of Education,* which I adopted as my text.[26] I then learned more about my distinguished teacher. Professor Broudy, who called himself a Classical Realist, was a modern Aristotelian. Then I understood why he kept on a steady course and did not latch on to the many current fads that often inflict themselves on education. I understood his responses to some of the clichés in education. When people said, "Everything is constantly changing and education, too, is constantly changing," Broudy would counter with "If everything is changing, then there has to be something that is changing." A true Aristotelian, he looked beyond the cliché to ask what it is that is changing. When people said, "Education is life," Broudy would ask, "If the school is life, why do we need it? Why not just live?" As a Realist, he saw the school as having a primary academic function—the cultivation of our intellect through an encounter with knowledge.

Broudy was committed to the proposition that all students had the right to a general academic education. Our civic democracy, like the Athenian *polis* of antiquity, required the shared and common understandings based on knowing what is real.

CONSTRUCTING YOUR OWN PHILOSOPHY OF EDUCATION

At the beginning of this chapter, you were encouraged to reflect on how Realism relates to constructing your own philosophy of education. Now that you have read and discussed the chapter, does Realism appeal to you as a philosophy of education? Are there elements in Realism that you plan to incorporate into your own philosophy of education? Are there aspects that you would definitely not include? Do you believe, like Aristotle, that reality is objective to us and is knowable, and that knowledge about it is our best guide to action? Do you agree that values are universal? Do you endorse a subject-matter curriculum and see the teacher's primary role as teaching these subjects?

Conclusion

This chapter introduced Realism as a philosophy of education. It began with Aristotle's Natural Realism—we live in an objective order of reality that we can know. Knowledge of this reality is our best guide to action. We examined Aristotle's ethics that encouraged moderation and MacIntyre's revival of Aristotelianism, especially his emphasis on virtues, traditions, and practices. We then discussed Theistic Realism, or Thomism, Thomas Aquinas's synthesis of Aristotle's philosophy and Christian doctrines in the Middle Ages.

After discussing Realism's Aristotelian origins and roots, we proceeded to examine Realism's philosophical principles and their implications for education. Among the most important educational implications are (1) a belief in universal truth and values; (2) an affirmation of the human being's inherent natural potentiality to reason; (3) knowing as a twofold process of sensation and abstraction; (4) that schools are academic institutions with the primary purpose of developing students' intellectual potentiality; (5) that the curriculum consists of conceptual systems organized into subject-matter disciplines; and (6) the proposition that teachers need to be committed to enhancing students' potentiality to reason and developing and using their practical wisdom; and (7) that instruction involves teaching a skill or subject to a learner.

Questions for Reflection and Discussion

1. Do you believe that Realism as a philosophy of education is too abstract and removed from the real problems of education to be relevant to today's teachers and students?
2. Why do Realists reject the assumption that values depend on situations and circumstances? What is your opinion on values? Are they general to all people everywhere? Or are they relative to different cultures, times, and places?
3. Is MacIntyre's emphasis on virtues in relation to practices relevant to education and teaching? Does the teaching profession emphasize virtues in relation to practices?
4. Do you agree or disagree with Realism that teaching involves a knowledgeable teacher instructing students in a skill or subject? Is the Realist concept of teaching adequate for contemporary education?
5. Do you find religiously based philosophies such as Thomism relevant to public education or should faith-based theories of education be reserved for private education?
6. What are the strengths and weaknesses of the Realist view of a subject-matter curriculum? Do you endorse, modify, or reject the Realist subject-matter discipline curriculum?
7. Do you believe that all educational experiences are equal or are some more important than others? Consider the Realist concept of a hierarchy of values as you frame your response. Defend your answer.
8. Aristotle believes that we live in a purposeful and meaningful world. Do you believe that there is an inherent purpose to human life or do we make our own purposes?
9. Do you agree or disagree with Aristotle that desired ethical behavior follows a mean of moderation between excess and repression? Consider your answer in terms of the standards of behavior found in contemporary American society and education.

Inquiry and Research Projects

1. Review the catalogue of your college or university. How is it organized? Would Realists agree with its organization?
2. Organize the students in your class as a focus group that is examining the issue of values in American society and schools. Ask such focusing questions as: Are values general to all people and universal to all places and times? Or are values based on personal preferences and social and cultural norms?
3. Access Web sites dealing with Realism. You might begin with the Stanford Encyclopedia of Philosophy at http://plato.stanford.edu/entries/realism. Locate the philosophers identified with Realism and their major philosophical ideas.
4. In outline form, design a secondary school curriculum based on the Realist principles of subject-matter disciplines and a hierarchy of generality.
5. Examine a textbook used in a course you are taking. Determine whether the book is organized according to Realist principles.
6. Examine the liberal arts and science requirements in your degree program. In a position paper, indicate how you think a Realist would react.

Internet Sources

For a discussion of Realism, access the Stanford Encyclopedia of Philosophy at http://plato.stanford.edu/entries/realism.

For Realism and education, access www.pdst.purdue.edu/georgeoff/phil_am_ed/Realism.html.

For a general overview of Aristotle, access www.iep.utm.edu/a/aristotl.htm.

For the Paideia Project, access www.paideia.org/content.php/system/index.htm.

Suggestions for Further Reading

Adler, Mortimer J. *Aristotle for Everybody*. New York: Touchstone, 1997.

___. *How to Think About the Great Ideas: From the Great Books of Western Civilization*. Peru, IL: Open Court, 2000.

Anagnostopoulos, Georgios. *Aristotle on the Goals and Exactness of Ethics*. Berkeley: University of California Press, 1994.

Barnes, Jonathan. *Aristotle: A Very Short Introduction*. Oxford, UK: Oxford University Press, 2000.

Blanchette, Olivia. *The Perfection of the Universe According to Aquinas: Teleological Cosmology*. University Park: Pennsylvania State University Press, 1992.

Broadie, Sarah. *Ethics with Aristotle*. New York: Oxford University Press, 1991.

Davies, Brian. *The Thought of Thomas Aquinas*. New York: Oxford University Press, 1991.

Fatula, Mary Ann. *Thomas Aquinas: Preacher and Friend*. Collegeville, MN: Liturgical Press, 1993.

Gilson, Etienne. *The Christian Philosophy of St. Thomas Aquinas*. Notre Dame, IN: University of Notre Dame Press, 1994.

Hall, Pamela M. *Narrative and the Natural Law: An Interpretation of Thomistic Ethics*. Notre Dame, IN: University of Notre Dame Press, 1994.

Kenny, Anthony J. *Aquinas on Mind*. New York: Routledge, 1992.

MacIntyre, Alasdair. *After Virtue: A Study in Moral Theory* (3rd ed.). Notre Dame, IN: University of Notre Dame Press, 2007.

Maton, Karl, and Rob Moore. *Social Realism, Knowledge and the Sociology of Knowledge: Conditions of the Mind*. New York and London: Continuum International Publishing, 2010.

McInerny, Ralph M. *Aquinas on Human Action: A Theory of Practice*. Washington, DC: Catholic University of America Press, 1992.

___. *A First Glance at St. Thomas Aquinas: A Handbook for Peeping Thomists*. Notre Dame, IN: University of Notre Dame Press, 1990.

Rankin, Kenneth. *The Recovery of the Soul: An Aristotelian Essay on Self-Fulfillment*. Montreal: McGill-Queen's University Press, 1991.

Reeve, C. D. C. *Practices of Reason: Aristotle's Nicomachean Ethics*. New York: Oxford University Press, 1992.

Scott, David. *Education, Epistemology, and Critical Realism*. Abingdon, UK, and New York: Routledge, 2010.

Selman, Francis J. *Saint Thomas Aquinas: Teacher of Truth*. Edinburgh: T&T Clark, 1994.

Spangler, Mary Michael. *Aristotle on Teaching*. Lanham, MD: University Press of America, 1998.

Swanson, Judith A. *The Public and the Private in Aristotle's Political Philosophy*. Ithaca, NY: Cornell University Press, 1992.

Tomuschat, Christian. *Human Rights: Between Idealism and Realism*. Oxford, UK, and New York: Oxford University Press, 2008.

Young, Michael. *Bringing Knowledge Back In: From Social Constructivism to Social Realism in the Sociology of Education*. Abingdon, UK, and New York: Routledge, 2008.

Verbeke, Gerard. *Moral Education in Aristotle*. Washington, DC: Catholic University of America Press, 1990.

White, Stephen A. *Sovereign Virtue: Aristotle on the Relation Between Happiness and Prosperity*. Stanford, CA: Stanford University Press, 1992.

Notes

1. G. E. R. Lloyd, *Aristotle: The Growth and Structure of His Thought* (Cambridge, UK: Cambridge University Press, 1968), 3.
2. E. W. Tomlin, *The Western Philosophers* (New York: Harper and Row, 1967), 62.
3. Jonathan Barnes, *Aristotle: A Very Short Introduction* (Oxford, UK: Oxford University Press, 2000), 30.
4. H. D. F. Kitto, *The Greeks* (Baltimore: Penguin Books, 1962), 169–194.
5. John Wild, *Introduction to Realistic Philosophy* (New York: Harper and Brothers, 1948), 441–468.
6. Alasdair MacIntyre, *After Virtue: A Study in Moral Theory*, 3rd ed. (Notre Dame, IN: University of Notre Dame Press, 2007), 52–53.

7. Ibid., 148.
8. Ibid., 148.
9. Ibid., 148.
10. Ibid., 110.
11. Ibid., 154.
12. Barnes, *Aristotle: A Very Short Introduction*, p. 3.
13. Ibid., 30.
14. Tomlin, *The Western Philosophers*, 62.
15. MacIntyre, *After Virtue*, xi.
16. Ibid., 162.
17. Ibid., 110.
18. Ibid., 191.
19. Ibid., 187.
20. William Cunningham, *Pivotal Problems in Education* (New York: Macmillan, 1940).
21. John W. Donohue, *St. Thomas Aquinas and Education* (New York: Random House, 1968), 58–64, 82–89.
22. Harry S. Broudy, *Building a Philosophy of Education* (Upper Saddle River, NJ: Prentice Hall, 1961), 3–20.
23. Ibid., 202–231.
24. Ibid., 45–50.
25. MacIntyre, *After Virtue*, 204.
26. Broudy, *Building a Philosophy of Education*, 243–250.

Pragmatism and Education

John Dewey (1859–1952), a leading American Pragmatist philosopher who developed Experimentalism.

CHAPTER PREVIEW

This chapter examines the origins of **Pragmatism**, an American philosophy that has had a worldwide impact on education. After focusing on John Dewey's Experimentalist or Instrumentalist version, it examines Pragmatism's major concepts and their implications for society, education, schooling, curriculum, and teaching and learning. It then identifies recent trends in Pragmatism. Dewey's philosophy of education is called **Experimentalism** because it sees human beings, who exercise their **social intelligence**, engaged in problem solving according to the scientific experimental method.

Instrumentalism means that people can use their ideas as instruments, or tools, to solve problems. Constructed on a theme of empiricist naturalism, Dewey's philosophy rejected traditional philosophies founded on metaphysics. When ideas rest on metaphysics, they cannot be tested because they are beyond human experience. In sharp contrast, Dewey argues that humans live in the natural environment and the social world they construct is built on the natural world. Ideas need to be tested in terms of the consequences they have for personal and social life. To determine the validity of an idea, its consequences need to be empirical—verifiable in human experience.

Dewey opposed the philosophical *dualisms,* like those of Aristotle, that portrayed human beings as divided into antecedent categories such as mind and body and that bifurcated education into theory and practice. He worked to remove the barriers that separated school from society, curriculum from community, and content from method. He discarded the doctrine of preparation that defines education as preparing for something in the future—the next stage in schooling, a job, or even a specific definition of nationality or citizenship. Integrating social life and education in the unifying concept of experience, Dewey redefined the school as a setting in which students, actively engaged in solving problems, added to their ongoing experience. Dewey reformulated the concept of the school from a strictly academic institution into a socially charged miniature community. Dewey's Pragmatism continues to be one of the world's leading educational philosophies. The following major topics are examined in the chapter:

- Pragmatism in the American experience
- John Dewey as a Pragmatist educator
- Experimentalism's philosophical bases
- Experimentalism's educational implications
- Pragmatism's Resurgence
- Pragmatism's philosophical opponents

As you read the chapter, reflect on how Pragmatism, especially Dewey's Experimentalism, relates to constructing your own philosophy of education. In your educational experience, have your encountered Pragmatist teachers, problem solving, and process learning? Does Pragmatism appeal to you as a philosophy of education? Are there elements of Pragmatism that you plan to incorporate into your own philosophy of education? Are there aspects that you would definitely not include?

Pragmatism: constructed by Charles S. Peirce, William James, and John Dewey, this philosophy emphasizes the practical application of ideas by acting on them to actually test them in human experience.

PRAGMATISM IN THE AMERICAN EXPERIENCE

Whereas Idealism and Realism date back to ancient Greece, Pragmatism developed in twentieth-century America. Whereas the older traditional philosophies rested on an antecedent metaphysical conception of reality in which truth is *a priori,* or prior to and independent of human experience, the Pragmatists contended that a "truth" is a tentative assertion based on human experience.

Experimentalism: Dewey's version of Pragmatism that asserts that socially intelligent individuals should use the scientific method of experimentation to solve their problems.

An American Challenge to Traditional Philosophy

Social Intelligence: the shared reflective experience of individuals, living in associated groups, in solving their mutual problems.

Instrumentalism: another name for Dewey's Pragmatism, which holds that ideas are instruments that can solve human problems.

The Pragmatists challenged traditional philosophical assumptions that a completed and perfect universe could be approached, only distantly and abstractly, through metaphysical speculation into the nature of ultimate reality. Rejecting the philosophical security provided by absolute and unchanging truth and values, the Pragmatists saw the world, much as Darwin did, as evolving and changing. People lived by successfully interacting with their environment and with each other in flexible relationships that could be examined, reappraised, and, when necessary, reconstructed. For the Pragmatists, ideas were not fixed in time and space as the universal and eternal reflections of an ultimate intelligence, as the Platonic and Hegelian Idealists believed. As human-made instruments, ideas are mental tools that could be used to solve the problems of real life. Ideas are to be judged by their consequences when acted on; truth is a **warranted assertion**, a tentative statement based on the application of hypotheses to solving problems; logic, following the scientific method, is experimental; values are experienced within the cultural contexts of ethical and aesthetic problems and issues charged by the unique features of particular situations.

For Aristotelian dualisms, see the chapter on Realism and Education.

For Plato and Hegel, see the chapter on Idealism and Education.

Warranted Assertion: the Pragmatist view of a "truth" as an idea or belief that is tentative and subject to further testing and revision.

Pragmatism was a philosophical expression of America's frontier experience in which westward-moving pioneers migrated through varying natural environments that they transformed, but that also changed them and their society. The frontier experience caused Americans to judge success in terms of the consequences that came from transforming the environment for human purposes. Over time, the openness of an expansive frontier was translated into a wider vision of an open universe, charged by the dynamics of constant flux, change, and movement. Pragmatism appeared at a time when science and industry were creating a new technological society, the outlines of which were still emergent and flexible. As the nineteenth century yielded to the twentieth, the scientific temperament was exalted as a positive force for making a better life on earth. The legacy of the old frontier of open land in the West and the new frontier of a scientifically functioning technology made the time ripe for the new, hardheaded pragmatic philosophy. Pragmatism proclaimed the American propensity to discard purely speculative philosophy as an empty metaphysical meandering.

Pragmatism's formulation overlapped with that period of energetic social, political, and educational reform known as the Progressive movement, from the late 1890s to the United States' entry into World War I in 1917. The pragmatic outlook, which argued that problems, if capable of definition, could be solved, fitted the social reformist attitude of Progressive Americans.[1] While Pragmatism's origins were in the American experience, it has shaped educational philosophy and practices throughout the world. The following pragmatic intellectual currents had an international impact: (1) The universe is an open and relative rather than a closed and fixed system; (2) individuals need to be open to change rather than fear it; (3) human experience is pluralistic in that lives are lived in cultural contexts; and (4) philosophy and education need to incorporate and make use of science, especially the scientific method.

Three Americans developed Pragmatism as a philosophy: Charles S. Peirce (1839–1914), William James (1841–1910), and John Dewey (1859–1952). The next sections discuss Peirce and James as originators of Pragmatism; a later section examines Dewey for his development of Pragmatism and an educational philosophy.

Charles S. Peirce

Charles S. Peirce, a mathematician and logician, has been called the "most original" of the Pragmatists.[2] Calling his new philosophy *pragmaticism*, Peirce rejected Plato's speculation that reality is universal, perfect, and unchanging. Rather, Peirce claimed our world was neither perfect nor imperfect, but was constantly changing. To make the best of this fluid situation, we need to use our "common sense" to solve life's practical problems. Our knowledge, Peirce claimed, is based on results, the empirically measurable and verifiable consequences of our actions. From our experience, we learn that certain of our actions are more likely than others to produce the results we want.[3]

Drawing on his mathematical expertise, Peirce designed a strategy for choice making and action that rested on probability and estimated results. When we act, we are basing our action on an estimate of the best hypothesis about something, namely, that our action will produce the results that we want. However, as estimates, we know these hypotheses will need to be revised to make them into more accurate tools or instruments that will improve our chances of getting the desired results. Instead of a certain and unchanging world in which truth is universal and eternal, as Plato claimed, Peirce's world is changing and in flux, and is indeterminate, not determined in advance. Because our world is indeterminate, our lives and our actions in it are also changing, relative, and undetermined. To make sense of a world in flux, Peirce argued that we need to do the best job with it that is possible. Possibility and probability, however, are not certainty. We need to estimate what we can do by using the theory of probability—what is likely to happen if we act in a certain way. Because certain actions bring about reactions in a way that can be quantified, we can estimate them. It is probable that similar reactions will occur in the future. It is necessary to understand, however, that actions and reactions in our personal and social lives never reoccur in exactly the same way. Our knowledge about something is probable rather than certain. However, probability provides us with a sense of intelligent direction and possible action.[4] With enough work, investigation, and thought, it is possible that we can formulate tentative generalizations—never ironclad laws—about how the world works.

For Peirce, our thinking is hypothetical in that it puts our tentative generalizations to the test of acting on them. Involved in our action is probability in that we expect consequences that are likely to be similar to, but not the same as, when we acted on related or comparable problems in the past. Further, it is possible to estimate these consequences. We can then measure if our estimates were correct or if they need to be revised. As we test our hypotheses, we can keep improving them by clarifying and revising them. For Peirce, this process of knowing is both a commonsense and a scientific way of dealing with problems.[5]

In education, especially in educational research and testing, there is an emphasis on statistical measurement of students' intelligence, readiness, learning similarities and differences, and academic results of the implementation of certain types of curricula and the use of certain instructional strategies. In educational planning, there is an emphasis on using statistics to devise educational innovation and change. This process assumes that the educator can use statistical information to predict what is likely to happen as a result of the implementation of a particular innovation. This kind of prediction, as Peirce advises us, is a guide, but not an ironclad one, to achieve the results that we want.

William James

Although he had studied for a career in medicine, James chose to become a university professor.[6] A psychologist turned philosopher, James was fascinated by the cultural and religious pluralism that he observed in human experience. Just as Peirce replaced metaphysical speculation with empirical experience, James took issue with the Idealist and Realist premise of a universal human nature. Human consciousness, like the variety in humankind's cultural experiences, was "a teeming multiplicity of objects and relations."[7] Unlike Peirce's mathematical reasoning, James thought in broader, more imaginative, and creative ways.

For the Idealist and Realist views of antecedent reality, see the chapters on Idealism and Realism.

James's broadly conceived Pragmatism celebrated the idea of human pluralism within an open and pluralistic universe.[8] His open universe can be contrasted with the Idealist and Realist concept of one that is already defined or antecedent to an individual's experience. Such an antecedent definition would result, for James, in a closed universe. James's emphasis on pluralism meant that there were many ways to live and express oneself. Pluralism represented a wide egalitarianism and not the grading of experience on a Platonic or Aristotelian hierarchy.

James's cultural pluralism resonates very well with contemporary multicultural education. Warning against the dangers of stereotyping and dogmatism, James advises us to extend our horizons beyond our own limited cultural, ethnic, and racial backgrounds and to see life from the perspective of other individuals and groups.

James regarded ideas as conjectural plans of action that humans formulated when they had to define and choose from possible alternative ways of acting in a situation. When we choose an alternative to act on, our choice, though it directs our action, is provisional and contingent. It is probable, as Peirce asserted, that we will need to revise our options as we encounter different situations in the course of life.[9] Our discussion of Pragmatism now turns to John Dewey's Experimentalism, or Instrumentalism. For Dewey, philosophy, like science, is experimental. Dewey is highly significant as a philosopher who concentrated much of his effort on educational problems.

JOHN DEWEY: PRAGMATIST EDUCATOR

John Dewey was born in Burlington, Vermont, in 1859, the year of the publication of Charles Darwin's *Origin of Species*. Dewey's father was a local businessman, and his family was active in the social and political life of the late nineteenth-century Vermont community, which was characterized by a spirit of democratic neighborliness.[10] Dewey's social philosophy would stress the significance of the face-to-face community in which people shared common concerns and problems. His democratic vision was shaped by the New England town meeting, where people met to solve their mutual problems through a peaceful and shared process of discussion, debate, and decision making. As he constructed his social and educational philosophy, Dewey embraced the concepts of democracy, the participatory community, and the application of the scientific method in his theory of social intelligence.

Dewey's religious upbringing as a Congregationalist shaped his social and ethical outlook. Evangelical Protestantism was being infused with the "social gospel," which emphasized a person's ethical responsibility of working for society's social and economic betterment. Although he would later end his formal adherence to organized religion, Dewey, like many Progressives, was a social reformer who believed that people had a mission to make the earth a better place in which to live, through reform and education.[11]

Dewey's Education and Career

Dewey attended the University of Vermont, where he received his bachelor's degree. He then taught school in Oil City, Pennsylvania, and later in rural Vermont. Dewey pursued doctoral studies at Johns Hopkins University, a graduate institution founded on the German research model. Also attending Johns Hopkins was the future political scientist, academic and political reformer, and U.S. president, Woodrow Wilson.

For the Hegelian sense of community, see the chapter on Idealism and Education.

As a graduate student at Johns Hopkins, Dewey studied the Hegelian Idealism of his mentor, George Sylvester Morris, which he would later abandon for Pragmatism. Although he moved away from Idealist metaphysics, Dewey's attraction to Hegel's theme of a unifying "great community" continued. For him, the Idealist ethic that accentuated human self-realization remained a guiding possibility, but he no longer believed that it was to be achieved in a spiritual realm.[12] Rather, Dewey believed that it would be achieved in human experiences transformed by larger transactions that embraced human relationships and democratic participation in the community.[13] Dewey's Experimentalism emphasized an optimism in the possibility of human progress that was influenced by a blending of Enlightenment science and Hegel's Idealism that saw humanity heading toward an ever better society.

After receiving his doctorate, Dewey began his career as a professor at the University of Minnesota in 1888. The following year, he joined the philosophy department of the University of Michigan, where he taught from 1889 to 1894.

In 1894, Dewey joined the faculty of the University of Chicago, which, under the leadership of William Rainey Harper, its president, was emerging as an internationally recognized institution for graduate research and study. At Chicago, Dewey served as head of the Department of Philosophy, Psychology, and Education. These three disciplines, then jointly organized in a single academic unit, held a special interest for Dewey, who studied and wrote on each of them.

Dewey's Association with George H. Mead

Dewey's Chicago years, from 1894 to 1904, were especially significant for his formulation of Experimentalism and for his educational experiment at the University Laboratory School. Early in his thinking, Dewey had forged a close relationship between philosophy and education.

Dewey's association with George Herbert Mead (1863–1931), a colleague in his department, and his involvement in Jane Addams's Hull House shaped his emerging Pragmatism. Mead argued that ideas and actions ought to be fused and directed toward social reform. Among Mead's ideas shared by Dewey were that (1) democracy, as an ideal, required a public that was educated to understand the social duties and responsibilities of political life; and (2) morality should be applied to the problems of daily life—to personal, political, social, and educational behavior.[14]

Like Dewey, Mead was interested in child development, particularly in early childhood education. Mead developed a theory of play as an activity whose purposes create connections to later activities, including work. Mead, who saw play as a natural way to learn, argued that the child's environment provided myriad opportunities for play.[15] Teachers should arrange the children's learning environment so that it stimulated interest and elicited activity. Mead also advocated experimental learning in which students engaged in field studies and laboratory work. His ideas were congenial to Dewey's thought and stimulated Dewey's philosophical and educational work at the University of Chicago.

University of Chicago Laboratory School

The University of Chicago Laboratory School, an experimental school Dewey established, had a profound influence on his evolving philosophy of education, especially its relationship to teaching and learning.[16] The school enrolled children ages four through fourteen and sought to provide experiences in cooperative and mutually useful living through the "activity method," which involved play, construction, nature study, and self-expression. These activities were designed to stimulate and exercise learners' active reconstruction of their own experiences. Through such activities, the school would function as a miniature community and an embryonic society. The children's individual tendencies were directed toward cooperative living in the school community.

Dewey's Laboratory School was an experimental school in which he tested his theories about education and learning. Educational hypotheses that were effective in aiding the students to reconstruct their experiences in terms of larger social outcomes could then be disseminated to a larger professional and public audience. In describing the Laboratory School at the University of Chicago, Dewey wrote:

> The conception underlying the school is that of a laboratory. It bears the same relation to the work in pedagogy that a laboratory bears to biology, physics, or chemistry. Like any such laboratory it has two main purposes: (1) to exhibit, test, verify, and criticize theoretical statements and principles; and (2) to add to the sum of facts and principles in its special line.[17]

Dewey's educational experiment emphasized the school's social function. As a "special social community," the complexity of the "social environment" was "reduced and simplified." According to Dewey:

> The simplified social life should reproduce, in miniature, the activities fundamental to life as a whole, and thus enable the child, on one side, to become gradually acquainted with the structure, materials, and modes of operation of the larger community; while upon the other, it enables him individually to express himself through these lines of conduct, and thus attain control of his own powers.[18]

The Laboratory School's curriculum integrated three of Dewey's concepts: critical reflective thinking, the scientific method, and the educative role of the group in constructing children's social intelligence. Unlike the conventional school curriculum organized around skills such as reading, writing, and arithmetic and academic subjects such as history, mathematics, and chemistry, the Laboratory curriculum focused on three broad sets of activities: making and doing, history and geography, and science. Making and doing referred to children's activities in their early years of schooling, the primary grades. To maintain continuity in their experience between home and school, children engaged in activities that grew out of their familiar experiences and interests and led them to the larger society's relationships and occupations. Making and doing was followed by history and geography, taught not as conventional school subjects but designed to expand children's perspectives into time and space. The curriculum's third stage, science, broadly meant investigating various subject-matter disciplines, not in isolation from each other, but for their instrumental interdisciplinary use in solving problems. Dewey's stages of curriculum are discussed more fully in the chapter's section on curriculum.

After testing his early ideas about education at the Laboratory School, Dewey constructed the philosophical scaffolding of Instrumentalism, or Experimentalism, his version of Pragmatism. Dewey's Laboratory School, which attracted national and international attention, still fascinates historians and philosophers of education. Despite the school's acclaim and perhaps because of it, Dewey ran into administrative conflicts, especially over his employment of his wife, Alice Chipman Dewey, as the school's principal. The University of Chicago's president, William Rainey Harper, began to challenge Dewey's administrative decisions.

Dewey's Chicago period, especially his Laboratory School, identified him with Progressivism as a social, political, and educational movement. He collaborated with Jane Addams (1860–1935), the founder of Hull House, a social settlement house on Chicago's west side, where Dewey was a consultant and lecturer. Dewey's conversations with Addams helped him to refine his philosophy. When he came to Chicago, Dewey still retained some ideas from his earlier Hegelian training that social change resulted from a synthesis of necessary social conflicts. Addams convinced him that conflict was unnecessary and often interfered with the socially intelligent cooperative solving of problems. Conflicts, according to Addams, generally arose when individuals interjected their personal biases and prejudices into a controversial issue. The genuine resolution of conflict, Addams advised Dewey, came when people collaborated to resolve a problem or issue.

While in Chicago, Dewey broadened his insights into the relationships between schools and children's learning. He collaborated with Colonel Francis Parker (1837–1902), a leading progressive educator, who was principal of the Cook County Normal School and the Chicago Institute of Education. He worked closely with Ella Flagg Young (1845–1918), the first woman to be a superintendent of a major urban school district. It was Young who encouraged him to put his ideas into practice at the Laboratory School.

Dewey left the University of Chicago to become a professor of philosophy at Columbia University in New York City in 1905, where he taught until he retired in 1930. At Columbia, Dewey was closely associated with such prominent Progressive professors of education as William Heard Kilpatrick (1871–1965), the founder of the project method, George S. Counts (1889–1974), the originator of social reconstructionism, and Harold Rugg (1886–1960), a pioneer in issue-based social studies.

For Kilpatrick, Counts, and Rugg, see the chapter on Progressivism and Education.

Dewey's Major Philosophical and Educational Works

Because Dewey was such a prolific author, we comment only on a selected number of his books that are most relevant for Pragmatism as an educational philosophy.[19] Dewey's *The School and Society* originated from lectures he delivered about the University of Chicago Laboratory School in 1899. Dewey, then in a highly formative stage of his career, began to implement his Experimentalist philosophy into education in the Laboratory school setting. He commented on the need for schools to assume a larger social function.[20] His *The Child and the Curriculum* (1902) examined the teacher's role in relating the curriculum to the child's interest, readiness, and stage of development.[21] Emphasizing experience as the basis for learning, Dewey recommended activities that encouraged the child's immediate and personal use of knowledge.

In 1910, Dewey's *How We Think* argued that thinking is experimental in that it involves a series of problem-solving episodes that occur as we attempt to survive and grow in an environmental context.[22] Employing the scientific method, thinking occurs when we conjecture hypotheses designed to make an indeterminate situation into a determinate one. Thinking, as defined by Dewey, had implications for a method of educational inquiry based on problem solving. (Later in the chapter, we shall comment more extensively on *How We Think* in relation to Dewey's epistemology.)

Democratic Environment: for Dewey, a democracy is a democratic society in an open environment where beliefs, ideas, and values can be examined, tested, revised, reconstructed, or discarded.

Democracy and Education (1916), Dewey's most complete rendition of educational philosophy, identified the foundational ideas of a democratic society and applied them to education.[23] Essentially, Dewey, who consistently rejected dualism, argued that genuine education proceeded more effectively in an open or **democratic environment** that is free of absolutes that block freedom of inquiry. In *Individualism, Old and New* (1920) he rejected the inherited notion of "rugged individualism" as an archaic historic residue.[24] In place of a competitive economy and society, Dewey urged social planning and action that would make the emergent corporate social order congenial to human growth and purposes. In *Art as Experience* (1934), Dewey elaborated an aesthetic theory asserting that art was properly a public means of shared expression and communication between the artist and the perceiver of the art object.[25]

Among Dewey's other major books were *Interest and Effort in Education* (1913), *Human Nature and Conduct* (1922), and *Freedom and Culture* (1939).[26] Through his writings, lectures, and presence on the U.S. and world scene, Dewey contributed to political and social liberalism that urged social reform based on pragmatic planning. His work stimulated the rise of an Experimentalist educational philosophy that profoundly influenced educational theory and practice in the United States.

Dewey and Progressive Education

For Progressive education, see the chapter on Progressivism and Education.

Although often called the father of progressive education, Dewey's identification with progressive education needs some qualifications. Dewey's influence on Progressivism came as he contributed to the general emphasis on social and educational reform. He agreed with many elements in progressive education and rejected others—especially the naive romanticism of the neo-Rousseaueans.

Although many Progressives were influenced by Dewey's Experimentalism, others were not. The Progressive Education Association (PEA), an umbrella organization, encompassed a variety of individuals and groups ranging from neo-Rousseauean, child-centered educators to neo-Freudians. The publication of many of Dewey's educational writings coincided with the Progressive education movement, and similarities existed between Dewey and the Progressive reformers who opposed a static conception of learning and schooling. Although Dewey and many Progressive educators agreed on the importance of experience, continuity, and the cultivation of the child's interests and needs, Dewey challenged the sentimental, romantic neo-Rousseauean Progressives who dogmatically asserted child-centered doctrines. Dewey's *Experience and Education* (1938) criticized Progressive educators for failing to elaborate a positive educational philosophy based on experience.[27] He cautioned educators against a simplistic categorization of educational theories and practices into "either-or" polar opposites. Challenging Progressives to move beyond merely opposing traditional school practices, he urged them to develop an affirmative educational philosophy rooted in human experience.

EXPERIMENTALISM'S PHILOSOPHICAL BASES

Dewey's Experimentalism held a special relevance for education. Among its philosophical bases are (1) Dewey's rejection of metaphysical absolutes; (2) the interaction of the organism and the environment; (3) Dewey's Experimentalist epistemology; (4) the complete act of thought; and (5) axiology as experimental valuation.

Dewey's Rejection of Metaphysical Absolutes

For their metaphysics, see the chapters on Idealism and Realism.

In earlier chapters on Idealism and Realism, we examined metaphysics as speculation about the nature of ultimate reality. In this section, we examine Dewey's attack on philosophical systems based on absolute metaphysical positions, dualism, and a quest for certitude. Pragmatists such as Dewey reject such speculation as unverifiable in terms of human experience.

Although *Democracy and Education* most completely stated Dewey's educational philosophy, the key to Dewey's system of thought is found in *The Quest for Certainty*.[28] Dewey argued against a dualistic conception of the universe, which he claimed was merely a human contrivance designed to postulate a theoretically unchanging realm of complete and perfect certitude. The more traditional Idealist, Realist, and Thomist philosophies, based on metaphysical propositions, grounded reality in a world of unchanging ideas for the Idealist or structures for the Realist. Based on these conceptions, Western thinkers had devised a bipolar, dualistic view of reality that divided it into ideational, or conceptual, and material dimensions. In these older philosophies, ideas and spirit are higher in the chain of being, and work and action are lower in the hierarchy. Priority is given to the immaterial and unchanging order. Thus, such classical dualisms as spirit–matter, mind–body, and soul–body came to permeate Western thought. These metaphysical dualisms had an impact on life and education in that they created distinctions between theory and practice, liberal and vocational education, fine and applied arts, and thought and action.

The bifurcation between theory and practice, or thought and action, was not only a matter for speculation by philosophers, but it also had an impact on educational practice. Philosophical dualism contributed to patterns of hierarchical curricular organization in which the most theoretical subjects were given priority over practical ones. Distinguishing between theory and practice, the traditional curriculum required learners to first master symbolic and literary skills such as reading, writing, and arithmetic. Learning these tool skills prepared children to study systematically such subjects as history, geography, mathematics, and science at the secondary and higher levels. In the traditional subject-matter curriculum, disciplines are organized deductively as bodies of principles, theories, factual content, and examples. Formal education became excessively abstract and bore little relationship to the learner's own personal and social experience. Furthermore, the subject-matter curriculum aimed to prepare students for future situations after the completion of formal schooling. According to Dewey's critique, the traditional subject-matter curriculum, based on the dualism between theory and practice, created additional bifurcations that separated the child from the curriculum and the school from the society.

Dewey's social conception of education is basic to his Experimentalism, which viewed thinking and doing as a unified flow of ongoing experience. Thinking and acting were not separable; thinking was incomplete until tested in experience. To understand Dewey's pragmatic philosophy, we need to examine his antagonism toward the dualism that supported traditional philosophical beliefs in a higher, transcendent, and unchanging reality.

According to Dewey, human beings inhabit an uncertain world that contains threats to survival. In their minds, human beings sought to create a concept of certainty to give them a sense of permanence and security. Because actual living contains risk, traditional philosophers differentiated between the uncertainty of everyday life and the security that came from an unchanging and perfect reality. Early religio-philosophical systems, such as Idealism and Thomism, created a worldview that posited reality in a perfect, unchanging, and eternal universal being. In this *Weltanschauung*, the inferior level of existence was mundane, changing, and uncertain, and the superior order was that which was beyond the scope of the empirical, experiential, and everyday existence, or, in other words, metaphysical, higher than and beyond the physical world.

Traditional philosophies, derived from Platonism, or Aristotelianism, were occupied with speculation about permanent, eternal, and self-sufficient being. According to the doctrines of an immutable good and fixed order of being, speculative philosophers were concerned with describing metaphysical systems of immutable and necessary truths and principles that lay beyond human experience. According to philosophical **dualism**, a higher realm of fixed and permanent reality existed in which truth was absolute; there was also an inferior world of changing objects and persons that was the realm of experience and practice.

Dualism: Dewey opposed dualism, or seeing the world in two dimensions—a superior one that is perfect, timeless, and unchanging and an inferior one that is temporary, finite, and changing.

Dewey emphasizes a changing and evolutionary universe in which the human situation is not to transcend experience but rather to use it to solve human problems. Rejecting dualistic epistemologies, Dewey emphasizes a continuum of human experience that relates rather than separates thinking and acting, fact and value, and intellect and emotion.[29] He argues that philosophy should recognize, reconstruct, and use experience to improve the human condition. In such a reconstruction of experience, theory and practice are fused and used in ongoing human activity. Derived from experience, theory is tested in action. Instead of a dualism between the immutable and the changing, experience is a continuum in which individuals and groups deal with a successive sequence of problematic situations. In such a sequence, theory is derived from and tested in practice; mind is a social process of intelligently solving problems rather than an antecedent and transcendent category; education is liberal, or liberating, as it frees human beings by giving them a methodology for dealing with all kinds of problems, including the social and vocational; and the distinction between the fine and useful arts is dissolved by integrating beauty and function. Dewey's thesis is that living is uncertain. To exist means to be alive and involved in a changing world. The human quest, Dewey advises, is not for certainty but rather for a means, or a method of controlling and directing the process of change insofar as this is possible in an imperfect world.

The Organism and the Environment

As indicated earlier, Dewey's birth in 1859 coincided with Charles Darwin's publication of the *Origin of Species.* The revolutionary implications of Darwin's biological theory reverberated throughout the late nineteenth and early twentieth centuries and continue to spark controversy in the twenty-first century. In education, the continuing controversy is about teaching the theory of evolution, Creationism, or Intelligent Design in the schools.

Initially, Darwin's evolutionary theory appeared to challenge the traditional Judeo-Christian narrative of creation, found in the Bible's book of Genesis, that God had created species in a fixed form. Those who accepted the literal version of Genesis as revealed truth, opposed Darwin's findings about the origin of species, especially human beings. For some fundamentalist Protestant Americans, Darwin's theory was a dangerous undermining of moral and religious values.

According to Darwin's thesis that species evolved slowly and gradually, members of the species, or organisms, lived, adjusted, and adapted to their environments to survive. Those species that succeeded in surviving did so because they possessed favorable characteristics that enabled them to adjust satisfactorily to environmental changes. The transmission of these favorable characteristics to their offspring guaranteed the particular species' continuation. Darwin's theory emphasized the competition of individuals for survival in a frequently challenging environment.

SOCIAL DARWINISM. To understand Darwin's impact on Dewey's thinking, we need to look briefly at the adaptation of evolutionary theory into a sociology of knowledge by Herbert Spencer (1820–1903). Spencer's **Social Darwinism**, the application of Darwin's findings to society, economics, and politics, had a pervasive influence of American education, especially in the late nineteenth and early twentieth centuries. For example, Spencer's argument that the curriculum should be based on health, economic, social, and political needs shaped the program in American high schools. Although Spencer and Dewey rejected traditional metaphysically based philosophies and agreed with Darwin's theory of evolution, there were sharp differences between them. In many respects, Spencer's Social Darwinism was a major obstacle to Dewey's Experimentalism and its residues still block progressive innovations in schools.

Social Darwinism: The application of Darwin's biological theory of evolution to other areas such as society, the economy, and politics.

Spencer viewed the human being as an individual social atom who is locked in a fiercely competitive struggle against other individuals. Through individual competition and initiative, some individuals adapt to the environment more efficiently than others. These intelligent and strong competitors climb upward in society to positions of social, economic, and political leadership. Unfit individuals, who are unintelligent in their behavior and unable to compete effectively or efficiently, descend on the rungs of the social ladder to become the dregs of society. For Spencer, competition is the natural order of life, with the prize going to the fittest individuals. Fighting against the Social Darwinist stress on individual competition, Dewey emphasized social cooperation as a key element in building social intelligence. In education, he accentuated the importance of group work and social interaction.

Spencer and his many followers in business and in academia regarded the laissez-faire economic and social order as the natural state of affairs and argued against tampering with nature's laws of competition. Society, they argued, is composed of independent, autonomous, and competitive individuals, who at the most direct level struggle for economic survival. In the Social Darwinist view, schools efficiently exercise their socioeconomic role by preparing individuals to succeed in a competitive world. Progress takes place as individuals invent and devise innovative ways of competing against each other in exploiting the natural and social environments. Dewey, in contrast, rejected Spencer's belief that the law of supply and demand was a natural law. For him, this laissez-faire attitude blocked needed social, political, and economic reform.

INTERACTION OF THE ORGANISM IN THE ENVIRONMENT. Darwin's theory of an evolutionary process exercised an important influence on Dewey. Using an organismic psychology, Dewey applied the terms *organism* and *environment* to human experience and education. For Dewey, the human organism is a living and natural creature, physiologically composed of living tissue and possessing life-sustaining impulses and drives. Every organism, including the human being, lives within an environment, or habitat, which has elements that both enhance and threaten its life.

For Dewey, human life is sustained through interactions with the natural and social environments. Rather than becoming one with nature, as Rousseau suggested, or being locked in struggle with nature, as Spencer argued, Dewey, using his empiricist naturalism, advised human beings instrumentally to actively use nature to transform parts of the environment to increase their life-sustaining possibilities. Through the application of scientific intelligence and through cooperative social activity, humans can use certain elements in nature to solve problems with other aspects of the natural environment.[30]

Dewey's emphasis on active human transaction with the environment challenged the more traditional philosophical orientation found in Aristotelian Realism that the human being is a spectator, albeit an intelligent observer of reality. Dewey wanted education to be transformed from merely training students to be passive observers or recipients of information into proactive learners who could effect environment change to improve the quality of life.

For the spectator and correspondence theory of knowledge, see the chapter on Realism and Education.

As the individual human being, or human organism, lives, he or she encounters problematic situations of an indeterminate character that interfere with the ongoing march of experience. Upon encountering such an indeterminate situation, the individual's activity is blocked or impeded until she or he can render the novel situation determinate and resume activity. The successful person is able to solve problems and add the elements of his or her solution to the reserves of experience. As a result of this network of interaction between the organism and its environment, the human being acquires experience. In Dewey's Experimentalism, the key concept of **experience** is best thought of as the interaction of or the transaction between a person and her or his environment. We know through our experiences, or environmental interactions; each experiential episode adds to our experience. When confronted by problematic situations, we examine our experience for clues, which suggest the means for resolving the present difficulty.

Experience: for Dewey, the interaction of the individual or group with the environment.

At this point, several basic components of Dewey's educational philosophy can be identified: (1) The learner is a living organism, a biological and sociological phenomenon, who possesses drives or impulses designed to sustain life; (2) the learner lives in an environment, or habitat, which is both natural and social; (3) the learner, moved by personal drives, is actively engaged in constant interaction with the environment; (4) environmental interaction causes problems that occur as the individual seeks to satisfy his or her needs; and (5) learning is the process of using experience as an instrument to solve problems in the environment.

SOCIAL EXPERIENCE: ASSOCIATIVE LIVING. From his days at the University of Chicago Laboratory School onward, Dewey emphasized the school's social function as a miniature community or embryonic society. Although holding that society was composed of separate and discrete individual human beings, he rejected Social Darwinism's competitive ethic of social atomism. For Dewey, human beings live in both a social and a natural environment. In striving to live, human beings found that group life, or human association, most effectively contributed to their welfare and survival. **Associative living**, or community, enriches human experience and adds to it as the group mutually engages in problem-solving activities.

Associative Living: the interaction (the sharing and participation) of individuals in a community.

Associative human experience provides individuals with a more complex set of experiences, or interactive episodes. Barriers to full human association block free interaction. They impede the opportunities of individuals and groups to contribute to cultural growth by mutual sharing experiences.[31] In the scope and varieties of interactions, a community should be democratic. It should be free of traditions, prejudices, and biases that block individuals from mutual association. As the school becomes more inclusive, the opportunities for social growth increase.

Although Dewey's model of experience arising from the interaction of the organism with the environment has often been interpreted in socio-educational terms, some scholars broaden the interpretation to include an ecological-educational dimension as well. According to this emphasis on Dewey's humanist Naturalism, the human organism is interacting then with "an integrated social and biophysical environment."[32]

This naturalistic element in Dewey's thought, while not romantic in the Rousseauean sense, argues against a dualism that sees human beings occupying two separate spheres of existence—one social and the other natural. It also rejects a crude Darwinism that sees human beings as combatants locked in struggle against nature. Such a broadened conception of environmental interaction encourages an ecological sensitivity to the earth as a biosphere, which opens the educational process to a wide range of world problems such as pollution, conservation of natural resources, preservation of endangered species, global warming, and ultimately arms control.

Dewey's Experimentalist Epistemology

Rather than having a preoccupation with metaphysics, Dewey focused on epistemology or how we construct our knowledge. For him, as well as other Pragmatists, knowing as an experimental and commonsense process followed the method of scientific inquiry. In the next section, we examine Dewey's concepts of intelligence and experimental inquiry and his integrating of the scientific method into the "complete act of thought."

In breaking with the more traditional Idealism and Realism, which rested on a metaphysical conception of antecedent reality, Dewey believed that these speculative philosophies had constructed a static theory of mind that was isolated from life's personal and social realities. Dewey proposed an active social conception of human intelligence, which, while conditioned by societal institutions, could dynamically affect social change.

For Dewey, intelligence is socially constructed as people cooperatively relate their experiences to the common problems that they face. Intelligence, the ability to define and solve problems, is developed through the experience of persisting and working through problem-solving situations. Within the problem-solving context, intelligence results from shared activity in making and using instruments, in fashioning plans of action, and in acting on hypotheses. Human beings use their intelligence to invent and fabricate instruments or tools. The more complex and sophisticated the society, the more instruments are available to use in solving problems. Unlike Rousseau's glorification of the primitive state of nature, Dewey found the savage or primitive human being to be limited by a paucity of instruments that could be used in solving problems. In contrast, civilized society possessed the instruments that enhanced group problem-solving efforts and cultivated and enriched social intelligence.

Dewey's view of the human being as a fabricator of tools, as an instrument maker, has important implications for education. Children in a civilized society need to develop familiarity with making and using instruments. Through schooling, they can experience in a relatively short time much of the human experience that is involved in making and using instruments.

HOW WE THINK. Dewey's insightful *How We Think* (1910) developed his Experimentalist epistemology, psychology, and logic. He argues that (1) philosophy's true purpose is to help people solve their real problems that arise in experience; (2) "truth" is not the result of metaphysical speculation but is constructed from our tentative "warranted assertions" that guide us in a constantly changing environment; and (3) we verify our ideas when we test them to see whether their consequences resolve our problems. Relating epistemology to teaching and learning, Dewey argues that we use our ideas as instruments to solve our personal, social, and political problems.

Dewey, in *How We Think*, introduces the concept of "reflective thinking," or **reflection**, that is a frequently used term in contemporary teacher education. Teachers are advised to be reflective practitioners who think deeply and draw inferences about their teaching methods, sense of social justice, and attitudes and behavior toward their students and colleagues.

Reflection: the process of thinking deeply and introspectively about something; as used in teacher education, to think deeply and to draw inferences from educational observations and experiences.

Relating reflection to the scientific method, Dewey defined reflective thinking as the "active, persistent, and careful" examination of our beliefs in terms of the evidence that supports them and the conclusions to which they lead. Reflection, for Dewey, is not daydreaming, listening to a teacher or professor lecture, or passive contemplation. Thinking is based on reflection during which the individual conjectures the consequences her or his ideas are likely to have when acted upon. When we think reflectively, our thoughts are "persistent," in that each element in them grows out of, relates to, and is connected in a chain, or continuum, to the preceding one. The term *careful* means the willingness to delay acting and to avoid jumping to hasty, unwarranted conclusions. It means taking time and expending the energy to collect the evidence needed to support a conclusion and to defer a judgment as we conjecture its consequences and test it. Reflective thinking, like the scientific method, does not take beliefs for granted because of custom, tradition, or opinion, but puts them to the test of critical inquiry and action.[33]

Dewey wrote *How We Think* to guide teachers in developing students' reflective or scientific thinking habits and skills. He believed that children's intrinsic curiosity, imagination, and activities mark the beginning of experimentation. Curious about their environment, children are eager to explore it; their explorations stimulate their thinking about what they are experiencing. Children's natural curiosity has a social and educational connection. Children learn to ask others—parents, friends, and teachers—to add to their experience. When they see something new, they ask, "What is that?" When they don't understand what something does, they ask, often repeatedly, "How does it work?" or "What does it do?" These important leading questions verbalize their thinking process and seek to engage others in moving it from an internal process to a social one with many educational possibilities. "What," "why," and "how" are the questions children use to begin what, if encouraged and properly guided, leads to complete, reflective, and scientific thinking. In this process of moving from curiosity to critical thinking, Dewey observed that the "teacher has usually more to learn than to teach."[34] Dewey encouraged teachers to use children's open and flexible interests as the avenue to reflective thought. Too often, he warned, dogma and routine blight the learning process.

Complete Act of Thought: Dewey's concept of thinking completely by using the scientific method, in which we are in a problematic situation, define it, research it, develop hypotheses to solve it, and choose and act on a particular hypothesis.

Problematic Situation: a person's encounter with something that is different from previous experience and blocks ongoing activity.

Complete Act of Thought

According to Dewey, genuine thinking means that the individual uses the scientific method to solve problems that arise when interacting with the environment. Dewey's concept of the scientific method is a broadly conceived procedure of scientific intelligence that is applicable to human affairs.[35] Dewey's problem-solving method, or **complete act of thought**—consists of five steps:

1. The **problematic situation**, in which the individual is involved in an incomplete situation of indeterminate character. In the problematic situation, the individual's

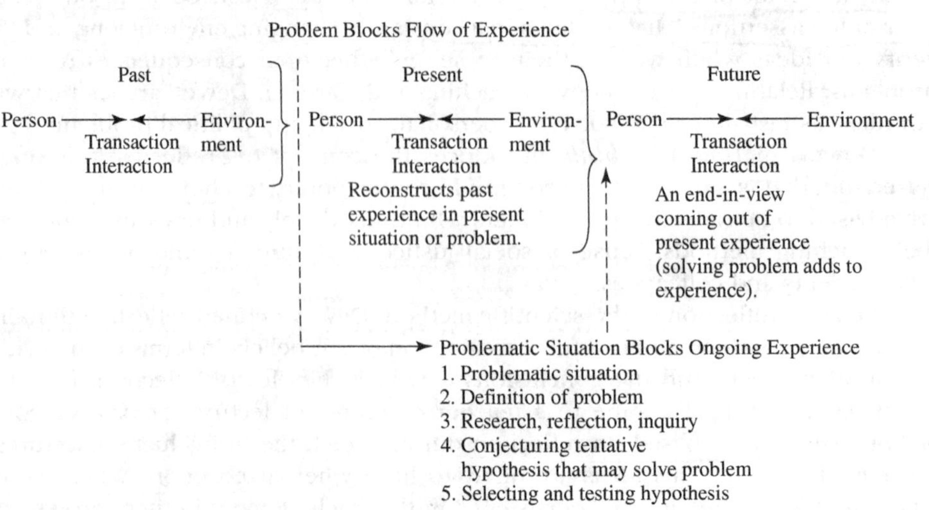

Pragmatic Continuum of Experience

ongoing activity is blocked by some unique situational element that deviates or is different from past experience.

2. In *defining the problem,* the individual examines the problematic situation and identifies that aspect of the situation, the deviant particular that is different from past experience and is blocking continuing activity.
3. *Clarification of the problem* involves a careful and reflective survey, examination, inspection, exploration, and analysis of the elements involved in the problematic situation. At this stage of inquiry, the individual systematically and reflectively researches the problem to locate the ideas, materials, and instruments that might resolve the difficulty.
4. By *constructing tentative hypotheses,* the individual establishes a number of generalizations—if–then statements—that are possible means of solving the problem. This process involves mentally projecting oneself into the future and conjecturing the possible consequences of action. As a result of hypothesizing and conjecturing, the individual frames tentative solutions that might resolve the difficulty and yield the greatest possibilities for producing the desired consequences.
5. This crucial step involves *testing the preferred hypothesis by acting on it.* If the hypothesis resolves the problem and brings the desired consequences, then the individual resumes activity until encountering another problem. If the problem remains, then another hypothesis is needed to resolve it.[36]

It is important to understand, as Dewey states, that reflective thought is an ongoing and cumulative process and not just a sequence of mechanical steps. Each phase in thinking through a problem builds from the preceding phase and is related and connected to the phase that follows. Amassing, reciting, and recalling facts as information is not reflective thinking. The facts, or evidence, need to be organized, referenced, and used. The process needs to point to an end: solving the problem that was identified and defined at the onset of the process. Having a direction means that the problem solver is flexible and alert to new leads on how to solve the problem. It also means that the learner needs the perseverance to stay with the project and not jump from one phase to another or to abandon it when it becomes difficult.

While reflective thinking often begins with children's instincts and impulses, it did not intend that teachers should stay with them. Rather, they are to guide the thinking process from impulsivity to reflection. Reflective thinking does not mean that children should jump to conclusions; rather, it means staying with the process, researching the problem, and conjecturing ways to solve it. Children become reflective thinkers when they learn to take their time, pause, step back, and reflect on the consequences of their actions. Encouraging reflective thinking also means that adults, particularly teachers who may be anxious that children get the right answer, are not to become impatient with the process and pressure children to get it done quickly. Education is truly progressive when children learn to think reflectively by formulating plans, gathering evidence pertinent to the problem, and avoiding being diverted into incidental and irrelevant matters.

Dewey's experimental epistemology provides the format for the method of problem solving in which the learner, as an individual or in association with others, uses the scientific method to solve both personal and social problems. Each problem-solving episode becomes an experimental situation in which learners apply the method of intelligence to real problems arising in their own experiences. For Dewey and his followers, the problem-solving method is transferable to a variety of problematic situations.

Dewey's fifth step, the testing of the hypothesis, represents the greatest departure from the learning pattern of the traditional subject-oriented school. Teachers and students in more conventional schools might explore problems and frame tentative solutions, but rarely do they attempt to solve these problems by acting on them directly. Although they might act on problems encountered in their chemistry and mathematics lessons, the solutions to these problems are predetermined. It is most unlikely that students would be encouraged to act on controversial social, economic, and political problems. Although such problems as war, poverty, and pollution might be discussed in the conventional classroom, the students' active attempt to resolve these problems is deferred to times and situations outside the school. It might, in fact, be deferred until the student reaches adulthood and becomes a voter. In contrast, Dewey held that the validation of an idea occurs only as it is tested in experience. Thought is incomplete until acted on and the consequences of action are assessed.

Axiology as Experimental Valuation

When Dewey abandoned Idealism for Pragmatism, he began to construct a nonmetaphysical value theory in which ethical and aesthetic sensibilities and actions come from human experience rather than a vision of ultimate reality.[37] Unlike the Idealist and Realist philosophers who proposed a hierarchy of values inherent in the universe, Dewey believed that values arose from human responses to varying environmental and cultural situations. For Dewey, a major defect of hierarchical value systems is that humans experience wide varieties of conflicting hierarchies, or what James would call *plural values.*

Dewey turned away from ethical and aesthetic theories where tradition and custom determine what is good, true, and beautiful. The validation of values by custom and tradition, Dewey believed, justified whatever exists at a particular time and place and becomes a rationale for preserving the status quo. In an interdependent modern world, a method of valuation is needed to resolve cross-cultural conflicts. In a technological society of rapid material change, customs and traditions lag so far behind social change that they are grossly inadequate in influencing value choices.

Dewey argued that the method of shared scientific intelligence should be applied to moral, ethical, and aesthetic issues. Evaluation should be based on the relationships of aims, means, and ends. Experimentalist valuation begins in human preferences, wants, wishes, desires, and needs. Evaluation arises when a conflict occurs in these raw materials of value. If a person has a single desire, then he or she will act to satisfy that desire. In the case of value conflict, it is necessary to unify the apparently conflicting desires. If the desires cannot be unified, then a choice needs to be made between conflicting alternatives. Choice is made by evaluating the possible consequences of acting on the chosen preference.

Dewey's method of valuation is designed to unify aims, means, and ends. When an end is attained, it becomes a means for the satisfaction of still another end. If a person desires a given end, it is necessary to ask questions about the appropriate and efficient means of attaining it.

Dewey's Democratic Ethics

Democratic Society: a social environment free of the dogma and absolutes that block truly experimental inquiry.

Although Dewey's value theory followed an experimental design, it also embraced a conception of democracy that held broad implications for society and education. Democracy means more than the political arrangements associated with representative, popular governments. It is both an ethical and a methodological necessity in Dewey's thought. A **democratic society** embraces the widest possible human sharing, participation, and involvement in institutional life and processes. Dewey's opposition to dualism in philosophy extended to dualisms in society in which individuals or groups are segregated and marginalized. Societies that practice segregation on the basis of class, race, sex, or ethnicity lose the opportunity for the growth of social intelligence and enrichment that comes from a sense of community life in which all people participate.

An earlier section of the chapter commented on Dewey's opposition to Social Darwinism's ethic of competitive individualism. Dewey's new or modern liberalism challenged older classical liberalism that was and still is a powerful ideology in the United States. Classical liberalism, associated with free enterprise capitalism, allied with Social Darwinism and argued that values are based on individual self-interest and are best realized in a market-driven economy free from government regulations. Dewey found that the older variety of liberalism exaggerated individualism and neglected human community and cooperation.

For Classical Liberalism, see the chapter on Liberalism and Education.

In Dewey's theory of democratic ethics, a necessary and reciprocal relationship exists between individuals and their community. In a democracy, all members of the community have an equal right and responsibility to participate in its processes and actions. Participation in the democratic community should take place in an open social and political setting guaranteed by freedom of inquiry, assembly, and communication.[38]

Dewey's concept of democracy is wholly egalitarian and fully operative in the public sphere. He rejected the idea that some people, because of their credentials, status, and position, should have more power than others in making decisions. He would have opposed the contemporary trend in American society and politics that empowers special interest groups over the entire polity.[39]

Democratic social arrangements are a methodological necessity for experimental inquiry. Such arrangements are free of philosophical absolutes that block inquiry into what are privileged as immutable first principles. They also are free of the restrictions to inquiry imposed by regimes that close off public discussion and debate.

Dewey's conceptions of democratic social arrangements and democratic education are related to a society that is willing to reform its institutions through careful experimentation. Not specific to the American form of government or to its political institutions, Dewey's conception of democratic education is rather an epistemological and sociological one characterized by the presence of an experimental temperament. In the experimenting society, citizens are free from the impediments erected by absolutist governments or *a priori* philosophies. Because educational institutions socialize the young in group values, genuinely democratic education occurs within the milieu of the experimental or inquiry-oriented school.

Dewey saw the school as a miniature society in which children engage in mutually shared activities that lead them to participate in an associative participatory democracy. In education, Dewey's democratic value theory encourages inquiring minds in an open classroom. Such openness carries with it the risk that long-standing ideas and values may be challenged, reconstructed, and possibly discarded. Openness, however, does not mean educational anarchy or naive romanticism. Rather, openness requires social arrangements conducive to using the method of intelligence, the experimental method, to deal with human issues.

EXPERIMENTALISM'S EDUCATIONAL IMPLICATIONS

The following section examines selected aspects of Dewey's educational philosophy. These include (1) education as conservation and reconstruction, (2) schooling and society, (3) the democratic society and education, (4) Experimentalist teaching and learning, (5) growth as the end of education, and (6) the experiential curriculum.

Education as Conservation and Reconstruction

In *Democracy and Education,* Dewey is primarily concerned with the relationship between society and education. Education occurs informally as children grow in the socio-cultural milieu and acquire the language, skills, and knowledge common to their group. In the more formal education in schools, education is a deliberate process of instructing children in symbolic and linguistic tools needed for group interaction and communication.

For Dewey, education has both conservative (preserving) and reconstructive (renewing) dimensions. It is conservative in that it provides cultural continuity by transmitting the heritage from adults to children, the group's immature members. In both its formal and informal aspects, education involves cultural imposition because it takes place within the context of a particular culture with its own language, beliefs, traditions, and customs. Although cultural imposition is always contextual to a given time and place, it provides individuals with the skills and instruments they need to communicate with and express themselves to other members of their group.

Dewey recognized that all learning is particular and contextual to a given time, place, and circumstance. Although cultural particularities impose themselves on learning, Dewey made a distinction between imposition and indoctrination. Imposition reflects the concrete contingencies of living in a particular culture and environment with its unique heritage and values, whereas indoctrination closes the mind to divergent thinking and alternative ways of acting.

As it transmits the cultural heritage from the older to the younger generation, education is the means by which the group reproduces its preferred kind of personality in its young members and perpetuates itself culturally. Children are socialized as they acquire and use the cultural instruments and values through association with the members of the group. Although he clearly recognized that the conservative aspects of education provide cultural continuity, Dewey saw education's purpose as broader and more dynamic than preserving the status quo. Cultural conservation, for Dewey, did not mean that adults in a society should use schools to simply reproduce traditional beliefs and values. Rather, it meant that the young are provided with the cultural skills, instruments, and processes that they can use to improve social conditions.[40] The very cultural instrumentalities such as the language and technology that are imposed on the young carry with them the possibilities for improving the inherited culture. In his pragmatic view of a constantly changing universe, Dewey believed human beings, using the scientific method, could direct the course of change.

Dewey gave the past an instrumentalist interpretation. Precedents—conclusions about past experiences—were instruments to use in analyzing present situations and issues rather than prescriptions to be followed dogmatically.[41] Humans could reconstruct historical precedents as part of the process of constructing new hypotheses to solve problems in the present.

Schooling and Society

The cultural heritage is a vast and myriad compendium of beliefs and values; it is derived from the general accumulated experience of the human race as well as from the more specific experience of particular groups. It includes the general and more specific elements of language, beliefs, knowledge, values, traditions, and customs. It is so large and unwieldy that it needs to be simplified and organized so that it can be presented to children in schools. Further, some aspects of the cultural heritage such as prejudice, violence, and crime should not be transmitted to the young. The cultural heritage then has elements that are both worthy and unworthy of transmission and perpetuation. Formal education in schools is one of society's means of selecting those aspects of the cultural heritage that are worthy of being passed on to the young.

Dewey defined the school as a specialized educational environment established by society to enculturate the young by deliberately bringing them into cultural participation. As a social institution, the school is a selective agency that, while transmitting the culture, also seeks to reconstruct it to meet contemporary needs. For Dewey, the school's threefold functions are to simplify, purify, and balance the cultural heritage.[42] **Simplification** means that the school, really curriculum makers and teachers as social agents, selects elements of the heritage and reduces their complexity into units of instruction that are appropriate to the learner's maturity and readiness. As a purifying agency, the school selects and transmits those elements of the cultural heritage that enhance human growth and eliminates unworthy aspects that limit it. Balancing the cultural heritage refers to integrating the selected experiences into a harmonious core.

Simplification: reducing complex cultural materials into smaller and simpler units in the curriculum.

Because a society, especially American society, is culturally pluralistic and composed of many diverse groups, children need guidance to understand and appreciate the contributions of members of groups other than their own. The genuinely democratic society as an integrated and balanced community rests on mutually shared understanding.

Group experience is based on shared participation in which all members share their individual experiences and mutually create a broader experiential network. The more individuals share their own experiences, their life stories, with others in the group, the more possibilities develop to enlarge the quantity and enhance the quality of the group's experience. Dewey believed that this broad sharing generates social intelligence.

Dewey understood that life in an industrial, urban, technological, and global society generated challenges for society and schools. The more complex the society becomes, the greater is the gap between children's immediate activities and the requirements of responsible adult life. He believed that a problem-based, activity-oriented school would develop skills and knowledge that would reduce the gap between children's experience and the larger society.

The Community, Education, and the School

Dewey emphasized the cooperative nature of shared human experience. His stress on human association embraced three key elements: the common, communication, and community. The **common** refers to the ideas, values, objects, instruments, and processes that are shared and used by members of a group in a given cultural context. In a school situation, the common would include the games, stories, books, activities, and tools that students share in their educational process.

Common: group identification generated by sharing objects and engaging in shared activities that leads to communication and community.

Communication occurs when people frame and express their shared experiences of the common in symbolic patterns in a common language. When individuals communicate, they use the common as a shared perspective with other persons to express meanings and construct reciprocal understanding with them. In the school where discussion is an important feature in learning, students, as they talk about their shared activities and problems, are constructing networks of communication. Communication thus develops a commonly shared context; this context, which includes the common and communication about it, lays the foundations of the community.[43] **Community** is the human association that results as individuals come together to discuss their common experiences and problems through shared communication.

Communication: using language to express shared experience in the common environment.

Community: the society that arises from common experiences and communication about them.

As already indicated, Dewey wanted the community to be democratic in that (1) no one was denied access to the common because of race, creed, gender, or class; (2) the means of communication—spoken, printed, or electronically transmitted—were available, open, and uncensored to all; and (3) its institutions and processes were open to all its members.

Dewey believed a community needed to rest on a like-minded commitment of its members to use experimental and democratic processes. His emphasis on building community consensus through shared experience avoided conformity. Although there was shared agreement about using experimental and democratic processes, the community was open to a pluralism of ideas and values. A genuinely democratic community honored cultural pluralism and diversity within a shared context.

In the debates over multicultural education, Dewey would see American society and culture as being composed of smaller communities within a larger encompassing community. Each of the smaller communities—racial, ethnic, gender—has its own common communication and sense of membership. Each has a potentially enriching contribution to make to the greater community. Viewing the genuine American as an international composite, Dewey stated that the American

> is not American plus Pole or German. But the American is . . . Pole-German-English-French-Spanish-Italian-Greek-Irish-Scandinavian-Bohemian . . . and so on . . . the hyphen connects instead of separates. And this means . . . that our public schools shall teach each factor to respect every other, and shall . . . enlighten us all as to the great past contributions of every strain in our composite make-up.[44]

For Dewey, the smaller cultural communities could be expected to differ with each other in terms of their customs, traditions, and interests. At times, there might even be a conflict in interests. It was crucial to the larger community, the great society, and especially to its democratic processes and values, that this conflict take place within and not outside of the generally shared communal framework. Communal conflicts should be resolved in a procedural, nonviolent, nondestructive way. The larger community, the greater society, is governed by commonly shared processes of conflict resolution. For Dewey, there is a communal, or communitarian, American core of beliefs and values. This core, however, rests on commonly agreed-on and shared democratic procedures.

Experimentalist Teaching and Learning

For Perennialism and Essentialism, see the chapters on Perennialism in Education and Essentialism in Education.

Although his Perennialist and Essentialist critics often accused him of encouraging disorderly permissiveness in schools, Dewey's views of the learner, like his relationships to Progressive education, need to be considered carefully. For Dewey, the learner's freedom is not anarchy or doing as one pleases without regard to consequences. Rather, freedom requires an open classroom environment that facilitates using experimental inquiry to examine and test beliefs and values.

Dewey's group problem-solving method differs from traditional classroom management in which instruction is based on the teacher's authority. Questioning externally imposed discipline, Dewey preferred an internal discipline designed to cultivate self-directing and self-disciplining persons. This kind of task, or problem-centered discipline, originates within the activity needed to solve the problem. Control comes from the cooperative context of shared activity, which involves working with instruments and people. Rather than *controlling* the learning situation, the teacher, as a resource person, *guides* it.

Intrinsic Aims: a sense of direction and a need to act based on a student's interest or the requirements of a task in contrast to extrinsic aims, which are external.

In Dewey's learning situation, the starting point of any activity is the learner's felt needs. Such intrinsic interest, related to a real concern, is effective in eliciting the effort needed to satisfy the need and solve the problem. Based on Dewey's conception of learning, educational aims are of two kinds: intrinsic and extrinsic. Internal to the learner's experience and interests, **intrinsic aims** arise from the problem or the task. In contrast, extrinsic aims are extraneous to the person's problem, task, or interest. For example, externally administered rewards or punishments, often used to motivate learning in traditional school situations, are extrinsic and often distort genuine learning. For Dewey, intrinsic aims are always superior to extrinsic ones because they are personal, problematic, and relate to the individual learner's own self-direction, self-control, and self-discipline. Intrinsic educational aims, arising within the context of the learner's own experience, are flexible, are capable of alteration, and lead to activity. Such an experimental aim is a tentative sketch, or plan of action, capable of being reconstructed and redirected.

In Dewey's problem-centered school, the teacher, as a resource person, guides rather than directs learning. The teacher's role is primarily that of guiding learners who need advice or assistance. Direction comes from the requirements of solving the particular problem. Educational aims belong to the learner rather than the teacher.

Teachers using the problem-solving method need to be patient with their students. Although coercion might force students to arrive at immediate results, it is likely to limit the flexibility needed for future problem solving. The teacher's control of the learning situation is ideally indirect rather than direct. Direct control, coercion, or external discipline fail to enlarge the learner's internal dispositions and do not contribute to the learner's becoming a self-directed person. Teachers, motivated by a false sense of instructional efficiency, often err when their anxiety about having students arrive at the "correct answers" in the shortest possible time causes them to bypass the procedural requirements of experimental inquiry. For example, teaching for tests, in which teachers direct instruction toward passing a test, leads to a false sense of educational efficiency. This falsity is compounded when the test is imposed by authorities from outside of the school and classroom.

As resource persons, teachers need to allow students to make errors and to experience the consequences of their actions. In this way, students are more likely to become self-correcting. Dewey did not mean that childish whims should dictate the curriculum, however. The teacher, as a mature person, should exercise professional judgment and expertise so that the consequences of action do not become dangerous to the student or to his or her classmates.

Growth as the End of Education

For Dewey, the sole end of education is **growth**, or that reconstruction of experience that leads to the direction and control of subsequent experience. Particular experiences should be assessed according to the degree to which they contribute to growth, that which leads to more experience. Valuable experiences lead to further experience, whereas undesirable ones inhibit and reduce the possibilities for subsequent experiences. Growth, in Dewey's context, means that the individual is enhancing his or her ability to understand the relationships and interconnections among various experiences, between one learning episode and another. Learning by experience, through problem solving, means that education, like life, is a process of continuously reconstructing experience.

Growth: Dewey's sole end of education, which means to have more experience, more problems, more resolutions to problems, and a greater network of social relationships that makes life more effective, meaningful, and satisfying.

Dewey's educational goal of growth rejects the traditional school's emphasis on the doctrine of preparation. According to the doctrine of preparation, students learn their lessons and master subject matter to get ready for situations that will occur after the period of schooling is completed. In contrast, Dewey argued that deferring action until after the end of schooling would prepare students for a world that would be very different from the one for which they had been prepared. For example, the pace of technological innovation is so rapid that specific training for it soon becomes obsolete. Instead of waiting for some remote future date, students should act on their interests and needs to resolve present problems. By using day-to-day experiences, students would internalize a method of intelligence that is situationally applicable to the present and future.

The Experiential Curriculum

Dewey challenged the traditional subject-matter curriculum that has been historically associated with formal schooling. Human experience is of a whole; it is not separated into isolated subjects such as history, geography, mathematics, science, and language. Instruction becomes abstract and remote from students when it is separated from their interests, needs, and experiences.

Making and Doing: Dewey's first level of curriculum, consisting of learning activities with materials that lead children from their immediate families and homes into the larger society.

Dewey closely related curriculum and instruction when, in *Democracy and Education,* he recommended three levels of curricular organization: (1) making and doing; (2) history and geography; and (3) organized sciences.[45] **Making and doing**, the first curricular level, is designed to construct "the common" in students' school experiences. Engaging students in activities and projects that arise from direct experience, it involves using and manipulating raw materials and tools. These activities, though centered in working with concrete materials, also contain intellectual possibilities. In discussing making and doing as occupations, Dewey said: ". . . the introduction into the school of various forms of active occupation" renews the "entire spirit of the school . . . . To do this means to make each one of our schools an embryonic community life, active with types of occupations that reflect the life of the larger society, and permeated throughout with the spirit of art, history, and science. . . ."[46]

History and Geography: Dewey's second level of curriculum designed to expand children's perspective into time and space.

Dewey regarded **history and geography**, the second curricular level, as two important educational resources for enlarging the scope and significance of the child's temporal (time) and spatial (space) experiences. They help to transport children, in a step-by-step graduated process, from their immediate home and school environments to the larger community and the world. For Dewey, history and geography should not be taught as discretely organized bodies of information but rather should begin with children's immediate environment and then be extended slowly in more distant vistas into time and place.

Science: Dewey's third level of curriculum; refers to the interdisciplinary nature of various subjects in problem solving.

Science, Dewey's third stage of curriculum, represents what can be called organized knowledge—the sciences, social sciences, humanities, and arts. In particular, the natural and physical sciences and social sciences contain information, findings, warranted assertions, and theories that are necessary in problem solving. However, human problems are not located in separate subjects, and they can only be resolved by using these subjects in an interdisciplinary way. The definition of a problem leads the problem solver to the knowledge area that contains the information and findings that can help to solve it, particularly in formulating hypotheses of possible action.

Dewey's Challenge to the Traditional Curriculum

Dewey challenged the traditional view of curriculum, embraced by Idealists and Realists, that knowledge is appropriately organized into academic subjects and that instruction takes place when teachers transmit this knowledge to students. He rejected the traditional curriculum that divided knowledge into separate subjects. Further, he opposed the Idealist and Realist conception that certain bodies of knowledge, or subjects, are intellectual and others are not. According to the Idealist-Realist view, also found in Essentialism and Perennialism, some subjects, such as the great books, are academic in that they have the power to make us think. In contrast, Dewey argued that all experience, whether labeled or catalogued as intellectual or academic, can generate thinking, not by its internal structure but by its power to stimulate inquiry and reflection.

For the more traditional subject-based curriculum, see the chapters on Idealism and Education, Realism and Education, Perennialism and Education, and Essentialism and Education.

Just as he opposed the subject-matter curriculum, Dewey rejected instruction in which a teacher transmitted knowledge to students. What was mistakenly called *knowledge* is really bits of information. Merely transmitting facts and information tells students what to think by having them memorize books, recite what has been memorized, and then regurgitate that information on a test. Of his efforts to rethink and reorganize curriculum and instruction, Dewey said:

> . . . I have attempted to indicate how the school may be connected with life so that the experience gained by the child in a familiar, commonplace way is carried over and made use of there, and what the child learns in the school is carried back and applied in everyday life, making the school an organic whole, instead of a composite of isolated parts. The isolation of studies as well as of parts of the school system disappears. Experience has its geographical aspect, its artistic and its literary, its scientific and its historical sides. All studies arise from aspects of the one earth and the one life lived upon it. We do not have a series of stratified earths, one of which is mathematical, another physical, another historical, and so on. . . .[47]

My Reflections on Philsophy of Education: Using Dewey's Concept of Interaction in Writing

As a professor of the history and philosophy of education, I have written several books about the lives of great educators such as Johann Heinrich Pestalozzi, Friedrich Froebel, Maria Montessori, and John Dewey, the principal subject of this chapter on Pragmatism. In analyzing the biographies of these educators, I have used Dewey's concept of experience, the interaction of the person with the environment. I can illustrate how I used this philosophical concept in my historical writing by turning to the life of John Dewey.

I began by establishing the general context (the historical environment) into which Dewey (1859–1952) was born and lived. He was born on the eve of the Civil War, lived through World War I, the Great Depression, and World War II, and died during the Cold War. During this time, the United States was transformed from an agrarian nation into an industrial and technological superpower. He lived during a time of great social, cultural, and intellectual change: Darwin's theory of evolution, Freud's psychoanalysis, the Progressive Movement, the rise of Pragmatism, and the advent of the nuclear age. Once I established the context, I positioned my historical figure in that context.

Again using Dewey's concept of the individual in interaction with her or his environment, I considered Dewey, my subject, as a person. I explored his childhood, education, and career. I tried to find out how he came to his beliefs and values. Then, I placed my subject within his historical context, his environment.

Developing a pragmatic interpretation, I attempted to analyze how my subject, Dewey, interacted with this context. How did he respond to it? What problems resulted from this interaction? How did he solve them? My analysis of my subject's interactions led me to his major ideas, writings, values, and contributions. As an educational historian, I tried to focus on how this interaction led to his educational philosophy.

Then, I came to my concluding question: What is the significance of the person's life, her or his series of interactions with the broad context? I approached significance from two perspectives: the historical and the contemporary dimensions. I asked what the person's significance was at the time, during the period in which he lived. What was Dewey's significance as an educator of the twentieth century? Then, I turned to the question: What is his significance today? Contemporary significance changes; it depends on the questions that we seek to answer in our own times.

PRAGMATISM'S RESURGENCE

Pragmatism, especially Dewey's Experimentalism, remains particularly important in education. In philosophy itself, Pragmatism has enjoyed a resurgence in the work of Richard Bernstein and Hilary Putnam.

Richard Bernstein

Richard A. Bernstein's *The Pragmatic Turn* provides a commentary on Pragmatism's origin and development within a philosophical and historical perspective that brings this philosophy into the contemporary world. Bernstein notes a "resurgence of pragmatic themes" has sparked interest in its founders—Peirce, James, and Dewey—and has stimulated a renewal of interest among contemporary philosophers such as Hilary Putnam and Richard Rorty.[48] He sees the Pragmatists as historically launching the critique of philosophies that rested on metaphysics, antecedent reality, grand all-inclusive worldviews, and dualism. While this critique has been continued, the Pragmatists, especially Dewey, challenged it. We continually need to reconstruct our beliefs and values in the light of ongoing human experience. We now turn to the contemporary Pragmatist, Hilary Putnam.

Hilary Putnam

Hilary Putnam's contributions to contemporary philosophy are extensive and highly significant. Like Peirce and James, Putnam takes a "this worldly" rather than a speculative "otherworldly" view of philosophy. Its role is "to integrate our various views of the world" and to aid individuals in establishing a "meaningful orientation in life."[49] For education, especially schooling, the implications of integrating our views of the world is highly significant. In the information age global society, we are impacted by multiple and often conflicting bits of information, some of which purports to be knowledge from the media, the press, the Internet, and social media as well as more conventional journals and books. Further, public schools have moved from a monolithic to a multicultural perspective of American society and culture. The challenge for education then becomes integrating these various perspectives into a meaningful rather than sporadic and chaotic view of the world. The pressing question then becomes: What principle of authority can be used in bringing about this integration? For Putnam this question is open rather than closed. We cannot base our beliefs on a metaphysical affirmation that they were, are, and will always be true. Rather, we will continually need to revise and reconstruct them.[50] The challenge facing us educationally is how to integrate our perspectives (our beliefs and values) about the world while simultaneously and continually revising them.

For Putnam, facts and values reflect not only our perspective on the world but also how we choose to construct our worldview. It is our choice of epistemology (of knowing) that integrates facts and values.[51] If we choose a democratic community as the context for our living, our choice, based on our values, will give us a much different perspective on society and politics than if we preferred a totalitarian arrangement. Because there are differences in individual and group perspectives, there will be differences in worldviews as well. There will be disagreements about the validity of some facts and the worthiness of some values. These disagreements are best worked out, revised, and reconstructed, as Dewey asserted, in the flexibility of an open democratic community. Putnam's argument that these differences need to be worked out in a democratic community means that (1) there is no objective metaphysical standard that exists to which our values should conform; (2) our knowledge and value claims are ethically relative; and (3) the flexibility of a democratic community provides a way to work out our agreements and disagreements about the relationship of facts and values and what is true and false and right and wrong.[52]

Putnam's Pragmatism carries some important implications for education, especially for the milieu and processes used in schools. Teachers should recognize that students bring with them different perspectives about the world, their society, and culture. These perspectives are shaped by differences in individual interests and particular group experiences. These differences will generate disagreements about what is true and what is right and wrong. Such disagreements can be identified, clarified, and examined. The democratic classroom provides a flexible but procedural way of dealing with disagreements in that it calls for a reasonable process of discussion in which different voices can be heard and different viewpoints expressed. Through discussion, some of the differences may be resolved or at least revised to create an ongoing democratic classroom dialogue.

PRAGMATISM'S PHILOSOPHICAL OPPONENTS

Although Dewey inspired Liberal and Progressive educators, his experimentalism also generated strong opposition. Philosophical opponents such as the Idealists and Realists, who remained committed to metaphysics, dispute Dewey's contention that we live in an open universe where everything is changing and relative to particular situations. They see Dewey and the other Pragmatists as undermining the true role of philosophy as a search for universal truth. For them, Dewey's dismissal of the *a priori* principles found in the metaphysics of Idealism, Realism, and Thomism was an attack on the concept that human beings are the rational inhabitants of a purposeful universe. Dewey challenged the older philosophies in his relativist argument that truth, goodness, and beauty are not absolutes, inherent in the nature of the universe, but are projects to be worked out in human experience. Human experience arises in concrete and particular events and situations; therefore, the values that arise in these experiences are also relative to particular situations, to people living and acting at a particular time, at a given historical moment, in a particular place. The ethical and moral relativism associated with Pragmatism provokes criticism from those who believe that action should be guided on universal ethical and moral standards. Instead of prescribing and proscribing behavior on universal standards as do Idealists, Realists, and Thomists, the Pragmatists argue that our values arise as we find satisfactory and satisfying ways to live that enrich our experience.

Dewey's Experimentalism encountered opposition from some Realists, especially Perennialists, who see it as negating the essential cultural heritage of Western civilization. Educational philosophers, especially the Perennialists—Jacques Maritain, Robert Hutchins, Mortimer Adler, and Allan Bloom—see Western civilization as carrying with it the importance of reason as a human universal. They see Dewey's blurring of the distinction between the theoretical and the practical as a dangerous anti-intellectualism. Regardless of changing times and circumstances, they believed that certain truths would be forever valid and certain values would be universally applicable. For them, good and bad and right and wrong do not depend on changing circumstances but are the moral standards that schools should perennially convey to each new generation. Dewey rejected Perennialist assumptions, such as those of Robert Hutchins, that education is everywhere the same or is intrinsically good. Rather, he reasoned that the quality of education depends on the quality of life of the group that establishes and supports the school.

For Hutchins and Perennialism, see the chapter on Perennialism and Education.

CONSTRUCTING YOUR OWN PHILOSOPHY OF EDUCATION

At the beginning of this chapter, you were encouraged to reflect on how Pragmatism relates to constructing your own philosophy of education. Now that you have read and discussed the chapter, does Pragmatism appeal to you as a philosophy of education? Are there elements in Pragmatism that you plan to incorporate into your own philosophy of education? Are there aspects that you would definitely not include? Do you believe, like Dewey, that our world is constantly changing and that the scientific method is our best guide to directing the course of change? Do you agree that values are cultural responses to different times and places? Do you endorse an experience-based, activity-oriented problem-solving curriculum and see the teacher's primary role as facilitating students' exploration of the environment?

Conclusion

Pragmatism represented a dramatic change in philosophy in that it focused on a changing universe rather an unchanging one as the Idealists, Realists, and Thomists had claimed. The Pragmatists, especially Dewey, waged a relentless struggle against the traditional philosophical dualisms that presented human beings as divided into antecedent categories such as mind and body and bifurcated education into theory and practice. Rejecting metaphysics, the Pragmatists emphasize what we know, how we think, and how we use our hypotheses as tentative plans to control and direct change. In particular, Dewey's Experimentalism suggested significant changes in American education such as using the scientific method as the basis of problem solving and using experience as the basis of activity. Dewey's Experimentalism is a broad-based philosophy of education that argues that education is directly related to democracy—an environment free of absolutes and dogmas that block inquiry. In a democratic society, individuals are free to use their social intelligence to devise strategies to solve their problems and improve their lives and society. Dewey worked to remove the barriers that separated school from society, curriculum from community, and content from method. Dewey's pragmatism continues to be one of the world's leading educational philosophies.

Questions for Reflection and Discussion

1. Do you agree with the Realists that we live in a purposeful universe or do you agree with Dewey that we construct our own purposes?
2. Consider Dewey's rejection of dualism. How does dualism operate in education? Have you encountered dualism in your own education? Why was Dewey so opposed to dualism in education?
3. Do you agree with Dewey that values are relative to time, place, and culture? Or do you agree with the Idealists and the Realists that values are universal and unchanging?
4. Do you prefer Dewey's experience-based curriculum or do you favor the subject-matter curriculum of the Idealists and Realists?
5. Some of Dewey's critics contend that he contributed to anti-intellectualism in education. Do you agree or disagree with these critics? Defend your answer.
6. Do you agree with Dewey that to have a complete thought we must act on it to test it? Explain your answer.
7. Apply Dewey's concepts of the common, communication, and community to the current debates over multiculturalism and bilingualism in education.
8. Do you think that most Americans are pragmatic and experimental?

Inquiry and Research Topics

1. Organize a panel discussion on the question: Is the American character still pragmatic and experimental?
2. Access William James's *Talks for Teachers* at http://www.des.emory.edu/mfp/james.html. Identify and analyze James's major ideas on teaching. What philosophy underlies his educational principles?
3. Access research, projects, and programs on John Dewey and progressive education at the John Dewey

Project on Progressive Education at the University of Vermont at http://www.uvm.edu/~dewey. Determine how these programs reflect Dewey's philosophy.

4. Access resources on John Dewey's life and philosophy at the Center for Dewey Studies, Southern Illinois University at http://www.siuc.edu/~deweyctr. Compare and contrast the treatment of Dewey's life and philosophy with the presentation in this chapter.
5. Read John Dewey's *How We Think*. Identify and analyze Dewey's view of thinking; then devise a lesson based on it.
6. Read John Dewey's *Experience and Education*. Then answer the following questions: Dewey says to avoid putting educational issues into polar opposites of yes and no. Why? Do you find polar opposites in education today? For example, on No Child Left Behind, teachers' unions, and merit pay and tenure?
7. Design a lesson plan that follows Dewey's complete act of thought method of problem solving.
8. Dewey stated that community arises from shared communication. Arrange a panel discussion on the statement: Social media is a form of shared communication that is building a larger sense of community in the United States and the world.

Internet Sources

Access Movietone News footage of John Dewey and audio excerpts on George Counts and Boyd Bode at the Education Museum at the University of South Carolina at http://www.ed.sc.edu/museum/.

Access William James's articles and books at http://www.des.emory.edu/mfp/james.html.

Access research, projects, and programs on John Dewey and progressive education at the John Dewey Project on Progressive Education at the University of Vermont at http://www.uvm.edu/~dewey.

Access resources on John Dewey's life and philosophy at the Center for Dewey Studies, Southern Illinois University at http://www.siuc.edu/~deweyctr.

Access the Pragmatism Archive, Oklahoma State University, John R. Shook, Director at www.pragmatism.org/archive.

Suggestions for Further Reading

Brandon, Robert B. *Perspectives on Pragmatism: Classical, Recent, and Contemporary*. Cambridge: Harvard University Press, 2011.

Brent, Joseph. *Charles Sanders Peirce: A Life*. Bloomington: Indiana University Press, 1998.

Conant, James, and Urszula M. Zegler. *Hilary Putnam: Pragmatism and Realism*. New York: Routledge, 2001.

Dewey, John. *A Common Faith*. New Haven, CT: Yale University Press, 1934.

___. *Art as Experience*. New York: Perigee Books, 2005. (Originally published by Minton, Balch, and Co., 1934.)

___. *Democracy and Education: An Introduction to the Philosophy of Education*. New York: Cosimo Classics, 2005. (Originally published by Macmillan, 1916.)

___. *Experience and Education: The 60th Anniversary Edition*. West Lafayette, IN: Kappa Delta Pi, 1998.

___. *Experience and Nature*. New York: Dover, 1958.

___. *Freedom and Culture*. New York: Capricorn Books, 1963.

___. *How We Think*. Introduction by Gerald L. Gutek. New York: Barnes and Noble, 2005. (Originally published in 1910.)

___. *Individualism: Old and New*. New York: Capricorn Books, 1962.

___. *Lectures on Ethics, 1900–1901*. Carbondale: Southern Illinois University Press, 1991.

___. *Liberalism and Social Action*. New York: G. P. Putnam's Sons, 1935.

___. *Logic: The Theory of Inquiry*. New York: Henry Holt, 1938.

___. *The Early Works: 1882–1898*. Edited by Jo Ann Boydston, 5 vols. Carbondale and Edwardsville: Southern Illinois University Press, 1969–1972.

___. *The Later Works: 1925–1953*. Edited by Jo Ann Boydston, 17 vols. Carbondale and Edwardsville: Southern Illinois University Press, 1981–1990.

___. *The Middle Works: 1899–1924*. Edited by Jo Ann Boydston, 15 vols. Carbondale and Edwardsville: Southern Illinois University Press, 1976–1983.

___. *The Public and Its Problems*. Athens: Ohio University Press, 1994.

___. *The Quest for Certainty: A Study of the Relation of Knowledge and Action*. New York: Minton, Balch, 1929.

___. *Reconstruction in Philosophy*. Boston: Beacon Press, 1957.

___. *The School and Society & The Child and the Curriculum*. Minneola, NY: Dover Publications, 2001.

___ and Evelyn Dewey. *Schools of Tomorrow*. Mineola, NY: Dover Publications, 2006. (First published by E. P. Dutton and Co., 1915.)

___ and James H. Tufts. *Ethics*. New York: Henry Holt and Co., 1932.

Diggins, John P. *The Promise of Pragmatism: Modernism and the Crisis of Knowledge and Authority.* Chicago: University of Chicago Press, 1994.

Feffer, Andrew. *The Chicago Pragmatists and American Progressivism.* Ithaca, NY: Cornell University Press, 1993.

Garrison, James W., and Ronald Podeschi. *William James and Education.* New York: Teachers College Press, 2002.

Hansen, David T., ed. *A Critical Engagement with Dewey's Democracy and Education.* Albany: State University of New York Press, 2006.

Haskins, Casey, and David I. Seiple. *Dewey Reconfigured.* Albany: State University of New York Press, 1999.

Hickman, Larry A. *John Dewey's Pragmatic Technology.* Bloomington: Indiana University Press, 1990.

Hoy, Terry. *The Political Philosophy of John Dewey: Towards a Constructive Renewal.* Westport, CT: Praeger, 1998.

Kadlec, Alison. *Dewey's Critical Pragmatism.* New York: Lexington Books, 2007.

Martin, Jay. *The Education of John Dewey: A Biography.* New York: Columbia University Press, 2002.

Menand, Louis. *The Metaphysical Club.* New York: Farrar, Straus and Giroux, 2001.

___. *Pragmatism: A Reader.* New York: Vintage Press, 1997.

Putnam, Hilary. *Philosophy in an Age of Science: Physics, Mathematics, and Skepticism.* Cambridge: Harvard University Press, 2012.

___. *Pragmatism: An Open Question,* Malden, MA: Blackwell, 1995.

Rorty, Richard. *Consequences of Pragmatism: Essays 1972–1980.* Minneapolis: University of Minnesota Press, 1992.

___. *Philosophy and Social Hope.* New York: Penguin Books, 1999.

___. *Philosophy on the Mirror of Nature: Thirteenth Anniversary Edition.* Princeton, NJ: Princeton University Press, 2008.

Ryan, Alan. *John Dewey and the High Tide of American Liberalism.* New York: W. W. Norton, 1995.

Tanner, Laurel N. *Dewey's Laboratory School, Lessons for Today.* New York: Teachers College Press, 1997.

Welchman, Jennifer. *Dewey's Ethical Thought.* Ithaca, NY: Cornell University Press, 1995.

West, Cornel. *The American Evasion of Philosophy: A Genealogy of Pragmatism.* Madison: University of Wisconsin Press, 1989.

Westbrook, Robert B. *John Dewey and American Democracy.* Ithaca, NY: Cornell University Press, 1991.

Notes

1. Lawrence A. Cremin, *The Transformation of the School: Progressivism in American Education, 1876–1957* (New York: Alfred A. Knopf, 1962), 105–126.
2. Richard J. Bernstein, *The Pragmatic Turn* (Cambridge, UK: Polity Press, 2010), 2; for a biography, see Joseph Brent, *Charles S. Peirce: A Life* (Bloomington: Indiana University Press, 1998).
3. Charles S. Peirce, "How to Make Our Ideas Clear," *Popular Science Monthly, 12* (January, 1878), 286–302.
4. Louis Menand, *The Metaphysical Club* (New York: Farrar, Straus and Giroux, 2001), 188–189, 222–223.
5. Richard J. Bernstein, *The Pragmatic Turn,* 36–37.
6. For James's writings, see Robert D. Richardson, ed., *The Heart of William James* (Cambridge, MA: Harvard University Press, 2010).
7. Richard J. Bernstein, *The Pragmatic Turn,* 57.
8. William James, *The Varieties of Religious Experience: A Study in Human Nature* (Toronto: University of Toronto Libraries, 2011). (First published in 1902). For William James's *Talks to Teachers* and *Pragmatism: A New Name for Some Old Ways of Thinking,* access William James at http://www.des.emory.edu/mfp/james.html.
9. Menand, *The Metaphysical Club,* 141–143.
10. Jay Martin, *The Education of John Dewey: A Biography* (New York: Columbia University Press, 2002).
11. Robert M. Crunden, *Ministers of Reform: The Progressives' Achievement in American Civilization, 1889–1920* (Urbana: University of Illinois Press, 1984), 56–57.
12. Robert B. Westbrook, *John Dewey and American Democracy* (Ithaca, NY: Cornell University Press, 1991), 42–43.
13. Walter Feinberg, "Dewey and Democracy at the Dawn of the Twenty-First Century," *Educational Theory, 43,* no. 2 (spring 1993), 199.
14. Crunden, *Ministers of Reform,* 34–38. Also see John D. Baldwin, *George Herbert Mead: A Unifying Theory for Sociology* (Newbury Park, CA: Sage, 1986).
15. Lawrence J. Dennis and George W. Stickel, "Mead and Dewey: Thematic Connections on Educational Topics," *Educational Theory, 31* (summer/fall 1981), 320–321.
16. Dewey's Laboratory School is discussed in the following sources: John Dewey, *The School and Society* (Chicago: University of Chicago Press, 1923); John Dewey and Evelyn Dewey, *Schools of Tomorrow* (New York: E. P. Dutton, 1915); Katherine C. Mayhew

and Anna C. Edwards, *The Dewey School* (New York: Appleton-Century-Crofts, 1936); Arthur G. Wirth, *John Dewey as Educator: His Design for Work in Education (1894–1904)* (New York: John Wiley & Sons, 1966); and Herbert M. Kliebard, *The Struggle for the American Curriculum, 1893–1958* (Boston and London: Routledge & Kegan Paul, 1986).

17. John Dewey, "The Laboratory School," *University Record, 1,* no. 32 (November 6, 1896), 417–422.
18. Ibid.
19. A useful guide to Dewey's publications is Jo Ann Boydston, ed., *Guide to the Works of John Dewey* (Carbondale: Southern Illinois University Press, 1970).
20. John Dewey, *The School and Society* (Chicago: University of Chicago Press, 1899).
21. John Dewey, *The Child and the Curriculum* (Chicago: University of Chicago Press, 1902).
22. John Dewey, *How We Think* (Boston: D. C. Heath, 1910); also see John Dewey, *Logic: The Theory of Inquiry* (New York: Henry Holt, 1938).
23. John Dewey, *Democracy and Education* (New York: Macmillan, 1916).
24. John Dewey, *Individualism: Old and New* (New York: Minton, Balch, 1930). Also see Christine L. McCarthy and Evelyn Sears, "Deweyan Pragmatism and the Quest for True Self," *Educational Theory* (spring 2000), 213–227.
25. John Dewey, *Art as Experience* (New York: Minton, Balch, 1934).
26. John Dewey, *Interest and Effort in Education* (Boston: Houghton Mifflin, 1913); *Human Nature and Conduct* (New York: Holt, Rinehart & Winston, 1922); and *Freedom and Culture* (New York: G. P. Putnam's Sons, 1939).
27. John Dewey, *Experience and Education* (New York: Macmillan, 1938), 25–31.
28. John Dewey, *The Quest for Certainty: A Study of the Relation of Knowledge and Action* (New York: Minton, Balch, 1929).
29. Hilary Putnam and Ruth Anna Putnam, "Education for Democracy," *Educational Theory, 43,* no. 4 (fall 1993), 364.
30. Feinberg, "Dewey and Democracy," 204–205.
31. Putnam and Putnam, "Education for Democracy," 364.
32. Tom Colwell, "The Ecological Perspective in John Dewey's Philosophy of Education," *Educational Theory, 35,* no. 3 (summer 1985) 257.
33. John Dewey, *How We Think,* introduction by Gerald Gutek (New York: Barnes and Noble, 2005), 6.
34. Ibid., 31–32.
35. Westbrook, *John Dewey and American Democracy,* 141.
36. Dewey, *Democracy and Education,* 163–178.
37. Feinberg, "Dewey and Democracy," 203–204. Also see Jennifer Welchman, *Dewey's Ethical Thought* (Ithaca, NY: Cornell University Press, 1995).
38. Richard J. Bernstein, *The Pragmatic Turn,* 72–73, 76.
39. Putnam and Putnam, "Education for Democracy," 367.
40. Ibid., 365.
41. Gail P. Sorenson, "John Dewey's Philosophy of Law: A Democratic Vision," *Educational Theory, 30,* no. 1 (winter 1980), 57.
42. Dewey, *Democracy and Education,* 22–26.
43. Sandra Rosenthal, "Democracy and Education: A Deweyan Approach," *Educational Theory, 43,* no. 4 (fall 1993), 377.
44. The quote is abridged from John Dewey, "Nationalizing Education," in *The Middle Works,* vol. 10, ed., Jo Ann Boydston (Carbondale: Southern Illinois University Press, 1985), 205, as quoted in Putnam and Putnam, "Education for Democracy," 362.
45. Dewey, *Democracy and Education,* 228–270.
46. John Dewey, *The School and Society* (Chicago: University of Chicago Press, 1899), 29–31.
47. Ibid., 107–108.
48. Bernstein, *The Pragmatic Turn,* 13.
49. Hilary Putnam, "Interview with Hilary Putnam," *Cogito, 314* (1997), 52, as quoted in Richard J. Bernstein, *The Pragmatic Turn,* 153. My discussion of Putnam relies heavily on Bernstein, "Hilary Putnam, The Entanglement of Fact and Value." Bernstein, *The Pragmatic Turn,* 153–167.
50. Hilary Putnam, *Words and Life* (Cambridge: Harvard University Press, 1994), 152, as quoted in Bernstein, *The Pragmatic Turn,* 154.
51. For the fact-value issue, see Hilary Putnam, *The Collapse of the Fact/Value Dichotomy* (Cambridge: Harvard University Press, 2002).
52. Bernstein, *The Pragmatic Turn,* 162–163.

Existentialism and Education

Søren Kierkegaard (1813–1855), the Danish philosopher whose ideas contributed to Existentialism.

CHAPTER PREVIEW

As a philosophy, Existentialism challenges traditional metaphysically based Idealism, Realism, and Thomism but also objects to certain features of Pragmatism. It questions the Pragmatist reliance on the scientific method as an exclusive way of empirically validating our ideas and also challenges Dewey's emphasis on the group. The Existentialists offer a different way of approaching education, schooling, curriculum, and teaching and learning. This chapter is organized into the following major topics:

- How Existentialism's rejection of systems differs from that of other philosophies
- Identification of the major Existentialist philosophers
- The human situation in the twenty-first century, especially the context of the global mass society
- Major Existentialist themes
- Existentialism's educational implications for curriculum and teaching and learning

Existentialism is a philosophy that encourages us to reflect on our life and situation. It sees reflection about education and teaching as not directed to constructing a complete and finished philosophy. Rather, reflection is intended to examine who you are as teacher, the choices that you make as an educator, and the meaning that you find as a teacher. As you read and discuss this chapter, consider whether Existentialism, in its entirety or in its parts, appeals to you as a teacher. Or, do you reject it or parts of it as possibilities in constructing your own philosophy of education?

NOT LIKE OTHER PHILOSOPHIES

Existentialism differs from Idealism and Realism and other more traditional philosophies. Choosing to not construct a philosophical system, Existentialists did not seek to answer traditional metaphysical questions about the nature of ultimate reality or the structure of the universe. They believed that metaphysical speculation avoids grappling with the real issues of how people choose to deal with the everyday situations of their lives. For them, the speculative philosophers, retreating into a metaphysical world, wrote many highly abstract and theoretical books about what, in the end, really doesn't matter to individuals living in the real world. The genuine pursuit of philosophers, as well as ordinary persons, is to philosophize, to reflect on, and determine for themselves what it means to exist, to be alive, in a concrete situation at a particular time in history. Philosophizing entails asking axiological questions about values, ethics, morality, and aesthetics. The real question is not about the ultimate structure of the universe but rather what it is that makes one's life valuable. How can a person live a life that is true, good, and beautiful? Although Existentialists asked these questions, they deliberately refrained from systemizing their answers into a unified system. Rather than writing a world script with the same lines for all the actors, they believed that each individual, each actor on the scene, is responsible for working out and telling her or his own story.

Because Existentialists did not systematize their philosophy, it is difficult to provide a succinct and ironclad definition of Existentialism. The dictionary provides some help as we begin to explore Existentialism, which it defines as a modern philosophical movement that encompasses a variety of themes. Among these themes are the beliefs that individuals exist and determine their essences; that human beings have absolute freedom of choice but no rational criteria serve as a basis for choice; that individuals live with **angst**, anxiety, and alienation in an absurd universe. When we go to the root of the word *exist*, the dictionary tells us that it means to have actual being, to have life, and to have being in the conditions of a specified place at a particular time in history.[1] Aided by the dictionary's definitions, we can stipulate some starting points for our discussion about Existentialism:

Angst: the German word for a deep Existential anguish that is felt when a person becomes conscious of freedom of choice in a world in which he or she is temporary.

1. Existentialism is a movement, albeit a sometimes disconnected one, about philosophizing.
2. Human beings first exist—come on the scene—living in a concrete place, a context, at a given time, and through freedom of choice, they construct their own essence, their own meaning of life.
3. Human choices, especially significant life-determining ones, are made freely without a guide that is outside of the person.
4. Individuals know that their existence is temporary and that they will disappear; living with this knowledge is a source of anxiety.

REJECTION OF SYSTEMS

Embracing a variety of philosophical perspectives, Existentialism is not a traditional systematic philosophy. It rejects both the desirability and the possibility of constructing an all-explaining architectonic or systematic philosophy that seeks to answer all questions. Existentialists especially distrust philosophical systems that seek to construct an all-encompassing worldview that categorizes human experience according to conceptions of antecedent reality that exist prior to the person's entry on the world scene. According to traditional views, the human being enters the world and is defined, catalogued, and assigned a role or place in it. For example, Aristotelian natural Realists assert the existence of an objective order of reality independent of human plans and purposes. The human being, a part of this reality, has an assigned place in it as a rational creature who possesses an intellect and naturally seeks to know. The descriptive assertion of human rationality also prescribes—asserts the value—that human beings ought to act or behave rationally. In countering Aristotle's premise, Existentialists contend that if reason is asserted as the primary element in defining the human being, then there is no genuine freedom in the human condition. If reason is an antecedent constituent and determinant of human nature, then humans cannot really choose reason as a value. In contrast, Existentialists contend that humans are choosing and valuing beings who can reason if they so choose. The Existentialist sees life as too varied, complex, confused, and unpredictable to be arranged in neatly structured philosophical categories.

For Aristotle's natural Realism, see the chapter on Realism and Education.

In abandoning the metaphysical system building of Idealists, Realists, and Thomists, the Existentialist examines the most significant and persistent doubts from the perspective of the individual human person. Existentialist involvement calls for individual philosophizing about the persistent human concerns of life, love, death, and meaning. Accepting the fact that we live in a physical environment as an evident fact of life, Existentialists view this world as an indifferent phenomenon, which, while it may not be antagonistic to human purposes, is nonetheless devoid of personal meaning. In this world, each person is born, lives, chooses his or her course, and creates the meaning of his or her own existence.

Reservations About the Scientific Method and Group-Based Learning

Existentialism questions not only the architectonic traditional philosophies but also Pragmatism's reliance on the scientific method. Dewey's Experimentalism stresses the efficacy of both the scientific method and social intelligence arising from shared human association. It stresses the individual's ability to use the empirical procedures of science as the exclusive means of establishing tentative truths. For Existentialists, the scientific method, so prized by Pragmatists, is only one of many ways in which individuals construct their own truth. Indeed, the scientific method can inform us only about the physical facts of the world, the "givens" that describe natural reality. The most important way to construct the truth is not through the scientific method but through personal, subjective choice. The person can choose to be scientific or not.

For Dewey's Experimentalism, see the chapter on Pragmatism and Education.

Dewey's Experimentalism asserts the importance of developing the individual's desire and competency to participate in meaningful group interactions. For Dewey, the individual develops social intelligence through group association and participation. Reiterating Dewey's emphasis on group-centered learning, contemporary education emphasizes the importance of collaborative learning.

Some Existentialists, however, do not share Dewey's enthusiasm for group-centered learning. As with the scientific method, there are many choices to be made about how to teach and how to learn. The waves of pedagogical enthusiasm often found in teacher education programs and in schools tend to see a particular method as a panacea that should fit all teachers and students. Enthusiasm that limits choice carries subtle limitations on freedom, which has some of the limiting consequences of more doctrinaire approaches to teaching and learning. For example, if you reflect on your group-based collaborative educational experiences, you might find that the "like-minded" group was a sometimes-coercive agency in which individual choice was subordinated to the group will or consensus. The group can overwhelm the individual who is pressured to accept its decisions "for the good of group so we can complete the assignment and get on with the project."

Contemporary education, especially multicultural education, emphasizes that we live in a culturally diverse and pluralistic society that is composed of different racial, ethnic, and language groups. It advises us of the importance that socio-economic class and gender play in shaping our cultural tradition, beliefs, and values.

Existentialists do not deny the significance that cultural group experience has in shaping our attitudes and values. They would endorse a multiculturalism that is exploratory rather than so inclusive that it becomes exclusive. Certainly, they say, the groups of which we are members are "givens" of our social, political, and economic lives that shape us but that do not define us. Regardless of class, gender, race, or ethnicity, the person is free to define himself or herself by making significant life choices.

Historical Perspective

Although early Existentialism appeared in the works of nineteenth-century writers Søren Kierkegaard (1813–1855), Friedrich Nietzsche (1844–1900), and Fyodor Dostoyevsky (1821–1881), its greatest philosophical impact came in the twentieth century, especially during and after World War II. Among the leading twentieth-century

Existentialists were the German philosophers Karl Jaspers (1883–1969) and Martin Heidegger (1889–1976), the Israeli philosopher Martin Buber (1878–1965), and the French philosophers Gabriel Marcel (1889–1973), who took a Christian perspective, and Jean-Paul Sartre (1905–1980), an atheist.[2] In addition, the eminent Protestant theologian Paul Tillich (1886–1965) examined the relationship between Christian theology and Existentialist philosophy. Like Kierkegaard, Tillich saw the human being facing the free but awesome choice of whether or not to enter into a personal relationship with God.

Phenomenological Method: in epistemology, an assertion that objects exist as perceptual phenomena in space and time.

Some Existentialists used Edmund Husserl's (1859–1938) **phenomenological method** as a point of entry in developing their philosophy. Husserl defined philosophy as a method of analyzing phenomena according to our conscious awareness in experience of how objects and events appear to us. This philosophical analysis occurs without limiting conditions imposed by metaphysical assumptions. For example, Heidegger studied with Husserl, and Sartre attended his lectures. Although he was not an Existentialist, certain of Husserl's themes such as ***human subjectivity, consciousness, perspective,*** and ***being in the lived world*** were congenial to Existentialism. The individual person, a subject, not an object in the world, through consciousness creates a perspective on the phenomena of the world in which he or she lives. Although we empirically hear, feel, and smell objects through our senses, it is our perspective, our consciousness of them that makes them meaningful to us.

For the Idealist and Realist views of reality, see the chapters on Idealism and Realism.

Husserl found that every conscious human act is directed toward or intended for another person or object that already exists in the world.[3] The meanings that we give to these persons and objects are not objective, determined by something outside of us, but depend on our individual perceptions, images, and memories of them. Thus, our concepts are not mirror images of reality as Idealists assert, nor do they correspond with the structure of objects in reality as Realists claim. Rather, they are perceptions built on our personal subjective experiences with them. Human consciousness, our awareness of phenomena, is the basis for our understanding and interpretation of our situation. The educational implications of Husserl's phenomenology are: (1) students' perceptions of their reality (their lived world) need to be emphasized in schools: (2) students need to be become conscious of the various ways to perceive the world; and (3) students should be open to perspectives of other individuals. This diverse and sometimes conflicting array of writers of literature and philosophy suggests that Existentialism was and is a philosophical perspective that examines common themes rather than a finished philosophical system of thought.

In discussing the Existentialists, we concentrate on two highly significant philosophers, Søren Kierkegaard, a nineteenth-century Dane, and Jean-Paul Sartre, a twentieth-century French author and playwright. These preeminent philosophers illustrate two varieties of Existentialism: Kierkegaard's Theistic, or Christian, Existentialism and Sartre's Atheistic Existentialism. In addition, we discuss other philosophers such as Gabriel Marcel and Simone de Beauvoir, who accentuated certain Existentialist themes. As our discussion enters more directly into education, we examine the contributions of two educational philosophers: Maxine Greene and Van Cleve Morris.

SØREN KIERKEGAARD

Søren Kierkegaard (1813–1855), an important founder of religious Existentialism, was born, educated, and lived in Copenhagen, Denmark. His memory of his childhood home and family was that of an unhappy place, drenched with gloom, guilt, and foreboding. His severe and authoritarian father, Michael Pedersen Kierkegaard, demanded unquestioned obedience. Soren's mother and five of his siblings died before he was twenty-one and he grew up feeling that death was a constant presence in the household.

Initially aiming for a career as a Lutheran minister, Kierkegaard studied theology and philosophy at the University of Copenhagen. Moving slowly through his courses, he took ten years to complete his program in theology and dissertation, *On the Concept of Irony with Constant Reference to Socrates* (1841).[4]

In his personal life, the highly introspective Kierkegaard, often called the "melancholy Dane," appeared to be drifting toward taking his place in the conventional upper-middle-class Danish lifestyle of the Victorian era. His engagement to marry Regine Olsen, the daughter of a well-connected government official, confirmed that he was on the path to a comfortable and respected social status.[5]

As his marriage drew near, Kierkegaard, ever more introspective, experienced feelings that his life was empty and meaningless. He felt that his coming conventional, middle-class marriage would seal his fate. Instead of conforming to respected Victorian social expectations, he ended his engagement to Regine.

Choosing to make a dramatic change in his life, Kierkegaard became a rebel with his own personal cause of choosing his own path to a self-defined and self-determined life. For the introspective young man, taking this path meant unrelenting probing of the question: What does it mean to exist? He decided against seeking an appointment as a pastor in the officially established Danish Lutheran Church. Just as he rebelled against conforming to middle-class social values, Kierkegaard deliberately challenged the official religion and Hegelian Idealism, the dominant intellectual authority.[6] Although highly critical of doctrinally institutionalized Christianity, Kierkegaard remained intensely religious, a person on a quest for his own redemption. He rejected the convention of being born into a religion. In Denmark at the time, with the exception of Jews, children were automatically made members of the Church at birth; this was supported through government funding. For Kierkegaard, automatic enrollment in a Church was being a Christian in name but not in faith.

For Hegelian Idealism, see the Chapter on Idealism and Education.

Kierkegaard argued that officially established state churches, such as the Lutheran Church in Denmark, enjoying their government support and subsidies, had substituted rote dogmas and empty ceremonies for what should be a vital personal faith in God. The ministers, paid members of the state bureaucracy, like all bureaucrats were most concerned with maintaining their privileged status rather than living according to Christ's Gospel. Kierkegaard suggested that the human search for spiritual meaning is an important personal goal that needs to be respected in education and schooling, but that this search can proceed without imposing doctrinal conformity on others. For him, genuine spirituality came from a "leap of faith," a personal conversion experience, to embrace and live by the truth, regardless of the consequences. For the converted person, faith, the experience of recognizing God's awesome majesty, was a total experience that united believing and thinking and feeling and hoping.[7]

REACTION AGAINST HEGELIAN PHILOSOPHY

Just as he rebelled against the state church, Kierkegaard reacted against Hegelian philosophy, which dominated intellectual life in nineteenth-century continental Europe. Kierkegaard's critique of the Hegelian domination of higher education can be applied to trends in education today that produce a mindset of allegiance to a dominant ideology or method. The list of pervasive approaches that dominate thinking in instruction is a long one. While standardized testing, multiculturalism, collaborative learning, service-oriented projects, magnet schools, and other approaches each suggest ways to improve education, Kierkegaard would advise us that they should not become doctrines of "true-believers" that there is one right way to educate, teach, and learn.

Kierkegaard, an iconoclast whom some regarded as an eccentric, challenged the religious and educational establishment. He became a prolific author of philosophical and theological books and articles that featured Existentialist themes. Among his most important books were *Either/Or* (1843), *Repetition* (1843), *Fear and Trembling* (1843), *Philosophical Fragments* (1844), *The Concept of Anxiety* (1844), *Stages on Life's Way* (1845), *Unscientific Postscript* (1846), *Sickness Unto Death* (1849), and *Training in Christianity* (1850).

Unconcerned with personal popularity and a personal risk taker, Kierkegaard battled against the powerful centers of conformity that he believed were stifling freedom of choice: He challenged the press—the popular journals and newspapers—that he believed had constructed a pervasive climate of opinion in which individual thinking was distorted into a conformist mass mind. Kierkegaard paid a price for challenging the media. *The Corsair,* a very popular weekly magazine with a large circulation, launched a series of scurrilous attacks on Kierkegaard, criticizing his ideas as the ludicrous ravings of a madman and running cartoons that caricatured his appearance.[8] Kierkegaard's challenge to the media resonates well today—a time when television and social media generate popular slogans and catchwords and -phrases that attract wide circulation and dominate expression for intense but relatively short intervals. It also is a challenge for "instant celebrity" that confuses a meaningful and useful life with the current cult of personality.

Kierkegaard's criticisms of his own society in nineteenth-century Copenhagen bear many parallels to twenty-first-century American issues. The contemporary mass media—television, motion pictures, radio, newspapers, magazines, and social media—often tell us the same story with the same sensational interpretation of events. This media-shaped message is repeated incessantly until the mantra-like refrain is echoed by members of the mass audience. The result is that what should be many voices, speaking independently of each other, becomes one mass voice that speaks slogans and clichés. Though no secularist, Kierkegaard, as indicated, had no sympathy for state-sponsored churches. He believed in the free exercise of religion, which for him was a private, not a public matter. Today, he would be likely to warn Americans against connecting churches to government. Institutionalized religion today often is geared to generate social conformism, especially when church leaders seek to influence politics and encourage their members to vote in a block on a single issue. Kierkegaard's admonition about the domination of intellectual life by a particular philosophy or ideology is an especially telling comment that applies to theory and methods of education, particularly when they become doctrinaire and dogmatic.

Stages of Becoming

Authentic Person: refers to authenticity, being original or genuine and not a copy.

In his *Either/Or* and *Stages on Life's Way,* Kierkegaard identified three spheres or stages in the process of becoming an **authentic person**: the aesthetic, the ethical, and the religious.[9] Although every individual who is becoming an authentic person can proceed through these stages, this movement to moral development does not take place for all individuals. Some people stay locked by their own inclination in a particular stage of arrested development and do not grow to moral fulfillment. The stages are not cumulative in that one variety of experience is subsumed into the next stage, as the Pragmatists would assert. Neither are the stages a dialectical synthesis of the thesis of one stage and the antithesis of the next stage into a still higher and more comprehensive synthesis as Idealists, especially Hegelians, would argue. Rather, for Kierkegaard, progression from one stage to another is not made by transitions; it is made only by a deliberate personal choice between incompatible alternatives.[10] Kierkegaard personifies each stage by using a model who exemplifies it: the

For Pragmatism and Hegelianism, see the chapters on Pragmatism and Idealism.

pleasure-seeking, adventurous lover Don Juan, who seeks immediate sensual pleasure and instant gratification, for the aesthetic stage; the inquiring and provocative Socrates for the intellectual stage; and the Biblical Abraham for the religious stage, that of complete fulfillment.[11]

Don Juan lives in the sphere of the immediate present to enjoy sensual delights. Morally irresponsible, he is unconcerned with the past and the future and lacks the sense that his actions will have consequences for himself and others. Living for the moment's instant gratification, Don Juan's interests are momentary excitements. His life is without continuity or direction. When it comes to enhancing his pleasures, however, Don Juan, the seducer, can be cunning and manipulative. Using persons as objects for his pleasure, especially unsuspecting young women, he has no concern for them as individuals. Uninterested in higher modes of intellectual and aesthetic experience, Don Juan rejects anything that may interfere with his insatiable appetite for pleasure.[12]

Socrates, the model for the intellectual stage, represents an individual who is growing toward authenticity. Unlike Don Juan, Socrates has developed a perspective on the past, present, and future. The intellectual person is capable of looking to the past to reflect on her or his misdeeds with an ethical sense of sorrow and repentance for having committed them. Ethical persons are willing to project themselves into the future with a sense of personal commitment and obligation to do the right thing as they conceive of it. For example, Socrates is willing to risk searching for truth regardless of where it will take him. His search put him up against the Athenian authorities, who punished his intellectual pursuit of truth by sentencing him to death. Although admirable, the intellectual stage is still not Kierkegaard's highest sphere.

For Kierkegaard, the spiritual "leap of faith" is the highest stage of personal authenticity. Intensely and intimately personal, faith is beyond rational explanations. To personify the religious sphere, Kierkegaard chose the Biblical character Abraham, whom God, in order to test his faith, called on to sacrifice his son, Isaac. Although he could find no justification for this act in religious principles, Abraham, standing alone before God, prepares to sacrifice his son. Seeing Abraham's "leap of faith" to unconditionally obey his Divine command, God no longer requires the sacrifice; He stays Abraham's hand and spares Isaac.[13] Abraham's act of faith ran counter to both his love for his son and all ethical proscriptions against taking an innocent life.[14] In the Biblical account, Abraham did not attempt to use theological or philosophical authorities to try to change God's command. He accepted God's command to sacrifice Isaac because of his faith. Because of his leap of faith, God released him from his dreadful task and spared Isaac. Kierkegaard's "leap of faith" provides a point of origin for other theistic expressions of Existentialism.

THEISTIC EXISTENTIALISM

For Theistic Existentialists, Kierkegaard's leap of faith provides a means by which the person can choose openness to and a willingness to commit to a caring God. Not explained by religious dogma, doctrine, or ritual, the leap of faith comes from the person's conversion to seek God.

Gabriel Marcel

Gabriel Marcel (1889–1973), a French philosopher and writer, was a resonant voice for Theistic Existentialism. Marcel was a contemporary of Jean-Paul Sartre, an atheist Existentialist. Sartre's philosophy will be discussed later in the chapter. At this point, we will differentiate Marcel's Theistic Existentialism from Sartre's position.

Whereas Sartre argued that a human being is born into a world without meaning, Marcel contends that human existence is a gift from God. He distinguished his Existentialism from Sartre's atheistic and semi-Marxist perspectives. A Roman Catholic, Marcel integrated his religious faith into his philosophy. Marcel and Sartre shared similar backgrounds in that they were poets and playwrights as well as philosophers. Marcel's *The Mystery of Being* (1950) and *The Philosophy of Existentialism* (1961) express his Theistic Existentialism.[15]

Unlike the angst and dread found in other Existentialists, Marcel emphasizes faith and hope in God's promises. Urging an abiding charity for human beings, Marcel warns against turning one's companions into objects or functions. In educational terms, Marcel's admonition against turning people into "others" is similar to arguments against "othering," a system of labeling and classifying children into categories in schools rather than seeing them as persons.

In *Man Against Mass Society* (1951), Marcel issued strong arguments against the pervasive conformity in modern mass society. He was especially critical of totalitarianism and materialism.[16] Marcel shared Sartre's abhorrence of totalitarianism, especially Nazism and Fascism, which Europe experienced in World War II. His book, written six years after the end of World War II, struck out against how the Nazi regime mobilized Germans into a collective mass mind controlled by one man, Adolph Hitler. Writing in the midst of the Cold War, Marcel saw Soviet totalitarianism as an equally pernicious force in the modern world. Totalitarian regimes sought total mind control as they whipped up hysteria against enemies relegated to the caste of the threatening outsider. For Hitler, the outsiders who threatened the Aryan race were the Jews. For the Soviet regime, the outsiders were the capitalists who surrounded the Soviet state and were determined to destroy it. Censoring all information and controlling the police, military, and schools, the totalitarian state sustained itself by denying freedom. Ironically, it proclaimed that worthy members of the state were to surrender their freedom to a supreme leader. The totalitarian state promotes a mass fanaticism that is exalted as faithful and good citizenship. Fanaticism is substituted for a consciousness about the reality of a situation.

Marcel's warning against fanaticism is especially relevant given the contemporary anxiety generated by the rise of religious fundamentalists and ethnic and racial purists worldwide. Fanatical terrorists resort to terror, bombing, maiming, and killing innocent people, whom they condemn as "others" who need to be eliminated. Ethnic cleansing in Bosnia, in the former Yugoslavia, and in Rwanda and Burundi in Africa are examples of extremism that turns people into others, potential victims, who are selected for killing or expulsion solely because they are members of a different ethnic or tribal group.

Materialism, the replacement of the spiritual by the lust for consumer products, operates in the global economy, fed by mass advertising. Materialism (denying the spiritual), and consumerism (exalting possession of things as the highest value) falsely appears to offer choices in an array of consumer goods. However, the choices are merely slightly altered duplicates of each other that deflect the person from recognizing the real and most important choices about how to live life. The mass society, constructed by a profit-driven economy and pervasive advertising, generates and sustains itself in a circular fashion. Advertising campaigns, using radio, television, and the World Wide Web, generate a blitz of commercials, often misnamed as "infomercials" that tell people what they need and should have. The individual, submerged in and conditioned by consumerism, reacts by wanting what is advertised and thereby creating a greater demand for it. Consumer demands, actually created by the forces that control the global marketing system, stimulate still another round of advertising, buying, and charging purchases on credit cards.

While warning of the dangers of the mass society, be it totalitarian or materialist, Marcel expressed an optimism that it was possible for human beings to choose to be free and overturn the conditions that jeopardize true personal authenticity. If we are educated to be conscious of the dangers to freedom posed by the mass society, it remains possible to create a community of free people. Marcel used the concept of *communion,* which has both a sacramental and a social meaning, to describe his hoped for community of personal freedom. Communion, in Marcel's Existentialism, conveys a spirituality in which individuals are in community with each other and also in their own personal communication with God. It means being in a society in which individuals have an abiding and nonexclusive mutual respect for each other so that no one is "demonized" as a dangerous outsider because of class, race, religion, ethnicity, or gender.[17]

Marcel's theistic Existentialism has important implications for education. Foremost is that each individual should be respected as a person, not as an accident in a world without meaning. Since each person is valuable, individuals should not be marginalized or categorized as outsiders or others. In general, education can raise consciousness about the threats to individual freedom generated by the webs of massive consumerism. Consciousness raising in educational institutions, however, will be deeply challenging because schools and curricula in a mass society tend, in mirror-like fashion, to reflect the images of the larger society. Schools have grown large, impersonal, and bureaucratic, with students categorized by ability or disability or marginalized by race, ethnicity, language, or socio-economic class. Older schools resemble industrial factories; newer schools, in affluent neighborhoods, may appear to be modern media centers or shopping malls, mimicking the information diffusion centers of the mass media, or mass consumerism. Neither of these types of schools, however, is designed to raise consciousness about the dangers that mass consumerism and consumer-generated tastes pose for individual choice and freedom. Educational outcomes are even described as products—units or credit hours to be accumulated—rather than as achievements of the goals of cultivating personal and social consciousness. Despite the limitations found in schools, Marcel argues that there is still the hope of overcoming them. Teachers and students can work their way through them and come to recognize them for what they are—ways of shaping behavior that are not freely chosen.

Marcel's analysis can be applied to creating educational settings, or spaces, in which teachers and students are willing to empower themselves by creating communities in which persons, respecting one another, are in communion. Public institutions can become centers of this kind of self-empowerment, but it is the faith-based private and parochial schools that have a unique opportunity to move beyond instilling doctrine to becoming places where students might make the leap to personal faith in God and in which they are in communion with their teachers and peers.

ATHEISTIC EXISTENTIALISM

In contrast to Theistic Existentialism, we now examine Atheistic Existentialism through the philosophies of Friedrich Nietzsche (1844–1900), a German philosopher, and Jean-Paul Sartre, the paramount voice of French Existentialism.

Friedrich Nietzsche

While Kierkegaard is regarded as the originator of Theistic, or God-centered, Existentialism,[18] Friedrich Nietzsche stands out for his challenge of Judeo-Christian theology and morality and Aristotelian metaphysics.[19] His attack on traditional

Western religion and philosophy was also a challenge to the educational authorities and structures that were based on these traditional foundations.

Regarded as an originator of atheistic, or at least agnostic Existentialism, Nietzsche, convinced that modern science had made belief in the supernatural irrelevant, proclaimed, "God is dead." Since there is no Divine plan at work in the universe, Nietzsche saw the purpose in life to be whatever an individual decides for himself or herself.

Tracing Judeo-Christian morality to antiquity, especially to ancient Greece and Rome, Nietzsche saw its origins situated in the relationship between the master, the ruler, and the slave, the ruled. While the master enjoys and is self-confident in his power, the slave, always reacting to his subordination, sees himself only in relation to his master.[20] Judeo-Christian morality, like the slave–master relationship, defines the person in relationship to God and makes morality a reactive response to following divinely sanctioned commandments.

PERSPECTIVISM. Nietzsche challenged the traditional metaphysical belief that an ultimate and true reality lies beyond the world that appears to us in our experience. He also challenged Aristotle's claim that our knowledge is true when our concepts correspond to objects as they exist in reality. Discounting that there is one true objective knowledge, Nietzsche argued that there are many ways of seeing things. Along with the scientific empirical view provided by the microscope or telescope, there is also the aesthetic or artistic insight into the relationships of persons, nature, and objects to each other. These multiple views of phenomena create our perspectives of what we make of our world. Instead of concepts we have percepts, our interpretations about ourselves in the world that come from our own point of view.

Perspectivism: Nietzsche's view that individuals construct their world through multiple points of view and not a single objective truth.

For education, Nietzsche's **perspectivism** means that there is not a single privileged view of reality. Questions do not have a single right and wrong answer. Instead of the true–false answer on a standardized test, there are multiple responses. Instead of a privileged method of instruction, there are many ways to teach and to learn.

Ubermensch: Nietzsche's ideal of an Over man or superman who creates himself through his own empowerment.[22]

THE WILL TO POWER. Nietzsche replaced Aristotle's dictum that "man is a rational animal" with "man is an evaluating animal." The human project, especially for the extraordinary person, the ***Ubermensch,*** is to create by free choice a life that is a noble and beautiful aesthetic self-construction.[21] In *Thus Spake Zarathustra* (1883) and *The Will to Power* (1901), Nietzsche argued that some exceptional individuals could, because of their own absolute freedom, create their own ethics and be accountable only to themselves.[23] These exceptional individuals use their will to power. Ignoring the other voices around them who preach conformity, they use their will to think and to feel for themselves.[24]

Although there are some chords in Nietzsche's philosophy that resonated well with Sartre's belief that individuals create themselves without reference, there was also a major historical by-product of Nietzsche that Sartre rejected. Hitler and the Nazis in Germany appropriated Nietzsche's idea of the *Ubermensch* and the will to power as an ideological justification for their totalitarian state. Sartre, in contrast, opposed the Nazi rationale for power.

JEAN-PAUL SARTRE

Jean-Paul Sartre (1905–1980), considered the leading twentieth-century Existentialist, held the center intellectual stage in France as the prominent author of plays and novels, as well as political and philosophical books and essays. A graduate of the prestigious

École Normale in Paris, Sartre taught philosophy, but left teaching for his preferred life as a writer. He followed his novel *Nausea* (1938) with *L'Imaginaire* (1940), his first book on philosophy. Sartre, a playwright and dramatist, related his philosophy to human imagination and aesthetic sensibility. He saw the human imagination as creating possibilities for personal choice and freedom. When France declared war on Germany in 1939, Sartre was mobilized into the French army, captured, and held as a prisoner of war. After his release, Sartre returned to Paris, then under German occupation, and joined the underground resistance movement.[25]

World War II, especially the Nazi conquest of much of Europe, painfully portrayed, not as fiction but in reality, modern humanity's existential predicament. Western Europe, especially France, was regarded as the citadel of culture, civilization, and rationality. Then, the rise to power of Hitler and the Nazis brought on the world scene a fanatical and ruthless totalitarianism that, boasting of its barbaric irrationality, demanded the total subjugation of the individual to the state. With the inherited traditions of Western culture and civility rendered meaningless by the irrationality of Hitler's new barbarianism, the Europe of the 1940s became a place of repression and the extermination of millions of people in technologically efficient death camps. It was in the chaos of the world turned upside down that individuals faced the choice of collaborating with Nazi totalitarianism, shutting their minds to it, or actively resisting it. Even in Nazi-occupied Europe, individuals still had a choice, often the ultimate choice between life and death: collaborating with or resisting evil.

Sartre's *Being and Nothingness* (1943) made him a paramount intellectual leader of the Existentialist movement that flowered in France after its liberation in 1945. Sartre's 1945 lecture, "Is Existentialism Humanism?" became a manifesto of the Existentialist movement. He proclaimed what became the leading principle of Sartrean Existentialism, "**existence** precedes essence." These three words signaled that individuals create their own essence, their own meaning and values, through their choices. Further, there was no authority to which to appeal other than the person who is making the choice.[26] Sartre answered his question affirmatively. Existentialism is humanistic because it focuses directly on the freedom of every person to create his or her own essence in light of the values chosen.

Existence: simply being present, or being there; as in being present in the world.

Although sharing some common themes with Kierkegaard's and Marcel's Theistic Existentialism, Sartre's version was essentially atheistic. Sartre examined the predicament of the human being in an absurd world devoid of meaning, except what people create for themselves. In coining the phrase "existence precedes essence," Sartre challenged the traditional philosophies that preached that human behavior is based on an antecedent definition of human nature. He rejected a predefined version of humanity. Unlike Aristotle's assertion that the human being is antecedently a rational creature who inhabits a purposeful, hence meaningful, universe, Sartre countered that each person exists—comes uninvited on the world scene—and creates his or her own meaning or essence. Because no universal truths, no absolute rules, no ultimate destiny exist to guide us, each person is totally free to choose. With this complete freedom comes total responsibility for our choices and actions.

Existence / Person is in the world → Precedes → Essence / Self-definition of the person

Precedes → Choices; Person is in the world → Choices → Self-definition of the person

Existentialist Creation of Essence

SIMONE DE BEAUVOIR

Simone de Beauvoir (1908–1986), Sartre's lifelong companion, had an illustrious career as a writer, playwright, novelist, and philosopher.[27] A graduate of the prestigious French educational institution, the École Normale Supérieure, she also taught in a *lycée*, a French academic secondary school. Her important book, *The Second Sex* (1949), provides a feminist perspective on Existentialism.

Beauvoir argues that human experience takes place in concrete contexts, lived in unstable and ambiguous situations. These contextual situations are the sites in which gender is constructed. She makes a distinction between a person's sex and gender. Sex is a biological given: A person is born as either a female or a male. However, the lived-in situation, the context, constructs what it means to be a woman or a man. For the female, becoming a woman is traditionally defined by men who are masters in patriarchal societies.[28]

Beauvoir attacks the mytho-history that portrays women as possessing a defining female essence that makes them what they are. Because of this alleged female essence, women are traditionally portrayed as passive personalities who are fulfilled by being a dutiful daughter, a loving wife, and a caring and nurturing mother. The traditional concept of the patriarchally defined woman is a clear example of essence preceding existence—men creating an *a priori* definition of what it means to be a woman. Historically, this definition has been constructed by men and imposed on women. Beauvoir argues that to accept this definition imposes a prior definition on women that severely limits their freedom to choose who they will be; in other words, it denies them the freedom to construct themselves through their own choices. Beauvoir argues further that the historical construction of the feminine can be deconstructed and socially, politically, and economically dismantled.[29]

There are many examples of women who, in their lives, challenged the concept of a male-defined feminism. Two stand out in particular—Jane Addams and Maria Montessori. In her autobiography, Addams tells of being the dutiful daughter of her respected father and of being encased in the strictures of a Victorian-era family and upbringing. Coming of age during a time when a young woman's expectations were determined by others—usually males—Addams eventually made the choices that led her to found Hull House, a pioneering social settlement. Montessori, too, had to run against the tide of the late nineteenth century in an Italian middle-class family structure and to challenge the conventional educational strictures. A single parent, she chose to define herself as one of Italy's first women physicians and to create the worldwide renowned method of early childhood education that bears her name.

MAXINE GREENE

Maxine Greene, a professor of education at Columbia University's Teachers College, created a multilayered Existentialism that is directed to the world of education, especially to teachers and students in school situations. She sees education as offering teachers and students the possibilities of creating an "always open world." Using her knowledge of the history and philosophy of education and literature and the arts, Greene uses "multiple modes of interpretation" to explore the Existentialist questions of existence, anxiety, authenticity, and freedom.[30]

Dewey's Experimentalism is examined in the chapter on Pragmatism and Education.

Just as she urges students to create their possibilities from multiple perspectives, Greene constructs her Existentialism from multiple philosophical perspectives. She finds Dewey's Experimentalist rejection of static antecedent definitions of human identity, his concept of growth as exploring and testing new possibilities, and of "mind" as dealing actively with the situations we encounter in our lives to be useful elements in an Existentialist education. Greene finds Sartre's idea of freedom—not an abstract ideal but as something to be earned—to be highly compatible with an Existentialist educational perspective. We earn our freedom when we become conscious of the conditions that limit our freedom of choice and self-definition and are courageous enough to resist and overcome them.[31] While some of these limitations may seem to be mundane, such as doing what is comfortable, following routines, yielding to peer group pressure, or doing what is needed to be economically secure, they may lead a larger climate of dependency on other people or situations. They become increasingly larger when they create a climate of yielding to the racial, class, and gender stereotypes that permeate many situations in schools.

As we try to interpret the world from our own perspectives, we encounter a variety of limiting obstacles blocking our course. Some of them are so embedded in society and schools that we may not even be conscious of them. There are the pervasive voices coming from the radio, television, and computer that tell us what we should desire, what will make us happy, and what we should buy. There are messages from "talking heads," educational experts, and spokespersons for special interests that tell us education should increase American economic productivity, be measured by standardized tests, follow a common core, and so on. Sometimes these limitations come from philosophies that tell us to conform to an objective reality; sometimes they come from those who see conformity as needed for social stability. Sartre warned that these limiting factors, whatever their source, can deflect us from facing and reflecting on our own situation—from creating our own perspectives and our own personal interpretation of the world.

Unlike some versions of Existentialism that seem to recommend escaping from where we are in our lives, Greene's Existentialism is not abstract or remotely out in space. She presents a situated philosophy that is contextually located in time and place. For her, human experience is situated in personal interactions and shared relationships between individuals living in community. Our community experience, she advises, is enriched in the larger human experience of culture, society, history, and literature. She presents us with the challenge of creating personal openings to freedom while we live in the contexts of social, political, and economic situations. Our reflections and perspectives are situated in these contexts.[32]

Greene's insights into the larger American community come from her progressive perspectives. For her, progressivism is a project for a forward-looking community that uses the past—especially the contributions of leading American thinkers such as Thomas Jefferson, Ralph Waldo Emerson, John Dewey, and Jane Addams—as providing points of departure to create communities with greater alternatives and possibilities for freedom. Greene finds the progressive themes that schools should be educational spaces where children are free to experiment, to be spontaneous learners, and to build their own embryonic communities to be highly congenial with an Existentialist education.

Progressivism is examined in the chapter on Progressivism and Education.

For Greene, dialectical relationships are present in every human situation and association. For example, the dialectic is present between a subject and an object, an individual and society, a parent and a child, and an individual and nature. These interactions create a network of multiple perspectives on what it means to be alive in the world.

Greene sees education as a means of opening individuals to move beyond that which limits them. Education is a way to examine life from multiple perspectives and to use these perspectives to raise consciousness about our situation; it provides a way to frame choices and take alternative courses of action, even risky ones, in creating our lives. Education, Greene suggests, should lead us to a variety of ways of interpreting the world, the situated world of our lives (the where, how, and why we live as we do).

Education as Authorship

Greene introduces the educationally intriguing concept of authorship that encourages students to become authors of their own world. Authorship brings to the student a "feeling of temporality, the sense of being in communication, the awareness of perspective in a constructed world."[33] The concept of students as authors encourages them to develop the perspective of their own time and place and understand how this perspective relates to their past. The interpretation of a personal past and present needs to be situated in a time and place where they live in relationship with the natural environment and in a community with other individuals and groups. As authors, students need to be conscious that their own their life story, their personal autobiography, is both their own but still related to their situations. Authorship, so conceived, carries the possibility and challenge of creating an open future that is and always will be an unfinished life project.

Throughout this book, you have been encouraged to reflect on your educational experiences and to construct your own philosophy of education. Greene's concept of authorship and a way to create meaning provides a strategy that can be used in writing your philosophy of education.

Imagination and Autonomy

Greene describes genuinely educated persons as autonomous individuals that she defines as being "self-directed and responsible" and capable of choosing and acting with "internalized norms and principles." Knowing their own histories and aware of their own impulses, individuals, as they become educated, become conscious of the manipulations, pressures, and limitations that outside forces seek to impose on them.[34]

To create choices and alternative ways of acting means that teachers and students need to recognize, value, and use their imaginations. Although using imagination is a key factor in early childhood education, especially kindergarten through the primary grades, the curricula and instruction in the upper grades and secondary and higher education tends to limit the use of imagination to certain subjects such as art and creative writing. Opposing the limiting of imagination to specific subjects and times, Greene would release its power throughout the entire curriculum. Every subject carries with it the possibilities of using the imagination, not only for self-reflection but also for classroom dialogue and critical thinking. In art, literature, drama, and dance, the imagination can create new forms of personal expression and creativity. In history, imagination can suggest the consideration of the counterfactual, as in: What if John Wilkes Booth had experienced a change of mind in his plot to assassinate President Lincoln? Or in the sciences: How has imagination led to new discoveries and breakthroughs? Or in technology and the electronic flow of information: What are new ways to involve more people, as with social media, in the exploration of issues and problems? Regardless of the subject, the imagination provides a way to project oneself forward in time and to contemplate the possibilities of being in the future. The imagination is a way of exposing teachers and students to new and multiple perspectives, enlivening consciousness, and creating new openings of life and community.

THE HUMAN SITUATION IN THE TWENTY-FIRST CENTURY

Existentialists argue that we need to philosophize in the concrete situations in which we live rather than speculate about metaphysical systems. We now examine the human context in the twenty-first century, especially identifying trends and forces that deter us from philosophizing about the importance of our free choice. These self-limiting trends can be examined historically in terms of the mass society created during the modern industrial period from the 1830s to the 1980s and the postmodern period from the 1980s to the present. This examination emphasizes that the trends of modernity and postmodernity represent a continuum rather than a sharp break in history from one period to another.

Modern Mass Society

Existentialism's philosophical origins coincided with disaffection against the nineteenth century's optimistic view of science, technology, and progress after World War I. The rise of a mass society and technological culture, causing the depersonalization of the individual, aggravated the feeling of alienation. The Industrial Revolution introduced innovative mechanisms that facilitated both efficient production and massive consumption. The logic of the machine age and the efficiency of the assembly line required that machine parts be both standardized and interchangeable. When a machine part wears out, it is replaced by an identical part that fits the machine and allows it to function effectively. The logic of interchangeable machine parts was gradually extended to individuals who are designated by their functions in the system. When such functioning individuals wear out or become obsolete, they are discarded and replaced by other standardized individuals who have been trained to perform the same functions. The logic of interchangeable parts and interchangeable people had profound implications for education, especially for schooling. The school, as a system, became an assembly line that turns out products—namely, graduates trained to perform specific functions for the larger corporate system.

The rise of mass production–consumption systems, technological innovations, and scientific engineering attitudes produced an urban, corporate, and mass society. At the root of the mass society is standardization, which, in turn, creates mass housing, communications, media, entertainment, and education. The thrust of the global corporate structure and its subsidiaries is to ascertain the material needs of the average person and persuade him or her to prefer certain goods. The global corporate structure both creates and caters to the needs of a standardized human being, a composite of statistical and sampling techniques. As a consumer and as a citizen, the private person is reduced to a standardized unit whose needs, desires, and wishes can be measured and quantified.

Modern technological society, created by applying science to industrial processes, emphasizes quantification over quality. The scientific method based on objective empirical verification deliberately minimizes the subjective and value-laden aspects of life. The demand for scientific objectivity has led to the quantification of human experience. Following the physical sciences, social science, sociology, social psychology, and behaviorism describe persons in empirically verifiable terms. The consequences of emphasizing science and de-emphasizing the humanities have led to the objectification and reduction of the human being to an entity or unit that can be weighed, measured, and quantitatively analyzed.

The public life of mass society now reaches far into the private sphere of life, a person's unique lifestyle. The impersonal forces of industrialization, standardization, and globalization isolate, detach, and erode personal relationships and meaning that come from the unique elements of human life. Uniqueness is labeled as eccentricity, as in the case of Kierkegaard, rather than as the means of achieving self-definition. Success is measured quantitatively in terms of power, possessions, or control. Standardization objectifies, quantifies, and reduces human beings to objects or functional adjuncts of the corporate mechanism.

The corporate and standardized features of a mass global society are not restricted to economic, political, and social life; they also extend into education. Assembly-line logic has extended into the educational complex serving the mass society as schools apply the logic and techniques of mass production to learning. The global corporate economy needs trained managerial and engineering elites who can apply their administrative expertise to stimulating increased production and consumption. The corporate managers have their counterparts in the administrators who staff the bureaucracies of school and university systems. Educational technology, or innovative media, has entered the school. Teaching machines, online instruction, multimedia instructional packages, computer-assisted learning, and standardized tests are some of the tools of educational technology introduced to make instruction controlled and efficient in the mass society's educational complexes.

The emphasis on standardization has had pervasive consequences for American students that begin in the elementary schools, run through the high schools, and continue on through colleges and universities. For school districts to receive federal funding, the *No Child Left Behind Act* requires that students be examined annually using standardized tests in mathematics and reading. Test data are used to determine whether teachers and schools are performing competently in achieving the prescribed standards in these skill areas. Schools that score below the standard may be remediated. One consequence of this requirement is that teachers spend more instructional time preparing students to pass the standardized tests and less exploring other subjects such as social studies and the arts. The kind of standardization required by the act also impacts classroom instruction. Standardized testing leads to standardized teaching methods that emphasize the specific requirements needed to pass the test. The primary and intermediate grades generally have been the years during which teachers have had the greatest freedom to recognize students' individual needs and to experiment with creative teaching methods. Existentialists warn that the teachers' emphasis on students' subjectivity and individual needs and the freedom to experiment with creative and innovative methods decreases proportionately to the increase of standardized expectations and outcomes.

When the educational system is based on the movement of students from lower to higher levels, the doctrine of preparing for the next level exerts strong pressure on the lower level. The higher level's entry requirements typically determine what skills and subjects are taught and what methods are used in instruction. For example, the entry requirements for law, medical, and other professional schools shape the undergraduate college curriculum; college and university entry requirements, in turn, determine the high school's curriculum and teaching methods. Secondary school requirements to a large extent shape the curriculum of the middle schools, and so on.

With the exception of some innovative and progressive schools, the pressure of the higher level on the lower level is found in educational systems worldwide. From an Existentialist perspective, is it possible to resist the power of the higher rung on the lower rung? Is it possible to resist this educational determinism that places students into school ranks and requires them to march in formation to the drum beat of preparation? Part of the answer is for teachers and students to challenge the system, at least at some times, and emphasize the unique features of personal experience that make it possible to do something that is different and not predetermined by the pressures of preparation.

EXISTENTIALIST THEMES

In this section, we examine philosophical themes that run through Existentialism. We consider Existentialism's relevance to education in the twenty-first century; its epistemology of appropriation; its perspective on space and time; its search for authenticity in group and school contexts and in ambiguous situations; and its concern for social justice.

Existentialism's Relevance

Some readers might argue that Existentialism's high tide is past and that the philosophy is no longer relevant in the twenty-first century. Others would consider Existentialism to be especially needed in a time of globalization, corporate marketing, mass information, and the ever-increasing standardization of society and education. Focusing on the living person engaged in coping with a concrete situational reality, its questions about how we can choose to live self-examined and self-defined lives in whatever situation or context we find ourselves are always relevant. It is especially relevant to philosophy of education because it raises the possibility of creating authentic learning experiences that can lead to personal freedom for students and teachers. It offers a different kind of philosophical experience as it engages individuals in examining and addressing what matters most—their personal lives—and taking responsibility for either acting or failing to act.

An Epistemology of Appropriation

In asking the question, "What does it mean to me?" Existentialists want the truth to be a personal **appropriation** that is chosen, lived, and acted on rather than a speculative abstraction in the Platonic sense. Knowing and learning, for Existentialists, means appropriating, choosing, and taking what is known or learned and making it one's own by giving it a personal meaning. This is very different from the Realist view that one's knowledge, to be valid and valuable, needs to correspond to the object that is external but knowable to the learner. It also differs from the Pragmatist concept that we can have tentative "truths" based on their probability of occurring in experience and that acting on them scientifically or empirically is likely to bring about predictable consequences. For Existentialists, knowing as appropriation is subjective, personal, and individualized, not objective, probable, predictable, or standardized.

Appropriation: an Existentialist epistemology in which a person chooses what is learned and gives it a personal meaning.

For their theories of knowing, see the chapters on Realism and Pragmatism.

Existentialists accept the validity or usefulness of objective or scientific information about the concrete world; it is up to the person to choose, appropriate, and determine how to use this information in his or her personal perspective of reality. For example, think of a road map with its major expressways and highways, its smaller and slower two-lane roads, or its meandering scenic back roads, the "blue roads," as providing objective information. If geographically plotted, the road map provides accurate information about distances and locations that may guide our choice of how to reach a destination, but the choice of which road to take constitutes the meaning of a journey and what we might encounter on our way. Our choice of which road to take reveals how we have defined space, time, and direction. However, in making the journey, there is also the possibility of encountering the unexpected, the surprise, which can be exciting, engaging, or dangerous. For the Existentialist, the traveler who chooses the road is creating a journey that is more meaningful than the logistical specificity of the map.[35]

Space and Time

The analogy of the map engages us in the issues of space and time. The map is a graphic representation of the places within a given space (e.g., a state, a country, or the world). Distances on the map require so much time to reach depending on our mode of transportation (e.g., walking, driving, or flying). We can think of the questions Where am I? Where am I going? and How long will it take to get there? as matters of practical logistics or in the broader sense of life determinations.

It is interesting to note that two primary goals of early childhood learning—to understand the meanings of space and time—are also important philosophical issues.

It is a striking coincidence that the way children learn to construct the meanings of space and time bear strong relationships to how Existentialists look at space and time. For children, the construct of space comes from where I am and where I live; for Existentialists, space is a concrete personal lived-in place. My personally meaningful construction of space is largely determined by how I choose to arrange my life. Note how the persistent issue between parents (usually mothers) and children (especially teenagers) is about how they keep their rooms. Notice, too, how your friends furnish and decorate their rooms and homes. In a school, observe how teachers have arranged and decorated their classrooms. These different patterns of arranging space mean more than moving chairs and desks. They reveal how a person has decided to make a space a personally lived-in place.

Similar to space, Existentialists define time as lived time rather than as the ticking of an impersonal mechanical clock or the inexorable passage of the months on a calendar. The value and meaning of the minutes, hours, days, months, and years of our lives are consequences of how we choose to live, use, and enjoy our time. Although we have no power over how much time we will have in our lives (i.e., we don't know the time of our death), we are free to choose to do what we wish with the time we have. Our decisions to put off, procrastinate about, and flee action or to seize the day as our own determines much of who we are. It is a matter of how we establish our temporal priorities.[36]

Becoming an Authentic Person

Sartre's short sentence "existence precedes essence" clearly states the basic Existentialist premise. It means that who you are (your meaning or essence) is the result of your choices in a concrete situation, in a time and space. Your essence is self-constructed, self-made; it does not come from being defined as an *a priori* category, as Idealists and Realists claim. Neither are you determined by and predestined to an inevitable future by some psychological, sociological, or political ideology. You are who you choose to be.

Authenticity: being real or genuine; not a copy or fake; being a self-directed person who is honest with himself or herself.

Existentialists hope that as individuals construct their own essence, they will make choices that lead to **authenticity**. The dictionary defines *authentic* as not false or copied, as being genuine or real; *to authenticate* means to establish something as genuine, valid, or authoritative. As well as being a writer, the word *author* also means being the maker or creator of something.[37] Using these definitions, the quest to be authentic means that the person needs to recognize and understand the human situation as one being lived in a concrete context, but to resist being defined by the historical, psychological, social, political, and economic aspects of that context. As we live in the context of a global mass society and attend schools that reflect it, we face pervasive and rampant standardization, conformity, and consumerism that make the challenge of becoming an authentic person perilous. The contemporary drives for instant notoriety on television that result in a parade of short-lived celebrities; bumper sticker slogans of religiosity and patriotism that claim to be moral dicta; and the belief that the big questions of life can be framed in a box on the computer screen, a PowerPoint program, or a textbook reduce life's mysteries to simplistic formulas.

Authenticity in Situational Contexts

Existentialists recognize that human beings live in situations, in contexts. These contexts set up the facts of our existences—who we are in terms of gender, race, socioeconomic class, ethnicity, and religious groupings. These bodies of facts, organized as the subjects of science, social sciences, history, and so forth, are important constituents of the formal school curriculum. Teacher education programs, too, are based on the historical, sociological, and psychological foundations of education that purport to describe, analyze, and predict students' development, behavior, and learning.

Situating Multiculturalism in the Group and Individual

Multiculturalism and multicultural education pose important considerations for Existentialism. We live situated lives in that our existence is within a group context. We are members of ethnic, racial, language, gender, and socio-economic class groups. We learn the beliefs, attitudes, values, and behaviors associated with our group life. Multicultural education celebrates the identity that group association provides to individuals. From an Existentialist perspective, it seeks to free us from the stereotypical limitations associated with being a member of a group. The traditional gender expectation that a young woman is predetermined by her sex to be a wife and mother, an elementary school teacher, or a nurse but not a physicist or a surgeon is an example of using a group stereotype to limit a person's freedom of choice. On the other hand, identity with the group should not override the quest for personal authenticity. For the Existentialists, membership in a group is part of living in a situated reality. However, group identification cannot be used as an excuse to avoid making critical choices, or to abandon these choices to others. While these contextual facts set the stage, they are not the determinants of our authenticity—they do not create us as persons. As authors of our own autobiographies, our evaluations and our choices make us who we are.

Being Situated in the School Milieu

Along with the formal curriculum, the hidden curriculum or the school milieu contains pressures that work against authenticity. Being situated in a school means constantly facing pressures to conform, think, dress, speak, and behave the same as everyone else. In junior and senior high school, the pressures to conform are intense because subgroups identify themselves by how they dress, how they talk, what clubs they join, the type of music they listen to, the movies they see, with whom they sit in the cafeteria, and with whom they text and email. It is all right to be different if that difference has the security of belonging to a group composed of other people who share and conform to that differentiating feature.

Existentialism runs against the strong currents of group conformity found in schools. Rather than accepting group designation as our primary identification, Existentialists urge us to recognize the facts in a situation but not to let them define us. An Existentialist education involves examining and becoming conscious of how the forces in the situation in which we live often impose definitions on us rather than being our genuine choices. It seeks to enliven our consciousness that we are our own authors, our own creators, and that we write our own story by welcoming and not dodging the choices, though often difficult, that we find in our situations. This kind of education leads us to face our excuses for not acting and our rationalizations for acting in other-defined ways that often disguise our fear of being responsible for our choices. It alerts us to the true meaning of the clichés of "following the crowd," "going with the flow," "not making waves," and "that's just the way things are." Acceptance of the clichés means that I have resigned myself to something, to some situation, that I don't want to think about. In creating a self-definition and meaning by making significant choices, the goal cannot be found in ends that are stipulated or proposed by others; it needs to be self-framed and self-defined. Becoming an authentic person is a challenge to be accepted, undertaken, and sustained, but most likely never really permanently achieved. Creating one's own agenda and purpose in life is dynamic and often filled with risks.[38] Existentialism challenges us to recognize and act on our self-defining, essence-creating choices. This requires us to be conscious of our situation, to know where we are and who we are, and to move forward in making ourselves into what we want to be. Being the author of our own story means that we need to recognize that while we are the principal character who makes the plot, the story is a continuous work in progress, an unfinished symphony that we write and rewrite as we face the choices that define us. Despite whatever context we find ourselves in, being alive also means that we have the possibility of moving through and beyond it.[39] An example of moving through and beyond the facts can be found in the life and choices of Helen Keller, who, though left blind and deaf by a childhood illness, moved beyond these givens to make herself into what she wanted to be—an independent person and a contributor to society. One also can think of Jane Addams, who recognized the facts of her Victorian era that limited women's choice but who went through and beyond them to define herself as the creator, or author, of Hull House in Chicago and to become a voice for women's rights and world peace.

Creating Meaning in Ambiguous Situations

Existentialism does not flee from ambiguity—the cognitive and evaluative awareness that individuals experience that they are free and not already defined, or determined. Ambiguity means that we do not have the security of being in a situation where everything is labeled, defined, and prescribed: It means working our way through a situation for ourselves. No matter who or what you are, you have the power to redefine yourself and to create your essence. The Existentialist openness to ambiguity strikes out against determinism. It rejects metaphysical systems that define the person as a being within a preordained, *a priori* system of reality. Unlike Aristotle, who defined the human being as rational, the Existentialist argues that rationality is a state of mind that the individual must define and freely choose. Arguing against economic determinism, which defines people as members of a class, Existentialists say that individuals are free to define themselves regardless of their economic status. An individual may be a citizen of a nation-state, yet he or she still may choose to remain a citizen or to redefine citizenship in personal terms. A classic example of redefining citizenship occurred when Henry David Thoreau acted on his belief in civil disobedience when he was jailed for refusing to pay taxes to support what he regarded as an unjust war, the war against Mexico. Although Existentialists recognize the importance of gender, race, ethnicity, and class to human beings, these are not the ultimate factors that define persons. The human being, an individual person, may be predisposed but is not predetermined. Predetermined social, economic, or philosophical theories fall before the ambiguity of life, which has many roads leading to many destinations. Indeed, ambiguity holds the promise of opening the way for the free choice that only the individual has the power to make.

In education, the recognition that the human being is continuously defining himself or herself in an undetermined life project means that the person is more than a composite of physical, social, economic, historical, and social forces. These forces are important conditioning factors in human choice but they are not fated or ultimate ones. We can study and be informed by the physical, natural, and social sciences for the information and insights that they provide for assessing our choices, but these fields, or subjects, cannot make the decisions for us.

AESTHETIC CHOICE. Sartre and Marcel employed Existentialist themes in their novels, plays, and short stories. The Existentialist emphasis on the dramatic element in human experience resonates well in the fine and dramatic arts, which make it possible to express our feelings and our creation of value. Existentialism, as Maxine Greene writes, is closely related to the fine arts—literature, drama, art, music, dance, poetry, and architecture. It is closely interwoven with literature, especially its style, meaning, and interpretation.

Many Roles but Only One Self

Formal, institutionalized education—elementary, secondary, and higher education—often emphasizes learning the different roles one plays in society, especially those being guided by expectations about social popularity and economic success. Those who master role playing can enter the right college or university, prepare for the right profession, marry the right partner, live in the right neighborhood, and enjoy the good things of life, especially consumer goods—a "MacMansion," a second home on the beach, several large cars, and so on. Playing roles means doing what is needed to satisfy the requirements to join a prestigious corporation and to become a member of a high-status country club. For the Existentialist, even though these roles are chosen by the role player, they are not defined by him or her. They are defined by others. The Existentialist wants individuals to be conscious that the human condition involves the need to navigate between the many social and economic roles and expectations taught in schools and to choose personal authenticity over role determination.

For Existentialists, the tyranny of role playing may lead to an unauthentic stage acting in which the person wears the mask, speaks the words, and exhibits the behavior required by the role rather than being true to himself or herself. The danger is an unintegrated personality, one who is constantly shifting roles and adrift—carried along by social eddies and currents rather than by self-direction. Without freely determined authentic choice, there is the danger that the roles will conflict and the individual will become an unhinged, disintegrated personality. The Existentialists constantly remind us we need to remove the masks that hide our true identity. We make our authentic identity by facing the reality that we are what we choose to be, not by retreating into a socially or economically determined success role. Taking off the mask can be risky—it may mean losing the job, the fancy car, and the mansion.

Ethics and Social Justice

Social justice issues are important ethical concerns in contemporary education. Commitments to social justice are found in the mission statements of educational institutions and professional societies. Existentialism has often been accused of being a selfish, hedonistic, self-centered philosophy that ignores social justice needs and ideas. It is true that Existentialists place primary responsibility on the individual person and warn that persons must look to their own choices to create their own essences. Indeed, Sartre warned that the "other person is hell." And yet, despite the charges made against it, Existentialism is concerned with social justice issues, especially those that deny human rights because of race, ethnicity, gender, socio-economic class, language, or disability.

Often accused of putting individual preferences before social needs, Existentialists respond that personal ethical conduct—not making speeches or writing polemics—reveals a person's true commitment to social justice. Sartre, for example, a determined anticolonialist, staunchly opposed European imperialism, especially French repression of the Algerian independence movement.[40] Acts of social injustice are perpetrated by oppressive regimes, but repression is not solely the consequence of an institutionalized political or economic system. It also needs to be seen in the subjective sense of the officials, who administer the instruments of repression, and the larger body of people who ignore it or condone it. This means that repression, marginalization, and other forms of oppression need to be seen as acts committed by individuals who are agents of such regimes, and as the responsibility of the larger public who support them through taxes. Oppression has a human face no matter how well it is hidden within a system.

Existentialists such as Sartre see the control and marginalization of one group by another as a serious cause of personal alienation in society. Those social, economic, and political factors that repress human freedom cause both the suppressed and the suppressor to be alienated from social justice. Alienation asserts that conditions of repression are necessary and that those who are repressed deserve this treatment because they are inferior or not like us. As part of the raising of consciousness needed for authentic choices, Existentialist educators encourage students to examine their social contexts—both the school community and the larger society—to identify conditions of repression and to expose the ideological factors that justify this repression.

Existentialists would make human rights and freedom a personal issue in that I as a person can be free only when you are free. This kind of freedom between persons means that other persons are not objectified or turned into the functions they perform. A teacher, physician, truck driver, and grocery checkout clerk are more than how they function in society or the economy. They, too, are persons who have the right to self-identification and self-determination.

Finally, Existentialists would resist the move to standardize social justice issues in much the same way that the curriculum has been standardized. It is insufficient to merely list social justice themes in the standards of professional societies and the mission statements of educational organizations and institutions. Justice between individuals is always personal and must resist being encased in standards or slogans that make one feel good but take away the responsibility of doing what is right.

EXISTENTIALISM'S EDUCATIONAL IMPLICATIONS

In this section, we examine Existentialism's implications for education. In particular, we consider its critique of educational trends and its suggestions for an Existentialist pedagogy and curriculum and for the relationships between teachers and learners.

An Existentialist Critique of Educational Trends

Philosophizing in the Existentialist mode provokes a critique of certain social and educational trends in contemporary society and schools. Among the trends that limit personal choice and self-definition are standardization, categorization, the inculcation of socio-economic roles, and the tyranny of the average.

As educational institutions emulate the global corporate system, they depersonalize the teaching–learning relationship. Various subdivisions of professional education, such as educational psychology, instructional methodology, measurement, and evaluation, borrow heavily from the social sciences of psychology, sociology, and political science as well as from statistics. Emulating the physical sciences, these various social sciences and their educational derivatives seek to predict and control behavior. Instruction is structured according to behavioral objectives so that outcomes can be measured to the degree that behavior has changed. Such a conception of learning views the learner as a social object or phenomenon and elicits responses that are quantified and rendered into measurable statistical and otherwise standardized responses.

Contemporary American education has become highly group centered as a result of the stress on shared activity and collaborative learning and because of the dominance of educational psychologies that emphasize social acceptance and adjustment. The aims of socialized education are such objectives as learning to cooperate with others, functioning successfully in group situations, and working as an effective collaborative team member. According to group-centered educational theories, the individual becomes more effective and efficient by identifying with and participating in group activities.

Existentialist educators are cautious about the glorification of the group. In the midst of crowds, human beings are still lonely and anxiety ridden. Some group-centered learning situations may become so coercive of the individual that personal authenticity may be sacrificed to the pressure to achieve consensus. When a person freely chooses to join and to participate in a group, opportunities still exist for authentic choice. However, many group-centered situations in schools are not freely chosen. Learning situations organized around groups should be such that they permit and encourage opportunities for individuals to assert the unique aspects of their personalities.

A very strong trend in contemporary education is setting standards for the teaching and learning of skills and subjects. Standardized tests, designed to measure student aptitude and achievement, are used to assign students to educational categories from which there is often little mobility. School records and reporting systems deal in categories that encourage little or no recognition of students' uniqueness and creativity. Mass-produced instructional materials, ranging from basal readers and textbooks to videos and computer programs, are geared to categories of students. For their organization, schools rely on routinized and standardized schedules. Although contributing to time on task efficiency, standardization in schools requires uniformity in materials and instruction. With this kind of standardization, it becomes increasingly difficult for teachers to deviate from set patterns in school routines. The movements lobbying for a common core of skills and subjects and for uniform standards in teaching them often are initiated by groups external to schools. For example, the standards movement that led to the No Child Left Behind Act identified specific skills (reading) and subjects (mathematics and science) as the essential curriculum components that every student needed to master. State legislatures and the U.S. Congress enacted legislation that mandates standardized testing of students to determine whether they have achieved a basic and minimal competency in these specified skills and subjects. The test results of mass student cohorts at specified grade levels are used as evidence that schools and their teachers are performing either adequately or inadequately. When students perform below the benchmark prescribed in the standard, this is used as empirical evidence of schools' and teachers' incompetence in teaching basic academic skills and subjects.

Devoted to preserving and enhancing students' personal individuality and uniqueness, Existentialists are suspicious of, and indeed apprehensive about, using standardized tests to determine teachers' and students' academic competency. The standards carry with them an expected desirable outcome, a benchmark to verify competence; however, the specific outcome determines the kind of instruction needed to meet the benchmark. The internal choice of teachers and students, which the Existentialists prize, is reduced to other-directed prescriptions that allegedly signify competency in academic instruction and learning. Because so much is riding on meeting the external standards, more time, effort, and resources are expended on the tested skills and subjects and less on other educational experiences, especially in the arts and humanities. Existentialists are concerned that the opportunities for expressive and creative experiences are being sacrificed as schools and teachers scramble to meet standards.

A consequence of the drive to reach externally imposed standards is that teachers focus instruction on preparing their students on the skills and subjects on which they will be tested. Their choices in designing and choosing different points of emphasis and different teaching strategies are limited to teaching specifically what is needed for their students to score well on standardized tests.

The general effect of externally imposed standards is to standardize what takes place in classrooms. Because a standard is uniform, classrooms, too, will become uniform. Uniformity means that uniqueness and difference have been eliminated and replaced by a new kind of lockstep approach in schools. Whereas Existentialists see ambiguity, openness, and indeterminacy as positive aspects of education, advocates of standards and standardization want instruction to be specifically related to achieving predetermined results. Standards emphasize specific academic expectations and outcomes that reduce ambiguity and bring closure to instruction. It is not only the school's impetus toward standardized efficiency that threatens students' self-definition. Students themselves, seeking the security that comes from group identification, often become conformists who eagerly consign their peers to categories. In the typical high school, students often identify peers who are studious academic achievers as "brains" or "grinds"; those who are athletes and cheerleaders as "jocks"; those who are on drugs as "freaks" or "druggies"; and then there are the "nobodies" without group identification. Once assigned to a school caste, the adolescent often is locked within that group. It becomes a risk to cultivate uniqueness or to appreciate others for their individual worth.

A pervasive but subtle factor that erodes the possibilities of human authenticity comes from the "tyranny of the average." The tyranny of dictatorial and authoritarian regimes and institutions is an obvious form of oppression. Less obvious, the tyranny of the average appears initially to be democratic, but in actuality it reduces individuals to measurable statistics. Mass media, art, and entertainment—television, radio, movies, newspapers, magazines, popular books—are also designed for the average person so that they attract the largest possible audience. These agencies of informal education both reflect and create popular tastes. In a mass society, deviations from the average do not sell well; uniqueness either becomes so expensive that it can be enjoyed only by a privileged elite or so unpopular that it is pushed to the margins of society.

It may be argued that standardization, categorization, role-playing, and the tyranny of the average are the inevitable by-products of a mass society and that contemporary schooling only mirrors these irresistible trends. An Existentialist educator would argue, however, that as society becomes more conformist, standardized, and categorized, it is the responsibility of teachers to expose these trends by having students examine and analyze them. This exposé is not merely for sociological interest; it is to raise students' consciousness so that they at least are aware of the dangers that a global technological society poses to authentic freedom.

Toward an Existentialist Education

The educational philosopher Van Cleve Morris wants education to cultivate an "intensity of awareness" in learners. Such an awareness means that students should recognize that as individuals they are constantly, freely, baselessly, and creatively choosing. Such an awareness carries with it the responsibility for determining how one wants to live and for creating one's own self-definition.[41]

Pre-Existential Period: the stage of human development, the years of childhood, when children are immersed in their direct experience of their environment rather than in making important personal choices.

Existential Moment: occurs during puberty when we become aware of our personal responsibility for defining ourselves.

In developing an Existentialist educational psychology, Morris identified a "pre-Existential" period of human development and the "Existential Moment."[42] During the **pre-Existential period** prior to puberty, the child, not really aware of his or her human condition, is not yet conscious of a personal identity and destiny. The pre-Existentialist years coincide with elementary education, when children learn to read, write, do arithmetic, and acquire physical, recreational, communicative, and social skills. Children also learn some subject matter and problem-solving skills.

The **Existential Moment** generally occurs with the onset of puberty when an individual becomes conscious of her or his presence as a self in the world. It brings with it an insight into one's own consciousness and responsibility for making choices and acting on them. At certain times, the adolescent experiences a feeling of self-empowerment and independence; at other times, the adolescent seeks to escape adult responsibilities and to return to childhood's dependence of parents and other adults.

According to Morris, the onset of the Existential Moment in a person's psychological development signifies a readiness to begin an Existentialist education. Such an Existentialist education would begin with entry into the middle or junior high school and continue through the senior high school and undergraduate college. Concerned with experiences that are subjective, personal, and affective, an Existentialist education emphasizes those that involve personal questions and choices about what is good or bad and right or wrong.

AN EXISTENTIALIST CURRICULUM

Attempting to describe an Existentialist curriculum presents a challenging paradox in that determining what teachers teach and students learn in advance of their engagement in the classroom limits freedom of choice. To deal with this paradox, we need to reflect on a possible curriculum from an Existentialist perspective. The following Existentialist themes are useful in our reflection:

- the need to arouse consciousness about the human situation;
- the need to maximize individual freedom and choice;
- the need to recognize the desirability of ambiguity;
- the need to refrain from turning persons into objects or functions.

In exploring Existentialist possibilities for curriculum, two broad areas, the "given" and the "open," are proposed.

The Givens

The Existentialists emphasize that our lives are situated in given facts of existence. We live in specific, concrete contexts—spaces—at a particular time. The term **givens** refers to the skills and subjects that describe and explain the physical, social, political, and economic realities of our local, national, and global situations. The givens are subjects such as the natural and physical sciences (e.g., biology, botany, chemistry, physics), mathematics, and the various social sciences (e.g., political science, sociology, and psychology) that provide knowledge about our contexts. The skills—reading, writing, languages, arithmetic, research competencies, and computer literacy—provide the means to access the information contained in the subjects. The givens as skills and subjects help explain our contexts. Since we need to know them as bodies of existing knowledge, the givens are a necessary part of our education. However, there is another part, the open areas of the curriculum, that is highly relevant to us in creating our self-definition, our essence, as persons.

Givens: skills and subjects that describe and explain our natural, physical, social, political, and economic contexts.

The Open Areas

For Existentialists, the important part of the curriculum for raising consciousness about the human condition and freedom and choice are the **open areas**, especially the humanities, literature, poetry, drama, music, dance, and other fine and expressive arts. The open areas include literature, music, dance, filmmaking and film studies, creative writing, autobiography, biography, art, drawing, painting, poetry, history, philosophy, and religion. These open areas, centered in ethical and aesthetic values, often tend to be neglected, given low priority, or squeezed out in schools and colleges by the more career-oriented saleable skills or mandated required subjects, especially those related

Open Areas: the humanities, fine arts, and expressive arts, which hold great potential for raising consciousness about the human condition and freedom of choice.

to meeting standards. For Existentialists, the humanities and the arts are of crucial importance in raising consciousness and encouraging self-definition because they are open-ended and offer multiple perspectives on the human condition.

The arts, designed to cultivate and express aesthetic experience, include music, drama, dance, creative writing, painting, and film. For Existentialists, aesthetic education's primary goal is not for students to imitate the styles of selected classical artists, although these might be studied, but rather to evoke their creative expression. Although not knowing what the learner will create, the teacher provides a variety of creative materials and media so students have the raw materials to create their own art. Students use the various media, materials, and instruments to portray the world as they experience it in their own consciousness and to create art from the center of their own private existence.

As Maxine Greene indicates, literature and the humanities are especially relevant in an Existentialist curriculum. Relevant for awakening the learner to the significance of choice making, literature portrays persons facing human issues in life situations. Through literature, drama, and film, students are enabled to engage their experiences and feelings in an author's story. Literature involves readers in profound human questions of love, death, suffering, guilt, and freedom. These questions provide openings for creating personal meaning in an apparently indifferent world.

My Reflections on Philosophy of Education: An Existentialist Review of *The Help*

I belong to a book club. At a recent meeting of the club, it was my turn to select a book and lead a discussion on it. I selected Kathryn Stockett's novel, *The Help,* which provides an apt illustration of how fiction portrays Existentialist themes. The best-selling novel, made into a popular movie, takes place in Mississippi in 1962. Although eight years have passed since the Supreme Court ruled racially segregated public schools unconstitutional, the historic patterns of racial segregation are deeply set in the Mississippi city that is the story's setting. These racial patterns are what Existentialists refer to as *situated life experience*. The novel's characters are born into and living in a historical, sociological, political, and economic world that they inherited but did not create.

The book's major characters, Skeeter, Abileen, Minny, and Hilly, are situated in this Mississippi town. Each of them illustrates how they create their essence, their own self-definition in their situated experience. Skeeter, a twenty-two-year-old recent graduate of the University of Mississippi who lives with her parents, has been hired to write a household column for the local newspaper. She faces unrelenting pressure from her mother and her friends to find a suitable man, get engaged, marry, and join the town's upper-class society. Skeeter has a choice to make: Fall in line with others' expectations or choose another path. She chooses another path—to write a book about the situation of the African American maids and caregivers who are raising the children of her white friends. Her choice is a risky one, even a dangerous one, since she is deviating from the expectations of her family, friends, and the dominant white society. From an Existentialist perspective, Skeeter is making a choice that has the possibility of liberating her and creating her own self-identity. She has put much at risk, however: family approval, a comfortable circle of friends, and the possibility of being shunned by her peers.

Skeeter enlists two African American maids, Abileen and Minny, who are the "Help" for her friends. Like Skeeter, Abileen and Minnie are situated in that they are living and working in a racially regulated society. Underpaid, overworked, and unappreciated, they live as subordinates in a world they are in but did not make. Hesitant to cooperate with Skeeter, Abileen and Minny reluctantly agree and are interviewed in clandestine meetings about what it is like to raise other people's children. They, too, are taking a risk in that they will lose their jobs if their activity is discovered. As the plot unfolds, the two women begin to write their own stories. Through their authorship, they face the risk of challenging the system that has defined them and begin to create their own self-definitions, what Sartre would call their own essences.

Skeeter, Abileen, and Minny are choosing their own paths to self-definition by being the authors of their own life story. They have to do this by challenging the system that defines what is expected of a young white woman and two middle-aged black women. The system they face is represented by Hilly, a friend of Skeeter who is the leader of the white women's club. A powerful and controlling presence, Hilly is determined to keep things as they are and not allow change. If change occurs, Hilly's dominance will be threatened and perhaps ended. She represents the controlling other in a controlled situation.

Existentialism and History

History as a subject presents an interesting issue for Existentialists because it is not really a science, yet not quite an art. The sources—the documents and artifacts—historians use to construct their version of the past need to meet the requirements of validity that is somewhat empirical. Written history is also literature, somewhat akin to the novel; the historical narrative, though purporting to be based on a recital of the facts of an actual event, tells a story of individuals, their conflicts, choices, successes, and failures. As with other subjects, teaching and learning history involve the appropriation of the narrative in which students can make it their own and either accept or reject the historian's interpretation of the meaning of the past.

In teaching history, Existentialists might use the strategy of **emplotment**, in which the student is encouraged to appropriate, internalize, and interpret the narrative's plot—as the unfolding story of individuals, who, facing their situation, seek to shape their destiny.[43] Through emplotment—the acts of appropriating and internalizing—students can consider and reflect on ideas, beliefs, and values from narratives about the past and either make them their own or reject them.[44]

Emplotment: teaching and studying history by appropriating, internalizing, and interpreting the narrative's plot.

For example, students might engage with the months immediate to the American Civil War, and consider the hesitation and inaction of President James Buchanan, Abraham Lincoln's predecessor, and the action taken by Lincoln when he became president. The process of emplotment involves the student's participation in reflecting on the choices made by the two men. The educational philosopher George Kneller wrote:

> The student should therefore learn to handle his history with passion, personal thrust, and in the manner of a stage director, talently manipulating the human scene, with all its heroes, villains, and plots.[45]

Existentialism, Philosophy, and Education

Philosophy	Reality	Epistemology	Axiology	Educational Implications	Leading Philosophers
Existentialism	Existence precedes essence; we live in concrete situations and define ourselves through our choices.	Choosing what we want to know by appropriating it; making it our own.	Living is a process of open-ended evaluation and the construction of values through our choices.	Curriculum and activities, especially in humanities and arts, to stimulate an awareness that each person creates a self-concept through significant choices.	Kierkegaard Sartre Marcel Morris Greene

EXISTENTIALIST EPISTEMOLOGY, HUMANIST PSYCHOLOGY, AND TEACHING AND LEARNING

In viewing an Existentialist classroom, we need to consider the relationship of epistemology and psychology to teaching and learning.

Existentialist Epistemology

For the human being as rational by nature, see the chapters on Idealism and Realism.

Traditional philosophies such as Idealism, Realism, and Thomism emphasize the human being as a thinking and reasoning being. For example, Plato's philosopher-kings were an intellectual elite who possessed the keenest powers of speculative abstraction; Aristotle, identifying the power to reason as unique to the human being, called the human being a rational animal. For Idealism and Realism, the overriding educational goal is the development of students' cognitive and rational powers. Existentialism, in contrast, has more varied and less specific goals. The person can be rational or irrational, thinking but also feeling, cognitive but also affective.

Existentialist epistemology assumes that individuals are responsible for constructing their own knowledge and process of knowing.[46] Knowledge is based on an individual's perspective of reality in that it is many-sided and multi-dimensional. Human situations have both rational and irrational components. What is true and good is determined by the meaning and value that a person gives to it. An Existentialist epistemology emerges from the recognition that human experience and knowledge are subjective, personal, rational, and irrational. Whereas Pragmatists emphasize using the scientific method of problem solving, Existentialists prefer to probe human aesthetic, moral, and emotional concerns as well as cognitive ones.

For using the scientific method to solve problems, see the chapter on Pragmatism and Education.

Humanist Psychology

Existentialism has influenced humanist psychology, which in turn has implications for educational psychology and counseling. Sartre and other Existentialists criticized deterministic psychologies that reduce human behavior to satisfying needs, instincts, and impulses and neglect the complexity of human freedom and choice. Arguing against psychological determinism, Sartre contended that human beings make their choice in situations that are unique to each person.

Abraham Maslow, Gordon Allport, Carl Rogers, and Rollo May have been the leaders in humanist psychology. Rogers, who developed client-centered counseling, emphasizes that the individual should be free to create his or her own self-concept. This creating of self-identity means that the person exists at the center of a changing world of experience, which, though it encompasses social interactions, is ultimately private and is self-formed rather than other-directed.[47]

Guided by humanist psychology, Existentialist teaching seeks to stimulate self-examination and definition, in the broadest sense. Maintaining the Existentialist classroom requires a delicate balance in which both teacher and students maintain their identities as persons. This means that the teacher must constantly struggle against falling into a situation in which students are defined simply by their age, academic ranking, status, or group membership. It also means that students need to be conscious that they, too, can define a teacher, not as a person but as one who performs custodial, instructional, and supervisory functions. This necessary but delicate Existential balance is jeopardized when teachers reduce students to objects or products and students reduce teachers to functions.

Existentialist Teaching and Learning

Although the Existentialist teacher may choose to use a variety of educational methods, none of these methods should replace or obscure the personal I–Thou teacher and learner relationship. The Socratic dialogue can be an appropriate method for

Existentialist teachers. The dialogue can raise questions about the meaning of life and the importance of choice. It can raise issues about the tension between freedom and conformity. Unlike the Idealist's use of the Socratic dialogue, the Existentialist teacher does not know the answers to the questions.

In an Existentialist method, the teacher seeks to stimulate an "intensity of awareness" in the learner, encouraging the quest for a personal truth by asking questions that concern life's meaning. It is the teacher's task to create a learning situation in which students can express their subjectivity. Only the learner can come face to face with his or her responsibility for self-definition. The creation of the intensity of awareness is as much the learner's own responsibility as it is the teacher's. Such an awareness involves the sense of being personally involved in the ethical and aesthetic dimensions of existence.

To create their own modes of self-expression, students should be free to experiment with artistic media and to dramatize their emotions, feelings, and insights in short stories, poems, plays, drawings, paintings, dances, and films. Educational technology such as videos, movies, and social media that enhances personal choice and freedom can also be useful in an Existentialist education. For example, students might benefit from expressing themselves by creating multimedia productions, videos, and movies. Prepackaged programs that create conformity in thinking and in accessing information, on the other hand, should be viewed with suspicion.

An Existentialist Lesson

Literature, history, drama, and film are especially powerful subjects in Existentialist teaching. One example might be a junior high school class reading *The Diary of Anne Frank,* the story of a young Jewish girl, her family, and others who hide in an attic in Amsterdam, which was under Nazi occupation during World War II. Anne and her family live in an absurd and dangerous world. They must hide to avoid being rounded up and sent to a German concentration camp. They are aided by several Dutch friends who are loyal to Anne's father, their former employer. Anne and her family find themselves in a situation, a context, that is fraught with the everyday danger of their arrest simply because they are Jewish. If sent to a concentration camp, they face extermination. The danger represents the Existentialist theme of the dread of eventual disappearance. Anne makes a choice to turn her cramped refuge into lived space and to use her time, in which night and day have no meaning, to write her diary, which records growing up as a teenage girl in a world that makes no sense. In the end, the family is betrayed by a collaborator. The Gestapo find the hiding place, and Anne and her family are seized and transported to the concentration camp in which Anne will die.

Students can consider the ethical meaning of Anne's situation. There are those righteous gentiles who, at the risk of their own lives, provided the Frank family and the others hidden in the attic with the food they needed to survive. Then, there is the choice made by the Nazi collaborator who revealed their hiding place. Students can ask themselves what they would have done under the circumstances. What choices would they make?

The lesson deals with an Existential situation being lived out in a concrete situation—the reality of surviving in a cramped attic. It crosses back and forth from history, biography, literature, and ethics. It uses the strategy of emplotment, by which students appropriate, internalize, and interpret the plot as the unfolding story of individuals facing the facts of their context and striving for meaningful action. Through emplotment, individuals can acquire beliefs, attitudes, or behaviors from external sources and make them their own by transforming them into personal attributes, values, or styles.

CONSTRUCTING YOUR OWN PHILOSOPHY OF EDUCATION

At the beginning of this chapter, you were encouraged to reflect on how Existentialism relates to constructing your own philosophy of education. Now that you have read and discussed the chapter, does Existentialism appeal to you as a philosophy of education? Are there elements in Existentialism that you plan to incorporate into your own philosophy of education? Are there aspects that you would definitely not include? Do you believe that we are responsible for defining ourselves?

Conclusion

Existentialist philosophy has made its mark on how we think and feel today. The Existentialist themes of mutual respect, the freedom to define oneself by making significant choices, and the idea that life and education are open-ended and indeterminate resonate throughout thinking on education. Contemporary efforts to resist conformity and standardization echo the arguments of Sartre, Marcel, de Beauvoir, Greene, and Morris. The contemporary search for a spirituality that is free from dogma is reminiscent of Kierkegaard's "leap of faith." The terms *choice, commitment, authenticity,* and *freedom* resonate throughout political, social, and educational discourse that runs counter to establishment thinking. Arguments that an authentic education means that students have the right to construct their own identities, write their own stories, and bring their lived-in situations into the classroom reflect the Existentialist argument that persons come before definitions and actions come before theories.

Most likely where the Existentialists part company with contemporary education is in their belief that persons are more than the sum of their social, political, economic, religious, class, race, ethnic, and gender parts. Although these aspects of living may illuminate who we are, we are not defined by them. In its abhorrence of determinism, Existentialism's assertion that we are a self-constructed human project flies in the face of the many determinist theories that are taught and preached in academic lecture halls and classrooms. A major difference that the Existentialists offer to us is facing up to and accepting our own responsibility for who we are and what we do.

Questions for Reflection and Discussion

1. Assume you are an Existentialist teacher. How would you respond to a student who asks, "What difference does it make to you that I am here in your classroom?"
2. A student says, "I want to make a difference." What would this statement mean to an Existentialist?
3. What does it mean to create your own self-definition without defining others?
4. Give some examples of antecedent definitions that define persons prior to their own individual existence. Do you find these examples present in contemporary schools?
5. Have you been involved with groups, especially in educational situations, that limited your freedom to define yourself?
6. Have you known an authentic person, one who is completely self-directed? Describe this person.
7. Reflect on current trends in education such as the standards movement, multiculturalism, women's studies programs, authentic assessment, the common core curriculum, and constructionism. Do these trends encourage or discourage Existentialist themes such as authenticity, cultivating an intensity of awareness, and self-definition?
8. Have you had teachers or professors who either encouraged or limited your freedom of choice? Identify and compare and contrast one model of encouragement or limitation from your educational experience.

Inquiry and Research Projects

1. Review a book by one of the following in which you identify the work's Existentialist themes: Søren Kierkegaard, Friedrich Nietzsche, Fyodor Dostoyevsky, Martin Buber, Jean-Paul Sartre, Gabriel Marcel, Simone de Beauvoir, Maxine Greene, or Van Cleve Morris.

2. Identify and review movies, television programs, and novels that portray Existentialist themes or situations.
3. Write a script for a short play that exemplifies an Existentialist teaching situation; invite your colleagues to portray the various characters in the play. If possible, videotape the play and then analyze it as a classroom activity.
4. Arrange a group discussion on the topic, "Is Existentialism a relevant educational philosophy?" After the discussion, have the participants reflect on pressures that they experienced from being involved in the discussion.
5. Identify and describe in a journal entry how specific situations in your school either encourage or discourage freedom of choice and expression.
6. Select a current trend in education such as the standards movement, multiculturalism, women's studies programs, authentic assessment, constructionism, service education, or the common core curriculum. Review the literature about this trend and determine how an Existentialist would relate to it.

Internet Resources

For a discussion of Existentialism, with commentary and quotes from Sartre, Marcel, de Beauvoir, and others, access "Existentialism Philosophy" at http://www.spaceandmotion.com/Philosophy/Existentialism.htm.

For a discussion of Existentialism's key concepts, access "Existentialism" at the Stanford Encyclopedia of Philosophy at http://plato.stanford.edu/existentialism/.

For an introduction to Existentialism, access www.allaboutphilosophy.org/existentialism.htm.

For Existentialism as a recent philosophy, access www.radicalacademy.com/adiphiexistentialism.htm.

Suggestions for Further Reading

Barrett, William. *Irrational Man: A Study in Existentialist Philosophy.* New York: Anchor Books, 1990.

Catalano, Joseph S. *Good Faith and Other Essays: Perspectives on Sartre's Ethics.* Lanham, MD: Rowman and Littlefield, 1996.

Crowell, Steven, ed. *The Cambridge Companion to Existentialism.* New York: Cambridge University Press, 2012.

Dall'Alba, Gloria, ed. *Exploring Education Through Phenomenology: Diverse Approaches.* New York: Wiley-Blackwell, 2009.

De Beauvoir, Simone. *The Ethics of Ambiguity.* New York: Citadel, 2000.

___. *The Second Sex.* New York: Knopf, 1989.

Dobson, Andrew. *Jean-Paul Sartre and the Politics of Reason: A Theory of History.* New York: Cambridge University Press, 1993.

Dreyfus, Hubert L., and Mark A. Wrathall, eds. *A Companion to Existentialism and Phenomenology.* Oxford, UK: Blackwell, 2006.

Flynn, Thomas. *Existentialism: A Very Short Introduction.* Oxford, UK: Oxford University Press, 2006.

Garff, Joakim. *Søren Kierkegaard: A Biography.* Princeton, NJ: Princeton University Press, 2005.

Golomb, Jacob. *In Search of Authenticity: From Kierkegaard to Camus.* London: Routledge, 1995.

Greene, Maxine. *Public School and the Private Vision: A Search for America in Education and Literature.* New York: New Press, 2007.

___. *Releasing the Imagination: Essays on Education, the Arts, and Social Change.* New York: Jossey Bass/Wiley, 2000.

___. *Variations on a Blue Guitar: The Lincoln Center Institute Lectures on Aesthetic Education.* New York: Lincoln Center, 2001.

Guignon, Charles, and Derk Pereboom, eds. *Existentialism: Basic Writings.* Indianapolis, IN: Hackett, 1995.

Kierkegaard, Søren. *Either/Or.* Translated by Alastair Hannay. London: Penguin Books, 1992.

___. *Papers and Journals: A Selection.* London: Penguin Books, 1996.

MacDonald, Paul S., ed. *The Existentialist Reader: An Anthology of Key Texts.* New York: Routledge, 2001.

Manno, Gordon, ed. *Basic Writings of Existentialism.* New York: Modern Library, 2004.

Marcel, Gabriel. *Man Against Mass Society.* Chicago: Gateway, 1970.

___. *The Philosophy of Existentialism.* New York: Citadel, 1961.

Peters, Michael A. *Heidegger, Education, and Modernity.* Lanham, MD: Rowman and Littlefied, 2002.

Pinar, William F. *The Passionate Mind of Maxine Greene: "I Am . . . Not Yet."* London, UK, and Bristol, PA: Falmer Press/Taylor & Francis, 1998.

Rasheed, Shaireen. *An Existentialist Curriculum of Action: Creating a Language of Freedom and Possibility.* Washington, DC: University Press of America, 2006.

Santoni, Ronald E. *Bad Faith, Good Faith, and Authenticity in Sartre's Early Philosophy*. Philadelphia: Temple University Press, 1995.

Sartre, Jean-Paul. *Being and Nothingness*. New York: Citadel, 1984.

___. *Existentialism Is a Humanism*. New Haven: Yale University Press, 2007.

Solomon, Robert C. *Existentialism*. New York: Oxford University Press, 2004.

Stewart. Jon, ed. *Kierkegaard and Existentialism*. Oxford, UK: Ashgate, 2011.

Westphal, Merold. *Becoming a Self: A Reading of Kierkegaard's Concluding Unscientific Postscript*. West Lafayette, IN: Purdue University Press, 1996.

Notes

1. *The Random House Dictionary of the English Language* (New York: Random House, 1968), 464.
2. Thomas Flynn, *Existentialism: A Very Short Introduction* (Oxford, UK: Oxford University Press, 2006), 17–20.
3. Alastair Hanny, "Søren Aabye Kierkegaard," in Ted Honderich, ed., *The Philosophers: Introducing Great Western Thinkers* (Oxford and New York: Oxford University Press, 2001), 149.
4. Patrick Gardiner, *Kierkegaard: A Very Short Introduction* (Oxford and New York: Oxford University Press, 2002), 8–9.
5. For a biography of Kierkegaard, see Joakim Garff, *Søren Kierkegaard: A Biography* (Princeton, NJ: Princeton University Press, 2005).
6. Flynn, *Existentialism: A Very Short Introduction*, 3, 10.
7. Ibid., 25.
8. Ibid., 90–91.
9. Gardiner, *Kierkegaard: A Very Short Introduction*, 52–53.
10. Flynn, *Existentialism: A Very Short Introduction*, 26–27.
11. Gardiner, *Kierkegaard: A Very Short Introduction*, 48–49.
12. Flynn, *Existentialism: A Very Short Introduction*, 34–36.
13. Gardiner, *Kierkegaard: A Very Short Introduction*, 60.
14. Gabriel Marcel, *The Philosophy of Existentialism* (New York: Citadel Press, 1961).
15. Gabriel Marcel, *Man Against Mass Society* (Chicago: Gateway, 1970).
16. Flynn, *Existentialism: A Very Short Introduction*, 90–91.
17. Thomas Baldwin, "Jean-Paul Sartre," in Ted Honderich, ed., *The Philosophers: Introducing Great Western Thinkers* (Oxford and New York: Oxford University Press, 2001), 245.
18. Biographies of Nietzshe are: Julian Young, *Friedrich Nietzsche:A Philosophical Biography* (New York: Cambridge University Press, 2010); and Jennifer Ratner-Rosenhagen, *American Nietzsche: History of an Icon and His Ideas* (Chicago: University of Chicago Press, 2011).
19. Walter Kaufmann, ed., *Basic Writings of Nietzsche* (New York: Modern Library, 2000).
20. Friedrich Nietzsche, *The Will to Power,* Walter Kaufmann, ed. (New York: Random House, 1968), 127–140,
21. For de Beauvoir's impressions of the French Existentialist movement, see Simone de Beauvoir, *The Force of Circumstances* (New York: Putnam, 1965); and Beauvoir, *All Said and Done* (New York: Putnam, 1974).
22. Nietzsche, *The Will to Power,* 500–507.
23. Flynn, *Existentialism: A Very Short Introduction,* 40.
24. Friedrich Nietzsche, *Thus Spoke Zarathustra* (Blacksburg, VA: Wilder Publishers, 2012), 220–227.
25. Jean-Paul Sartre, "Is Existentialism a Humanism?" in Walter Kaufmann, ed., *Existentialism: From Dostoevsky to Sartre* (New York: Penguin Books, 1988).
26. For Nietzsche, see Friedrich Nietzsche, *The Anti-Christ, Ecce Homo, Twilight of the Idols: and Other Writings* (Cambridge, UK: Cambridge University Press, 2005); and Nietzsche, *Beyond Good and Evil* (Cambridge, UK: Cambridge University Press, 2001).
27. Flynn, *Existentialism: A Very Short Introduction*, 98–99.
28. Ibid., 101–102.
29. My analogy of the map is derived from Flynn's discussion of Kierkegaard's "fork in the road" commentary on truth in Flynn, *Existentialism: A Very Short Introduction*, 9–10.
30. Maxine Greene, *The Dialectic of Freedom* (New York: Teachers College Press, 1988), xi–xii.
31. Ibid., 3–6.
32. Ibid., 21.
33. Ibid., 22–23.
34. Ibid., 118.
35. Flynn, *Existentialism: A Very Short Introduction*, 5–7.
36. *Random House Dictionary of the English Language*, 91.
37. Flynn, *Existentialism: A Very Short Introduction*, 24–25.
38. Ibid., 65–67.

39. Ibid., 92.
40. Van Cleve Morris, *Existentialism in Education* (New York: Harper and Row, 1966), 110.
41. Ibid., 116–117.
42. For discussions of history, meaning, and memory, see Peter N. Stearns, Peter Seixas, and Sam Weinburg, eds., *Knowing, Teaching and Learning History: National and International Perspectives* (New York: New York University Press, 2000).
43. James Wertsch, "Is It Possible to Teach Beliefs, as Well as Knowledge About History?" in Peter N. Stearns, Peter Seixas, and Sam Weinburg, eds., *Knowing, Teaching and Learning History,* 38–50.
44. George F. Kneller, *Existentialism and Education* (New York: John Wiley and Sons, 1966), 129–130.
45. Morris, *Existentialism in Education,* 120–122.
46. Frank Milhollan and Bill E. Forisha, *From Skinner to Rogers: Contrasting Approaches to Education* (Lincoln, NE: Professional Educators, 1972), 98–113.
47. Ibid.

Postmodernism and Education

Michel Foucault (1926–1984), a French philosopher whose ideas were highly influential in the development of Postmodernism.

6

CHAPTER PREVIEW

Postmodernism is a much-discussed contemporary philosophy in both general conversation and academic discourse. We often hear that we live in the postmodern, postindustrial, and poststructural era that followed the modern period of history. The term **postmodern condition** is used to describe the cultural changes caused in the contemporary information age society. Among academics, postmodernism exerts a strong influence in literature, architecture, education, humanities, and the arts as well in multicultural, feminist, and gender studies. To take a closer look at postmodernism, we begin with two terms, *post* and *modern*. The prefix *post* means coming after some event, such as being a postgraduate, meaning after one graduates, or postsurgical, the recovery period needed to recuperate after surgery. *Modern* as an adjective has been applied to Western history from the Renaissance through the end of the Cold War, roughly from the fifteenth through the twentieth century. Postmodernists, in their critique of modernism, focus on the period from the eighteenth-century Enlightenment to the end of the twentieth century. Postmodernists are especially critical of the emphasis in Western history and culture that is given to the Enlightenment as the "age of reason" as well as its consequences for scientific discovery, European exploration and imperialism and industrialism, the two World Wars, the Cold War, the nuclear era, and the current trend toward globalization. The chapter examines the following aspects of Postmodernism:

- Postmodern Philosophers
- Postmodern Themes
- Postmodern Education

As you read about and discuss Postmodernism, use it to critique your ideas about education, schooling, curriculum, and teaching and learning. Consider whether Postmodernism, in its entirety or in its parts, appeals to you as a teacher. Do you plan to incorporate Postmodernism in your philosophy of education? Or do you reject it or some parts of it as possibilities in constructing your own philosophy of education?

POSTMODERNIST PHILOSOPHERS

Rather than pointing to a particular founder of Postmodernism as we did with Plato for Idealism, Aristotle for Realism, and Dewey for Pragmatism, we will examine the ideas of several philosophers. Postmodernism's origins are traced to the philosophers Nietzsche and Heidegger; contemporary Postmodernism is associated with such theorists as Jacques Derrida and Michel Foucault.

Postmodern Condition: the cultural changes caused by the end of the modern period and the rise of the contemporary information and service society and economy.

Nietzsche and Heidegger are discussed in the chapter on Existentialism and education.

Antecedents of Postmodernism

While we discussed how Nietzsche and Heidegger contributed to the origins of Existentialism in the previous chapter on Existentialism and Education, here we consider how their ideas also stimulated Postmodernism. Friedrich Nietzsche (1844–1900), an iconoclastic German philosopher, attacked traditional philosophical assumptions that metaphysical speculation could discover the universal truths of ultimate reality.[1] For Nietzsche, metaphysics was merely a human construction designed to fill the void when ancient myths and supernaturalism imploded because of modern science. Metaphysicians—Idealists, Realists, and Thomists—had constructed an unchanging otherworld of certitude that is always good, true, and beautiful. Their cosmic invention provided a philosophical tranquilizer for anxious people who could not accept the reality of a world that was incomplete, changing, and always in the ferment of becoming. Postmodernist philosophers agreed with Nietzsche that metaphysical statements were human-made rationales constructed at a given time in history that could be traced genealogically to their origins in historical, psychological, economic, sociological, and educational situations.[2] Further, Postmodernists agreed with Nietzsche that all ideas, freed from metaphysical constraints, are open and flexible. Certain heroic individuals, "the supermen," Nietzsche claimed, celebrate the absence of absolutes and the incompleteness of life, by making their own rules on how to live.

Martin Heidegger (1899–1976), another German philosopher, elaborating on the ideas of Nietzsche and Husserl, constructed a philosophy called *Existentialist Phenomenology*. Heidegger dismissed the metaphysical idea of pre-existing universal truth and values. Rather, we are here in a world in which we reconstruct our own "truths" from our perspectives—from our intuitions, perceptions, and reflections—of how we experience phenomena. Borrowing from Heidegger, Postmodernist philosophers are highly suspicious of the claims of an objective reality and objective claims of knowing it.

Karl Marx

Karl Marx's ideas are examined in the chapter on Marxism and Education.

Postmodernism has been influenced by the ideas of Karl Marx, a nineteenth-century German philosopher. (Our discussion of Marxism here comments on its relationship to Postmodernism. Marxism is examined in greater depth in a later chapter.) Although Postmodernists would question Marx's universalizing dialectical materialism and his claims about the inevitability of class war, revolution, and the eventual construction of a classless society, his ideas inform aspects of their philosophy. French Postmodernists sought to construct a version of Marxism that was free of the earlier connections between Marx and Soviet Communism. One important Marxist concept that influenced Postmodernism was **false consciousness**, a pervasive misinformation deliberately constructed by dominant classes and conveyed by their media and educational agencies to mislead oppressed people from recognizing who and what was exploiting them.

False Consciousness: the Postmodernist appropriation of Marx's concept that dominant classes deliberately use misinformation to delude oppressed groups from forming a true consciousness about their exploitation.

An example of false consciousness, from the Marxist perspective, is the false belief that everyone can achieve the "American dream" of wealth if they go to school, work hard, overcome setbacks, and win by following the competitive rules of the corporate economic game. Marxists contend that the rules of the corporate economy are controlled by the upper economic classes.[3] False consciousness is instilled, according to Marx, by the capitalist-controlled information systems—the media, entertainment, religious, and educational institutions and processes. Peter Sloterdijk identifies "enlightened false consciousness" as a pervasive symptom in postmodern society's ways of thinking.[4] In education, those holding political and economic power construct a curriculum of "official knowledge," the approved subjects that are transmitted to the young to indoctrinate them in this false consciousness. Unless they are conscious that they are being indoctrinated, subordinate groups may mistake this imposition as a valid rendition of their situation. Later in this chapter, we examine how Postmodernists would deconstruct false consciousness.

Leading Postmodern Philosophers

In this section, we discuss the ideas of two major Postmodern philosophers, Jacques Derrida and Michel Foucault.

JACQUES DERRIDA. Jacques Derrida (1930–2004), an Algerian-born French philosopher, is often identified as a major originator of Postmodernism, especially poststructuralism. He is known for his method of **deconstruction** for analyzing texts. To understand Derrida's deconstruction, we first need to understand how he views the construction of philosophical and other texts in Western civilization. The term *construction* is important. If the parts of something have been put together, or constructed, to build a structure, they can be taken apart or dismantled, or deconstructed.

Deconstruction: Derrida's method of penetrating and disassembling texts to analyze their origins and meanings to determine why they are officially privileged.

Examining Western philosophy's origins in ancient Greece, Derrida found that philosophers such as Plato and Aristotle, and their later disciples, sought to discover the general original source of existence, or **logos**, in which, they believed, were the inherent purposes that ordered and governed the universe. As the source of all meaning and significance, every description of what something meant and how the universe functioned and every prescription on how society should be organized came from the logos, the original and permanent principles that governed reality. For example, Plato claimed that the logos was the Form of the Good, the great unifying metaphysical principle of truth and goodness that gave order, purpose, and meaning to the universe. He then used this principle as the **logocentric** foundation or center on which to construct his entire philosophy. For Christian theologians such as Thomas Aquinas, God is the Creator, the Originator of the universe, who established the patterns and the rules that govern the universe and society.

Logos: the universal principles that traditional philosophers claim are at the origin and center of the universe

For Plato's philosophy, see the chapter on Idealism and Education.

Logocentric: the philosophical rationale that reality rests on the principles at the center of the universe.

Derrida advises us that the metaphysical center of Plato's philosophy is not a reality but only a man-made construction. Further, Plato's ideas of an epistemology of reminiscence and political philosophy in *The Republic* can be deconstructed and pulled apart.

Using these classical Greek origins, later philosophers continued to search for universal principles of rationality, inherent in an ultimate reality. They saw philosophy as going back to and searching for the original center of truth and values. They believed that the human being, as defined by Aristotle, possessed a reasoning mind that made it possible to discover the logi, the universe's rational principles, and act according to them.

Despite continued attacks on metaphysics by Pragmatists, some Existentialists, and Postmodernists, Derrida finds that metaphysical assumptions about rational principles, the logi, remain deeply embedded in Western culture. Indeed, meaning in Western cultures is logocentric, centered in and often controlled by these inherited metaphysical principles.

Although Pragmatists like John Dewey rejected metaphysics, they were still haunted by Plato's ghost in that they continued to attempt to center their philosophy on some kind of unifying principles. If no center exists, then philosophers like Dewey sought to create one. For Dewey, these central principles became the scientific method, democracy, and community. According to Derrida, there is no central or logocentric principle of rationality in the universe. All there is are the constructions of how philosophers represented the logos in their writings, their texts.

Now, the term *text* becomes important for Postmodernists, because authorities are represented in words, in language, in documents such as the Bible, the U.S. Constitution, the U.N. Charter, a Papal Encyclical, the No Child Left Behind Act, the Common Core Standards, Plato's *Republic,* or John Dewey's *Democracy and Education.* Although a text has historically been a written document or a published book, it can take other forms in the technological and digital era. Texts may be oral dialogues, or movies, videos, plays, or other forms of cultural representation. In education, a text can be a curriculum guide, a syllabus, a video, or a book, including a textbook like the one you are now reading.

Canon: an official text that has authority in a culture, political order, society, religion, or learned discipline.

Deconstruction is a method of getting inside and penetrating texts to explore different shades of meaning in addition to those designated as an officially sanctioned **canon**. A particular text becomes a canon when it is regarded as a privileged authority that defines and sets standards in a particular field. Getting inside the text means to (1) identify its logocentric principles; (2) trace the origin and development of meanings conveyed, with special sensitivity to justification by appealing to the logi; and (3) determine how the knowledge claims, meanings, and interpretation in the text affect our ideas, beliefs, interpretations, and meanings. The aim of deconstruction is not simply to engage in language analysis but to understand how texts, rather than reflecting metaphysical principles, are historically and culturally specific constructions that involve political power relationships. The idea of power as an instrument of control is a persistent theme in Postmodernist philosophy.

For Derrida, philosophers need to liberate themselves from metaphysics and end their futile efforts to construct new centers, colossal worldviews, and new world orders that claim to be based on some kind of universal principles. What they can do is to conduct a rigorous analysis, a deconstruction, of the language used to provide the theoretical foundations for social, cultural, political, economic, and educational institutions. These supposed foundations are conveyed in discourses—oral and written narratives—that promise to explain reality and are used to justify allegiance to existing institutions and situations. What we need to examine is how the authors, the originators and users of the discourses, have interpreted reality. Because interpretation comes from a person's experience, we need to examine how individuals and groups have used language to construct meaning, to interpret reality, and to justify their position in society in order to use and keep power.

The philosopher's task is to deconstruct ideas about institutions and culture in order to uncover the rationale builder's underlying assumptions, presuppositions, and meanings. These rationales, often referred to as the foundations of culture, are expressed in the language of a text and assume the authority or special status of a canon. All discourse, including philosophical, historical, and scientific discourse, is presented in texts. A text, itself, is not reality, but rather an author's representation. Deconstruction involves identifying and explaining the author's meaning, her or his version of reality, as well as what the reader brings to the text in terms of experience. To deconstruct a text means to identify and analyze, "unpack" the author's assumptions and meanings as they are expressed by word choices, examples, metaphors, and puns.[5] In other words, deconstruction involves analyzing language as it is used in social relationships; it is a socially charged study in grammar.[6]

Differance: Derrida's term that the meanings conveyed by language are different rather than similar and that meanings are so fluid that they are never final.

Derrida coined the term **differance,** to combine the words *difference* and *defer.* The efforts to deconstruct language involve identifying and analyzing the differences in how people understand and use language. To deconstruct requires us to find the differences in meanings and relationships in the various voices engaged in discourse. Language is a complex body of differences and nuances in which the meaning of a word can be determined only by comparing it and contrasting it with other words. Establishing meaning requires the act of interpreting—using other words to tell us what it is not.[7] At the same time that the search for meaning takes place in its various shades and nuances, there is a need to defer final definitions in establishing a central meaning because of the complexity, fluidity, and drift of language—how it is used at different times in different places.[8]

Derrida does not want us to get locked into closed language boxes that use fixed definitions. Fixed definitions freeze meanings at a given time in history. Consider this sentence, "A woman, by her nature, is suited to be a wife, mother, nurse, or elementary school teacher." These descriptors of what is appropriate for a woman were often used in the nineteenth century, especially in the Victorian era. The sentence confines women to certain defined and prescribed roles. For Derrida, our words should be flexible and open to different shades and nuances of meaning.

MICHEL FOUCAULT. Michel Foucault (1926–1984), a French social philosopher and historian, shaped Postmodernism through his analyses of history, society, culture, politics, economics, and education. Foucault argues that notions of ***truth*** are not universal, but arise in historical contexts and express power relationships in society, politics, economics, and education. To understand Foucault's philosophy, we begin with three of his major working premises: (1) the relationship of truth and power; (2) **regimes of truth**; and (3) the use of discourse.

Regimes of Truth: according to Foucault, the ideologies, institutions, and practices by which people control, regulate, govern, and even define each other at different periods of history.

Foucault, like Derrida, dismisses the possibilities of universal truth, based on traditional metaphysical speculation, and also the claims of the eighteenth-century Enlightenment that science and social science can provide objective and unbiased truths. Foucault rejects the Enlightenment assumption that rational individuals, using the scientific method, can discover the truth as objective knowledge. He also discounts the Enlightenment premise that this kind of objective knowledge is open to all and that it can fairly and equally benefit all people.[9] The various social and behavioral sciences that originated in the Enlightenment and were developed in the modern period—sociology, economics, political science, anthropology, psychology—profess to be objective, empirical, and scientific ways of describing and examining human behavior. Note how much of modern educational theory and practice rests on these social sciences. From this allegedly objective research, social scientists developed prescriptions, guidelines that told how "normal," socially sound, good citizens—men, women, and children—should behave. Modern social sciences rest on probability and predictability—which in turn rest on the human being as a complex of observable, predictable, and measurable behaviors. For example, the Pragmatists, especially Peirce, who discounted metaphysics as empirically unvariable, claimed that probability should provide people with a sense of predictable direction. Postmodernists like Foucault believed that using statistical predictability to guide instruction and shape behavior can lead to controlled and manipulated, rewarded and punished behavior. For example, the results of standardized achievement tests can be used to identify "competent" and "incompetent teachers" and "achieving" and "underachieving" schools. Competent teachers can be rewarded with merit pay increases; incompetent ones can be remediated or terminated.

For Peirce's theory of probability, see the chapter on Pragmatism and Education.

The social sciences categorize people into roles and functions based on a standard of the normal, which lead to norms or rules of behavior. Just as there are approved and rewarded norms, there are also disapproved deviant behaviors. Foucault examined how institutions such as law courts, hospitals, prisons, and asylums are controlled by the officially sanctioned norms established by experts.[10] Legal norms determine who is innocent or guilty of crimes (indeed what constitutes a crime); medical norms determine who is healthy or sick and how patients should be treated; psychiatric norms determine who is sane or insane, and so on. Depending on the degree of deviancy from the norm, individuals in these categories can be remediated, rehabilitated, or reeducated and, if need be, institutionalized in hospitals, asylums, and prisons. Individuals can be classified into those who meet the norm and act appropriately and those who do not and behave inappropriately. The categories of "the others" are those who need to be confined, helped, corrected, or remediated.

Schools, too, fit the patterns of other institutions. In their institutionalized settings, age-specific cohorts of children and adolescents are assigned to historically determined grade levels. Then, they are often sorted into groups according their readiness and ability levels based on assessments determined by school authorities who use tests developed by educational experts. Teachers determine acceptable and unacceptable behavior, who should be promoted or retained, and who should be rewarded or remediated.

Rather than analyzing institutions from the perspectives of the experts who control them, Foucault analyzes them from the viewpoint of those who are subjected to the experts' norms—prisoners, patients, plaintiffs, and students. Schools should be analyzed from the perspectives of students—children and adolescents.

Foucault's Postmodernist analysis provides an alternative to the officially privileged way of looking at institutions that is typically found in schools of business, law, social work, and education. For him, expert knowledge and professional standards setting, associated with modern institutions, represent the establishment's exercise of power to categorize, manipulate, and control others, especially those in marginalized groups. The texts, standards, and certificates of the power holders represent the discourse, "regime of truth," used to justify the status quo. Foucault examines how claims of a group, such as modern experts, that they have the objective or scientifically verified "truth" are used to legitimate what is really a power relationship. When a particular group asserts that it knows the truth, they are asserting a claim to knowledge that privileges them over others who do not know it. At certain historic periods and in certain places, Foucault asserts that the truth–power formula favors, or empowers, some groups over others. For example, in Plato's dialogues, the true intellectuals are privileged over the society's practitioners; in the Middle Ages, the scholastics are favored over the tradesmen and serfs.

Episteme: according to Foucault, the dominant intellectual assumptions that govern a culture during a particular historical period.

As a historian of ideas, Foucault seeks to identify the **episteme**, the regnant intellectual assumptions that govern the official outlook of a society in a particular historical period. In doing so, he is making the case, as did the Existentialists, that knowledge claims are not universal but are situated in time and place. These ruling assumptions condition how people view their society, its social and economic conditions, its institutions and power relationships. They set the guidelines on how discourse, debate, and discussion are to take place. Most importantly, they determine what questions can or cannot be asked. For example, in the medieval period, church-approved doctrines set the framework for discourse. In the Soviet Union under Communism, Marxist-Leninism set parameters for discussion. To be discussed, a topic had to fit the parameters set by the episteme. These truth–power relationships produce "regimes of truth," the ideologies, institutions, and practices by which one group controls, regulates, governs, and even defines another. The truth–power regime implies that those who hold and use power have a right to do so because they know or possess truth, unknown to others. Texts, especially those sanctioned as containing official knowledge, rationalize and justify the relationships that empower or disempower certain individuals and groups.[11] By deconstructing the texts, the power relationships can be stripped to their essentials—of who is exerting power and why they are doing so. Foucault advises us that power relationships are present despite the power holders' claim to be fair, objective, or unbiased.

Like other Postmodernist philosophers, Foucault challenges those who claim to know universal truth to be altruistic in its application and to justify their actions on universal principles. Instead of one truth that is universally manifested, he argues that there are many claims to truth, found in all societies, and in all situations. As there are multiple perspectives, there need to be multiple discourses with open questions. Discourses can justify one group's claim to truth but also can be used by another group to resist it.[12] The relationships between groups regarding regimes of truth are constantly shifting, with one group's claim ascendant and the other's suppressed or inarticulate. The interplay of discourses, each representing a truth claim by some groups, can be examined. Members of marginalized groups can use analysis to deconstruct the official knowledge that justifies the power of dominant groups and liberate themselves.

POSTMODERNIST THEMES

This section identifies some general themes that run though Postmodernism, especially those that have a bearing on education.

Deconstructing Universal Principles

Postmodernist philosophers emphasize the need to redirect our thinking away from the patterns of traditional philosophies such as Idealism and Realism that have long influenced Western conceptions of knowledge. They especially attack the belief in universal metaphysical principles that transcend particular cultures and times. They want to depose the philosophies of education that claim to be based on eternal truths that are neither limited by nor dependent on time, and universal truths that are not bound by place or culture. Such claims to foundation on universal and eternal truths and values actually create philosophical fogs, "cover-ups" of social conflict that justify the power of one group or class over another subordinated group at a particular time in history.

For Postmodernists, such revered philosophical texts as Plato's *Republic,* Aristotle's *Nicomachean Ethics,* and Aquinas's *Summa Theologiae* are **meta-narratives** constructed by a ruling group at a particular time in history rather than universal, totalizing, metaphysical explanations of reality, truth, and values. Plato's Idealism, for example, provided a conservative rationale against the rival Sophists who represented a more democratic, but materialist, culturally relative orientation in Athens. Postmodernists argue against proponents of the belief that there should be a required cultural core based on the great and enduring texts in Western civilization. They would also question the imposition of the Common Core Curriculum on students and teachers.

Meta-narratives: the universalizing and legitimizing grand texts of theology, philosophy, science, politics, economics, and education that constitute "official" knowledge.

Postmodernists challenge the grand philosophical systems purported to explain reality as an architecture of the universe and the metaphysical assumption that an ultimate ground of being, a transcendent cosmic reality, exists beyond and above the physical world. Postmodernists challenge the **binary** or dualist view of the traditional philosophies that there is a sphere of reality, the sphere of truth, which is higher, purer, and better than the one that we know through our everyday experiences.

Binary: a set of two concepts or terms in which one is privileged over the other because it is closer to the universal principles at the center of reality.

In traditional philosophies, our everyday experiences constitute an inferior empirical world of experience that we need, as Plato said, to transcend to get to the

For Dewey's attack on dualism, see the chapter on Pragmatism and Education.

"real" metaphysical truth. John Dewey and the Pragmatists launched a similar attack on dualisms that elevated theory over practice and the liberal arts over vocational education.

Postmodernists add another dimension to the attack on dualism. They see the traditional rationales for a binary or dualistic world as privileging the theoretical over the practical; those who claim expertise in knowing the eternal and the universal have an exalted claim to power over those who do not have this expertise.

For the Realist premise of an objective reality, see the chapter on Realism and Education.

Postmodernists make a strong attack against the Realist assertion that an objective reality exists and is knowable and our knowledge of it should guide human conduct. They argue that traditional philosophies such as Realism that rest on metaphysical foundations are not explanations of ultimate reality. Rather, they are the discourses—the written texts—produced by the intellectuals of a given period of history that rationalized and explained the knowledge that gave power to some but denied it to others.[13]

Postmodernists attack binary, or dualist positions in which traditional philosophers, like Plato and Aquinas, enjoin us to think deeply, to search for, to speculate, and to penetrate the surface of culture to find the ultimate, logocentric, metaphysical nature of reality. Such binary thinking privileges the "ultimate" over the natural and the human. In opposition, Postmodernists say there is no ultimate nature or center of reality to find. Their reaction discounts those (e.g., Plato, Aristotle, Aquinas, and Emerson) who looked for a deeper metaphysical understanding that penetrates the surface to reach the true nature and meaning of underlying reality. These traditional philosophers misled people by proclaiming grand universal metaphysical designs, labeled by Postmodernists as meta-narratives, which argue that there are universal and timeless principles that are superior to personal, group, and cultural norms.[14] We do not need to try to find some deeper hidden reality that lies beneath the surface of our experiences, such as Plato's "Form of the Good" or Emerson's Oversoul, because we can trust ourselves in our personal and communal relationships.

For Plato's "Form of the Good" and Emerson's Oversoul," see the chapter on Idealism and Education.

For the Pragmatists, see the chapter on Pragmatism and Education.

Postmodernism is not the first philosophy to reject metaphysics. Earlier in the twentieth century, the Pragmatists—William James, Charles Peirce, George H. Mead, and John Dewey—had abandoned metaphysics as empirically unverifiable "nonsense." Dethroning metaphysics, the Pragmatists put their trust in the scientific method, to either verify or disprove the claims to "truth," now reduced to a probability or a warranted assumption rather than a universal. The scientific method, derived from Enlightenment thinking, was proclaimed to be a public, dispassionate, and objective process of solving problems. Postmodernists, unlike the Pragmatists, reject the claims that the scientific method is really objective. It is "scientific" and "objective" only for those who share the commitment to use its terminology. Scientific knowledge is merely what is acceptable to a particular group, the circle that shares a commitment to it.[15]

Postmodernists look with disdain at philosophers who try to seek the universalizing authority of grand metaphysical narratives, single processes of empirical verification, or the development of an all-embracing social consensus. They are highly skeptical of meta-narratives, the universalizing and legitimizing bodies of theology, philosophy, and scientific theory.

Postmodernist contend that the issue of meta-narratives is highly important in education. They ask: Who is proclaiming that something is official knowledge or a standard in the curriculum and why are they doing so? For example, the Declaration of Independence, the U.S. Constitution, and James Madison's *Federalist Papers* are regarded as canonical texts about the political origins of the United States. There are heated controversies about the "intent" of the founding fathers, especially about the role and relationship of religion to government. These controversies have been felt in the selection of history texts and in discussions of how history should be taught in schools.

Meta-narratives concern what constitutes the cultural core in the curriculum, especially in multicultural and social justice education. The concern is that you or members of a particular group do not fit in or have a place in the meta-narrative and are marginalized by it. Also, think about the power of those who proclaim a meta-narrative, such as the Common Core Curriculum, as official, legitimate knowledge and have the means to disseminate it.

Instead of grand, universalizing meta-narratives, Postmodernists look to the specific discourses or local narratives constructed by individuals in their immediate relationships in their groups and communities—the different expressions found in the varieties of human experiences. Each of these different expressions exists freely without a need to constrain experience by conformity to some contrived universal principles.

The Postmodernist call to celebrate the different expressions of human experiences in ourselves and local communities (racial, ethnic, and gender groups) has important implications for education. It relies on an Existentialist orientation to live and let live and not to fear those who are different from us as threats, but to learn about and respect them. The Postmodernist antagonism to universalize—be it in the guise of metaphysics, empiricism, or consensus—contributes to multicultural education that celebrates and respects the differences among ethnic, racial, and gender experiences. Rather than being deduced from some grand metaphysical system or exclusive reliance on a single method of inquiry such as the scientific method, the curriculum should be constructed from the "lived experiences," the autobiographies of persons and groups. The school, in the Postmodernist scenario, is the gathering site for members of the local community to voice their experiences and share their life stories. The school should be locally managed by its teachers, administrators, students, and community members.

Critique of the Enlightenment

Postmodernists are highly concerned with deconstructing, actually deflating, the claims of scientific objectivity that stem from the Enlightenment. You may well ask: Why give such attention to critiquing a long gone historical period such as the Enlightenment? In education, especially in the ideology of American public schooling, the Enlightenment has had a pervasive impact. The Enlightenment philosophers believed that it was possible for people to improve their lives—their society, politics, economy, and education—if they applied the scientific method to solve problems. It was possible for human society to be progressive and look to a better future. Education needed to be scientifically based, forward looking, and progressive and not tied down to the past's obsolete classical and religious dogmas. Pragmatism, the philosophy, and Progressivism, the ideology, which were so important in shaping modern American education, were permeated by the belief in progress and the scientific method.

For Progressivism, see the chapter on Progressivism and Education. Ideology is discussed in the chapter on Ideology and Education.

Although the liberal Enlightenment ideology proclaimed "liberty, equality, and fraternity," Postmodernists allege that it was subverted to become the political and economic justification for a new capitalist ruling class, the bourgeoisie or middle class, which had overturned the privileged political position and ascribed social status of landed aristocrats. Science combined with technology generated the nineteenth-century Industrial Revolution, which continued through the twentieth century and now drives globalization. Science, touted as an objective mode of inquiry, was applied to technology, which generated a spiraling cycle of new techniques to exploit natural resources and produce goods for a mass market of consumers. Linked together, the

Enlightenment ideology, scientific rationales, and technological discoveries gave the capitalist class the economic power to control society and politics and to dominate other classes and groups either through the domestic structures in their home countries or through imperialism and colonialism in other countries, especially those in Latin America, Africa, and Asia. The capitalists, now the ruling class, constructed canons, the various texts that through philosophy, ideology, politics, literature, and education served as rationales for their taking of power and subordinating other groups such as the working class in their own countries or indigenous people, usually of color, in their colonies overseas. Postmodernists are especially interested in critically examining, or in deconstructing, the canons, which pass for philosophical or ideological rationales, that justify, often in universal terms, the control of one class over another. Now that we have moved from the modern industrial to the global postmodern information age, they are concerned with who writes, produces, disseminates, and controls a text—how information is selected and transmitted by the media and by the school in a curriculum.

De-Enlightening the Enlightenment

In the Postmodernist critique, the Enlightenment theorists wrote the texts that represented modern philosophy and ideology. Enlightenment philosophers argued that humans using reason, enlightened by science, can discover the natural laws on which the universe, the world, and society operate. Enlightenment philosophers claimed that the scientific method, relying on empirical discovery and verification, is the most accurate instrument to discover the laws and the principles that govern humankind's physical and social worlds. The application of these principles to society, politics, economics, and education will bring about continuing progress. Note that the Enlightenment prospect that individuals and groups could reform and construct a better society in the future sharply contrasts with the premodern, classical, and medieval view that the historically transmitted traditional social order was a permanent reality.

Although many Enlightenment theorists rejected traditional philosophical metaphysics, they constructed a new meta-narrative proclaiming that reasonable people, by using science, can discover the principles that govern the universe and by doing so can bring about progress. Postmodernists see the Enlightenment philosophers' turn to reason as a mechanism of social and political control. By asserting that certain knowledge claims are reasonable and scientific, the Enlightenment theorists also ruled that other claims are unreasonable and unscientific. Those who do not follow the rules of reason and science are non-rational and can be either ignored, marginalized, or purged. Certainly, prescientific thinkers should not hold power. Postmodernists assert that the scientific method is but one of many methods of constructing one of many "truths." Further, they argue that the prescriptions for human behavior are established by groups, not nature, and are contested between dominant and subordinate groups. The groups or classes in control of society at a given time, as during the Enlightenment, try to set standards and values that they claim are universal but, in reality, are a specific means of social, political, and educational control.

Postmodernism, like Pragmatism, rejects universal, absolute, and eternal truths and values. For Postmodernists, the claim of any statement to be true or valuable depends on the culture, time, situations, and conditions in which it is made. The claim to be representing what is true or valuable is necessarily communicated by language—words used in speech, writing, or texting—in the form of a text. The language that conveys the claim can be deconstructed or "unpacked" to reveal the time and setting in which it was stated and its author's socio-economic and political status and motivations. Thus, much Postmodernist deconstruction looks for clues that explain motivation such as the author's sex, race, class, or ethnicity. For example, is the statement being made by a male or female, a person of color or a white, a member of the upper or lower socio-economic class? Whereas a universalist such as an Idealist, Realist, or Thomist says that the truth is what it is regardless of who states it, the Postmodernist argues that what is claimed to be the truth depends on who is making the statement. In education, the "official knowledge" conveyed through the school's mandated and approved curriculum represents the opinion of those in control of educational institutions rather than those outside the corridors of power.

The Postmodernist holds that no universal knowledge exists but rather that there is a variety of claims to knowledge, which arise in different cultural and social contexts. Although certain cultures may claim to be superior to others, the argument for preferential treatment is a fiction. In the variety of cultures, no one is better or preferred. Even within a particular society or country such as the United States, various groups are contesting for control of the social, political, and educational systems. Those who base the curriculum on one culture, such as Western culture, in reality are using schools to dominate other cultures. Postmodernists argue that the variety of different cultures in American society should be recognized in a celebration of multicultural differences, with respect for local and long-suppressed views and voices.[16]

Canons and the Canonical

For Postmodernists, canons, privileged texts, are regarded as definitive authorities in a particular area of knowledge. A discussion of the genealogy of a canon's meaning illustrates how it has been used as a rationale for authority and power. The claims to authority, expressed in a canon, have an interesting origin that explains how canons are used to rationalize power relationships. In ancient Greece, a canon (*kanon*) was a rod used to measure something, especially property. Measurements based on the *kanon* were regarded as legally accurate in establishing property boundaries. By the fourth century, the term *canon* had taken on a broader meaning as an authoritative rule or a law that was to guide and govern correct interpretations and practices. During the Middle Ages, the term *canonical* was used to designate an authentic religious text, officially sanctioned by the church. For example, the governing legal code of the Roman Catholic Church is referred to as *canon law*. Over time, a more general use of *canon* developed to refer to the great texts that have official acceptance and carry authority in a culture, political order, or in a learned discipline. It means that whatever is done in a particular field needs to be measured against the canonical or regnant definitions and standards in a field.

A canon gives something authority. In education, it claims that a particular interpretation in an academic discipline or subject matter is correct; if that interpretation is correct, then alternative versions are likely to be incorrect. Note that a great deal of teaching in traditional schools is devoted to correcting what is incorrect in students' work. This correcting is done so that students' work corresponds to the canon—to the correct interpretation. In other words, a canon sets a standard.

Going back to the word's origins, a canon marked something off and established a parameter or a boundary. It indicated what belonged within a boundary and what did not. First used to mark property boundaries, the concept of a canon was extended to set the definitions and boundaries of bodies of knowledge. In the traditional curriculum, these boundaries set off one subject from another and identify who is an expert in that subject and what texts are the canons, the bases of official knowledge. Postmodernists attack the concept that disciplines and subjects are demarcated by boundaries and that to do their work properly, teachers and students have to stay within boundaries. In contrast, Postmodernists urge teachers and students to freely cross these arbitrary boundaries erected by academic elites.

If we think of the curriculum as a contested area, as the Postmodernists do, we can see how the construction and deconstruction of canons operate. There have been many arguments about the need for a cultural core in education. Some advocates of a core curriculum refer to the core as containing those ideas or subjects that are indispensable to an educated person. Some proponents of a cultural core in the curriculum base their argument on what they identify as the major ideas that have shaped Western civilization. Still others call for a core that represents what they call "traditional American values"—family, home, and country. Postmodernists reject the proposals for a cultural core in the curriculum as a device not only to set boundaries between subjects but also between people. They see them as representing male-dominated, **Eurocentric** Western culture, which takes on an added capitalist dimension in the United States. They contend that these canons have no intrinsic authority or value over alternatives. It is time, they argue, that the works of underrepresented groups—African, Asian, Hispanic, and Native Americans; feminists; those in the so-called third world; and gays and lesbians—be included in the curriculum.

Eurocentric: official knowledge, constructed by white people of European ancestry, that emphasizes their cultural, political, and economic achievements.

The Council of Chief State School Officers (CCSSO) and the National Governors Association Center for Best Practices launched an initiative for a common core curriculum in 2010 that is gaining momentum across the United States. It identified as core subjects English language arts, history and social studies, mathematics, science, and selected technical subjects, and it specifies standards for the teaching and assessment of these subjects. Postmodernists would apply the same method of deconstruction to this new core as they do to all core assumptions. They would ask: Who are the authors of this text? Whom do they represent? What are their motives? Does this core, this text, empower some and disempower others? Does this core respect local communities and school sites? Since the Postmodernists see canons as historical constructions by a given group or class in a particular place and time, they can be analyzed, or deconstructed. Postmodernists want to know the criteria being used to establish some but not other works as canons. They argue that the criteria for analyzing and appraising a canon are internal to the work. There are no legitimate external—spiritual, natural, or universal—criteria for giving a canon a privileged authoritative status in a culture and society. In deconstructing a canon, or text, Postmodernists ask: What events and situations gave rise to the canon? Who gives a canon a privileged status in a culture or society? Who benefits from the existence and acceptance of a canon? Why do lists of canons in a particular culture exclude those who are underrepresented and marginalized in a given society?

Discovering or Constructing Knowledge—Epistemological Questions

Important for epistemology and methods of teaching and learning is the question: Do we discover or do we construct our knowledge? For example, Realism, especially Scientific Realism, asserts that what we know is objective, or outside of us. Realists say that our knowledge is based on what we discover through our observations and that, as the Enlightenment philosophers claimed, by using science we can discover the structures, functions, and patterns of how nature works. For example, we can discover how the blood circulates through the body and the patterns of bird migration during the year. The popular film *March of the Penguins*, for example, which documents the nesting, birth, and nurture of generations of emperor penguins, was a way to discover this bird's patterns of behavior. In teaching and learning, the "discovery method" is based on the assumption that there is something outside of us, outside of our minds that we can know if we use the correct methods.

For knowing as discovering and for Scientific Realism, see the chapter on Realism and Education.

Postmodernism argues against traditional philosophies' metaphysical claims that we can know objects as they correspond to reality. Rather than looking outside of human experience and history for truth, we need to look within the human past and present to see how claims to truth have been constructed and expressed. What people claim to be true is meaningful only when it is expressed in conceptual and symbolic form through language. Concepts do not correspond to objects existing in some supernatural or metaphysical realm, as the Realists claim; rather, they are human constructions based on experience. Knowledge claims are constructions used to explain and control human life and institutions. Claims to knowledge, the constructions that explain and control, are expressed symbolically using sounds, signs, gestures, words, and language.[17] These language-expressed and language-bound claims of truth can be approached, dissected, decoded, or deconstructed by "unpacking" what is asserted to be true. Working through language reveals that what purports to be knowledge is a human-made construction. The language that a group uses to express its knowledge beliefs is a construction, a text that involves how the language is to be expressed and used. Language expression and use have been used historically to define knowledge and give control to those who purport to understand and interpret it. Historically, certain texts or meta-narratives—religious and philosophical works, great books, the classics—have been given a prominent privileged status as speaking of universal truths to a universal audience that is trans-generational. Challenging these universalizing claims, Postmodernists contend that they, too, are the constructions of once-powerful historical elites that are still used to empower new elites by investing them with the old order's signs and symbols of authority. Instead of one way, there are many ways to describe human experience, each of which has its own validity.

Closely related to the attack on meta-narratives is how the Postmodernists conceive of language. The meta-narratives in the Western cultural tradition, especially in philosophy, history, and literature, assert that the relationship between the great texts and the world reflects the structure of reality, civilization, and art. Postmodernists reject the assumption that words that describe this reality are valid definitions that mirror and accurately explain an objective reality. Instead, Postmodernists argue that the traditional language used to express beliefs about the universe, the world, society, politics, economics, and education are not accurate statements that correspond to reality but are social constructions arising from how a group decides to use them. Words are meaningful only in terms of the cultural systems of which they are a part.[18]

Deconstructing or decoding the text is a relentless effort to discern meaning and relationships. Deconstruction assumes that all claims to truth are relative and dependent on the intellectual and cultural outlook of the individuals or groups making the claim. Because claims that something is true are conveyed by language, Postmodernists are highly engaged with analyzing language. They reject the assumption that the meanings of words (their definitions) are fixed, final, and definitive. All statements require further statements and definitions. Language is variable, contextual, and shaped by its users. Indeed, every knowledge claim or statement can be deconstructed by looking at who is making the claim, what the context is for its use, and how it is being used. What did the text mean at the time of its origination or construction? What groups established and used the meaning of the text at its origination? What has the text come to mean over the course of history? What does the text mean at the present time for different groups? Turning to formal education, these questions focus on how curriculum is constructed. What texts represent official knowledge in the curriculum? How are these texts interpreted to establish and maintain the power relationships among different groups? What texts, meaning what experiences, are included or excluded? Postmodernists see the curriculum as a locus of struggle, a cultural war, between contending groups to establish knowledge claims and to assert power.

In contrast, "to discover," "to construct," as in constructionist psychology and instruction, means that we construct, make, or build what we know through our own explorations of our environment. As a construction, our knowledge is personal, subjective, and temporary, in that we keep revising it as we have more experiences. Unlike the discovery of knowledge, the construction of "knowledges" (note the plural use of the term) means that there is no one true knowledge, but rather a variety of knowledges, each of which is meaningful to the person or group that constructs them.

Philosophy of History

For Postmodernists, history is constructed by individuals and groups who write it in terms of their experience. It is not the unfolding of the Absolute over time as Idealists contend, nor can it ever be an objective account of what has happened. Although revisionist histories may detect and attempt to revise earlier historical accounts, they, too, are subject to the same errors that plague all efforts to construct a "truthful" and "more accurate" account. This occurs because history, for Postmodernists, is a set of competing stories, laden with myths and metaphors, that is more like literature, especially novels with fictional plots created by historians, than empirically grounded or documented accounts of the past. The sources on which history is based, primary sources and documents, are texts that can be deconstructed and have multiple meanings and interpretations. The past is simply what historians say it is and what they say can be disputed, reinterpreted, accepted, or rejected.

Dominant groups use history to validate their past actions and to apply that interpretation of the past to legitimate their present practices and future projects. Dominant groups tend to impose their view of the past on others, especially marginalized groups. History, written by historians of the dominant group and made part of "official knowledge," can be used to maintain and extend the privileged position to exert control over marginalized people who are put in the historical situation of being a member of the "other" group. Historical accounts can be binary in that they set up a dichotomy between us and them—between members of lesser, more primitive, less developed (i.e., "less civilized") peoples and people in technologically developed societies. Concepts such as the "other," the "primitive," the "less technologically developed," and the "non-Western" reveal a stereotypic view of society in which the alternatives to these terms are regarded as higher and better, and those included in these categories as subordinate and placed at the margins of institutions and society.[19]

Still another example of the use of history to construct a false consciousness comes from the "official" history of American public education. For example, the educational establishment's history of public education in the United States celebrates it as open to the children of all the people and as creating socio-economic mobility and opportunity for all groups. In reality, Postmodernists would contend that public education's hidden history is as much as or even more about maintaining the socio-economic status quo and of upper- and middle-class domination of lower socio-economic classes. As Foucault argued, history examines the use of power in specific contexts. We study history by constructing a "genealogy" of the use of power and control. A genealogy provides meanings from within specific historical events, from the perspective of **eventualization**. Discounting the principle of uniformity of events, eventualization examines breaks in the historical flow—those distinct and separate occurrences that are significant in how we define ourselves and organize our relationships. Events have multiple causation. Rather than looking for universal causal factors or forces to explain history, the challenge is to look for multiple influences within historical events or periods. Power is found in the manner in which people conduct and govern themselves and how they perceive and define themselves and the society in which they live. Situations such as power regimes that pass themselves off as necessary and historically determined are not the result of inevitable destiny, but rather of human invention within specific historical contexts.

Eventualization: the distinct, separate, and multiple historical events that define us and organize our relationships.

Postmodernists see a relationship between historical knowledge and power—whoever controls the interpretation of the past sets the standard for the present. They see traditional historical narratives—with a beginning, middle, and end—as constructions expressed by language that conforms to its own rules. For Postmodernists, the past has no beginning, middle, or end; it has no meaning except that imposed by historians. Historiography is an attempt to impose meaning on a meaningless past. Postmodernism questions historians' claims to be able to stand as unbiased observers outside of the flow of history. All historical accounts and interpretations are positioned and politicized. With its method of deconstruction, Postmodernism calls attention to sources, particularly to the questions of the conditions of their production and how they are used. Historians construct interpretations. but never the past.[20]

For Postmodernists, genuine history, especially historical narratives or stories, comprises personal, local, and group accounts of past-lived experience. There is no standard that exists "out there" such as reliance on historical method. The most genuine judgment that can be made is the meaning that the local story has for those who tell it. This assertion presents a different way of reading, writing, teaching, and learning history than has been done traditionally.

As a local story, history begins at the grassroots, in the lives of students, in their families, and in their racial, ethnic, and language groups. What purports to be a national history, such as the history of the United States or France, is often a glossed-over presentation of selected events, designed to create an "official" and "privileged" account of the past that either ignores or marginalizes local stories.

Philosophy of Science

Postmodernists are more concerned with culture, literature, philosophy, and history than science. Unlike the Pragmatists who share their relativism, Postmodernists are suspicious of the motives of those who emphasize the scientific method and empirical verification as objective and unbiased ways to construct warranted claims to truth. Dewey's insistence that the scientific method is the most reliable test of "truths" (i.e., warranted assumptions) for them is another effort to create a methodological metanarrative. Given their opposition to claims that truth is objective and "out there," Postmodernists are skeptical of scientists (e.g., Scientific Realists) who claim to construct theories describing reality. In particular, they attack the claims of Scientific Realists that (1) they can objectively describe the physical phenomena that surround us and (2) scientific investigation is an unbiased, objective, and universal explanation of reality.[21] Postmodernists see scientific inquiry not as completely objective but as rooted in the cultural and ideological locations and orientations of the scientist. For them, there are as many candidates for truth as there are individuals and groups who make truth claims. They are alert to how scientists are funded by powerful corporate elites who use the findings of science and technology to advance agendas of economic profit and international globalization. Scientists, especially those committed to empirical experimentation and public verification, contend that the validity of scientific claims needs to be free of politics and ideology. The question of what is science has important implications for science education. Should science be taught as a quest for empirically verified and testable assertions about reality, or should it be seen as highly influenced by politics, ideology, and economics?

Scientific Realism is discussed in the chapter on Realism and Education.

Philosophy of Technology

The Postmodern era is called the time of the information society and of the technological revolution. Throughout society, politics, and education, technology has brought about a revolution in how information is defined, accessed, stored, retrieved, and disseminated. State and professional education mandates require that teachers and students be computer literate and that schools be linked electronically to the Internet and the World Wide Web. Postmodernists do not distrust technology and electronic information retrieval as a process, but they are suspicious of those who simplistically regard technology as an instrument of liberated communications. While it provides a means, such as social media, for like-minded people to share information about oppressive conditions and to organize to liberate exploited people, technology, as an instrument, can be used to either empower or dominate. It is important to understand that what is conveyed electronically is a text that needs to be deconstructed. Much of what purports to be information is, in reality, a formula for manipulative image making by those in power to create a mass consumer-oriented society.[22]

Information conveyed by the media in terms of the "news," "factoids," interviews, and "infomercials," including visual images on the television or computer screen, is typically screened, selected, interpreted, and manipulated. Key questions are: Who decides that something is newsworthy? How much time should be allotted for its presentation? and When should it be transmitted? The events that we see on our television or computer screens or read about in print, though presented as unfolding on the scene as actual events, are often semifictionalized narratives, selected and edited for political or commercial purposes.[23] They are distorted by corporate business sponsors. Further, in the capitalist system, media control is concentrated in a few wealthy and powerful persons. The result is manipulated news, based on selected visual images, reaching a manipulated audience of consumers steeped in false consciousness. The mass audience, so conditioned by the mass media, seeks not to work at a more accurate portrayal of information but rather to buy television sets with larger screens with multiple images or software that makes it possible to download programs more rapidly.

Postmodernists are alert to dangers that a mass technology presents when it is controlled by dominant groups; they also see that this technology, if critically used, can be an instrument of liberation. The World Wide Web and the Internet provide a means for persons to join in critical dialogues about their own uncensored analysis of issues and conditions in their communities. The "blogosphere," if used critically, can communicate a wide variety of opinions and transmit these opinions to other bloggers in almost any part of the world. The Internet, at this time, is an open forum for the free expression of ideas about any subject.

The educational issues created by a technologically manipulated mass society are myriad. It is difficult for teachers to resist being caught up in the manipulative web of a managed technology. The same issues that relate to the impact of technology in the larger society also affect its entry and use in schools. Students typically spend a large amount of time, outside of school, viewing television or computer programs or texting each other. These out-of-school experiences are subject to the entry of the false consciousness that is often found in the production and dissemination of mass electronically generated information and entertainment programming. The programs are vividly and dramatically presented to them. Critical examinations of issues in schools pale in comparison!

POSTMODERNISM AND EDUCATION

In this section, we move from Postmodernism's more general philosophical themes to those that relate more specifically to education and schooling. As indicated in earlier sections, Postmodernism emphasizes education as a critique of existing social institutions and conditions so that people can free themselves from domination.

False Consciousness Versus Lived or Authentic Consciousness

The Postmodernist critique of education involves the deconstruction of the texts of official knowledge or approved subjects that transmit and rationalize the status quo. Official knowledge is mandated by educational authorities, which for public elementary and secondary schools are state legislatures and authorities, local boards of education, school administrators such as superintendents and principals, and curriculum committees. For higher education, the authorities are boards of trustees, university presidents, vice presidents, deans, and often committees of tenured faculty who approve degree requirements. The texts, conveying official knowledge, find their way into schools and colleges from state mandates and through textbook publishers. Teachers are accountable for successfully transmitting the official knowledge to students. Successful transmission is registered on standardized achievement tests. When teachers succeed in transmitting the official knowledge, they are designated as competent by their supervisors in the educational bureaucracy; when they fail, they are judged incompetent and require remediation to improve their performance. Educational technology, such as computerized learning programs, is designed to enliven the transmission of official knowledge to students by making it current, rapid, dynamic, and colorful. Regardless of the method used, the aim is the same—to transmit official knowledge.

Official Knowledge as False Consciousness

The transmission of official knowledge in schools provides the rationale that justifies the position of the dominant class or group; it states the reasons why this class's position is historically, economically, socially, politically, and often religiously valid and justified. Official knowledge in the curriculum is "privileged" in that it is accorded a high status in the curriculum as better—more accurate, more scientific, more objective—than other academic subjects or educational experiences. Further, privileged or official knowledge is hierarchically ranked in priority—given more funding, more instructional time, and greater value than other subjects or experiences. Recall that Idealists and Realists argue that the subjects in the curriculum should be arranged hierarchically in terms of their generality, their abstract nature.

See the chapters on Idealism and Education and Realism and Education.

Regardless of students' interests or a group's needs, privileged knowledge has official preference and sanction. The subjects that convey official knowledge are typically history, literature, political science, economics, sociology, and psychology. From these subjects, elementary and secondary curriculum areas such as language arts, social studies, consumer education, and history are derived. Although they are part of the official curriculum, mathematics and the natural and physical sciences are less likely to carry the official ideology. However, the illustrations, cases, and examples used in mathematics and the sciences may do so.

The transmission of official knowledge has the effect of creating a sense of false consciousness in the minds of students who are members of dominated groups. All countries and societies have dominant and dominated, or subordinate, groups: Those dominated in American schools tend to be women; African, Asian, Native, and Hispanic Americans; and the economically impoverished. According to the Postmodernist critique, the transmission of official knowledge creates false consciousness by: (1) reiterating universals and absolutes that distract from genuine lived reality; (2) maintaining and transmitting social and cultural consensus shaped by the dominant group; (3) maintaining the traditional curriculum; and (4) relying on "scientific" testing and standards to reinforce the academic mastering of mandated subjects.

Reiterating Universals and Absolutes

For the great ideas and great books approach, look ahead to the chapter on Perennialism and Education.

For Postmodernists, the curriculum is a contested area that various groups seek to control. However, the dominant groups—typically white male, Euro-American, and upper and upper-middle classes—have controlled it historically. The contemporary arena of curriculum making has seen a struggle, a "cultural war" over what constitutes its required official core. The battle lines have been drawn between those who want to perpetuate a Western cultural tradition and those who want a variety of multicultural experiences represented. Postmodernists take issue with the Western civilization canon that argues that education's major objective is to transmit to the young the cultural heritage of great ideas, derived from the cultures of ancient Greece and Rome and Western Europe. Schools and colleges that mandate, or privilege, a curricular core derived from the canons of traditional Western philosophy, theology, literature, and history that claims their universal validity and applicability are engrafting "false consciousness" on the minds of their students.

The aim in asserting the supremacy of Western civilization is to form the intellectual matrix of the young and to root it in what are claimed to be universal truths and values. Some educators who argue for these universal canons are sincerely committed to them; they, nonetheless, are fostering a false consciousness on the young. Others, realizing these universal canons are obsolete and archaic, continue to indoctrinate the young in them to maintain their institutional positions of power and control.

Postmodernists argue for a multicultural perspective that cuts across, broadens, and integrates the humanities and social sciences to focus on what they call the voices of dominated peoples. They want schools to tell the stories of the experiences of women, working people, and underrepresented ethnic and racial groups. They want a world narrative in history and literature that includes the peoples of Africa, Asia, the Middle East, and Latin America along with Europe and North America. Rather than portraying a Western model, the curriculum is to reflect a variety of human experiences. With the canons of Western superiority deconstructed, every culture is represented as having its own coherence, integrity, and logic. There is an equality of experience rather than the hierarchically designed stratification of experience that privileges Western above African or Asian, or male above female.

Maintaining and Transmitting Social and Cultural Consensus

A pervasive element in American public education, especially in public schools, is that it reflects a national consensus and, in turn, promotes, or maintains, a general social consensus that is needed to unify a multicultural nation. Common-school leaders in the nineteenth century such as Horace Mann, Catharine Beecher, and Henry Barnard argued that public schools would be the welders of a great American feeling of national identity. They would be the shapers of an all-embracing social consensus—an overarching agreement on the role of government, society, and the economy and on what constitutes appropriate behavior. The theory of consensus operates in two ways in the public school philosophy/ideology. First, the presence of a consensus is regarded as necessary for the establishment, continuance, and support of public schools as well as other institutions of government, industry, and society. People need to agree that public schools are necessary for the common good, especially to educate people who will be committed to American political, social, and economic institutions and processes. Second, public schools, once established, act as agencies that contribute to maintaining a national consensus—a shared agreement—on what to believe and how to act as Americans. The Postmodernist critique of consensus in public education is that it masks serious contradictions and conflicts in American society between dominant and subordinate classes and groups. Although many public school administrators and teachers know that the boasted consensus is false, they continue to give public allegiance, or lip service, to it, while harboring private doubts. The idea of a national consensus patches over and suppresses differences of class, gender, race, and ethnicity.

Maintaining the Traditional Curriculum

Still another instance of transmitting an "enlightened false consciousness" comes from those—often politicians, parents, organizations, and teachers—who seek to keep, maintain, and transmit the traditional curriculum. Those who oppose curriculum and instructional innovation often point to education in the "good old days" when parents knew what the schools were teaching, when teachers controlled their classrooms, and when students obeyed, studied, and learned. Some define the traditional curriculum as the basics—reading, writing, arithmetic, history, geography, language (especially and often exclusively English), wholesome and uplifting literature, and science. The school milieu is charged with traditional values that reflect the family, patriotism, and the free enterprise economy.

In addition to the "good old days" approach, there is also another way of maintaining the traditional curriculum that is vested in the educational establishment—especially administrators and many teachers. The traditional curriculum is built around reiterating consensus values about American history and society throughout the system. The traditional curriculum presents "official knowledge" according to the school's curriculum guide, state mandates or standards, and required core skills and subjects. The transmission of the official curriculum constitutes passing on and engulfing students in a false consciousness that minimizes their lived experiences or the experiences of their group. It becomes an "enlightened false consciousness" when teachers who understand that the established curriculum represents official knowledge that is often irrelevant for students continue to require it as a rite of passage through the school system. They do so for a variety of reasons: because they are committed to it by their own unexamined false consciousness, to protect their positions and fields, because they are uncomfortable with change, or because they no longer care.

Relying on Standardized Tests

Still another instance of creating false consciousness comes from transmitting and requiring students to learn the "information," "subjects," or "knowledge" that purports to be the truth and then testing them to determine whether they have "mastered" the officially approved doctrines. With the standards movement and No Child Left Behind, standardized tests touted to be "fair," "objective," and "scientific" are administered to students. The test results are then used to indicate the degree of students' academic achievement and their teachers' competency in effectively transmitting official knowledge. The outcome is that false consciousness is legitimized as scientifically validated knowledge. While the answers to the questions on the tests may be true in terms of what is being examined, the result is that a particular kind of information is privileged as official knowledge. Supporters of this type of standardized testing, including educators, do so because they may be perpetuating an embedded false consciousness that, once learned, is difficult to unlearn. Although some educators may realize that the "official knowledge" is skewed, archaic, or inauthentic, they nonetheless publicly endorse and teach it as a comfortable way to maintain the status quo that ensures their position and authority.

The use of mandated standards and standardized testing illustrates the impact of a politically generated false consciousness on educational practice. It also illustrates how a canon is used to validate the mandate. The discourse used to validate the standards movement, especially No Child Left Behind, states as truth that: (1) all children in a democratic society such as the United States have a right to an excellent education and no child should be left behind; (2) an excellent education, a qualitative concept, is one in which students achieve academically; (3) academic achievement can be measured fairly and objectively by standardized tests; (4) these tests will identify those students who are achieving a quality education and those who are being left behind; (5) the tests will identify the schools that have a high record of academic success as well as those whose students fail to score well on the tests; (6) schools with high failure rates can be remediated; (7) if the remediation is unsuccessful, students in these schools can transfer to schools with higher test results with the assumption that this transfer will enable them to have an excellent education.

Using Postmodernist deconstruction, we can analyze the canon and the false consciousness that operates in using standardized tests to assess or measure an excellent education. While Postmodernist educators would not argue against an excellent education, they want to know how the term was used by the framers of the Act and what it means in its application to schools and children. Specifically, who defines what an excellent education is, and is the standard of excellence the same for all students? The general claim quickly shifts, however, to an assertion that standardized tests provide objective, scientifically unbiased findings, presented in impersonal statistics, about who is meeting academic standards and who is failing to meet them. A qualitative goal, the right to an excellent education, is being measured quantitatively by standardized test results. Are these test results the same as the right to an excellent education? The Postmodernist educator, in deconstructing the No Child Left Behind Act, asks: Who is setting the standard? Who is mandating the testing? Who is making up the test? Who is interpreting the test results? How will the results be used? What roles do politicians, parents, teachers, and students play in setting standards and using tests to verify whether they have been met? What are the consequences of the Act's implementation on teachers and students? These questions can also be used to deconstruct the Common Core State Standards Initiative that was developed and is currently being promoted by the Council of Chief State School Officers and the National Governors Association Center for Best Practices.

Based on the canon of scientific objectivity, the statistics about meeting or failing to meet the empirically measurable and verified standard discount the importance of individual specificity about the students taking the test. It discounts the importance of race, ethnicity, gender, and socioeconomic class.

Curriculum

Postmodernists critique the ways in which the curriculum has been organized in Western (including American) schools, according to which knowledge has been separated into either Aristotelian categories or on demarcations derived from Enlightenment science and social science. According to the Aristotelian categorization of knowledge, subject matters, reflecting metaphysical reality, correspond to the objects as they exist in reality. Further, those subjects that are more theoretical and more abstract are more important, located higher in the curriculum hierarchy, and given greater priority in instruction than those that are more direct and immediate. For Postmodernists, Aristotelian categorization, though premodern, has had a lingering historical power in Western thought. Subjects are not an accurate representation of reality but rather represent how classical and scholastic elites constructed knowledge. For several thousand years, this Aristotelian categorization contributed to the control of formal education by dominant political aristocracies and religious elites.

See the chapter on Realism and Education for the hierarchical concept of curriculum.

In addition to rejecting premodern metaphysics, Postmodernist educators also reject the modern scientific construction of knowledge that began with the Enlightenment. Growing out of their search to discover the natural laws that governed the universe and society, eighteenth-century theorists turned to empiricism, as in the case of John Locke, rather than to metaphysics as did the earlier Aristotelian Realists and Thomists. However, modern science and social science, too, represented a construction of knowledge by new elites—scientists, economists, and political scientists. The scientists of the Enlightenment and post-Enlightenment periods claimed that to be used correctly, the scientific method had to be used in a neutral, uncommitted, and objective manner. Modern versions of science in the social studies, psychology, and education also claim to be scientific and objective. Postmodernists argue that scientific claims to objectivity are either a delusion or contrived. Claims to knowledge, they allege, are never neutral but represent the establishment of a relationship of power between those who claim to know the truth and those on whom they impose their version of the truth. For Postmodernists, the modern construction of knowledge, along with the language used to convey it, represents the strategy of modernizing elites to take and keep power.

Both the premodern Aristotelian metaphysical categories and modern sciences and social sciences remain encased and encoded in subject-matter disciplines. The controlling elites have constructed "canons," texts that contain definitions, cases, and illustrations that demarcate subjects, boundaries, or borders, where a subject begins and ends. Like any boundary, these canons give a sense of ownership to the experts who control them and to the interests they serve. In academic institutions, the experts in each subject matter have constructed theoretical moats that act as impenetrable boundaries that protect their power and their "turf."[24] Often, educational reforms and efforts at change are weakened by academics who fight boundary wars to protect their subject matters and prevent curriculum reconstruction.

The dominant elites, once colonialist, have constructed a neocolonialist curriculum that is Eurocentric, patriarchal, and class based. By deconstructing the canons of the vested subjects, these canons can be revealed as historically constructed rationales that justify dominant groups' racial, gender, and class biases. Once they are seen as rationales rather than as descriptions of universal or scientific truths, these canons can be deconstructed so that the purposes of those who originated them and use them can be examined. Further, the canons and the texts that convey them can be unmasked as the representation of a dominant class or group rather than having a larger, broader, universal legitimacy. With such official knowledge dethroned, it becomes possible to replace it with the representations of those groups, the marginalized, whose voices have been excluded by those who constructed what was passed off as official knowledge.

For Postmodernist educators, the relationship between a discourse and the exercise of power is an important issue in curriculum and instruction. A discourse is a set of related, interlocking, and mutually supporting statements that define and describe a particular subject. In curriculum, a discourse describes a subject matter. It is based on the belief that some authorities possess expert knowledge to set boundaries between subjects, describe their structures, define their terms, construct appropriate interpretations and explanations, and select appropriate examples and illustrations. Such expertise gives the authority the power to define what belongs and what does not belong to a subject. More important, the authority has the power to determine what is an appropriate or an inappropriate question in a subject. The power to set the range of questions determines the answers. For example, historians have the expertise to tell us what history is and political scientists to tell us what politics is. Literary critics tell us what literature is, and so forth. What is implied is that for each subject, there is a cadre of experts who have the authority to set standards for a field. To construct an authentic education, it is necessary to deconstruct and to restructure the curriculum. The Postmodernist educator is suspicious of certain catchwords or-phrases such as *objective, unbiased, scientific*, or *neutral* that are used to justify the existing curriculum. Postmodernists attack the idea that the curriculum subjects are a means of introducing students to the bodies of knowledge that represent humankind's funded or refined experiences. Rather than inducting young people into the officially approved culture, the curriculum should feature experiences in which teachers and students unpack, deconstruct, and resist the transmission of approved information and knowledge. The teacher of history, for example, does not see history as a chronology with approved meanings. History is a "constructed" rather than an unbiased narrative about the past. It is important to ask whose past and whose interpretation are being conveyed in the history text or whose story is being told in the literature course. The goal of Postmodernist teaching is to engage students to be authors in constructing their own history or writing their own literature. The science teacher will represent science not as a body of objective propositions about physical and natural reality, but rather as a set of constructed propositions about the world that we are part of rather than one that exists apart from us. Scientific theories, like all theories, are human constructions.[25]

For the student as author, see Maxine Greene on "authorship" in the chapter on Existentialism and Education.

Instruction involves representation, a Postmodernist term that has a larger meaning for any kind of cultural expression or discussion. **Representation** refers to the "processes" that individuals and groups "use to interpret and give meaning" to their experience; this meaning is conveyed by "language, stories, images, music, and other cultural constructions."[26] Much teaching, especially the transmission of the official curriculum, involves making representations to students through language as teachers purport to provide students with descriptions of reality. However, the official curriculum—the approved representation—is only one version of reality, usually that of the dominant group in society. Teachers need to become conscious of the powerful role that they exercise and critical about the representations that they make. The official curriculum neglects the experience of marginalized groups, especially African, Hispanic, and Native Americans; women; and gays and lesbians. Rather than the transmission of officially approved knowledge, the process of representation needs to be used critically and reflectively to present a wider range of perspectives.[27]

Representation: the language individuals and groups use to interpret and give meaning to their experience.

In curriculum and instruction, Postmodernism and constructivism are compatible. Knowledge and subjects are constructed by human beings and are not a set of objective facts, concepts, or laws independent of the knower that are waiting to be discovered. Humans make knowledge rather than discover it. To express our constructions, we use language, which is also a construction.[28] Not universal or eternal, knowledge, as a human construction, is always fluid and flexible and is continually being reconstructed. Human understandings are tentative, incomplete, and imperfect, even though all of them may not be equally imperfect.

An important principle shared among Idealist and Realist educators (especially in the humanities, literature, art, and music) is that students can elaborate on aesthetic expression by first studying and emulating the classical rendition of existing forms. In other words, aspiring student writers study the novels of important authors—Twain, Wharton, Cather, Steinbeck, Hemingway, and others who have been recognized in their genre—and find in their writing styles models that they can imitate, revise, and extend in their own writing. In the same way, aspiring artists are exposed to and study the important genres of art developed over time in order to imitate and extend them to their own modes of artistic appreciation and creation. This approach—a going through the classic works of art—differs from constructionism. Postmodernists would regard the designation an "important novelist" and "an important period of art" to be a form of privileging art that is similar to privileging knowledge. Some expert in an elite group of literary or art critics has made a determination that a novel, a painting, or a musical composition is significant enough to be designated as a canon and as a model to be followed by students. In contrast, Postmodernists would regard the necessity of going through the models in aesthetics to represent a domination by imposing a standard on the aspiring artist's freedom to create his or her new style and mode of expression. New forms should not be regulated by older forms of artistic expression and aesthetic critique. There are myriad forms and modes of expressing the aesthetic sense. Further, there is no privileged standard for judging it.

Schools and Schooling

Postmodernists would take a critical look at schools, especially how they are organized and controlled. As educational institutions, public schools in the United States are agencies of the official social, political, and economic system. The canons that are part of the public school ideology purport that schools educate the children of all the people, provide for upward social and economic mobility, and are necessary to maintain and continue American democratic political processes. In deconstructing the public school ideology, Postmodernists contend that schools, especially as part of publicly controlled systems, exemplify places that represent official knowledge and maintain it by instilling it into the young. However, schools, like other institutions, are used to reproduce a social order that is patriarchal in that it favors male dominance of women. They are Eurocentric in that what is represented as official knowledge is actually constructed by white people of European stock. They are capitalist in that private property and the corporate attitude are enshrined in the free market ideology. Given these official foundations, the dominance of white European males is approved, reinforced, and reproduced in institutionalized education. Other groups (e.g., people of color, many women, and gays and lesbians) are excluded from the official narratives and pushed to the margins of the schools and society.[29]

The organization of public schools typically is hierarchical, with rules, regulations, and procedures coming down from centralized educational bureaucracies to local schools and classrooms. The more schools are centralized and run by top-down bureaucracies, the more pervasive are the strategies for official control.

Postmodernism argues that schools should be local educational spaces in which local community experience is at the heart of constructing an informed consciousness of the people directly involved. In these local sites, students are to use their own voices and their own situated knowledge to understand and shape their own lives.[30] The educator's role is to help people to learn to use their own voices. Postmodernists want schools to be decentralized as local educational spaces in which local communities—children, parents, teachers, and neighbors—decide what they want to learn, why they want to learn it, and how they will learn it—without the monitoring of administrators, experts, and consultants to make sure that external standards are being enforced.

Foundations of Education

Especially pernicious, contend Postmodernists, is the claim that scientific objectivity can be extended from the natural and physical sciences to the social sciences and education. Some experts in fields such as psychology, sociology, political science, and education claim that they can approach their areas of inquiry with scientific objectivity and arrive at disinterested knowledge claims. Postmodernists believe that such claims are feigned or false. All knowledge claims and the texts that convey them represent power relationships. Claims to objectivity are used to deflect critical analysis.

Postmodernism questions the possibility of foundations—the bodies of knowledge, usually history, philosophy, psychology, and sociology—that are designated as the theoretical base of educational practice. Rather than explanatory foundations, the real meaning of education is found in the subjective encounters of persons—teachers and students—in classrooms and schools. The foundations of education should be approached genealogically, with attention to the situations that gave rise to them—historically, philosophically, psychologically, and sociologically.

My Reflections on Philosophy of Education: A Controversy over Power in Historical Representation

Throughout this book, I have challenged readers to reflect on their educational experiences to begin the process of constructing their own philosophy of education. As I was writing this chapter about Postmodernism, I recalled an episode in my own teaching that caused me to reflect on historical representations and how history is a source of power. I was teaching a course in the history of Western Education and had finished lecturing about the ancient Egyptians and Greeks. My representation generally followed the conventional historical interpretation that I had learned as a student, that ancient Egyptian civilization was a highly static despotism and that its major cultural legacy was its great architectural monuments. My interpretation saw Greek culture, especially Athenian democracy, as the cradle of Western civilization.

At this point, an African American student objected to my interpretation, saying that it had been challenged by the historian Martin Bernal, who claimed that the Greeks had appropriated many of their concepts about government, philosophy, the arts, sciences, and medicine from ancient Egypt.[31] Furthermore, the student said, the Egyptians, geographically located in North Africa, were an African people, and that we need to look for the origins of Western culture in Egypt rather than in Greece. Although they recognize the interactions between Egyptians and Greeks, Bernal's critics contend that he greatly overemphasizes Egypt's influence on ancient Greece. The student also said that how we represent and interpret history is a means of exercising power. Bernal's interpretation would empower those who argue for a broader interpretation of Western history and education and would be a rationale for an Afrocentric curriculum. At this point, I admitted that I knew little about Bernal's interpretation and suggested that the topic was important enough to warrant further investigation. The students and I investigated Bernal's claims. I found a video documentary that examined Bernal's thesis and the counterarguments of his critics. We found that the Bernal thesis had generated a heated debate among historians. Some tentative findings indicated that Egyptian–Greek cultural contacts, particularly at Crete, introduced the Greeks to Egyptian mathematics and art. This intriguing historical controversy has important ideological significance. Whoever interprets the past, as the Postmodernists contend, gains the power of illuminating and shaping the present.

This episode, an event in my own interactions with students, brought to mind the Postmodernist argument that there is a relationship between discourse and power. It demonstrated how a discourse leads to related, interlocking, and mutually supporting statements that define and describe a particular subject. It also illustrated how knowledge becomes "official." I was transmitting the interpretation of ancient Egypt and Greece as I had learned it from my teachers and professors and from the textbooks that they had selected.

I thought, if Bernal is correct, then the conventional underpinnings about the origins of Western civilization need to be rethought and revised. At question is the issue of who is to construct interpretations and explanations in history.

CONSTRUCTING YOUR OWN PHILOSOPHY OF EDUCATION

Now that you have read and discussed the chapter on Postmodernism, will you use it in constructing your own philosophy of education? Will you use it to deconstruct and critique other philosophies of education? Will you examine curriculum and instruction as contested arenas of schooling? Will you see issues in education as representing conflicts between dominant and subordinate groups? Do you see Postmodernism as a possibility for infusion in your own philosophy of education or do you reject it?

Conclusion

Postmodernism is a provocative philosophy whose influence pervades contemporary thinking in philosophy, literature, art, the humanities, and education. It has support among some feminist theorists and multicultural educators. Simultaneously, it has sparked a sharp negative reaction by those who argue against its relativism and its often dense and repetitive language.

Those who endorse Postmodernism see it as having a liberating power in its questioning of philosophical, political, social, economic, and educational systems that set the boundaries for our social roles. They endorse its challenge to the dominance of the boundaries, definitions, prescriptions, and proscriptions that the systems establish. Postmodernism has opened up and freed our thinking about gender, race, sexual orientation, and ethnicity. Its demands for the recognition and celebration of differences and the acceptance of others in society have shaped multiculturalism in education. In its relativist pluralist discourse, it warns against allowing one frame of reference to dominate education.

Critics see Postmodernism leading to a kind of social mitosis in which groups continually split off, go their own way, and construct their own systems of meaning without regard for any social or political commonalities. In such extreme pluralism, it becomes impossible to talk about community based on the common good because the idea of a common is a universal that carries with it the repression of those who are uncommon. Because of the fear of domination, it becomes virtually impossible to create a common government and a common school system or establish the means to adjudicate disputes according to some kind of common law. Without a central method of authority for adjudicating disputes, groups are left in isolation, living in their own spaces, and weaving their own conceptions about community and society.

Questions for Reflection and Discussion

1. Compare and contrast the concepts of "modern" and "postmodern." Are you a modern or a postmodern person?
2. Examine the statement "Some societies are advanced and others are primitive" from Modernist and Postmodernist perspectives.
3. Do you accept or reject the Postmodernist argument that the curriculum is a contested area? Explain your answer.
4. Do you agree with the critics of Postmodernism who regard it as failing to establish the common values that a society needs to function?
5. Reflect on the courses that you are taking or have taken at your college or university, especially in literature, political science, sociology, and education. Do you find evidence of Postmodernism in the way these courses are represented?
6. Reflect on courses dealing with women's education or multicultural education that you are taking or have taken at your college or university. Do you find evidence of Postmodernism in the way these courses are represented?
7. Do you accept or reject the Postmodernist argument against claims that purport to have universal truth and values?
8. In your education courses, do you find examples of what Foucault calls a "regime of truth"?
9. What are the rules or guidelines that are followed in discussions in your education courses? Are they examples of "official knowledge"?

Inquiry and Research Projects

1. Using deconstruction, examine a syllabus in a course in teacher education at your college or university.
2. Examine a textbook in world history, at either the secondary or higher level. Is the general interpretation Modernist or Postmodernist?
3. Do some research on the Common Core State Standards Initiative developed by the Council of Chief State School Officers and the National Governors Association Center for Best Practices. Using deconstruction, try to determine the genealogy of the Initiative: Who supported it? Why was it developed? What is the definition of a "common core"? What kind of power relationships does it establish?
4. Visit elementary and secondary school classrooms. Observe the kinds of teacher representations that are taking place. How might a Postmodernist evaluate these representations?
5. Research the mission statement of the NCATE or another accreditation document relating to the teacher education program at your college or university. Using deconstruction, determine the genealogy of the statement. What kinds of power relationships does it express? Does it endorse an "official" or "privileged" knowledge?
6. Watch the same television news station for a week and keep a log of what is covered and how much time is devoted to the particular coverage. Determine what kind of consciousness this representation creates.
7. Access information about Postmodernism at http://artandpopularculture.com/Postmodernism. Survey Postmodernism's influence on art, literature, architecture, and other forms of aesthetic expression and criticism. Do you think that Postmodernism has had a wide influence these fields?

Internet Resources

For the origins, key ideas, and bibliography of Postmodernism and a discussion of deconstruction, access http://plato.stanford.edu/entries;postmodernism/.

For its history, reactions to Modernism, critics, and Web links, access "Postmodernism" at New World Encyclopedia at http://www.newworldencyclopedia.org/entry/Postmodernism.

For Foucault's ideas and a glossary, bibliography, and links to Web sites, access the Foucault Web page at Michel-Foucault.com.

For an overview of Postmodernism, access www.allaboutphilosophy.org/postmodernism.htm.

Suggestions for Further Reading

Aronowitz, Stanley, and Henry A. Giroux. *Postmodern Education: Politics, Culture, and Social Criticism.* Minneapolis: University of Minnesota Press, 1991.

Ball, S., ed. *Foucault and Education.* London: Routledge, 1991.

Best, Steven, and Douglas Kellner. . *Postmodern Theory.* New York: Guilford, 1991.

Butler, Christopher. *Post-Modernism: A Very Short Introduction.* Oxford, UK: Oxford University Press, 2002.

Cahoone, Lawrence E. *From Modernism to Postmodernism: An Anthology.* Oxford, UK: Blackwell, 1996.

Carr, D., ed. *Education, Knowledge and Truth: Beyond the Postmodern Impasse.* London: Routledge, 1998.

Cole, Mike. *Marxism, Postmodernism and Education.* Oxford, UK: Taylor & Francis, 2007.

Cooper, David E. *A Companion to the Philosophy of Education.* Malden, MA, and Oxford, UK: Blackwell, 2006.

Cooper, David E. *World Philosophies: An Historical Introduction.* Oxford, UK, and Cambridge, MA: Blackwell, 1996.

Derrida, Jacques. *Of Grammatology.* Baltimore: Johns Hopkins University Press, 1976.

Doll, William E., Jr. *A Post-Modern Perspective on Curriculum.* New York: Teachers College Press, Columbia University, 1993.

Edwards, Richard, and Robin Usher. *Postmodernism and Education: Different Voices, Different Worlds.* New York: Routledge, 1994.

Foucault, Michel. *The Archeology of Knowledge and the Discourse of Language.* New York: Pantheon Books, 1972.

___. *Power Knowledge.* Translated by Colin Gordon, Leo Marschall, John Mepham, and Kate Sopher. New York: Pantheon, 1980.

Giroux, Henry A. *Postmodernism, Feminism, and Cultural Politics: Redrawing Boundaries.* Albany: State University Press of New York, 1991.

Hardy, Tom, ed. *Art Education in a Postmodern World: Collected Essays.* Bristol, UK: Intellect Ltd., 2006.

Hill, Dave, Peter McLaren, Mike Cole, and Glenn Ritkowski, eds. *Postmodernism in Educational Theory: Education and the Politics of Human Resistance.* London: Tufnell Press, 1999.

Jencks, Charles. *The Post-Modern Reader.* London: Academy Editions, 1992.

Kincheloe, Joe L. *Toward a Critical Politics of Teaching Thinking: Mapping the Postmodern*. Westport, CT: Bergin & Garvey, 1993.

Lyotard, Jean-Francois. *The Postmodern Condition: A Report on Knowledge*. Translated by Geoff Bennington and Brian Massumi. Minneapolis: Minnesota University Press, 1984.

___. *Toward the Postmodern*. Edited by Robert Harvey and Mark Roberts. Atlantic Highlands, NJ: Humanities, 1993.

Rosenau, Pauline M. *Post-Modernism and the Social Sciences: Insights, Inroads, and Intrusions*. Princeton, NJ: Princeton University Press, 1992.

Slattery, Patrick. *Curriculum Development in the Postmodern Era*. New York: Garland, 1995.

Smith, Richard. *After Postmodernism: Education, Politics, and Identity*. Oxford, UK: Taylor & Francis, 1995.

Stronach, Ian, Margaret MacLure, and Maggie MacLure. *Educational Research Undone: The Postmodern Embrace*. Buckingham, UK: Open University Press, 1997.

Notes

1. Friedrich Nietzsche, *The Will to Power*, trans. Walter Kaufmann (New York: Vintage, 1967).
2. David E. Cooper, *World Philosophies: An Historical Introduction* (Oxford, UK, and Cambridge, MA: Blackwell, 1996), 467.
3. Christopher Butler, *Post-Modernism: A Very Short Introduction* (Oxford, UK: Oxford University Press, 2002), 29.
4. P. Sloterdijk, *Critique of Cynical Reason*, trans. M. Eldred (Minneapolis: University of Minnesota Press, 1987), xi, 5.
5. George R. Knight, *Issues and Alternatives in Educational Philosophy* (Berrien Springs, MI: Andrews University Press, 1998), 86.
6. Jacques Derrida, *Of Grammatology* (Baltimore: Johns Hopkins University Press, 1976).
7. Cooper, *World Philosophies: An Historical Introduction*, 473.
8. Howard A. Ozmon and Samuel M. Craver, *Philosophical Foundations of Education* (Columbus, OH: Merrill/Prentice Hall, 1999), 356.
9. Knight, *Issues and Alternatives in Educational Philosophy*, 86–87.
10. Butler, *Post-Modernism: A Very Short Introduction*, 45.
11. Jennifer M. Gore, "Enticing Challenges: An Introduction to Foucault and Educational Discourses," in Rebecca A. Martusewicz and William M. Reynolds, *Inside/Out: Contemporary Critical Perspectives in Education* (New York: St. Martin's Press, 1994), 110.
12. Ibid., 114.
13. Cooper, *World Philosophies: An Historical Introduction*, 476.
14. David E. Cooper, "Postmodernism," in *A Companion to the Philosophy of Education* (Malden, MA, and Oxford, UK: Blackwell, 2006), 208.
15. Cooper, *World Philosophies: An Historical Introduction*, 476.
16. Cooper, "Postmodernism," 210.
17. Rebecca A. Martusewicz and William M. Reynolds, *Inside/Out: Contemporary Critical Perspectives in Education* (New York: St. Martin's Press, 1994), 11–13.
18. Butler, *Post-Modernism: A Very Short Introduction*, 17–18.
19. Edward K. Berggren, "Deconstruction and Nothingness: Some Cross-Cultural Lessons on Teaching Comparative World Civilization," in Rebecca A. Martusewicz and William M. Reynolds, *Inside/Out: Contemporary Critical Perspectives in Education* (New York: St. Martin's Press, 1994), 24–25.
20. Peter Seixas, "Schreiber! Die Kinder! Or, Does Postmodern History Have a Place in the Schools?" in Peter N. Stearns, Peter Seixas, and Sam Wineburg, *Knowing, Teaching and Learning History: National and International Perspectives* (New York: New York University Press, 2000), 19–37.
21. Butler, *Post-Modernism: A Very Short Introduction*, 37–38.
22. Ibid., 3.
23. Ibid., 110–111.
24. Martusewicz and Reynolds, *Inside/Out: Contemporary Critical Perspectives in Education*, 3–4.
25. Cooper, "Postmodernism," 212.
26. Elizabeth Ellsworth, "Representation, Self-Representation, and the Meanings of Difference: Questions for Educators," in Rebecca A. Martusewicz and William M. Reynolds, *Inside/Out: Contemporary Critical Perspectives in Education* (New York: St. Martin's Press, 1994), 100.
27. Ibid., 100–101.
28. John A. Zohorik, *Constructivist Teaching* (Bloomington, IN: Phi Delta Kappa Educational Foundation, 1995), 11.
29. Angeline Martel and Linda Peterat, "Margins of Exclusion, Margins of Transformation: The Place of Women in Education," in Rebecca A. Martusewicz and William M. Reynolds, *Inside/Out: Contemporary Critical Perspectives in Education* (New York: St. Martin's Press, 1994), 152.
30. Michel Foucault, *Power/Knowledge*, trans. Colin Gordon, Leo Marshall, John Mepham, and Kate Soper (New York: Pantheon, 1980), 81–83.
31. Martin Bernal, *Black Athena: The Afroasiatic Roots of Classical Civilization: The Fabrication of Ancient Greece 1785–1985* (New Brunswick, NJ: Rutgers University Press, 1987), 2–3.

Ideology and Education

Paulo Freire (1923–1997), a Brazilian educator, who originated Liberation Pedagogy and asserted that all education is ideological.

7

CHAPTER PREVIEW

We examine ideology and its educational significance as an introduction for the chapters in which we discuss particular ideologies, their general role in policy formulation, and their impact on education. Ever since the eighteenth-century Enlightenment, ideologies have been and remain potent forces for shaping and expressing social, political, economic, and educational programs. The American Revolution in 1776, the French Revolution in 1789, the Bolshevik Revolution in 1917, the Chinese Communist Revolution in 1949, and the Arab Spring in 2011 were, in large part, caused by ideology. A particular ideology, for example, Nationalism, Liberalism, Conservatism, or Marxism, carries with it a portrait of the preferred person. In painting this portrait with an ideological brush, the ideologist uses strokes that are historical, sociological, political, and economic. In reproducing the preferred person, the ideologist relies heavily on education. Informal educational agencies, especially the media—the press, movies, radio, television, the Internet, and social media—are used, as well as the formal educational agency, namely, the school, which recreates the prototype through the milieu (hidden curriculum) and the curriculum, the official and explicit program.

Since the rise of the modern nation-state, ideology has influenced policy making and policy implementation in many areas, including economics, science, technology, and education. Educational policies, and the programs and practices that they engender, have a direct impact on schooling.

Ideology serves to give theoretical legitimacy to a group's outlook, aspirations, program, and action. Rather than appearing to be based on personal or group special interests, ideological justification or legitimacy appeals to a higher and seemingly more generalizable, hence more applicable, authority. Often, the appeal to myth or history is used to legitimize policies and actions.

Ideology is also used to justify and determine the power relationships among contending groups. For example, contemporary educational policy in the United States has tended toward inclusiveness rather than exclusiveness; that is, it has worked to make educational opportunities more available to groups, such as African Americans, Native Americans, Hispanics, women, and people with disabilities, who were excluded in the past.

The impact of ideology on modern education is as profound as that of the traditional foundational disciplines of philosophy, history, psychology, and sociology. Since the eighteenth-century Enlightenment, individuals and societies have inhabited an ideological world. After the sociopolitical theorists of the Enlightenment and the revolutionaries in Great Britain's American colonies and in France challenged control by absolute monarchies, there was a period of time during which numerous ideologies emerged and then competed for the loyalty of individuals, groups, and nations

For a discussion of power relationships, see the chapter on Postmodernism and Education.

throughout the world. With the advent of nationalism and the rise of modern nation-states, schools were organized to function as parts of national systems of education. Further, the rise of social-class consciousness, stimulated by industrialization, also engendered competition between socio-economic and political groups over the control of nation-states and their governmental and educational systems. As a result, much institutionalized education, or schooling, has been shaped by ideological outlooks and programs.

Ideology is so pervasive in our lives, in our group identification and membership, and in shaping our behavior that we are all touched by it. Consciously or unconsciously, we all share and are shaped by ideologies. To begin our discussion of ideology, we describe and analyze the concept so that we can identify and recognize the various ideologies and determine how they function in society and education.

As we study the concept of ideology, we need to recognize that we have been and are influenced by ideology in general and by specific ideologies in particular. To analyze the concept of ideology, we need to examine how an ideology originates, functions, and is sustained. As teachers, we need to recognize and examine both the conscious and unconscious ideological assumptions that people use to interpret and to guide their social, cultural, political, economic, and educational behavior. The chapter is organized into the following topics:

- Ideology's ambiguity
- Historical origins of ideology
- Contributors to the analysis of ideology
- A stipulated definition of ideology
- Social change and ideology
- The use of ideology to create consensus
- Ideology's permeability and flexibility
- Ideology, education, and schooling
- Ideology and instruction
- Ideology and philosophy

You might consider how the concept of ideology or particular ideologies often resembles and relates to philosophies of education. Many educational policies are based on an ideology, or they combine elements of ideology and philosophy. You might consider how ideology has shaped your ideas about education and how these ideas relate to your thinking about philosophy of education.

IDEOLOGY'S AMBIGUITY

Ideology: the shared ideas and values that create group identity and meaning, especially in politics, society, economics, culture, and education.

Ideology is a slippery and ambiguous term that arouses strong reactions in people. Although some people see ideology as a generally negative term, the same people are likely to be strongly committed to a particular ideology such as Conservatism or Liberalism. For these reasons, a stipulated definition is deferred until the history and background of ideology have been examined. But so that we have some initial terminology for our discussion, we begin with a preliminary working definition of ideology.

Ideology is often defined as the belief system of a group, usually based on a rendition of its past, which carries prescriptions for policy. Group beliefs arise primarily in historical, social, political, and economic contexts, however, rather than in a metaphysical system that seeks to transcend such cultural particularities. The ideological interpretation of the past also suggests how this past has shaped the individual's and the group's present situation; from this interpretation comes a theory of social stasis or social change that seeks to define, predict, and ensure the course of the social, political, and economic order. Ideologies are prescriptive in that they recommend policy guidelines for programs to move society in the desired direction.

Action-oriented, rather than merely theoretical, ideology is used to guide political, social, economic, and educational policies. Insofar as institutionalized education, especially schooling, is used as an instrument of achieving these policies, education follows an ideological direction.

Although some ideologists sought to create a worldview that appears to transcend a particular cultural context, their abstractions are generally historically derived and represent the desire to give worldwide validity to a particular interpretation of the past. Indeed, the particular cultural heritage of a group influences its construction of an ideology. For example, the interpretations and reinterpretations of Marxism in the People's Republic of China and the policies based on it reflect the Chinese cultural heritage and geopolitical conditions. The revolutions against authoritarian regimes in Tunisia, Egypt, and Libya in the Arab Spring in 2011 reflected a fusing of Arabic cultural and Islamic religious heritages that may take a more definite ideological form or may give rise to conflicting ideologies in the future.

HISTORICAL ORIGINS OF IDEOLOGY

In this section, we examine the historical origin of the concept of ideology in the eighteenth-century Enlightenment and the rise of contending ideologies in the nineteenth century. The section includes an analysis of Karl Marx's critique of ideology.

The Origins of Ideology in the Enlightenment

In the eighteenth century, the *philosophes* of the French Enlightenment originally used the term *ideology* as an epistemology to explain how groups generate and use ideas. In contrast to theology and metaphysics, the *philosophes* hoped to create a science of ideas. For example, the French *philosophe* Étienne Bonnot de Condillac (1715–1780), denying Plato's assertion that ideas were innately present in the mind, claimed that sensation was the source of all human ideas. In relation to the development of ideology, Condillac and other *philosophes* asserted that human ideas did not originate in a metaphysical realm that was prior to human experience but rather originated with the human being's sensory experience in the environment.

For the theory of innate ideas, see the chapter on Idealism and Education.

Antoine Destutt de Tracy (1754–1836) used the word *ideology* to designate his efforts to create a science of ideas that examined how people originated and used ideas to create institutions and to regulate their behavior.[1] Like the other *philosophes*, de Tracy believed that ideology could be an empirical science rather than metaphysical speculation. As they fashioned a nontheological and nonmetaphysical explanation of the origins of human knowledge, the *philosophes* attempted to develop a social science that replicated the scientific investigation of physical phenomena.

For a critique of the Enlightenment project refer to the previous chapter on Postmodernism and Education.

Ideologues: French Enlightenment theorists who sought to develop an empirical theory of how people formed their ideas.

In the case of the Enlightenment **ideologues**, ideas about creating an improved society eventually led to actions to change social, political, economic, and educational institutions. If the *ancien régime* of the French Bourbon monarchy rested on scientifically untenable propositions such as the divine right of kings or the theory of absolute monarchy, then the *philosophes* reasoned that these obsolete and erroneous political and social residues should be overthrown and replaced by scientific ones. Enlightened persons could use the scientific method to investigate social phenomena in the same way that Isaac Newton and others had investigated physical phenomena. A genuine social science could uncover the natural order of society. Once the natural laws of social, political, and economic life were discovered, they could be used to create a new and scientifically legitimate social and political order. In eighteenth-century America and France, the Enlightenment ideology stimulated two major revolutions that shook the foundations of the Western political order and ushered in republican governments, which, supporters claimed, conformed to natural laws. The theory that natural laws applied to social, political, and economic life and institutions, as proposed by the Enlightenment ideologues, had profound educational implications. In the past, individuals had been indoctrinated by archaic structures of religious or classical education to accept a static view of society. A new education needed to be constructed to instruct a rising generation of republican citizens who could establish representative institutions and govern themselves according to reason and science.

Social and Economic Change, Ideology and Education

In the late eighteenth and nineteenth centuries, those who sought to design the ideal social and political order disagreed on the ideological plan for creating the "heavenly city" on earth. Social theorists and politicians devised alternative and often contradictory models of the good society. John Locke's contract theory of government based on natural rights of life, liberty, and property became the ideology that guided liberal politics in the United Kingdom. In the United States, Jefferson shaped Locke's ideological principles as justification for the American Revolution. In France, in the years following the revolution that dethroned the Bourbons, moderate monarchists, republicans, socialists, and communists proposed a plethora of politically conflicting political designs. These ideological designs for creating a new perfect social order included educational strategies to create the new social and political citizen for the new world.

The nineteenth and early twentieth centuries experienced the economic and social transformation generated by industrial and technological modernization. Machine power, the mass production of the factory system, and the availability of inexpensively manufactured products dramatically transformed the economies and societies of Western Europe and North America. The Industrial Revolution spurred the growth of large cities, urban populations, and the development of transportation systems. These material changes were reflected in ideology and education.

Industrialization generated socioeconomic class antagonisms. In the nineteenth century, the middle classes, consisting of industrialists, bankers, professionals, and commercial entrepreneurs, were the rising emergent class that challenged the supremacy of the older landed gentry and traditional aristocracy of birth and blood. Those who labored in the factories, mills, and mines—the working class, the future industrial proletariat—would eventually challenge the political and social control of the middle class in the twentieth century.

The material changes caused by industrialization and technology generated new social, political, and educational theories. Ideology, in particular, became oriented toward a social and economic class orientation that, in turn, raised the following issues that continue to engage educational policy analysis:

- How does education reflect particular class interests?
- Should education reflect or seek to change society?
- Do dominant classes use education to reproduce themselves?
- Is educational policy making an arena of class conflicts?
- Do dominant classes use the school as an agency of social control over subordinate classes?

For issues of power and control, see the chapter on Postmodernism and Education.

Recall that these issues of dominant and subordinate classes, the use of power, and social control were again raised by the Postmodernists in the late twentieth century and early twenty-first century.

The Rise of Contending Ideologies

As the nineteenth century unfolded, social and economic components were added to political ideology. The middle class—the bourgeois—found a congenial and supportive political ideology in the **Liberalism** of Locke and other proponents of individualism. To Lockean individualism was added the free trade laissez-faire theories of Adam Smith, David Ricardo, and Thomas Malthus. Later, more reformist social, political, economic, and educational ideas were incorporated into liberal ideology.

Liberalism: an ideology that emphasizes the freedom of individuals to form a social contract to protect their natural rights of life, liberty, and property.

Communitarian socialist theorists such as Saint-Simon, Fourier, Owen, Cabet, and others developed a counterideology to correct what they regarded as Liberalism's erroneous interpretation of socio-economic conditions. These visionary reformers condemned what they saw as the dismal theories of classical Liberalism that justified working-class repression and exploitation. Communitarian Socialism argued that the emergent forces of industrialism, urbanization, and technology could be planned and patterned in a rational way to alleviate human misery and suffering.

Socialism took another turn with the organization of labor-based political parties such as the Social Democrats in Germany, the Labour Party in the United Kingdom, and the various Socialist parties in France, Italy, and the Scandinavian countries. In the United States, Eugene V. Debs and Norman Thomas led a Socialist Party, which functioned as a third party. The Socialist parties sought to create a welfare state that protected the rights of the working class: to organize trade unions, to have safe working conditions, to have access to state-supported educational systems, and to have guaranteed health and old-age services and pensions. Depending on the particular Socialist party, the degree to which industry, transportation, and other services would be nationalized—run as public agencies—varied.

Another important variant of Socialism was the Marxist or Communist parties that rejected the parliamentary approach to gaining political power by elections. Communists argued that genuine social change could come only by an organized proletariat overthrowing the capitalist classes who held power.

Whereas classical liberal ideology sought to explain, to justify, and to rationalize middle-class supremacy, and whereas Communitarian Socialists challenged these assumptions, the defenders of the old order—the landed gentry, the wealthy establishment, and the traditional aristocracy—developed the counterrevolutionary Conservative ideology. The principles of **Conservatism**, ably articulated by the British theorist Edmund Burke, sought to preserve an older and more settled traditional way of life.

Conservatism: an ideology that emphasizes the role of tradition and historically derived institutions as the foundation of culture and society.

After World War I, totalitarian movements developed on the extreme right and left, namely, Fascism in Italy and Spain, National Socialism in Germany, and Communism (Marxist-Leninism) in the Soviet Union. According to totalitarianism, either of the extreme right or left, all power was organized in the state and its leader. With one monolithic political power in place, the state was to regulate all social, cultural, economic, and educational institutions and processes. People (e.g., the Fascists in Italy and Nazis in Germany or the proletariat in the Soviet Union) were to surrender their freedom to the totalitarian state in exchange for the promise of a regenerated and glorious future in which their nation or class would be triumphant.

Through the twentieth and into the twenty-first centuries, the ideologies that originated in the late eighteenth and nineteenth centuries have worked their way through human life, society, and education. They have become interrelated and interconnected clusters of ideas that have shaped our worldviews, cultural outlooks, political programs, and educational policies. They have also spawned political conflicts, hostilities, and world wars.

Ideologies are often classified on a continuum that ranges from the political and cultural right with Fascism at the far right, then Conservatism, moving to Liberalism at

Nationalism: an ideology that identifies the nation as the focus of group life and nationality as the primary mode of personal identification.

the center, and to Socialism at the left and Communism at the far left. This ideological continuum, though of limited use, needs frequent recalibrations. **Nationalism**, a pervasive ideology based on the nation as the focus of group life and on nationality as the primary mode of personal identification, blurs the continuum. Nationalism has penetrated into the other ideologies. Extreme nationalism, or chauvinism, was a prevalent feature of totalitarian movements. Conservatives esteem love of country as a cherished traditional value. Nationalist impulses also entered into Liberalism and Socialism.

Although the general categorizations provide a useful way of locating an ideology on the ideological spectrum, they need to be reclassified in terms of the variety of ideologies that have developed as either new or from the restructuring of older ones in the twenty-first century. The question is where to locate newer ideologies such as the Green environmentalist movement, feminism, multiculturalism, Libertarianism, the peace movement, religious fundamentalism, globalization, "Occupy Wall Street," and the "Tea Party."

Consider feminism, for example. Some would argue it is the women's rights movement or an academic area of study rather than an ideology. However, others regard it as an ideology that expresses the shared ideas and values of a group that wants to raise women's consciousness about their situation in a male-dominated society and construct avenues of greater freedom and choice for women. As ideologists, feminists construct their history by describing the efforts of the suffragettes and other pioneers of women's rights in the nineteenth century and identify such leaders as Elizabeth Cady Stanton and Lucretia Mott. They regard gender as the crucial element and focus on how women have been subjugated or disempowered in a male-dominated patriarchal social, economic, and educational system.[2] One issue in locating and interpreting feminism is whether it is an independent, freestanding ideology or it is connected to larger ideologies.

Multiculturalism raises many of the same issues as feminism. Should it be seen as a movement or an area of study? Or is it an ideology? Several sets of questions can be raised regarding ideology. Note that many of the major ideologies on the left-to-right continuum, including Marxism, originated in Western Europe. They were then transported to Asia, Africa, and Latin America. Multiculturalism argues that world social reality consists of a pluralism of racial, ethnic, and language groups, each of which is culturally equal to the other. It sees social justice, for instance, as based on pluralistic equality rather than domination. It can be viewed as a counterideology to those that assert that Western cultures are more culturally and technologically advanced and that those in non-Western regions need to be raised to the Western standard.

Religion and Ideology

The relationship of religion to ideology raises serious issues, especially in the contemporary world. Religions are based on theologies that examine profound questions about the nature of God and the relationship of God to the universe and to human beings. Theology is much like philosophy, especially philosophies grounded in metaphysics. The major world religions, especially those identified as Abrahamic, are based on sacred authoritative texts (holy books) that contain the word of God (the truth), revealed to special agents (the prophets). For Judaism, the book is the Bible; for Christians, too, it is the Bible, but including both the Old and New Testaments; for Muslims, it is the Koran revealed to the prophet Mohammed.

With the exception of Conservatism, the origins of the major ideologies that developed in the nineteenth century were secular. Liberals generally sought to separate the state from church control and to separate the church from state control.

Marxists were antireligious, seeing religion as a smoke screen to distract the workers from their wretched condition on earth with the promise of an afterlife.

The strong currents of religious fundamentalism in the contemporary world represent the mixture of religious and ideological beliefs. Although religions are theologically rather than ideologically based, some of their adherents may merge religious and ideological principles. For example, what is called the "religious right" in the United States draws many of its members from fundamentalist churches and is allied with Conservativism. The "religious right" has definite views on social and educational policies. For example, the religious right wants to include the teaching of Creationism or Intelligent Design in the school science curriculum along with or in place of Darwin's theory of evolution. It wants abstinence taught in sex education courses along with or in place of contraception. Islamic fundamentalism is a variant of Islam that has ideological overtones. Politicized Islam has a religiously motivated political agenda that blurs distinctions between religion and ideology.[3] It seeks to overthrow or change moderate Islamic or secular states that have a predominantly Muslim population and instead establish a strict interpretation of Islamic law. In Iran, for example, a council of clerics has authority to revise or nullify actions by the country's legislative body. The council also can set and enforce cultural norms as to acceptable dress and public behavior.

CONTRIBUTORS TO THE ANALYSIS OF IDEOLOGY

So far in our discussion of ideology, we have examined the historical origins of ideology and how it relates to society and education. Ideology, like philosophy, is a dynamic field of study in that standing contributions to these fields are restated and revised. Newly developed ones are proposed to replace older ones. Our discussion now turns to a consideration of those who have shaped the meaning of ideology.

Marx's Critique of Ideology

In the chapter on Postmodernism and Education, we introduced the concept of **false consciousness**. We again return to Marx as we consider false consciousness in terms of his critique of ideology. In *The German Ideology,* Karl Marx and Friedrich Engels critiqued Idealism, then the dominant philosophy in Germany. They began their critique by attacking the Idealist metaphysical claim that ideas had a pure and transcendent existence, accusing it of creating an illusory false consciousness.[4] Marx and Engels moved their critique from Idealism when they said that false consciousness was an ideology. Whereas the eighteenth-century French *philosophes* Condillac and de Tracy saw ideology as advancing the course of human knowledge, Marx condemned it as the source of false consciousness about social and economic reality. For Marx, ideology was more than misguided fairy tales about society; it was the tool that the dominant economic class, the capitalists, used to control social, political, economic, and educational institutions. To maintain their control, the capitalists indoctrinated the subordinate working classes into accepting **false ideology** as a true picture of reality.

False Consciousness: Marx's description of ideology as a misleading form of consciousness contrived to block true consciousness.

The chapter on Marxism and Education provides an extended discussion of Marx's ideas; here we consider his ideas on Ideology.

Refer to the chapter on Idealism and Education for German Idealism.

This capitalist strategy claimed that ideas about religion, politics, society, law, and education existed in their own spheres independent of the material base of society, the means of economic production and control. Marx and Engels, in contrast, argued that the classes who controlled the economy also controlled society and social institutions. The true consciousness recognized the power of economic control. Schools, controlled by the dominant classes, were key agencies that indoctrinated the children of oppressed classes in the ideology that justified and sustained upper-class

False Ideology: a Marxist term that argues that the capitalists, the dominant class that controls the superstructure of society, manipulate subordinate classes into believing that cultural illusions are real.

domination. For instance, teachers were to indoctrinate students to accept the beliefs and values that sustained the status quo.

Despite Marx's critique, the nineteenth and twentieth centuries saw a proliferation of ideologies. Marx, the genius of what would be termed Scientific Socialism, hurled his theoretical invective against all of these ideologies and denounced them as theoretical smoke screens designed to cloud the vision of the exploited working class. According to Marx, the various ideologies, such as Liberalism, Conservatism, and even Communitarian Socialism, each generated its own version of false consciousness to delude the working classes and preserve the power of the exploiting classes. This brief examination of Marx's analysis of ideology is useful in explaining how *ideology* came to take on a negative connotation. In terms of historical development, the Marxist conception of history and the good society became another ideology that competed for people's hearts and minds. Marx's critics used his arguments against his position, claiming that Marxism was but another ideology, one of many competing for believing adherents.

The Marxist critique did not kill the concept of ideology, but rather made it a field of greater study. Because ideologies circulated and contended with each other, they had important consequences in political, social, economic, and educational life. Historians, philosophers, economists, and sociologists made them an area of academic study.

Karl Mannheim

Karl Mannheim (1893–1947), a pioneering sociologist, analyzed how ideologies gained credence and functioned in society. As a sociologist, Mannheim looked to society for the origins and workings of ideology. He found that ideology, as a social and political process, was relevant to how people identified themselves as group members.[5] Discounting Marx's view that society was an arena of two conflicting classes—the capitalists and the working class, Mannheim argued that society was much more complicated in that it comprised many groups and subgroups, each of which had its own ideology. Mannheim's grounding of ideology in society raises important questions for education. Is there a general ideology that shapes educational ideas, policies, and practices in a particular society? Is there a general ideology about the role and functions of public education in the United States? What are the subgroups in a society, what are their ideologies, and how do these ideologies influence that group's ideas about education? Is subgroup ideology in congruence with or in conflict with the general ideology and other subgroup ideologies? Do Euro-, Hispanic, and African Americans have common or different ideological views of education, its purposes, and its functions?

Mannheim observed how a group's beliefs about itself are embodied in its histories, myths, and stories, as well as how its ceremonies, rituals, and observances filter into an ideology. For example, think about the American holiday of Thanksgiving and how its observance carries with it a mytho-history about the relationships of the English settlers and the Native Americans, about how the Puritan religious beliefs were conveyed as an act of thanks given to God, and how the historical event has been replicated and ritualized around the American dinner table on a designated Thursday in late November. This kind of observance affects the person at both the social and the psychological levels. There is a socially approved norm for celebrating the event as well as a psychological good feeling about being with family and friends at this celebration.

Mannheim raised the issue of how an ideology relates to social stasis or maintenance and to social change. The power holders in a society construct an ideology to justify and rationalize (to conserve) the social, economic, political, and educational institutions that support their position. Depending on the degree of their alienation from the dominant ideology, other groups may develop a counterideology that seeks to change or modify institutional arrangements or to overthrow them. All groups—ranging from conservatives seeking to preserve the status quo, liberals seeking to modify it, or revolutionaries seeking to overthrow it—see their ideology as providing the way to the good life within the good society. Mannheim applied the term **utopian** to ideologies that seek to create a society based on their vision of how things should be.[6]

Utopian: ideologies that seek to create a society based on their vision of how things should be in the future.

Mannheim drew inferences from his analysis of ideology to the role of the intelligentsia, the intellectuals and artists, in a society. For him, the intelligentsia as a group is able to interpret the world to the members of their society. As a society, such as that of the United States, became more mobile and better educated, the intelligentsia came from broader and more varied social and economic backgrounds.[7] Because of their education, they were able to become more independent of their class origins and were able to present a fairer and more unbiased interpretation of social realities.

We can apply Mannheim's concept of the intelligentsia to educators, professors, and teachers. Teachers in the United States come from a broad range of racial, ethnic, socio-economic, and cultural backgrounds. Because their work is not directly related to the agencies of production and consumption of goods or dependent on being elected to political office, teachers can have a fairer and more unbiased interpretation of social institutions and processes. They can interpret society for their students.

Antonio Gramsci

Antonio Gramsci (1891–1937), an Italian Marxist and anti-Fascist, analyzed ideology from a neo-Marxist perspective. Redefining Marx's original definition of ideology as an illusory false consciousness, Gramsci enlarged the scope and meaning of the term from economics and politics to the larger culture, including the media, art, and education. He developed the concept of **hegemony**—the control of and domination of one group by another—that is so important in contemporary Neo-Marxism, Postmodernism, and Critical Theory.

Hegemony: Gramsci's concept of the social control of and domination of one group by another.

Gramsci saw ideology as signifying a large and complex network of ideas that are cultural as well as economic and political. Ideology shapes group ideas about religion, politics and law, and culture. Ideological influences come from the family and media as informal educators and particularly from formal educational institutions such as schools, colleges, and universities. It includes the broad network of cultural, ethical, and moral beliefs and expressions that are disseminated through the mass media, educational institutions, and social media. Gramsci revised and broadened Marx's concept of how the bourgeoisie, the middle classes, dominated society. According to Marx, because of their control of the economic base, the bourgeoisie also controlled the state and its military, police, and legal apparatus, using them to enforce its rule and domination of the working class. Gramsci broadened the concept of hegemony to mean the social control of the culture and how culture was expressed. He argued that the culture was consciously manipulated by the dominant class to create a pervasive and permeating climate of opinion in which the oppressed classes, deceived into thinking they were free, actually were diverted from and remained unconscious of their oppressive situation.[8]

For their views of hegemony or social control, see the chapters on Postmodernism, Marxism, and Critical Theory.

Gramsci's concept of hegemony applies to educational institutions and processes. The bourgeoisie-controlled school determines what should be included in the curriculum and designates it as official knowledge; it then establishes mandates and sets standards for instructing (indoctrinating) students in the approved ideology. This domination of institutions led to schools being used to reproduce the knowledge and values of the dominant group while controlling the subordinate group.

Paulo Freire

Paulo Freire (1921–1997), a Brazilian educator, developed Liberation Pedagogy while working to educate Brazil's impoverished, illiterate peasants and urban poor. As an educator, Freire did not skirt the edges of ideology but went right to its core. He argued that education, schooling, teaching, and learning are never objective or neutral but always involve ideological commitment and imposition.

Freire's interpretation of ideology was influenced by Marxism, Existentialism, and Liberation Theology. Although Freire used Marx's argument that economic conditions shape human relationships, he did not believe that human reactions to these conditions are determined.[9] He rejected Marx's determinism that our future, like our past, is caused by historical inevitability. Like the Existentialists, he rejects the view that the human being is predefined at birth as to status and condition. Drawing on Existentialism, he sees the person as an incomplete and unfinished presence in the world. Freire's literacy campaigns were supported by Roman Catholic social action groups that worked among the poor. Part of his thinking was shaped by Liberation Theology, a belief popular in Central and South America that Christians should be socially and politically active in working to change conditions of oppression.[10]

Freire sees ideology as highly contextual in that the cultural, social, political, economic, and educational conditions are historically derived and are the ongoing reality in which people find themselves. As people develop a true consciousness of their social reality, they can interpret their situation and understand the personal and social conditions that either repress or liberate them.

Freire clearly distinguishes Liberation Pedagogy, as a radicalizing ideology, from other ideologies that distort history and rely on myths to create a sense of false consciousness in the oppressed. Freire, who constructed his ideas in the Latin American context, faced the opposition and repression of right-wing reactionary ideologies that were supported by vested oligarchic economic elites and militarist regimes. He was imprisoned and then exiled by the military regime in Brazil. He criticizes Conservatism as an ideology that fears change and tries to "slow down the historical process" by constructing a protective official history that seeks to legitimize the ruling elite's privileged position in the name of traditional values.

Conservatism is discussed in the chapter on Conservatism and Education.

Freire finds Liberalism to be a particularly insidious ideology. Although Liberalism, especially the Neo-Liberal variant associated with economic globalization, promises eventual equality of opportunity and socio-economic mobility, it establishes institutions and procedures that create new elites, usually bureaucratic and corporate ones.

Liberalism is discussed in the chapter on Liberalism and Education.

Although they portray themselves as working to improve the condition of minorities and the lower socio-economic classes, Liberals use institutions, including schools, to maintain and reproduce their privileged status. Avoiding transformative reform to change the exploitative economic conditions from which they profit, Liberals offer the poor transactional piecemeal reforms that create the illusion of change, but that, in reality, maintain their own privileged social and economic status. Even the Liberal notion of welfare and assistance, benignly intended to aid the poor, creates a dependency that locks the dependents into the system rather than liberating them from it.[11]

Even though he advocates a radical transformation of society, Freire rejects what he calls doctrinaire left-wing sectarian ideologies. Leftist sectarian ideology justifies its actions, even if violent, in the belief that its desired end justifies the means to reach it. True to his Existentialist learning, Freire is highly suspicious of radicals who base their actions on inevitably establishing a predetermined perfect state of society, a utopia. For the leftist sectarian, the future is "inexorably pre-ordained" rather than existentially indeterminate and arising from immediate contexts, as Freire argues.[12]

To think critically means to be empowered to penetrate the ideological mists of false consciousness—the myths, theories, and rationales that others, especially the oppressors, have constructed to confuse and indoctrinate dominated groups. These rationales, derived from the oppressor's ideology, are designed to indoctrinate the oppressed to accept uncritically the oppressive conditions in the social environment as being "right," "just," "the standard," or "in the nature of things." Thinking critically requires the ability to see these rationales for what they are—the constructions of an oppressive group. For Freire, educational institutions and processes are never free of the conditions and situations—the contexts—of which they are a part. They are never ideologically neutral or scientifically objective. All educational systems, like all social, political, and economic systems, are ideologically conditioned. Education either convinces the younger generation to accept and conform to the power relationships of the existing system or it becomes a pedagogy of liberation. Education, committed to liberation, implies raising people's consciousness, encouraging them to reflect critically on social reality, and empowering them to transform the conditions and the contexts that shape their lives. Freire's contextualism is similar to that found in Postmodernism, which asserts that all societies exhibit relationships of power that empower some and subjugate others. Freire, like the Postmodernists, is most concerned with the marginalized people of the earth.

Postmodernism is discussed in the chapter on Postmodernism and Education.

A STIPULATED DEFINITION OF IDEOLOGY

As you can see from the preceding discussion, ideology has had a long and somewhat tortuous history. It has had a variety of definitions, meanings, and uses since it was coined by the French *philosophes* who were trying to create a science of ideas. Because its definition is contested, I am stipulating a definition of ideology that we can use in the rest of the chapter. Ideology is defined here as a set of related ideas held by a group that explains its past, examines its present, and gives direction to its future. Based on this definition, we can consider the following ideological elements: (1) an ideology provides an orientation for a group in time and space by interpreting its history; (2) the ideology then explains the group's present social, economic, political, and educational circumstances; (3) the examination of the past contributes to a conception of social change; that is, it attempts to predict what can be expected to happen in the future based on the interpretation of patterns that occurred in the past; and (4) the ideology is policy generating in that it presents a blueprint for the future that indicates to the group which policies are needed to attain certain desired ends or goals; in this way, an ideology becomes programmatic or action oriented. To attain the group's goals, the ideologue recommends political or educational action.

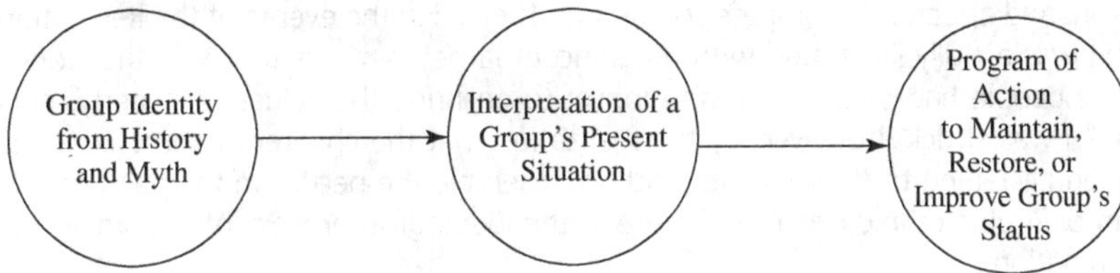

Ideological Clusters of Ideas

Ideology As an Interpretation of the Past

First of all, an ideology constructs a perspective on a group's past. The group may be the citizens of a nation, such as the German or the Russian people; the group may be a racial or ethnic subgroup such as Euro-, African, Native, Hispanic, or Arab Americans in the United States. The group may refer to the members of a socio-economic class such as the upper, middle, or lower classes. The group may consist of members of a profession such as teachers, clergy, librarians, or physicians. Its membership may be based on a special interest such as the Sierra Society, the National Rifle Association, or the American Association of Retired Persons. The ideologue examines the group's past to develop a historical interpretation that provides the group with a perspective in time and place and a sense of identification, solidarity, and meaning.

This historical perspective provides the group with a way of arranging historical time in its contexts (its spaces or places). This perspective is selective in that it arranges persons and events into an understandable (often simplified) and metaphorical or allegorical story, as it merges fact with fiction, especially **myth**. This rendition of the past is presented in narratives and stories that easily engage listeners or readers.

Myth: a legendary story, often concerned with actual, but embellished or imagined significant events in a group's past.

The way a group interprets its history serves to construct its collective memory. Group memory, like personal memory, provides a perspective that answers questions such as: Who are we? How did we get to this place and time? Where do we want to go? The historical narrative, the story, in a group's memory provides identity and location in time and place. The mental snapshots stored in the mind, like a family photo album, connect individuals to the group. An individual's autobiography becomes linked to the group's history. These historical snapshots, images of our past, always tell only part of the story because they emphasize some aspects of the past while minimizing other aspects. The snapshot is about us and is a selected image that sets us apart. For example, the image of George Washington and his troops at Valley Forge and the video that shows the collapse of the twin towers of the World Trade Center in New York on September 11, 2001, are part of the collective memory of Americans; and the images of police in Selma, Alabama, using dogs and tear gas against civil rights marchers, along with the voice of Martin Luther King, Jr., giving his "I have a dream" speech in Washington, D.C., form the collective memory of African Americans. These are dramatic events; collective memories are also constructed through many

My Reflections on Philosophy of Education: Encountering an Ideologically Oriented School Trip

While recently visiting the City Museum in Paris, I was struck by the power of narrative in forming group identity, especially in constructing a collective national identity. I encountered a teacher leading a school field trip through the exhibits on the French Revolution. The teacher—white, well spoken, and apparently competent—was well versed in the events of the Revolution. Further, the exhibit was artfully illustrated with magnificent large paintings that told the story, especially of how the people had overthrown absolutism to enshrine the values of "liberty, equality, and fraternity." I was struck, however, by the realization that the children, engrossed in viewing the paintings and listening to their teacher, did not resemble the people in the paintings. Most were of African or Arabic ethnic origin and were in the ideological process of becoming members of the French nation.

As the teacher led her students though the exhibit, she stopped before each painting, describing the scene and explaining its meanings. As they saw the storming of the Bastille, with the red, white, and blue tri-color flag standing over barricades, and viewed the portraits of the leaders of the republican revolution, the children were involved in a mixture of myth and history designed to make them into French citizens.

smaller but more personal events such as ethnic celebrations, photograph albums of families, and so on. The interpretation of the past helps to assess the present situation that, in turn, suggests ways to shape the future we want.[13]

Just as our personal memories may not always be a true version of our past, the ideological interpretation of the past may or may not be historically accurate. The ideologist often uses the past to justify a policy or program in the present. The desire for historical justification leads to "presentism," the use of history as an explanation or rationale for action in the present. Past events may be shaped to fit a preconceived thesis that justifies a present or future program. For example, consider how the American Founding Fathers, the framers of the U.S. Constitution such as Washington, Adams, Hamilton, and Madison, are used to support a particular political policy or agenda. The same "Founders" are used by those who hold opposing viewpoints on issues such as separation of church and state, federal aid for education, and immigration policy.

HISTORICALLY GENERATED BELIEFS AND VALUES. In constructing a perspective on a group's past, ideology is descriptive: It sets forth and disseminates a statement of beliefs that describe and interpret social, political, economic, cultural, and educational situations. The descriptions, which tell the story of how things came to be, argue that the processes that made them such can and should be maintained or changed. What should be done to maintain or change the context—the conditions with which the group lives? The question of social continuity or change raises "should" or "ought" value issues. Thus, ideological descriptions and interpretations of the past also generate moral and ethical issues about human action, reaction, or inaction. For example, the concern for social justice issues relates to ideological descriptions of a just or unjust society and how schools and teachers should react to these issues. Philosophies raise similar but much more general issues about social justice; ideologies attempt to deal with these issues in a more specific way politically and socially in the contexts in which they arise.

The merging or the blurring of descriptions (explanations of reality), prescriptions (appropriate behavior), and proscriptions (inappropriate behavior) pervades a society's culture, especially its symbols. The symbols are cultural representations of both cultural reality and values. Note how the American flag is a symbol of the United States. When schoolchildren pledge allegiance to the flag, they are affirming loyalty to the republic for which the flag stands; it symbolizes the nation and its republican political processes. It also symbolizes commitment to the nation's values, "liberty and justice for all." Also, consider the symbolic meaning of a yellow ribbon to show support for troops, the red cross for aid during disasters, and so on.

THE PRESENT SITUATION AND IDEOLOGICAL INTERPRETATION. Once the ideologist has used the past to create a sense of group solidarity and identity, then it is possible to assess the group's contemporary social, political, economic, and educational situation. For example, the liberal middle-class value orientation that emphasizes individualism, competition, property rights, and representative government can be explained and justified in terms of the middle class's struggle against oppressive aristocratic and monarchical governments that repressed these values.

Another example of using the past to explain a present situation can be seen in the conceptions that certain "oppressed people" have developed. For example, the Basques of Spain reckon themselves to be a people who once had a great and noble history. Historic events have caused this once great culture to be submerged by the Hispanic culture that surrounds it. Thus, part of the movement for Basque freedom, or autonomy, derives from their view of the past. The historically or mythically derived idea that a particular racial or ethnic group has been repressed in the past and is now

Ethnonationalism is discussed in the chapter on Nationalism, American Exceptionalism, Ethnonationalism, and Education.

seeking to secure its lost freedom is an important driving force in the contemporary reassertion of ethnonationalism. An important part of the ideology of ethnonationalism is that the sense of a "lost greatness or grandeur" be nurtured and kept alive in the young until the moment comes for liberation from the oppressors.

In this linking of the past with the present, educational processes became significantly important. Informal sources of education, such as the media and social networking, become the means for forging the links between what was, what is, and what ought to be. Institutionalized education in the schools functions to create a sense of group identification in the minds of the children, the immature members of the group, that connects them to the past. In such a linkage, myths, stories, and heroic portrayals are particularly useful. In India, for example, the story of Gandhi's struggle for Indian independence provides a figure of heroic dimension that in a dramatic way links the young Indian with both his or her past and present. Additionally, the figure of Martin Luther King, Jr., becomes a heroic figure who exemplifies values that are worthy of imitation by the young African American. In a more advanced school situation, at either the upper grades of the elementary school or in secondary education, the selection of both historical and literary works cultivates a means of linking the individual with the past in such a way that the present situation acquires an added significance that is meaningful to group identity.

SOCIAL CHANGE AND IDEOLOGY

Ideology represents an interpretation of history and social change. History is interpreted contextually; change, too, is viewed in terms of the need to preserve and maintain or to reconstruct or even to destroy existing institutions. The idea of social change itself is screened and interpreted through the lenses of the competing ideologies. For example, think about the following qualifiers that are used with change: *gradual*, *orderly*, *radical*, *transformative*, *transactional*, *utopian*, *revolutionary*, or *planned*. *Gradual* and *orderly*, for a Conservative, are likely to mean slow, natural, or unhurried. *Radical*, *transformative*, and *revolutionary* is likely to be seen as socially dangerous for a Conservative but socially desirable for a Critical Theorist. *Transactional*, in the sense of being limited, negotiated, and defined is likely to be socially, politically, and educationally desirable for Liberals. The word *utopian* can be highly charged. It can mean a vision of the future for some, whereas Conservatives, Liberals, and Marxists tend to view it with suspicion. For Conservatives, it conjures up a dangerously idealized future used to justify any means to reach an end; for Liberals, it may mean ignoring existing contexts and step-by-step methods; and for Marxists, it can mean ignoring the necessity of class conflict and struggle.

For the Conservative view of change, see the chapter on Conservatism and Education.

How an ideology interprets the meaning of change is a key to how it seeks to socialize the young. The general Conservative suspicion of change encourages seeing existing social institutions as being grounded in some higher source that stands outside of but guides the legitimate principles operating in the context. The assertion that the United States is founded on Christian principles or that the U.S. Constitution should be strictly construed using the original meaning that the founders of the republic gave to it are examples of historically ordained contexts. These principles are to be enshrined in the minds of the young so that they will maintain these governing and guiding principles.

For the Liberal emphasis on process, see the chapter on Liberalism and Education.

In contrast, the Liberal approach to socializing the young is to build familiarity with and to practice democratic methods to use discussion and clarification in regard to issues and even values. Rather than being perceived as immutable givens, values are subject to clarification, discussion, and revision. The revisions are to follow procedures that operate within prescribed channels and don't spill out of them to create "dangerous" situations. The *modus operandi* is that of constant reconsideration and revision.

Ideologists are rarely content to have their interpretation of the past and assessment of the contemporary situation remain at the level of academic discussion. The conception of the past and the assessment of the present often imply a desire to fashion values and to shape behavior. In other words, ideologies possess elements that are both descriptive and prescriptive. The descriptive phase of an ideology arises from the explanation of the past and the examination of the present. The view of the past, especially when portrayed by heroic models, is used to reinforce the concept of what constitutes proper behavior in the present. Such behavior is also designed to guide future action. Depending on the particular ideology, the prescriptive element may be a set of simple behaviors that characterize the good member of the group. Or it may become an elaborate social, political, and educational code. A particular approved behavior in ideological terms can be illustrated by a brief examination of Classical Liberal attitudes. The child who is being raised in the milieu of Classical Liberalism learns that he or she is an individual who has certain rights and certain responsibilities. For example, he or she learns that it is important and desirable to compete against peers and to win. Competition and winning are defined in personal and individual terms. If there are winners, then there are also losers. Winning the spelling bee, the track meet, the essay contest, or the musical competition requires that effort be expended to discipline oneself and to acquire the skills needed to win. It is important to be a winner.

For a discussion of Classical Liberalism, see the chapter on Liberalism and Education.

Further, the value of competition is presented as being socially useful as well as personally fulfilling. Competition leads to discovery, invention, and human progress. In fact, the liberal tradition of progress by means of individual effort is a linking device that connects past, present, and future. It becomes a linear theory of social change. The progress of humanity depends on individual initiative within a social, political, economic, and educational milieu that emphasizes competition.

For a discussion of Marx's revolutionary change, see the chapter on Marx and Education.

The Marxist historical interpretation and assessment of the present offers a very different theory of social change from Classical Liberalism. For Marx, the economic class rather than the individual is important. Personal values are determined by one's relationship to the means and modes of production. In a pre-revolutionary situation, members of the working class need to identify with their class and to struggle for its liberation. In a post-revolutionary situation, members of the society are to work to realize Marxist goals by cooperating for the good of the state. Beyond this, Marx developed a theory of social change based on history's dialectical pattern. Throughout history, Marx argued, economic classes struggled to control the means and modes of production. In the course of historical evolution, the proletariat will come to control both the economic base of society and the political, social, and educational superstructure that has been erected on it. Marx and his followers preached that the proletariat's coming victory was historically destined and irreversible.

Ideology as Policy Generating and Programmatic

Although ideologues may use academic devices, they rarely expend their energies in the pursuit of knowledge solely because of its intrinsic value. Ideologies, embracing theories of social change, become instruments for achieving a desired social goal or even a new social order. The programmatic element in ideology stems from the prescription that arises regarding the contours of the desired social order.

Ideologies are prescriptive in that they make social, political, economic, and educational assessments or judgments. These assessments, identifying what is good or bad, lead to prescriptive policies. If the assessment is favorable to the status quo, then the ideological policy is conservative in that it seeks to preserve it. If unfavorable, then it seeks to bring about change in ways that may range from the evolutionary to the revolutionary. Indeed, ideologies are action oriented or programmatic.

Ideologies are aimed at the public political and educational arena and, in seeking to garner public support for a program, are in conflict with each other. They encompass large (macro) principles and also smaller, more specific (micro) ones. A key challenge for maintaining ideological coherence is to avoid letting specific aims splinter the ideology. For example, consider the related issues of immigration and illegal aliens in the United States. American Conservatives want to maintain a traditional cultural core that includes English as the official language and to secure U.S. borders to prevent illegal aliens from entering the country. Consequently, some Conservatives favor enforcing greater security at the border, especially with Mexico, constructing a massive fence at the border, ending medical and educational services for illegal aliens, and deporting illegal aliens from the country. However, some businesspeople, who argue that free enterprise and competition are key Conservative principles, rely on immigrants as a source of plentiful and inexpensive labor. The issue for Conservatives is how to relate their general principles on American culture and economics with the specific issue of immigration.

The Ideological Continuum and Educational Policy

The concept of the ideological continuum illustrates how ideology impacts education. Ideology operates as a continuum that encompasses the following: (1) the origins of the belief system based on a view of the past that may be mythic or historical or a combination of both; (2) an instrumental interpretation of the past intended to make certain aspects of it operational in the present (this attempt to operationalize an ideology results in policy formulation—the design of a plan to bring about some action in the present that will shape the future); and (3) action, based on the policy guidelines, that will bring about the desired results.

The ideological continuum contains both descriptive and prescriptive elements. For example, we might consider the formulation of educational policy in the United States to illustrate the functioning of the ideological continuum.

A vital and continuing policy issue is how schools are and should be funded. Funding education is always an important political issue in states across the nation as legislatures debate various funding formulas. Boards of education and school administrators frequently engage in campaigns to convince voters to increase taxes for schools. Internal arguments occur among board members over establishing budgets and setting spending priorities for educational programs. The inequality in school funding is well known and extensively documented. For example, in *Savage Inequalities*, which described inequalities in America's public schools, Jonathan Kozol found wide disparities between facilities and programs in the poorest inner-city communities and schools in the wealthier suburban communities. Kozol examines how the unequal funding of schools relates to social class divisions, racism and classism, isolation and alienation of students and staff within poorer schools, the physical decay of buildings, and the health of students. Funding based on local property taxes means that more affluent school districts, usually suburban ones, can generate more revenue for schools than urban and rural ones are able to. Groups in lower economic levels such as African and Latino Americans tend to live in the inner areas of large cities that generate lower revenues for schools because of declining property values. This unequal funding leads to inferior schools and creates a wide disparity between schools in the poorest and wealthiest communities. Isolation of students, staff, and the community is a direct result of the inequities in funding.[14]

The education issues of how to spend funds and who should pay the bill is obviously a practical fiscal problem. However, behind the problem is ideology. The longstanding traditional pattern is to pay for education through a combination of state aid and revenue generated by property taxes in the local school districts. This pattern has minimal federal support, usually around six percent of the total. The ideology supporting the traditional pattern is that of local and state rather than federal responsibility. It draws from Conservatism as well as from Liberalism, but to a more limited extent. To maintain local control and avoid federal intervention, defenders of the traditional pattern are willing to accept disparities in funding. A result is the unequal funding of schools that Kozol decries. Further, the unequal funding works to favor economically advantaged groups and classes. Neo-Marxists and Critical Theorists see inequalities in funding as a deliberate effort by advantaged groups to maintain their privileged status. The tax on property to support schools, however, can be seen from a Liberal perspective as a way to provide some equity in funding without radically tampering with the economic system.

Because revenues generated by the property tax vary considerably from district to district, some analysts have proposed using more revenues from income taxes or from sales taxes. If the income tax were graduated, those in higher brackets would pay more and would be supporting the education of lower income groups. This kind of tax is progressive and so would likely garner support from Liberals, especially when combined with the property tax. It is the kind of policy that Liberals could be expected to endorse. However, a sales tax would be regressive, placing the same burden on all income brackets. Although it is an equal kind of taxation, a sales tax is not equitable in terms of social justice.

Finally, there are those who argue that education should be privately controlled and paid for by those who use the schools and not by the general public. The ideological issue here is whether education is a public or a private good.

National Reports

A Nation at Risk, Action for Excellence, and many national reports on education were based on an interpretation of the U.S. educational present.[15] This perspective expressed such beliefs as: (1) U.S. preeminence as a leading technological, economic, and military power had been established, at least in part, by the nation's educational system; (2) other nations are threatening to overtake the United States and surpass it as a preeminent technological and economic power; and (3) the U.S. educational system, especially the public schools, are in crisis because of poorly defined goals; a soft, nonacademic curriculum; declining scholastic standards; permissiveness; inadequately prepared teachers; and myriad other causes of educational malaise. Although some educators, including philosophers of education, questioned the accuracy of the analysis, it nevertheless was accepted as accurate by large segments of the public, media commentators, and policymakers in Congress, and state governors, legislators, and many local school boards.

The interpretation that came from the analysis of the condition of U.S. education led to a generalized policy that stated: U.S. education was in a state of crisis that could be resolved by strengthening the academic components of schools by setting standards, especially in reading, mathematics, and science, and by restoring discipline to the schools. Various states and local boards developed specific policies to resolve the crisis. Among them were the following proposals: increase the length of the school day and school year; require competency examinations to guarantee that students master basic skills; establish teacher competency examinations to ensure that teachers possess adequate skills and knowledge; and reduce expenditures for nonacademic aspects of schooling.

The policy proposals were designated as educational reforms by their proponents, who anticipated improvement in mathematics and science teaching and competencies in particular, along with higher standards of achievement in other academic subjects. Some proponents of "reform" believed that the restoration of discipline would lead to a decrease in juvenile delinquency and drug abuse, as well as an affirmation of political and moral values. Ultimately, the proponents of reform believed that schooling, conceived of as the rigorous study of academic subjects, would substantially aid the efforts of the United States to regain its economic and military preeminence as a world power.

STANDARDS MOVEMENT. The criticisms voiced in *A Nation at Risk* further stimulated the standards movement, which endorsed a policy to improve American education by creating high standards, or benchmarks, that can be used to assess students' academic achievement through standardized tests. The standards movement affected schools throughout the United States as states enacted legislation requiring standardized testing to measure student academic achievement and teacher competency. Further, it had a ripple effect as it stimulated professional "learned" organizations such as the American Historical Association to work to establish standards in their disciplines that could guide how subjects were taught in the school curriculum.

The standards movement led to significant policy developments at the federal level, when the Elementary and Secondary Education Act of 2001, the No Child Left Behind Act (NCLB) endorsed by President George W. Bush, passed Congress. The Act assumes that there are necessary basic skills, such as reading and mathematics, and that students' academic achievement in these skills can be assessed objectively by standardized tests. Further, the Act implies that students' scores on standardized tests indicate how well schools and teachers are doing to meet stated outcomes. To qualify for federal aid under the terms of NCLB, states must establish annual assessments in reading and mathematics for every student in grades 3 through 8. Proponents of NCLB contend that these test results will identify schools in which large numbers of students fail to achieve to the standard.[16] The law holds school districts accountable for improving the performance of disadvantaged students as well as the overall student population. Schools and districts failing to make adequate yearly progress are to be identified and helped. If the schools fail to meet standards for three years, their students may then transfer to a higher performing public or private school.[17]

My purpose in commenting on the national reports and the standards movement is neither to debate the validity of their analyses of American education nor to assess their results. Rather, this discussion is intended to illustrate how ideology shapes educational policies and classroom practices.

THE USE OF IDEOLOGY TO CREATE CONSENSUS

Ideology, which gives identity to a group, is used to create a sense of shared ideas, goals, and commitments. It functions to form group identity and to sustain group cohesion by generating a "we-feeling," or sense of group solidarity. Assumptions about the world and the society that are embraced by the particular ideology are publicly expressed and used to develop togetherness, solidarity, and agreement among group members.

Consensus: a feeling of shared goals, aspirations, and commitments generated by group identification and solidarity.

As a molder of **consensus**, ideology functions in the society as a whole and also in its informal and formal educational agencies. Informal educational agencies, especially the media, express and reinforce ideological commitments. Formal agencies, such as schools, likewise build a sense of group identification, or a "we-feeling," in the young through the school milieu—the hidden curriculum—and through certain components of the formal or explicit curriculum, such as literature and history. All school systems work to cultivate a sense of national identity and loyalty in the young; they also function to cultivate a sense of social consensus, an adherence to the group's dominant values.

The origins of the public, or common, school system in the United States provide a clear example of how education was used to construct consensus. Horace Mann, Henry Barnard, Catharine Beecher, and other proponents of common schools viewed them as agencies to construct a common American society marked by widespread consensus, or agreement on the political processes that should govern the United States and the ethical values that should govern individuals' public and personal behavior. They wanted to create a system of state-funded and controlled public schools that could be used to mold a society in which ideologically homogeneous citizens shared a commitment to common beliefs and values.[18] They saw public schools, especially their administrators and teachers, as public agents to transmit an official version of American culture.[19]

Once constructed and maintained by dedicated educators, the official consensus was to absorb and Americanize immigrants, reduce class conflicts, and develop a national community, a society united by shared interests, commitments, and values. They especially worked to use the public consensus to guard against counterideologies that might fragment American social, cultural, and political unity. Even as the overarching consensus could be peripherally revised to incorporate new groups, such as European immigrants and African Americans freed from slavery, the consensus would retain its core features.

Ideology and Outlook

As part of the process of forming social consensus, ideology shapes a person's outlook on self and society. The use of *outlook* is deliberately imprecise. It refers to the way in which we intellectually organize or "put together" our ideas about social, political, economic, and educational concepts, events, and trends. It creates a view of the world in which we live and seeks to answer the following questions: Who am I? What are my origins? What is the role of society and my place in the social order? What are the requirements and responsibilities of citizenship? How should I function in the economic system? Outlook, broadly defined, is shaped by formal and informal educational agencies. A major part of the schooling process is devoted to shaping a person's social, political, and economic perspective and to developing skills and knowledge for functioning in the society, the economy, and the political process.

Shaped by ideology, a person's outlook not only affects external relationships with social, political, economic, and educational systems, but it also shapes a person's interior sense of being or self-identity and esteem. How an individual ultimately relates to these systems determines the attitude he or she takes about identity, roles, functions, aspirations, and destiny. Ideology, through both the hidden curriculum of the educational milieu and the formal curricular components of schooling, serves to organize the various roles and functions of persons both in school and in future social, political, and economic (employment) situations. In its origins, an ideology is contextual, that is, formulated by a group in a society. Many adherents of an ideology are content to keep it in the place and among the people who originated it or to see it as so contextual that it is special to them and cannot and should not be exported elsewhere. This was the case with American isolationists who wanted no involvement with people or situations elsewhere in the world. However, there is a tendency for advocates of an ideology to see it moving from the contexts of origin to a broader field of operations. Ideologies that strive to be transcontextual develop a *Weltanschauung*, an all-encompassing outlook that interprets the world for its adherents. For example, the Marxist ideology has a set of explanations and procedures for socio-economic and political change that they believe are universally operative.

It has been argued that American democratic institutions and processes can be exported to and implemented in other countries such as Iraq and Afghanistan, for example. This policy stance represents a belief that American political institutions are universally applicable.

IDEOLOGY'S PERMEABILITY AND FLEXIBILITY

Ideologies contain patterns of related and interconnected combinations and clusters of cultural concepts. A key to understanding an ideology lies in recognizing how the concepts are arranged and determining which are at its core and which are adjacent. Core concepts need to be stable, whereas adjacent ones can be revised and adjusted. In both Liberal and Progressive educational thinking, respect for the child's individual needs, interests, and differences is a core concept. At the same time, Liberals and Progressives are concerned about children's socialization, their ability to work democratically and collaboratively in groups. The issue for teachers in these perspectives is to develop strategies that maintain the core concept—children's individuality—with related concepts of working in groups. If the group becomes paramount rather than related, it can coerce the individual as in authoritarian situations.

For the Liberal and Progressive views of individual differences and group socialization, see the chapters on Liberalism and Progressivism.

Ideologies are permeable; that is, they can absorb concepts from other ideologies, from philosophies, and from religions and use them to reconstruct their conceptual pattern. This **permeability** is a feature of an ideology's functional flexibility. An illustration is provided by American Conservatism. A core feature of Conservatism is the authority given to tradition as a source of group wisdom and guidance. Conservatives often assert the need to maintain traditional family values. In its contemporary format, American Conservatism has absorbed concepts from Classical Liberalism, especially the emphasis on individualism and private property. Conformity to traditional values remains at the Conservative core but individualism has found its own place there. Critics of Conservative ideology, especially Liberals, contend that conformity to what is defined as traditional values can seriously limit individual freedom and expression. American Conservatism has also absorbed religious beliefs from Evangelical Protestants about what constitutes appropriate family values. What emerges from the relationship of Conservatism with Evangelical Protestantism is a definition of marriage as monogamous, between a man (the husband) and a woman (the wife) who are legally married; and the family as the husband and wife and their children, living in a unit. The concept of family values, so defined, becomes religiously sanctified and culturally justified.

Permeability: an ideology's ability to absorb concepts from other ideologies, philosophies, and theories and to rearrange them in terms of its core and peripheral beliefs and values.

In building consensus and commitment, ideologies vary in their functional flexibility. The efficacy of an ideology in building consensus ranges between those ideologies that encourage or tolerate pluralism and those that are monolithic. Throughout U.S. history, there has been continuous debate about how new immigrant groups were to function in society. Antagonists in the debate were divided between those who argued for Americanization of immigrants and those who argued for cultural pluralism.

According to the ideological orientation of the "Americanists," the American past was largely the history of the contributions and achievements of white, English Protestants. The development of institutions of representative government, judicial practices based on the common law, and the nation's rise to an industrial world power were interpreted as achievements of the dominant English-speaking Protestants of the older stock of Americans. The study of history and social studies reinforced the ethos of the dominant group by portraying historic heroic models from the dominant group.

Anticipated results of the Americanization policy were to enculturate immigrants—the great majority of whom were neither English nor Protestant after 1880—into a monolithic national character. For Americanists, this policy would preserve the national character and institutions. Educational policy conceived according to such a monolithic ideological interpretation shaped both the school's milieu—the hidden curriculum—and the formal or explicit curriculum. The school's milieu—namely, the rules, regulations, etiquette, and student-teacher relationships—emphasized values associated with the Protestant ethic: punctuality, orderliness, frugality, industriousness, and respect for private property. These values were also congenial to training a disciplined workforce for an emerging industrial society.

The educational policy of the Americanization ideology used certain components of the formal curriculum to create a monolithic society. The language of instruction, reading, and literature was English. Non-English-speaking children were to learn English and abandon their own languages to become like the dominant group.

In contrast to a monolithic conception of the American character, those who subscribed to the ideology of cultural pluralism saw the American past in a broader and more varied perspective. Many groups and peoples contributed to the still-emerging and evolving American character—Native Americans, African Americans, Hispanics, Asians, and Europeans from both southern and eastern Europe as well as the British Isles and northern Europe. Such a culturally pluralistic interpretation of the American past was multilingual, multisocial, and multiethnic. The consensus-generating power of cultural pluralism, though less specific than the Americanist version, possessed a vitality that had the capacity to unite various groups into a larger American identity that respected and did not jeopardize other group identifications. In other words, the core beliefs of cultural pluralism could be shared without eradicating distinctive characteristics of ethnic or language groups. For example, a policy designed to encourage bilingual education rests on the assumption that the use of English as well as another language enhances a student's development in both the linguistic-ethnic subgroup and the larger society.

Just as a monolithic ideology has implications for the school milieu and the curriculum, so does a cultural pluralistic ideology. In terms of the school milieu, language, ethnic, and racial differences are valued. The school's value orientation would emphasize multicultural understanding. The formal curricular components, especially literature, history, and civic education, include the contributions of various ethnic and racial groups to the common heritage. It should be noted, however, that the dominant contemporary U.S. public school ideology, while culturally pluralistic, continues to emphasize commonalities related to government, law, and property. The delicate balance in a culturally pluralistic ideology and society is that of maintaining a commonly shared framework of experience and belief in which cultural differences can exist and flourish.

IDEOLOGY, EDUCATION, AND SCHOOLING

When held by a dominant group and represented as official knowledge, ideology exerts the following influences on education, especially on schooling:

1. It leads to the expression of the dominant group's educational policies, expectations, and goals as official standards and mandates.
2. It uses the school milieu or environment to reproduce and reinforce dominant group attitudes and values.
3. It emphasizes the dominant group's selected and approved skills and knowledge through the formal curriculum, the school's official and explicit program.

Educational Policies, Expectations, and Goals

In examining ideology's influence on schools, we need to examine the interplay, or the relationship of ideological views about society, politics, and the economy to education. Ideologies typically operate as systems of beliefs that are mutually interdependent.

In any given society, a range of ideologies is likely to exist. If we use the United States as an example, we can identify a variety of ideological perspectives. The two major U.S. political parties—the Democrats and Republicans—operate from ideological bases that include views of the past with their own heroes. Republican heroic figures are Abraham Lincoln and Ronald Reagan. For Democrats, Thomas Jefferson and John Kennedy are highly honored. Every four years, the Republican and Democratic national conventions approve a platform that states the party's policy plans for the future. Like the national political parties, other groups—the American Federation of Teachers, the National Education Association, the American Medical Association, the National Farmers Union, the National Association of Manufacturers, the Urban League and many others, for example—present an array of ideological shadings. Despite this spectrum of ideologies, the dominant ideology in the United States appears to be based on middle-class conceptions of knowledge, values, and standards of behavior that influence educational policies, attitudes toward schooling, and measures of educational success. This middle-class ideology influences education, schools, and the curriculum.

Values Conveyed by the School Milieu

School Milieu: the atmosphere or environment that pervades a school in terms of rules, regulations, styles, behaviors, and relationships.

The **school milieu**—the environment in which teaching and learning take place—shapes teachers' and students' social and intellectual attitudes and values. In calling the school milieu the "hidden curriculum," Michael Apple refers to the inculcation of "norms, values, and dispositions" that occurs as students experience the school's institutional expectations, incentives, routines, rewards, and punishments.[20] The milieu reflects ideological factors that enter the school from the larger society as well as those that are internal to it as an institution. Power, prestige, and status, as determined by the dominant or official ideology's criterion of success, shape not only educational goals but also teacher and student behavior.

Ideology and Curriculum

In terms of the formal curriculum, ideology seeks to answer the questions: What knowledge is of most worth? Most worth to whom? To national policies and priorities? To personal goals and expectations? For participation in the society and the group? For preferred social and economic positions? Does the policy emphasize the mathematical and scientific knowledge needed for technological development? Or does the curriculum reflect the literary and artistic styles and tastes of a leadership elite? As these questions are answered, often in terms of an ideological perspective, the curriculum takes shape.

IDEOLOGY AND INSTRUCTION

The role of ideology in instruction has been controversial, especially to those who claim that ideologically referenced education leads to indoctrination of students. Opponents of ideologically based instruction contend that it leads to indoctrination because: (1) its history is so selective that it presents only one side of the past; (2) it wants to implement a particular agenda; (3) it seeks to persuade students rather than to examine issues in a critical and unbiased way. Critics contend that instruction based on ideology is designed to persuade students to accept the teacher's ideological commitments.

Those who defend ideology's role in curriculum and instruction argue that by its nature, all education is ideological. They contend that education is contextual and is particular to a place and time; it imposes the knowledge, beliefs, and values of those who live in a place at a given time in history. There are also defenders of the role of ideology who contend that the argument for objective and disinterested curriculum and teaching is a strategy for those who hold power to use schools to maintain the status quo. This guise is used to block consideration of alternative ideologies by claiming that the one already in place represents genuine or real truth and values.

IDEOLOGY AND PHILOSOPHY

Although it is difficult to distinguish between philosophy and ideology, we will attempt to do so. The traditional philosophies discussed earlier, namely Idealism, Realism, and Thomism, were based on a metaphysical view of reality. These philosophies, which explained reality in terms of universal being or essence, are therefore abstract in the sense that they answered the question "What is real?" in general and universal terms. In contrast, ideologies are **contextual** and concrete. By contextual we mean that they are heavily related to time, their historical point of origin, and to place, a geographical, economic, political, sociological situation. Most philosophies, especially the traditional systematic ones, seek to transcend time and place; ideologies, in contrast, are essentially contextual.

Contextual: ideology's relationship to specific places and historic periods; the belief that ideas and values arise in contexts, particular places at particular times.

Philosophers are concerned with the truth of their claims about reality, the moral and ethical rightness of the values they prescribe, and the coherence, or logical validity, of their arguments.[21] Much philosophical writing probes for inconsistencies in other philosophies. Philosophers ask general questions such as: What is reality? What is true? How do we know? What is valuable? What makes this position or set of beliefs or arguments consistent and coherent? They would examine such concepts as "social justice," a key concept in many teacher education programs, in terms of: What is the meaning of the terms *social* and *justice*?

Operating at a high level of generality, philosophies seek to explain what is real, how we think, and how we assign value. In terms of valuing, in ethics and aesthetics, philosophies are also prescriptive. All philosophies, in attempting to explain the most general human concerns, seek to establish meaning. For example, the Experimentalist's analysis of the interaction of a human organism with the environment seeks to explain and make meaningful to us the nature of experience. The Existentialist is more concerned with the private and subjective meaning that we give to ourselves by choosing to act in the most significant situations that we encounter.

Ideologies, while also a quest for meaning, look more to economics, politics, and society for meaning. Meaning in these contexts comes from an interpretation of the past, which is either historical or mythological, or a combination of the two, and from an interpretation of policies and programs. In contrast to the speculative detachment or analytical reflection of philosophy, ideology, oriented to action, is often a rationale for explaining a particular program and persuading individuals to act to implement it.

Philosophers, seeking to extend their ideas outside of their own contexts, use language that is much more abstract and general than ideologists, who are more context-related. At times, there are similarities in expression. To make their ideas understandable, philosophers often provide examples that are made concrete by locating them in a context. Ideologists, in seeking to give their ideas greater transference from one context to another, may attempt to universalize their language. However, to enlist group loyalties for a specific program, ideologists, unlike philosophers, need to restore the concreteness that was developed in a context. Ideologies often rely on concepts that carry specific meanings but can enlist broad support, that can be descriptive but also highly emotional, that can be expanded but also simplified. Such concepts are conveyed by terms that are specific and direct but also expansive such as *family, race, gender, ethnicity, language, class, property*, and so forth.

In contrast to philosophy's speculative or analytical quest for meaning, ideology functions to create loyalty to the vision of the group's past and sense of historic destiny and to mobilize people and resources to achieve desired programmatic goals. In creating loyalty and commitment, ideologists use a variety of persuasive techniques that range from the rational to the emotional. Ideologies also possess a rhetorical or journalistic element, a persuasive means for fostering commitment and bringing about mobilization, which is generally absent from philosophy.

CONSTRUCTING YOUR OWN PHILOSOPHY OF EDUCATION

Now that you have studied ideology, do you believe that your educational ideas have been shaped by ideology? Can you identify this ideology? Have you observed ideological features in your education experiences, especially in history, social studies, and literature? Do you plan to relate ideology to the construction of your own philosophy of education?

Conclusion

This chapter analyzed ideology as the belief system of a group and the source of group identification. It discussed how groups use a selective interpretation of history to construct their identity, to explain social change, and to formulate policies and programs of action. Because of the ambiguity of the term, a definition of ideology was stipulated that enabled us to examine how ideology is used to create consensus. Ideology shapes the school milieu, especially the hidden curriculum. It also serves to formulate educational policy, such as the current standards and common core curricula movements. Although similarities exist between philosophies and ideologies, philosophies are more general and abstract, whereas ideologies are more contextual and action oriented.

Questions for Reflection and Discussion

1. Reflect on your political and economic beliefs and values. How have they been influenced by ideology?
2. Reflect on the groups of which you are a member. How has your group identity been shaped by ideology?
3. Reflect on your family's beliefs and values and determine whether they have been shaped by ideology.
4. Mannheim believed that intellectuals, including teachers, can be objective enough to act as mediators of different groups' beliefs and values. Do you agree or disagree?
5. Freire claimed that all education and all schooling are ideological. Do you agree or disagree?
6. Reflect on your own schooling. Did it involve learning to respond to ideological signs and symbols?

Inquiry and Research Projects

1. Visit a public school and a private school and compare and contrast how their environments, their milieus, have been shaped by ideology. Note any signs and symbols and paintings and decorations that carry an ideological meaning.
2. Access the Web sites of the American Federation of Teachers and the National Education Association. How do these organizations build group identity in their members? How do they portray the meaning of American education and schools? Does ideology play a role in these organizations?
3. Look through your family's photo albums. Do you think these photographs serve to create a collective family memory? How has this family memory shaped your beliefs and values?
4. Based on your school and classroom experiences, what scenarios have you observed on how children are taught the myths and symbols that carry ideological meanings?

5. In your clinical and teaching experiences, have you found a hidden curriculum? If so, describe how the hidden curriculum shapes teachers' and students' beliefs and behaviors.

6. Research your institution's teacher education program. Do you find evidence of ideological assumptions in the program?

As you begin to read the next chapters on Nationalism, Liberalism, Conservatism, and Marxism, you might wish to refer back to this overview table.

Overview of Ideologies and Education

Ideology	Past	Present	Future	Educational Implications	Proponents
Nationalism	Is based on the history and myths of a particular nation.	Is the ongoing historically derived achievements of a particular national group.	Is the extension of the national group in time and place, renewing its national heritage and extending it.	An emphasis on national history, literature, stories, myths, symbols, and ceremonies. The learning of a national language and literature.	Depends on particular nation. In American experience, Webster and others.
Liberalism	Importance of the Enlightenment—application of reason and science to society. Locke's inalienable rights; parliamentary government.	Application of democratic and scientific processes; continuation of parliamentary processes; separation of church and state.	Directed peaceful and nonviolent incremental change; reform of existing institutions when needed.	Academic freedom; use of scientific method and open processes; objectivity and impartiality. Cultivating commitment to democracy.	Locke Jefferson Mill Dewey
Conservatism	Affirmation of traditional and customary wisdom. Protection of historically evolved institutions and values.	Maintenance and protection of historically evolved institutions from radical change. Restoration of traditional values.	Maintain the cultural heritage and traditional values. Acceptance of only gradual necessary change.	Transmitting the cultural heritage and values; emphasis on patriotism, civility, and tradition.	Burke Reagan
Marxism	Class conflict over control of the means and modes of production. Dialectical and predictable conflict.	Organize to resist economic and political domination. Engage in consciousness raising and oppressed class militancy.	After the proletarian revolution, the coming of a classless society that will be without oppression.	Study of objective economic conditions; exposing false consciousness; developing critical consciousness.	Marx Engels

Internet Resources

For Professor Jim Riley's "Introduction to Political Ideologies," access http://www.academic.regis, edu/jriley/introide/htm.

For an introduction to the relationships of ideology to philosophy, sociology of knowledge, and bibliography, access Encyclopedia Britannica at http://www.britannica.com/EBchecked/topic/281943/ideology.

For the "State of American Political Ideology" from a Progressive orientation, access the Center for American Progress at http://www.americanprogress.org/issues/2009/03/t/progressive_quiz.html.

For sources and resources on ideology, access www.intute.ac.uk/socialsciences.

Suggestions for Further Reading

Balkin, J. M. *Cultural Software: A Theory of Ideology*. New Haven, CT: Yale University Press, 1998.

Ball, T., and R. Dagger. *Political Ideologies and the Democratic Ideal*. New York: Longman, 1999.

Bartolome, Lilia I. *Ideologies in Education: Unmasking the Trap of Teacher Neutrality*. New York: Peter Lang, 2008.

Debray, Elizabeth H. *Politics, Ideology & Education: Federal Policy During the Clinton and Bush Administrations*. New York: Teachers College Press, 2006.

Freeden, Michael. *Ideologies and Political Theory: A Conceptual Approach*. Oxford, UK: Clarendon Press, 1996.

___. *Ideology: A Very Short Introduction*. Oxford, UK: Oxford University Press, 2003.

Freire, Paulo. *Letters to Cristina: Reflections on My Life and Work*. London: Routledge, 1996.

___. *Pedagogy of Freedom: Ethics, Democracy, and Civic Courage*. Lanham, MD: Rowman and Littlefield, 1998.

___. *Pedagogy of Hope, Reliving Pedagogy of the Oppressed*. New York: Continuum, 1995.

___. *Pedagogy of the Oppressed*. Translated by Myra Bergman Ramos. New York: Continuum, 1984.

Gadotti, M. *Reading Paulo Freire: His Life and Work*. New York: SUNY Press, 1994.

Gramsci, Antonio. *Selections from Prison Notebooks*. Edited by Q. Hoare and G. Newell-Smith. London: Lawrence & Wishart, 1971.

Heywood, Andrew. *Political Ideologies: An Introduction*. Basingstoke, UK, and New York: Palgrave/Macmillan, 2012.

McCullough, H. B. *Political Ideologies*. New York: Oxford University Press, 2010.

McLaren, Peter, and Peter Leonard. *Paulo Freire: A Critical Encounter*. New York and London: Routledge, 1993.

Morrow, Raymond A., and Carlos Alberto Torres. *Reading Freire and Habermas: Critical Pedagogy and Transformative Social Change*. New York: Teachers College Press, Columbia University, 2002.

Oliker, Michael A., and Walter P. Krolikowski, eds. *Images of Youth: Popular Culture as Educational Ideology*. New York: Peter Lang, 2001.

Picciono, Anthony G., and Joel Spring. *The Great American Education-Industrial Complex: Ideology, Technology, and Profit*. New York: Routledge, 2012.

Spring, Joel. *How Educational Ideologies Are Shaping Global Society: Intergovernmental Organizations, NGOs, and the Decline of the Nation-State*. Oxford, UK: Taylor & Francis, 2004.

Taylor, P. *The Texts of Paulo Freire*. Buckingham, UK: Open University Press, 1993.

Vincent, A. *Modern Political Ideologies*. Oxford, UK: Blackwell, 1995.

Watt, John. *Ideology, Objectivity and Education*, New York: Teachers College Press, 1994.

Weis, Lois, Cameron McCarthy, and Greg Dimitriadis. *Ideology, Curriculum, and the New Sociology of Education: Revisiting the Work of Michael Apple*. New York: Routledge, 2006.

Zamudio, Margaret, Christopher Russell, Francisco Rio, and Jacquelyn Bridgeman. *Critical Race Theory Matters: Education and Ideology*. New York: Routledge, 2010.

Notes

1. Michael Freeden, *Ideology: A Very Short Introduction* (Oxford, UK: Oxford University Press, 2003), 4.
2. Ibid., 99–100.
3. Ibid., 101–102.
4. Ibid., 5.
5. Ibid., 12–13.
6. Ibid., 13.
7. Ibid., 14–15.
8. Ibid., 19–20.
9. Donaldo Macedo, "Foreword," in Paulo Freire, *Pedagogy of Freedom: Ethics, Democracy, and Civic Courage,* trans. Patrick Clarke (Lanham, MD: Rowman & Littlefield, 1998), xxiv.
10. Although its origins are in Catholic action groups, the recent popes, John Paul II and Benedict XVI, have condemned what they say are the Marxist orientation and overt politics of Liberation Theology.
11. Macedo, "Foreward," in Paulo Freire, *Pedagogy of Freedom, Ethics, Democracy and Civic Courage,* xxviii.
12. Paulo Freire, *Pedagogy of the Oppressed,* trans. Myra Bergman Ramos (New York: Continuum, 1984), 21–23.
13. For an analysis of the "interpretational component," see Stanley E. Ballinger, *The Nature and Function of Educational Policy* (Bloomington, IN: Center for the Study of Educational Policy, Department of History and Philosophy of Education, Indiana University, 1965); also see Richard Pratte, *Ideology and Education* (New York: David McKay, 1977), 49–51.
14. Jonathan Kozol, *Savage Inequalities: Children in America's Schools* (New York: HarperPerennial, 1991), 67–74.

15. Among the national reports are: National Commission on Excellence in Education, *A Nation at Risk: The Imperative for Educational Reform* (Washington, DC: Government Printing Office, 1983); Task Force on Education for Economic Growth, *Action for Excellence* (Denver, CO: Education Commission of the States, 1983).
16. No Child Left Behind (Washington, DC: U.S. Government Printing Office, 2001), 1.
17. Ibid., 8–9.
18. Kathryn Kish Sklar, *Catharine Beecher: A Study in American Domesticity* (New York: W. W. Norton & Co., 1976), xii.
19. The concept of "cultural interpreter" is developed by Kathryn Kish Sklar, *Catharine Beecher: A Study in American Domesticity,* xiii.
20. Michael W. Apple, *Ideology and Curriculum* (London: Routledge and Kegan Paul, 1979), 67
21. Freeden, *Ideology: A Very Short Introduction,* 67.

Nationalism, American Exceptionalism, Ethnonationalism, and Education

Children pledging allegiance to the American flag and "to the republic for which it stands," which develops a sense of national identity.

8

CHAPTER PREVIEW

Nationalism, American Exceptionalism, and ethnonationalism are all variations on the nationalist theme. Nationalism is based on a commitment to the nation as a person's primary source of identification, commitment, and loyalty. American Exceptionalism, an American version of nationalism, views the United States as unique among the countries of the world. Ethnonationalism focuses on the ethnic group as the source of primary allegiance. The chapter examines how these related ideologies have shaped education, schooling, curriculum, and teaching and learning. The chapter discusses the following major topics:

- Definitions of nationalism, American Exceptionalism, and ethnonationalism
- The connections between nationalism, the nation-state, and school systems
- Nationalism's major ideological themes
- Constructing national identity
- Education as cultural transmission
- American Exceptionalism
- Ethnonationalism
- Nationalism, American Exceptionalism, ethnonationalism, and multicultural education

Because nationalism is so pervasive in society and education, reflect on nationalism and how it relates to the construction of your philosophy of education. How does nationalism, especially American Exceptionalism and ethnonationalism, relate to your view of education, schooling, teaching, and learning?" Did you encounter it in courses in history and literature or in commemorative events? Reflect on and ask if nationalism or some aspects of it are meaningful to you. What aspects of nationalism do you especially like or dislike? Are there aspects of nationalism that you plan to incorporate into your philosophy of education?

DEFINING NATIONALISM

This chapter examines nationalism, an ideology that is paradoxically disarmingly simple and direct, but also highly complex. We can illustrate nationalism's paradoxical nature by reviewing some definitions. The dictionary defines **nationalism** as "national spirit or aspirations" and "as devotion to the interests of one's own nation." That definition seems very direct if we take it to mean that we are devoted to the interests of the United States and possess the American spirit. Then, we look up

Nationalism: an ideology that asserts the importance, value, and worth of belonging to a nation.

Nation: a body of people, living in a particular territory, that is sufficiently conscious of its unity to seek or to possess a government of its own.

the root, **nation**, from which nationalism is derived, and find that it means "a body of people, associated with a particular territory, that is sufficiently conscious of its unity to seek or to possess a government peculiarly its own," "the territory or country itself," and "an aggregation of persons of the same ethnic family, often speaking the same language or cognate languages."[1] To complete our definitions, we look at how Steven Grosby, a leading scholar, has defined nationalism. He says it refers to a set of beliefs about the nation, focusing on its value and worth and the desirability of belonging to it. For him, a "nation is a territorial community of nativity," which has evolved through historical processes, into which a person is born or naturalized as a citizen.[2]

Now, our initial discussion of nationalism has become more complex. We are faced with two paradoxes: (1) Although Americans are conscious of their unity and have their own government, they are not of the same racial and ethnic family; (2) although the majority of Americans speak English, many of them also speak other languages.

In examining nationalism, we have an ideology that is simple and emotional in that it evokes love of our country. The nation's symbols, its flag and anthems, stir our emotions. Even if we cannot deconstruct or analyze nationalism, we can feel it because we have been taught from childhood to be inspired by it. Simultaneously, nationalism is highly complex: It is not limited to our emotions only but penetrates into other areas. It can cross over to and override other group identifications such as socio-economic class, gender, ethnicity, and race. How often have we heard, especially in times of crisis, such phrases as "united we stand; divided we fall," or "we are all Americans"? To begin to unpack the bundle of emotions as well as the complex relationships of nationalism to our lives and institutions, we can focus on several leading questions:[3]

- Why do people separate themselves from other people in nations?
- What does the existence of nations and nationalism tell us about people?
- What role do education and schooling play in this separating of peoples and creating of nations?

American Exceptionalism: the pervasive belief that the United States is a unique country and that Americans are a special people, blessed by Providence and with a mission in the world.

Ethnonationalism: nationalism that is based on identity and membership in a race or ethnic group that may or may not be co-terminus with a nation-state.

Throughout modern history, nationalism has been a significant ideology in constructing the primary identification in which we distinguish "us from them" and in mobilizing the people of nation-states.[4] In particular, nationalism penetrates the school systems of nation-states. In the United States, nationalism is often expressed as **American Exceptionalism**, the belief that the United States is an exceptional country and that Americans are a special people. Throughout history, the ethnic and racial group has had a profound effect in shaping cultural identity, character, and social commitments. At times, ethnicity and race have promoted nation-state nationalism. At other times, they have weakened the sense of nation-state nationalism. In the twenty-first century, **ethnonationalism**, based on ethnicity or race, is a powerful global force. Ethnonationalism, an old and a new way of viewing one's cultural identity and affiliation and of distinguishing "us from them," raises profound issues for education.

Nation-State: an independent country that occupies and is sovereign over a particular geographical territory and has its own political, social, economic, and educational institutions.

CONNECTING NATIONALISM, THE NATION-STATE, AND SCHOOLING

A direct connection exists between nationalism, as an ideology, and the school, as an institution of formal education. The connection comes through the nation-state, a country such as the United States, France, or Japan. A **nation-state** occupies a particular geographical territory over which it has sovereignty that has its own political, social, economic, and educational institutions.

Nationalism as an Ideology

Ideology	View of the Past	Present Program	Curriculum	Instruction	Issues
Nationalism	Uses history and myth to construct a shared national consciousness or memory.	To reinforce national identity through education, commemorative events, and definitions of citizenship.	National themes reflected in an official history, language arts, and literature. Patriotic events commemorated in school programs and activities.	Education as cultural transmission.	Should there be a national cultural core? An official language? Bilingual-bicultural education? Multicultural education?

A nation is composed of a group of people, its citizens, who live within its political boundaries and participate in its cultural, political, religious, and educational institutions. Based on the concept of the nation as the primary unit of identification, nationalism manifests the sense of belonging to and sharing in common membership in the country. This identification manifests itself further in the group's national ethos or patriotism. The idea of citizenship in the nation is based in nationality, that is, being designated an official member by being born in the country or naturalized in it as a citizen.

Historic Origins of Nation-States

Racial, ethnic, and language groups such as the ancient Greeks, Hebrews, and Egyptians identified themselves as a distinct people before the rise of the modern nation-state. However, the modern nation-state, stimulated by nationalism, developed in the late eighteenth and early nineteenth centuries. Key events that generated nationalism's rise were the American Revolution in 1776 and the French Revolution in 1789. The emerging nationalism of the American rebels against British colonial rule was born of their sense that they were no longer Englishmen and women connected to the mother country, but were becoming a distinct people, living in their own territory and developing their own American culture. As Jefferson asserted in the Declaration of Independence, Americans had the inalienable right, as a people, to create their own self-governing and sovereign nation-state.

In 1789, the second great revolution occurred in France in a popular insurrection against the monarchy and aristocracy. The revolution proclaimed that the French people, not the Bourbon monarch, constituted the French nation. Napoleon's efforts to conquer Europe and remake it into a system of French satellite states generated a counternationalist tide among the British, Russians, Spanish, Germans, and other national groups. In the nineteenth century, the idea of the country as a nation-state rather than a realm of a dynastic monarch took hold in Europe. Throughout the nineteenth century, the major European powers, especially France, England, and Germany, stimulated by nationalist rivalries, colonized much of Africa and Asia. Two additional ideologies—imperialism and colonialism—both with significant educational implications, developed. Imperialism was based on the belief that powerful nation-states such as the United Kingdom, France, and Germany had the right to occupy foreign territory and control other peoples such as the Indians, the Indo-Chinese, and the Africans and to exploit them in the interest of the imperial nation. Colonialism held that certain people, usually individuals of color in Africa and Asia, were inferior and needed to be controlled and tutored by the imperial nation. Nationalism caused the tensions, armaments races, and military alliances and counteralliances that led to World War I and World War II.

European imperialists unconsciously exported the nation-state model of political organization to South America, Asia, and Africa. When Spain's Central and South American colonies revolted and became independent sovereign states, they adopted the nation-state model of organization. When the British, French, Dutch, and Portuguese colonies gained independence in the twentieth century, they, too, adopted the model of the nation-state organization as independent and sovereign nations.

Nationalism and Nation-States' Structures

As indicated, the nation-state connects with and is the location for the nation. A nation-state such as the United States, the United Kingdom, or Brazil creates institutional structures—governments, parliaments and other legislative bodies, courts, police and armed forces, and school systems—designed to preserve and promote the nation's territorial integrity, survival, maintenance, and interests. The nation-state exercises sovereignty over its territory through laws that relate its members, its citizens, to each other.[5] The citizens of nation-states establish governments with presidents, prime ministers, parliaments, congresses, and courts to manage their internal political affairs. They establish treasuries, banks, and taxation agencies to support the nation-state financially. They maintain police and military forces—armies, navies, air forces—to protect their nation-state's security and maintain its borders. They create diplomatic services to conduct their nation-states, international relations with other countries. They create school systems to educate their children and young people, especially to socialize them in the ideology and processes that sustain the nation-state and reproduce it for future generations.

Nation-States and Schools

National School System: a system of schools organized, supported, maintained, and administered by the government of a nation-state.

In the nineteenth century, nation-states began to establish **national school systems**. In the 1830s in the United Kingdom, Parliament gave financial grants to voluntary school societies to promote primary education. France, under the leadership of François Guizot (1787–1874) established national primary schools. Although not creating a national or federal system of education, the individual states of the United States established locally controlled common, or public, school systems. Though not an official national system, the fifty state school systems have many characteristics of a national system, including the facts that the books and materials they use are similar and their teachers generally have a similar preparation. In some countries, national schools either cooperated with or replaced existing religious schools. In France and Mexico, there were prolonged conflicts between state and religious authorities for control of the schools. Just as nation-states are found throughout the world, so are national school systems. As new nation-states appeared in the twentieth century after winning independence from colonial powers, they, too, established some version of a national school system. National, state-operated schools became key agencies in constructing a sense of national identity and in bringing about political socialization in the young. Often building on nationalist themes, political socialization instills patriotic and civic values in the young. The close relationships among nationalism, nation-states, and national school systems raise serious implications for education. For much of the nineteenth and twentieth centuries, national school systems fostered a patriotism in the young that glorified their own country over all others. Now that we have made a connection between nationalism and schooling, we can turn to a more thorough analysis of nationalism as an ideology.

Nationalism in the Foundations of Education

In the foundations of education, the early studies of nationalism's effect on education were conducted by Isaac L. Kandel (1881–1965), a comparative educator, and Edward H. Reisner (1885–1937), a historian of education. Kandel and Reisner studied nationalism within the political context of particular nation-states such as France, Germany, Italy, and Russia. They examined nationalism as a force in creating an individual's identity with the nation-state and in mobilizing the people of these nation-states for politically based agendas such as defense, war, imperialism, and modernization. These pioneer educational theorists identified nationalism with modernization as a force that eroded residues of feudalism, localism, and provincialism. Kandel and Reisner concluded that (1) nationalism was a powerful emotional force for constructing an individual's primary identification and social cohesion with the nation-state; (2) modern national school systems, supported by nation-states, were educational agencies designed to deliberately cultivate national identity and social and political cohesion; and (3) the modern curriculum, dating from the early nineteenth century, was a medium for instilling national sentiments, loyalties, and values. Kandel's and Reisner's pioneering studies assessed nationalism's power in mobilizing nation-state energies, examined its uses in education, and identified the ideology's emotional aspects.

After World War I, tension developed in educational theory about nationalism's nature and impact on children's political socialization. Whereas nationalism was seen as necessary to the modern nation-state and in schooling for the nation-state, internationally minded educators condemned extreme nationalism, especially when chauvinistic, as generating conflicts among nations that endangered world peace. The educational problem then became how to use nationalism as a constructive force in building nations while reining in and circumscribing those conflict-generating elements that threatened world peace and security. This tension between nationalism's constructive and destructive potentialities remains an important and unresolved issue in education.

NATIONALISM'S IDEOLOGICAL THEMES

In this section, we turn to an analysis of nationalism's most important ideological themes. We consider how history, joined with myth, forges a national memory; how national political socialization generates a "we feeling" that makes one people feel different from another; and how a homeland, or territory, is based on a nationalist interpretation of space and time.

For definitions of ideology, see the chapter on Ideology and Education.

History, Myth, and Memory

All nations have historical beginnings and processes of development. For example, the United States' historical beginnings were as thirteen British colonies on the Atlantic coast of North America. The history of the United States taught in schools recounts the story of these colonies' settlement, their struggle for independence, and the creation of a new republic by American heroes such as George Washington, Benjamin Franklin, and Thomas Jefferson. Interwoven with the historical account are images and myths about the Pilgrims, especially the first Thanksgiving, which they celebrated with the Native-Americans. The myth is carried by many symbols—Pilgrim girls in white caps and aprons and Indians in tribal regalia, wearing headbands of brightly colored feathers. Go to any elementary school classroom in the United States in November and you will see pictures of the Thanksgiving feast drawn by children that replicate the scene, which becomes encased as a powerful myth in the individual and national memory. Equally important are the values that the combination of history and myth carry—images of a family, sitting with their heads bowed in prayer at a dinner table laden with turkey, dressing, sweet potatoes, and pumpkin pies. The scene carries the economic values of an American bounty, the social values of family togetherness and sharing, and the religious values of a people thanking God. It creates the very powerful image of the United States as a bountiful, exceptional nation that has been especially blessed by a providential God. The blending of history and myth works to create a **collective memory** in which certain symbols of a nation get the same response throughout the republic. The history of the settlement of the American west, the movement of the line of settlement from the Atlantic to the Pacific Ocean, is conveyed through the images and stories of the mountain man, the pioneer, the cowboy, the settler, the wagon train, and so on. Instilled in the account are the mixed and unresolved tensions of rugged individuals but also of people traveling in groups and building communities together. To the degree to which history and myths are filtered, so are these memories. The earlier images and memories of a filtered **official history** of a blessed nation under a benevolent God, conveyed by the Thanksgiving story, may be challenged and even shattered by other, often submerged alternative histories about African American slavery, the war with Mexico, and the oppression and forced resettlement of Native Americans. However, the earliest images of the nation, like the earliest images of God, have great staying power in memory and are likely to remain despite contrary evidence. In other words, the facts often do not matter.

Collective Memory: the shared remembrances of past events that are pertinent to a group's identity, membership, and meaning.

Official History: the standard or approved version and interpretation of history that is mandated in school.

Making People Different from Each Other

As our national psyche is shaped through shared or collective memories, history becomes more than facts and events, and myth becomes more than imagined stories and images. It weaves the fabric of a national consciousness that is different from the national consciousness of other peoples.[6] Every nation—Japan, China, Russia, France, Israel, and the United States, for example—has its own understanding of its past as a national narrative that is different and distinctive from that of other peoples.

The past, however, is not a completed set of episodes, relegated to history. The past is moving and alive; it flows like a current into the present and helps shape it. It transcends the narratives about historical and mythical episodes and heroes and enters into a group's collective consciousness. It constructs a "we-feeling" that distinguishes and separates us from them. It makes Americans interpret themselves as a people different from the Chinese, Egyptians, French, or Russians.

SCHOOLING FOR DIFFERENCE. Schooling, especially in nation-state school systems, is a powerful force in building the collective national consciousness of being a different people. We preface our discussion of how children are schooled to be different in terms of their national identity by stating what is important but also overtly obvious. Human beings are, with some slight genetic differences, essentially alike; children are born biologically alike. Political socialization, an important part of schooling, is the process that makes them different in their national identification. Children learn to speak, read, write, and listen in the language of their particular nation. The language, in turn, carries the beliefs and values and the laws, rules, and customs particular to the nation. When children begin to perceive of themselves as being like those who share the same history, myth, and memory, they become participants in the common collective national self-consciousness and memory. As these beliefs and values are shared with others in the national community, the individual child becomes socially and politically related to others and acquires the feeling of being an American. The sense of being an American makes the person understand himself or herself as being different from other people. As individuals take on this common collective self-consciousness, they construct a political and cultural national identity or "we-feeling." Along with identifying with those who are like us, those who are different are the others, the outsiders.

Space and Time

Two important concepts developed in a child's education are the meaning and relationships of space and time. These two key concepts in interpreting the world are of special significance in developing a child's collective national self-consciousness. We have already discussed how the sense of time, in terms of nationalism, is developed through history and myth. Now, we turn to space, or territoriality, another key component of constructing national identity and consciousness. When it merges with the mythical and historical sense of the past, a national territory is replete with rich and heightened meanings. The lyrics of well-known songs, such as "from sea to shining sea," "this land is your land; this land is my land," "God bless America, my home sweet home," which are all known by children and sung at school ceremonies, designate space, place, and territoriality. The particular people have a land, a place, a space called the homeland. In some countries, the homeland, personified as a parent, is lovingly called the "motherland" or the "fatherland."

The sense that our homeland belongs to us and not to them is important: After the terrorist attacks on the World Trade Center in New York City on September 11, 2001, Americans rallied to the defense of the homeland. The United States Congress, on the recommendation of the President, established a federal Department of Homeland Security.

The national space or homeland is much more than an area on a map; it is a place filled with relationships—between a spatially situated past and a changing present—that creates an almost spiritual sense of being there that is expressed in such phrases as "the indomitable and unconquerable American spirit." Thus, time and space are connected in the spirit of past and present generations in the American homeland.

The nation occupies the space of a territorially distinct people that is formed by its memories and its historically based institutions, along with its sense of civic belonging and membership.[7] The nation becomes a set of social, political, and emotional relationships that are temporally interwoven in a collective memory based on history and myth and spatially reinforced by the living place of those who share this consciousness. More important, the nation, when perceived as a territorial space, generates the values of "possession" and "attachment." As conveyed by the lyric, "this land is my land," the member of the nation has a sense of possession or ownership in the nation. Attachment means being connected to the territory across time. The past generations prepared and defended the homeland, as with the celebrated World War II "greatest generation," for the present generation, which, in turn, is responsible for transmitting the cultural inheritance to future generations. Based on the sense of a collective cultural consciousness and memory, developed by history and myth, and a national space, or homeland, the following generalizations can be stated regarding a nation. It has a:

- territory, bounded by borders that keep others out.
- name that designates it as a particular territory, such as the United States or the United Kingdom.
- capital, a center, in which is located its major government institutions and national monuments (e.g., Washington, DC, or London).
- history that expresses its existence over time.
- relatively common culture, institutions, political processes, and laws.[8]

NATIONALISM AND CONSTRUCTING NATIONAL IDENTITY

Nationalism, an ideology identified with the nation-state, is used to construct a sense of primary identification, a collective consciousness of being and feeling French, English, Italian, Chinese, Israeli, Egyptian, or American, for example. The chords of national identity arise through the shared participatory experience of speaking a common language, worshiping in a common religion, and possessing common culture.

A Common Language

A common language is instrumental in instilling national history and myths into the individual's collective consciousness. A common language is a means of everyday communication, and yet its cultural meaning is much more powerful than being a simple tool. Its words express the meaning of time and space and the values of honesty, loyalty, beauty, friendship, politeness, and family in a unique national and cultural context. The language describes a shared version of self and the past and prescribes what should be in the future.

Many countries have a standard official language in their schools. By learning a shared language, individuals also become immersed in the nation's cultural context. Speakers of the common language are identified as being like us. A common language unites people by constructing shared meanings and understandings—ideas, beliefs, and values—about themselves as a group and their relationships to others who, not speaking the same language, are different from them. Indeed, the ancient Greeks denigrated non-Greek-speaking people as barbarians.

School curricula, throughout the world, give priority in time and resources to teaching the national language. In the primary or elementary schools, reading instruction and language arts as central activities command much instructional time and resources. A child's academic access to and success at the secondary and higher level of education is often determined by how well she or he has mastered the national language. As children learn language, their ideas, beliefs, and values become more contextualized and more specific to the national setting.

Nationalism endorses a common language and its teaching in nation-state schools, but language instruction itself is often emotionally and politically charged, as with bilingual education in the United States. In earliest childhood, before commencing school, children are socially learning the language of their family and their immediate social group. With spoken and heard (listened-to) language already ingrained in their early socialization, they enter school—a social and often national educational agency that emphasizes language learning. As the child begins formal language instruction in school, an important question is: Is the language of instruction the same as or different from the language that the child already knows? If the same, the school reinforces the linguistic and cultural traditions the child already has.

In monolingual and monocultural nation-states such as Iceland and Japan, the educational issues relating to language instruction are much simpler and basically pedagogical than in multilingual and multicultural countries. Their focus is on devising and implementing methods to teach the national language more effectively, easily, and efficiently. In multiethnic, multiracial, and multilingual nation-states, especially in India and Nigeria but also to a degree in the United States, language learning is much more complicated because it involves political decision making and power relationships as well as pedagogical concerns. The basic political issue is that of having or not having an official language. If there is an official language, what is that language? The inclination in nation states has been to have an official language and to impose that language of those who do not speak it.

Patriotism

Instilling patriotism, love of country and the nation, is an important goal of education in national or state-operated school systems throughout the world. **Patriotism** indicates a primary identification with the nation and a commitment to its territory, the homeland. Schools instill patriotism by bringing children into the national consciousness by transmitting an official language and history, promoting a literature that exemplifies the national story and character, and embracing ritual ceremonies that celebrate the nation and the significant events in its history. In the United States, Independence Day, the Fourth of July, is commemorated with parades, speeches, and fireworks that engage the young. In France, on Bastille Day, July 14, the posting of the tricolor flag, the singing of "La Marseillaise," and parades invoke historic national memories. In Israel, Holocaust Remembrance Day commemorates the genocide of six million Jews by the Nazis during World War II. Each nation has particular ceremonial events, heroes and heroines, and days of commemoration. In schools, these ceremonial events, with their songs, stories, and patriotic reenactments, are part of the process of political socialization and identification of students in nationality and the nation-state. Similar to religious rituals, these patriotic ceremonies and symbols elicit an almost automatic response in the person.

Patriotism: a love, commitment, and desire for the well-being of the nation and its territory.

Whereas most educators have little problem with patriotism as an educational goal, they debate its meaning and how it should be cultivated in schools. Some Conservatives have argued that too many public schools in the United States emphasize cultural relativism and ignore the importance of instilling patriotic values. They point to countries that are splintered by racial and ethnic hatreds and warn that it could happen here if public schools do not require solid core subjects in the curriculum that promote patriotic values. In contrast, Liberals and Critical Theorists argue that narrow patriotism can become chauvinistic and that patriotism should be redefined in more pluralistic, multicultural, and international terms. They do not want schools either to encourage a monolithic view of America or to generate prejudice against people of other countries.

For their view on political socialization, see the chapters on Conservatism, Liberalism, and Critical Theory.

Nationalism and Religion

Another element in constructing national identification in many countries is a common religion, often an "official church." The relationship between religion and nationalism is historically very complex. Where the observance of a particular religion is territorial, religion and nationality coincide. When it is the religion of the land, religion helps to give spiritual support to nationalism and nationalism gives political and economic support to religion. In Eastern Europe—Russia, Serbia, Romania, and Bulgaria—and in Greece, for example, Orthodox Christianity was an important historical force in the emergence, unification, and cohesion of nationality and is a force for cultural homogeneity.[9] In Italy, Poland, Ireland, Portugal, and Spain, Roman Catholicism provides a religious and cultural sense of belonging. In Israel, Judaism is the religious and cultural link. In Egypt, Pakistan, Malaysia, Afghanistan, Iraq, and Iran, Islam is deeply embedded in the culture. In Thailand, Buddhism is embedded in the culture.

Historically, the origins of formal education, or schooling, can be traced to temples, churches, mosques, and synagogues. In many countries, churches and religious institutions remain powerful informal educational forces. In many countries, the teaching of religion, especially that of the official church, takes place in the state-operated schools. In the United States, where church and state are separated constitutionally, the government does not sponsor or sanction religion, nor does it interfere with its free exercise. Religiously as well as culturally pluralistic, the United States is home to a variety of Protestant denominations as well as to Roman Catholics, Orthodox Christians, Jews, Moslems, and other religious denominations.

The role of religion in American national life and education, however, has really never been settled. There have been religious issues in American education since the common or public schools were established in the nineteenth century. Although the Enlightenment influence in the American tradition, especially in Jeffersonianism, emphasized separation of church and state and, correspondingly, separation of public schools from religious control, evangelical Protestantism identified American institutions with a generalized Protestant cultural ethos. Today, there are concerted campaigns, especially on the part of cultural conservatives allied with fundamentalist Christians, to fashion American institutions, especially schools, on Christian beliefs and values. These groups define the United States as "a Christian nation," founded on Christian principles.

For the relationships of Conservatism and religion, see the chapter on Conservatism and Education.

Common Culture

Nationalism, manifested in identification with a common cultural heritage, finds expression in the art, history, literature, poetry, drama, music, and architecture that exemplifies a national ethos. As far back as the ancient Greeks, cultural symbols and artifacts were used to construct ethnic and cultural identity in the young. Homer's epic poems, the *Iliad* and *Odyssey,* gave the young Greeks a sense of what it meant to be a Greek hero. The Parthenon on the Acropolis in Athens was a visible monument to Greek culture, religion, and architecture. Writing about the Greeks, the historian Herodotus wrote, "We are one in blood and one in language; those shrines of the gods belong to us . . . all in common, and the sacrifices in common, and there are our habits, bred of a common upbringing."[10]

Certain cultural works and artifacts convey the sense of nationalism. In the United States, the novels of James Fenimore Cooper, Henry James, Herman Melville, Edith Wharton, Ernest Hemingway, and F. Scott Fitzgerald and the essays of Ralph Waldo Emerson, Henry David Thoreau, and Mark Twain exemplify American literature. The poetry of Emily Dickinson, Walt Whitman, and Robert Frost portrays the American mood in verse. The architecture of Louis Sullivan and Frank Lloyd Wright expresses American design. The White House, the Washington Monument, the Statue of Liberty, Mount Rushmore, the Lincoln Memorial, all evoke American consciousness.

For Germans, the literary masterpieces of Johann Wolfgang von Goethe and Friedrich Schiller and the music of Ludwig van Beethoven and Richard Wagner evoke the sense of being a German. Wagner, who composed some of the world's greatest operas, was also a strident nationalist. In France, nationalist themes were conveyed by Alexander Dumas and Victor Hugo, especially the latter's literary masterpiece, *Les Misérables.* The epic murals in the Louvre and the Chamber of Deputies portray glorious events in French history. The stirring strains of "La Marseillaise" and vistas of the Eiffel Tower and Arc de Triomphe elicit vivid images of France. For Italians, Giuseppe Verdi's dramatic operas portray Italia. Frederic Chopin's stirring Polonaise inspired Polish patriots to rally for their country's freedom. In China, the Great Wall, the Forbidden City, Tiananmen Square, and Mao's tomb tell the story of that country's cultural heritage. In India, the Red Fort, the statue of Gandhi in Bombay, and the Taj Mahal are physical symbols of the Indian past.

These works of art, literature, music, and architecture are aesthetic references in the psyches of those who share a common national consciousness. In the school curriculum, these great works are used to bring the young into contact with their national heritage. Courses in literature, music, art, and drama as well as field trips are used to introduce the young to the monuments of their national culture so that they will recognize, participate in, and appreciate it.

EDUCATION AS CULTURAL TRANSMISSION

Formal education and schooling for nationalism, particularly curriculum and instruction, take the form of transmission of the national cultural heritage, developing patriotism and loyalty to the nation, instilling the proper performance of national ceremonies and rituals, and creating a national collective consciousness. As indicated, nationalism rests on the shared collective consciousness that the individual shares membership with other nationals or citizens of the nation-state. The cultural consciousness is constructed through shared memories based on history and myth. In constructing cultural consciousness, the schools' primary role is to transmit the elements of the national culture to the young.

An important political issue that has strong educational implications regards the questions: What is the culture? Who determines what it is? Is the culture a completed or an ongoing project? In answering these questions, the different educational philosophies, ideologies, and theories line up on opposing sides. Conservatives and Essentialists see the national culture as already existing and construe **cultural transmission** as having the goal of molding people to fit into the existing culture.

Cultural Transmission: the view that a major purpose of education is to transmit the culture from adults to children in order to maintain it from one generation to the next.

Liberals, Pragmatists, Social Reconstructionists, and Critical Theorists, in varying degrees, see American culture as an unfinished project and argue that education is more than merely transmitting what is claimed to exist; it is designed to reshape and reconstruct American culture.

Conservatives and Essentialists reply, in rebuttal, that an American cultural tradition exists and, in order for it to be sustained, it needs to be transmitted to the young. Otherwise, they contend, the cultural relativism advocated by their opponents will erode core knowledge and values. They want an American cultural core at the vital center of curriculum and instruction. An American cultural core would consist of:

- English as the language of instruction
- American history and government
- American literature

For Conservatism, see the chapter on Conservatism and Education; for Essentialism, see Essentialism and Education.

For their cultural perspectives, see the chapters on Liberalism, Pragmatism, Social Reconstruction, and Critical Theory.

American History

Transmitting a national history plays a critical role in developing national consciousness. This is particularly true in the United States where American Exceptionalism, the belief that the United States is a special nation populated by an exceptional people, is a powerful influence on national consciousness. In transmitting a national history, an official version is used to construct a sense of American nationality and identity.

Such an official history is often highly generalized, emphasizing American progress, achievements, and victories. According to historian Gary Gerstle, "nationalism demands that boundaries against outsiders be drawn, that a dominant national culture be created or reinvigorated, and that internal and external opponents of the national project be subdued, nationalized, vanquished, and even excluded or repelled."[11]

The content and interpretations of the history taught in schools have been continually contested. What is the official history? Who decides what it is? There are alternative interpretations of versions of the past and alternative versions of the culture. The issue becomes: What is the preferred version? A preferred version raises the further question of preferred by whom? For nationalists, culture and history are raw materials used to mold and create the myths that vivify and sustain the preferred interpretation. The construction of an official culture and version of history requires decisions about what is to be consciously remembered and what is to be repressed or excised from the official version of the national memory.[12] Alternative histories develop under the surface and at the margins of the official history and struggle to replace or revise it.

AMERICAN EXCEPTIONALISM

The belief that the United States is a "shining city on a hill," "a beacon to the world," a special country blessed by Providence, and a country with a Manifest Destiny expresses an American version of nationalism called American Exceptionalism. Proclaiming that the United States is an extraordinary, unique land that is very different from and, indeed, better than other countries, American Exceptionalism is embedded in both American history and culture and in the public school philosophy.

Alexis de Tocqueville, a young French intellectual, spent 1831 and 1832 traveling throughout what was then the United States. In his insightful account of his experiences, *Democracy in America* (1835), Tocqueville detected the origins of American Exceptionalism in the young country. He wrote, "Everything about the Americans, from their social condition to their laws, is extraordinary; but the most extraordinary thing of all is the land that supports them."[13] He observed that Americans "have an immensely high opinion of themselves and are not far from believing that they form a species apart from the rest of the human race."[14]

As the U.S. frontier moved westward to occupy the vast territory between the Atlantic and Pacific Oceans in the nineteenth century, many Americans believed they had a **Manifest Destiny** to occupy the North American continent. The term *manifest destiny* was coined by publicist John Sullivan, in his article, "The Great Nation of Futurity." Sullivan wrote that,

Manifest Destiny: the belief that it was the God-given right of Americans to occupy the North American continent.

> our national birth was the beginning of a new history, the formation and progress of an untried political system, which separates us from the past and connects us with the future only; and so far as regards the entire development of the natural rights of man, in moral, political, and national life, we may confidently assume that our country is destined to be the great nation of futurity.

Emphasizing that the United States is a nation blessed by Providence, Sullivan claimed, "We are the nation of human progress, and who will, what can, set limits to our onward march? Providence is with us, and no earthly power can."[15]

Resting on the ideology of American Exceptionalism, Manifest Destiny proclaimed that Divine Providence, in bestowing a vast continent with immense expanses of land and an abundance of natural resources on Americans, had favored them above all other peoples. Protected from hostile and less deserving nations by the great Atlantic and Pacific Oceans, Americans had created the best of all possible political systems—a republican government, democratic institutions, and a free enterprise economy. As the recipients of Providence's blessings, Americans had a mission in the world. The United States, an exemplary and exceptional nation, was to be a beacon light of freedom and democracy for people in less favored lands.

Influencing both culture and politics, American Exceptionalism shaped American beliefs and attitudes about education. The public schools Americans established were agencies for constructing a sense of identification with and loyalty to the United States. The public schools, like the country they served, were unique institutions established to educate the sons and daughters of an exceptional people. Originally called common schools, they differed from old Europe's class-based educational institutions. Unlike old Europe's schools, American public schools were the great social equalizers that were open to all children. While European schools reflected a socio-economic class organization that benefited the children of aristocrats, American public schools brought children from all classes into one egalitarian institution. Whereas Europe's schools reproduced the socio-economic status quo, American public schools gave students the gift of upward social and economic mobility. In the public education ideology, common schools are special, unique institutions, created by an exceptional people.

ETHNONATIONALISM

We now turn to ethnonationalism, an important contemporary ideology that is generating major changes in the relationships among people, especially in multiethnic nation-states. Nationalism generates a sense of identification with the nation-state; ethnonationalism unites the members of the same racial, ethnic, or tribal group in a sense of ethnic identity with their group.

At first glance, nationalism and ethnonationalism may appear similar. In the nation-states where there is a single racial or ethnic group such as Japan and Iceland, nationalism and ethnicity converge and are mutually reinforcing. In multiethnic, multitribal, or multiracial nation-states, however, ethnonationalism may cause groups within the nation-state to diverge and often oppose each other.

Whereas Nationalism constructs primary identification and cohesion with the nation-state, ethnonationalism instead focuses primary identification and loyalty on one's particular racial and ethnic group. Ethnonationalism rests on the belief, often embodied in a powerful myth, that an individual is a member of a unique group because of descent from common ancestors and a blood relationship shared only with those similarly descended, as is the case of Serbs, Croats, Quebecois, Ibos, or Basques, for example.[16] Those sharing their perceived common ancestry may address each other as brothers or sisters. Ethnonationalism sees the members of the group as related through kinship. Not dependent on genetic verification, the belief in common ancestry is mythic and emotional. Myth, as used here, refers to a powerful sense of meaning that may be partially historical or pseudohistorical but nonetheless is the reference point for belief in a common ancestral identity. Although the mythic ideology supporting ethnonationalism is emotional and subconscious, it creates ethnic group self-identification. For ethnonationalist identity, the scientifically correct description of ethnic group membership is not paramount; what the group believes to be historically and contemporaneously true is of utmost significance.

The various enthnonational groups have strong traditions and narratives, often epics, about the particular group's origins, history, triumphs, and adversities. Many ethnonational groups trace their origins to a creation story or epic. For example, the ancient Israelites believed they were descended from Abraham and the Romanians from the ancient Latinized Dacians.[17] The collective memory of Serbs is stirred by commemorations of their defeat at the Battle of Kosovo in 1389, in which they were led by the heroic Prince Lazar. The transmission of the group's language and heritage from the older generation to the younger takes place through informal as well as formal education. In situations in which the particular ethnic group is suppressed by a more dominant group, its ethnic heritage may be passed on informally or even secretly. Whereas nationalism seeks to focus on the nation as a larger and more encompassing entity, ethnonationalism, especially in multiethnic and multiracial nation-states, may erode larger commitments and replace them with more particular racial or ethnic identification.

In Africa, ethnonationalism takes the form of tribalism. In countries such as Nigeria, Burundi, Rwanda, the Sudan, and others, the primary identification is often to the tribe rather than to the nation-state. In Nigeria, for example, the political and educational situation has been tortured by attempts of Yorubas, Hausas, and Ibos to gain hegemony over each other. In the Sudan, the dominant group, supported by the state, has repressed and conducted a campaign to remove the African minority.

In the Western world, ethnonationalism has asserted itself in political and educational conflicts in Canada where the French-speaking Quebecois energetically seek to maintain their language and culture against Anglicization; in Belgium, where the Flemish resist Walloons; and in Spain, where the Basques seek greater autonomy. For international education, especially peace and conflict-resolution education and multicultural education, the contemporary rise of ethnonationalism poses immense challenges.

Nationalism, resting in the nation-state or country, and ethnonationalism, resting in the ethnic group, poses a contemporary world dilemma. In some instances, the nation-state and the ethnonational group are in violent confrontation and conflict. Some subordinated ethnic groups such as the Kurds in Iraq, Iran, and Turkey; the Chechens in Russia; and the Albanians in Kosovo have resorted to armed conflict to win independence or more autonomy. As an emergent or reemergent international trend, ethnonationalism is a significant force in multiethnic nation-states that range from technologically developed countries such as Canada and Belgium to former Soviet-bloc countries in eastern Europe such as the constituent republics of the former USSR and the former Yugoslavia to less technologically developed nations such as Somalia, Nigeria, Rwanda, and Sri Lanka. Ethnonationalism is a worldwide trend as the preponderant number of nation-states are multiethnic, and ethnic consciousness has been rising rather than diminishing.

Throughout the world, there are signs of ethnonationalist conflict and a recognition that political and ethnic boundaries rarely coincide. A list of conflict areas illustrates this point: Russia and the other republics of the former Soviet Union; the successor states of the former Yugoslavia; tribal conflict in Nigeria, Burundi, Uganda, and Somalia; ethnic and racial conflict in Tibet and other border regions of the People's Republic of China; communal strife in India, especially among Muslims, Hindus, and Sikhs; language conflict in Belgium between Flemings and Walloons; conflict in Mexico between mestizos and Indians; ethnic and language conflict in Canada between English- and French-speaking groups, particularly in Quebec. The issue among the Quebecois, the French-speaking people of Quebec, is whether they consider themselves to be Canadians or to be a different people. The issue illustrates ethnonationalism in a multiethnic country such as Canada. What is the language? What is the history? What is the culture? The list of conflict areas where ethnonationalism is the root cause is a long one.

Ethnonationalism and Education

As indicated, education, especially schooling, is a process that creates group identity and the sense of "we-feeling." Informal education—living in a particular ethnocultural milieu of family, church, media, and community—socializes children into that particular ethnic group. In instances in which the particular ethnic group is dominant, schools, too, continue the process of ethnic socialization. In instances in which the particular ethnic group is subordinant, however, the group's children may attend schools where the language of instruction and the curriculum reflects the dominant group's culture rather than its own. Historically, the process of Americanization in the United States represented the use of schooling to impose the dominant white, English-speaking, Protestant culture on subordinated groups. The process, if successful, erodes the subordinant culture and assimilates its members into the dominant culture. Some of the controversies over bilingual, bicultural, and multicultural education in the United States reflect ethnonational issues.

In some countries, ethnonational issues are interwoven with language issues. Is there to be an official language or are there to be several languages used in government and education? When ethnonational issues come to the surface in education, they involve: (1) using the ethnic group's language rather than the dominant group's official language; (2) including the ethnic group's traditions, literature, and history in the curriculum; and (3) constructing a school milieu that celebrates and reinforces ethnic group membership and identity. Defenders of the nation-state as the central focus of identity contend that using several languages and literatures rather than the dominant national one is divisive and weakens the nation-state. Those who seek ethnonational recognition, autonomy, or independence, in contrast, argue that each group has the right to ensure its ongoing existence. In education, conflicts between multiethnic state and subgroup ethnonational identity occur over control of schools, curriculum, and language of instruction. Cases of such conflict have occurred in Canada, where the Quebecois have resisted Anglicization; in Belgium, where the Flemish have resisted the imposition of French; and in India, where non-Hindi speakers have opposed the imposition of Hindi. Ethnonationalism creates resistance to cultural and educational impositions by other groups, but it also uses education positively to preserve and extend the particular ethnic group's identifying characteristics. Among these characteristics are (1) the use of the ethnic mother tongue as the medium of instruction rather than the official national language; (2) the inclusion of the ethnic group's literature, history, and traditions in the curriculum to create a sense of group identity; and (3) the use of the hidden curriculum to reinforce a sense of "we-feeling" by cultivating a group response to ethnonational symbols.

In educational policy studies, the concept and force of ethnonationalism need analysis. Education, in its organized form as schooling, has traditionally (1) transmitted the cultural heritage from the adult members of the particular society to the children; and (2) since the late eighteenth century, been a force for creating national identity through the teaching of a national language, literature, and history in the school curriculum. Although they involve some degree of imposition, these two large goals have shaped educational programs in modern nation-states. American educators have debated the degree to which the school and the curriculum should transmit and cultivate both a common cultural identity and also encourage recognition and cultivation of more particular racial, ethnic, and language identities. Multiculturalism has been an American educational response to cultural, racial, ethnic, and language diversities. Unlike immigrant and racial groups in the United States, the ethnonational groups throughout the world tend to be located in particular regions within nation-states that they consider their traditional ancestral cultural preserve and homeland.

My Reflections on Philosophy of Education: A Nationalist, American Exceptionalist, Ethnonationalist, and Multicultural Episode

As I reviewed this chapter, I recalled an event that took place when I attended a program sponsored by a local Czech and Slovak genealogical society. I am a third generation Slovak American; like many of my generation, I have lost many of my ethnic roots and am trying to rediscover them. The program, which featured presentations on Czech, Slovak, and Moravian cultures and traditions, took place at an old but well-maintained Bohemian restaurant. It was in a large room that contained two huge wall murals—one of Prague, the capital of the Czech Republic, and the other of George Washington. I was struck to see Washington, kneeling in prayer, in the snow at Valley Forge. I was impressed to see this image that so strongly conveys American Exceptionalism in a Bohemian restaurant.

A feature of the program was a performance by children from a Czech dancing school. The children, mostly girls dressed in traditional costumes, sang and danced to Czech and Slovak songs. Their songs and dances illustrated ethnonationalism, the identification with an ethnic group.

Then, the most moving aspect of the program occurred. A young girl, probably about age seven, sang the Czech national anthem. The audience stood and some of the older people joined in the singing. It was a bit emotional, but what impressed me the most was that the girl was a bi-racial child. Her mother, a Slovak American, accompanied her on the piano. When she had finished, her father, an African American, picked her up and hugged her. So what began with American Exceptionalism, moved through ethnonationalism, and culminated in a multicultural celebration of a shared human experience.

NATIONALISM, ETHNONATIONALISM, AND MULTICULTURAL EDUCATION

Throughout history, nationalism has posed serious challenges to education for international understanding. Today, the resurgence of ethnonationalism has made these challenges even more pressing. The dilemma for educators is that nationalism and ethnonationalism can lead to positive personal identification and group solidarity, but also to destructive rivalries. Today, education in the United States and other countries is infused with multicultural programs that seek to cultivate the positive aspects of ethnicity without accentuating the negative aspects of rivalry, antagonism, and conflict. Multicultural education emphasizes that although human beings belong to diverse racial, ethnic, and language groups they all share a common humanity with the same needs, hopes, and fears. Multicultural education seeks to expose and examine racial and ethnic stereotyping and bigotry.

The history of life on earth is one of magnificent cultural achievements but also of the gross inhumanity of people toward each other. Throughout the world, this inhumanity has taken the form of violence by one national, racial, ethnic, or religious group against another. From the time of the great Oriental empires of Egypt, Mesopotamia, India, and China, purges and extermination of people who were different have occurred.

Violence of group against group reached its extreme form during World War II when the Nazis operated concentration camps in which millions of Jews, Slavs, gypsies, and others were systematically exterminated. The Nazi racial ideology regarded those who were being exterminated as subhumans who were to be eliminated so that the favored "Aryans" would rule the earth. Part of the process of extermination involved deliberate efforts to dehumanize the victims, as occurred in the infamous Warsaw ghetto. When one group looks at another as so different that they are not members of the same human family, the danger of violence and genocide occurs.

Since the end of World War II, multiculturalism and its inclusion in the school curriculum have become a worldwide educational movement. Internationally, it is possible to identify several cases in which multicultural education is either being implemented or needs to be implemented. Although some nations may appear to be homogeneous at first glance, on closer examination they are likely to have multicultural populations. Nations that have been settled by large-scale immigrations invariably exhibit multicultural situations. Among such nations are the United States, Australia, Canada, New Zealand, South Africa, Chile, Argentina, and other Latin American nations. In addition to the immigrant population in these nations, there is also a native indigenous population that was present before the immigrants arrived. In the United States, the indigenous people are the Native American population. In Australia, it is the native Austroloid peoples, and in New Zealand, the Maoris. In these nations, multicultural education examines immigrant–indigenous cultures and relationships.

A second kind of multicultural issue arises in nations, often former colonial countries, that have a large number of ethnic, language, and perhaps racial groups. In Asia, India presents an example of a nation with seventeen major languages, several large ethnic divisions, particularly those of Aryan and Dravidian stock, and major religions such as Hinduism, Islam, and Sikhism. Nigeria in sub-Saharan Africa, with its more than 400 languages and dialects, is still another example of a nation in this category.

A third type of multicultural issue can be found in eastern and central Europe, including the former Soviet Union, where different ethnic and language groups are included in the same nation-state. In these nations, ethnic and language tensions have a long history. Since the end of Soviet control, many supposedly dormant ethnic tensions have been rekindled. For example, the former Yugoslavia, especially Bosnia and Kosovo, which are composed of Serbians, Croatians, and Slavic Muslims, is a region of ethnic, language, and religious hostilities. Ethnic and language tensions are also present in Slovakia between Slovaks, Hungarians, and Roma; in Bulgaria between the Bulgar majority and the Turkish minority; and in Romania between the Romanian majority and the Hungarian minority. In addition to ethnic rivalries in central and eastern Europe, the region has a long history of anti-Semitism, especially in the former Soviet Union and Poland.

In western Europe, the former homogeneity that characterized nations such as the Netherlands, France, Germany, and the United Kingdom has been eclipsed by immigration to these countries. In the United Kingdom, there has been immigration of peoples from Britain's former colonies in Asia, such as Pakistan and India, in Africa, and in the Caribbean. In France, immigrants have come from Indochina and North Africa. In the Netherlands, there has been immigration from Indonesia. These former colonial rulers are experiencing the need for multicultural education. The United Kingdom, for example, had made concerted efforts at multicultural education, especially in its larger cities, where there is significant cultural, ethnic, racial, and religious diversity. Still another kind of immigration in western Europe has been that of workers and their families from countries such as Turkey and Poland who have settled in technologically developed nations such as Germany, Switzerland, and Sweden. With the implementation of the European Economic Community in 1992, Europe is becoming increasingly multinational and cross-cultural as persons from the participatory nations freely move across borders for economic, professional, educational, and cultural reasons.

School administrators and teachers throughout the world are now experiencing the need to develop multicultural sensitivity and pedagogical skills to educate diverse groups. The awareness of the need for multicultural education has become so significant that James A. Banks, a leading authority on the subject, has called it "an international reform movement."[18]

Today, the world is full of ethnic, religious, and racial violence and atrocities. The list of acts of ethnic, racial, and religious intolerance and violence goes on and on. This violence takes the form of terrorism, repression, and at its extreme, genocide.

CONSTRUCTING YOUR OWN PHILOSOPHY OF EDUCATION

At the beginning of the chapter, you were asked how nationalism, as an ideology, might relate to your own philosophy of education. As you reflect on your education, do you recall if certain subjects such as English language and literature and American history carried a nationalist or American Exceptionalist impulse? Do you identify with a particular racial, ethnic, or language group as a primary or secondary source of identification? Now that you have read the chapter and discussed it with your colleagues, will nationalism, especially American Exceptionalism, have an influence in shaping your ideas of education, schooling, teaching, and learning?

Conclusion

This chapter examined the ideology of nationalism and the related ideologies of American Exceptionalism and ethnonationalism and their implications for education. It explored how national identity and collective consciousness are constructed from history and myth. It then considered how school systems are related to nation-states and are agencies for developing primary identification with the nation. National school systems were examined as agencies to deliberately instill the sense of nationalism in the young as a means of their political socialization in the nation-state. American Exceptionalism was examined as an ideology that has given Americans a belief that they are a unique, indeed, an exceptional people. Ethnonationalism was examined as a revival of an old but submerged ideology that makes the racial or ethnic group the focus of an individual's primary identification.

The world is organized into nation-states, independent, sovereign countries, each of which uses nationalism to create and maintain a sense of national identity. National school systems socialize that nation's children into its citizens. How this socialization takes place is vital for our future. It can involve both identification with one's own country and also respect for the people of other countries. Or it can take the form of chauvinism, which exalts one's country over all others. Extreme nationalism has led to world wars and conflicts. Ethnic identification too can be a force of group pride and self-esteem. It can be a positive celebration of one's ethnic heritage that also respects the racial and ethnic heritages of other people. If, however, ethnic identification becomes a strident assertion of one group's superiority over others, it can lead to suspicion of and violence toward other groups. Strident ethnonationalism can degenerate into ethnocentrism, the belief in the inherent superiority of one's group and seeing members of other groups as inferior.

Questions for Inquiry and Discussion

1. What is a collective consciousness? Do you believe you share a collective consciousness? If so, how did your upbringing and schooling help to form this consciousness?
2. Think about the relationship of history and myth in forming a collective national memory. Did you encounter this relationship in your education? Do you find examples of it in schools today?
3. Do you find examples of American Exceptionalism in your own educational experience? Did you find aspects of American Exceptionalism in your courses in English language and American history and literature?

Did you find it in school-related ceremonies and commemorations? Do you find it operating in schools and society today?

4. Reflect on the idea that schools should transmit the American cultural heritage. How do you conceive of the American cultural heritage? Is your version the same as that presented in the school curriculum? What does this mean for curriculum and instruction? Do you favor or oppose the concept of transmitting the cultural heritage?
5. In your own education, did you encounter special activities related to a national commemorative holiday or observation? What did you learn? Has this learning had an impact on your national consciousness?

Topics for Reflection and Inquiry

1. Reflect on your national identity. How did you become conscious of your nationality or ethnicity? Write a short autobiography that focuses on your national identity, especially the role played by your community, schools, and teachers in shaping your identity.
2. Begin a clippings file of newspaper and magazine articles that deal with the contemporary debate over immigration. After you have collected a number of articles, analyze them for elements of nationalism, American Exceptionalism, ethnonationalism, and multiculturalism.
3. Interview international students from various countries who are studying at your college or university. Invite them to discuss education, schooling, and the forming of national character from their own perspectives. Then analyze your findings.
4. If you are teaching or planning to teach in the primary and intermediate grade levels, examine the books and materials used in the language arts. See whether you detect elements relating to constructing a national identity.
5. If you are teaching or planning to teach at the secondary level, examine the books and materials used to teach history and literature. See whether you detect elements relating to constructing a national identity.
6. Begin a clippings file of newspaper and magazine articles that deal with the contemporary debate over bilingual and bicultural education. After you have collected a number of articles, analyze them for elements of nationalism, American Exceptionalism, ethnonationalism, and multiculturalism.
7. Debate the topic: "Resolved, that English should be the official language of the United States."
8. Visit a cultural center or heritage museum of a racial or ethnic group. Determine whether the exhibits at the center or museum have ethnonationalist elements.
9. Access Nationalism in the Encyclopaedia Britannica at http://britannica.com/EBchecked/topic/405644/nationalism. Then compare and contrast African and Asian Nationalism with American Exceptionalism.

Internet Resources

For definitions of a nation, nationalism, Internet resources, and a bibliography, access "Nationalism," Stanford Encyclopedia of Philosophy, at http://www.Plato.stanford.edu/entries/nationalism/.

For cultural, European, Asian, and African Nationalism, access the Encyclopaedia Britannica at http://britannica.com/EBchecked/topic/405644/nationalism.

For nationalism in the "Regents Prep" for New York state, access http://www.regentsprep.org/Regents/global/themes/.

For discussions and debates about nationalism, access the "Nationalism Project" at http://www.nationalismproject.org/what.htm.

For the theory of nationalism, access www.dmoz.org/Society/Politics/Nationalism/Theory.

Suggestions for Further Reading

Brass, Paul R. *Ethnicity and Nationalism: Theory and Comparison*. Newbury Park, CA: Sage, 1991.

Connor, Walker. *Ethnonationalism: The Quest for Understanding*. Princeton, NJ: Princeton University Press, 1994.

Diamond, Larry, and Marc F. Plattner. *Nationalism, Ethnic Conflict, and Democracy*. Baltimore, MD: Johns Hopkins University Press, 1994.

Eriksen, Thomas H. *Ethnicity and Nationalism: Anthropological Perspectives*. London, UK, and Boulder, CO: Pluto Press, 1993.

Farnen, Russell F., ed. *Nationalism, Ethnicity, and Identity: Cross National and Comparative Perspectives*. New Brunswick, NJ: Transaction, 1994.

Gates, Henry L., Jr. *Loose Canons: Notes on the Culture Wars*. New York: Oxford University Press, 1992.

Gellner, Ernest. *Encounters with Nationalism*. Oxford, UK, and Cambridge, MA: Blackwell, 1994.

___. *Nations and Nationalism*. Ithaca, NY: Cornell University Press, 2008.

Gillis, John R., ed. *Commemorations: The Politics of National Identity*. Princeton, NJ: Princeton University Press, 1993.

Grosby, Steven. *Nationalism: A Very Short Introduction*. Oxford, UK: Oxford University Press, 2005.

Hutchinson, John, and Anthony D. Smith, eds. *Nationalism*. New York: Oxford University Press, 1994.

Ignatieff, Michael. *Blood and Belonging: Journeys into the New Nationalism*. New York: Farrar, Straus, and Giroux, 1994.

Kammen, Michael. *Contested Values: Democracy and Diversity in American Culture*. New York: St. Martin's Press, 1995.

Nieto, Sonia. *Affirming Diversity: The Sociopolitical Context of Multicultural Education*. New York: Longman, 1992.

Reimers, Fernando, and Noel McGinn. *Informed Dialogue: Using Research to Shape Education Policy around the World*. Westport, CT: Praeger, 1997.

___. *Nationalism*. Cambridge, UK, and Malden, MA: Polity Press, 2010.

Takaki, Ronald. *A Different Mirror: A History of Multicultural America*. Boston: Little, Brown and Co., 1993.

Notes

1. *The Random House Dictionary of the English Language* (New York: Random House, 1968), 886.
2. Steven Grosby, *Nationalism: A Very Short Introduction* (Oxford, UK: Oxford University Press, 2005), 7.
3. Ibid., 4–5.
4. In introducing his subject, Steven Grosby uses the phrase "us and them" as a basic feature of nationalism. See Grosby, *Nationalism: A Very Short Introduction,* 1.
5. Ibid., 22.
6. Ibid., 8.
7. Ibid., 10–11.
8. Ibid., 26.
9. Ibid., 83.
10. Herodotus, *The History,* quoted in Steven Grosby, *Nationalism: A Very Short Introduction* (Oxford, UK: Oxford University Press, 2005), 2.
11. Gary Gerstle, "Liberty, Coercion, and the Making of Americans," *Journal of American History, 84* (2) (1997), 524–588; quote from p. 555.
12. Linda S. Levstik, Chapter 17: "Articulating the Silences: Teachers' and Adolescents' Conceptions of Historical Significance," in Peter N. Stearns, Peter Seixas, and Sam Wineburg, Eds. *Knowing, Teaching, and Learning History: National and International Perspectives* (New York: New York University Press, 2000), 284.
13. Alexis de Tocqueville, *Democracy in America,* J. P. Lawrence, ed. (New York: Perennial Classics// Harper-Collins, 2000), 280.
14. Ibid., 374.
15. John L. Sullivan, "The Great Nation of Futurity," *The United States Democratic Review, 6* (23), 426–430.
16. My definition of ethnonationalism relies heavily on Walker Connor, *Ethnonationalism: The Quest for Understanding* (Princeton, NJ: Princeton University Press, 1994), xi.
17. Grosby, *Nationalism: A Very Short Introduction,* 12.
18. James A. Banks, *Multiethnic Education: Theory and Practice,* 2nd ed. (Boston: Allyn & Bacon, 1988), 3–4.

Liberalism and Education

John Stuart Mill (1806–1873), English Utilitarian and Liberal philosopher who argued for individual liberty and freedom.

CHAPTER PREVIEW

Liberalism, an important Western and American ideology, as an "ism" is derived from the word *liberal.* Open to change, liberals believe in progress and oppose restrictions on individual liberties. Opposing repressive political regimes, liberals support representative, parliamentary, democratic government. They believe that people should enjoy the greatest possible individual freedom and that this freedom should be guaranteed by due process of law and protection of civil liberties. In education, liberals, not bound by tradition, believe in the free flow of ideas and the testing of human experience. Liberalism, based on its Enlightenment origins, is optimistic about the possibility of the progressive improvement of human culture and society.

At the beginning of our discussion, we examine the concept of "liberal education." In its ancient Greek origins, a liberal education was an education for free persons (almost always men) in contrast to training for slaves. As the concept developed in Western education, liberal education came to mean a grounding in the arts and sciences. While Liberals may see education as liberal in the sense of the arts and sciences, Conservatives, too, endorse this kind of education. Liberalism in education means more than the arts and sciences curriculum—it also describes certain beliefs, attitudes, values, and especially procedures.

The chapter discusses the following major topics:

- Liberalism's Historical Antecedents
- John Locke as a founder of Liberalism
- Jeremy Bentham's and John Stuart Mill's Utilitarianism
- Modern American Liberalism
- Liberal Ideology's Key Elements
- Liberalism's educational implications

As you read the chapter, reflect on your own educational experiences. Determine if you experienced Liberalism in your own education. Since Liberalism is an important social, political, economic, and educational implications, consider its impact on American society generally. Did you have teachers and professors who were Liberals? How did you react to them? As you read and discuss this chapter, determine if you agree or disagree with Liberalism. Will you incorporate aspects of Liberalism in your own philosophy of education?

LIBERALISM'S HISTORICAL ANTECEDENTS

Liberalism originated in the late sixteenth and early seventeenth centuries when medieval feudalism was disintegrating as a political system in Europe. The emergent commercial class of shopkeepers, bankers, lawyers, and other professionals began to challenge the old landed aristocracy for social and political power. The established class structure at the time of the middle class challenge in Western Europe consisted of the feudal aristocracy and the peasantry. Aristocrats held land, and with it, political power and social status. Membership in the aristocracy was ascribed because a person had to be born into aristocratic families. The same was true of the peasants who tilled the soil—their situation was largely ascribed. **Ascription** means that a person's role is defined at birth; a person typically stayed in the class into which he or she was born.

Ascription: a term meaning that a person's social and economic role is defined by the class into which he or she is born.

Educationally, if a person's role is known at birth, educational decision making is already done for the person. The son of an aristocrat will be educated to exercise his father's role as a landowner; the daughter will be educated to be the wife of an aristocrat. Children of peasants will be trained, largely by doing tasks, to be farmers. Although this socio-economic condition prevailed during much of the Middle Ages, it began to erode as new classes of individuals emerged that were neither aristocrats nor peasants. Occupying a position on the social ladder between the aristocrats and the peasantry, these new middle classes were called the **bourgeoisie**. The middle classes came to their position through their use of economic power; they earned or merited their status. In the early eighteenth century, their political role was still undefined and being shaped—largely through their own efforts. Their educational situation, too, was ambiguous because they needed to create their own kinds of schools.[1]

Bourgeoisie: the French word for members of the middle class.

By the eighteenth century, liberals were constructing an evolving ideology that challenged the absolutism of the divine right of kings and aristocratic lords. The rationalism of the Enlightenment, or Age of Reason, nourished liberal ideology. French *philosophes* such as de Tracy and Condillac, who had initially articulated the concept of ideology, sought to replace the dogmas of the church and the traditional authority of absolutism with what they believed were the empirically grounded truths supporting a new society. The *philosophes* believed they could construct a social science, an empirical way of studying society and politics that replicated how scientists investigated natural and physical reality. Once they had discovered the natural laws of human growth and social development, they could begin a twofold mission of guided reform. First, existing ideas, especially those supporting institutions such as absolutist monarchy, could be either removed or reconstructed; next, new, more rational and scientifically based institutions could be created. If this were done, humankind's future, unlike its past, would be better and more progressive. In this Enlightenment project for a progressive future, existing educational institutions—schools and universities—needed to be reappraised and transformed. Existing schools served their aristocratic and clerical masters in that they taught blind tradition and superstition as unquestioned "truths." Using dogmatic catechetical rote learning in schools and prescientific Aristotelian scholasticism in universities, educational institutions maintained the old order's intellectual stagnation rather than the new progressive scientific outlook.

For the French philosophes, see the chapter on Ideology and Education.

Liberalism was very much an ideology that came out of the intellectual, social, political, economic, and educational change generated by the Enlightenment. It inspired the middle classes to throw off domination by absolute monarchs and privileged aristocrats. Culturally, Liberals looked to individual initiative and innovation to develop new social and educational structures and processes. An interesting feature of the Liberal cultural agenda is that it is always unfinished and remains incomplete.

JOHN LOCKE: A FOUNDER OF LIBERALISM

This section examines the contribution of the English philosopher John Locke (1632–1704) to Liberal ideology. Our discussion of Locke is divided into three parts: (1) a short biographical sketch, (2) a discussion of his ideas on epistemology and education, and (3) an analysis of his *Two Treatises on Civil Government* (1690), which established Liberalism's essential political principles.

Locke's Biographical Sketch

Locke was the son of John Locke, an attorney and small landowner. Locke's family members were nonconformist Puritans who dissented from the established Church of England. For the first fourteen years of his life, Locke was home-schooled by his father.[2] From 1646 to 1651, John Locke attended Westminster School, a renowned preparatory institution, where he studied traditional Latin and Greek classics to prepare for entry into Oxford University. In 1652, at age 20, Locke was awarded the Bachelor of Arts degree and he received his master's degree in 1658. In 1660, he became a lecturer in Greek, rhetoric, and moral philosophy. He then studied medicine. Although Locke did not complete a medical degree, he was a respected physician.

Locke's overriding interest was political philosophy rather than medicine. His appointment as secretary and personal physician to Lord Ashley, Earl of Shaftesbury, in 1667 involved Locke with British politics. He also served as tutor to Ashley's son.

While Ashley was Lord Chancellor of England, from 1672 to 1674, Locke held several government appointments. When Shaftesbury fell from power during the Stuart restoration, Locke went into exile as an expatriate in Holland. While in exile, Locke completed his *Treatises on Government*. With the Glorious Revolution of 1688 and William and Mary's accession to the English throne, Locke returned to England where he served as Commissioner of Appeals. In ailing health, Locke retired from government service in 1700 and died four years later.

Locke made important contributions to Liberal ideology in his *Two Treatises of Government* (1689) and *A Letter Concerning Toleration* (1689). His works on philosophy, *An Essay Concerning Human Understanding* (1690) and *Of the Conduct of the Understanding* (1706), contributed directly to empiricist epistemology and indirectly to sense-based process learning. Locke's *Some Thoughts Concerning Education* (1693) dealt specifically with issues of teaching and learning.

Locke on Epistemology and Education

Locke's *An Essay Concerning Human Understanding* (1690) became a classic statement of empiricist epistemology.[3] He began his analysis by attacking the Platonic theory of innate ideas, which asserted that human ideas originate in fundamental concepts present in the mind at birth and prior to sensory experience. In attacking Platonic assumptions, Locke sought to establish the empiricist view that human knowledge originates in sense perception. At birth the mind is a **tabula rasa**, a clean slate, a white paper, on which the data of experience are impressed. These ideas are either simple or complex. If complex, they are relational and arise from mental faculties that enable us to compare, contrast, abstract, and remember them.

For Plato's epistemology of reminiscence, see the chapter on Idealism and Education.

Tabula Rasa: a Latin phrase meaning a blank or clear slate or table. In Locke's epistemology, the mind, too, is blank, or clear of ideas, prior to sensory experience.

Locke's theory challenged the exclusive reliance on tradition, custom, and authority based on immutable first principles. His **empiricism** emphasized using the scientific method. Locke's epistemology suggests that knowledge and human character are shaped by a person's experience. While there are no innate ideas in the mind, individuals, however, have different mental potentialities.

Empiricism: an epistemology that holds that human ideas are derived from sensory experience.

Locke's epistemology argues that we construct our concepts of knowledge through the cognitive process of building ideas from our sense experience. Every human being possesses this power of generating ideas through experience; therefore, knowing is an individual matter. It is not limited to a group or class of people such as an aristocracy or a gifted elite who have an innate power of knowing more than others. Locke's epistemology individualized and equalized the process of knowing. Individuals have the freedom to act on their ideas and to accept the consequences for their actions.

Locke's *Conduct of the Understanding* reiterated the empirical epistemological arguments made earlier in *An Essay Concerning Human Understanding* and applied them to education. Locke warned that the belief in innate ideas gave an unwarranted power to elites who claimed that they had privileged insight into the truth and that their pronouncements were authoritative. Locke identified the following procedures as necessary in critical thinking: (1) a careful examination of how one's ideas had originated in sensation; (2) reflection and analysis of how the data of sensation were rendered into clear and distinct ideas; (3) skill in using language to express our ideas clearly and precisely; (4) civil discussion of ideas that avoids reliance on traditional biases and prejudices. Locke also introduced the concept of "indifferancy," which John Stuart Mill would develop further. Indifferancy meant that the person, not motivated by a special interest, could be impartial and unbiased in considering different opinions and making an informed judgment.[4]

Locke's *Some Thoughts Concerning Education* (1693) was a guide to an English gentleman's education.[5] The goal of education is to develop the habits of reasonable thinking in children's minds and to develop their bodies physically. Locke urged teachers to guide instruction toward achieving four major outcomes in students:

1. Virtue, the practice of self-denial, which inhibits impulsive behavior and resists temptation; cultivating virtuous habits facilitates leading a life governed by reason.
2. Wisdom, the shrewd and practical skill that enables a person to manage affairs and property successfully and to be prudent in human relationships.
3. Good breeding, which ensures that a person will be socially responsible.
4. Studying morality, politics, civil society, government, law, and history as a preparation for participation in representative institutions.

Locke's ideas introduced themes that became associated with Liberal pedagogy. Reinforcing the emphasis on individualism, Locke advised teachers to recognize and respect children's individual differences and to use these interests to motivate each child's learning. Teachers should encourage their students to develop their own self-esteem and to value the self-esteem of other persons. Emphasizing the middle-class preference for utilitarian and practical over classical and ornamental studies, Locke recommended a curriculum of such useful subjects as reading, arithmetic, writing, accounting, geography, geometry, science, and history. Anticipating the Liberal emphasis on orderly decision-making procedures, Locke stressed the importance of civility, which meant respecting the rights of others while expecting them to observe the rules that governed the group behavior.[6]

Locke on Government

Locke's *Two Treatises of Government* exercised a powerful influence on the development of Liberal ideology. His concepts that the individual possessed inalienable natural rights of life, liberty, and property and that governments are created as representative institutions to protect these rights expressed Liberalism's germinal ideas. This section examines these concepts and their educational implications.

Locke's social contract theory contributed to a new conception of the polity—a commonwealth of self-governing individuals. Locke's **natural rights theory** and contract form of government had the greatest impact on the American Liberal theorists, especially Thomas Jefferson and the framers of the Declaration of Independence.

Natural Rights Theory: the belief that individuals possess inherent rights; for Locke, these were life, liberty, and property; for Jefferson, life, liberty, and pursuit of happiness.

Locke and Human Rights

In 1690, Locke's *Two Treatises of Government* not only justified Britain's Glorious Revolution of 1688 but also elaborated a new ideological perspective. Finding the general principles governing human association in the original state of nature, Locke claimed that "no one ought to harm another in his life, health, liberty or possession." Each person, like every other individual, equally possessed inherent natural rights to life, liberty, and property. When these natural rights were in jeopardy, individuals in common association formed a social contract in mutual defense against those who transgressed these natural rights. Individuals entered into political society to form a government to protect these natural rights. According to Locke, individuals who unite in one civil body have agreed to "a common established law" and can appeal to a judiciary to which they have given "authority" to settle "controversies between them" and to punish offenders.[7]

For Locke, individuals are free, equal, and independent, and no one can deprive them of property or subject them to another's political power without their consent. Arising from the mutual agreement of those who form the civil society, government relies on majority rule, the fairest way of formulating policy and making political decisions. According to Locke, every person, by agreeing to form a government, enters "an obligation to everyone of that society to submit to majority rule."[8] While all the members of the society agree to the general processes of the social contract, some will agree and others will disagree on specific legislation. Majorities and minorities that arise over specifics are temporary and shifting. Based on the mutual respect of the individuals who comprise the civil society, the rights of both the majority and the minority are to be respected.

In Locke's version of civil society, the three branches of government—legislative, judicial, and executive—are calculated to achieve a balance of power. This threefold division of powers is clearly apparent in U.S. political institutions. In Locke's social compact, a known common law arises from common consent through elected representatives in the legislature. The executive of the commonwealth enforces the common law; the judiciary renders objective decisions based on its interpretation of the common law. For Locke, and for Liberals in general, the legislature is at the heart of representative government. Members of the legislature, coming from the ranks of the people who have joined in the social contract, represent these people. Crucial to the principle of a representative government is the process of election by which citizens elect their representatives to the legislature.

The legislature is created by the individuals who enter into the social contract; its power to enact laws is given to it by the members of society. The elected members of the legislature are subject, as are other individuals, to the laws they enact. Whereas the enacted legislation grows into a cumulative body of law that is subject to revision, the composition of the legislature itself is temporary, its members serving fixed terms. When its work is done in a particular session, the members of the legislature return to their various constituencies.

In addition to its political prescriptions, Locke's Liberalism held significant implications for education. First of all, Locke's prescription of representative institutions directly challenged the doctrine of the "divine right of kings," which held that authority descended from God to the king, then downward to a hereditary aristocracy, and then further downward until it reached the masses of the population. In the divine right of kings theory, no check existed on the sovereign except that which came from God.

In the class structure based on the divine right of kings theory of government, three political castes existed: (1) the reigning monarch and aristocracy of birth, (2) the clergy, and (3) the so-called third estate, which included all other people. Members of all three classes were educated according to the doctrine of social class appropriateness. Because the social roles of both the members of the aristocracy and the masses were ascribed at birth, the type of education that they were to receive depended on, or was appropriate to, their membership in a hereditary social class. Each hereditary socio-economic class had political and economic duties that were also ascribed on the basis of birth. For the prince who was expected to succeed his father to the throne as king, there was instruction in statecraft, diplomacy, and royal etiquette. The prince's education was to prepare him to rule and to exercise authority. The aristocracy received the appropriate education to serve as the monarch's subordinates, magistrates, and officers. They were prepared to be generals in the army, administrators, or diplomats. The hereditary aristocrats were educated in the rubrics of court ceremony. Conversely, the masses of the population were trained as tradesmen, manual workers, farmers, and soldiers. Their civic duties were to hear and obey the commands of hereditary superiors.

The education of the hereditary aristocracy was based on ascribed political and economic roles. Leaders were born to rule and then prepared to exercise their authority. Likewise, followers were born to follow and then conditioned by their training to follow with docile obedience. Because a person's political role was ascribed, civic education was based on performing a specifically defined role rather than participating in the general political process.

Contract Theory: Locke's concept of government as a contract between the government and the governed.

In contrast to the divine right of kings theory, Locke's **contract theory** of government and the evolving Liberal ideology created a change in education. To be sure, the political implications were evident much earlier than the educational ones. Representative government meant that any citizen could be elected to the commonwealth's legislature. The flow of political authority was no longer downward through a hierarchical pattern as in the model of the divine right of kings; rather, it arose from the people—from the governed—who, in forming the social contract, created the government. Because service in the legislature was not hereditary but temporary, civic education was no longer determined by membership in a particular class. Instead, civic education was necessary for all citizens of the commonwealth so that they could cast informed ballots in elections and be prepared to serve in the three branches of government: the legislature, executive, or judiciary.

According to Lockean ideology, the members of the commonwealth needed to be educated as political generalists rather than specialists. An individual's civic destiny was not specifically defined at birth but was influenced by many factors. The elective process defined every citizen as a voter and a decision maker; this meant that a person's civic education should be general and include: (1) the principles of contract government based on the recognition of fundamental human rights, (2) knowledge about the organization and functions of government institutions based on the division of power, (3) knowledge and skill in exercising the procedures of representative institutions, and (4) cultivation of civic attitudes and values that were committed to sustaining representative institutions and processes. The educational implications of Locke's political theory, especially in the United Kingdom and the United States, generated a new conception of civic education.

Locke and the Right of Revolution

In his *Two Treatises of Government,* Locke argued that the government's purpose was to protect the inherent natural rights of its citizens. He sought to justify the revolt of 1688 that overthrew the Stuart monarchy and established William and Mary as constitutional monarchs, subject to parliamentary rule, on England's throne. When a government—such as that of the Stuarts—sought to subvert basic human freedoms, then the people had the right to revolt to regain their original liberty and to establish a new government, thus renewing the social contract.

Thomas Jefferson, in writing the Declaration of Independence, used Locke's arguments to justify the American Revolution against King George III and English rule. Accusing the British monarch of violating the social contract and of depriving the American colonists of their natural rights, the Americans, Jefferson argued, had a right to overthrow and replace Britain's colonial rule with a new republican government. In appealing to natural rights theory, Jefferson proclaimed the self-evident truths that "all men are created equal, that they are endowed by their Creator with certain unalienable rights, that among these are life, liberty, and the pursuit of happiness."

By repressing these self-evident truths, George III had violated the contract between the government and the American colonists. Jefferson affirmed the colonists' right to revolt and to establish a new government to renew the social contract and to secure the people's unalienable rights:

> Whenever any form of government becomes destructive to these ends, it is the right of the people to deter or abolish it, and to institute a new government, allying its foundation on such principles, and organizing its powers in such form as to them shall seem most likely to effect their safety and happiness.

Both Locke and Jefferson identified liberty as one of the three inalienable human rights. Liberty meant freedom to frame alternatives, to choose between them, and to fulfill them through political, social, economic, religious, intellectual, and educational action.

Classical Economic Liberalism

In the nineteenth century, the United Kingdom and the United States experienced the industrial revolution with the harnessing of machine power in the factory system of mass production. A highly influential group of economists, called the Manchester school, added a strong economic rationale to Locke's Liberal ideas on politics and society. This economic rationale became known as **Classical Liberalism**.[9]

Classical Liberalism: the economic theory developed by Adam Smith and others of the Manchester school that government should not interfere with commerce and should encourage free trade in an open market.

Classical Liberals emphasize the right of individuals to possess property and engage in free trade with little or no government interference or regulation. The designation of Classical Liberalism is used to differentiate it as the authoritative nineteenth-century statement of Liberalism from the modern and social welfare Liberalism that developed in the twentieth century. Classical Liberalism has taken on a contemporary significance as the historical source of what is called the Neo-Liberalism of the twenty-first century. (These varieties of Liberalism will be discussed in more detail in later sections of the chapter.) Adam Smith (1723–1790), the foremost theorist of the Manchester school, endorsed a completely free trade or laissez-faire economic and political position. Smith argued that society prospered when its economy was free from government interference and regulations. A free market, Smith believed, is the most efficient mechanism in satisfying human needs and in using natural and human resources most productively. He argued that a natural law of **supply and demand** works on its own to regulate the economy.

Supply and Demand: the classical Liberal argument that the economy is self-regulating by supply and demand; when goods are scarce there is a demand for them in the market; when plentiful, a declining market.

When there is a need (a demand) for a particular product, enterprising entrepreneurs will establish businesses (factories) to manufacture and sell that item. After a time, the need for that item will be satisfied and a surplus will result. As the demand for the item falls, so will the price; factories manufacturing the item will either close or be converted to other areas of production; workers making the item will be laid off, become unemployed, and retrained to make other items. According to Smith, government subsidies to businesses, payments to unemployed workers, or "bailouts" interfere with the economy's natural operations. They are doomed to fail and are economically and socially useless and counterproductive.

Individuals should be encouraged to establish businesses and to compete with other individuals to make profits. To maximize their profits, they will invent new processes of making products more efficiently and more cheaply. These profits will result in investments in business expansion that employ more people and will trickle down to benefit the entire society. Government efforts to regulate the economy, supervise business and working conditions, or interfere with the natural law of supply and demand will only result in bureaucracy that stifles economic innovation and growth. Smith's theory was very powerful in shaping economic policies and attitudes in the United States in the nineteenth century. It provides core ideas to the Neo-Liberal economic theory of the early twenty-first century that serves as a rationale for globalization, namely, that governments should reduce tariffs and other trade barriers, and also privatize social and often educational programs.

David Ricardo (1772–1833) and Thomas Malthus (1766–1834) provided added support to Classical Liberal economic theory. Ricardo, the proponent of the iron law of wages, provided industrialists with an economic rationale for low wages and long hours of work.[10] If wages rose above the subsistence level, workers, Ricardo claimed, would use their increased income to have more children. More children would lead to a labor surplus that would cause workers to either work for lower wages or be "laid off" from their jobs. A far better use of profits would be for more capital investment by industrialists and bankers to build more factories and purchase more machinery to make products more efficiently and at a lower cost. Economic growth would make more products available to more consumers, which, in turn, would create more jobs.

Reverend Thomas Malthus, in his influential *Essay on the Principle of Population as It Affects the Future Improvement of Society* (1798), argued that population has a constant tendency to increase beyond the supply of food. If war or disease did not check population growth, famine would reduce it to manageable levels that could subsist on the food available. Malthus's thesis was used as an argument against government-sponsored social welfare programs to improve working conditions in factories and mines and the sanitary and living conditions of the poor. Malthus joined Smith and Ricardo in arguing that like the inevitable workings of the invisible law of supply and demand, the human condition, too, could not be improved by well-intentioned but misguided "do good" social reformers.

In Classical Liberalism, individuals are the foremost actors in society, economics, politics, and education. Classical Liberals believe that a just society is one in which individuals are free to maximize their personal talents and resources.[11] They would oppose what they would call "unwarranted and unnecessary meddling" to engineer some kind of artificial social equality. Human relationships, like market relationships, are exchanges to satisfy individual interests.

Herbert Spencer's Social Darwinism

In the mid-nineteenth century, the British sociologist Herbert Spencer (1820–1903) revivified the Classical Liberal economic theory of Smith, Ricardo, and Malthus. Popular and widely disseminated, Spencer's opinions on society, politics, economics, and education attracted a receptive audience in the United Kingdom and especially in the United States. Applying Charles Darwin's theory of biological evolution to human society, Spencer constructed the ideology of **Social Darwinism**. Darwin's hypothesis that plants and animals had slowly evolved as a result of a process of natural selection was especially congenial to Spencer, who adapted it to his own social theory. Spencer

Social Darwinism: the transfer of Darwin's biological theory of evolution to society, economics, politics, and education.

provided Classical Liberalism with what appeared to be a modern scientific rationale grounded on evolution.

According to Spencer, evolution was the dynamic process that affected all natural and social phenomena. The most adaptable individuals, in the human as in all species, would adjust quickly to challenges in the natural and social environment. The most intelligent persons, armed with scientific knowledge, would be able to make an efficient adjustment to changes in the environment. It would be foolish and futile to attempt to change society by revolution, legislation, or even by education. Social reforms, regardless of their altruistic humanitarian intentions, would inevitably lead to a larger, more costly, and bureaucratic government that invaded individual rights and liberties.

Spencer, in his essay "What Knowledge Is of Most Worth?" (1855), asked if some subjects rather than others generated useful knowledge and if these useful subjects should be given more time and effort in education. Answering his own queries, Spencer determined that the curriculum should be based on useful activities that related to (1) health, (2) earning a living, (3) raising and educating children, (4) maintaining social and political order, and (5) providing for enjoyment and recreation.

Endorsing private and voluntary education, Spencer opposed state-run schools. For him, the best kind of education emphasized science, the most useful knowledge. Science was most useful in that intelligent individuals could apply it to industry, engineering, and technology. It was important that the fittest individuals came forward and, through competition, climbed to society's upper rungs. Driven by competition and the will to survive, the fittest, by their inventiveness and innovation, would create a better and more efficient and productive society.

Neo-Liberalism

At this point in the discussion, we introduce the ideology called **Neo-Liberalism**. Although it is a twenty-first century ideology, it is positioned here near its nineteenth-century Classical Liberal and Social Darwinist antecedents. Although the prefix *neo* means new, Neo-Liberalism needs to be distinguished from Modern or Social Reform Liberalism, which is discussed later in the chapter. It also needs to be noted that some Conservatives have appropriated many Classical Liberal and Neo-Liberal ideas and accommodated their ideology to them.

Neo-Liberalism: a twenty-first-century version of Classical Liberalism that supports free market ideas in the global economy.

Neo-Liberalism is associated with the twenty-first century worldwide process of **globalization**. Like the nineteenth-century Classical Liberals, contemporary proponents of globalization argue that countries, especially less technologically developed ones in Latin America, eastern Europe, and Africa, need to restructure their governments to reduce regulations and subsidies to inefficient economic sectors such as small farmers, eliminate tariffs and restrictions on free trade, and create representative political institutions. The Neo-Liberal proponents of a worldwide free market economy argue that globalization's long-term benefits will reduce production costs and make goods available to more buyers in an expanding global marketplace. Similar to the arguments of laissez-faire economic theorists in the nineteenth and early twentieth centuries, the proponents of free trade globalization contend that the elimination of tariffs and other trade barriers, erected by individual nation-states, will make production more efficient and bring jobs to more people, especially in less technologically developed countries.

Globalization: the twenty-first-century development of worldwide, global economic, information, entertainment, and educational networks.

Postmodernists, Critical Theorists, and Neo-Marxists have attacked Neo-Liberalism as the rationale that justifies corporate capitalism's economic exploitation of people throughout the world. These critics contend that Neo-Liberalism represents the linking of corporate capitalism with the pretense of establishing democratic institutions throughout the world for exploitative profit-making purposes. Globalization's critics see it as a strategy to exploit the world's poor by turning the earth into a global factory whose engines are driven to give wealth and power to corporate elites.

Liberalism's Internal Tensions

As laissez-faire economic policy became a standard feature of Liberalism throughout the nineteenth century, Liberal political theorists continued to stress freedoms of speech, press, assembly, and religion against a powerful state's interference. Economically, socially, politically, and educationally, Liberals sought to fashion and bring to power an ideology that asserted the rights of individuals and safeguarded the property rights, free markets, freedom of contract, and other interests of the rising middle classes.[12]

Dissatisfied with inherited traditional political, religious, social, and educational systems, Liberals argued for reforms. Determining how to bring about that change was a major issue that divided Liberals into two related but internally divided camps: laissez-faire Classical Liberals and Social Darwinists on one side and those who advocated a government role in bringing about social and political reforms on the other.

UTILITARIANISM

Liberals of all ideological hues continued to agree on Locke's premises that individuals and their natural rights to life, liberty, and property precede and exist independently of society; however, they began to experience an internal tension about the nature of social change and reform, especially government's role. The Classical Liberals—the followers of Smith, Malthus, and Ricardo—and Spencer's Social Darwinists—thought that people could not legislate change, especially economic change, as it was governed by natural, not enacted laws. However, they did believe that government had a role in eliminating the inherited obstacles from the past that attempted to control and regulate the free market economy. For example, government could remove tariffs and trade barriers between nations and prevent combinations of people such as labor unions from strikes that interfered with production. The Classical Liberal and Social Darwinist rationale for free trade continues in contemporary Neo-Liberalism.

Diverging from Classical Liberalism, other Liberals, especially Jeremy Bentham's Utilitarians, believed that the state (government) could legitimately enact limited incremental reforms to improve society.[13] The Utilitarian viewpoint marked a gradual but significant transition in Liberal thinking that would grow into the movement toward modern Liberalism. It moved Liberals away from the natural law thinking of Smith and Spencer and into the belief that laws are social constructions. It developed criteria for judging personal and social actions on how they contributed to the greatest good for the greatest number of people.

Jeremy Bentham (1748–1832) was the son of a wealthy London lawyer. An intellectually gifted child, nicknamed "the philosopher," Bentham was educated at Westminster, a venerable English public school, and Oxford University. Although prepared for a career in law, he devoted himself to philosophy. Using his training as a lawyer, Bentham saw the state as a kind of gardener who removed the weeds so that the useful beneficial plants could grow. Bentham believed that too much of English common law was based on archaic and obsolete encumbrances from the past. He believed that England's judicial system needed to be reformed according to rational principles. Bentham's *Rationale of Judicial Evidence* (1827) proposed to replace Britain's cumbersome legal system based on precedent with a new legal code of easily applied basic regulations.

Utilitarianism: Bentham's philosophy of utility based on calculating pleasure and pain and maximizing pleasure by reducing pain.

Bentham's *Introduction to the Principles of Morals and Legislation* articulated his Utilitarian philosophy. He called his philosophy **Utilitarianism** because it rested on the principle of utility, which meant, for him, maximizing pleasure and minimizing pain. He believed that an individual could calculate, or estimate, the likely degree of pleasure or pain that a particular action would produce. Social actions, too, could be evaluated by the principle of "the greatest good for the greatest number of people." Bentham's procedure of calculating and estimating the consequences of an action anticipated the theory of probability found in Pragmatism.

For Peirce's theory of probability, see the chapter on Pragmatism and Education.

Bentham's Utilitarianism inaugurated the shift among some Liberals from a natural rights theory to a social policy orientation. His emphasis on an action's usefulness in bringing about predicted consequences began to guide some Liberal policymakers and legislators. Bentham's method of calculating a law's or program's anticipated consequences and then measuring these expectations against actual results was a forerunner of the proposition that everything that exists can be measured.

Bentham's Utilitarianism retained but broadened the central Liberal concept of individualism. Although individuals still acted in their own self-interest, they could unite their individual self-interest with that of others. This uniting of interests had the social benefit of promoting the good, the welfare, of those who had conjoined their interests. This broadened concept of individualism marked Liberalism's transition from an exclusive concern for individual self-interests to broader social issues related to the general welfare. Existing institutions, laws, customs, traditions, and conventions could be reevaluated. If they did not produce the greatest good for the greatest number, they could be reformed. The idea that society could be reformed or improved, reiterating the Enlightenment ideal of progress, emerged as an important proposition in modern Liberalism.

Liberals, in general, both Classical Liberals and Benthamite social reformers, were active politically. True to Locke's original Liberalism, they believed in both elected representative government and checks and balances. Classical Liberals wanted policies that would establish free trade, protect private property, and ensure competition. They were adamantly opposed, however, to government social programs. Utilitarians, in contrast, believed a limited government role was needed in areas such as education, police, firefighting, and sanitation. A contagious disease would not be confined to a single individual but could spread through the entire population. The burning of a single building could spread to adjacent buildings. Some specific conditions of life needed to be considered for their general impact on the entire community. The question was then (as it is now): Should these more general interests be dealt with privately or publicly? For example, is health care in the United States best provided by government or private for-profit insurance companies?

Advocating moderate, measured, gradual, and nonviolent reform, Utilitarianism relied heavily on education to cultivate an informed public opinion. Bentham saw popular education as the means by which individuals would know their true self-interests and could participate in forming the public interest. Under the leadership of Bentham and other Utilitarians, the University of London was established in 1828 to emphasize social philosophy and social science to educate people about the process of reform.

John Stuart Mill

John Stuart Mill (1806–1873) was a proponent of Liberalism in philosophy, social policy, and education.[14] Mill's reconceptualization of Liberal ideology, based on a revision of Jeremy Bentham's Utilitarianism, moved Liberalism in the direction of humanitarian social reform.

For Mill, personal freedom and the free expression and circulation of ideas were necessary conditions for a life and society of quality. In *On Liberty,* Mill expressed his belief in human progress through the exercise of freedom of thought. According to

Mill, "the only purpose for which power can be rightfully exercised over any member of a civilized community, against his will, is to prevent harm to others. His own good, either physical or moral, is not a sufficient warrant."[15]

Mill based his emphasis on individual liberty on his belief that a society benefited from the presence of critically minded individuals who challenged conventional wisdom and originated new ideas. Liberty and criticism were utilitarian or useful to a society because they made it possible to express divergent opinions and test new ideas. Mill obviously opposed authoritarian and despotic government that used overt power to censor ideas. However, equally dangerous to intellectual freedom was the power of conventional thinking, tradition, and customs that impeded free expression. Intellectual freedom meant freedom of expression—the freedom to communicate ideas in speech, in print, in the classroom, and today through social media on the Internet. This meant that the school should not be an agency to impress conventional wisdom and the status quo on the young but rather an agency to foster individual intellectual initiative, especially the power of critical thinking.

Mill's political philosophy rested on the Liberal ideological commitment to an elected representative government in which legislators are responsible to the voters who elected them. He believed civil liberties are best secured and defended by self-government. Representative government required that the people, the electorate, have a civic education that made them conscious of the need to safeguard their liberties and to elect legislatures that act to promote individual freedom.

Mill prophetically anticipated what he feared was the construction of a mass mind, a generalized and pervasive mentality, that might be generated through mass media that catered to sensationalism rather than to critical thinking. In the nineteenth century, the best-selling newspapers appealed to the largest readership, which was not necessarily constituted of critically minded individuals. To attract this readership, the reporting of news and human-interest features was directed to the widest possible audience, a mass audience. To capture the largest possible audience, the media geared their reporting of information and presenting of entertainment to what it believed the majority wanted. Although he favored a free press, Mill feared the power of a press that thrived on sensationalism and catered to puerile readers. If he were alive today, Mill would fear the power of the mass media and mass entertainment—television, movies, and even the Internet—to orient their presentations to the appetites of the largest possible audience. Instead of providing choices, the mass media creates a sameness in which most programs, oriented to the average audience, end up being the same in a kind of self-induced censorship that generates its own pervasive conformity.

For similar fears about mass society, see Gabriel Marcel in the chapter on Existentialism and Education.

Tyranny of the Majority: Mill's fear that in a mass society, the majority may impose prevailing opinions on the minority.

Just as Mill feared the **tyranny of the majority** might reduce standards to the average, he feared that representative institutions might be subverted when special interest groups (lobbies) promote legislation to advance their causes rather than those of the greatest number of persons. Mill looked to education, especially the education of a disinterested group of citizens, who could resolve the dilemma of special interests.

Disinterested Participant: Mill's concept of a participant in politics and society who is unbiased and not motivated by the desire for personal profit and thus can evaluate an issue objectively.

For Mill, a group of well-educated persons, or **disinterested participants**, might be able to stem the tide of the tyranny of the majority as well as reconcile the contentions of conflicting special interest groups. A disinterested person is neither biased by personal interests nor motivated by the desire for personal profit. Although unprejudiced, the disinterested person is nonetheless a participant in social, political, and educational processes and not aloof from them. Unlike the member of the special interest group, the disinterested person would not be motivated to seek special privileges or advantages. The quality of disinterestedness implies having an educated perspective that makes it possible to evaluate an issue objectively. Educated people,

Mill reasoned, would be concerned with the general good rather than special class interests. Mill's concept of disinterested objectivity held important implications for education, especially for teaching and learning. It implies that teachers can and should present instruction, including discussions of controversial issues, in a fair, open, and unbiased manner. Essentialist educators would concur with Mills on the need for objectivity. However, proponents of other ideological perspectives would strongly disagree. Postmodernists, Marxists, Social Reconstructionists, and Critical Theorists would contend that all instruction, all teaching, proceeds from a point of view or an ideological commitment.

For their perspectives on objectivity, see the chapters on Postmodernism, Marxism, Essentialism, Social Reconstructionism, and Critical Theory.

Mill argued in *On Liberty* that new ideas that express human inventiveness and creativity advance individual and social progress. In a social and political climate of freedom of thought and opinion, alternative ideas will be expressed and compete with each other. From the competition of ideas, truth will emerge and new policies will be formulated.

CRITICAL THINKING. Mill's concept of the disinterested participant and the competition of ideas signaled the importance that Liberals give to critical thinking as a process in decision making. Critical thinking is a much-used term in education. Like most frequently used terms, it has different meanings that often vary with the user. As indicated, Liberals, like Mill, see critical thinking as approaching an issue or a question with an open mind and weighing the evidence before reaching a conclusion. However, Idealists would claim that critical thinking means discovering the truth through reflective introspection. Realists would contend that critical thinking means to think about something so that our ideas correspond with objective reality. Postmodernists, who see ideas as the means to power, would strongly disagree with Mill's concept of disinterested participation. Postmodernists would argue that when we think critically we are deconstructing a text. Pointedly, unlike Mill, Critical Theorists would argue that critical thinking does not take place in an unbiased vacuum; it means that we are approaching an issue or a question from a perspective that opposes oppression and oppressors.

For these differing philosophical perspectives on truth, see the chapters on Idealism, Realism, Postmodernism, and Critical Theory.

Bentham's and Mill's Utilitarianism gradually moved Liberalism to a social reformist orientation. Not only was it an ideology that sought to safeguard individual and civil liberties but now it reunited with the Enlightenment Project that society could be progressively improved. The social reformist strain in Liberalism split Liberal ranks. Some Liberals remained loyal to the Classical Liberal doctrines of noninterference by government and laissez-faire in the economy. In the United States, these Classical Liberal doctrines were appropriated into the Conservative ideology (which is examined in the following chapter). Other Liberals saw the state as a necessary agent of social reform. Not revolutionaries, the new Liberals believed that reform should take place through carefully considered incremental transactions and bring a gradual improvement that restored existing institutions to an efficient and good working order instead of overturning them. Bentham and Mill had a definitive Utilitarian educational model in mind. To be well educated the Utilitarian would (1) be open-minded and willing to assess all ideas—both longstanding and new ones, (2) avoid utopian or revolutionary appeals for sweeping change, and (3) be unbiased but methodologically committed to critical discussion and decision making that followed agreed upon procedures.

A Utilitarian would see schools as necessary and socially beneficial institutions. However, over time, schools, like other institutions, had become too formal and traditional. The curricula and methods of teaching might have become static and separated from social realities and issues. They might not reflect scientific discoveries and technological innovations. When this happens, the schools themselves need to be reformed. The curricula and teaching methods can be reformed to incorporate new areas of knowledge. Indeed, some new subjects and skills might need to be added and obsolete ones removed. Such a process of incremental reform would make schools more utilitarian, more relevant, and more efficient. This kind of reform would work for the good of the greatest number of students and teachers as well as for social improvement.

CONTEMPORARY AMERICAN REFORM, OR MODERN LIBERALISM

Modern Liberalism: a transformation in Liberalism in which the government became responsible for social welfare and health programs such as ending racial segregation, promoting integration and affirmative action, aiding persons with disabilties, and alleviating poverty.

In this section, we examine contemporary American Liberalism, which is sometimes called **Modern Liberalism**, Reform Liberalism, or Social Welfare Liberalism to distinguish it from Classical Liberalism. To simplify terminology, we shall refer to American Modern Liberalism as Reform Liberalism. In the United States, John Dewey's Experimentalism and the Progressive movement incorporated Liberal ideas and methods into their agendas for social and educational reforms.

Progressivism and Liberalism

For Progressivism, see the chapter on Progressivism and Education; for John Dewey, see the chapter on Pragmatism and Education.

From the 1890s through the early 1920s, Progressives worked to reform American politics, society, economics, and education. The impetus for reform was stimulated by investigative journalists such as Upton Sinclair, who exposed the unsanitary conditions in the meatpacking industry in *The Jungle*, and Ida Tarbell, in her exposé of the Standard Oil Company monopoly in the oil industry. Progressive investigative journalists' articles appeared in popular journals such as *McClure's Magazine* that had a large readership. Progressive political leaders such as President Theodore Roosevelt (1858–1919), President Woodrow Wilson (1856–1924), and Senator Robert LaFollette (1855–1925) supported legislation to reform government, curb economic monopolies, and conserve natural resources. The Progressive process of reform followed the Liberal approach in that it (1) identified a social, political, or economic problem where representative institutions were malfunctioning due to manipulation by special interests or lack of adequate support and regulation; (2) raised consciousness about the problem area through investigative journalism and public hearings; (3) used experts to research and provide empirical, often statistical, findings about the problem and its consequences; (4) structured possible policies designed to remedy the situation and fix the malfunctioning sector; and (5) enacted legislation to solve the problem and to regulate the area to ensure that it functioned efficiently and that those responsible for operating in the particular area were held accountable to the general public.

Progressivism transformed American Reform Liberalism. It gave a large role to education—both through informal agencies such as the media and press and through formal ones such as schools and universities. The expert advice of academics, especially professors who were authorities in economics and sociology, often aided those drafting legislation. It also gave the government or state a regulatory power to ensure that matters were functioning in the public interest. For example, federal inspectors were to make periodic checks to ensure that food and drugs were being processed safely and hygienically. It gave inspectors the authority to inspect mines and factories to ensure that working conditions were safe. Reform Liberalism's regulatory power had moved American Liberalism far from the classical laissez-faire position of little or no interference with the economy to its regulation. It was at this juncture that the Classical Liberal ideas of the free marketplace and a limited government role in the economy were appropriated by American Conservatism.

For the Conservative appropriation of Classical Liberalism, see the chapter on Conservatism and Education.

Progressive reformist Liberals initiated legislation to restrict child labor and to make schooling compulsory for certain age groups. They argued that compulsory education would improve people's lives in that it made them more informed citizens and improved their career prospects. Importantly, it would improve the national economy and society. Many states passed laws that made attendance at school compulsory between the ages of six and fourteen. In true liberal fashion, the Progressive efforts for compulsory school attendance laws were incremental and additive but not transformative. They were based on existing patterns of state and local control of public schools that were established in the nineteenth-century common school movement. They were intended to make schools more inclusive of the general population. They were incremental in that they simply added more years to the time children spent in school.

The tendencies in Reform Liberalism led reformers, like the Progressives, from one area of needed reform to another. For compulsory school attendance laws to be effective, there also needed to be a restriction on school-aged children in the work force. Jane Addams and other American Progressives organized the National Child Labor Committee in 1904 to lobby to remove children from the workforce. In 1916, Congress passed the Keating-Owen Child Labor Act to restrict child labor. However, in 1918, the U.S. Supreme Court, relying on Classical Liberal precedents, ruled the law unconstitutional because it violated freedom of trade in interstate commerce.[16] The movement to restrict child labor and require compulsory school attendance in the United States reflected the tension between Classical and Reformist Liberalism. Enforcement of compulsory school attendance meant that regulations had to established and enforced. Thus, the position of the truant officer was created as part of the American school system. Opponents of compulsory attendance argued that the requirements were an infringement on the prior rights of parents and that it was a stratagem for the middle class to take social control of schools.

The New Deal and Liberalism

In the 1930s, President Franklin Roosevelt's New Deal developed myriad reforms to bring the United States out of the Great Depression. Roosevelt (1882–1945) used the federal government to provide relief to millions of unemployed people and their families by establishing programs to stimulate recovery and enacting laws that would reform the system. Roosevelt's New Deal, like the earlier Progressive movement, was an effort at internal reforms to save the American political and economic system by incremental changes rather than by radically transforming or overthrowing it. The important point in the New Deal is that it used the federal government as the major agency of reform. This change was diametrically opposed to the Classical Liberalism position that wanted a small government with limited powers.

During the Depression era, several leading American educators, including John Dewey, called for the creation of a New Liberalism. Dewey wanted the New Liberalism to be an active ideology that promoted a cooperative society that provided for the social welfare and education of all people. George S. Counts, a Reconstructionist educator, called on teachers to join with other Progressive groups in working for a more planning, collaborating, and sharing society. Harold Rugg called on the schools to prepare people to use the new technology for social betterment. Educators like Counts and Rugg argued that the economic Depression of the 1930s was caused by the laissez-faire economy left over from Classical Liberalism. They wanted government to become the central agency for social and economic planning.

For the emphasis on planning, see the chapter on Social Reconstruction and Education.

President Johnson's Great Society Program

President Lyndon B. Johnson's Great Society and War on Poverty programs enacted in 1965 illustrate American Reform Liberalism's basic premises. Johnson (1908–1973), whose ideological formation took place when he served as a National Youth

Administrator during the New Deal, wanted to be known as the "Education President." Johnson took a broad view of the federal government's socio-economic and educational role.[17] A former teacher and school principal, he was earnestly committed to a larger federal role in education.

Johnson saw education in broad socio-economic terms that connected it to progress in society. He envisioned education as an important component in a comprehensive federal policy to eliminate poverty and promote social welfare and economic growth. Federal programs would be used to stimulate and diffuse innovations throughout the nation's schools.[18]

Johnson relied on the Liberal-Progressive strategy of expert opinion, often from social scientists, to provide evidence that supported his program. Numerous experts, many of whom were university professors in tune with Liberal ideology, argued that America's big cities, particularly their urban ghettoes, and some rural areas, such as Appalachia, were blighted by poverty, especially high unemployment and little economic investment. In his *Affluent Society*, liberal economist John Galbraith had called attention to the existence of pockets of poverty, a residual problem in an otherwise seemingly prosperous economy. Liberal economists linked poverty to two conditions: the residual factor, identified by Galbraith, and structural adjustment, unemployment due to low or inappropriate workers' skills in a technological economy. Johnson's War on Poverty sought to correct these deficiencies by eliminating poverty in its residual pockets and by implementing training and educational programs to prepare the workforce for technological changes in the economy. Liberals, taking a view that human beings are essentially good, attributed higher crime rates and drug abuse in urban ghettoes to structural weaknesses in the urban environment that could be corrected. If the social environment, the communities in which people lived, were improved, individual behavior also would improve.

Johnson's War on Poverty programs required community participation on advisory and other kinds of boards and committees. These requirements were designed as community-building, consensus-generating strategies. Events in the late 1960s, however, would replace his ideas of consensus with conflicts as angry students demonstrated on campuses against the war in Vietnam and the inner cities exploded in urban disorders.

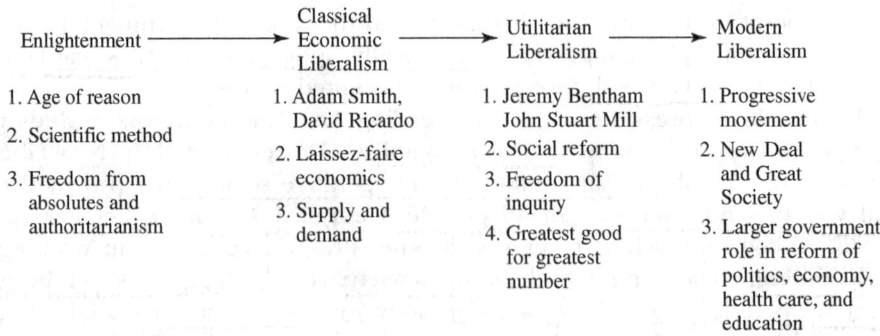

Liberalism's Transformation

Liberalism's Transformation

As a result of Progressivism, the New Deal, and the Great Society, American Liberalism was transformed into modern or social welfare Liberalism. Liberals still prized the freedom of the individual, as well as civil rights and liberties, but they now extended their ideological perspective to give government a greater role. Government, especially at the federal level, was to improve the general welfare by providing old-age pensions, health care, social security, and aid to hitherto disadvantaged groups; ending racial segregation and promoting integration, affirmative action programs, equal opportunities for persons with disabilities, aid to people at the poverty level, and environmental protection. Importantly, liberals believed that education was about more than learning basic skills and subjects. Public schools were redefined as agencies to promote social and economic change. They were to provide compensatory education to help economically disadvantaged children; to devise means of ending racial segregation and creating racial integration; to mainstream children with disabilities into regular classrooms; to provide early childhood education; to develop programs addressing sex education, drug and alcohol abuse, and AIDS education; and to create a climate that fostered multiculturalism and environmentalism. The new Liberal agenda made schools into much more than just academic institutions. They were to act as multipurpose and multifunctional institutions that were involved in treating social ills and solving social problems. Modern American Liberalism worked to equalize economic and gender opportunities and to promote respect for cultural and religious diversity within a framework of shared operational procedures.

LIBERALISM'S CORE ELEMENTS

The following section identifies and examines core elements in Liberalism. Among them are the Liberal perspectives on property and the economy, human nature and reason, secularism, the individual, progress, representative institutions, process, and social change. An understanding of these concepts at Liberalism's core provides a framework for examining its perspectives on education and schooling.

Property and the Economy

In its origins, Liberalism appealed to the property-owning professional and business middle classes. Locke, for example, asserted that the possession of property was a natural inherent right of individuals. Liberal policymakers promoted laws to safeguard the individual's freedom to compete in the economy and acquire property. Economic initiative and competition satisfied individual needs arising from self-interest and would lead to general economic prosperity.

The Liberal rights of property involve freedom of contract—that employers have the right to hire, employ, and dismiss employees and that investors have the right to earn income, decide how to invest their money, and make a profit, a financial dividend. They also face the prospect of losing their investment because of poor investment strategies or the vicissitudes of the market. This self-motivated economic interest stimulates people to invest their time and money in education, hoping to learn saleable skills and marketable expertise to enter and advance through the corporate economic ranks.

Although agreeing on the core right of individuals to hold private property, Liberals disagreed on the extent to which the economy should be regulated. Laissez-faire Classical Liberals, insisting that government should not interfere in the economy, would restrict the state's role in regulating business. For them, the government should encourage a free enterprise climate and a competitive marketplace in which the natural laws of supply and demand functioned. Conversely, Reform Liberals wanted the government to function as a regulatory agency to protect the health and safety of workers and consumers, to regulate the hours and conditions of work, and to protect the environment.

As Reform Liberals embraced social welfare policies, they revised the principle of the individual's right to property. While still asserting that the right to own property is a fundamental individual right, they increasingly used the Utilitarian principle of the "greatest good for the greatest number" to justify an enlarged sphere of state activity in the society and economy. The Reform Liberal agenda included the following roles for government: (1) assisting individuals in the lower socio-economic classes, especially at the poverty line, with the resources—food, health care, low-cost housing, and job training—to help them improve their situation; and (2) encouraging and requiring affirmative action programs to give preference in college and university admissions and in employment positions to members of underrepresented minority groups.

Reform Liberals argued that individuals in higher income groups should have a higher rate of taxation, a progressive tax, to generate the needed revenues for social, health, and educational services. They asserted that the right to own property stands as an individual right, but the property owners should be taxed to contribute to the general welfare by paying for public schools, health care, and subsidized low-income housing. At this juncture, Classical Liberalism, now part of American Conservatism, and Reform Liberalism diverged. Liberal economic theory has an impact on educational policymaking. Education is seen as an input, an investment that prepares individuals for economically productive careers and occupations. When education is seen as an economic investment, it leads to debate over how funds for education should be used. Should they be directed to training in saleable skills, to develop technological competency, to enhance American competition in the global economy, or for other kinds of programs? Liberals, both Classical and Reformist, insist that individuals should be free to choose their own occupation or profession. Liberals contend that completing high school and college will lead to higher paying jobs. However, educational policies, especially those related to the economy, have consequences in that they may or may not lead to employment. Classical Liberals predict employment needs based on supply and demand. Reform Liberals weigh educational policies in terms of their likelihood to improve the society and the economy.

For Neo-Conservatism, see the chapter on Conservatism and Education.

For a discussion of the Neo-Conservative appropriation of Classical Liberal economic theory, see the chapter on Conservatism and Education.

Ideologies are permeable in that concepts from one ideology may be appropriated and used by another ideology. In the United States, this has occurred with Neo-Conservatism, which appropriated key principles from Classical Liberalism. Neo-Conservatives seek to deregulate the economy by removing or reducing Reform Liberal regulatory controls over businesses, banks, and the corporate sector. They also seek to eliminate affirmative action guidelines designed to provide reserved proportional places in higher education and employment for members of underrepresented minority groups, on the grounds that it unfairly limits individual initiative and merit. Some Neo-Conservatives would privatize schooling by issuing vouchers that parents could use to select educational alternatives to public schooling.

RATIONALITY AND THE POWER OF REASON

The major intellectual impetus for Liberalism came in the eighteenth century with the Enlightenment, the Age of Reason. A powerful intellectual force, the Enlightenment transformed European and American worldviews. The Enlightenment's key ideas were voiced by the *philosophes*, a circle of French intellectuals that included Denis Diderot and Etienne Condillac. They believed that human beings, by their nature, possessed the power to reason. For them, reasoning took an empirical direction. By using the scientific method, people could observe and examine natural and physical phenomena. They also sought to construct a social science that would enable individuals to examine society, politics, and education in much the same way that scientists investigated the natural and physical worlds. Social science, they believed, would find the natural laws that were meant to apply to social, political, economic, and educational institutions. If these natural laws were permitted to function, human life and society could be reformed, improved, and perfected. However, powerful special interests and institutions were entrenched, blocking the needed inquiry and the projected reforms. Among the institutions that blocked reform were the monarchy, in which a king ruled with unquestioned authority by the grace of God; members of an aristocracy who occupied the places of influence and privilege, not by merit, but simply by their birth into noble families; a Church that emphasized the unquestioning acceptance of its dogma; a society and economy based on rigid social class divisions and the proposition that the "poor would always be with us"; and schools and teachers who indoctrinated students to believe that "they lived in the best of all possible worlds." The *philosophes'* unrelenting criticisms of the established social, political, religious, and educational institutions undermined them and contributed to the American Revolution of 1776 and the French Revolution of 1789.

Liberalism asserts the human power of using reason to solve problems and improve life and society. What interfered with the free exercise of reason were the residues of superstition and ignorance. Once the channels of free inquiry were cleared of the debris of an unenlightened past, human intelligence would lead humanity to a better future on this earth. James Mill (1773–1836), the father of John Stuart Mill and a committed Utilitarian Liberal, argued that reasonable individuals could "weigh evidence" to make their decisions. Believing in the power of the majority to make correct decisions, he claimed that the greatest number of such reasonable persons would "judge right."[19] John Dewey, a modern Reform Liberal, moved the cause of free intelligence further when he argued that the scientific method of inquiry could be applied to life's myriad social, political, economic, and educational problems.

The Liberal assumptions that human beings are rational and that most people can be reasonable have enormous educational implications. In informal education, especially in the media, publishing, and social media, there needs to be freedom to access and disseminate information. As John Stuart Mill argued, freedom of speech, press, and assembly encourages competition in the marketplace of ideas.[20] School libraries and computer programs need to be free of censorship. Teachers need to use methods, especially the scientific method, that liberate and use intelligence.

John Dewey, in *How We Think*, provides a useful examination of how thinking, or reasoning, occurs. His discussion of epistemology illustrates the Liberal emphasis on the efficacy of human reasoning and its application in schools. Like Mill and earlier Liberals, Dewey identified the conditions that interfere with critical and problematic thought, or reasoning. Existing conditions, especially customary beliefs, may block inquiry. In resisting change in society and schools, the belief that something should remain as it has always been has a staying power that blocks critical inquiry. To encourage critical thinking in schools, students need to learn how to use scientific thinking to challenge customs that interfere with growth.[21] Perpetuating the existing curriculum simply because it is already in place or using the same teaching methods because teachers are comfortable with them when alternatives might improve learning shows how unexamined traditions can block educational innovation.[22]

For Dewey, as for many Liberals, reflective thinking is a method that requires (1) doing research about an issue by defining it and finding the facts, the evidence, that relates to and explains it; (2) using the evidence to construct hypotheses, tentative solutions that may resolve the issue or solve the problem; (3) conjecturing, thinking about, what would be the consequences if we acted on a particular hypothesis; (4) choosing a particular hypothesis as a plan of action; and (5) acting on the hypothesis to see if it works, if it produced the consequences that resolved the issue or solved the problem.[23]

There is a similarity between Dewey's method of critical or reflective thinking and James Mill's "weighing the evidence." Reflecting on or weighing the evidence needs to take place in a tentative attitude in which the person deliberately pauses from taking action to assess the validity of the facts and inferences based on them. It involves a conscious inquiry into the nature, conditions, and bearings of the evidence.[24]

Dewey's method of reflective thought transfers and translates into critical thinking in education. Like other Liberals, Dewey sees the process as highly methodological in that it is a way to resolve issues and problems. It provides a group or collaborative process in which individuals move through the same phases of resolving an issue or solving a problem together. Shared critical thinking carries over into democratic civic practices.

SECULARISM

Although they might be religious in their personal lives and be members of churches, Liberals generally oppose state efforts to enforce religious conformity and support officially established churches. In France and Mexico, Liberals worked to disestablish the Roman Catholic Church as the official religion. In England, Liberals, often members of dissenting or nonconformist churches, wanted to free both political and educational life from domination by the official Anglican Church.

Thomas Jefferson, a founding father of the American republic, sought to separate church and state.[25] In particular, he wanted to disestablish the Church of England as Virginia's official church. Jefferson believed that officially established churches denied citizens liberty in the free exercise of religion as well as the objective pursuit of knowledge. Jefferson's "Bill for Establishing Religious Freedom" in 1779 stated that ". . . God . . . created the mind free, and manifested his supreme will that free it shall remain by making it altogether insusceptible of restraint." Arguing against religious tests as a basis for citizenship and for public office, Jefferson asserted that "civil rights" do not depend "on our religious opinions."[26] The Constitution of the United States prohibits the establishment of religion by the government, guarantees the free exercise of religion to its citizens, and prohibits a religious test to vote and to hold public office.

The role of religion in American politics, society, and education is still controversial and continues to divide Liberals and Conservatives. Although many of the republic's founders shared Jefferson's belief in **separation of church and state**, others such as Benjamin Rush believed that the nation's origins and purpose reflected Christianity. In the nineteenth and twentieth centuries, the U.S. Supreme Court generally upheld separation of church and state and separation of religion from public education. In the twenty-first century, most American liberals argue for maintaining separation of church and state. However, the strict separation of church and state is questioned by Neo-Conservatives and Christian fundamentalists, who want prayers in public schools, publicly funded vouchers for their children to attend religious schools, and Creationism included in the science curriculum.

Separation of Church and State: the liberal proposition that the church and state should be separate; that is, the state should not establish a religion or interfere with its free exercise.

For Liberals, religious identification and church membership are personal rather than public matters. Individuals should be free to practice their religion, but they are not free to impose their beliefs on others through state-ordered observances, ceremonies, or financial aid. There should be no religious test for citizenship or for seeking and holding public office. For Liberals, church and state and church and public schools should be separate. Harkening back to Jefferson's warning that state-sanctioned religious dogmas can interfere with freedom of inquiry, Liberals assert that public schools need to be free from the control of churches. They oppose religious instruction, religious observances and prayer, posting the Ten Commandments, and the teaching of Creationism and Intelligent Design in public schools.

The Liberal principle of separation of religion from public education has generated strong and persistent controversy in the United States. Among the leading opponents are Christian Evangelical Fundamentalists, often associated with the Neo-Conservative ideology. Some Roman Catholics, too, believe that the doctrine of separation of church and state has been overextended from the founders' original intent, and they want state aid for Roman Catholic schools.

Christian Evangelical Fundamentalists argue that the United States was founded on Christian principles. They contend that Liberals, while denying the right of others to religious observance and instruction, have imposed their own secular humanist philosophy on public education. They argue that Secular Humanism encourages moral relativism in which truth and values are seen as temporary and variable human constructions rather than as universal principles ordained by God. Moral relativism, associated with Secular Humanism and Liberalism, has eroded the values of honesty, civility, and patriotism and has produced an "anything goes" attitude and behavior. Fundamentalists believe the restoration of religious values in schools will remedy the decline in moral values and behavior caused by relativism.

INDIVIDUALISM

An important original Liberal core concept is that individuals possess inherent human rights that the state can neither give nor take away. Rather, government arises from a contract to promote and protect these individual rights. For example, Locke proclaimed and Jefferson reiterated that the individual person possesses unalienable natural rights of "life, liberty, and property" that government is created to protect and maintain. The "Declaration of the Rights of Man and the Citizen" proclaimed in the French Revolution asserted that "all men are born and remain free and equal in rights." In these early statements of Liberal individualism, the person's rights exist prior to the social and political order and remain regardless of the particular social and political order in which he or she lives. The thoughts and activities of individuals are private and as free as possible from government interference or regulation.

By the early nineteenth century, Classical Liberals interpreted the priority of the individual as the person's right to unrestricted economic competition. The Social Darwinist Herbert Spencer asserted that individual competition was nature's means of selecting the fittest for survival. Even in John Dewey's Pragmatic interpretation of Darwin, the individual is prior to the group. While social intelligence is generated as individuals interact and participate in the group, the group is made up of individuals who can work together to build social consensus. Clearly, the Liberal impulse is to advance the individual's freedom and development. In education, Liberals, concerned with the individual student's progress, sought to recognize individual differences in the context of group socialization. Some Liberals, such as Herbert Spencer, saw education as preparing individuals for a competitive world; others, such as John Dewey, stressed cooperative group participation as the basis of social intelligence. In its development, Liberals, though agreeing on individualism as a necessary core concept, differed on the individual's relationship to society. This tension still affects how Liberals relate to society and to education. Reform Liberalism reaffirms individual rights and freedoms, often framed as human rights and civil liberties, but simultaneously emphasizes the importance of human association in government, society, and education. For Liberal principles to function in society, there needs to be a commonly held social **consensus** to use agreed-on political and educational processes.

Consensus: for Liberals, a pervasive social agreement to be committed to representative and agreed upon processes.

Procedural or process-oriented consensus relies on a social contract to uphold certain working premises and to follow agreed-on methods. In the history of the American common school movement, Horace Mann, Henry Barnard, and other leaders saw public education as constructing a broad consensus that embraced a commitment

Representative Institutions: institutions, usually political ones, that are governed by elected officials who represent the people.

to **representative political institutions** and processes, respect for private property, a strong work ethic, and patriotic values. Public schools, in their mission statements, still reflect this commitment to consensus building.

In American public schools, there is a simultaneous emphasis on both the individual and the group. In classrooms, individual students are instructed in group settings. In the relationship of individuals to the group, teachers face two equally compelling premises: (1) they are to identify and respect the needs and interests of each student as an individual person; and (2) they are to encourage individuals to function well in group activities, especially collaborative learning, as an effective and socially enriching way to learn. As members of a group, students are encouraged to express and share their ideas with their colleagues in the group; they are then expected to cooperate with other students in reaching consensus in a collaborative way that enables the group to meet its goals, solve its problem, or complete its project.

Further, the tension between Classical and Reform Liberalism surfaces over competition and cooperation in schools. Children are encouraged to be creative, even competitive; to do their own work; and to respect private property and the property of others. At the same time, they are also encouraged to be good group members, to take turns and to share, to use collaborative learning to solve group problems, and to be team players.

These ideological paradoxes in schools mirror tensions in the larger society between the individual and the group. Individual competition and initiative is prized, but so is being a team player and an effective member in business corporations and an active joiner and participant in community projects.

Progress

Progress: the belief that society can be reformed and improved.

Since the Enlightenment in the eighteenth century, Liberals have believed that the liberation of human intelligence will lead to **progress**, the improvement of human life on earth. Liberals developed the "Enlightenment project," which emphasized using science and technology to improve education, eliminate superstition and ignorance, raise literacy rates, reduce poverty, fight disease, and facilitate communication and travel. Unlike traditionalists or Conservatives, Liberals, optimistic about the prospects of creating a better future, did not look back to a "golden age" in the past.

As Liberalism developed ideologically, Classical and Reformist Liberals began to differ on how progress would occur. Both Liberal camps agreed that it was necessary to remove obstacles such as political absolutism and religious establishment that interfered with progress. Once these obstacles were removed, Classical Liberals believed that natural laws of supply and demand would spur competition and produce scientific discoveries and technological innovations. Government should ensure freedom of competition but otherwise limit its scope of operations. Reform Liberals, however, believed that progress needed to be stimulated and directed.

Utilitarians such as Jeremy Bentham and James Mill believed it was possible to calculate and plan the reforms that would bring the greatest happiness to the greatest number of people. American Progressives believed it was possible to create a "Great Society" in which all Americans could share in the good things of life. Woodrow Wilson would design plans for the ending of World War I by means of an international parliament such as the League of Nations. In general, Liberals believed that society was dynamically changing for the better and human intelligence could create a good society by means of reform.

They are not utopians who believe that the world can be dramatically transformed and made perfect. Rather, they see progress as a continuum of small incremental steps forward. If a social or institutional imbalance or strain appears, then specific reform is needed to apply the necessary remediation or regulation so that the institution will function more effectively and efficiently.[27]

REPRESENTATIVE POLITICAL INSTITUTIONS

Liberalism brought change in western Europe and in the United States to the way people thought about the purpose, role, and function of government. Historically, Liberalism grew out of the protest and, in some cases, the revolt of the middle classes against states that ruled them but in which they had either no voice or only a very limited one. In England, liberals challenged the Stuart monarchs' attempts to rule by divine right. In Britain's thirteen American colonies, the colonists rebelled against British colonialism and established their own republic. In France, the revolutionaries overthrew the Bourbon monarchy and aristocracy.

Although these political actions differed somewhat because of the contexts in which they occurred, a common thread ran through them—the desire to establish political institutions and processes that would empower middle classes with the right to govern themselves. The revolutionaries, now in positions of power, established legislative bodies that would represent the citizens who elected their members. In the United Kingdom, the legislative body is the House of Commons, in the United States the Congress, and in France the Chamber of Deputies. Eligible voters elect the members of these legislative bodies for fixed terms. After serving in Congress, for example, elected representatives return to the people. An important point is that the terms of these members are for a fixed duration and not for life. Further, they are elected and do not gain their seats by ascription—by inheritance because they were from noble families. The Liberal formula of representative institutions recognizes that the state needs power to implement the will of the majority. However, it requires that power be exercised through approved procedures, through due process, and that it be as limited and restrained as possible. Those who exercise power are accountable for its use and for following representative political processes.

Liberalism's emphasis on process, gradual reform, and limited change established a concept of the state that functions by means of elected legislative bodies. The interests of the people are identified with the power of the state through a government in which elected representatives are responsible to the electorate. Liberalism's political processes, especially in England and in the United States, emphasized the power of numbers and the roles of majorities and minorities in the process. With the creation of parliamentary government, revolution left the street and entered the legislative chamber where it became institutionalized in peaceful parliamentary processes. In such a system, the majority is not to abuse its power; the minority has the right to work for change through legislative processes. Further, majorities and minorities are temporary and will change as their members shift their positions on specific issues.

Further, within the Liberal state, constitutional guarantees of civil rights protect the individual against arbitrary government action. The U.S. Constitution, adopted in 1788, illustrates the process. According to the U.S. Constitution, the state machinery is based on the principle of popular sovereignty; the Bill of Rights protects and guarantees civil liberties, and the Constitution may be amended peacefully.

Liberal political processes emphasize the freedom of individuals to make their own choices about electing candidates for public office. Hopefully, the choice is an informed one; however, if not informed, it is nonetheless the right of the individual to make the choice and to be responsible for the consequences of that decision. This freedom of choice applies to voting for candidates for public office, choosing a college or university, choosing a career, and a range of other life options.

Education for General Citizenship

The Liberal emphasis on representative political institutions has profound implications for civic, or citizenship, education. As noted, in an absolutist political state or in one ruled by hereditary aristocrats, the person or persons who will govern the state are well known in advance of their actual taking of power. They can be given the prescribed and specific education that prepares them to rule. For example, the education for a prince is appropriate to his being king; for a princess to be queen; for an aristocrat to be a member of a ruling elite. In these situations, there is no need for aptitude tests or career guidance. What is in place is the doctrine of education that is appropriate to a known future. In a system of representative institutions, however, it is not known in advance who will be a president, a governor, or a member of Congress, for example. The often cited adage, "A student in this class may become President of the United States," is true.

The proposition that citizens of the country elect their leaders and legislators carries with it a need for general citizenship education that will (1) provide a knowledge base and understanding of how the political system works; (2) provide citizens with the skills to make informed decisions about those they will elect to office; (3) provide future elected officials with the knowledge and skills they need to be responsible and responsive representatives of the citizens who elected them; and (4) build a value commitment to respect and use the system and its processes.

THE NEED FOR A GENERALLY EDUCATED PUBLIC. Historically, Liberals have supported state school systems to cultivate a generally educated public. These schools provide a civic education in the belief that the responsibilities of citizenship such as voting in elections and serving on juries requires a literate and generally educated citizenry. The assumption underlying general education policies and programs is that citizens will be called on to make decisions in areas other than the specialties related to their occupations or professions.

Still another argument for general education is the need to have educated persons who can be disinterested decision makers. John Stuart Mill believed that disinterested decision making was important to maintain the fairness and objectivity that was needed in making political, social, economic, and educational decisions.

Liberals believe that an educated citizenry should have a general interest in the problems and issues of the society and also a methodological commitment to the representative processes designed to resolve these issues. In addition to this general interest, individuals and groups have special interests. For example, teachers may have a special interest in the design of the curriculum but also a general interest on foreign policy or energy issues. In making decisions about a general interest, individuals can be disinterested (not having a special interest) in resolving them. On any given issue, a body of disinterested citizens can be expected to deal with the issue objectively.

CIVIC EDUCATION. In addition to general education, Liberalism emphasizes a particular kind of civic education that relates to the cognitive and affective development of future citizens. In the cognitive dimension, civic education seeks to develop knowledge of the institutions, structures, and processes related to representative institutions. This includes a historical perspective on the organization and development of these institutions and an analysis of their functions in contemporary society. For example, the civic education of a U.S. student would involve an examination of federal, state, and local government and of the executive, legislative, and judicial branches of government. Civic education also seeks to cultivate values that encourage a commitment to participate in the political process.

The affective dimension of civic education, according to Liberalism, involves a public overview and accountability. The holders of public office are expected not only to fulfill the requirements of the position but also to maintain the integrity of the representative process. An important cognitive and attitudinal blending is found in the Liberal notion of civility. As indicated, Liberals emphasize process or procedures both in politics and in education. They assume that individuals need to know what the process is, how it came to be, and how it works. The process of raising issues and then defining, discussing, and resolving them is to take place in a reasonable, nonviolent, procedural fashion in which the participants agree to the process, follow it, and exercise civility in doing so. For Liberals, civility means to respect but not necessarily agree with the opinions of others and to follow the rules of orderly discussion and decision making. Obviously, Liberals in education would stress learning and playing by the rules.

Constitutional Literacy

In a manner similar to the Liberals' emphasis on civic education, Toni Marie Massaro recommends constructing a core curriculum around the theme of the U.S. Constitution and cases related to its interpretation, especially those concerned with rights and due process. Massaro argues that (1) there is an "American paideia," a concept of formative education that brings persons into civic understanding and participation; (2) schooling is a powerful force of cultural transmission and formation; (3) a curricular core that emphasizes that constitutional literacy can revitalize schooling's central mission in U.S. society; and (4) such a constitutional curricular core can develop a consensus to accommodate both political and procedural commonalities and cultural conflicts.[28] Massaro's emphasis on constitutional literacy reiterates Liberal arguments that in order to maintain and renew itself, a society needs agreed-on processes that can keep conflict within a communal framework. When the framework does not exist or has eroded to the degree that it is ineffective, disagreements may become noncommunal to the extent that the society can no longer maintain and renew itself in a peaceful, nonviolent way. Necessary to agreed-on processes is the building and creation of a consensus—a shared commitment to accept and use the processes. Liberals, historically, have been consensus builders. They seek to create a middle, moderate, or centrist position in politics, society, and education that can accommodate pluralisms within a shared framework of processes or procedures.

Massaro's argument for constitutional literacy takes a middle position in debates over multiculturalism and a cultural core. Proponents of a national core curriculum, such as E. D. Hirsch, Jr., Allan Bloom, Arthur M. Schlesinger, Jr., and others, argue that cultural commonality, its consensual core, is disintegrating and needs restoration. Proponents of a national core curriculum attribute this cultural disintegration to both a declining historical and political public literacy and a deliberate disuniting of the strands of American cultural identity by extremist multiculturalists. Critics of a national core curriculum, preferring cultural diversity and multicultural pluralism, counter that the public school curriculum should no longer transmit a monocultural version of American cultural identity, as it did in its assimilationist past. Rather, it should encourage racial, religious, gender, and ethnic pluralism.[29]

Seeking to build consensus, Massaro proposes a synthesis to unite contentious factions in a procedural framework. She argues that (1) a national core curriculum is needed; (2) such a curriculum can embrace both the commonality that unites Americans as well as the diversity and pluralism that enriches their society; and (3) the U.S. Constitution, with its rights and processes, provides the content for constructing the curricular core and for cultivating a sense of constitutional processes. Massaro contends that the Constitution and its legal interpretation offer a coherent framework for a core curriculum that can be used to educate a constitutionally literate populace that is sensitive to the issues of freedom of religion and expression, and equal protection of the law. Her analysis confronts what she regards as Liberal democracy's essential educational paradox—promoting "neutrality among competing versions of the good life while trying to instill . . . the principles of the liberal democratic state, among them the nonneutral preference for critical deliberation."[30]

Meaningful conversation, informed by constitutional literacy and undertaken within a consensual framework of shared processes, will encourage productive explorations about religious, racial, ethnic, gender, class, and other differences. With a constitutional core in place, teachers and students then can critically examine America's continuing multicultural issues—its racial, religious, ethnic, gender, and class conflicts.

PROCESS-ORIENTED CHANGE

Once it had evolved from its revolutionary origins in the early nineteenth century, Liberalism came to emphasize a cautious, moderate, and balanced approach to solving social, economic, and political problems. Liberalism's process for change involves limited objectives in which problems can be solved incrementally. They avoid utopian grand designs that promise to solve all social problems in one broad transformational sweep. Liberals, including modern Social Welfare Liberals such as John Dewey, were suspicious of large-scale hypotheses for social transformation. Large transformative agendas broke the continuity of testable experience often by making utopian leaps into untested, uncharted, and remote waters.

As indicated earlier in the chapter, Classical Liberals believe that government is best that governs least. Classical Liberals, who preferred that government maintain its role of a passive watchdog and avoid entering into social reform, believed social engineering only confuses and worsens the condition it seeks to remedy.

Reform Liberals, in contrast, want government to exercise regulatory and ameliorative functions to promote the general welfare. Where social and economic abuses or injustices exist, the government should correct them. Furthermore, only government can furnish needed social services such as providing sanitation services, supplying water, inspecting the safety of drugs, regulating working conditions, licensing drivers, maintaining schools, and so on. In approaching problems, however, modern Liberals usually deal with specific issues rather than transformative social reconstruction.

Liberalism encourages an intellectual outlook that recognizes change as an evolutionary process. The Liberal procedure for reform, or a limited change, is to investigate a problem; collect statistics, data, and evidence; design and enact reform legislation; and establish regulatory mechanisms to ensure the reform is being implemented.

Gradualism, moderation, balance, and the absence of a sweeping grand designs all characterize the Liberal temperament. Liberals are process oriented in their emphasis on using the scientific method to solve problems. While the end result is important, it is crucial that those who use the process be committed to its methodological requirements and to implementing its recommended outcomes. Results, however, are never finished but provide the means to use the process once again to solve new issues and problems.

In curriculum and instruction, Liberal educators, especially in the United States, tend to emphasize process-centered education. Both John Dewey and William H. Kilpatrick exalted democratic processes in education. Kilpatrick's "project method" was designed so that children would work in collaborative groups to solve specific problems. Learners would not only solve the specific problems but also concomitantly acquire experience in using group-centered democratic procedures.

For the project method, see the chapter on Progressivism and Education.

Collaborative learning, a contemporary revival of the project method, encourages instruction being enriched by students cooperating in learning skills, sharing information, and working as teams. Collaborative learning, in some respects, is a pedagogical counterpart to Reformist Liberal participatory democracy. Liberals emphasize process and participation in decision making. Using the processes of the scientific method and following democratic procedures give individuals a degree of control over their destinies. Human intelligence is to chart the progressive course toward a better future. Not bound by longstanding traditions, Liberals want to deal with problems unencumbered by dogmas.

For more on process and project learning, see the chapter on Progressivism and Education.

LIBERALISM'S EDUCATIONAL IMPLICATIONS

This section examines Liberalism's major educational implications. Among them are Liberalism's promotion of universal education, process-oriented teaching and learning, and the defense of academic freedom.

Universal Education

When Liberal political parties in the United Kingdom, the United States, France, and Mexico won power in the nineteenth century, they gradually established universal education systems. A universal system of education provides formal schooling, usually government mandated and supported, to a broad section of the population, typically children and adolescents. These school systems transformed Liberal knowledge beliefs, political processes, and values into educational content and processes. In particular, they emphasized civic (citizenship) education. Often, they were directed toward constructing children's identification with the nation-state and in cultivating a political socialization that features Liberal processes and values. School climates came to reflect the Liberal emphasis on the value of literacy and training, commitment to republican civic processes, and the need to maintain public order and practice scientific processes. The Liberal interpretation of civic sensibilities and productive economic individualism replaced more traditional religious beliefs and values.

In the United States, common school leaders such as Horace Mann and Henry Barnard followed the American Whig party's general Liberal orientation. They saw public education as a necessary corollary of republican civic institutions and political processes. Universal public education provided an investment against misinformed mobs that might be manipulated by demagogues. For example, Horace Mann's emphasis on property and individual initiative reflected the developing merchant and industrialist capitalism in the United States in the nineteenth century. Mann believed that business leaders had the social and educational responsibility to be the stewards of wealth and society. The taxes they paid to support schools were an investment in the future of their community and their country that would be repaid in the dividends of social stability, political order, and economic productivity.

In addition to the Liberal arguments on the relationship of universal education to government, business leaders, especially industrialists, wanted schools to train young people to be industrious workers and efficient managers. The leaders of business and industry, aided by their allies in politics and education, believed that schools could train a modern, skilled workforce. Thus, Liberals in Western Europe and in the United States could be counted among the friends of organized systems of state-supported and managed schools. While some Liberals were altruistic, others regarded schools as instruments for social control of the unruly elements in society.

Educational Policy in a Liberal System

In a Liberal system, policy development and implementation are often slow and uneven. This is especially true if one considers two Liberal prescriptions, namely,

(1) that the concentration of power should be limited and diffused through a system of checks and balances and (2) that it is important, socially and politically, to maintain a vital center, or sense of balance. Although U.S. education is constitutionally a state responsibility, educational policymaking is also done by the federal government and local school boards. In particular, the U.S. historical tradition supports locally controlled school policies. The process of making educational policies, then, is slow and uneven, depending on a variety of policy-making authorities. This diffusion of power protects schools from monolithically imposed policies but also slows down efforts for educational change and innovation.

In public education, various individuals, groups, and associations have agendas for policy formulation. These organizations include such diverse groups as the National Education Association, the American Federation of Teachers, parent-teacher associations, the National Association of Manufacturers, the American Legion, and many others. In addition to these organizations, there have been development and growth of "policy think tanks," supported by foundations. Some of these foundations operate from an ideological orientation that shapes their policy reports and recommendations. The result of these many policy-recommending voices has been a plethora of proposals, often conflicting ones, for educational reform. Modern Reformist Liberals have moved increasingly toward a larger federal educational role. State and local control and funding of schools has created inequalities in education. For example, in *Savage Inequalities*, Jonathan Kozol documented wide disparities between facilities and programs in the poorest inner-city communities and schools in the wealthier suburban communities. Liberals, though not endorsing a national school system, have supported federal initiatives, particularly federal aid, to reduce these inequities.[31]

My Reflections on Philosophy of Education: Serving on a Local Board of Education

In reviewing and editing this chapter, I thought about the Liberal emphasis on following procedures, having open discussions, making decisions based on votes, and being publicly accountable. These features of process-oriented decision-making caused me to reflect on my service as a member of a local elementary school board in a suburb in the Chicago area. What I learned as a school board member is that the position brings you very close to the citizens of the local community. The board, at that time, had to deal with very difficult issues such as trying to balance the school budget during a time of declining revenues due to decreasing enrollments and working to establish priorities between maintaining the mandated curriculum and extra-curricular activities. As I served on the board, I learned that these issues were not easy ones to resolve. The public, including parents, as well as my colleagues on the board, had different opinions, strongly held, about what was a priority in the district's educational program.

As we tried to solve the district's problems, I learned directly how public schools function at the local level. I learned that there are processes, which Liberals would call procedures, that needed to be observed. All board meetings had to be announced publicly; the meetings were open to the public; a time was set aside at each meeting for members of the public to voice their opinions; the board members were expected to state their positions on a particular issue; after discussion, the board members voted. In Illinois, there are seven members on a local school board. For a proposal to pass, it had to carry a majority of votes. Many of our decisions were based on votes of four to three.

As I reflected on the process of the local government of schools, I thought that Jeremy Bentham, John Stuart Mill, and John Dewey, though they might disagree with some of our decisions, would agree with our processes.

PROCESS-ORIENTED INSTRUCTION

The Liberal conception that life should be lived, especially socially and politically, according to well-defined and mutually accepted procedures has a particular relevance for teaching and learning in schools. Both early childhood education and primary education can establish and reinforce procedural habits such as respecting other children's property, taking turns and waiting to use certain items or playthings, and respecting other students as persons.

The concept that the group should establish its own rules of governance and conduct is also a Liberal derivation found in some classrooms. The assumption underlying this kind of discipline is that such rules will be more readily accepted and adhered to by members of the group if they arise out of common consent and consensus. In U.S. secondary schools, a wide variety of student organizations, clubs, and associations exist, each having its own elected officers who conduct meetings according to parliamentary processes.

It is anticipated that these procedural behaviors, learned by participating in the school milieu, will become habitualized standards of behavior that will transfer to the larger out-of-school society. Membership in school clubs or associations provides experience and may lead to the skill of working well with others, which can contribute to successful social and working relationships. Participation in school activities is expected to reinforce a civic outlook that sees voting in elections, running for office, and serving on juries as an ethical responsibility. These predispositions arising in the school milieu are also designed to create an attitude that disputes and conflicts should be settled according to nonviolent and fair procedures.

The distinction between schools as separate from explicit political ideology and yet reflective of and encouraging of attitudes, values, and methods supportive of a Liberal civic outlook is a difficult and delicate one. In the Liberal orientation, the methodology associated with decision making in the broader society is also compatible with academic freedom within the school. Critics, especially Critical Theorists, however, allege that the school in a liberal democracy is a servant of the reigning political ideology.

For the Critical Theorist critique of Liberalism see the chapter on Critical Theory and Education.

LIBERALISM AND ACADEMIC FREEDOM

This section examines Liberalism and academic freedom—the freedom to teach and the freedom to learn. First, we consider how the Liberal view of **negative freedoms** has shaped academic freedom. By negative, we mean the elimination of those situations that interfere with teaching and learning. We then examine how Liberalism has positively defined academic freedom.

Negative Freedoms: laws that restrict government from interfering with speech, press, assembly, and religion.

Negative Freedom and Education

Historically, Liberalism, as a largely middle-class ideology, opposed the absolutism and traditionalism of the old aristocratic political order, especially its limitations on individual freedom. It sought to remove restrictions on freedom by limiting an absolutist state's authority. For example, among these liberal negative freedoms are that there shall be no restrictions on freedom of speech, press, and assembly; there shall be no taxation without representation; there shall be no interference with free exercise of religion. The concept of negative freedoms can be extended to education, schooling, and teaching and learning in the classroom.

FREEDOM FROM A RESTRICTIVE PAST. Liberalism does not ignore the past but rather wants it to be instructive for interpreting the present and planning for the future.

History can be instructive but can also be restrictive when the past is seen as the source of customs, traditions, and practices that need to be routinely followed in the present and safeguarded for the future. Everyone has had educational experiences and almost everyone has attended school; therefore, ideas about education, teaching, and learning are derived from these past experiences. The important Liberal qualification is that the past be revisited and revised but not be an ironclad straitjacket on thinking, innovation, and change. A restrictive sense of the past does not allow traditions to be questioned. For example, the past-based traditional view that schools should limit their curriculum to basic skills such as reading, writing, and arithmetic limits curricular innovation, reconstruction, and change. In societies worldwide, there are many traditional prohibitions and prescriptions on women and their education—on what they can or cannot be taught and on what careers they can or cannot pursue. Gender equality requires that the past be examined to find the origin of restrictions on women and that it be reconstructed to eliminate these impediments to freedom.

FREEDOM FROM INDOCTRINATION. Historically, Liberals sought to separate church and state. In doing so, they ran into the reality that historically schools were organized and supported by churches. Church-supported schools taught the religious doctrines, beliefs, rituals, and values to the young so that they could become participating members of the church. Today, many church-related schools continue to introduce the young members of a particular religion to its doctrines and rituals. In this sense, ***indoctrinate*** means to lead to and instill doctrines. Liberals, such as Jefferson and Mill, opposed indoctrination as closing the mind to considering alternative beliefs. For example, some Christians reject Darwin's theory of evolution as contrary to the Bible and do not want it taught in schools.

In the twentieth century, the Liberal view of indoctrination broadened to include prescriptions against what they regarded as closed totalitarian ideologies, such as Fascism, Nazism, and Communism. These ideologies insisted that they possessed political truth and that other political alternatives should be eliminated. According to these totalitarian ideologies, students were to be indoctrinated with their political beliefs. Now, Liberals faced a dilemma—should teachers who were members of totalitarian political parties such as the Communist Party be allowed to teach?

FREEDOM FROM CENSORSHIP. For Liberals, among the negative freedoms of individuals is that there shall be no restriction on the free and open exchange of ideas. In schools, this means the freedom of teachers to teach within their area of academic competence; it also means the freedom of students to learn, even if it means questioning tradition. The Liberal view of **academic freedom** is that critical thinking is valued and encouraged in schools. However, there are many times when academic freedom is threatened even in a Liberal society. There are those—both individuals and organizations—that do not want some topics such as evolution and contraception taught, discussed, and studied in schools.

Academic Freedom: the freedom of teachers to teach and students to learn, without having their freedom curtailed by censorship or arbitrary controls.

A POSITIVE STATEMENT OF ACADEMIC FREEDOM. From a negative statement that opposed limitations on academic freedom, Liberals developed a positive conception of academic freedom. Schools should be places of academic freedom, where teachers are free to teach and where students are free to learn, without having their freedom curtailed by censorship or arbitrary controls. The curriculum should be open to new ideas and to methods of inquiry in which students are free to ask questions that may challenge the status quo. Libraries should not be censored but should include controversial books on their shelves. Teachers should encourage critical exploration and discussion of ideas in which students can question and share thoughts and opinions.

ACADEMIC FREEDOM AS PROCESS. In their approach to politics, society, and education, Liberals value the processes of using appropriate methods or procedures to do things fairly, effectively, and efficiently. Their devotion to process originated in the Enlightenment project of using the scientific method, observing due process in law, and using parliamentary procedures in enacting laws.

In schools, academic freedom means that teachers and students (1) are free to examine and discuss issues, even controversial ones; (2) apply the same procedures to all participants; and (3) accept decisions but also are open to changing them by using the same process by which they were established. What is important is the tentativeness of knowledge and values; they are reached by examination and discussion and are not imposed by an authority figure or by being derived from some a priori principles. For the process to work, those who use it need to be committed to it and know how to use or work it. All members of a class have the right to participate and be listened to as long as they follow the rules that apply equally to all of them.

CONSTRUCTING YOUR OWN PHILOSOPHY OF EDUCATION

Now that you have read about Liberalism, reflect on how this ideology has either influenced or not influenced your thinking about politics, society, change, reform, and education. Have you experienced aspects of Liberalism in your education? Were some of your teachers and professors Liberals? If so, what made them a Liberal? Determine whether you find Liberalism compatible with your educational experiences and efforts to construct your own philosophy of education. Are there elements of Liberalism that you plan to include in your philosophy?

Conclusion

This chapter examined Liberalism as an ideology and discussed its social, political, economic, and educational implications. It treated Liberalism as a historically evolving ideology that developed from its origins in John Locke's contract theory, through Classical economic theory and Utilitarian reform, to modern Social Reformist Liberalism and contemporary Neo-Liberalism. Liberalism's affinity for process, procedures, and gradual, moderate, incremental change was discussed, and the way this tendency relates to education as a process was examined. Particular emphasis was devoted to a discussion of Liberalism and academic freedom.

Questions for Reflection and Discussion

1. Do you believe that Liberalism is a relevant ideology in contemporary American politics, society, and education? Explain your answer.
2. Critics contend that the Liberal claims of objectivity and fairness are false and cover up special interests. Do you agree or disagree?
3. Consider how Liberals define academic freedom. In your educational experience, is this how teaching and learning were treated in schools you attended?
4. Reflect on your experiences in schools both as a student and as a teacher. Did you find that academic freedom was encouraged or discouraged by your teachers and other students? How is it treated by teachers and students in the school in which you are teaching?
5. Reflect on John Stuart Mill's fear of the "tyranny of the majority." Do you believe that there is a tyranny of the majority operating in contemporary American life and education?
6. Do you believe that the idea of moderate incremental change is adequate for the problems facing American society and education?

7. How would Liberals react to the following requests made to a high school principal? (a) a group of Christian students ask the school administration to provide a room for after-school discussion of the Bible; (b) a student group wants to invite a rapper, known to use profanity in her performances, to sing at an after-school function; and (c) a group of students who oppose global businesses are organizing a boycott to protest the presentation of a manager of a large retail store that features low-cost clothing made in less technologically developed countries at your school.

Topics for Inquiry and Research

1. In a survey of the students in this class, determine what they identify as major Liberal principles.
2. Access "Liberalism" at the Stanford Encyclopedia of Philosophy at http://plato.stanford.edu/entries/liberalism. Then analyze its statement on Liberal ethics and values.
3. Examine the syllabi and textbooks in several courses in teacher education at your college or university. Do you find a tendency toward Liberalism in your analysis of this material?
4. Examine the procedures at your college or university that deal with students' rights and due process. Do these procedures reflect a Liberal orientation?
5. Interview several experienced teachers about the innovations or reforms that they have experienced in schools. Determine what kind of change these reforms or innovations have generated. Is it additive or transactional change in the Liberal sense or is it a broader transformational change? Or is it no real change at all?
6. Research the policies of a particular high school regarding co- or extracurricular student organizations or activities. Are these policies compatible with Liberal principles?
7. Research the guidelines that apply to the student newspaper or television or radio station at a high school or college. Does the institution have guidelines that limit what the newspaper or stations may cover?

Internet Resources

For distinctions between Classical and New Liberalism, a discussion of ethics and values, and bibliography, access "Liberalism" at the Stanford Encyclopedia of Philosophy at http://plato.stanford.edu/entries/liberalism.

For Liberalism's characteristics, a discussion of Classical and Modern Liberalism, a bibliography, and websites, access "Liberalism" at the Encyclopaedia Britannica at http://www,britannica.com/EBchecked/topic/339173/liberalism.

For Liberalism's development, divisions, and contemporary situation, access Citizendia at http://citizendia.org/Liberalism.

For a wide spectrum of Liberal perspectives, access the homepage of the Liberal International at http://www.liberal-international.org.

Suggestions for Further Reading

Carlisle, Janice. *John Stuart Mill and the Writing of Character*. Athens: University of Georgia Press, 1991.

Donner, Wendy. *The Liberal Self: John Stuart Mill's Moral and Political Philosophy*. Ithaca, NY: Cornell University Press, 1991.

Garforth, Francis W. *Educative Democracy: John Stuart Mill on Education in Society*. Oxford: Oxford University Press, 1980.

Gray, John. *Two Faces of Liberalism*. New York: New Press, 2000.

Hardin, Russell. *Liberalism, Constitutionalism, and Democracy*. New York: Oxford University Press, 2003.

Holmes, Stephen. *Passions & Constraint: On the Theory of Liberal Democracy*. Chicago: University of Chicago Press, 1995.

Jackson, Julius. *A Guided Tour of John Stuart Mill's Utilitarianism*. Mountain View, CA: Mayfield, 1993.

Johnston, David. *The Idea of a Liberal Theory: A Critique and Reconstruction*. Princeton, NJ: Princeton University Press, 1996.

Kerner, George C. *Three Philosophical Moralists: Mill, Kant, and Sartre*. New York: Oxford University Press, 1990.

Kurer, Oskar. *John Stuart Mill: The Politics of Progress*. New York: Garland, 1991.

Massaro, Toni Marie. *Constitutional Literacy: A Core Curriculum for a Multicultural Nation*. Durham, NC: Duke University Press, 1993.

Rawls, John. *Political Liberalism*. New York: Columbia University Press, 1993.

Ryan, Alan. *The Making of Modern Liberalism*. Princeton: Princeton University Press, 2012.

Sandel, Michael J. *Liberalism and the Limits of Justice*. New York: Cambridge University Press, 1998.

Strasser, Mark P. *The Moral Philosophy of John Stuart Mill: Toward Modifications of Contemporary Utilitarianism*. Wakefield, NH: Longwood Academic, 1991.

Wolfe, Alan. *The Future of Liberalism*. New York: Vintage Books/Random House, 2010.

Notes

1. This historical account is deliberately simplified to indicate the early differences between a society based on ascription and one based on merit. The social structure during the Medieval period was complex if one considers the role and power of the clergy.

2. Richard I. Aaron, *John Locke* (London: Clarendon Press, 1963), 2; M. V. C. Jeffreys, *John Locke: Prophet of Common Sense* (London: Methuen, 1967), 21.

3. John Locke, *An Essay Concerning Human Understanding,* ed. Raymond Wilbur (New York: E. P. Dutton, 1947), 8, 65, 106, 145, 253.

4. Amy M. Schmitter, Nathan Tarcov, and Wendy Donner, "Enlightenment Liberalism," in Randall Curren, ed., *A Companion to the Philosophy of Education* (Malden, MA: Blackwell, 2006), 83–85.

5. John Locke, *Some Thoughts Concerning Education* (Cambridge: Cambridge University Press, 1902), 419.

6. Schmitter et al., "Enlightenment Liberalism," 82–83.

7. John Locke, *Two Treatises of Government, 1690,* from the 1823 edition of Locke's works published in London by Thomas Tegg and others, in *Communism, Fascism and Democracy: The Theoretical Foundations,* ed., Carl Cohen (New York: Random House, 1972), 399.

8. Ibid., 399.

9. Brad Stetson, *Human Dignity and Contemporary Liberalism* (New York: Praeger/Greenwood, 1998), 26.

10. Michael J. Gootzeit, *David Ricardo* (New York: Columbia University Press, 1975).

11. Michael Freeden, *Ideology: A Very Short Introduction* (Oxford: Oxford University Press, 2003), 68–69.

12. Ian Adams, *Political Ideology Today* (Manchester, UK: Manchester University Press, 2001), 20.

13. J. Salwyn Schapiro, *Liberalism and the Challenge of Fascism: Social Forces in England and France* (New York: McGraw-Hill Book Co., 1949), 43–59.

14. For his autobiography, see John Stuart Mill, *The Autobiography of John Stuart Mill* (New York: Columbia University Press, 1944). Among biographies of Mill are: Alan Ryan, *John Stuart Mill* (New York: Pantheon Books, 1970); Peter J. Glassman, *J. S. Mill: The Evolution of a Genius* (Gainesville: University of Florida Press, 1985); and Richard J. Halliday, *John Stuart Mill* (London: Allen and Unwin, 1976).

15. Schapiro, *Liberalism and the Challenge of Fascism,* 281.

16. Michael McGeer, *A Fierce Discontent: The Rise and Fall of the Progressive Movement in America: 1870–1920* (New York: Free Press/Simon & Schuster, 2003), 108–109.

17. For Johnson's programs, see James MacGregor Burns, *To Heal and to Build: The Programs of President Lyndon B. Johnson* (New York: McGraw-Hill Book Co., 1968).

18. Hugh Davis Graham, *The Uncertain Triumph: Federal Education Policy in the Kennedy and Johnson Years* (Chapel Hill: University of North Carolina Press, 1984), 60–61.

19. J. Salwyn Schapiro, *Liberalism: Its Meaning and History* (New York: D. Van Nostrand Co., 1958), 44.

20. Ibid., 44–45.

21. John Dewey, *How We Think* (Mineola, NY: Dover, 1997), 45.

22. Ibid., 20–21.

23. Ibid., 5–6.

24. Ibid., 12–13.

25. Gordon C. Lee, ed., *Crusade Against Ignorance: Thomas Jefferson on Education* (New York: Bureau of Publications, Teachers College, Columbia University, 1961), 10–11.

26. Jefferson, "A Bill for Establishing Religious Freedom," in Julian P. Boyd et al., eds., *The Papers of Thomas Jefferson,* II (Princeton, NJ: Princeton University Press, 1950), 545–547.

27. D. J. Manning, *Liberalism* (New York: St. Martin's Press, 1976), 20–23.

28. Toni Marie Massaro, *Constitutional Literacy: A Core Curriculum for a Multicultural Nation* (Durham, NC: Duke University Press, 1993).

29. For examples of the debate, see Henry L. Gates, *Loose Canons: Notes on the Cultural Wars* (New York: Oxford University Press, 1992); Dinesh D'Souza, *Illiberal Education: The Politics of Race and Sex on Campus* (New York: Free Press, 1991); Arthur M. Schlesinger, Jr., *The Disuniting of America: Reflections on a Multicultural Society* (Knoxville, TN: Whittle Direct Books, 1991); and James A. Banks, *Multiethnic Education: Theory and Practice* (Boston: Allyn & Bacon, 1994).

30. Massaro, *Constitutional Literacy: A Core Curriculum for a Multicultural Nation,* 73.

31. Jonathan Kozol, *Savage Inequalities: Children in America's Schools* (New York: HarperPerennial, 1991), 67–74.

Conservatism and Education

Edmund Burke (1729–1797), British orator, political leader, and philosopher, who articulated Conservatism's leading principles.

10

CHAPTER PREVIEW

Conservatism, as an ideology, has had a contemporary revival in the United States and Europe. The word's root, *conserve*, means to keep, maintain, preserve, and prevent loss or decay. Conservatism originated as a reaction of the landed gentry and established churches in Europe against what they decried as the excesses and violence of the French Revolution. Conservatism reacts against rapid change but accommodates to gradual change by incorporating selected new social, political, economic, and educational elements into its cultural outlook. Like Liberalism and other ideologies, Conservatism has accommodated to selected innovations, especially economic and technological ones, but retains its core principles. For example, it has been sufficiently permeable to appropriate Classical Liberal economic principles into its core beliefs. American Neo-Conservatism has had a significant impact on contemporary education, especially in the standards movement to restore basic skills and subjects to the curriculum. The chapter is organized into the following major topics:

- Edmund Burke as an originator of Conservative cultural civility
- The principles of Classical Euro-American Conservatism
- Contemporary American Neo-Conservatism
- Conservatism's implications for education, schooling, curriculum, and teaching and learning

As you read the chapter, reflect on your own educational experiences. Did you encounter Conservatism in your own education? Did you have teachers and professors who emphasized Conservative principles, such as transmitting the cultural heritage? As you read and discuss this chapter, see whether you agree or disagree with Conservatism and if you will incorporate it in your philosophy of education.

BURKE AS AN ORIGINATOR OF CONSERVATIVE CULTURAL CIVILITY

In this section, we consider Edmund Burke (1729–1797) as a leading originator of Conservatism, especially the principles of cultural transmission and civility. Burke, a graduate of Trinity College in Dublin, was a distinguished British statesman and political philosopher. Elected to the House of Commons in 1765, Burke became a leader of the Whig party. Opposing the absolutist royal policies that he believed were forcing the thirteen American colonies into rebellion, Burke urged conciliation between Britain and its rebellious American colonies. Although he supported gradual and moderate

Historically Evolved Institutions: institutions that have evolved slowly over time and have acquired defining primary roles.

reforms, Burke believed that traditional political, social, religious, and educational institutions manifested and transmitted humanity's historically evolved wisdom.

Burke's interpretive principles of **historically evolved institutions**, enduring wisdom, and cultural transmission are especially relevant to education, schools, and instruction. For him, institutions such as the state, the church, and the school have evolved slowly over time. Having stood the test of time over the centuries, these institutions should be maintained and protected. As each new generation comes into the world, it is civilized, socialized, and inducted into society through these institutions. Because they are so important, proposals to change or reform these institutions must be moderate and carefully considered. These institutions organize, maintain, and transmit historically evolved knowledge to each generation.

Burke wrote on philosophical and political themes. His *Vindication of Natural Society* (1756) was a satire against political rationalism and religious skepticism. Burke's *Philosophical Enquiry into the Origin of Our Ideas of the Sublime and Beautiful* (1756) examined aesthetics from a romanticist perspective. He expressed his antagonism against the violence and excesses of the French Revolution in *Reflections on the Revolution in France* (1790), which remains a classic statement of Conservative ideology.

Utopian End: an unrealistic goal that is not based on and does not arise from historical reality.

Reacting against the French Revolution's violent turn, Burke saw the revolutionaries as sacrificing the bulwark of tradition to a **utopian end** that justified any action, no matter how reprehensible, on the pretext that it was necessary to create a better world. The trial and execution of the king and queen, decimation of the aristocracy, and attack on the church had undermined France's primary institutions that had once provided core stability to French society. Without these traditional institutions to maintain society and channel gradual change, the Revolution had been taken over by a dictatorial gang of conspirators who had usurped the legitimate prerogatives of the natural elite of birth and breeding. The conspiratorial elite, led by Robespierre, had embarked on a "reign of terror," with mass trials and purges, which anticipated the crimes that other totalitarian despots such as Hitler and Stalin would commit in the twentieth century in the name of a utopian future. Robespierre and other zealots of the French Revolution believed that the end justified the means as they attempted to create a perfect society on earth. Their orders for mass executions were justified by the Revolution's true believers as the necessary steps in eliminating those who stood in the way of creating a perfect republic. Burke warned that such **counsels of perfection** and revolutionary excesses were doomed to fail. Human beings, who themselves are imperfect, cannot possibly create a perfect society. Burke's *Reflections* warned against revolutionary change and social engineering that undermined civilization and civility.

Counsels of Perfection: misguided plans to create a utopian society on earth.

For Burke, the traditional cultural heritage was a repository of humanity's time-tested achievements. He saw the social, political, religious, and educational institutions—the family, state, church, and school—as cultural edifices that had evolved through centuries of human experience. These historically defined institutions have the following definitions and primary purposes:

- The family, composed of a man, the husband, and a woman, his wife, lives in a legally and religiously sanctioned marriage, with the purpose of rearing their children.
- The state, the government, through its various forms of power, is to maintain order, law, and stability.
- The church, transmitting divinely revealed truths, is to act as an intermediary between people and God.
- The school is to transmit and, thereby, maintain the civilized cultural heritage from generation to generation.

Standards of civility, as well as moral and ethical values, represented the fundamental wisdom of the human race.[1] A Burkean educational ideology stresses the need to cultivate in the young a sense of awe and respect for cultural institutions.

Education involves inculcating traditional wisdom and standards of behavior and civility in the young. Ideologically, Conservatives, following Burke's ideas, would be highly suspicious of proposals for transformative radical change, seeing them as a threat to civilization and civility.

The following tenets constitute Burke's major contributions to Conservative ideology: (1) institutions form a complex framework of customary practices and historically evolved rights and duties; (2) ethical and moral standards are developed within the historically evolved institutional system; (3) the wisdom of the past is a cultural inheritance to be transmitted from one generation to the next; (4) human culture and institutions represent a continuum of tested experience that should not be broken by untested innovation, revolutionary action, or social engineering; and (5) tradition is the repository of a collective social intelligence. To be educated according to these Burkean principles meant that the young were to be enculturated in the traditions of their parents, who in turn had been nurtured in the traditions of their parents. Thus, the heritage was passed on and kept alive over time.

Burke, who distrusted John Locke's emphasis on individual interests and government by majorities, believed that decisions are best made by an elite of well-educated persons, an aristocracy, not necessarily by birth, but certainly of culture and civility. Burke did not believe that the genuine interests of a nation and a people could be determined by opinion polls or adding up the numbers of voters. He feared that Liberalism would lead to a society of selfishness where decision making would fall to narrow special-interest groups. Burke believed that Conservative leadership and decision making should come from a public-spirited elite, who, steeped in tradition, would represent the entire nation's enduring interests.

For Locke's principles, see the chapter on Liberalism and Education.

Burke's assumption that society should be governed by the elite was an important original Conservative principle that had serious educational implications. Throughout history, the belief in rule by an elite has had many proponents, the most prominent of whom was Plato, who, in the *Republic*, argued that the philosopher-kings, an aristocracy of intellectuals, should rule. While there is a common human nature, there are likely to be some variations in a person's particular physical and mental constitution. Further, differences in how individuals realize their human potentiality result from the social milieus into which they are born, reared, and educated. Plato and Burke would agree that being raised as a member of a "good family," having a proper upbringing, and a receiving a well-grounded liberal education go a long way in giving a person the credentials needed for leadership. A contemporary example of an elite governing class is that of the graduates of England's famous public schools (really private preparatory schools) such as Eton, Rugby, Winchester, and Harrow, who, after completing university studies at either Oxford or Cambridge, join the country's governing elite. This British elite, historically deriving from the gentry, was, by birth and breeding, destined to rule. Their education in the classics, languages, history, and sportsmanship was designed to make them the bearers of traditional outlooks and values.

For a discussion of Plato's philosopher-kings, see the chapter on Idealism and Education.

Elitism in the Burkean sense rejected as fiction both Locke's and Rousseau's ideas of equality in the state of nature. If attempts were made to implement equality in society, the results would be a disastrous leveling, a dangerous utopianism, or mob rule. The good society, in Burkean terms, recognized and prized uniqueness or differences. The better educated, the more prudent, and the more expert were to protect and guide the less educated, the weaker, and the inexpert. Educationally, the traditional Conservative society, in the European sense, would prepare the culturally gifted to rule and prepare those of lesser ability to respect, support, and follow their rule.

Burke's vision of society, like Plato's, was not one in which those who were governed were suspicious of or rebellious against their rulers. Guided by an altruistic paternalism, the traditional Conservative society resembled a great extended family, where love and loyalty, emanating from an inherited shared past, washed over the entire community. This community was deeply rooted in a shared sense of identity, membership, and duty. Burke moved Conservative sensibility and sentimentality to a consciously articulated ideology.

THE PRINCIPLES OF CLASSICAL EURO-AMERICAN CONSERVATISM

In this section, we move from Burke's originating expression of Conservatism to examine the major principles of classical European and American Conservatism. In the early American republic, Conservatism found a home in the Federalist Party, especially in the political theories of Alexander Hamilton and John Adams, who, though republicans, still believed that government should be entrusted to a principled, educated, and resolute leadership elite. Although certain principles in Classical Conservatism are preserved in modern Neo-Conservatism, the new Conservatism has modified and revised some of its themes, especially in its American expression.

An Imperfect and Flawed Human Nature

Classical Conservatism, approximating the doctrine of humankind's fallen and sinful nature due to original sin, sees the human being as imperfect, flawed, and weak. Because of this inherent imperfection, individuals are inclined toward egotism, selfishness, idleness, and incivility. Given humankind's flawed nature, it is impossible to create a perfect society on earth. Those who promise to do so mislead people into a false utopianism in which the ends justify the means.

We become civilized when we learn to control our instincts and channel them into constructive rather than destructive behavior. A good human character can be formed by the correct upbringing as a member of a family, by attendance at church, and by being educated in an effective academic school. The family, defined as a religious and legal union between a man (the husband and father), his wife, and their children, is the setting in which traditional values are transmitted in an intimate, personal, and nurturing way from parents to their children. The church, as a foundation that is intertwined in the culture, promotes and interprets moral and ethical values in a religiously charged context. Schools, emphasizing an academic curriculum, cultural core, and traditional values, build on and extend the value formation begun in the family and the church. These primary institutions transmit the traditional core of knowledge and values, protecting against individual alienation and social instability.

Conservatism and the Past

For Conservatives, the past is the source of the traditions that shape historically evolved social institutions and personal human relationships. From the past, people acquire a sense of cultural identity and belonging as members of a distinct community, a nation that is rooted in a given place at a particular time in history. At a moment in human history, a person's presence is not transitory but rather is part of a continuum that binds the past and the future. From the past, a people, a particular society, inherits a collective wisdom based on lessons learned over time.

The Conservative reverence for the past and the historic sense are to be cultivated through education, especially the study of history, literature, and religion.

Today, the incessant mobility and social change associated with modern life have produced a feeling of rootlessness in which people find themselves without a sense of place or belonging. Conservatives argue that education should create a feeling of cultural identity in the young by emphasizing the literature and history that builds connections with a great and vital past. Language, literature, and history should celebrate the achievements of the past, the major events in a group's collective life, and the heroes and heroines who best exemplify its values and aspirations. Indeed, when such a heritage and its values are reinforced by religious observance and ritual, they are dramatically encased in the psyches of the young.

TRADITION, HISTORICALLY EVOLVED INSTITUTIONS, AND CHANGE

The Conservative worldview emphasizes a reliance on tradition as a source of cultural and moral authority, the need to maintain and fortify historically evolved institutions, and a cautious and limited approach to change.[2] Conservatism emphasizes the civilizing power of **tradition** in providing sociocultural cohesion and stability. Tradition is the legacy, the repository of humankind's collective and tested wisdom, that maintains social stability and continuity from one generation to the next. Tradition builds a sense of identity and meaning that gives people a sense of belonging to a culture or to a nation.

Tradition: the historically evolved beliefs and values that are foundational to customary ways of action; the past, through customs, asserting itself in the present.

Historically Evolved Institutions

Conservatives believe that institutions are historically evolved and perform necessary primary roles in society. Human institutions, each with a primary purpose, have been shaped by a continuum of historical experience. A primary role is original, basic, or essential to an institution. Basic institutions—the home, family, school, state, and the church, for example—have evolved over time. This continuum, this historical continuity, should not be broken by revolutionary actions or untested innovations and social experimentation. Social experimentation will only cause moral confusion, weaken the safeguards provided by civility, and bring about social disequilibrium and cultural disarray. For example, marriage is the primary institution for a man (a husband) and a woman (a wife) to live together in wedlock. Conservatives believe that the primary function of marriage is sacred and that other relationships, such as a man and woman living together without wedlock or a same-sex "marriage," distort and violate the moral, social, and cultural purpose of this institution. The family has the primary purpose of providing the home environment in which a married man and woman raise their children. For Conservatives, so-called alternative family styles distort the family's primary role and function as an institution.

Schools have the primary purpose of providing an academic education that brings children into participation in their cultural heritage. Conservatives dispute what Progressives claim is the residual function of the school. The residual function means that when an institution can no longer perform its function, then another institution can assume it. If families, for example, do not perform their function of properly bringing up children, then the school is to assume that neglected function. If families do not inform their children about sex, then the school is to take on the function of sex education. Conservatives disagree. When schools assume nonacademic custodial, therapeutic, and social functions, they dilute, weaken, and distort their **primary role**. When institutions are uncertain about their primary role or interfere in the roles of other institutions, the process of historical evolution is disrupted. For example, Conservatives believe that schools as historically evolved educational institutions have the primary role of transmitting the cultural heritage, often prescribed as a core curriculum of academic skills and subjects and the values of civility to the young. When

For the school as a multifunctional institution, with a residual function, see the chapter on Progressivism and Education.

Primary Role: the belief that each institution exists to perform the single, most important function that defines it.

schools cross over and assume the roles of other institutions, they dilute their primary role. Conservatives want to keep institutions functioning according to their primary and traditional purposes.

Ideologically, Conservatism functions in two ways regarding institutions: (1) to maintain and preserve those institutions that are functioning according to their intended original or primary purpose; and (2) to restore their primary function to institutions that have been altered or changed so that they no longer perform their traditional original role. If schools have assumed nonacademic custodial, social, and therapeutic functions, these functions should be removed so that schools can regain their original, traditional, and historic academic functions. Teachers are to teach academic skills and subjects to students and not dilute or distort their traditional roles by trying to be babysitters, therapists, counselors, or social workers. Time spent on nonacademic functions takes away time and energy from the primary academic purpose for which schools were established in the first place.

Conservatism's Alliance with Organized Religion

Conservatives in Europe were historically allied with religion, especially with established churches. In Europe, Conservatives favored an establishment of religion by the state. For example, the Church of England, or Anglican Church, is the official state church in England and the monarch is the titular head of the church. The Russian Orthodox Church was the official religion in Tsarist Russia. In Norway and Sweden, the Lutheran Church was the official state church. For European Conservatives, an officially sanctioned and state-supported church identifies individuals in an integrating cultural heritage that binds earth to heaven.

Contemporary Conservative alliances with religion give a supernatural sanction to political, social, economic, and educational beliefs.[3] When the cultural core is seen as originating in a higher supernatural providential source, it becomes much more than a human construction. It is a covenant between humankind and God. This covenant is usually not generalized to the whole human race but is presented as a special relationship between God and a particular group of believers—those who have the true faith. For example, Christian fundamentalists tend to see the United States as a nation founded on a Christian covenant. Orthodox Jews see the covenant between God and the Hebrew people. Fundamentalist Moslems see it in the Koran.

Change

The Conservative worldview has a decided preference, indeed, a longing, to maintain historically evolved institutions in a way that is true to their original primary purposes. Relying on tradition as a source of authority, Conservatives are cautious about change. They endorse the saying, "The more things change, the more they stay the same." Conservatives recognize the reality and importance of scientific and technological change; however, their point is that these kinds of changes in the material realm—that of science and technology—must be subordinated to and put into historical perspective by traditional cultural controls. Changes will inevitably occur, and they need to be accommodated and incorporated into the traditional cultural heritage rather than changing the heritage to fit the areas of change. Although their applications may be adjusted to changing circumstances, the principles on which they are based remain the same.

Although economic and technological changes affect society, Conservatives want this change to be correctly channeled in order to preserve traditional institutions and values. Conservatives want to maintain an essential cultural core that is rooted in the knowledge and values of Western civilization and of the American heritage. Conservatives are open to programs of renewal that promise a restoration of traditional values.[4] For them, acceptable natural change is a gradual organic growth like the development of a child into an adult. Cultures and societies, too, experience this kind of gradual historical growth and development. Natural developmental change is gradual, cumulative, and orderly. It is not rapid and disruptive. Conservatives strongly oppose attempts to transform society as radical, revolutionary, and utopian. For example, the supposed radical change of the French and Russian revolutions was utopian and destined to fail. The French Revolution led to the reign of terror and to the rise of Napoleon. The Russian Revolution led to Stalin's massive repression, gulags, and the purges.

Conservatives are particularly opposed to attempts to engineer social change through the schools. With their piecemeal, incremental changes, Liberals are continually undermining the academic purpose of the schools. Their various additive changes such as anti-poverty, healthy diet, and recycling programs whittle away at the school as an academic institution.

For their emphasis on directed social change, see the chapter on Social Reconstructionism and Education.

Conservatives are especially opposed to Social Reconstructionism that seeks to use schools to build a new social order. This kind of **social engineering** puts schools into the hands of radical ideologues who would use classrooms for political indoctrination. Social Reconstructionists want schools to be agencies that promote social planning for a planned society. This kind of planning, the Conservatives say, undermines individual freedom. Social engineering programs are disruptive, disjointed, and disconnected from the school's primary and historically legitimate purpose. Schools should be agencies that preserve the cultural core that gives balance and ballast to society.

Social Engineering: the theory that society can be planned and that policies can be established and implemented to accomplish the plan.

Schools that function according to a Conservative ideology would not be centers of social change or cultural reconstruction. Rather, their foremost goal is to cultivate a social stasis and continuity. Determined to preserve the traditional curriculum, Conservative educators are suspicious of educational innovations. They point to the history of education to illustrate the fleeting insignificance of many highly publicized educational innovations such as team-teaching, competency-based learning, the discovery method, the "new mathematics," collaborative learning, and whole language reading. What persists over time, they argue, are the essential skills and subjects, especially those that exemplify cultural roots, such as literature and history.

Despite their reservations about educational innovations, Conservatives recognize that from time to time certain material technological changes occur that impact culture and society. It is important that technological innovations be integrated into the heritage so that they are connected to it and do not disrupt cultural continuity. An example of such a technological innovation is the computer. Conservatives would use computers as instruments to make instruction in the traditional subjects more efficient rather than employ them to transform or radically alter the curriculum. Examples of societies that have integrated technology into a strong culture core are Singapore and South Korea, where the new technological elements have been positioned into a traditional Confucianist core.

The Conservative Sense of Community

For Conservatives, the community is highly important and necessary in integrating individuals into a common culture. The individuals residing in a community participate in historically evolved institutions such as the family, church, and school. Picture the community as being set in a place, a town, where families have lived across generations. A place where children attend the same churches and schools as did their parents and grandparents. Place and time give the members of the community identity, meaning, and a sense of belonging. The church has a special place in this community in that it is intertwined in its cultural life; it promotes supernaturally sanctioned moral and ethical values and celebrates the major events—baptisms, marriages, and funerals--in a person's life. The family is the setting in which traditional values are transmitted in an intimate and personal way from the old to the young. The school, as a social agency, builds on and extends these values that originate in the family and church. These primary institutions—family, church, and school—transmit the traditional core of knowledge and value so that the community is perpetuated and protected against change that might jeopardize the community's cultural and social stability.

For discussion of individual self-interest, see the chapter on Liberalism and Education.

Conservatives contend that the Liberal exaggerated emphasis on individualism leads to a selfish atomistic society in which people act to satisfy their self-interests without regard to the historically evolved community. Equally undesirable to the Conservative is the mass society with its mass culture and mass-produced tastes that result in social leveling rather than a hierarchy that recognizes quality, good taste, and talent.

For discussion of the alienation of marginalized groups, see the chapters on Marxism, Postmodernism, and Critical Theory.

Conservatives want individuals to be integrated into the culture and society and not feel separated or alienated from it. They are especially opposed to those who view society through the Marxist lens of alienation, such as the Postmodernists and Critical Theorists. For Marx, human alienation from the existing society and economy is caused by the capitalist lust for profits at the expense of workers. Alienation means that the workers' time and the products made are taken from them and sold for a profit that they do not get to share.

For Marxists, the institutional superstructure in a capitalist society—school, church, state, and media—are economically controlled by the dominant class. Institutions are dependent on the owners of property. Marxists and Critical Theorists argue that education should raise the consciousness of exploited people so that they understand the cause of their alienation and exploitation. Conservatives believe that what Marxists and Critical Theorists call *consciousness-raising* is their method of indoctrinating people in a false reading of history. The purpose of education, for Conservatives, is to bring people into the culture by transmitting cultural values to them.

CONTEMPORARY AMERICAN NEO-CONSERVATISM

Neo-Conservatism: new or modern Conservatism.

Our discussion of Conservatism so far has focused on its origins and development in the Western, especially the European, cultural tradition. At this point, we discuss American Conservatism, especially the rise of contemporary **Neo-Conservatism.**

American Conservatism's Political Context

From the Roosevelt New Deal in the 1930s until the late 1960s, Liberalism was the dominant political ideology in the United States. Conservatism was the minority

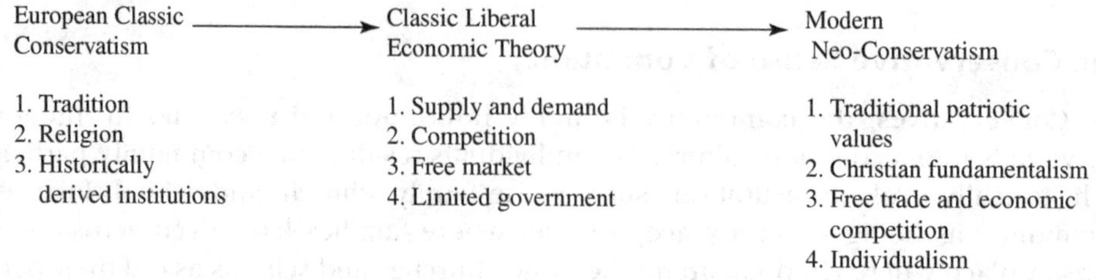

American Neo-Conservatism

ideology, espoused by some traditional Republicans, such as Robert Taft, who wanted to curb what they considered to be the excessive growth of the federal government. In academia and journalism, Conservatism had articulate spokespersons such as Russell Kirk (1918–1944) and William Buckley (1925–2008), but they were in the minority. In 1964, Barry Goldwater (1909–1998), the Republican senator from Arizona and presidential candidate, launched a more popular and less academic Conservative movement in his book, *The Conscience of a Conservative* (1960). With the election of Ronald Reagan (1911–2004) as president in 1980, Conservatism in the United States was on a political ascendancy, and it enjoyed a strong revival as Neo-Conservatism, the new Conservatism. In the election of 1988, the victorious Republican candidate for president, George H. Bush, continued the policies of Neo-Conservatism. In the elections of 2000 and 2004, George W. Bush was elected and reelected as a "compassionate Conservative."

A Neo-Conservative Interpretation of the American Past

Our discussion of general Conservative principles emphasized that Conservatives look to the past, to history, as the source of cultural and moral authority. Contemporary American Neo-Conservatives, too, look to American history as the source of American traditional beliefs and values. As is true of ideologies such as Liberalism, Neo-Conservatives have their own interpretation of the past. As with other ideologies, Neo-Conservatives' interpretation of history is a selective analysis. Their interpretation highlights the theme of American Exceptionalism, the belief that Americans are a unique and special people, living in a land providentially blessed with natural resources and abundant land. Eliciting sentiments of patriotism and loyalty to the nation, it presents a nationalist story of American greatness and rightness.

For the interpretation of the past, see the chapter on Ideology and Education.

For American Exceptionalism, see the chapter on Nationalism and Education.

Americans are a good people, ordained by Divine Providence to settle in a new world, tame the wilderness, and establish a republic, governed by law and civility. While some historians would question the accuracy of this version of the past, for an ideology, that is not the point. In creating a preferred interpretation of the past, myth becomes entwined with history.

The thirteen colonies were settled by people from Great Britain and northern Europe who came to the new world to create a better life in which they would be free to govern themselves and practice their religion. The Pilgrim and Puritan founding fathers, seeing their new country as the fulfillment of the biblical "city on a hill," formed a special covenant with God. This special covenant made the United States a Christian nation. The War for American Independence marked the beginnings of American patriots fighting for a just cause. The founding fathers at the Constitutional Convention established a government based on the original Christian principles that had inspired the Puritans. As in the days of the ancient Hebrews, when Mosaic Law was regarded as a covenant between the Jews and God, Neo-Conservatives see American government, too, as a covenant in which the people adopted a constitution as their instrument of self-government. For them, the Constitution rests on the tradition of essential Christian principles and precedents from Anglo-American common law. The Neo-Conservative interpretation of American history emphasizes the United States as a faith-based and religiously inspired nation. Selectively choosing one's founding fathers, it does not emphasize the Deist beliefs of some of the leaders of the early republic, such as Thomas Jefferson, who urged separation of church and state.

The Neo-Conservative interpretation of American educational history emphasizes how public schools, in the past, functioned to create a common American identity. For example, Noah Webster (1758–1843), a leading educator and lexicographer in the early national period, is seen as working to create a distinctive, but standardized, version of the English language.[5] Public schools, like the common schools, should resist maintenance of bilingual and bicultural programs that use languages other than English in instruction. While these programs might be used to transition non-English-speaking students into using the English language, they should be temporary and not permanent.

Catharine Beecher (1800–1878), a pioneer teacher educator, held ideas that contemporary Conservatives would endorse. Endorsing Evangelical Christianity as a part of teacher education, Beecher saw teachers, especially women, as missionaries of Western culture and civility.[6] Women teachers, serving as moral exemplars, were to use their "sensibility" to teach a common language and curriculum that brought literacy and civility to the western frontier.

Still another Neo-Conservative educational hero is William Holmes McGuffey (1800–1873), the author of the widely used McGuffey Readers, which affirmed the values of literacy, hard work, diligence, punctuality, patriotism, and civility.[7] McGuffey Readers emphasized the moral values of white, middle-class, Protestant Americans.

The westward-moving American frontier brought historically based institutions—the home, town, church, school, farm, and small business—to the wilderness. These institutions gave the growing nation a sense of stability, marked by political order and economic prosperity. In the frontier settlement of the western territories that became the United States, the settlers were community builders. As soon as they had constructed their crude cabins, the next structures to be created were the town meeting place, the church, and the school. These institutions were the historically evolved institutions that were transplanted as agencies of civility on the western frontier. For Conservatives, the American West was settled by rugged individuals, who through their own courage and initiative conquered a hostile environment. They and their families stood on their own two feet and did not seek government handouts. The rifle and the handgun were the necessary instruments they used to protect themselves against hostile Indians and outlaws. For some American Conservatives, an important part of their version of the past is "rugged individualism," which differs from the European version of Conservatism. The right to keep and to bear arms is affirmed as an important safeguard provided by the Constitution's Second Amendment.

The United States became a modern industrial nation because individual creativity and inventiveness were not shackled by an intrusive government. Inventors such as Alexander Graham Bell (1847–1922) and Thomas Edison (1847–1931), and industrialists such as Andrew Carnegie (1835–1919) and Henry Ford (1863–1947) built a great nation. Today, it is still possible for enterprising individuals such as Bill Gates and Warren Buffett to amass wealth. The economic development of the United States is presented not as exploitative but as representing an opportunity for those who have the ingenuity and energy to compete. All have a chance to earn and to learn and through their own merit to share in a great nation's prosperity. The Neo-Conservative interpretation of American economic history appropriates much from Adam Smith's classical liberal free market economics; in the free market economy, enterprising entrepreneurs are free to compete in producing and selling goods and services without government regulation.

For Classical Liberalism, see the chapter on Liberalism and Education.

Neo-Conservatives see the United States as a country of immigrants, of people who came to America to find the personal and religious freedom and economic opportunity that the country's original settlers found in the settlement of the New World. When the immigrants arrived, they found an American cultural and political tradition already in place. Established by the nation's founders, the characteristics of this tradition were (1) English as the "official" language in government, business, and education; (2) a willingness to work hard and be thrifty and industrious as a reflection of the generalized Puritan or Calvinist ethic; and (3) respect for the Constitution and obedience to the law. But for immigrants to succeed, they needed to be **Americanized**, that is, learn to speak the English language, practice civility, and be law-abiding and industrious contributors to American culture. Their role was to join the American national community and not try to change it into a version of the countries that they left behind. Conservatives would argue that today's new immigrants from Asia, the Middle East, and South America should emulate the patterns of the earlier European immigrants and Americanize themselves to function in the society of their adopted country.

Americanized: the end result of the Americanization ideology and policy used in public schools in the nineteenth and early twentieth centuries.

The Conservative version of how immigrants were successfully assimilated into American life, politics, and society has important educational implications. Foremost is that there already exists a completed model of American culture that was defined in the early decades of the republic. New generations, be they native born or immigrants, are to absorb and be assimilated into this model. The model is not open-ended and changing—it is rooted in the American cultural heritage and tradition. Education, then, is to further the process of assimilation into the model. Schools are to transmit an American cultural core to students so that they can adopt and adapt to the model. This means that the English language should be the language of instruction rather than other languages, as in bilingual programs. Schools should impart a solid cultural core based on American history and literature rather than multiculturalism. The values inculcated by the school need to focus on respect for legitimate authority, hard work, diligence, and civic responsibility.

Immigration has been a persistent area of controversy in the United States since the Know-Nothings of the 1850s sought to restrict immigration to the United States. Today, immigration is a highly controversial political, cultural, and national security issue. The debate, shaped by contrasting versions of history, carries ideological overtones. Contending that immigrants, especially illegal aliens, are an expensive burden on the country's educational, health care, social services, and security systems, Neo-Conservatives want laws to restrict immigration and stop illegal immigration. They argue that the movement of illegal immigrants across U.S. borders threatens national security, especially in the war on terrorism.[8]

In terms of foreign policy, Conservatives think of the United States as a good country, inhabited by morally good people, who do the right thing internationally. The United States represents a model of democratic government and human rights that other countries should emulate. Some Conservatives, in the past, were isolationists, believing that the United States, as a democratic fortress protected by two great oceans, should, as George Washington advised, avoid entangling alliances with other countries. Two world wars, the Cold War, and the war against terrorism have eroded the older isolationist view. Neo-Conservative foreign policy is driven heavily by an ideology that sees world issues in terms of moral right and wrong. For example, in the Cold War, President Reagan saw the Soviet Union as "an evil empire." President George W. Bush called the governments of Iran, North Korea, and Iraq (before the fall of Saddam Hussein) "an axis of evil." Neo-Conservative ideology argues that when other countries refuse to take the moral high ground, the United States has the right to make unilateral decisions in world affairs.

The Neo-Conservative Christian Fundamentalist Alliance

Christian fundamentalists, referred to as the "religious right," are often affiliated with Neo-Conservatism. For them, the morally righteous society builds its institutions and values on religious foundations. For them, the United States, as a nation, rests on a generalized Christian ethic, which is summed up nicely by "in God we trust." Although some Christian Conservatives would challenge the doctrine of separation of church and state, many would argue that the doctrine has been incorrectly interpreted by the courts. According to strict construction of the Constitution, the government is not to establish an official religion. Other faith-based initiatives such as government support of churches that provide child care, education, health care, and other social services do not violate the Constitution. Neo-Conservatives want a conscious affirmation by government and educational authorities that America's institutions rest on a religious—a Christian—core of values.

Christian Conservatives are fearful that some trends in modern society are undermining fundamental values. They assert a need to restore "family values." Religious Conservatives—Christian Fundamentalists and Roman Catholics—are especially opposed to the Supreme Court's decision in *Roe v. Wade*, which gave women a legal right to have abortions. Conservatives say that abortion denies the unborn child's right to life.

Christian Conservatives have an educational agenda that they believe is needed to restore religious values to schools. They contend that many public schools subscribe to secular humanism, a kind of secular religion based on Pragmatism and Liberalism, that sees truth as relative and situational. Neo-Conservatives want the public schools to reflect what they believe are the country's abiding traditional Christian values. They favor moments of silence for quiet reflection, the posting of the Ten Commandments, and permission for student groups to meet for prayer in public schools. Sex education programs need to be carefully monitored so that they emphasize abstinence from sexual relations before marriage and do not encourage other kinds of birth control such as the use of condoms.

A long-running issue between Christian Conservatives and their Pragmatist, Liberal, and Progressive opponents is the teaching of Darwin's theory of evolution in the science curriculum. In 1859, Charles Darwin (1809–1882) in *The Origin of Species by Means of Natural Selection* established the theory that all existing plants and animals had evolved by gradual modifications that, if they contributed to survival, were passed on to their offspring as inherited characteristics.[9]

Darwin's theory of evolution provoked deep controversies in religion, philosophy, and education. For many Christians, evolution challenged the biblical account of Creation, in Genesis, that God created all species as they now exist.[10] Although some theologians interpret Genesis allegorically, Christian Fundamentalists, taking a literal view of the Bible, reject Darwinian evolution.

The Scopes Trial in 1925 in Dayton, Tennessee, dramatically illustrated the tension generated by the teaching of evolution in the schools. John Scopes, a high school science and mathematics teacher, was tried for violating the Butler Act, which prohibited the teaching of evolution in Tennessee's public schools.[11] Although Scopes was convicted and fined a minimal one hundred dollars, the prosecution case was more of a symbolic victory than a real one.[12]

Intelligent Design: the theory that life is so complex and ordered that it has to be the work of an Intelligent Being, Creator, or Designer.

Today, the issue is framed as the teaching of Evolution versus Creationism or **Intelligent Design** in the science curriculum. Christian Fundamentalists, who argue that evolution is a theory rather than a factual account, want equal attention given to Creation Science or Intelligent Design. Creation Science argues that there is sufficient scientific evidence to support the biblical account of Creation. Intelligent Design argues that life is too complex to have developed without the intervention of an intelligent outside power.[13] Neo-Conservative Christian Fundamentalists seek to have these alternative views included in the curriculum.

Although Christian Conservatives continue their struggle for an alternative to Darwinian evolution in the science curriculum, they have been unsuccessful in the courts. The U.S. Supreme Court has ruled that local school boards and state legislatures cannot legally prohibit the teaching of evolution, nor require the teaching of Creationism, either alongside evolutionary theory or in place of it. For example, the Supreme Court ruled (in 1968) that a 1928 Arkansas law that made it a crime to teach evolution in a public school or state university violated the First Amendment's Establishment Clause in that it had a religious purpose to prevent students from being instructed in a position opposed by fundamentalist Christians.[14]

In 1982, Federal District Court Judge William Overton, in *McLean v. Arkansas Board of Education*, ruled against the "Balanced Treatment for Creation-Science and Evolution-Science Act," which required creation science to be taught alongside evolution. Overton ruled that the Arkansas law violated the Establishment Clause and that creation science was not science but based wholly on the biblical account of Creation. Therefore, the teaching of creation science clearly advances religion and entangles it with the government. In a similar case, the Supreme Court in *Edwards v. Aguillard* (1987) struck down a Louisiana law that forbade the teaching of the theory of evolution in public schools unless it was accompanied by instruction in creation science.[15] In *Kitzmiller v. Dover Area School District* (2005), Federal Judge John E. Jones III ruled that the board's decision to include Intelligent Design in the town's high school science curriculum violated the Establishment Clause.

Still another approach to instruction of subjects such as evolution, global warming, and cloning has been to identify them as areas in which there are conflicting opinions. In dealing with these controversial subjects, some states have enacted various "academic freedom laws" to protect the rights of teachers to challenge existing scientific theories. For example, the Louisiana Science Education Act (2008) safeguards the rights of teachers to present alternative opinions and materials to these scientific theories. Critics contend that this and similar laws represent another effort by opponents of the theory of evolution who are using academic freedom as an argument to weaken its teaching in the science curriculum. It is expected that the laws such as the Louisiana Act will be challenged in the courts in the future.

These court rulings apply to the teaching of Creationism in science courses but not in other courses such as in literature or world religions classes. The Supreme Court ruled that "the Bible may constitutionally be used in an appropriate study of history, civilization, ethics, comparative religion or the like."[16]

Neo-Conservatives hope that judges in the future will be appointed to the Supreme Court and other federal courts on their concurrence that the Constitution should be strictly interpreted. They believe that strict constructionists will not interpret the law liberally and that the decisions on abortion and evolution may yet be overturned.

Ideological Permeability: the process by which an ideology appropriates concepts from another ideology into its theoretical framework; as with American Neo-Conservatism's appropriation of Classical Liberal economic ideas.

Neo-Conservative Economic Beliefs

In considering the economic beliefs of Neo-Conservatives, it is necessary to return to the concept of **ideological permeability**, which means that ideologies often appropriate the ideas of other ideologies.[17]

For ideological permeability, see the chapter on Ideology and Education.

Neo-Conservative Appropriation of Classical Liberal Economic Theory

Neo-Conservatism has appropriated the Classical Liberal laissez-faire economic theories of Adam Smith and David Ricardo, which were developed in the early nineteenth century. Classical Liberal economists argued that (1) government should not interfere with the free market economy; (2) the natural law of supply and demand would make necessary corrections to the economy, without the need for external regulation; and (3) economic productivity results from competition that brings about new inventions

For Classical Liberal economic theory, see the chapter on Liberalism and Education.

and innovations. In applying classical liberal economic doctrines to contemporary globalization, Neo-Conservatives want trade barriers between countries removed, national economies deregulated, and government-provided social services reduced or eliminated.

NEO-LIBERALISM. This contemporary revival of Smith's and Ricardo's economic theories is also called Neo-Liberalism, or new Liberalism. Neo-Liberalism, like Nationalism, blurs ideological distinctions in that it is endorsed by some Conservatives and some Liberals. Neo-Liberalism needs to be separated from the Modern or Social Welfare Liberalism that permeates American liberal ideas, especially those associated with John Dewey. In contrast with the Neo-Conservative appropriation of Classical Liberal economic ideas, Social Welfare Liberalism has been shaped by the economists John Maynard Keynes, John Kenneth Galbraith, and Robert Reich.

The American and European Neo-Conservative appropriation of Classical Liberal economics has been very influential in domestic as well as in global economies. Ideas that were once directed to business entrepreneurs and industry are now applied to the larger and more interconnected corporate economy. Recall that in the previous chapter, it was emphasized that Modern Liberals have profoundly revised these ideas and prefer a larger government role to provide more social services. In opposition to the Modern Liberal social welfare state, American Conservatives advocate an open market, free trade, supply and demand, competitiveness, and the deregulation and privatization of social services and some educational programs. A free and competitive marketplace, they argue, will encourage the most industrious and able individuals to achieve and produce without having to carry the less productive on their economic shoulders. Neo-Conservatives believe that government intervention in the economy leads to higher taxes and inefficient bureaucracy. It is important to restore the economy to its free-flowing condition by deregulating it, that is, by removing the controls of government regulatory agencies.

In their appropriation of Classical Liberal economic theory, American Neo-Conservatives have abandoned the older European Conservative sense of paternalism, in which the upper classes were responsible for the well-being of less-favored classes. For Neo-Conservatives, the modern Liberal social welfare state has made the poor into a dependent underclass. Conservatives charge that government social welfare programs have perpetuated a dependent underclass. For Neo-Conservatives, the economically disadvantaged, especially the unemployed, need to be self-motivated to improve their own situations. Rather than government-regulated programs, Neo-Conservatives prefer private voluntarism in which individuals, by their private philanthropy, aid educational and health care institutions. The idea of private philanthropy and voluntarism can be combined with church-sponsored programs to uplift the disadvantaged.

According to Neo-Conservatives, modern welfare Liberals have enacted bureaucratic regulations that have weakened American economic productivity. For example, administrators and teachers in public schools have to spend far too much time meeting bureaucratic requirements and filling out countless forms that take them away from their real job—teaching basic skills and academic subjects. It is these skills and subjects that are vitally needed to revive American economic productivity. They have replaced the tried-and-true traditional values of hard work, diligence, respect for authority, and patriotism with Progressive and Liberal so-called innovative tinkering and experimentation with the curriculum. Rather than preparing the well-trained workforce and managers needed in an increasingly technological global economy, public schools, too often controlled by misguided Liberal educationists, have miseducated children.

In addition to reforming public schools by restoring their primary academic role, some Neo-Conservatives argue that the public school system is a tax-supported educational monopoly. As in a monopoly, it resists competition among schools. Competition among schools would reveal the more effective academic schools and, in a free educational market, students would be attracted to them. Conservatives believe there should be greater freedom of education that permits parents to place their children in better performing schools. A program of government-subsidized vouchers would enable parents to choose their preferred public or private school. In such a competitive educational arena, it would be possible to distinguish the most effective and efficient schools from mediocre ones. Effective schools would attract academically inclined and motivated students. Thus, the voucher system, a form of educational privatization, would improve education by opening schools to challenging competition.

Neo-Conservativism's Response to Confrontations

Neo-Conservatism is a protective ideology that reacts against attacks on its core beliefs and values, especially from a counter-ideology such as Liberalism or a counter-theory such as Critical Theory. The Conservative strategy is to assemble a defensive array of counter-concepts, a conceptual "circle of the wagons" directed against whatever or whomever appears to be threatening its version of the good society.[18] For example, in the abortion controversy, a "woman's right to choose" is countered by "the right to life." In health care, federal medical insurance is countered with the freedom and privacy between doctor and patient. The teaching of Darwin's theory of evolution in the science curriculum is countered with the teaching of Intelligent Design. A multicultural curriculum is countered with a core curriculum based on Western culture.

CONSERVATISM'S IMPLICATIONS FOR EDUCATION, SCHOOLING, CURRICULUM, AND TEACHING AND LEARNING

We have commented on Conservatism's and Neo-Conservativism's ideas about education throughout the chapter. We now turn to a more specific commentary on their implications for education, schooling, curriculum, and teaching and learning.

American Neo-Conservatives have a definite educational agenda. They want to restore the school to what they argue is its primary function—the transmission of the cultural heritage by deliberately organized instruction in academic skills and subjects in a climate of traditional moral values. For them, restoration is needed because decades of miseducation by Dewey's Pragmatists, Liberals, Progressives, cultural relativists, and secular humanists have disrupted the school's academic mission and eroded its cultivation of moral values.

For their perspectives on the educational and moral purpose of schools, see the chapters on Pragmatism, Liberalism, Progressivism, and Critical Theory.

Education

For Conservatives, education is the transmission of the cultural heritage, the essential aspects of the culture, from generation to generation so that the culture is preserved, perpetuated, and maintained. The cultural heritage means the important elements in the culture—historically tested traditional knowledge and values, as well as the historically evolved institutions—that comprise a culture. **Cultural transmission**, which avoids social disruption, provides the young with the correct idea of how institutions function and informs them that each institution has a primary function. Education, both informally and formally, through schooling, should create a perspective on time (past, present, and future) that is transgenerational (understood by both old and young) and of place, as constituting a homeland.

Cultural Transmission: the inter-generational process of deliberately passing on the culture (beliefs, attitudes, customs, and traditions) from generation to generation.

Schools

Schools, as historically evolved social and cultural institutions, have the primary role of introducing and transmitting the cultural heritage to the young by educating children and adolescents in academic skills and knowledge that are esteemed as culturally, socially, politically, and economically valuable. They promote cultural continuity through teaching language, history, literature, and the arts. Educators are to safeguard and protect the traditional curriculum from those who want to experiment with, add nonacademic frills to, and impose nonacademic functions on schools and teachers. They warn against being deluded by panacea-like promises that the introduction of a new subject or method will make teaching and learning easy and effective. From time to time, certain changes occur such as the introduction of computers and electronic information technologies. The educational challenge is to use these technologies so that they are linked to and reinforce the cultural heritage. Computers can be used to transmit the cultural heritage in a more dynamic and efficient way. For example, Ken Burns's series on the Civil War renews interest in a dynamic way about an important event in America's past. In *A Nation at Risk,* computer literacy is identified as a new basic, along with the traditional language, mathematics, science, and history. Computer literacy, a necessary skill in the global economy, is given a place along with the traditional skills and subjects.

ORDER AND CIVILITY. Conservatives argue that schools have been moving in the wrong direction regarding values and character education. Misguided by Dewey's Pragmatism, Liberalism, and Progressivism, the moral climate of schools has been eroded by hedonism, permissiveness, irresponsibility, and inappropriate language, dress, and behavior. In the past, teachers were respected persons in society and schools were respected institutions. This kind of respect was earned by emphasizing the tried-and-true historically validated moral values—patriotism, diligence, hard work, respect for private property, and the practice of manners and civility—that made the United States into a great and prosperous nation. It is time to reassert these core values in schools so that they have clear and unambiguous educational and moral purposes. Schools should be places in which students learn to respect their country, their teachers, and each other.

Curriculum

For Conservatives, the curriculum is historically derived and validated. It consists of skills and knowledge that contribute to cultural survival, have met the test of time, and remain necessary and useful in the culture. The traditional tool skills of reading, writing, composition, speaking, and listening, and the added skill of computer literacy contribute to a culturally sustaining and useful literacy that is important in reaffirming, maintaining, and reproducing the cultural heritage. Arithmetic is important for its generative power in higher mathematics and the sciences. Geography, a subject neglected in contemporary education, needs to be reestablished so that Americans are no longer geographically illiterate. It is useful in creating knowledge about location and place. The secondary curriculum is organized as subjects, each of which has clearly defined boundaries, and which should be taught by teachers who have knowledge of what they are teaching. Border crossing between subjects, as suggested by Critical Theorists, blurs the concept that each subject is about a particular area of knowledge.

For border crossing between subjects, see the chapter on Critical Theory and Education.

The education of knowledgeable teachers is grounded in the liberal arts and sciences. Too often, liberal education has been sacrificed in teacher education programs for courses in methods—on how to teach but not on what to teach. Science, mathematics, history, language, and literature, as indispensable subjects, must be taught by teachers who know their content. The content of these subjects should be taught in an orderly and sequential way.

A CULTURAL CORE. Conservatives believe that schools need to transmit a **cultural core** that is rooted in Western civilization and American culture. The heritage of Western civilization, as Conservatives define it, is based on the great ideas of Plato, Aristotle, Jesus, Aquinas, Luther, Calvin, Locke, Burke, and others, as well as the major events of European history such as the Renaissance, Reformation, and Enlightenment.

Cultural Core: featuring a core of subjects that reflect the key beliefs and values of a particular culture. For Conservatives, the core is centered in English language and American history and literature.

In addition to the core of Western civilization, Conservatives want the schools to emphasize what they identify as the core knowledge and values of American culture. This means that students should be taught American history and literature and should be expected to know the important persons and events that shaped the United States. It should not be taught in a way that downgrades American patriotism and minimizes the great achievements Americans made in creating their nation. It should emphasize knowledge of the Constitution, along with respect for law and duly constituted authorities. Conservatives would oppose what they regard as an extreme multiculturalism that minimizes American core values and represents the United States as a nation of unassimilated racial and ethnic groups.

Language, literature, and history should celebrate the achievements of the past, the major events in the group's collective life, and the heroes and heroines who best exemplify the group's values and aspirations. History is presented in terms of a tradition that is the basis of culture and a defensive rationale to be used against opponents. It is presented as a cumulative wisdom from the past that today's students need to inherit to remain stable and law-abiding citizens. Economics is interpreted in laissez-faire, free market terms.

My Reflections on Philosophy of Education: A Perspective on the Founders

The founders of the United States—Washington, Adams, Jefferson, Hamilton, Madison, and others who wrote the Constitution—occupy an important role in American history. I have observed how the same founders are used to support different ideological and political agendas. Liberals and Conservatives see the founders from different perspectives. When I have discussed the founders of the Republic with Conservative friends, I find that they use the following interpretation: (1) the founders established a system of checks and balances to limit the powers of the federal government; (2) while a few of them may have been Deists, most of the founders were Christians, who saw government in a religious way as a covenant between God and the American people; (3) the founders regarded the Constitution as protecting freedom of speech, press, assembly, and the right to keep and bear arms.

Then, the voices of the founders are used in considering contemporary issues. The interpretation of some of my Conservative associates is that the founders, favoring a limited federal role, would oppose the involvement of the federal government in education. Some of them would argue that the federal Department of Education should be abolished as an intrusion on the rights of the states and local districts. They might say that the strict separation of church and state is not what the founders intended. They would oppose laws that restrict gun ownership. Interestingly, their Liberal opponents would go to the same founders and, citing the Declaration of Independence and the Preamble to the Constitution, make differing interpretations.

RESTORING ACADEMIC STANDARDS. The contemporary standards movement and the federal No Child Left Behind Act mark a Neo-Conservative effort to restore academic standards to the school. The standards movement was inaugurated by the Reagan administration with *A Nation at Risk* (1983), which sought to reverse the nonacademic undermining of the schools. This national report called for a curriculum of academic basics—the English language, mathematics, science, language, social studies and history, and computer literacy. The Reagan administration developed a strategy that encouraged the states to enact legislation that added requirements in the basics, especially in English, mathematics, and science. It also encouraged them to use standardized testing to determine students' academic competency at specific grade levels. The initiative stimulated by *A Nation at Risk* led to the standards movement in education that asserts that schools need to be held accountable for the academic instruction that they are supposed to provide. The only way to really determine academic competency is to require standardized testing that measures students' academic achievement, especially in the key areas of reading and mathematics at specific grade levels. The Education Act of 2001, the No Child Left Behind Act, sponsored by the George W. Bush administration, requires states to implement standardized testing in reading and mathematics, in grades three through eight, in order to receive federal funds.

The Conservative Teacher

The teacher in the Conservative educational setting is an agent who transmits the cultural heritage to children and youth so that they can incorporate it into their intellectual outlooks and characters. Such teachers should be people who cherish the cultural heritage, who know it well, and who reflect the culture's traditional values in their personalities and behavior. Like the Idealist teacher, they are character models that students can imitate. Although they may use educational technology to transmit the tradition more effectively, Conservative teachers are not agents seeking to change or reconstruct society. Nor do such teachers encourage cultural alternatives and diversity. In a world that has grown increasingly unstable because of social and technological change, incessant mobility, and moral relativism, Conservative teachers use the school as a stabilizing agency. Their task is to maintain the cultural heritage as a repository of the enduring achievements of the human race by introducing it to the young so that they can absorb it and perpetuate it.

Conservativism's Philosophical and Ideological Relationships

For many Neo-Conservatives, U.S. public schooling has been moving in the wrong direction. They believe that Dewey's Pragmatism, Progressive education, and Critical Theory have caused the schools' miseducative problems. These philosophies and theories have brought about a decline of academic standards, an increase of indiscipline and incivility in both schools and society, an erosion of traditional ethical values, and a decline in U.S. economic productivity. To remedy these perceived defects, Neo-Conservatives have called for restorative educational reforms. *Restorative* means to return to a past greatness that needs to be revivified in the present for the future.

For their educational perspectives, see the chapters on Liberalism and Progressivism.

Many of the reforms of the 1980s stimulated by *A Nation at Risk* were designed to revivify the skills, subjects, and values that Neo-Conservatives believed had made American schools strong academic institutions in the past. Similar to Idealists and Realists, they argued that schools have a primary function: to foster basic skills and competency in traditional academic subjects, namely, mathematics, science, language, and history. To return to fundamental skills and subjects, the curricular residues of Liberalism and Progressivism needed to be removed. For example, they challenge the Liberal concept that the school is a multifunctional community service institution. **Multifunctionalism**, Neo-Conservatives assert, weakens the schools' primary academic role.

Multifunctionalism: the concept that an institution, such as a school, performs many, not just one, function.

Neo-Conservatives, especially those inclined toward Perennialism, see the schools as transmitting a knowledge and value core derived from the Western cultural experience. They see the classical Greco-Roman, Medieval, Renaissance, Reformation, and Enlightenment eras as presenting a needed cultural frame of reference that orients the young to the cultural heritage. Within this framework are the languages, literatures, history, and arts that were developed in Western civilization. Encased within the larger Western heritage is the American experience in which European settlement is highlighted. Also, for many Neo-Conservatives, the issue of the language of instruction in the schools is highly significant. Some would end bilingual and bicultural programs, claiming they erode an English-language-based cultural core.

For their emphasis on Western culture, see the chapter on Perennialism and Education.

Neo-Conservatives, similar to Essentialists, argue that schools are tied to the country's economic growth and productivity. Using studies that compare the academic achievements of U.S. students in mathematics and science with those of students from other countries, Neo-Conservatives claim that U.S. productivity has been declining in the face of foreign competition. Neo-Conservatives have supported reforms in the state legislatures to mandate increased requirements in mathematics and science that they hold as necessary for their application to applied areas such as engineering, technology, industry, medicine, national defense, and so on.

For their emphasis on economic productivity, see the chapter on Essentialism and Education.

The Neo-Conservative agenda in education includes both Perennialist and Essentialist arguments. It appropriates the Perennialist position that schools need to identify and transmit a stable cultural core that links generations in an inherited tradition. From Essentialism, it argues that the efficient and effective teaching of key skills and subjects has a positive impact on economic productivity. Neo-Conservatives decry what they perceive to be declining standards of morality and civility in society and schools. The failure of schools to impart a stable cultural core and universal ethical standards to the young, they contend, has resulted in violence, immorality, and mediocrity, which are all symptomatic of cultural rootlessness. Further, the schools' failure to hold up worthy personal models that young people can emulate further compounds the moral malaise besetting a relativist society. Some Neo-Conservatives, especially those who identify with Christian fundamentalism, look to a revival of traditional religious values to remedy what they see as moral decline. They advocate prayer in the schools, religious observances, and religious education. Other Neo-Conservatives see moral and ethical decline as the result of cultural relativism and situational ethics in education. For them, the remedy is to return to the Western heritage, especially those aspects of it that assert universal, eternal truths and values.

See the chapters on Perennialism and Essentialism.

CONSTRUCTING YOUR OWN PHILOSOPHY OF EDUCATION

Now that you have read the chapter, do you agree or disagree with Conservatism? Do you think that education should transmit the cultural heritage? Should it preserve or change the culture and society? Should there be a required cultural core in the curriculum? Do you plan to include Conservatism, or some aspects of it, in your own philosophy of education?

Conclusion

This chapter examined Conservatism as an ideology. It discussed its origins with Edmund Burke, as a reaction against the French Revolution. It then identified and analyzed Conservatism's key principles, which focus on the preservation, maintenance, and reproduction of the cultural heritage. Contemporary American Neo-Conservatism was examined as an ideology that has influenced the revival of the academic subject-matter curriculum and the standards movement, especially the testing of competency in basic skills and subjects. The chapter also examined Conservatism's implications for education, schools, curriculum, and instruction.

Questions for Reflection and Discussion

1. Do you consider Conservatism to be a relevant ideology in American society, politics, and education?
2. Do you find a pro-Conservative or anti-Conservative orientation in the courses, especially the Education ones, that you have taken or are taking for your degree?
3. Think back on the various courses that you took in American history in high school and college. Were these courses ideologically neutral or were they influenced by a Conservative or Liberal bias?
4. Critics of American Neo-Conservatism contend that it misrepresents American culture in order to use it as a rationale for its policies. Do you agree or disagree? Do you think this charge can be leveled against other ideologies as well?
5. Reflect on the concept of alienation. You have encountered it in the chapter on Existentialism and will encounter it in the next chapter on Marxism. What is alienation? Do you consider yourself alienated? How might a Conservative react to your considerations about alienation?

Topics for Inquiry and Research

1. In class discussion, identify the leading contemporary contributors to Conservative thinking.
2. Read a leading newspaper for a week. Make a reference file of the articles and the frequency with which Conservatism is mentioned.
3. In class discussion, examine the meaning of the term *traditional cultural values.* What are traditional values? What impact do traditional values have on teaching?
4. Debate the immigration issue in contemporary American politics and society. Assign students to argue from a Liberal and Conservative position.
5. Do an analysis of several high school texts in American history on the chapters that deal with recent history from the 1960s to the present. Do you find these texts to have an ideological bias? How do they treat the Neo-Conservative revival?
6. Access "Education Goals" at Advocates for Academic Freedom at http://advocatesforacademicfreedom.org/resolutions.asp. Select a particular goal and describe how it is defined from a Conservative perspective. Do you agree or disagree with the goal?
7. Access Peter R. E. Viereck at http://www.proconservative.net. Compare and constrast American Conservatism with its expression in the United Kingdom, France, and Japan.

Internet Resources

For an identification of Conservative educational goals, access "Education Goals" at Advocates for Academic Freedom at http://advocatesforacademicfreedom.org/resolutions.asp.

For historical and comparative perspectives on Conservatism, access Peter R. E. Viereck at http://www.proconservative.net/.

For the characteristics, history, bibliography, and websites related to Conservatism, access "Conservatism" at Encyclopaedia Britannica at http://www.britannica.com/EBchecked/topic/133435/conservatism.

For modern American Conservatism, access Lee Edwards, "The Origins of the Modern American Conservative Movement" at the Heritage Foundation at http://www.heritage.org.

For a discussion of the ideas of Russell Kirk, a leading American Conservative theorist, access www.townhall.com/.

Suggestions for Further Reading

Abbott, Pamela, and Claire Wallace. *The Family and the New Right.* London and Boulder, CO: Pluto Press, 1992.

Bennett, William J. *The De-Valuing of America: The Fight for Our Culture and Our Children.* New York: Simon & Schuster, 1992.

Buckley, William F. *God and Man at Yale: The Superstitions of "Academic Freedom."* Washington, DC: Gateway/ Regnery Pulishing, 2002.

Cheney, Lynne V. *Telling the Truth: Why Our Culture and Our Country Have Stopped Making Sense—and What We Can Do About It.* New York: Simon & Schuster, 1995.

Frohnen, Bruce. *Virtue and the Promise of Conservatism: The Legacy of Burke and Tocqueville.* Lawrence: University Press of Kansas, 1993.

Garry, Patrick. *Conservatism Redefined: A Creed for the Poor and Disadvantaged.* New York: Encounter Books, 2010.

Goldwater, Barry M. *The Conscience of a Conservative.* Princeton, NJ: Princeton University Press, 2007.

Gottfried, Paul. *The Conservative Movement.* New York: Twayne, 1993.

Kekes, John. *A Case for Conservatism.* Ithaca, NY: Cornell University Press, 2001.

Kirk, Russell. *Academic Freedom.* Chicago: Henry Regnery Co., 1995.

———. *The Conservative Mind: From Burke to Eliot.* New York: BN Publishing, 2008.

Mullen, Jerry Z. *Conservatism: An Anthology of Social and Political Thought From David Hume to the Present.* Princeton, NJ: Princeton University Press, 1997.

Regnery, Alfred S. *Upstream: The Ascendance of American Conservatism.* New York: Simon & Schuster, 2008.

Scruton, Roger. *The Meaning of Conservatism.* New York: Palgrave Macmillan, 2002.

Stanlis, Peter J. *The Best of Burke: Selected Writings and Speeches.* Chicago: Regnery, 1999.

Notes

1. Edmund Burke, *Writings and Speeches,* vol. VII (London: Bickers & Sons, 1865), 93–95.
2. Glenn D. Wilson, ed., *The Psychology of Conservatism* (New York: Academic Press, 1973), 13.
3. Michael Freeden, *Ideology: A Very Short Introduction* (Oxford, UK: Oxford University Press, 2003), 88.
4. Ibid., 50, 88.
5. Harlow Giles Unger, *Noah Webster: The Life and Times of an American Patriot* (New York: Wiley, 1998).
6. Catharine E. Beecher, *An Essay on the Education of Female Teachers* (New York: Van Nostrand & Dwight, 1835), 19.
7. John H. Westerhoff, *McGuffey and His Readers: Piety, Morality, and Education in Nineteenth-Century America* (Nashville, TN: Abingdon, 1978). See also James M. Lower, "William Holmes McGuffey: A Book or a Man? Or More?" *Vitae Scholasticae* (Fall 1984), 311–320.
8. Close Up Foundation Civics Education/U.S. Immigration Policy, www.howstuffworks.on/ immigration8.htm. (1-1-2007).
9. Jonathan Howard, *Darwin* (New York: Oxford University Press, 1982). Also, see Michael Ruse, *The Darwinian Revolution* (Chicago: University of Chicago Press, 1979).
10. Neil C. Gillespie, *Charles Darwin and the Problem of Creation* (Chicago: University of Chicago Press, 1979).
11. The Scopes Trial continues to fascinate Americans. *Inherit the Wind,* a drama about the trial, was a popular play and motion picture.
12. *The Scopes Trial: A Photographic History,* introduction by Edward Caudill (Knoxville: University of Tennessee Press, 2000), 1–20. Also, see Edward J. Larson, *Summer for the Gods: The Scopes Trial and America's Continuing Debate over Science and Religion* (New York: Basic Books, 1997).
13. David Masci, "From Darwin to Dover: An Overview of Important Cases in the Evolution Debate," Pew Forum on Religion & Public Life (September 22, 2005).
14. Ibid.
15. Ibid.
16. Ibid.
17. Freeden, *Ideology: A Very Short Introduction,* 63–64.
18. Ibid., 89.

Marxism and Education

Karl Marx (1818–1883), the nineteenth-century philosopher, who developed Marxism, an ideology that emphasizes economically caused class conflict.

11

CHAPTER PREVIEW

Marxism, an ideology named for its founder, German philosopher Karl Marx (1818–1883), has been and continues to be important in economic, social, political, and educational critique and analysis. We now discuss its basic doctrines and their implications for education, schooling, curriculum, and teaching and learning. Whether or not we reject Marxism as an ideology, we need to recognize the power that Marx gave to economic factors in shaping society, politics, and education. In education, especially the foundations of education, Marxism and Neo-Marxism exert a significant influence on some educational theorists. The designation **Neo-Marxist** refers to new or contemporary Marxists, who have revised Marx's ideology in terms of the modern situation. Marxist themes also can be found in Postmodern philosophy and in Critical Theory.

The chapter is organized into the following major topics:

- Karl Marx as a revolutionary ideologist
- Marxism's basic doctrines: Dialectical and historical materialism
- Marx's analysis of Capitalism
- The proletariat as the revolutionary destined class
- Between philosophy and ideology: Marxism's philosophical and ideological relationships
- Marxism's educational implications
- Schools in a capitalist society

As you read this chapter, reflect on your own educational experiences. Did you encounter Marxism, Neo-Marxism, or anti-Marxism in your courses? Did you have teachers and professors who were Marxists or Neo-Marxists or who used Marxist interpretations in their teaching? See if you will include Marxism, or aspects of it, in your philosophy of education.

KARL MARX: REVOLUTIONARY EDUCATOR

Karl Marx, the son of a prominent lawyer, was born in 1818 in Trier, Germany, into a middle-class family of Jewish ancestry. Home-schooled until age twelve, Marx was heavily influenced by his father, who believed in the Enlightenment project.[1] The young Marx was also influenced by Baron von Westphalen, his future father-in-law, who encouraged him to read the books on history, philosophy, and literature that filled the shelves of his library.

Neo-Marxist: a theorist, who while using Marx's ideology, has reinterpreted aspects of it to apply to the contemporary situation.

For Marxist themes in Postmodernism and Critical Theory, see the chapters on Postmodernism and Critical Theory.

For Hegel's Idealism, see the chapter on Idealism and Education.

For Kierkegaard's rejection of Hegelianism, see the chapter on Existentialism and Education.

Marx's formal schooling began in Trier, where he attended the local *gymnasium*, or academic secondary school. He received a classical humanist education, studying Latin, Greek, French, religion, mathematics, and history.

Intending to become a lawyer like his father, Marx entered the university at Bonn in 1835, where he studied philosophy and literature as well as law. After spending a year at Bonn, he transferred to the more prestigious University of Berlin. There, Marx studied Hegelian Idealism, the philosophy that dominated German intellectual life at the time. Although he would ultimately reject Hegelianism's Idealism, Marx incorporated Hegel's dialectical process into his philosophy of dialectical materialism.

In addition to Hegel, Marx was influenced by Ludwig Feuerbach, author of *Theses on the Hegelian Philosophy.* Like some other nineteenth-century European intellectuals such as Soren Kierkegaard, Feuerbach was reacting against Hegelian Idealism. Rejecting the Hegelian concept that historical events were caused by the unfolding of a spiritual force, the Absolute Idea, Feuerbach asserted that human history was a product of material conditions, the economic factors that existed at a particular time. Nonmaterial elements such as art, literature, and other cultural forms were not independent entities but reflected the underlying economic reality. Impressed by Feuerbach's arguments, Marx later united the concept of materialism to the Hegelian dialectical process in his synthesis of dialectical materialism.

Marx later studied at the University of Jena, where he completed his doctorate in philosophy in 1841. Unable to find a position in higher education, he accepted a job as editor of a liberal Rhineland newspaper, the *Rheinische Zeitung*. Marx's evolving ideology was influenced by Moses Hess, the publisher of the *Rheinische Zeitung*, who combined traditional Judaism and humanitarianism with Hegelian Idealism. From Hess, Marx came to view private property as the source of all human ills. As a humanitarian, Hess wanted to organize an international society based on a collective economy. As a result of his association with Hess, Marx came to emphasize economic influences in shaping historical and social forces. He also stressed the need for an international revolutionary organization.

As editor of the *Rheinische Zeitung*, Marx attacked the Prussian government's conservative policies. In 1843, the government suppressed the journal's publication. Unemployed, Marx, who had married Jenny von Westphalen in 1843, emigrated to France. He went to Paris with his young wife to write for the German-language periodical, *Deutsch-Französische Jahrbücher*. He had already formulated some basic ideas that would be expressed in his synthesis of scientific socialism, such as the premise of a material universe, dialectical processes of social change, and the coming class struggle.

Utopian Socialist: a socialist who believed that a cooperative society could be created without violence or revolution; a position Marx condemned.

As an exile in France from 1843 to 1845, Marx completed his ideological transformation and became a convinced socialist. During his French exile, Marx encountered Saint-Simon and other **Utopian Socialist** theorists. He agreed with Saint-Simon that economic relationships determined the course of history, which was largely the record of the conflict of competing economic classes. Saint-Simon's belief that the government should be in the hands of a small group of expert scientists and technicians contributed to Marx's emphasis that the coming revolution should be led by an elite vanguard of the proletariat. However, he rejected what he regarded as the naive views of Fourier, Owen, and other Utopians that social and political change could be attained without revolutionary violence.

While in Paris, Marx became a lifelong collaborator with the wealthy German radical Friedrich Engels. Devoting himself to theory and writing, Marx and his family lived in near poverty. Engels provided the funds that enabled Marx to concentrate on his writing.

In 1847 and 1848, Marx was still in exile from his native Germany, living in Brussels, Belgium. He developed his basic ideological themes, especially on economic determinism and historical inevitability during that time. Marx believed that economic forces, the means and modes of production, were at the base of society. Historical processes and events were caused by history's inevitable and inexorable course. These economically directed historical forces would lead to the inevitable triumph of the proletariat, the working class.

Marx's theorizing was broken by the momentous revolutions that swept Europe in 1848. This revolutionary situation stimulated Marx and Engels to write their famous *Communist Manifesto*, which begins: "A specter is haunting Europe—the specter of Communism," and concludes:

> The Communists disdain to conceal their views and aims. They openly declare that their ends can be attained only by the forcible overthrow of all existing social conditions. Let the ruling classes tremble at a Communist revolution. The proletarians have nothing to lose but their chains. They have a world to win. Workingmen of all countries, unite![2]

When the uprisings of 1848 failed to overthrow the reactionary Prussian government, Marx spent the rest of his life in London, researching and writing his monumental work, *Das Kapital*, an extensive analysis of economics.

MARXISM'S BASIC DOCTRINES

This section examines Marx's basic ideological doctrines. Among them are **dialectical materialism** and his theory of economically determined history. Particularly significant are the concepts of economic determinism and class conflict.

Dialectical Materialism: Marx's concept of reality in which the essential dynamic in the universe is matter in motion.

Dialectical Materialism

Marx sees the basic force in the universe as matter in motion. Philosophically, he took the concept of matter, found in materialism and realism, and combined it with the Hegelian Idealist idea of dialectical change. Marx enlarged the meaning of materialism from the physical, concrete objects found in nature to include observable human activity, especially human beings' practical interactions, their work within their environment.[3]

THE HUMAN BEING. Marx defined human beings as natural, social, economic, and historical individuals. They differ from animals in that they use the material conditions in their environment to produce their own economic means of subsistence. The **human being** is a material physical creature with physiological needs and drives, who possesses a brain that enables thought, a voice that enables speech, and limbs, arms, and hands that enable work. Living in a material world, humans work to produce goods or commodities that they need to survive. How and what they produce determine how they organize themselves politically, socially, and economically and how they use education.[4]

Human Being: in Marxism, a physical creature with physiological needs and drives, who possesses a brain that enables consciousness and is a producer of commodities and services.

Society

Marx challenges the traditional Idealist and Realist view of society in which human beings are what they are because they share a common essence, human nature, and in which human societies arise as organizations of individuals who share in this essential common humanity. Marx challenges the Liberal view of society, which is more

See the chapters on Idealism, Realism, and Liberalism.

closely associated with capitalism, that a society is atomistic and composed of discrete individuals, social atoms, who join associations for self-protection, either in the literal Darwinism sense of self-preservation or to defend their inalienable rights as asserted by John Locke.

Society: for Marx, a developing, expanding, and changing network of economically generated and economically determined human relationships.

Marx sees **society** as a developing, expanding, and changing network of human relationships that are the results of the economic means and modes of production but that, in turn, have economic consequences. The means and modes of production connect the biological, sociological, cultural, political, and educational aspects of group life with its economic foundation.[5] Group life and social cooperation have a material or economic base that rests on the production of commodities. Social events are caused by the need to keep expanding and further developing the means of production—the industry, machinery, and technology that make it possible to produce products.

A Marxist analysis of the social, philosophical, and cultural foundations of education focuses first on the material or economic conditions in a society.[6] If the analyst begins with the social composition of students attending a particular school, for example, she or he is soon led to the students' socio-economic class. If the issue is the difference in resources among schools in inner cities and suburbs, the difference will have an economic cause such as disparities in revenues generated for education. If the issue is differences among groups in high school completion or college attendance rates, their cause will be based on socio-economic class status.

The Dialectic

Marx, who had studied Hegelian Idealism as a university student, continued to rely on Hegel's principle of the dialectic. When he abandoned Idealism, Marx retained the idea of the dialectic but transferred it from the realm of ideas, where Hegel had located it, to material reality—to the means and modes of production. For Hegel, all ideas came forth from the mind of the Absolute Idea, the universal idea that contained all other subordinate ideas. History, for Hegel, was the unfolding of these ideas on earth over time, and historical change was the result of the resolution, the creation of new syntheses, in this realm of ideas. Every idea stated a thesis that, while it embodied a partial truth, also held its contradiction. From the conflict of thesis and antithesis emerged a newer and higher idea, a synthesis, a new and more integrated composite or compound idea that, as a new thesis, generated a new conflict and continued the dialectical process. Borrowing Hegel's dialectical process, Marx transferred it to his own strictly material or physical version of reality. Instead of a conflict of ideas, Marx saw human history as a ceaseless struggle between conflicting economic classes for control of the economic base of society. History is a process of conflict and resolution between opposing economic classes for power and control in society.

Dialectical Epistemology: for Marx, dialectical thinking that immerses individuals in an ongoing process of class conflict.

Dialectical Thought: for Marx, an idea (a thesis) generates its contradiction that eventually will be reconciled into a synthesis, a new thesis.

DIALECTICAL EPISTEMOLOGY. Marx's dialectical way of thinking, or **dialectical epistemology**, portrays the human situation as immersion in a process of continuing class conflict and struggle. In **dialectical thought**, there are always two opposing sides and two conflicting sets of arguments. These opposites are contradictory stages that eventually will be reconciled in a synthesis, a new thesis. Neo-Marxists continue to use dialectical reasoning to analyze social, political, and educational issues in terms of contradictions or conflicts. Although less certain that history is determined than are orthodox Marxists, Neo-Marxists still consider the dialectic to be useful in social and educational analysis.

The dialectical process functions in history by eliminating some aspects in the older and prior economic stage but also transmitting and transforming some parts of it in the new stage. This historic change is based on economic developments that involve the movement of productive processes from the older to the newer stage. Operating in history, the dialectic moves inevitably and relentlessly forward. The economically dominant class is caught up in the process in that it seeks to increase the output of production. However, in doing so, it is bringing about consequences that it does not understand.

Marx's Philosophy of History: Historical Materialism

Marx constructed a detailed interpretation of history called **historical materialism**. Marx's narrative of past events is primarily a historical interpretation of economically generated social, political, and educational change. Building his theory on the scaffolding of dialectical materialism, Marx saw history's forward course as determined, inevitable, and inexorable. According to his ideological predestination, past, present, and future are the results of the dialectical process as contending socio-economic classes struggle to control and possess the means and modes of production. Following its predetermined course, the dialectical process relentlessly creates new syntheses from the clash of thesis and antithesis. Marx argued that historically identifiable stages such as slavery in the ancient world and feudalism in the medieval period along with the emergence of capitalism made the future predictable. Today, he would probably say globalization is a stage in worldwide capitalism as dominant economic classes seek to maintain their supremacy in global production, marketing, and consumption.

Historical Materialism: Marx's philosophy of history in which history follows a dialectical materialism path to a determined end.

History originated when human beings began to produce the goods, the commodities, the food, clothing, and other products needed to sustain life. The first major historical event, in the broad sense, was the human construction of material life—what needs to be done and how life needs to be organized to satisfy basic survival needs. Each satisfaction of needs generated additional needs in an ongoing continuum of production of goods. Throughout much of history, social control—the domination of one class over another—was based on the material condition of land, especially land suited for agriculture. People were agricultural, tilling the soil, planting and harvesting crops, and raising livestock during the ancient Greek and Roman and the European medieval periods. A strong group of warriors, the medieval knights, created the European feudal system, in which they owned the land and forced others, the serfs, to work it for them. In addition to their brute physical force, which directly oppressed the agricultural workers, the knightly landlords used the church as an agency of social control to convince the oppressed that life on earth was fated to be this way and life in heaven would be better. The social and religious patterns of medieval culture created a **false consciousness** in the serfs that deluded many of them from understanding their true condition and the sources of their oppression.

False Consciousness: an erroneous set of beliefs and values into which subordinate classes are indoctrinated by the dominant class.

Agricultural production eventually created a surplus of wealth. This surplus led to the formation of a new class, the bourgeoisie, or the middle class, which left agriculture and took up other economic pursuits such as trade, banking, and the professions. In the Industrial Revolution of the early nineteenth century, machines were invented that produced goods on a mass scale. Some of the middle class invested their capital in the new industries to create the factory system of mass production and the economy of mass consumption.

For Marx, modern industrial society is composed of two classes: the **capitalists**, who own the factories—the means and modes of production—and the **proletariat**, the workers who produce goods but who do not own the machines on which they work. For Marx, economic class is our primary identification. Our social relationships are based on our economic situation and condition. The economic class that controls the economy, the means and modes of production, also controls society's institutional **superstructure**.

Capitalists: in a modern society, members of the dominant economic class who own the means and modes of production.

Proletariat: the industrial working class that is historically determined to revolt and seize power from the capitalists.

Superstructure: institutions, resting on the economic base of society, such as the state, church, schools, courts, and so on, that are controlled by the dominant class.

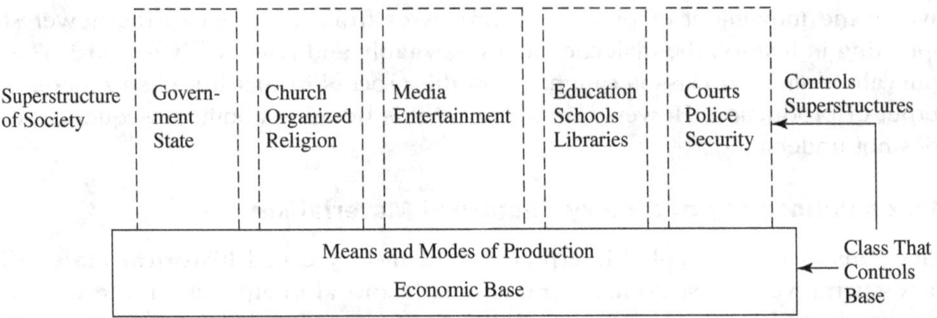

Marxist Means and Modes of Production: Economic Base

Among the institutions in the superstructure are the state (the government), the church (organized religion), the courts (the legal system), the police and military (the arms of state power), the media (agencies of information), and the school (the agency of organized education). The exploiting class also constructs a highly usable false ideology, designed to mislead and miseducate the workers so they are not conscious of their true situation as exploited victims.

At this point, we can comment on how Marx's dialectical interpretation of history relates to education and to schools. Schools are part of the superstructure. Their role and functions are determined economically. The socio-economic class that controls the means and modes of production will also control the schools—determining their philosophy, purposes and goals, curriculum, and instruction. Schools will be used as agencies to ensure that the dominant class maintains its position and the subordinant class stays in its position. The curriculum will be used to transmit officially approved "knowledge" and values mandated as standards and requirements by the power holders.

We now turn to Marx's analysis of capitalism, the historical stage when he constructed his ideology in the mid- and late nineteenth century. It is Marx's analysis of capitalism that engages most of his interpreters today. Then we return to Marx's prediction of the inevitable proletarian revolution and the creation of a classless society.

MARX'S ANALYSIS OF CAPITALISM

Capitalism: an economic theory and system in which property, especially in manufacturing, distributing, and selling products, is privately owned by individuals, companies, and corporations.

See the chapters on Liberalism and Conservatism for the Classical Liberal rationale for capitalism.

Marx wrote an extensive analysis of capitalism, an economic system he believed was doomed to fail because of its own internal contradictions. **Capitalism** is a market-driven economic system of private ownership and production. Marx's detailed critical analysis identified capitalism's key elements as commodities and production, private ownership of property, money, capital, labor, surplus value, accumulation, and crisis. He saw capitalism as an expansive force, much like globalization today, that, in seeking new markets and larger profits, would move beyond its place of origin in western Europe and North America to universalize itself and to spread across the earth.

For Marx, society is organized into classes that, in turn, are based on what they own or do not own. Capitalism's origins began with the rise of the bourgeoisie, the middle class, in the nineteenth century and with that class's emphasis on the right of individuals to own private property. The middle classes, as Marx understood them in the nineteenth century, were composed of the business, commercial, and professional classes, who stood in the middle of the old social order between the aristocracy and the peasantry. For the middle classes, their right to hold their own property was, as John Locke stated, an inalienable natural right. In the late nineteenth and early twentieth centuries, the Industrial Revolution had generated new forms of property and ownership that had changed the economy and society. Industrialism, especially the factory system of production, had generated a new class—the proletariat, the industrial workers. According to Marx's conflict theory, modern history had reached the stage where the middle-class industrial capitalists, the thesis in the historical dialectic, were locked in conflict with the proletariat, their antithetical adversaries.

Producing Commodities

Under capitalism, as well as the earlier agricultural modes of production, a **commodity** is something material produced by human labor to satisfy human needs. In a capitalist economy, commodities are produced by workers who are paid wages for their labor. Every commodity has both a "use" and an "exchange" value. How something is used satisfies a human need so that a customer wants to buy it. Exchange value determines the value of a particular commodity, such as a computer or an iPad, in relation to other commodities.[7] Commodity production (e.g., manufacturing automobiles) is geared to exchange value. Work or the labor needed to produce a commodity is analyzed as "concrete labor" and "abstract labor." **Concrete labor** refers to the skills needed to produce a particular commodity. **Abstract labor** refers to the general expenditure of human labor in producing commodities.

Commodity: a product made by human labor to satisfy human needs.

Concrete Labor: the expenditure of specific labors needed to produce a particular commodity.

Abstract Labor: the general expenditure of human labor needed to produce commodities.

Concrete labor can be measured as the wage that an employer pays to his workers; also the products made can be sold, again for money. Concrete labor is the source of abstract labor. The socially average time needed to produce a commodity becomes Marx's labor theory of value.[8] When exchange value is greater than the other factors of production, surplus value is created, which is expropriated by capitalists as profits.

ILLUSION IN MARKETING COMMODITIES. In the capitalist economy, marketing and advertising are used to stimulate consumers' desire to purchase commodities. Illusions are used to sell commodities by appealing to the sensual or the emotional rather than to real needs. In capitalism, these marketing illusions are beauty, empowerment, and sexual attraction. For example, think about the marketing of shampoo to young women. Television commercials tell them that buying and using a particular shampoo will improve their appearance and make their hair lustrous. This, in turn, will attract the glances and attention of males and lead to relationships between a beautiful young woman and a handsome young man. Or, for young men, owning a luxury car will make them the envy of their male rivals and attractive to beautiful women.

Maintaining and Extending the System

The capitalist strategy for power and profit has both conservative and innovative dimensions. The two-pronged strategy requires that the capitalists (1) maintain, defend, and reproduce the social, political, and educational institutions that ensure their domination and (2) develop new productive technologies to increase their profits, extend their property holdings, and enlarge their power. In this capitalist strategy, education functions to reproduce the dominant class by educating its children in well-funded, high-quality, academic schools. In schools, managed and controlled by the dominant class, working-class children are indoctrinated in the officially approved and mandated "knowledge" and values. The indoctrination of working-class children creates what Marx calls a "false consciousness" that dulls their sense of oppression. Informal education through media advertising, "infomercials," and video and Internet games adds to this false consciousness.

MAINTAINING, DEFENDING, AND REPRODUCING THE CAPITALIST SOCIAL ORDER. Marx calls the social, political, and educational agencies that arise from the economic base in capitalism the **superstructure of society**. It can be compared to the upper stories of a building that are most evident to a person's view. However, the crucial element in holding the upper stories in place securely is the foundation on which it rests. For Marx, the necessary foundations of society are the economic means and modes of production. He reasoned that whoever controlled the means and modes of production also controlled and determined the structure, purposes, and functions of the institutions and agencies in the superstructure. In a capitalist society, the capitalists own the means and modes of production as their private property. They constructed the superstructure to cover and protect the economic foundation that gives them their power. Social agencies and institutions are not independent, free-standing entities; their existence depends on the economic foundation or base on which they are erected. The class that controls the material conditions, the economy, will also control the superstructure.

Superstructure of Society: institutions that arise from and are dependent on the economic base of society.

The modern nation-state (the government and its agencies) is the principal agency in the social superstructure. The federal government in the United States has a president and legislative branch, the Congress. It has security agencies (military and police forces); a court or legal system; and the prison system. Although the government may appear to be democratic and elected, in reality, according to Marx, the major political parties differ primarily in name and stand for the same thing—enacting and enforcing the laws that protect and benefit the dominant class. The security agencies enforce and arrest those who threaten the continuation of the system. The courts try them and the prisons incarcerate them.

Further, state (government-controlled) school systems indoctrinate young working-class children to accept the status quo by transmitting a false ideology to them. Neo-Marxist educators would extend Marx's concept of the working class to include marginalized people such as members of racial and ethnic minority groups, gays and lesbians, and the poor and homeless. In both informal education via the media, and schooling, the role played by false ideology is crucial in defending a capitalist society. Although the dominant classes will proclaim their ideology to be true, Marxists label it false. A **false ideology** is one that purports that the institutions and agencies in the superstructure are freestanding and independent of those who control the economic base. The church, an agency in the superstructure, gives supernatural sanction to the status quo that protects capitalism; it promises eternal happiness in the afterlife to those who accept their situation in this life on earth. For example, religion, dealing with the human relationship to God, seeks to create a separate realm of thought, theology, to explain this relationship. The religious emphasis on a supernatural heaven and an afterlife, Marx felt, was the "opiate of the masses" that deluded them from understanding their true economic condition.

False Ideology: an unexamined acceptance of the beliefs of the dominant class that purport to be the truth.

Another example of false ideology can be found in education, especially among Liberals, who claim that they can be objective and can take a "disinterested" or neutral position on specific controversial social and political issues. For Marx, the Liberal assertion to objectivity is another example of falsity. For the Marxist, there is no neutral position in which to hide. You are either on the side of the oppressors or on the side of the oppressed.

For an example of disinterested objectivity, see the section on John Stuart Mill in the chapter on Liberalism and Education.

Contemporary Neo-Marxist educators continue to focus attention on who controls the superstructure. They point out that schools are controlled by the capitalists and often serve the interests of the international business corporation and the large banks, especially in the global economy. For them, it is necessary to examine the actual economic conditions in which an institution functions. If you want to cut through the sentimental fog of false consciousness that proclaims that public schools are agencies of equality of opportunity, you have to examine how local schools function in their communities. You have to study the material conditions of schools in the inner cities and analyze the impact that poverty, homelessness, unemployment, gang violence, and drugs have on education. This kind of analysis cuts through the fog of false ideology and replaces it with true ideological consciousness.

The superstructure also consists of informal educational agencies—the media, newspapers, television, the Internet—that mold what is called "public opinion" and formal educational agencies such as schools, colleges, and universities. These agencies play the role of "informing and educating the public," which Marx would say is deluding the public by generating disinformation and diffusing miseducation. Media programs include an incessant marketing and advertising of the commodities, the products produced by the system, that enlarge capitalist profits. The news of the day is reduced to sensational stories about prominent entertainers rather than important national and international issues. It is selected and programmed as quick, colorful, and superficial items that generate false consciousness by blurring the distinctions between entertainment and information.

Schools, colleges, and universities in a capitalist society play the role of creating a mind-set, a mentality that is favorable to and exalts the inventions, discoveries, and innovations of capitalism as human progress. At the same time, the schools are structured and organized to reproduce the class structure. Although a public school system has been extablished in the United States, there are, within it, schools attended predominantly by children of economically affluent classes and those attended by the disadvantaged. There are schools whose enrollments consists largely of students from the same class and race. The end result reproduces the existing class structure.

To illustrate the Marxist analysis of the superstructure, we can examine the teacher education program approval process. In the United States, each state approves teacher education programs and certifies teachers. The states, institutions in the superstructure, have established boards or divisions of education to approve programs to prepare teachers. The approved programs designate officially mandated requirements (courses and experiences) in a teacher education program. Colleges and universities, part of the superstructure, offer teacher education programs. Teachers with certification from approved programs can be employed to teach in that state's public schools—still another link in the superstructure's institutional chain. A Marxist analysis of the teacher approval process would penetrate the superstructure to reach the source of real power: the means and modes of production at the economic base. The holders of economic power establish the standards and set the requirements that control entry into teaching. These standards are designed to reproduce the status quo, which enables the economically dominant class to maintain their favored position.

DEVELOPING NEW PRODUCTIVE TECHNOLOGIES. Despite its emphasis on maintaining and reproducing the capitalist economy and society, capitalism is not static; rather, it is dynamic in that technological innovation is used to increase production and maximize profits that sustain and expand the system and continue to empower the dominant class. But the need for ever-increasing profits generates more production innovations. These technological developments, however, do not stay lodged in the economic realm but infect and reshape social, political, and educational relationships. Marx and the Marxists do not oppose technological innovation and development; they oppose the expropriation of technology for the profits of one group and the exploitation and alienation of another.

Examples of a technological innovation that generates still more technological innovation include the computer, the Internet, the World Wide Web, e-mail, and the iPhone. As soon as a new computer program is developed, it becomes technologically obsolete and is rapidly replaced by another, which is sold through intensive marketing. The computer and electronic data information are used by national and international airlines, banks, business firms, and other enterprises worldwide. The Web and Internet become tools to sell products and disseminate information, often disinformation. Electronic surveillance becomes an instrument of police and security forces. Computer and electronic data messaging and retrieval enhance capitalist economic dominance; they also produce social, political, and educational changes that impact societal relations, both nationally and globally. They give groups opposed to capitalism, especially globalization, a means of networking and organizing. Social media provide people with a means of communication outside of the capitalist-controlled media. For example, protesters in Tunisia, Egypt, and Libya used social media and networking to communicate with each other to bring down the authoritarian regimes in those countries in the Arab Spring of 2011. Occupy Wall Street demonstrators used social media in the United States in 2012 as they protested against the large financial firms and banks. In schools, computer-assisted instruction, like most technologies, by itself is pedagogically neutral. It may enhance instruction, be used to indoctrinate, or provide an opening for students beyond the control of school officials.

Colonialism, Imperialism, and Globalization

When Marx constructed his ideology in the nineteenth century, the major European nations—Great Britain, France, and Germany—and even the smaller ones—the Netherlands and Belgium—were in a race to build far-flung worldwide empires. They established colonies in Africa and Asia. The United States, too, claimed overseas colonies in Hawaii and the Philippines. They were locked in a race for colonies that led to the armament buildup that was one cause of World War I. Marx viewed imperialism and colonialism as consequences of the capitalist race for new markets and profits. The capitalist nations would seize and occupy other nations, and turn them into colonies that would supply raw materials—minerals, foodstuffs, rubber, fibers, and oil—that would be used to produce commodities in the capitalist nation, which were then exported back for sale in the colony and on the world market. Marx predicted that the capitalist nations would clash and destroy themselves in a struggle of their own making. Marxists saw the Bolshevik, or Communist, Revolution in Russia in 1917 as the beginning of a worldwide proletariat revolution. The international revolution did not occur. After World War II, nationalist movements achieved independence in the former colonies in Asia and Africa.

GLOBALIZATION. Contemporary Marxists see the globalization and global economy of the twenty-first century as a new form of imperialism and colonialism. For them, globalization is a worldwide economic process that is reducing the earth to a global factory. Multinational business and financial corporations, rather than nation-states, are the chief agents of globalization. Raw materials are extracted from some countries, processed in others, and used to produce commodities in still others. The owners and managers of the corporations locate their factories in countries where the workforce in underpaid, where benefits are low and working conditions poor or unregulated, and where environmental protections are not enforced. Workers in countries such as the United States and in western Europe where wages and benefits are higher often are displaced and lose their jobs. The advocates of globalization claim that its economic benefits will eventually trickle down to all people; Marxists and other opponents see globalization in its capitalist form, as another more advanced and technologically driven force for profits. However, the multinational corporations, like the imperialists before them, obsessed by profits, fail to understand that they are actually creating new productive relationships that will lead to their destined and inevitable demise.

Alienation

For Marx, human alienation is economically caused by the capitalists' insatiable greed for more profits made at the expense of workers. Remember, however, that capitalist avarice is caused not only by personal greed but also by the fact that the capitalists are being pushed by impersonal economic forces that will lead to their inevitable destruction. **Alienation** means that the worker's time and the products of her or his labor are owned and sold for a profit that the worker does not enjoy. At the root of this estrangement is the capitalist fiscal system, private property, exchange, and competition that separates the workers, the producers, from the products they make. The worker is trapped in an inevitable repetitive economic cycle.

Alienation: in a capitalist economy, the separation of workers from the product they are making; the expropriation of the workers' labor, time, and product by the capitalist employer.

The factory system of the nineteenth century, when Marx penned his ideology, marked the origin of mass production. The aesthetic sense of craftsmanship, enjoyed by the artisans of earlier times, was now a relic of the past. The repetitive work of the assembly line, in which the worker performed the same task over and over, had destroyed it. The wholeness of creating an object of which the craftsman felt ownership had been torn apart by the assembly line's repetition, minuteness, and staccato. The harder the laborers worked and the more commodities they produced, the poorer they became. Ground down by the wheels of production, the worker was reduced to a commodity to be bought and sold. As the capitalist exploited his labor, the worker became separated, disenchanted, or alienated from his work. Marx's argument struck home for all those who felt exploited, unappreciated, and alienated in their jobs.

THE FUTILITY OF TRYING TO BE PART OF THE SYSTEM. In capitalist economies, the capitalists use a variety of strategies to defuse workers' alienation by trying to delude them into believing that they are part of the system. Parliamentary government, democratic elections, and representative institutions, including educational ones, in a capitalist society and economy are a chimera, a false siren or image that distracts workers from their true interests and the revolutionary measures needed to end them. The primary purpose of government, the state, in a capitalist society is to secure the existing economy and the ownership of private property. The rationales for private ownership in the capitalist system find their way into the school curriculum in courses in civics, government, social studies, and consumer education. All politics, all government, like all society, originates in the material conditions of life. Educational institutions, like governmental ones, too, originate in the economic base of society. Whoever controls the economic base—the means and modes of production—controls institutional life. Schooling in a capitalist society provides a sedative that lulls the workers and their children into believing that political change can end economic alienation through piecemeal palliatives; for example, student loans, with support of the federal government, can provide workers' children with access to higher education, leading to better-paying jobs and higher social status. This palliative mechanism really will not change anything, but will perpetuate the system that requires student loans, and will, in fact, make the students indebted to the system.

Alienation and Resistance in Schools

Marx's analysis of alienation can be applied to schools, teaching, and learning. When the results of schooling are defined as products or commodities to be attained by students, such as learning saleable skills or academic subjects that contribute to economic production and consumption, then the educational process is commoditized.

A more direct feature of commoditization occurs when skills and subjects are defined as necessary to the economy and measured by standards imposed by others who are external to the educational process. Like the factory system, the teachers and students, although responsible for meeting quantity standards, have not determined these standards. They do not have ownership in the educational product they are expected to produce. They are alienated not only from the product but also from the process—from schooling and instruction. The process, like the product, is imposed on them much like the routines of the assembly line are imposed on workers. The goals and ends of instruction have been determined outside of the classroom and imposed on those within it. Schooling takes on more features of the industrial factory system in that what is supposed to be the educational process—teaching and learning—is monitored or supervised by a set of managers, school bureaucrats, who make certain that approved processes are being followed by teachers and students. This kind of alienation has several consequences for teachers and students. First, they accept the system and enter into it by competing with other schools, teachers, and students for higher test scores. In other words, they work to exceed the anticipated outcome much like factory workers seek to exceed production quotas. In their acceptance, however, they have shifted learning from something internal to something that is external. Second, they become more and more passive, trying to meet set production goals, without enthusiasm or interest. The educational process sinks into deadening routine. Third, they begin to understand what is happening to them and grow in consciousness of their true situation and find ways to resist it. They engage in activities that are not mandated or standardized. Teachers, in particular, may organize themselves in unions to resist commoditization of education. In this stage, the Marxist educator plays a significant role in exposing false consciousness, arousing true consciousness, and organizing for resistance and change.

THE PROLETARIAT AS THE REVOLUTIONARY DESTINED CLASS

At this point, we examine the proletariat, the working class, which Marx predicted was destined to revolt against and overthrow capitalism. Without property and without true representation, the proletariat is a universally suffering class, exploited and victimized. The proletariat is the destined revolutionary class that because of its exploitation and repression, will organize, arise, revolt, and overthrow its capitalist exploiters.

Capitalism, with its insatiable appetite for profits, is destined to sow the seeds of its own destruction. Its demands for more markets and more consumer goods will lead to spirals of overproduction, which, in turn, lead to recurring economic crises of inflation, recession, and depression. Capitalists will be forced to reinvest profits to increase production without being able to guarantee the consumption of commodities produced. As the ranks of unemployed grow because of "economic restructuring," more people will need goods and services but will be unable to purchase them. Wars will result as capitalist nations seek to control raw materials such as oil. Unemployment, once periodic, will become chronic, and conditions will grow ripe for revolution.

Institutionalizing the Revolution

After the revolution, all instruments of production will be centralized in the proletarian state created by the victorious workers. The dictatorship of the proletariat will be established to bring about the transformative changes needed in a classless society. The state apparatus will be taken over and redirected to ensure the working-class consolidation of power and control. After the remnants of the old capitalist regime have been obliterated, a classless society will appear, in utopian fashion, in which there is no repression. The means and modes of production underlying the industrial-technological base of capitalism would then be possessed by the people as a whole rather than just the capitalist class. With the elimination of the private ownership of property, the new society of the future would be without classes and without alienation. Importantly, because the new communist society is without classes, class conflict will end. The old history of class warfare will end and a new history will begin.[9]

Contemporary Neo-Marxists are likely to reject or seriously revise Marx's original premise of historical inevitability. They may still think in dialectical terms that involve the clash of opposing classes and see society as an arena of competing class interests, yet they are unlikely to accept the premise that a working class triumph is inevitable. The struggle will be long, with many temporary setbacks along the way.

Marx saw history moving in a predetermined and inexorable way toward the establishment of the communist society. This future was inevitable and, once realized, irreversible. Whereas orthodox Marxists hold to this view of predestined change that leads to an end, neo-Marxists and those whose ideas are influenced by Marxism such as Postmodernists and Critical Theorists downplay or dismiss Marx's historical inevitability. Conservatives and Liberals can agree that the perfect society promised by Marx is dangerously utopian and provided a cause, a justification, for ideologically driven zealots to take any action, any means, they think will lead to the promised perfect society. The leaders of the Soviet Union, especially Lenin and Stalin, justified their massive repressions, gulags, concentration camps, and purging and execution of perceived opponents to be necessary steps, justified by the utopia at the end. Pragmatists, especially Dewey, regarded Marx's claim that he had constructed a "scientific socialism" as a very unscientific method that closed rather than opened the process of scientific inquiry because it had a predestined end or goal.

For their views of historical change and inevitability, see the chapters on Postmodernism, Critical Theory, Pragmatism, Liberalism, and Conservatism.

BETWEEN PHILOSOPHY AND IDEOLOGY: MARXISM'S PHILOSOPHICAL AND IDEOLOGICAL RELATIONSHIPS

Marx was a philosopher who constructed an ideology, and Marxism lies between being a philosophy and an ideology. In its generalizations, it appears, like other philosophies, to offer universal explanations. However, its origins, lodged in a critique of western European nineteenth-century capitalism, are contextual. Marx sought to analyze capitalism as a universal global force and his alternative, Marxism, leading to the inevitable classless society, too, was described in universal terms.

For Marx, speculative philosophies such as Idealism and Thomism, like religion, led to false consciousness. Realism, especially its scientific variety, could be used to gain an accurate picture of reality when incorporated with Marxist dialectical materialism. Ideologies such as Liberalism and Conservatism were also part of the defensive armor of dominant groups to control subordinant ones. Certain aspects of Utopian Socialism, Marx believed, provided a useful analysis but a muddle-headed strategy for social change. Thus, Marx saw part of his task as consigning the philosophies and ideologies that contributed to false consciousness to the trash heap of history.

Like the Reconstructionists, Marx redefined philosophy and its purpose. Philosophers such as Plato, Aristotle, and even Hegel had attempted to speculate about the nature of reality and to describe it in metaphysical terms. Because their description is metaphysical, the reality of their speculations cannot be tested empirically. The universality found in the traditional philosophies came from an *a priori* definition of the human being as endowed with a defining human nature that was part of a universal architecture. For example, the Idealist would argue that the Universal Mind, or God, is a spiritual idea and that the individual's identity as a human being

For their views on universality, see the chapters on Idealism, Realism, and Social Reconstruction.

comes from sharing in this spirituality or intellectuality. The Aristotelian Realist would argue that in a purposeful and rationally organized universe, human beings are what they are because they are reasonable. Marx challenged this traditional view of universality and sought to replace it with another kind of universality, labor as its source. Human beings are universal, not because of their nature, but by their activity as producers. Human beings everywhere are producers; therefore, it is possible to look to a universal interpretation of history to see how production changed and socio-economic classes developed.[10]

Marx retained the idea that the philosopher's task is to interpret reality. But the reality he described and interpreted was material, not metaphysical; it was the means and modes of economic production. However, Marx gave the philosopher a new and added role—to change reality by acting on it. Unlike the Pragmatist who saw action as the person's interaction with a changing environment, the Marxist view of change and action meant that the individual was able to identify and join with the movement of history.

Marx's evolutionary use of philosophy as "practical-critical activity" is directed to a goal—to changing society.[11] It is philosophy with an agenda, to make a revolution, which more traditional philosophers would say moves philosophy to ideology.

Marxism and Communist States and Parties

Communism, Marxism's political face, draws it even closer to ideology. *The Communist Manifesto* in 1848 moved Marx's theory from dialectical materialism drawn from philosophy and history toward revolutionary political organization and action. During Marx's life, Communist political parties had been organized but nowhere was Communism implemented as a political and economic system.

In the twentieth century, Marxism was implemented as the official state ideology in the Soviet Union, the Soviet satellite nations in eastern and central Europe, the People's Republic of China, Vietnam, Cuba, and North Korea. Although Marxism was supposed to transcend and move through varying national and social contexts, it became contextualized in the nations and societies where it was implemented. In these countries, Marxism was codified into the reigning political and educational system and reinforced by monolithic repressive police states. From 1917 to 1989, Marxist-Leninism, or Communism, was redefined by Nikolai Lenin and Josef Stalin as the official ideology of the Soviet Union and the Soviet-controlled nations of eastern Europe. With the collapse of the Soviet system, Marxist-Leninism lost its official status and fell into disrepute in the former Soviet Union and in eastern and central Europe. The People's Republic of China (PRC) was established as a Communist nation in 1949. Chairman Mao Tse-tung, reinterpreting Communism as a peasant-based revolutionary movement, conducted the failed "great leap forward" and the cultural and educational purges of the Cultural Revolution. Although Communism formally remains as the PRC's official ideology, state and private capitalism is practiced as the country experiences unprecedented economic growth. In Cuba, Fidel Castro revised Marxism into an ideology that mixed Communism with the Latin American style of the personalist "great leader" dictatorship. Castro's Cuba remains a nation in which Marxism is the official state ideology.[12] In North Korea, Communism, merged with the idolization of the country's leader, stands as a repressive and isolated political and educational system.

Marxism's critics contend that it has led to dictatorship and authoritarian repression wherever it has been implemented and see it as a failed and discredited ideology. Marxism's defenders say that it was never really implemented as Marx had designed it and that the Soviet version of Communism was really authoritarian statism rather than true Communism.

My Reflections on Philosophy of Education: Visiting Communist Czechoslovakia

In 1974, I was teaching at the Loyola University Rome Center. Being in Europe, I decided that it was time to visit Czechoslovakia. I am of Slovak ethnicity and wanted to visit the place of my family's origin. When we had the fall break in Rome, I decided to make the trip. With me were my wife, Patricia, my seven-year-old daughter, Jennifer, and my four-year-old daughter, Laura. We took a train from Rome to Vienna and then a bus from Vienna to Bratislava, the capital of Slovakia.

As soon as we crossed the Austrian-Czechoslovak border, I knew that the trip was a mistake. Armed soldiers, with police dogs, got everyone off the bus and searched them. We got back on the bus and arrived in Bratislava. We took a taxi, with a silent driver, to our hotel. I got a strange and very disconcerting feeling of being in a place where no one would look you in the eye. We got to the hotel, a large, once grand hotel, but now in shabby condition. Although the hotel was virtually empty, with the only other group there being the Bulgarian soccer team, we were told our room was not ready. I had mistakenly given the hotel porter a large tip because I was not yet able to translate dollars into Czech crowns. As soon as he reported this to the staff, our room became instantly ready.

For four days, we were virtual prisoners in the city. I had naively expected to rent a car and visit the sites in Slovakia from which my grandparents had immigrated. I was told that this could not be done. The city was drab and gray; the people walked with their heads down, avoiding eye contact. The highlights of our visit were attending Mass at a church that was full despite the government's anti-religious policy, going to the Slovak canary show, and buying some pastries at a bakery. When the bus came, we were on it and got back to Vienna. I felt like a ton of bricks had been lifted from my shoulders.

I reflect on this experience as I think about Marxism. In 1974, Czechoslovakia was controlled by the Soviet Union. In both countries, the official ideology was Marxist-Leninism. I had studied Marx and Marxism, Russian and Soviet history, and foreign relations. I knew something about the ideological and political situation in eastern and central Europe. However, my direct encounter with the ideology caused me to reconstruct my thinking. I realized that there can be sharp differences between theory and practice; that the translation of a theory into practice is highly significant; and that it depends a lot on who is interpreting the theory. My neo-Marxist colleagues in philosophy of education would probably tell me that what I experienced was not true Marxism but a distorted Soviet misrepresentation. I find Marxism to be very significant historically; and I find some of it to be highly useful as a tool of social and educational analysis. But I have concluded that there are many ways, in addition to an economic one, of looking at life, culture, society, and education. Marxism is but one of them.

MARXIST EDUCATIONAL IMPLICATIONS

Marx was more directly concerned with economic and political themes than with education. When he wrote about education in the formal sense, as schooling, he saw it as the content and methods that contributed to the person's intellectual and physical development. He emphasized **polytechnical education** that related his theory of scientific socialism to the knowledge and skills needed for production in modern industrial society. The foremost values in polytechnical education related to socially useful labor—work done to benefit the entire society and not just a few. Marx argued that, in contrast to capitalist indoctrination, polytechnical education, as a genuine education, developed a critical consciousness that eradicated false consciousness.

Polytechnical Education: education that develops the skills, knowledge, and values needed for economic production in a modern industrial economy that benefits the entire society.

Rather than schooling, Marx dealt more with informal education to raise the consciousness of the proletariat about the real economic conditions that exploited them.

As informal educators, Marxists were to write pamphlets and tracts, organize protests and demonstrations, and inform the public in any way possible about the causes of exploitation.

Marx's interpreters, especially in the foundations of education, have developed many of the ideology's educational implications, especially analyzing schooling in a capitalist society.[13] They call for an education that creates a critical consciousness in students. They argue that the dominant class controls schools as well as other social institutions and uses them to socially control the oppressed classes.[14] Many Marxist-influenced contemporary educators take a broader and more comprehensive examination of the causes of class domination than Marx's original focus on economic factors. They see capitalism as a cultural as well as an economic system. Capitalist culture, reflected and reproduced in schools and other institutions, is hegemonic as the dominant group imposes its ideological beliefs and values on subordinate groups. In addition to analyzing the economic factors that impact schools, they examine how schools reproduce ideological, social, and political relationships that reflect dominant group interests.[15] Marxist teachers are to work at raising their students' **critical consciousness** by examining the real economic, political, and social conditions that impact their lives. Much of their analysis focuses on **classism**, the control of one class by another; on racism, discrimination and oppression because of one's race; and sexism, the oppression of women in a male-dominated patriarchal society.

Critical Consciousness: knowing and understanding the socio-economic conditions that either exploit or liberate people.

Classism: the control of one class by another.

They call on teachers to examine critically the material conditions in which schools function—the surrounding neighborhood and its conditions of unemployment, the scarcity of health care, and the lack of hope. This kind of critical examination helps to expose and combat the false ideology of consumerism, promoted by capitalists, and raise the consciousness of students about the true nature of the exploitative conditions in which they live. Teachers are to undertake a critical examination that reveals who owns much of the economy. They are to examine how large, modern business corporations, the capitalist successors of the older industrialists, control politicians through campaign contributions, manipulate the media through paid advertising, and use the courts to legitimate their exploitation. Modern society, for them, remains an arena of conflicting economic interests. They would broaden the contours of class struggle to enlarge Marx's proletariat to include oppressed racial and ethnic groups, women, the homeless, and the poor. It is the ownership and exploitation of the economy, the material conditions of society, that cause racism, sexism, and other forms of discrimination. Neo-Marxist educators would call for a thorough and critical examination of economic control.

Space and Time

Marxism provides insights on space and time, two major constructs people develop and use to order their living, working, and social relationships. Much education is concerned with developing children's concepts of space and time. Marx's discussion of space and time refers to how these constructs are organized in capitalist society and in schools.

For Locke on property, see the chapter on Liberalism and Education.

SPACE. Private property is given highest priority in the middle-class capitalist value schema. In Locke's liberalism, property is an inalienable natural right of the individual that cannot be taken away by government. In capitalism, the ownership of private property defines the middle classes. The capitalist school strives to instill in children a respect for and an appreciation of the value of private property. The little child's unwillingness to share a toy, for example, often expressed as "This is mine," means "I possess it and it is not yours." The concept of space is developed through the hidden curriculum, the values in the school's milieu. Children have their own chair at the table in the nursery school, their own desk in the elementary grades, and their own locker in the high school. Personal space is delineated, borders are set around it, and others are not to invade it.

TIME. One of the most frequent clichés in the capitalist lexicon is "time is money." Like most clichés, it is very true. The workers are selling their time to the employer and, indeed, the employer owns the workers' time, which means they do not own their lives during their working hours. In a time-driven workplace, the stress on increasing unit production turns into human stress. Unit production, in the modern technological workforce, is quantitatively determined and measured. For the physician and the nurse in a capitalist controlled hospital, unit production means the number of patients diagnosed and treated; for teachers, it is the number of students instructed and tested. When nurses and teachers say that they are "stressed out" or "burned out," it means that they are worn out by the physiological and psychological consequences of meeting production quotas in health care and education.

Delivery of curriculum and instruction in American education is organized around time. In schools, colleges, and universities, instruction in organized into the school year. In high school, the movement toward graduation is determined by the number of units—a given amount of time devoted to a subject—completed by the student. In colleges and universities, the movement toward graduation is based on semester or quarter hours completed.

Schooling, which is heavily scheduled and programmed, prepares individuals to lead time-programmed lives. It accentuates the Calvinist origins of honored school values such as being on time, using time effectively and efficiently, and not wasting time. It also reduces instruction to time on task. Efficient teachers are those who can teach basic skills to large numbers of students, who in turn receive high scores on standardized tests.

Vanguard of the Proletariat

Marx and his chief collaborator, Friedrich Engels, were not members of the proletariat, the working class. A university graduate from a middle-class family, Marx worked as a journalist. If individuals are defined by their economic class, how could Marx, himself, have escaped being enculturated in middle-class ideas and values? Answering this question, Marx reasoned that the **vanguard of the proletariat**, a small intellectual elite cadre of dedicated revolutionaries, steeped in scientific socialism and knowing history's predestined course, could raise workers' consciousness of their exploitation and marginalization, organize workers' groups and demonstrations, and lead the coming proletarian revolution.

Vanguard of the Proletariat: the enlightened elite who work to create the Marxist society.

Because they were removed from the actual means of production, this group of theoretical activist intellectual ideologists could escape their economically determined class position. The vanguard plays an educational as well as an action-oriented mission. It is to (1) study the true course of history as a dialectical process generated by economic class conflict; (2) organize the workers and raise their consciousness about the true conditions of their exploitation; (3) lead the revolution at the correct revolutionary moment; and (4) organize the new classless society destined to replace the fallen capitalist economic order.

In orthodox Marxist ideology, especially Leninism, the vanguard, a secretive conspiratorial group following a rigid strategy, was the revolutionary elite. However, contemporary educational philosophies, ideologies, and theories influenced by Marx, such as Neo-Marxism, Liberation Pedagogy, and Critical Theory, have revised the concept and strategy of the vanguard.

See the chapter on Critical Theory.

Contemporary Marxist-influenced educators have revised Marx's original concept of the vanguard from an elite group into a broad-based popular front of marginalized racial, ethnic, and gender groups, the economically disadvantaged, and those working for social justice and equality. Are teachers part of the vanguard? The socio-economic origins of teachers may be from oppressed and marginalized groups but also from the middle and upper socio-economic classes as well. Because of their higher education, professional preparation, and role in instruction, teachers, although they may identify with the industrial working class, are not factory or manual laborers. For teachers, their connection to the means and modes of production is not direct as it is with businessmen and businesswomen and workers. Because of this indirect connection, teachers can, like the vanguard, be ideological theorist-activists. Using the schools in which they teach, teachers can inform themselves about economic power in society. They can analyze the socio-economic situation in their school and the community in which it is situated. Importantly, they can raise their students' consciousness about empowerment, dominance, marginalization, and social justice.

False Ideology: erroneous "knowledge" and values about social and economic conditions imposed on subordinated classes by the dominant class.

FALSE IDEOLOGY. An important goal of Marxist-inspired education is to expose the **false ideology** constructed to support and defend capitalism and to replace it with the true ideology of Marxism. In a capitalist society and educational system, children of oppressed groups are indoctrinated into a false ideology that denies them the opportunity to critically examine the social, political, and economic conditions that cause their subjugation. Marxist educators, in the vanguard of the proletariat, have the challenge of raising the revolutionary consciousness of the masses of people. This consciousness raising requires (1) a realistic examination of the economic conditions that cause exploitation in society; (2) an exposure of the "false ideology" into which students are indoctrinated in a capitalist consumer-driven society; (3) a discussion of what can be done to organize oppressed groups to improve their economic, political, social, and educational situation; and (4) development and implementation of strategies of transformative action.

Marxism as Critique

Marxism has appealed to some scholars in the foundations of education, especially in the history, philosophy, and sociology of education. Of course, it appeals to orthodox Marxists who are guided by the original ideology and to Neo-Marxists who reinterpret it in light of the contemporary situation. It also appeals to some Critical Theorists who find the writings of Antonio Gramsci and the Frankfurt School to be cogent analyses of society, politics, and education. A relevant question is why does Marxism, a nineteenth-century ideology linked with failed state systems such as the Soviet Union, continue to exert this attraction? Why does it continue to resurface, especially in the foundations of education?

Perhaps, the answer lies in Marxism's power to critique existing systems. Marx once wrote that "we have to accomplish" a "ruthless criticism of all that exists" without fearing where this will take us or whom it might offend, regardless of their power over us.[16] Marxism lends itself to the idea that education involves social and cultural criticism.

For education as criticism, see the chapters on Realism, Pragmatism, Postmodernism, Liberalism, Conservatism, Perennialism, Progressivism, Social Reconstructionism, and Critical Theory.

The idea that education should exercise a critical function is not new, however, nor is it unique to Marxists and those scholars influenced by Marxism. Renaissance humanists such as Erasmus asserted education's critical role. Other, more contemporary scholars in the educational foundations—Pragmatists, Progressives, Liberals, and Conservatives—accept the role of social and educational critics. However, the criteria for criticism is non- and often anti-Marxist. For Realists and Perennialists, for example, criticism is an exercise of reason, a power inherent by nature in the person. For the Pragmatist, criticism is experimental and necessary for executing the scientific method and is methodological rather than based on antecedent definitions. There is a further distinction of criticism between academic and Marxist-action–oriented criticism. Educational critique as academic criticism is much like literary, artistic, and cinematic criticism, which evaluates an author, actor, or director in terms of genre, style, effect, and performance. Educational critique as academic criticism is an activity educators do as peer reviewers of colleagues in the field.

Unlike academic criticism, Marxism analyzes social, economic, political, and educational conditions in terms of a criterion based on analytical concepts such as commodity, property, labor, ownership, class conflict, and alienation. As a method of criticism, Marxism specifically focuses on concepts such as class, gender, race, and ethnicity when they are interpreted as sources of oppression by dominant groups, generally economically favored ones, over marginalized economically disadvantaged ones. Unlike the temperamental coolness of dispassionate academic criticism summed up by "don't let your emotions cloud your judgment," Marxist criticism is deliberately meant to raise consciousness and a sense of oppression, indignation, and resistance in those who are exploited and marginalized.

Neo-Marxists and those influenced by Marxism have selected aspects of Marx's theory as analytical tools. They have broadened Marx's concept of the proletariat, the working class, as the originally dispossessed and oppressed class to include other marginalized groups in American society such as women, African and Latino Americans, homosexuals and lesbians, the homeless, and others.[17] Drawing on Marx's themes of capitalist imperialism and colonialism, Marxist critique is also applied to globalization and global economics. Critiques based on Marxist analysis are intended to raise the consciousness of the dispossessed groups and inspire resistance to the exploiting ideology in order to bring about transformative social, economic, political, and educational change.

Conflict Theory in Education

In Marxism, the origin of socio-economic classes and inevitable class conflicts are economically determined by the class's relationship to the means, modes, and ownership of production. According to Marx, the capitalists and the proletariat are modern society's major conflicting classes. Subgroups that appear, at first glance, to be outside of these classes in socio-economic reality are satellites or appendages of the two major conflicting contenders for power. The lower middle class—small-business owners, self-employed craftspeople, and even adjunct professors—is destined to sink gradually into the proletariat because they cannot resist the force of globalization. The idea of class conflict, refined into conflict theory, is an important concept of Marxist-influenced education. It interprets the school, curriculum, and the relationship between teachers and administrators in terms of conflict theory.

In **conflict theory** Marxist-influenced educators argue that schools, like other social institutions, are places where contending groups struggle for power and control.[18] The essential struggle is between the dominant groups—the white upper and middle classes, who enjoy a favored economic status—and the dominated, oppressed groups—racial and ethnic minorities, the unemployed and underemployed, and women. To understand group dominance and subordination and to raise students' critical consciousness, **Neo-Marxist** educators seek to (1) examine the nature of class and class culture; (2) determine how power is distributed among the classes; (3) examine the social control mechanisms that the dominant class has developed to subordinate the dominated class; and (4) examine how the dominant class uses schools as agencies of social reproduction and control.

Conflict Theory: Marx's idea of class conflict in which contending groups struggle for power and control.

Neo-Marxist: new or contemporary Marxists who revised Marx's ideology in terms of the contemporary situation.

Marxist educators see schools in a capitalist society as agencies used by the dominant class to reproduce the existing class structure that favors their interests. Schooling reproduces the ideological, social, political, and economic relationships based on dominant class interests. The school's location reflects the material conditions of the society. If it is located in a predominantly white, affluent, upper-middle-class district, with a high tax base and a low crime rate, the climate within the school will reflect these material conditions of the larger society. However, if it is located in a predominantly African American, lower income district with a high rate of unemployment, the school, too, will reflect these material conditions. The school's curriculum will reflect how the dominant class conceives of and uses knowledge. What is selected in the curriculum will reinforce existing beliefs and values for the children of the dominant class and will be used to convince children of subordinated classes that this curriculum is also valid for them. Within the school, administrators employed by the dominant group will claim that they are using standardized tests as an objective measure of students' academic achievement. However, Marxists will allege that these so-called objective instruments are framed in class-referenced ways that work for the benefit of the dominant class. Students then will be grouped according to test results. What really is happening, however, is that the tests are used as a sorting device to arrange groups in the school that mirror and reproduce the class situation in the larger society outside of the school.

Rather than being the institutions that they claim to be in a capitalist society, schools are agencies designed to reproduce, ensure, and perpetuate the control by the dominant group. They do not implement equality of opportunity and social justice but rather reinforce and reproduce existing inequalities. They educate those who are in a favored position to stay in that position by preparing them for prestigious colleges and universities so that they can take their parents' places in the corporate sector. Simultaneously, the children of the less favored, dominated classes are also prepared to stay in their places at the bottom of the social and economic scale.

SCHOOLS IN A CAPITALIST SOCIETY

In a Marxist analysis of schools in a capitalist society, it is necessary to consider the general impact of economic factors on education both in and out of schools. The questions Marxists would ask are: What economic forces that affect schools are at work in the larger society? What economic forces are operative in schools that affect the official curriculum and instruction and the informal school environment?

The School in the Larger Society

For a Marxist analysis of schools in a capitalist society, it is necessary to begin in the communities (the school districts) in which a school is located. The socio-economic, racial, and ethnic composition of the community has an impact on what takes place in the school. Children in a particular local school district typically attend the school in their attendance area, which is based on their residence. Although there are exceptions such as magnet and specialized schools that enroll students throughout a district, a board of education's designated attendance area determines the school most children will attend. In other words, for most American children, where a child lives determines the school she or he attends.

Since school attendance for most students is based on residence, a Marxist analysis would include an examination of residential housing trends in the United States. Since 1980, there have been increasing differences in income levels in the United States. Residential segregation by income has increased significantly in the past thirty years, throughout the country, especially in the nation's twenty-seven largest metropolitan areas. Specifically, lower income households dwelling in lower income residential areas increased from 23 to 28 percent since 1980. At the same time, upper income households in upper income residential areas increased from 9 to 18 percent. This growing income inequality has led to a decrease in the households in middle-class residential areas from 85 percent in 1980 to 76 percent in 2010. In this thirty-year period, lower income households residing in lower income areas have increased from 12 to 18 percent; upper income households in upper income residential areas have increased from 3 to 6 percent.[19] When these income-based housing trends are related to school attendance areas, they indicate that a larger number of children will attend schools in economically segregated communities. Typically, schools in lower economic districts have inferior educational facilities and services. However, the community in which the school is located plays a large role in the school's internal education functions. James S. Coleman's *Equality of Educational Opportunity* (1966) examined racial desegregation and integration in terms of the relationship of school resources and facilities to students' academic achievement. Finding a more limited relationship between academic achievement and school facilities and staff, Coleman identified family, neighborhood, and socio-economic class as the more important determinants of students' achievement. According to Coleman:

> . . . schools bring little influence to bear on a child's achievement that is independent of his background and general social context; . . . this very lack of an independent effect means that the inequalities imposed on children by their home, neighborhood, and peer environment are carried along to become the inequalities with which they confront adult life . . . .[20]

Coleman's finding that children's achievement was dependent on their family and socio-economic background has important implications for schools in light of recent trends toward income-based residential segregation. Differences in achievement among children correlated highly with the socio-economic status of their peer group in the school.

The Impact of Socioeconomic Conditions on Schools

Neo-Marxist educational theorists such as Samuel Bowles, Herbert Gintis, and Michael Apple have applied a revised Marxist analysis to education in the contemporary United States. In *Schooling in Capitalist America*, Bowles and Gintis describe schools as people production agencies marked by capitalist demand for economic profit and social and political control.[21] They point out that serious contradictions exist in American political and economic systems. While political processes emphasize majority decision making and the protection of minority rights, a small elite controls the economy.

The modes of production in the economic sector are organized into a hierarchical division of labor. Each productive rung in the corporate ladder is organized and stratified at that level and managed bureaucratically.[22] Hierarchical economic stratification influences how the middle class determines its educational goals. To gain entry and to advance in the corporate economic system, the middle class wants education that will give it technological and managerial knowledge and skills.[23]

Schools are used as agencies to reproduce and legitimate economic disparities between socio-economic classes, the hierarchical structure in the corporate economy, and the domination of the capitalist class. The institutionalized educational system maintains and reproduces the class structure. The school, as a meritocratic mechanism, uses educational tracking based on competitive testing and assessment to assign students to particular programs that will take them to unequal economic positions in the hierarchical corporate economic sector. Success in the school and the economic structure depends on the student's ability to acquire technical and cognitive skills.[24]

Using the criterion of objectivity and fairness, educational policy setters both within and outside of schools legitimate the testing, grouping, and selecting processes used to prepare individuals for positions in the corporate structure. For example, it is claimed that standardized achievement testing is fair to all students in that it is not biased based on race or class. The test results can be used to group students on their assessed levels of competence. The Neo-Marxist theorists contend that homogeneous grouping in schools in a capitalist society reproduces the existing socio-economic class structure. The reproduction of social strata in the school, allegedly based on academic ability, implies that membership in a particular group or track is determined by an objective and competitive meritocratic system. In reality, Marxists would argue that the identification of a student with a particular track is economically based. Schools reproduce the existing socio-economic structure and condition students to accept the legitimacy of that structure.

Through curricula and instruction, schools prepare the future workforce.[25] The school's role in preparing the country's workforce is to identify, select, and prepare individuals for positions in the various rungs in the capitalist corporate ladder. It trains people for the specialties that make the division of labor possible. It prepares people to be consumers of the products of a capitalist economy. Based on premises of economic inequality, such schooling is a determinant, albeit a partial one, of the rewards and penalties that its graduates will receive. In effect, it perpetuates the economic inequalities of the society and maintains the status quo.

Bowles and Gintis and other Neo-Marxist educational theorists have analyzed the role of schools in reproducing the dominant capitalist culture. In a capitalist society such as the United States, the very location of the school, whether it is in an affluent suburb or in the economically depressed inner city, reflects and reproduces the attitudes and values of the surrounding locality. Neo-Marxists relate curriculum and instruction in schools to the larger culture and society. The officially approved skills, subjects, behaviors, and values in capitalist schools' curricula shape, confirm, maintain, and reproduce the dominant class ideology. The curriculum (both overt and hidden), methods of instruction, and testing are part of the capitalist strategy to reproduce itself as a dominant class.

Within a school the grouping and instructing of students reproduce the social, political, and economic status quo. The school mirrors the essential class divisions of the larger society and, rather than changing them, hardens these divisions by perpetuating them in the young.[26]

The interests and values of the capitalists, the dominant class, frame their special interests as being for the common good. For example, the values of respect for private property, hard work, patriotism, and respect for law and order have been traditional public school values since the time of the common schools. According to the Neo-Marxist critique, these traditional values are designed to protect the property of the dominant moneyed class. By encasing these class-centered values in a framework that extols the common good, the school is bending the minds of the young to accept their society as the best of all possible worlds.

When a privileged and dominant class has managed to entrench its thought-ways and values among subordinated suppressed classes, it has established ideological control over them.[27] Rather than being a place where ideas contend in an open market, as Liberal apologists assert, the school in a capitalist society is closed to alternative viewpoints that may threaten the hegemony that the dominant class enjoys over the lower class. Capitalist-dominated hegemony is established when members of subordinant groups express the opinions and values of the dominant class.

For the liberal competition of ideas, see the chapter on Liberalism and Education.

Contemporary Neo-Marxists, such as Michael Apple, have revised Marx's bipolar model of historically destined class conflict between the capitalists and the proletariat. Apple contends that the class structure within modern capitalism is more complex than it was when Marx wrote in the nineteenth century. Class structure, "the organization of social relations" is based on class interests. Class formation, the "organized collectivitics" within the structure, relates not only to economic forces but also to cultural, political, and social patterns and trends.[28] The formation of class cultures is further complicated in multiculturally diverse countries like the United States. In addition to economic conditions, class cultures also reflect racial, ethnic, and gender histories, relationships, and conflicts.[29] Apple argues that seventy percent of working-class occupational positions are filled by women and members of minority groups. Thus, an analysis of class formation needs to consider patriarchal and racial dominance themes.[30]

HIDDEN CURRICULUM. In addition to the overt or official curriculum, Neo-Marxist theorists refer to the "hidden curriculum," informal or milieu learning that takes place in the school's context. The hidden curriculum involves the informal relationship between administrators and teachers, teachers with teachers, and teachers and students. It refers to the beliefs and values that enter the school from the larger culture and society. According to Apple, the hidden curriculum "reinforces basic rules" regarding conflict and its uses. It establishes a "network of assumptions" that reinforces legitimacy and authority.[31] The hidden curriculum underscores the norms and values of the dominant group in such a pervasive way that challenges to it are rendered illegitimate.

For example, the emphasis on private property is reinforced as a value by assigning certain school spaces to particular individuals. Punctuality and the efficient use of time are also values reinforced by the school scheduling process. These attitudes and values, held to be characteristics of the effective school, are also conducive to the functioning of a capitalist economy.

CONSTRUCTING YOUR OWN PHILOSOPHY OF EDUCATION

Now that you have read and discussed the chapter on Marxism, you may wish to reflect on its relevance in constructing your philosophy of education. Marxism has been and continues to be an important mode of economic, social, political, and educational critique and analysis. Have you encountered Marxism or Neo-Marxism teachers and professors in your education? Has the reading of this chapter caused you to reappraise Marxist interpretations of education and schooling? Do you plan to use Marxism or some aspects of it in constructing your own philosophy of education?

Conclusion

This chapter described and analyzed the key ideas used by Karl Marx in his construction of Marxist ideology. It examined such Marxist concepts as dialectical materialism, the means and modes of production, production of commodities and alienation, class struggle between the capitalists and the proletariat, false consciousness, and the role of the vanguard of the proletariat. It discussed the role of Neo-Marxism on educational theory, especially foundations of education. It considered the Marxist critique of education and schools in a capitalist society and Neo-Marxism's view of schools as contested sites in the class struggle. It introduced the role of teachers as agents in raising students' consciousness about the impact of economic conditions and class on school and society.

Questions for Reflection and Discussion

1. Critics of Marxism contend that it exaggerates the economic factors in society and aggravates class conflicts. Do you agree or disagree with these critics? Why?
2. Do you agree or disagree with Marx that the superstructure of society—the government, church, media, and school, for example—rests on an economic base and is controlled by those who own this base? What evidence or experiences support your answer?
3. Why do you think that Marxism has influenced theories in the foundations of education? What is your opinion of this influence on educational theory?
4. Do you agree with Marxists who say that the school is a contested site between those who have power and those who do not? Why? Do you have examples or experiences that support your answer?
5. Do you agree with Marxists who claim that the capitalist economic system creates consumer desires through the manipulation of illusions in marketing? Defend your answer.
6. From a Marxist perspective, what is the role of teachers in the class struggle? Do you agree or disagree with this perspective? Why?
7. Have you taken courses in which instructors have used such terms as *hegemony, power, marginalization*, and *empowerment?* How would a Marxist analyze these terms?

Topics for Inquiry and Research

1. In your classroom observations, identify aspects of the hidden curriculum and describe how they function to establish patterns of behavior and control.
2. Analyze several textbooks that are used in the teacher education program at your college or university. Do you find comments about the impact of socioeconomic class on educational expectations and academic achievement? Would a Marxist agree or disagree with these comments?
3. Reread either the chapter on Liberalism or Conservatism. Apply a Marxist critique to one of these chapters.
4. Based on your classroom observations and clinical experiences, identify, describe, and analyze classroom situations that reproduce socio-economic relationships, attitudes, and behaviors from the community in which the students reside.
5. Visit several schools and determine whether the economic situation of the neighborhood in which the school is located has an impact on the curriculum, instruction, and teacher-student relationships.
6. Access http://www.marxists.org/subject/education/index.htm. Explore the site and read an article on Marx's ideas on education.

Internet Resources

For the ideas of Marx, Marxist education in the Soviet Union, and related items, access www.marxists.org/.

For Neo-Marxism, access www.markfoster.net/struc/NM.html.

For Marx on cultural institutions, access www.sociology.org.uk/as4i4cl.pdf.

Suggestions for Further Reading

Agostinone-Wilson, Faith. *Marxism and Education Beyond Identity: Sexuality and Schooling*. New York: Palgrave Macmillan/St. Martin's Press, 2010.

Anyon, Jean. *Marx and Education*. New York: Routledge, 2011.

Apple, Michael W. *Ideology and Curriculum*. London: Routledge, 1990.

Blumerberg, Werner. *Karl Marx*. New York: Verso, 2000.

Bowles, Samuel, and Herbert Gintis. *Schooling in Capitalist America*. New York: Basic Books, 1975.

Brosio, Richard M. *A Radical Democratic Critique of Capitalist Education*. New York: Peter Lang, 1994.

Churchich, Nicholas. *Marxism and Morality: A Critical Examination of Marxist Ethics*. Cambridge: James Clarke, 1994.

Cole, Mike. *Marxism, Postmodernism, and Education*. New York: Routledge, 2007.

Gottlieb, Roger S. *Marxism, 1844–1990: Origins, Betrayal, Rebirth*. New York: Routledge, 1992.

Green, Anthony, et al., eds. *Renewing Dialogues in Marxism and Education: Openings*. New York: Palgrave Macmillan/St. Martin's Press, 2007.

Jones, Peter E., ed. *Marxism and Education: Renewing the Dialogue, Pedagogy, and Culture*. New York: Palgrave Macmillan/St. Martin's Press, 2011.

Lefort, Claude. *Complications: Communism and the Dilemmas of Democracy*. Translated by Julian Bourg. New York: Columbia University Press, 2007.

Majab, Shahrzad, and Sara Carpenter. *Educating from Marx: Race, Gender, and Learning*. New York: Palgrave Macmillan/St. Martin's Press, 2011.

McLellan, David. *Karl Marx: Selected Writings*. Oxford, UK: Oxford University Press, 2000.

Osborne, Peter. *How to Read Marx*. New York: W. W. Norton & Co., 2006.

Torrance, John. *Karl Marx's Theory of Ideas*. New York: Cambridge University Press, 1995.

Van Parijs, Philippe. *Marxism Recycled*. New York: Cambridge University Press, 1993.

Wheen, Francis. *Karl Marx: A Life*. New York: W. W. Norton & Co., 2001.

Wood, Ellen M. *Democracy Against Capitalism: Renewing Historical Materialism*. New York: Cambridge University Press, 1995.

Notes

1. David McLellan, *Karl Marx: His Life and Thought* (New York: Harper & Row, 1973), 2–6.
2. Karl Marx and Friedrich Engels, "Manifesto of the Communist Party," in Carl Cohen, Ed., *Communism, Fascism, and Democracy: The Theoretical Foundations* (New York: Random House, 1972), 80, 89.
3. Peter Osborne, *How to Read Marx* (New York: W. W. Norton & Co., 2006), 22, 24.
4. Ibid., 33–34.
5. Ibid., 37.
6. Kenneth Strike, *Liberal Justice and the Marxist Critique of Education: A Study of Conflicting Research Programs* (New York: Routledge and Kegan Paul, 1988), 23.
7. Osborne, *How to Read Marx,* 11–12.
8. Ibid., 13.
9. Ibid., 79.
10. Ibid., 54.
11. Ibid., 31.
12. Samuel Farber, *The Origins of the Cuban Revolution Reconsidered* (Chapel Hill: University of North Carolina Press, 2006).
13. Frank Margonis, "Marxism, Liberalism, and Educational Theory," *Educational Theory, 43* (4) (Fall 1993), 449.
14. Michael Apple, "Education, Culture, and Class Power: Basil Bernstein and the Neo-Marxist Sociology of Education," *Educational Theory, 42* (2) (Spring 1992), 127.
15. Ibid., 128.
16. Osborne, *How to Read Marx*, 59.
17. For a discussion of race and gender, see Shahrzad Majab and Sara Carpenter, *Educating from Marx: Race, Gender and Learning* (New York: Palgrave Macmillan, 2011).
18. Walter Feinberg and Jonas Soltis, *School and Society* (New York: Teachers College Press, 1985), 43–44.
19. Paul Taylor and Richard Fry, "The Rise of Residential Segregation by Income," Pew Research Center. http://pewsocialtrends.org/2012/08/01/the-rise-of-residential-segregation-by-income/, 1–3.
20. James S. Coleman et al., *Equality of Educational Opportunity* (Washington, DC: U.S. Government Printing Office, 1966).
21. Samuel Bowles and Herbert Gintis, *Schooling in Capitalist America: Education Reform and the Contradictions of Economic Life* (New York: Basic Books, 1976), 53–56.
22. Ibid., 102–105.
23. Apple, "Education, Culture, and Class Power," 134–135.
24. Bowles and Gintis, 125–126, 131–133.
25. Ibid., 103–105, 125–126, 131–133.
26. Feinberg and Soltis, *School and Society,* 49.
27. Ibid., 50–52.
28. Apple, "Education, Culture, and Class Power," 137.
29. Ibid., 139.
30. Ibid., 143.
31. Michael Apple, *Ideology and Curriculum* (London: Routledge & Kegan Paul, 1979), 87.

Theory and Education

Theory based on practice, illustrated by a still from the motion picture *Freedom Writers*, in which students' autobiographical writings generate common features of their shared life experiences.

12

CHAPTER PREVIEW

In this chapter, we consider the relationships between theory and education. *Theory* is an often used but elusive term. In our everyday speech, we use it to mean that we have constructed some ideas that explain something, or we have a hypothesis about something, or that we have conjectured some cause-and-effect relationships (e.g., if I diet and exercise, I am going to lose weight). A theory represents a cluster of ideas that we can generalize about and apply to other situations. For example, if other people diet and exercise, they, too, can be expected to lose weight. You can test this kind of theory empirically, or scientifically, by standing on a scale and weighing yourself before and after you have completed your regimen of diet and exercise. However, there are other kinds of theories that we cannot verify empirically. For example, our beliefs about God, the supernatural, and the spiritual are not amenable to empirical testing. Those who hold these faith beliefs would say that the supernatural is higher than and above the empirical. We can also consider the Realist theory that the study of the liberal arts and sciences cultivates a person's power of reasoning. This kind of theory lies between those that can be tested directly by using empirical evidence and those that cannot be tested directly by such means. It is based on an *a priori* philosophical premise that the human being is rational by nature. However, the claim that studying the liberal arts and sciences improves reasoning processes needs further verification. In education, we find instances of both kinds of theory—the empirically verifiable ones and those that elude scientific verification. The word *theory*, however, is used constantly in education, and as we move through this chapter, we shall examine various uses of the word. The chapter includes the following topics:

- Defining theory
- Studying theory
- Theory as a bridge between philosophy and ideology and practice
- Theory as derivation
- Theory as reaction
- Theory arising from practice

Constructing your philosophy of education inevitably brings you to theorizing about education, school, curriculum, instruction, and the relationships between teachers and students. The act of constructing means that you are intellectually engaged in and generalizing about education. As you read the chapter, reflect on some of the theories that you have about education and how theory relates to your philosophy of education.

DEFINING THEORY

Theoria: the Greek word for intellectually contemplating, considering, or conjecturing something.

The word *theory* is derived from the ancient Greek word, **theoria**, which means intellectually contemplating, considering, or conjecturing something. It could mean comparing and contrasting objects and relating them to each other, as Aristotle did in his system of classifications. Or it might be thinking about how change occurred, as he did in his theory of the four causes. The ancient Greeks often dichotomize theory from practice. For example, Plato and Aristotle regarded theory—abstract thought about the nature of things—to be a higher, more elevated, and more rational activity of the mind than actual practice, or doing something or making something. In contrast to Plato and Aristotle, John Dewey, in his Experimentalist philosophy, challenged the Greek dualistic way of thinking and argued against separating theory from practice. He insisted, instead, that we construct our theories from our experiences and test them by acting on them as we have problems in our ongoing experience.

See the chapters on Idealism and Realism for Plato and Aristotle.

For Dewey, see the chapter on Pragmatism and Education.

At this point, we can consider several meanings of *theory* that have implications for education. As a hypothetical set of ideas or principles that can guide practice, theories can be turned into "if–then" statements: If I do this or act in this way, then the following is likely to happen. Theorizing can refer to the act of forming generalizations—plans that we can replicate in varying situations—based on how something is done successfully in a given field such as medicine, law, or education, for example. In this instance, theory arises from observing or performing similar actions that cause results that can be anticipated. Here, the process of forming the generalizations is inductive; the reasoning and logic used goes from the specific instance to the general case. For example, a football coach, who has had experience in the sport, can frame a number of plays or strategies that the team can use successfully in certain situations in a series of games. In education, especially in instruction, a teacher, who has had experience in teaching reading or mathematics, can identify those exercises and activities that have succeeded and those that have failed to bring about the desired outcomes. The teacher can generalize about those that work and arrive at a set of principles that can guide instruction. The guiding principles, derived from a particular experience, can be generalized and applied to other teaching situations. Further, a group of teachers can collaboratively share their experiences in teaching a particular skill or subject or dealing with a particular issue or problem and generalize to a set of operating principles—how and when to teach something or what methods to use in a given teaching situation.

Theory can refer to a general abstract conceptual frame of reference that can be used to guide practice. Such a frame of reference includes (1) a set of generalizations, or explanations, about the subject or field; (2) strategies on how to apply the generalizations as guiding principles in action; and (3) hypotheses, conjectures, or expectations about what is likely to happen when the generalization is applied in a specific instance. Such a frame of reference can be created in at least two ways: (1) based on experience that arises from practice, as discussed earlier, or (2) deduced from another set of generalizations as in the case of putting a philosophy or an ideology into practice. In the latter instance, the theory is formed by deductive reasoning in which the guiding principles are extracted from the broader and more comprehensive body of thought and applied to given situations. For example, a lawyer, using the common law, will look for precedents, earlier decisions, that can be used to support her or his argument in a particular case. A teacher can look to a philosophy such as Idealism or Realism or an ideology such as Liberalism or Conservatism to draw forth for them goals to be implemented in the classroom. Here, the problem is taking the abstractions provided by the philosophy or ideology and rendering them into a format or strategy by which they can be implemented in practice.

Still another meaning of theory is our beliefs, ideas, and concepts about phenomena—the objects, people, and situations—that we observe and with which we interact. Kerlinger, for example, defines a theory as "a set of interrelated constructs (concepts), definitions, and propositions that present a systematic view of phenomena by specifying relations among variables, with the purpose of explaining and predicting the phenomena."[1] It is what we attribute to be the origin and nature of something and the actions and reactions that take place. This kind of theorizing occurs when we try to make sense and give meaning to our situations and the actors, objects, and occurrences in these situations. It is a way of generalizing about our experience so that we construct some explanations about it. An important characteristic of a theory is the interrelationship of its parts and how it is possible to deduce one proposition from another.

In the case of all of these meanings of theory, the important point is that theory is a guide to practice. However, further questions remain: Are the assumptions in the theory valid? If the assumptions are valid, can they be successfully transferred and applied to other situations? Will implementation confirm or invalidate the theory's working generalizations? Or is the failure to transfer the theory due to faulty implementation rather than to inadequacies in the theory? For example, consider the following assumptions given as a rationale for the No Child Left Behind Act:

> We know from business practices that if we want to boost performance, we must set clear, measurable goals and align our systems to them. In education, academic standards is the foundation of a performance-based system. High standards do not just help teachers; they also encourage children, because children tend to perform to meet the expectations of adults. If these expectations are low, children can miss their true potential. When expectations are high, progress can be amazing. . . .
>
> Creating clear and rigorous academic standards is an important first step in improving our schools. We will never know, however, if we are reaching those standards unless we measure student performance."[2]

STUDYING THEORY

Individuals find themselves in constantly changing situations or events. Each situation is unique in that the setting and the actors, the other people, and the issue or problem may be different. However, in these situations, there are some common elements. It is the recognition and the clustering together of these common elements that are the foundations of theorizing. For example, at the beginning of each school year, a teacher will find that she or he has a class of new and unfamiliar students. However, with experience, the teacher will have built up a repertoire of strategies for engaging students. It relates to the question that all teachers have—what do I do on the first day of school? The teacher can recognize that students' needs and abilities fit into patterns that are found in each class of students each new year. From this recognition, the teacher can generalize about the similarities and differences found in various groups of students and create plans of action—strategies—to use in instruction. Further, teachers can collaborate with each other and discuss common successes, weaknesses, and issues and formulate some generalizations about teaching. These generalizations, when clustered and organized together, are the basis of a theory of teaching. Such theoretical underpinnings are the basis of methods of instruction.

Theory also relates to the larger issue of teacher professionalization. In contrast to a trade, which consists of the mastery of a set of techniques, a profession rests on a theoretical foundation—informed hypotheses, based on knowledge, about why as well as how something is done.

For example, in the first chapter in this book, we discussed the theory of reflective teaching in which teachers construct a conceptual framework for teaching. In other words, they construct a philosophy of education. While there are certain techniques that are followed in teaching, teaching itself implies more than using these techniques. It is informed by concepts from learned disciplines such as philosophy, history, sociology, and psychology that provide a theoretical foundation—an examination of why something is done in its larger contexts.

Theory as a Bridge Between Philosophy and Ideology and Practice

This chapter on theory and education can be thought of as a bridge that carries the reader from the more abstract chapters on philosophies and ideologies to five theories of education: Essentialism, Perennialism, Progressivism, Social Reconstructionism, and Critical Theory. As indicated in our definition of theory, these five theories (1) operate from a coherent set of generalizations and explanations about the purpose of education, the organization and structure of schools, and the processes of teaching and learning; (2) contain guiding hypotheses or working principles about how curriculum and instruction should be organized and conducted; and (3) indicate projected outcomes that will follow if the theoretical assumptions are applied in practice. In the next sections, we examine theories (1) that are derived from or deduced from other larger and more abstract bodies of thought such as philosophies and ideologies; (2) that develop as educational or school-centered responses to larger social, economic, cultural, or political problems and issues; and (3) that arise as generalizations or hypotheses from practices within schools and classrooms. It should be pointed out that in some cases a theory may include all three elements: derivations, responses, and generalizations from practice.

THEORY AS DERIVATION

Educational Theory Derived from Philosophy: deducing a theory of education—ideas about education—from a more general philosophy.

In this section, we consider how education is derived from another area, discipline, or field of inquiry. Specifically, we examine **educational theory that is derived from philosophy** and from ideology.

Philosophical Derivation

Part I of this book examined the philosophies of Idealism, Realism, Theistic Realism, Pragmatism, Existentialism, and Postmodernism. Of these, Idealism, Realism, and Theistic Realism are based on a grand, large, metaphysical structure that provides a kind of architecture of the universe and the human being's place in it. These older, more traditional philosophies are systematic in that they expound on what is real (metaphysics), how we know (epistemology), and what is right and beautiful (ethics and aesthetics). Education—especially schooling, curriculum, and instruction—is dealt with in these larger systems and subsumed as areas that are included and explained by the larger and more comprehensive worldview. Throughout history, these metaphysically based philosophies have attracted adherents who sought to apply their principles to culture, society, politics, and education. Educators, who look to eternal and universal truths, seek to apply them to education and to base a curriculum on what they believe is always good, true, and beautiful. For example, Essentialism exhibits strong elements of Idealism and Realism, and Perennialism draws heavily from the Realism of Aristotle and Aquinas.

See the chapters on Idealism, Realism, Essentialism, and Perennialism.

More modern philosophies such as Pragmatism, Existentialism, and Postmodernism rejected the metaphysical base of the older philosophies as unverifiable speculation and turned their attention to epistemology, meaning, and other issues. Dewey's

See the chapters on Pragmatism, Existentialism, and Postmodernism.

Experimentalism, a variety of Pragmatism, influenced Progressivism, which sought to apply the concepts of democracy, community, social intelligence, the scientific method, and problem solving to education, schooling, and instruction. Postmodernism, which borrowed some Existentialist and Marxist themes, has a strong influence on Critical Theory.

Ideological Derivation

Educational Theory Derived from Ideology: deducing or extrapolating a theory of education—ideas about education—from an ideology.

Educational theories are also derived from ideologies such as Nationalism, Liberalism, Conservatism, and Marxism. Schools in countries throughout the world are organized into national systems of education. In these systems, strong elements of Nationalism are used in children's political socialization and are designed to construct their primary identification. For example, public schools in the United States seek to create a sense of American identity and citizenship in students.

See the chapter on Nationalism and Education.

The content of the school curriculum is often a contested area on a number of grounds—some political, social, cultural, and economic and others methodological. Liberals, Conservatives, and Marxists differ on the goals of education, the purpose and function of schools, curriculum content, and styles of teaching and learning. Conservatism, with its emphasis on traditional knowledge and values, has influenced Essentialism and Perennialism. Liberalism, with its emphasis on flexibility and innovation, has influenced Progressivism. Themes from Marxism and Liberation Pedagogy such as class domination, control, and conflict are evident in Critical Theory.

See the chapters on Liberalism, Conservatism, and Marxism.

THEORY AS REACTION

Educational Theory as Reactive: a theory of education—ideas about education—based on a reaction to social, political, economic, and educational situations, issues, problems, and crises.

Educational theory as a reactive response to a crisis has often occurred in the past. Theories have been developed as reactions to social, political, economic, and educational situations, issues, problems, and crises. Reactive educational theories are designed to remedy a problem that occurs in the larger society or in schools. For example, childhood obesity has been diagnosed as a serious problem in contemporary American society. In reaction, it has been proposed that school lunches be composed of healthy foods, such as more fruits and vegetables, and eliminate fast food items; that physical education be increased for students; and that the curriculum include units informing students about healthy diet and exercise. The various components—healthy diet, physical exercise, and information—in the response, or reaction, to this issue indicate the formation of a theory. If these things are done, the anticipated result will be a reduction in the incidence of obesity in children.

An example of an educational theory in reaction to a school-based problem is programs designed to end bullying. Long an issue in schools, bullying has persisted despite attempts to end it. In addition to physical and psychological abuse inflicted on their victims by bullies, some of them now use the Internet and social media to harass their victims. In reaction to the problem of bullying, programs are being designed and implemented to inform students about the consequences of this behavior on all members of the school community—on bullies, their victims, students who are by standers and don't try to stop the harassment, teachers, and other school personnel such as bus drivers. Teacher educational programs are featuring units that examine the causes of bullying, how to recognize it, and the steps to intervene to prevent it. When these various aspects are generalized and related to each other, they will constitute a theory on the prevention of bullying.

An extended example of how educational theories have developed as reactions to issues is provided in the rise of environmental education. This educational reaction came in response to a growing concern about global warming and the degradation of the environment because of industrial and fossil-fuel emissions, depletion of the rain forests, and the hunting of endangered animal species. Environmental concerns contributed to the establishment of courses in environmental education that emphasize conserving natural resources, learning to use alternative energy sources, and recycling of items—paper, glass, and plastic—that could be collected and reused. These courses also emphasize the personal, social, and ethical responsibilities regarding protection of and respect for conserving the natural environment. They also emphasize the aesthetic sense of natural beauty that comes from a healthy planet. When environmental issues are scrutinized and taken to their global implications, they can be generalized to include questions about the role of industrialized nations such as the United States as a major pollutant, about the socio-economic disparities between the wealthy nations of the Northern Hemisphere and the poorer ones of the Southern Hemisphere, about the negative effects of economic globalization by multinational corporations, and about strategies for sustainable development. At this juncture, the theory of environmental education, which originated as a response, was juxtaposed with other philosophies, ideologies, and educational theories and reformulated. For example, Marxists see the multinational business corporation as a modern form of capitalism that exploits the poor of the less technologically developed nations. Freire and Illich argued that literacy programs tied to small-scale, grassroots, and sustainable development projects will empower the poverty-ridden classes in these countries. These themes of empowerment are also embraced and voiced by Critical Theorists.

Incidents of violence have increased in schools in the United States. Some students, in locations across the country, smuggled guns into schools, shooting and killing their classmates and teachers. One of the most tragic cases of in-school violence took place at Columbine High School near Littleton, Colorado, when two male students, using guns and bombs, killed twelve of their classmates and two teachers. These incidents clearly signaled that the nation faced a major problem. Educators responded with programs to create safe schools with zero tolerance for those who endangered the lives of others. Part of the response included programs in conflict resolution and in identifying and providing therapy to bullies, social isolates, and other students with social and psychological problems. As a result, a theory of nonviolent safe schools developed. Once again, this theory that arose as a response soon was juxtaposed with other ideological positions. Conservatives claimed that the problem of violence in schools mirrored the moral breakdown in the larger society. Rap music, videos, and games that used violence as a theme had eroded and weakened traditional social morals and engendered a climate that was prone to violence. Permissiveness and values clarification programs in schools had created a climate of ethical relativism that lacked universal moral standards. Perennialists called for a reaffirmation of universal values found in the Judeo-Christian religious tradition and in the Aristotelian philosophical tradition. Conservatives called for a return to strict discipline and moral standards along with zero tolerance school management. Religious Conservatives called for the posting of the Ten Commandments in the schools as a reminder of universal moral values and responsibility. However, at the same time, many Conservatives oppose gun control as violating what they consider to be the Constitution's right of citizens to keep and bear arms.

Another tragic incident of gun violence in schools occurred at the Sandy Hook School in Newtown, Connecticut, in 2013, when an armed intruder killed twenty children and six teachers and staff members. This tragedy, like the Columbine massacre, renewed the discussion of how to prevent it from occurring again. However, in the case of Sandy Hook, the perpetrator came from outside of the school. In reaction, the discussion has developed around the issues of gun control and mental health. Whether a comprehensive theory develops that can be implemented to protect teachers and

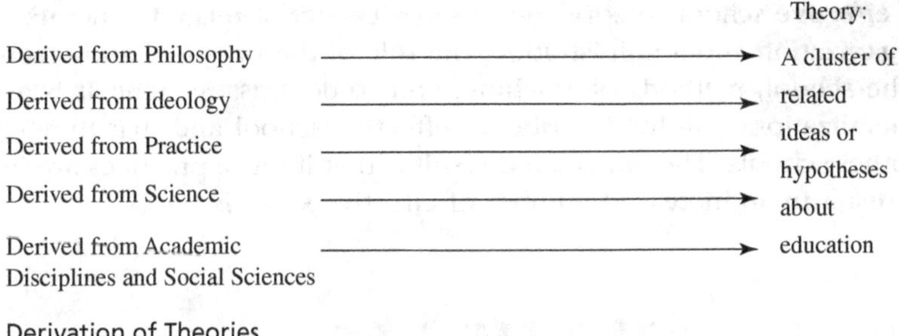

Derivation of Theories

students from gun violence remains to be seen. Among the hypotheses presented are if federal gun control laws, including a registry of gun owners, are enacted, then the incidence of gun-related violence in schools will be reduced; if teachers are armed with hand guns, they can protect their students from dangerous persons with guns; if comprehensive mental health requirements are required for owning a hand gun, the incidence of gun-related violence will be reduced in society and in schools. In addition to these hypotheses, a response to the problem is further complicated, as was the response to the tragedy at Columbine High School by political and ideological issues.

THEORY ARISING FROM PRACTICE

Educational Theory Arising from Practice: an educational theory—ideas about education—that is generated from classroom practices.

In many instances (e.g., in medicine, nursing, and education), **educational theory arises from practice**. In this scenario, the practitioner in a field has the experience of dealing with a number of similar instances. For example, a pediatrician may have dealt with a number of ear infections in children and as a result can form generalizations about their cause and treatment. These generalizations provide the physician with a set of hypotheses about the prevention and treatment of these cases. Or a foreign-language teacher, who has taught a course in Italian for several years to secondary school students, may have identified the situations that facilitate or impede learning the language for most students. She or he then reflects on these situations and arrives at some generalization to guide instruction. These generalizations then form a theory that can guide a method of teaching the language.

An example of theory being generated from practice can be found in the "effective" schools movement. Certain schools, their principals, and teachers are identified as especially competent educators whose students have demonstrated high levels of academic achievement. After analyzing specific practices that contributed to effective schools, the U.S. Department of Education, in *What Works: Research About Teaching and Learning*, arrived at the following generalizations:

- Belief in the value of hard work, the importance of personal responsibility, and the importance of education itself contributes to success in school.
- Children learn science best when they are able to do experiments, so they can witness "science in action."
- Teachers who set and communicate high expectations to all their students obtain greater academic performance from those students than do teachers who set low expectations.
- The most important characteristics of effective schools are strong instructional leadership, a safe and orderly climate, schoolwide emphasis on basic skills, high teacher expectations for student achievement, and continuous assessment of pupil progress.[3]

The effective schools theory consists of a cluster of related generalizations about school organization and administration, the role of the principal and teachers, the climate of the school, methods of teaching, and student assessment. It is assumed that these generalizations validly describe an effective school and that they can be replicated in other schools. The anticipated result is that if these practices are implemented they will result in an increased number of effective schools.

My Reflections on Philosophy of Education: An E-mail Discussion About Theory

I received an interesting e-mail from a student who was using my book on philosophy of education. The student raised some questions about my use of the term *theory.* He indicated that he was a major in one of the natural sciences and had learned that a theory is a hypothesis that can be tested empirically and either proved or disproved through experimentation. I wrote this reply to the student in an e-mail:

Thank you for your e-mail. You make important points about scientific theories and their verification. I hope that you will share your ideas with the other students in the course. If my book should have another edition, I'll make every effort to emphasize scientific theory in the chapter.

I am not sure if your class is reading the entire book or just the chapter on theory. Essentially, the book is divided into three parts: philosophies, ideologies, and theories. I try to show relationships between the three areas. My intention in the chapter on theory was to give a descriptive sample of the term *theory* and its importance and use in educational philosophy and policy. Education in the United States is a public concern, vested in the states, and therefore, nonspecialists—legislators, parents, students—will be propounding theories as well as teachers and professionals.

Textbook writing is difficult in that authors are always pressed by publishers to include more items but to use fewer pages. In my chapter, I tried to highlight theories as they are often used in education—arising from experience, especially classroom experience, or coming from, being derived from, a more speculative philosophy or ideology. Some theories used in education, such as that supporting *No Child Left Behind,* can be verified, if you accept standardized test scores as a validation. However, other educators would hold that such empirical tests are incomplete in that you cannot test empirically for affect. An interesting exercise might be to contrast how the two theories of Evolution and Intelligent Design are debated in education and politics. Theory is a slippery, varied, much-used term. It can be used as Plato used it as speculation and application of the insights from speculation. Or as Aquinas used it as a plan of action derived from higher theological and metaphysical truths or doctrines. In education, a much-used word is *policy*—a theory of actions that will achieve desired results—as in effective schools theory. Then there is the very important kind of theory that you emphasize in your e-mail—scientific theories that are subject to empirical verification.

Your definition of theory is the standard one used in the physical and natural sciences—predictability based on testable data and applied or replicated in legitimate situations. Today, however, in the philosophy of science, the standard model of scientific theory is regarded as problematic. There is the contention that the very observations we wish to account for are themselves "givens" in the assumptions of the theory; there is the issue of under-determination in which contradictory data can be equally well explained by the extant theory. These issues are explained in the excellent work on scientific theory by Larry Laudan, *Science and Relativism: Some Key Controversies in the Philosophy of Science,* University of Chicago Press, 1990. You may want to read Laudan's arguments about theory.

I want to thank you for your intelligent and well-crafted statements in your e-mail. I'll try to do a more complete job if I have the opportunity to do another edition of the book. Best wishes on your career in education. —Gerald Gutek

CONSTRUCTING YOUR OWN PHILOSOPHY OF EDUCATION

Now that you have read and discussed the chapter on theory, reflect on your theories of education. How did you develop these theories? How have your theories evolved and changed? Do you plan to use the ideas expressed in the chapter about theory in your philosophy of education?

Conclusion

This chapter examined the relationships between theory and education. Theory was defined as a set of ideas or principles that are derived from a larger body of thought such as a philosophy or an ideology, are responses to issues, or are generalized from experience. It was emphasized that teachers, as they reflect on their experiences and use them to create teaching strategies, are theory builders.

A theory can be seen as a guide or a map that leads us through the educational terrain. It can take us from a set of ideas that point to action to the various dimensions of education such as schools, curriculum, instruction, teaching, and learning. It may arise from practice in these areas and lead to transferable generalizations about them.

Questions for Reflection and Discussion

1. How would you define an educational theory? Do you have any theories about effective education?
2. What expectations do you have about teaching as a career? How did you develop these expectations, and do these expectations form a theory?
3. In your opinion, what constitutes a competent teacher? Do your ideas about teacher competency constitute a theory of education?
4. When you enroll is a course in education, do you have some preconceptions about or anticipated outcomes for the course? What is the basis for these preconceptions? Do these preconceptions constitute a theory?
5. In class discussion, identify some of the major issues in American society. What educational theories have been proposed as reactions to these issues?

Topics for Inquiry and Research

1. Examine the requirements for your degree as presented in your institution's catalogue. Are these requirements based on a theory of education?
2. Interview several experienced teachers. As a result of your interviews, see whether there are some common features in their experiences that can be generalized into a theory of teaching and learning.
3. Obtain a copy of your state's guidelines for the approval of teacher education programs. Analyze the guidelines and determine whether they reflect an underlying theory of education.
4. Do some research on a recent trend in education such as standards, common core, authentic assessment, or constructivist movements. Determine whether these movements rest on a theory of education.
5. Access http://www.education.com/reference/article/theoriesoflearning/ and analyze the discussion of the relationship between theory and practice.

Internet Resources

For Constructivism, Behaviorism, and other learning theories, access http://crescentok.com/staff//education/theories.htm.

For the relationship between theory and practice, access http://www.education.com/reference/article/theoriesoflearning/.

For discussions of theory and practice in education, access http://www.teachersgarden.com/professionalresources/learningtheorists.html.

As you begin to read the next chapters on Essentialism, Perennialism, Progressivism, Social Reconstructionism, and Critical Theory, you might wish to refer back to this overview box.

Overview of Theories of Education

Theory	Aim	Curriculum	Educational Implications	Proponents
Essentialism (rooted in Idealism and Realism)	To educate useful and competent persons	Basic education: reading, writing, arithmetic, history, English, science, foreign languages, mathematics	Cultural maintenance and subjects that transmit the cultural heritage and contribute to socio-economic efficiency	Kandel Bagley Bestor
Perennialism (rooted in Realism and Thomism)	To cultivate rationality through exposure to the great works of Western civilization	Curriculum skills and subjects based on liberal arts and sciences, especially the great books of Western civilization	Introduce all students to the cultural heritage	Hutchins Adler Maritain
Progressivism (rooted in Pragmatism and Liberalism)	To educate individuals according to their interests and needs	Activities and projects	Instruction that features problem solving and group activities; teacher acts as a facilitator	Dewey Kilpatrick Johnson
Social Reconstruction (rooted in Pragmatism, Liberalism, Socialism)	To engage schools, teachers, and students in building a new society	A curriculum infused with social, political, economic, and environmental issues	To raise consciousness about the issues society faces and to bring about engagement in solving these issues	Counts Brameld Rugg
Critical Theory (rooted in Neo-Marxism and Postmodernism)	To raise consciousness about issues of marginalization and empowerment	Autobiographies about oppressed people; issues about marginalization and exploitation	Focus on local, site-based learning—that examines the real conditions impacting a school and its community	Freire Illich McLaren Giroux

Suggestions for Further Reading

Anyon, Jean. *Theory and Educational Research: Toward Critical Social Explanation.* New York: Routledge, 2009.

Archer, Margaret S. *Realist Social Theory: The Morphonetic Approach.* New York: Cambridge University Press, 1995.

Chambliss, J. J. *Educational Theory as Theory of Conduct.* Albany: State University of New York Press, 1987.

Collins, Randall. *The Sociology of Philosophies: A Global Theory of Intellectual Change.* Cambridge, MA: Harvard University Press, 1998.

Feinberg, Walter. *Understanding Education: Toward a Reconstruction of Educational Inquiry.* New York: Cambridge University Press, 1983.

Hare, William. *What Makes a Good Teacher: Reflections on Some Characteristics Central to the Educational Enterprise.* Ontario, Canada: Althouse Press, 1993.

Jackson, Philip. *Life in Classrooms.* New York: Teachers College Press, 1993.

Shunk, Dale. *Learning Theories: An Educational Perspective* (6th ed.). New York: Addison Wesley, 2011.

Silver, Harold. *Good Schools, Effective Schools: Judgments and Their Histories.* New York: Cassell, 1995.

Notes

1. Fred N. Kerlinger, *Foundations of Behavioral Research* (New York: Holt, Rinehart, and Winston, 1973), 9.
2. U.S. Department of Education, Office of the Secretary, *Back to School, Moving Forward: What "No Child Left Behind" Means for America's Communities* (Washington, DC: U.S. Department of Education, 2001), 6–7.
3. *What Works: Research About Teaching and Learning* (Washington, DC: U.S. Department of Education, 1986), 7, 17, 23, 45.

Essentialism and Education

William C. Bagley (1874–1946), a professor of education, who articulated the Essentialist position.

13

CHAPTER PREVIEW

Essentialism, a significant educational theory, has had remarkable staying power in American schools. This chapter discusses Essentialism's historical origins and philosophical relationships, the ideas of its major proponents, and its implications for education, schooling, curriculum, and teaching and learning.

We begin with some focusing definitions. The dictionary defines *essential* as absolutely necessary or indispensable, as something's essence, or as a basic or necessary fundamental element. The dictionary further defines Essentialism in education as a "doctrine that certain traditional concepts, ideals, and skills are essential to society and should be taught methodically to all students, regardless of individual ability, need, etc."[1] The words *necessary, indispensable, basic, traditional*, and *methodically* provide clues as to what we will be discussing as we analyze Essentialism. *Etcetera*, however, provides us with an open-ended exploration of the Essentialist terrain.

Essentialism, sometimes called basic education, is a rather straightforward theory that argues that schools are academic institutions and that their curricula should consist of fundamental generative skills and subject-matter disciplines. It specifies the school's primary function as preserving culture and society by transmitting the basic elements of human civilization. It emphasizes (1) a curriculum of basic skills and subjects; (2) learning as mastery of these skills and subjects that is monitored by consistently high verifiable standards; (3) schools as places of order, discipline, and efficient and effective instruction; and (4) the goal of organized education to prepare people to be productive, civil, and patriotic individuals. Currently, the standards and common core movements, the use of standardized tests to measure student academic achievement, and the No Child Left Behind Act provide evidence of Essentialism's continuing influence on American education and schooling. The chapter is organized into the following major topics:

- Essentialism's historical and philosophical rationale
- Essentialism's historical and philosophical roots
- William C. Bagley and Arthur E. Bestor, as leading Essentialist theorists
- The reaction against life adjustment education
- The relationships between Neo-Conservatism and Neo-Essentialism
- Philosophies and ideologies that either support or oppose Essentialism
- Essentialism's implications for education, schools, curriculum, and teaching and learning

CONSTRUCTING YOUR OWN PHILOSOPHY OF EDUCATION

As you read and discuss this chapter, reflect on your own educational and school experiences. Did your teachers emphasize basic skills such as reading, writing, and arithmetic? Did they emphasize subjects such as science, history, mathematics, and language and literature? Did they emphasize the need to be prepared for the next grade level? Do you find evidence of Essentialism in your own education and in your observations of the school curriculum and instruction? Are there aspects of Essentialism that appeal to you as a teacher? Do you plan to use Essentialism or some aspects of it in constructing your own philosophy of education?

ESSENTIALISM'S HISTORICAL AND PHILOSOPHICAL RATIONALE

Essentialism asserts that education properly involves learning the basic skills, arts, and sciences that have been useful in the past and will remain useful in the future. It forcefully argues that a genuine education requires learning the basic literary, mathematical, and technological skills needed to function effectively in civilized society and in studying the liberal arts and sciences to appreciate, understand, and participate in the culture. Historian Diane Ravitch attributes the term **essentialism** to Michael Demiashkevich (1891–1938), who in his *Introduction to the Philosophy of Education* (1935) contrasted Essentialism and Progressivism.

Essentialism: a theory that asserts education's primary mission is to transmit the civilized cultural heritage by teaching essential skills and subjects to students.

Essentialism, which Demiashkevich endorsed, aims to transmit the essentials of the social and cultural heritage by teaching students subject-matter disciplines such as mathematics, natural sciences, and history and forming their moral and ethical character. In contrast, Demiashkevich asserts that Progressivism encourages students to develop their own interests in whatever appears to be interesting and useful at the moment. For Demiashkevich, the Progressive goal of individual "growth" disconnected education from the cultural heritage's reservoir of the humanities and sciences.[2] Throughout the chapter, we shall use the historically derived term *Essentialism* to refer to the theory that education and schools should emphasize a curriculum of basic skills of literacy and mathematical computation and subject matter derived from the liberal arts and sciences.

Basic Education: a version of Essentialism that calls for a return to basic skills and subjects in the school curriculum.

Essentialism is sometimes called **basic education** in that the basics constitute essential learning. In arguing for Essentialism, Clifton Fadiman asserted that basic education emphasizes skills and subjects that have "generative power," or the potency to endow students "with the ability to learn the higher, more complex developments of these master subjects as well as the minor or self-terminating" ones. Such generative subjects deal with "language, whether or not one's own; forms, figures, and numbers; the laws of nature; the past; and the shape and behavior of our common home, the earth."[3]

Essentialism's basic educational themes are (1) the elementary curriculum should emphasize basic tool skills that contribute to literacy and numeracy; (2) the secondary curriculum should include history, mathematics, science, literature, and language; (3) a safe, orderly, and well-managed school environment is necessary for systematic learning; (4) students need to respect legitimate authority and practice civility, both in school and in society; (5) learning a skill or a subject requires effort and diligence on the part of students; and (6) teachers must have a thorough knowledge of the skills and subjects they teach and need to know how to transmit them effectively and efficiently to students.

ESSENTIALISM'S HISTORICAL AND PHILOSOPHICAL ROOTS

This section positions Essentialism in the back-and-forth movement, the curricular pendulum, in the history of American education. Then it discusses how Essentialists view the history of curriculum. After providing a historical perspective on Essentialism, the section discusses its philosophical roots.

In the history of American education, two longstanding polar positions are evident in the school curriculum. The metaphor of the pendulum, like that of a clock, can be used to illustrate these positions. At one pole of the pendulum are educational theorists, like the Essentialists, who argue that schools are primarily places for students to learn organized academic skills such as reading, writing, arithmetic, computer literacy, and civility, along with basic subjects such as history, mathematics, science, and English and foreign languages. At the other pole are theorists, such as Progressives, who counter that schools are multifunctional sites where children should be encouraged to grow and develop through experiences, process and collaborative activities, and projects. The multifunctional view contends that schools are places for children's and adolescents' socialization as well as academic learning. Schools in the United States today incorporate aspects from both poles of the curricular pendulum and include both academic and multifunctional aspects in their programs. As the curriculum pendulum swings to and fro, however, either the Essentialist academic perspective or the Progressive multifunctional socialization orientation has been dominant at different times.

For the multifunctional perspective, see the chapter on Progressivism and Education.

Essentialism and Public Education

Historically, Essentialists root their theory in the European liberal arts and science tradition that was transported to the United States and implemented in secondary schools such as the Latin grammar schools, the academies, and the academic high schools. They envision the origins of public education in the nineteenth-century common schools, which, for them, emphasized literacy—reading, writing, listening, spelling, and basic mathematical computation—as the essential version of elementary schooling that should continue today. In addition to cultivating essential skills, the common schools, through the teaching of American history, literature, natural science, music, and art, provided children with an essential cultural foundation. This foundation, commonly shared across generations, was necessary to construct an American national identity and develop an understanding of the origins and processes of political democracy. The common cultural foundation created a shared source of morals and ethics that, in public schools, was manifested by civility. The Essentialist curricular orientation also related education and schooling to economic productivity and to the United States' ability to compete successfully in the world economy.

In American education's recent history, Essentialism appears, if challenged, to retreat, to readjust to change, and then to reappear, as in the case of the basic education, standards, and common core movements. Although its name may change and there might be minor variations of its theme, Essentialism's core principles remain fundamentally constant and consistent. Despite challenges from educational reformers such as Pragmatists, Postmodernists, Liberals, Progressives, Social Reconstructionists, and Critical Theorists, Essentialism continues to influence curriculum and instruction in schools.

See the chapters on Pragmatism, Postmodernism, Liberalism, Progressivism, Social Reconstructionism, and Critical Theory.

In the nineteenth century, Essentialists emphasized the "three R's" (reading, writing, and 'rithmetic), Americanization of immigrants, patriotism, and mental discipline (the theory that certain subjects trained or disciplined the mind). In the 1930s, a group of educators opposed to Progressive education, led by William Chandler

Bagley, spearheaded the Essentialist movement. In the 1950s, Essentialism was voiced by educational theorists such as the historian Arthur E. Bestor, Jr. (1908–1994), who called for a return to the teaching of fundamental intellectual disciplines. In the 1970s and 1980s, the Council for Basic Education stimulated a revival of basic education. In the 1980s, the U.S. Commission on Excellence in Education's *A Nation at Risk*, reasserting basic Essentialist themes, added computer literacy to the list of basic skills and subjects. In the early twenty-first century, the **standards movement**, based on identifying benchmarks to measure academic progress, has exerted a profound impact on schools, curriculum, and instruction.

Standards Movement: a movement to specify levels of academic achievement, or benchmarks, to measure students' academic competencies.

Scholarly organizations such as the American Historical Association and the National Council for the Teaching of English, for example, have identified standards that signify a necessary knowledge base in their fields for students. Setting standards, the states mandated standardized testing in basic subjects such as reading and mathematics. In 2001, the No Child Left Behind Act required states to use standardized testing in reading as a requirement for local school districts to qualify for federal aid. In 2010, the Council of Chief State School Officers (CCSSO) and the National Governors Association for Best Practices (NGA Center) endorsed Common Core State Standards that emphasize the essential knowledge and rigorous content needed for students' academic success. Among the skills and subjects endorsed by the Partnership for 21st Century Skills are English, reading, language arts, world languages, arts, mathematics, economics, science, geography, history, government, and civics. Essentialists, from across history's decades, could agree with the Partnership's subject-matter orientation.

Essentialism: A Theory Derived from Practice and Reaction

For theory as a reaction and arising from practice, see the chapter on Theory and Education.

The earlier chapter on Theory and Education described theories derived from school situations and those derived as a reaction to events, trends, and movements. Essentialism's basic concepts—transmission, skills, subjects, sequence, order, discipline, and effort—are based on what Essentialists regard as effective schools, a well-structured curriculum, and academically sound methods and classroom practices. From these school-based practices, Essentialists have constructed an educational theory that, they believe, can be applied to all schools. The following generalizations are key elements in their theory (1) schools succeed when they have well-defined academic goals; (2) students need basic skills to succeed in education and life; (3) a subject-matter curriculum is the most effective way to transmit the cultural heritage; (4) teachers need to know their subject and how to teach it; and (5) students need to work hard at learning basic skills and subjects.

Essentialism has been a traditional reaction, a countertheory, against Progressivism and Social Reconstruction. It presents a skill and subject matter rationale against those who propose alternatives to traditional education such as project-based learning, an interdisciplinary curriculum, and collaborative activities. As a reaction against cultural and ethical relativism, Essentialists call for the renewal of traditional values of civility, hard work, and patriotism. As we proceed to discuss Essentialism as a theory of education, note how it arises from practice and is a reaction against certain trends in society and education.

Essentialism's Philosophical Roots

Although Essentialism is derived primarily from a historical perspective on education, it also can be examined philosophically. As a theory of education, Essentialism is heavily influenced by the importance of the liberal arts and sciences in Western education. It was also shaped by a history of curriculum that sees a valid curriculum organized into skills and subjects and valid instruction as primarily the transmission of the cultural heritage to the young.

In examining Essentialism philosophically, we can consider its root in the term **essence**, a concept found in the metaphysics of traditional philosophies such as Idealism and Realism.[4] Essence means that which is necessary to and indispensable about something—a human being, an object, a discipline, or a subject, for example. Essence refers to the intrinsic, fundamental, or basic character of something rather than its accidental, temporary, or incidental features. Related to education, what is necessary for a person to be educated and to have an education? Essentialists such as Bagley and Bestor answered this question more historically than philosophically—finding what is essential to education in the liberal arts and science tradition in the Western heritage. Essentialism asserts that certain basic ideas, skills, and bodies of knowledge, over the course of history, have proved essential to human culture and civilization and need to be transmitted to oncoming generations. Basic skills and certain bodies of knowledge can be formulated and organized into subjects that can and should be taught by adults to the young. Deliberate instruction as the **transmission** of basic skills and subjects from one generation to the next guarantees the maintenance and perpetuation of civilization. These fundamentals or essentials are the skills of literacy (reading and writing), computation (arithmetic), and using the computer. (Contemporary Essentialists would add computer skills to the essentials.) With these skills are the subjects of history, mathematics, science, languages, and literature. (A more extended discussion of the Essentialist curriculum follows later in the chapter.) Essentialists would argue that disengaging from this necessary cultural transmission, as suggested by Progressives, Reconstructionists, and Critical Theorists, places civilization in peril.

Essence: that which is necessary for something to be what it is; the intrinsic structure or core that defines a human being or an object.

Transmission: curriculum and instruction that deliberately transmits or passes along essential skills and subjects from one generation to the next, thereby maintaining a literate and civilized society.

For their alternatives to transmitting the traditional curriculum, see the chapters on Progressivism, Social Reconstructionism, and Critical Theory.

Essentialists want this cultural transmission to take place efficiently and effectively through methods that have stood the test of time. Because there is much to learn and a limited time in which to learn it, teachers should plan, organize, and present lessons carefully and efficiently. Schools, then, are academic agencies established by society to transmit basic skills and knowledge to its children and youth.

Philosophically, Essentialism's premise that schools should transmit an existing body of knowledge, the arts and sciences, rests on a concept of antecedent reality. *Antecedent* means that this knowledge exists before we, as individuals come on the scene. In other words, knowledge, organized into skills and subjects, exists before the students enter the school in kindergarten. The curriculum is about this **antecedent knowledge** and the school's purpose is to transmit it.

Antecedent Knowledge: subject matter that exists prior to a student's learning of it; knowledge that is already there to be learned.

It does not depend on whether students are interested in learning it; it is important for them to learn it, just as it was for the students who preceded them in school and in society. Although teachers can motivate students to study this antecedent knowledge, they cannot ethically abandon their historical mission when the going gets tough. Essentialists are opposed by an array of adversaries who decry their theory as traditionalism. Pragmatists, Progressives, Postmodernists, and Critical Theorists all oppose Essentialism. For Pragmatists, antecedent knowledge is not based on the learner's experience, nor does it relate to the problems of life. Progressives contend that the Essentialist curriculum ignores children's interests and needs. Postmodernists and Critical Theorists see Essentialist curriculum as imposing the privileged "official knowledge" mandated by a dominant group on marginalized people.

We shall return to the discussion of Essentialism's philosophical and ideological relationships later in the chapter. At this point, we discuss the educational ideas of two leading Essentialist theorists: William Chandler Bagley and Arthur E. Bestor, Jr.

WILLIAM CHANDLER BAGLEY

In his definitive biography of William Chandler Bagley, J. Wesley Null calls him "one of the most invisible of the truly prominent educators of the twentieth century."[5] Because of Bagley's commitment to social progress, Null positions him within

For Kilpatrick and Counts, see the chapters on Progressivism and Social Reconstruction.

Progressivism but qualifies him as a "disciplined progressive" for insisting that academic disciplines are central to education and schooling. Bagley opposed what he considered to be extreme Progressives, such as William H. Kilpatrick, who substituted projects for academic subjects and Reconstructionists, such as George S. Counts, who wanted schools and teachers to build a new social order.

Bagley, who devoted his career to teacher education, was a professor of education at Montana State College, Oswego Normal School, the University of Illinois, and Teachers College, Columbia University. Progressives such as Kilpatrick and Reconstructionists such as Counts and Harold Rugg, closely identified with John Dewey, were among Teachers College's leading professors. Bagley, in the company of the comparative educator Isaac Kandel (1881–1965), found himself in the minority.[6] Bagley and Kandel shared a vision of teacher education that integrated a knowledge core in the liberal arts and sciences and professional education studies in the historical, philosophical, comparative, and psychological foundations of education. Teaching methods, for them, properly integrated the content of subjects such as mathematics, science, English, and history with the methods of instruction that related to that subject and to students' prior academic knowledge.

Bagley was the spokesman for a like-minded group of Essentialist educators who met at the convention of the American Association of School Administrators (AASA) in February 1938. In outlining the "Essentialist Platform," Bagley stated that (1) U.S. elementary school students were failing to meet the "standards of achievement in the fundamentals of education" attained in other countries; (2) U.S. secondary school students academically lagged behind the eighteen-year-olds of other countries; (3) increasingly large numbers of high school students were essentially illiterate and could not read effectively, and because of deficiencies at the primary and intermediate grade levels, remedial reading programs had to be instituted in many high schools; (4) in addition to declining literacy, notable deficiencies existed in mathematics and grammar; and (5) despite increased educational expenditures in the United States, there was a noticeable increase in the rates of serious crime.

Bagley identified two specific causes of the United States' educational malaise: (1) dominant educational theories, such as extreme Progressivism, were "essentially enfeebling," and (2) the relaxation of academic standards in many school systems had led to the policy of widespread "social promotion." Bagley chastised Progressives who overemphasized the child's freedom, interests, and play, and sacrificed discipline, effort, and work. For Bagley, Progressive education had contributed to the "complete abandonment in many school systems of rigorous standards of scholastic achievement for promotion from grade to grade, and the passing of all pupils 'on schedule.'"[7] Instead of a curriculum based on systematic and sequential learning and consecutive, cumulative, and orderly academic development, the Progressives had substituted an undifferentiated program of activities, projects, and incidental learning. Bagley's condemnation of social promotion was similar to today's arguments that students should master minimal competencies before being promoted to a higher grade or being awarded a diploma.

Bagley was joined by other professional educators such as Michael Demiashkevich, Walter H. Ryle, M. L. Shane, and Gary M. Whipple, who, calling themselves Essentialists, urged U.S. schools, teachers, and administrators to return to the basic skills of recording, computing, measuring, U.S. history, health instruction, natural science, and the fine and industrial arts. In taking their stance, the Essentialists asked:

> Should not our public schools prepare boys and girls for adult responsibility through systematic training in such subjects as reading, writing, arithmetic, history, and English, requiring mastery of such subjects, and, when necessary, stressing discipline and obedience?[8]

Arguing that Progressive education had created discontinuity between the generations, Bagley urged U.S. educators and schools to provide each generation with "possession of a common core of ideas, meanings, understandings, and ideals representing the most precious elements of the human heritage."[9]

Bagley as an Educational Theorist

Bagley's theory of education needs to be examined from two related perspectives: (1) the elementary and secondary school curriculum and (2) teacher education. Bagley, as an educational moderate, deliberately avoided what he regarded as extreme positions. For Bagley and his colleague Kandel, education's vital center rested in the liberal arts and sciences, the traditional core of undergraduate study in colleges and universities. Bagley, similar to the Perennialists, distinguished between a general education (the education that everyone should have) and vocational education (the education that some people need for a specific occupation).[10] A general education for all rested on the liberal arts and sciences. The elementary curriculum's generative skills of language—reading, writing, listening, and composition—were the necessary processes that students need to learn to approach the secondary school's academic subjects—mathematics, history, sciences, languages and literature, geography, and civics.

For general education, see the chapter on Perennialism and Education.

Standing at education's vital center, the liberal arts core needed to be maintained and transmitted as a body of indispensable and necessary skills and subjects. Reacting against extreme Progressivism, Bagley defended the schools' primary academic function as transmitting the cultural core. Dogmatic, child-centered Progressives, Bagley believed, sacrificed teaching necessary skills and subjects because of their naïve anti-intellectual view that children's interests should determine the curriculum. In their attempts to replace skills and subjects with children's interests, well-meaning but misguided educational sentimentalists and romantics were jeopardizing the school's necessary role in transmitting the cultural heritage. While teachers should not ignore children's interests, Bagley advised them to be guided by what students really needed to know—the essential skills and subjects.

For Bagley, Social Reconstructionism constituted another extremist position. Reconstructionists, such as Counts and Rugg, would politicize schools by indoctrinating children in a utopian ideology that sought to remake society. Bagley reasoned that students should study history and government; however, politically ambitious theorists should not distort these subjects into ideological pieces to accomplish goals external to education. Bagley's arguments against extreme educational positions did not make him popular with Progressive and Reconstructionist professors at Teachers College. If Bagley were alive today, he would most likely find Postmodernism and Critical Theory to be a contemporary extremist assault on the liberal arts core that stood at education's vital center.

Throughout his professional career, Bagley was a teacher educator. His approach to teacher education was based on (1) the school as the transmitter of the liberal arts and science heritage and (2) educating teachers who had studied the liberal arts and sciences and were highly skilled in transmitting this educational and cultural heritage to students. Teachers needed to be trained to prepare students to learn by motivating them and creating a readiness and desire to learn. While children learn many things incidentally in their daily experiences in and out of school, a teacher's primary function in the school is to stay focused on essential skills and subjects. Teachers must know the essential skills and subjects before they attempt to teach them—how they developed, their key concepts and vocabularies, and their structural logic as intrinsic bodies of knowledge. They need to know how the arts and sciences, as the repository of civilized knowledge, inform and contribute to society, economy, and culture. Then they need to know how to teach them effectively and efficiently. This means that teachers need to develop methods that enable them to transmit the skills and subjects in an orderly and cumulative **sequence** to students. Bagley believed that methods of instruction needed to be integrated with the skill and subject and not be separated from them as some Progressives insisted. As a teacher educator, Bagley believed that teachers should study the history, philosophy, and psychology of education as a necessary foundational base for their profession.

Sequence: instruction organized on the internal logic or chronology of a skill or subject that is taught in an orderly fashion.

THE CONFLICT BETWEEN ESSENTIALISTS AND PROGRESSIVES. Bagley, using an almost Hegelian format of thesis and antithesis, analyzed the "crux of the conflict" between Progressives and Essentialists.[11] His analysis illustrates the derivation of Essentialist theory as a reaction against Progressivism. Bagley argued that whereas Progressives emphasized children's interests in learning, Essentialists stressed the need for effort in mastering lessons; whereas Progressives stressed freedom to learn, Essentialists supported the need for discipline; whereas Progressives exalted individual experience, Essentialists prized the experience of the human race over time. Further, Progressives emphasized the psychological organization of the curriculum in contrast to the Essentialists' emphasis on the logical and chronological organization of subjects. Finally, Progressives emphasized learning through activities and projects; whereas Essentialists maintained the need for subject-matter organization. After outlining the polar opposites, Bagley then sought to reconcile them in a Hegelian-like synthesis. He argued that interest may lead children to problems, but they need effort to pursue them to their solution. Further, not all interests are equally important. Some are more important than others because they lead to matters of permanent concern. The view that some areas of the curriculum are related to permanent cultural matters was a serious contention between Progressives and Essentialists. Another important difference centered on the role of teachers. Bagley argued that the teacher, as an adult representative of the culture, is to guide learners to a definite goal, in contrast to the Progressives' ambiguous concept of "open-endedness."[12]

Essentialism's Revival in Neo-Essentialism

Although Essentialist practices prevailed in many schools, Essentialism was either dismissed or relegated to a footnote in the history and philosophy of education. It now enjoys a revival in Null's biographies of Bagley and Kandel and in Diane Ravitch's interpretation of American educational history.[13]

Bagley's assessment of educational deficits in late 1930s America would be reiterated several times in the following years. Arthur Bestor, Jr., and other critics in the 1950s and the proponents of *A Nation at Risk* in the 1980s would mount similar arguments. Critics would compare American students' academic achievement with those of other countries; find deficits in the American students' achievement, often attributed to Progressive education; and then call for a standardized skill and subject-matter curriculum for all students. Among these educational deficits, identified by the Essentialists and echoed by Bestor and the proponents of basic education and the standards movement were:

- American students' academic achievement rates were lower than those of students in other industrialized countries.
- The de-emphasis on logic, chronology, system, and sequence in the curriculum has caused a decline of academic standards in the United States.
- Social promotion policies promoted students who were often functionally illiterate and unprepared for the next higher levels of education.

THE REACTION AGAINST LIFE ADJUSTMENT EDUCATION

The Essentialist opposition to Life Adjustment Education illustrates how educational theory arises as reaction to a counter movement or trend. In the late 1940s and early 1950s, the decades after World War II, Life Adjustment sparked a controversy in education that resembled the reoccurring debate between Progressives and Essentialists. It needs to be noted that some Progressives, especially those associated with Dewey's Experimentalism, did not regard life adjustment as a genuine assertion of Progressive education. For these Experimentalist Progressives, genuine education required much more than an adjustment to society; it involved a transaction between individuals and their natural and social environments.

Life Adjustment Education

In 1945, Charles Prosser (1871–1952), a long-time leader in vocational education, inaugurated the life adjustment movement. Arguing that 60 percent of American secondary school students were underserved by existing academic college preparatory and vocational education programs, Prosser called for **life adjustment education**. For Prosser and his life adjustment colleagues, it was the time to restructure the high school into a broad-based multifunctional institution where adolescent growth and development were related to salable vocational work skills that would lead students to a socially satisfying and economically productive adulthood. The emphasis on academic subjects would be replaced by different curricular linchpins—students' personal, social, economic, health, and recreational needs.

Life Adjustment Education: a curriculum based on students' practical and immediate interests, needs, issues, and problems that leads to a satisfactory adjustment to living and working.

Prosser and the other life adjustment educators did not intend that a new course called life adjustment be merely added to the traditional curriculum. They wanted life adjustment at the heart, at the vital center, of the secondary school curriculum. This plan to replace the liberal arts and science core raised the ire of Essentialist defenders of traditional subject matter. Life adjustment educators often used the term **infusion**. Infuse life adjustment into the entire curriculum, they said. To get the new curriculum in place required serious modification of existing courses and the creation of new ones. All existing courses, including language, mathematics, science, and history, would need to be revised to deal with the real problems of living rather than academic preparation for college. With the curriculum so broadened to include all areas of life, then the nature of the school itself, and the teacher, would need to be expansively reconceptualized. The school was to be a multifunctional agency that addressed all areas of human life, including, but not exclusively limited to, academic ones. The school of the future would deal with education in very broad terms that were social, personal, civic, and economic, as well as academic. Further, because the concept of adjustment involved much that was psychological and emotional as well as intellectual, the life adjustment school had to deal with the students' total well-being, especially their healthy adjustment to society.

Infusion: to integrate a concept or process throughout the entire school curriculum so that it affects all skills, subjects and experiences.

The 1950s and early 1960s saw a strong and concerted reaction against life adjustment. Unlike the earlier Essentialist reaction against Progressivism that came primarily from a group of professors of education led by Bagley, the reaction against life adjustment came largely from critics outside of professional education. For example, Hyman Rickover, a leading critic, was an admiral in the U.S. Navy, and Arthur E. Bestor, Jr., was a history professor.

Admiral Hyman G. Rickover

Admiral Hyman G. Rickover (1900–1986), a U.S. Navy officer, was a persistent national critic of American education. Known as the "father of the atomic submarine," Rickover had supervised the scientists and engineers who developed the first U.S.

nuclear-powered submarine, the Nautilus.[14] Because of his interest in national defense and military technology during the Cold War, Rickover was especially concerned with the academic preparation of mathematicians, scientists, and engineers. This interest led him to examine mathematics and science education in American secondary schools. Reiterating some of the earlier Essentialist criticisms, Rickover found American secondary schools were failing to educate students well in mathematics and science. Comparing U.S. schools to those in other countries such as Switzerland, Germany, and the Soviet Union, Rickover found American students lacking the mathematical and scientific knowledge needed in a technological era. While American high school students were being infused with life adjustment courses, European secondary students were engaged in the rigorous academic study of history, mathematics, and the sciences. In contrast to American students, European students, upon completion of secondary school, had mastered not only their own native language but also knew one or two foreign languages.[15] Rickover criticized public schools for failing to provide challenging academic curricula for intellectually gifted students.[16] Anticipating academic specialty magnet and charter schools, Rickover proposed establishing model schools for the top 20 percent of academically talented students.

Arthur E. Bestor, Jr.

A leading critic of life adjustment education was historian Arthur E. Bestor, Jr. The son of Arthur E. Bestor, Sr., the director of the famed Chautauqua Institution in New York, Bestor was a scion of a distinguished academic family. At the time of his major critiques of American education, Bestor was a history professor at the University of Illinois in Urbana, where he taught courses in American history, historical methods, and U.S. constitutional history. Although advocating a new approach to Essentialism, Bestor, like Bagley, was not a political conservative. Similar to Bagley's identification with the broad progressive movement, Bestor was a liberal on academic freedom and civil rights. A member of the American Civil Liberties Union, he served on its Illinois board of directors. He was also a member of the National Association for the Advancement of Colored People. In education, however, he was a traditionalist. Bestor was a major figure in the Council for Basic Education, serving as its first president in 1956–1957. His most important books on education were *Educational Wastelands* (1953) and *The Restoration of Learning* (1955).[17]

In *The Restoration of Learning*, Bestor, like Bagley, identified the school's primary purpose; it is an academic institution, a place of thorough and disciplined intellectual development. He argued that life adjustment education had spawned an anti-intellectual ideology that diverted schools from their primary academic purpose to "trivial" aims that separated the curriculum from "the disciplines of science and scholarship."[18]

According to Bestor, (1) academic standards in U.S. public schools had declined because of an anti-intellectual educational ideology that separated schools from the scientific and scholarly disciplines, and (2) a narrowly educated group of professional educators, administrators, and department of education bureaucrats at the state level controlled entry into the teaching profession by manipulating certification requirements. Bestor urged that the trend to anti-intellectualism be reversed and that the public school curriculum be based on the intellectual disciplines of English, foreign languages, history, mathematics, and science.

Intellectual Discipline: Arthur Bestor's argument that the curriculum should consist of the fundamental disciplines, historically developed in Western culture.

Like Bagley's Essentialist rationale, Bestor's educational theory was historically rather than philosophically based. Both Bestor and Bagley emphasized the importance of the liberal arts and science core. However, Bagley, grounded in teacher education, constructed a strategy that integrated subject content with methods of instruction.

In *The Restoration of Learning*, Bestor established a criterion based on **intellectual disciplines**. Embedded in Bestor's theory is a conception of American democracy that emphasizes the rule of reasonable and intelligent citizens. An intelligently functioning democracy is a government of law, orderly parliamentary processes, and due process guarantees for all citizens. Bestor expressed an Essentialist theory of basic education that provides:

> sound training in the fundamental ways of thinking represented by history, science, mathematics, literature, language, art and other disciplines evolved in the course of mankind's long quest for usable knowledge, cultural understanding, and intellectual power.[19]

Bestor's terms "fundamental ways of thinking" and "mankind's long quest for usable knowledge" reveal his disciplinary and historically grounded approach to educational theory. Historically validated intellectual disciplines are fundamental in the school curriculum since they are basic to civilized life. In the elementary school, reading, writing, and arithmetic provide indispensable generative skills. A generative skill produces an effect that can be transferred and used in other operations. For example, reading as a skill can be transferred to many other reading-related functions such as reading books, newspapers, magazines, and information found on the Internet. Skill in using a keyboard, which originated in using a typewriter, can be used electronically on a computer or iPad or by texting on a smartphone.

For Bestor, the essential subjects in the secondary school curriculum are science, mathematics, history, English, and foreign languages. These intellectual disciplines, originating in the liberal arts and sciences, provide knowledge, insights, and methods for understanding the culture and for solving personal, social, political, and economic problems.

Bestor's Theoretical Rationale

Bestor's rationale began with his concern that American public education was failing to provide the intellectual disciplines needed in a democratic society. He attributed this deficiency to an erroneous view of democratic education advanced by some professional educators. (To understand Bestor's rationale, it is important to distinguish educators by type. There are liberal arts and science professors like Bestor. Professional educators are professors of education and educational administrators.) According to Bestor, some professional educators believed that the subject-matter emphasis on intellectual disciplines was an undemocratic legacy from the past when only a small elite had attended secondary schools and colleges and universities. Since the intellectual disciplines were once reserved for aristocratic elites, professional educators developed an educational alternative. Their serious mistake was that of sorting students into tracks in which the intellectually brighter students went to the academic track and other students were placed in non-academic general or vocational tracks. In their misapplication of the past to the present, professional educators had failed to realize that the requirements of the modern age made an intellectual education the democratic right of all.

Bestor charged that professional educators, no longer content to deal with teaching methods, had usurped and monopolized curriculum making. Curriculum construction, he argued, is best exercised by the scholars and scientists who are experts in their academic disciplines. According to Bestor, some professional educators had distorted Progressive education into "regressive education." By introducing life adjustment education, they had weakened the great intellectual disciplines. As a consequence, too much of public education had become antidemocratic and anti-intellectual.

Bestor's educational agenda emphasized two fundamental principles: (1) providing disciplined intellectual education to every future citizen and (2) providing opportunity for advanced study to all who possessed a genuine intellectual capacity and a willingness to develop their intellectual powers.[20] These two principles served as the basis of the school's primary responsibilities of: (1) providing a standard program of intellectual training in the fundamental disciplines geared to the needs of serious students and the capacities of the upper two-thirds of the school population; (2) providing advanced learning opportunities for academically gifted students; (3) providing programs for the highest third of the school population that are balanced with adequate remedial programs for the lowest third, the slow learners; (4) providing physical education for all children that is distinguished from interschool athletics; and (5) providing a diversity of offerings to include certain areas of vocational training.[21]

Bestor's Proposed Curriculum

With intellectual disciplines at the core, Bestor developed an Essentialist, or basic, education curriculum. He prescribed the same curriculum for all students. There is no tracking of selected students into non-academic areas.

During the first four, five, or six years of elementary school, reading, writing, and arithmetic are the necessary generative tool skills. The elementary school student should also be introduced to the structures and methods of the natural sciences, geography, and history.[22]

Junior high school, the grades from six or seven to nine, marks the beginning of the organized and systematic study of the academic disciplines. Commencing with algebra, students begin a transition to more abstract mathematical reasoning. History is organized chronologically. From the generalized natural science studied earlier, students make a transition to the separate disciplines of biology, physics, and chemistry. Instruction in foreign languages moves forward to more analysis of grammar.

Senior high school students are to use increasingly abstract reasoning as they systematically study a subject. Mathematics is continued through advanced algebra, plane and analytical geometry, trigonometry, and calculus. The systematic study of chemistry, physics, and biology creates the necessary knowledge base in science. History's chronological pattern and structure are emphasized. Students learn to use the English language with accuracy, lucidity, and graceful style. One foreign language is mastered and a second begun.[23]

Once they have mastered the prescribed academic essential subjects, students can choose to enter college or a vocational program. Training in the liberating disciplines prepares a person for intellectual life, citizenship, a vocation, and a profession.

My Reflection on Professor Bestor as a Teacher

As I reflect on my own education, I have had teachers who were traditionalists and Essentialists and also those who were Progressives and Reconstructionists. For example, my doctoral adviser and dissertation director was Archibald Anderson, a leading Progressive historian of education. I also completed courses offered by William O. Stanley, a noted Reconstructionist educator. However, to illustrate Essentialism, I reflect on my memory of Professor Arthur E. Bestor, Jr., as a teacher.[24] As a graduate student in history at the University of Illinois in the late 1950s and early 1960s, I enrolled in two courses offered by Professor Bestor: Historical Methods and American Constitutional History. Professor Bestor's approach to teaching illustrates his theory of education as centering on intellectual disciplines.

Professor Bestor consistently came to these courses meticulously prepared with an antecedent view of what he would teach. The syllabi for the courses were precise and specific, and they clearly told students his expectations for their work. There were no open spaces in the course where we would put aside the planned sequence to discuss a current event. As a teacher, Professor Bestor stayed on course and expected us to stay on it with him.

The course on historical methods was designed to prepare us to be historians; it dealt with primary sources and documents and how these sources were to be identified, read, analyzed, and interpreted. Bestor was not a presentist who read the past in terms of the present. Rather, the past needed to be seen as events that occurred as people were in an actual situation in human experience. Part of the course was lectures, but another part consisted of individual work with primary sources. We were to interpret a set of documents from the early nineteenth century that dealt with the controversy between Robert Owen and William Maclure at New Harmony, Indiana, over their financial obligations. Bestor, at the time, was writing what would become an award-winning book, *Backwoods Utopias,* about Robert Owen's community at New Harmony. Later in my career, as I was doing my own research on the educators at New Harmony, I found out that Bestor had undertaken the challenging work of organizing the documents at the site into an archive that he and other scholars could use. I was grateful that he had done his work so well.

Another individual exercise required me to prepare a thesis proposal, with a projected outline and a tentative bibliography. I wrote a proposal for a thesis on George E. Brennan, a rather obscure Illinois Democratic leader in the 1920s. Each student had an individual conference with Dr. Bestor. He critiqued my proposal as not being historically significant (Brennan was a very minor figure) and advised me that the sources were too few to do solid historical analysis. In providing this critique, there was no exchange of pleasantries—no real questions about why I wanted to do this study. The professor stayed on task and criticized the project as a mentor, senior experienced historian, advising a novice. I dropped my plan. I would later write my doctoral dissertation on George S. Counts, a highly significant educator. I later revised my dissertation into two books on Counts.

While Bestor used lecturing and individual critiques, there was also a field trip in the course. We went to Springfield, Illinois, the state capital, to visit the state historical archives, where the staff led a tour of the building and the collections. I was excited to see actual documents related to the events of the past, especially to Abraham Lincoln.

Bestor's course on American Constitutional History was done entirely by lecture. He was always meticulously prepared and well organized. The main points of the lecture were consistently clear and presented with sufficient supporting background to establish the context for a particular judicial decision and a perspective on its significance in American law. I do not recall students asking questions or there being discussions. There was a body of knowledge, a subject, that the professor was expert in and transmitted to us.

Professor Bestor left the University of Illinois and I went on to study the history and philosophy of education. Maybe coincidently or perhaps because of my work on the New Harmony project that Bestor had given us, I found myself interested in education at New Harmony. I encountered an educational pioneer by the name of Joseph Neef, who had studied with the noted Swiss educator, Johann Heinrich Pestalozzi (1747–1827). Neef wrote one of the first books on teaching methods to be published in English in the United States in the early nineteenth century. Early in my career as a historian and philosopher of education, I decided to write a biography of Neef, but needed support for travel expenses to use the New Harmony's archive that Bestor had been instrumental in organizing. With some trepidation, I wrote to Dr. Bestor, requesting a letter of support for a grant that I was applying for from the National Humanities Foundation. Bestor wrote the letter of support, I received the grant, and I wrote a book about Joseph Neef.

NEO-ESSENTIALISM, BASIC EDUCATION, AND NEO-CONSERVATISM

Essentialism's revival, as Basic Education, had significant implications for contemporary American education at the end of the twentieth century and into the twenty-first century. In the 1980s, Neo-Conservatives appropriated some aspects of Basic Education. The resulting mixture of Neo-Essentialism and Neo-Conservatism set the stage for

For Neo-Conservatism, see the chapter on Conservatism and Education.

A Nation at Risk, which, in turn, led to the standards movement and to the No Child Left Behind Act. Neo-Conservatism had been gathering momentum since the turbulent 1960s and was victorious with Ronald Reagan's election as U.S. President in 1980. Like the earlier theories of Bagley and Bestor, the Basic Education movement emphasized skills and subjects. However, its ideological relationships to Neo-Conservatism differed from the orientation of Bagley and Bestor. Although Bagley's Essentialists in the 1930s were concerned with the effects on American democracy of the economic Great Depression and the rise of totalitarianism in Europe, they argued against politicizing schools. Bestor, a liberal, saw his version of basic education as advancing democracy in the general sense, rather than with a particular political ideology.

The Basic Education revival began as a rather amorphous movement that attracted people from outside of schools rather than professional educators. The slogan "back-to-the-basics" covered wide-ranging criticisms about public education, such as:

- Overly permissive Progressive educators, by neglecting the basics, had weakened American education, causing functional illiteracy and ethical indifference.
- Values clarification and secular humanism in public schools had undermined traditional values of industriousness, honesty, and patriotism.
- Schools and teachers need to be held accountable not only for students' academic success but also for their failure.
- A plethora of so-called curricular innovations such as the "new math," "new science," and "new social studies," process-learning, and constructivism had replaced the necessary basics.
- Social promotion policies move children and adolescents through the public schools without adequate assessments to determine their academic competencies.
- Using schools for social engineering rather than teaching academic skills and subjects had confused the purposes of education, especially at the high school level.

Supporters of the revived basic education had mixed motives in that they knew what they were against, but not always what they were for. For example, some business organizations claimed that academically deficient public schools were not training students in the skills and competencies needed in a technologically changing economy. Other organizations, decrying increasing property taxes for schools, wanted school budgets trimmed by eliminating what they called "unnecessary frills and fads." Of growing ideological importance were the arguments of individuals who wanted to return to an idealized version of schooling, in which public schools provided instruction in clearly defined skills and subjects and instilled traditional values of patriotism, telling the truth, hard work, competition, and abstinence from sex until marriage. They charged that Liberals, Progressives, Reconstructionists, and other radicals who supported values clarification, cultural relativism, and secular humanism had confused the meanings of knowledge and values. The United States, with its rising rates of teen pregnancy, violence, crime, and drug addiction, desperately needed a return to traditional values.

The values issue generated major criticisms of public schools from what became known as the "religious right," a group largely made up of fundamentalist Christians, but also including members of other religions. The ascendancy of faith-based politics saw demands for prayer in public schools, the teaching of Creationism and Intelligent Design in science courses parallel to Darwin's theory of evolution, and the freedom of educational choice through state-paid vouchers that could be used in private and parochial schools as well as public schools.

Educational issues took center stage in American politics. Some conservative politicians campaigned for office as champions of basic education. They attacked declining academic standards and the lack of discipline in the schools, and emphasized the need to restore academic quality in public schools. Some also drew support from the religious right by urging prayer in the schools along with an emphasis on teaching "sound moral values." Ronald Reagan, keenly aware of the power of education as a national issue, kept it in the forefront of his administration, from 1981 to 1989.

A Nation at Risk

Reagan, guided by his effective Secretary of Education, Terrel Bell (1921–1996), advanced an educational agenda that integrated themes from Essentialism and basic education with Neo-Conservatism. Reagan's agenda sought to (1) improve the public schools' academic quality by emphasizing a basic subject curriculum; (2) encourage effective schools with strong principals and high teacher expectations; (3) relate education to national economic productivity; and (4) reduce indiscipline and violence in classrooms by insisting on high standards of behavior and performance.

In August 1981, Bell appointed a National Commission on Excellence in Education, chaired by David L. Gardner, President of the University of California. The Commission undertook a comprehensive review of the quality of education in the country's schools and colleges, did a comparative study of academic performance in the United States and other countries, examined the relationships between college admission requirements and the high school curriculum, and made recommendations to restore excellence to American education. In 1983, the Commission issued *A Nation at Risk.*

Similar to the earlier Essentialist Platform and Rickover's and Bestor's calls for a return to rigorous academic standards, *A Nation at Risk* warned that "the educational foundations of our society are presently being eroded by a rising tide of mediocrity that threatens our very future as a Nation and a people."[25] The National Commission on Excellence reported its findings:

- Secondary school curricula have been homogenized, diluted, and diffused to the point that they no longer have a central purpose.[26]
- In many other industrialized nations, courses in mathematics (other than arithmetic or general mathematics), biology, chemistry, physics, and geography start in grade 6 and are required of all students. The time spent on these subjects, based on class hours, is about three times that spent by even the most science-oriented U.S. students, i.e., those who select 4 years of science and mathematics in secondary school.[27]
- In many schools, the time spent learning how to cook and drive counts as much toward a high school diploma as the time spent studying mathematics, English, chemistry, U.S. history, or biology.[28]

Emphasizing a content-oriented subject-matter curriculum, the Commission recommended

> that State and local high school graduation requirements be strengthened and that, at a minimum, all students seeking a diploma be required to lay the foundations in the Five New Basics by taking the following curriculum during their 4 years of high school: (a) 4 years of English; (b) 3 years of mathematics; (c) 3 years of science; (d) 3 years of social studies; and (e) one-half year of computer science. For the college-bound, 2 years of foreign language in high school are strongly recommended in addition to those taken earlier.[29]

The Commission also recommended

> that schools, colleges, and universities adopt more rigorous and measurable standards, and higher expectations, for academic performance and student conduct, and that 4-year colleges and universities raise their requirements for admission. This will help students do their best educationally with challenging materials in an environment that supports learning and authentic accomplishment.[30]

A Nation at Risk stimulated other national reports and educational recommendations that emphasized basic skills and subjects. For example, the Task Force on Education for Economic Growth, in *Action for Excellence,* stressed basic skills and competencies for productive employment in a structurally and technologically changing society. The College Board, in *Academic Preparation for College,* identified the basic academic competencies or "broad intellectual skills essential to effective work" in college as reading, speaking and listening, writing, mathematics, reasoning, and studying. Added to this conventional list of tool skills was a knowledge of computer processes, terminology, and application.[31] The College Board identified the basic academic subjects that provide "the detailed knowledge and skills" for effective college work as English, the arts, mathematics, science, social studies, and foreign languages.[32]

The Standards Movement

The essential theme of the standards movement is that the improvement of American education requires high academic standards, or benchmarks, to measure students' academic achievement. For example, an empirical measurable goal should be predetermined to indicate whether a student is reading at grade level or has reached a specific level of achievement in mathematics and science. Students are assessed by using standardized tests to determine whether they are achieving at the set standard in the subject or below or above it. Using statistics based on the performance of students in a given school, that school could be judged to be performing at, above, or below the set standard. Advocates of setting standards and measuring them by standardized tests argue that student performance in a particular school could be used to determine the competency of the teachers and administrators in that school. Progressives and Critical Theorists contend that using standardized tests forces teachers to "teach for the test" rather than to genuinely educate students. The standards movement gained a strong footing in many states. A pronounced endorsement of standards came with the enactment of the federal Education Act of 2001, No Child Left Behind.

For their views on testing, see the chapters on Progressivism and Critical Theory.

No Child Left Behind

The No Child Left Behind Act, promoted by President George W. Bush, rested on the premise running through the standards movement—students' academic achievement could be measured by using standardized tests. Schools in which large numbers of students failed to perform at the set standard of achievement could be identified and remediated to improve performance. If this comparative identification of school performance were left undone, children in low-performing schools would be left behind academically. The rationale for the Act followed the usual Essentialist–Basic Education strategy of identifying deficiencies and prescribing measures to correct them. Among the deficiencies identified were:

> Today, nearly 70 percent of inner city fourth graders are unable to read at a basic level on national reading tests. Our high school seniors trail students in Cyprus and South Africa in international math tests. And nearly a third of our college freshmen find they must take a remedial course before they are able to even begin regular college level courses.[33]

Although the Act as comprehensive legislation deals with many areas of education, certain key features, reflecting the standards movement, reinforce a Neo-Essentialist–Basic Education approach. It identifies the key basics as reading and mathematics and requires using standardized tests to determine students' achievement in these essential subjects. The Act mandates that to qualify for federal aid, school districts must establish annual assessments in reading and mathematics for every student in grades three through eight. It holds school districts accountable for improving the performance of disadvantaged students as well as the overall student population. Schools and districts failing to make adequate yearly progress are to be identified and remediated. If the schools fail to meet standards for three years, their students may then transfer to a higher performing public or private school.[34]

A Common Core Curriculum

The Council of Chief State School Officers (CCSSO) and the National Governors Association Center for Best Practices (NGA Center) launched the Common Core State Standards Initiative in 2010.[35] Although the standards and core are somewhat eclectic, the Initiative reflects certain Neo-Essentialist themes. The Core State Standards are "aligned with college and work expectations," are "focused and coherent," "include rigorous content and application of knowledge through high-order skills," and are "internationally benchmarked so that all students are prepared to succeed in our global economy and society." These standards closely resemble Essentialism and Basic Education in that they emphasize: (1) skill and content learning (a subject matter curriculum); (2) education as preparation for something in the future such as college or work; and (3) productivity in the global economy. Again following an Essentialist pattern, the standards have "grade specific end-of-the-year expectations" and a "cumulative progression of skills and understandings."

The Common Core Standards Initiative establishes standards for English Language Arts, Mathematics, History and Social Studies, Science, and Technical Subjects. The similarities with earlier Essentialist theory can be illustrated by the English language and mathematics standards. Like the proposals from earlier Essentialists, especially Bagley, English Language Arts standards are skill based in reading, writing, speaking and listening, and language. The mathematics standards, similar to Bestor's "intellectual disciplines," reflect the "mind of a mathematically expert student." Like Bestor's secondary curriculum, the Common Core Standards Initiative includes Algebra and Geometry but adds Statistics and Probability.

Neo-Essentialist Scholarly Advocates

Essentialism reappeared in the arguments of scholars such as E. D. Hirsch, Jr., Chester Finn, and Diane Ravitch, who contend that public schools are failing to impart the knowledge needed for cultural and political literacy. For example, E. D. Hirsch, Jr., argues that the average American's declining cultural literacy—the lack of a shared body of common knowledge—is jeopardizing a sense of a national cultural identity and ability to communicate effectively with other Americans. Because the contemporary school curriculum does not deliberately transmit a core to develop cultural literacy, many students complete their formal education without the necessary contextual background that enables them to reference and interpret materials crucial for both public communication and effective functioning in the workplace. A core curriculum designed to promote cultural literacy, Hirsch contends, is needed if citizens are to participate in the institutions and processes of political democracy.[36]

Arguing from a historical perspective, Diane Ravitch wants schools and teacher education to be intellectual and academic. She contends that some strains of Progressivism contributed to anti-intellectualism in education. In *Left Back*, Ravitch attributes the failure of many educational reforms in the twentieth century to some Progressive educators who weakened the schools' primary academic function. As they created different curricular tracks for different students, Progressives weakened

My Reflections on Philosophy of Education: My Essentialist Moment

I would like to describe an Essentialist moment that I had while teaching a graduate course in philosophy of education. All of the students were pursing master's degrees in Education. I was discussing Progressivism and Progressive education. In analyzing the concept of "Progress" I referred to the eighteenth-century Enlightenment and the French Revolution. I incorrectly assumed that the students and I shared the same historical frame of reference. When a student asked what the Enlightenment and the French Revolution were, I was surprised. When I queried the class, several other students said that they were not familiar with these terms. I then backtracked and put the Enlightenment in historical perspective and related it to the concept of Progress, which is an important concept in understanding Progressivism. What I learned from my Essentialist moment was that I needed to make sure that the students and I were on common ground. I also wondered how many other areas were falling through transgenerational cracks.

My Essentialist moment caused me to reflect on E. D. Hirsch, Jr.'s argument that the average American's declining cultural literacy, the lack of a shared body of common knowledge, is jeopardizing our ability to communicate effectively with each other. Hirsch's contention that the contemporary school curriculum does not transmit a core to develop cultural literacy seemed to fit my experience in teaching about the Enlightenment's concept of Progress. Several students lacked the contextual background to reference and interpret the Enlightenment. I reflected on how understanding the Enlightenment was necessary in order to understand the Liberalism and Progressivism that endorsed it. It was also needed to understand the Postmodernism and Critical Theory that opposed the Enlightenment Project.

the schools' mission to provide all students with academic skills and subjects. For her, the true leaders in American education were often-neglected Essentialist educators such as William C. Bagley and Isaac Kandel, rather than Progressives such as William H. Kilpatrick and George S. Counts.[37] Although she once supported No Child Left Behind, Ravitch now opposes the Act's reliance on standardized testing to identify, rate, remediate, and close schools that fail to meet standards. She also thinks that the teaching and learning process is too complicated to use standardized test results to assess teachers' competencies.[38]

ESSENTIALISM'S PHILOSOPHICAL, IDEOLOGICAL, AND THEORETICAL RELATIONSHIPS

Because Essentialism emphasizes traditional education, it has few friends but many philosophical, ideological, and theoretical adversaries. In this section, we identify and discuss its philosophical, ideological, and theoretical allies and adversaries.

Essentialism's Allies

For their metaphysics, see the chapters on Idealism and Realism.

In earlier chapters, we encountered the term *essence* in our discussions about the metaphysics of Idealism, Realism, and Thomism, which assert the existence of an underlying ultimate and universal being or nature in reality. These traditional philosophies contend that human beings, by their nature, possess the power to be intelligent, as Idealists claim, or rational, as Realists assert. Essentialism, too, as its name indicates, is based on the idea that education has an essence, or essential characteristics. Essentialists agree that humans, as intelligent and rational persons, are capable of being educated and, indeed, need to be educated. For Essentialists, education is to bring the human being into contact with knowledge by transmitting it to each generation. Metaphysically, Idealists and Realists assert the existence of an antecedent reality that exists prior to each individual person's encounter with it. Every person can approach and know this reality, which the Realists assert is the best guide to human conduct. Essentialists, such as Bagley and Bestor, argue that historically there is a corpus of antecedent knowledge, found in the liberal arts and sciences, that constitutes what people need to know to be intelligent and rational. For the traditional philosophies as well as the Essentialists, this knowledge basc is organized into subjects, which Bestor called intellectual disciplines.[39] The school should transmit this historically validated disciplinary curriculum to each generation.

Although often linked and compared, there are important differences, in their historical origins, between Essentialism and Perennialism. While they share some common features, they exhibit some educational differences. Perennialism is heavily rooted in Realism, especially the philosophies of Aristotle and Thomas Aquinas. Whereas Essentialism is historically based, Perennialism has a metaphysical or philosophical foundation. Perennialists, like the Realists from which they originate, argue that there is an objective reality that is antecedent to us, but that we can come to know. It further asserts that as rational beings, we can use our power of reason to understand, to know, this reality and to base our ethical and practical conduct on its natural laws. Religious Perennialists such as Maritain, guided by Thomas Aquinas, see this reality as having spiritual and natural dimensions that human beings can approach through faith and reason. Because reality is objective, truth about it is also objective; because reality is eternal, truths about it are eternal; and because it is universal, truth, too, is universal and does not depend on contexts and circumstances of time and place.

For Perennialism, see the chapter on Perennialism and Education.

While Essentialists and Perennialists agree on the importance of the liberal arts and sciences, they do so for different philosophical reasons. For Essentialists, the liberal arts and sciences have been developed over time, historically, as the best, or most civilized body of thought in Western civilization. For Perennialists, the liberal arts and sciences speak to human beings about universal and unchanging truths. For both Essentialism and Perennialism, the school's primary function is academic and intellectual and curriculum should focus on basic skills and subjects. While Perennialists base their educational rationale on the Aristotelian-Thomist concept of a rational human nature, Essentialism is more historically than metaphysically grounded. It looks to the past, rather than to human nature, to identify the skills and subjects that have contributed to human survival and civilization.

Contemporary Essentialism, especially the basic education and standards aspects, has become aligned with Neo-Conservative ideology. This alignment was absent in in the earlier versions developed by Bagley and Bestor, who sought to keep education clear of ideology. Contemporary Neo-Conservatives and Neo-Essentialists agree that schools should be academic institutions with a well-defined curriculum of basic skills and subjects and that they should cultivate traditional values of patriotism, hard work, effort, punctuality, respect for authority, and civility. They argue that schools and colleges should stress a required core based on Western civilization and traditional American values. Members of the religious right, especially fundamentalist evangelical Christians, argue that Western and American traditional values are based on Christianity and that the United States is essentially a Christian nation. In addition to the congruence of Neo-Essentialism and Neo-Conservatism on traditional educational principles, they also concur that schools have an important economic role in enhancing U.S. economic productivity in a highly competitive global economy.

Essentialism's Philosophical and Ideological Adversaries

Essentialism meets strong opposition from philosophies such as Pragmatism, Existentialism, and Postmodernism; from ideologies such as Marxism; and from theories such as Progressivism, Social Reconstructionism, and Critical Theory. Liberals, depending on their particular ideological orientation, are somewhat critical of Neo-Essentialism, particularly its current association with religious fundamentalism.

For Dewey's rejection of antecedent reality, see the chapter on Pragmatism and Education.

Pragmatists, such as Dewey's Experimentalists, find much to oppose in Essentialism, especially its emphasis on antecedent knowledge, on the school as an exclusively academic institution, on subjects as knowledge, and on teaching methods embedded in subject matter. Experimentalists reject the concept that knowledge is antecedent and exists prior to the learner's experience. For them, antecedent knowledge implies that it is a finished and completed body of knowledge that can be transmitted and learned. Experimentalists, in contrast, see knowledge as fluid and changing, arising as individuals and groups interact with their environment and as they solve problems in that ongoing experience. Experimentalists reject the notion that the school is primarily an academic institution. They consider this academic definition of a school too inflexible and limiting. Rather, schools are community agencies and, like communities, frequently redefine their functions. Nor do some subjects have an academic character whereas others do not. For the Experimentalist, a subject is a body of tentative findings about an area of human experience such as history, chemistry, or biology that can be approached instrumentally, redefined, or reconstructed, and then used to solve problems. It is not necessary to master an entire subject; rather, we can take what we need from it to solve a current problem. Pragmatists oppose the Essentialist assumption that the curriculum can be defined as *a priori* subjects to which students are led. To them, the curriculum is open ended, like experience, and grows out of students' needs and interests. An important disagreement relates to methods of instruction. For Essentialists, methods are plural in that they are embedded in and specialized in subjects, such as the historical method or the scientific method. Experimentalists believe that the scientific method is applicable to all areas of problem solving.

For the Progressive rejection of tradition as forming the schools' curricular core, see the chapter on Progressivism and Education.

Progressives, echoing many of the Pragmatist objections to Essentialism, oppose Essentialism's emphasis on tradition as the core of knowledge and its neglect of students' needs and interests. Essentialists, such as Bagley and Ravitch, argue that education is based on a traditional historical conception of the liberal arts and sciences and that the school's primary function is academic and intellectual. Progressives resist the authority of tradition, the past, over the changing needs of the present. Kilpatrick, for example, attacked what he called bookish education as ignoring the interests and needs of learners. Whereas Essentialists like Bagley argued that students needed to expend effort to learn what was not immediately interesting or might be difficult, Progressives counter that children's interests are immensely educative in that they might lead anywhere, into new and uncharted expanses of human experience. Essentialists see the teacher as an adult authority figure, representing society, who teaches skills and transmits subjects to students; Progressives redefine the role of the teacher as a facilitator who guides rather than controls students' learning. Essentialists assert the necessity of a curriculum organized into subjects; Progressives, decrying it as inert information, argue for experience-based learning, especially projects.

Existentialists find much to oppose in Essentialism, which they believe imposes an externally defined rather than a self-constructed education on students. Like Experimentalists, they oppose the Essentialist reliance on a prior or antecedent knowledge as a necessary condition of education. A *necessary condition* for education means that there is no choice about the matter. Teachers and students need to be free,

Existentialists would say, to take what they want from a subject and appropriate it by making it their own. Whereas Essentialists would argue that there are correct or incorrect answers in subjects, Existentialists would not look to external authorities to ascertain the rightness or wrongness of an answer. It is up to students to pose their own questions and construct their own answers. The contemporary Neo-Conservative and Neo-Essentialist emphasis on academic standards and academic testing would raise the ire of Existentialists. For them, standardization reduces the uniqueness of personal experience. Standardized curriculum, instruction, and assessment lead to standardized teaching and learning.

Postmodernists see Essentialism's claims to transmitting civilization via a required curriculum, based on the liberal arts and sciences, to be a dated Eurocentric historical rationale that once ensured the education of favored socio-economic groups and classes. Indeed, they contend that Essentialists are elevating the scientific, historical, and literary works that comprise the liberal arts and sciences to the status of meta-narratives—representations of human culture that are taken out of context and given a totalizing prominence. The liberal arts and sciences are Eurocentric and patriarchal, and they are designed to give educational legitimacy to some ideas but not to others.

Critical Theorists, similar to Postmodernists, find the Essentialist mandate for basic skills and subjects to actually be a guise for reproducing the socio-economic status quo and locking students into predetermined class-based situations. Although Essentialists such as Bagley and Bestor assumed that what they were advocating was nonideological, Critical Theorists contend that their subject-matter curriculum is based on a Eurocentric and patriarchal ideology that presents knowledge as constructed by white males of European ancestry and ignores the experiences of marginalized groups such as Africans, Latinos, and Native Americans and women. It presents knowledge as something completed by scholars among the elite groups (Bestor's intellectual disciplines) that is to be mastered by students and that reproduces the status quo. Especially repugnant to Critical Theorists is the contemporary linkage between Neo-Conservatives and Neo-Essentialists, who, in the name of objectivity, impose the standards of the dominant group on all others.

Liberal Neutrality

So far, we have discussed philosophies, ideologies, and theories that either support or oppose Essentialism. We now consider Liberalism, which approaches Essentialism, especially its affirmation of the liberal arts and sciences, with some neutrality. For Liberals, the liberal arts and sciences have an important but not exclusive place in education; they form part but not all of the curriculum. There also needs to be room for less structured, experimental, creative, and process-oriented learning. Is it not possible to have a curriculum with various components? On the other hand, Liberals would reject the contemporary alliance of Neo-Conservatism and Neo-Essentialism as imposing what is too much of a closed view of knowledge rather than an open one. They would oppose school prayer and the teaching of Creationism as serious breaches of separation of church and state.

ESSENTIALISM AND EDUCATION, SCHOOLING, CURRICULUM, AND TEACHING AND LEARNING

While Essentialists share many generalizations about education, schooling, curriculum, and teaching and learning, there are also shades of difference between the various manifestations of the theory in American education. The next section examines some general features of Essentialism and Basic Education.

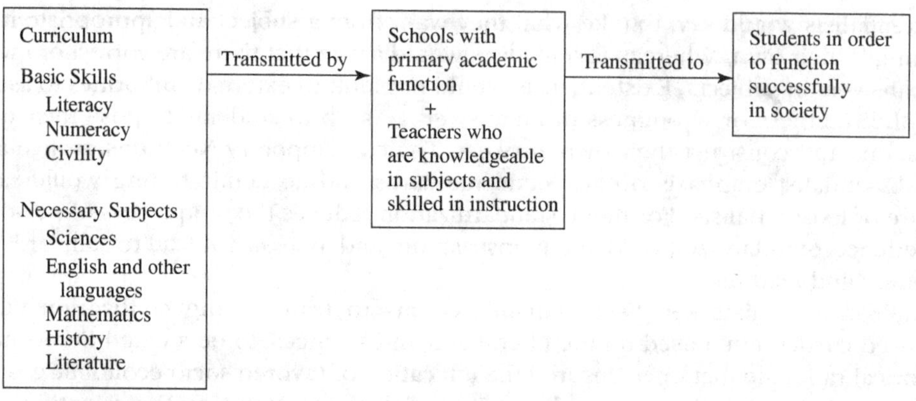

Essentialist Education

Education

Essentialism's view of the purpose of education, as the transmission of the culture through academic skills and subjects, is historically based. For Bagley and Bestor, in particular, education is to transmit the liberal arts and sciences from one generation to the next. Beginning with the ancient Greeks and Romans and developed and refined during the Medieval, Renaissance, Reformation, and Enlightenment periods, the liberal arts and sciences represent humankind's repository of knowledge. This knowledge has a past and a tradition but is dynamic and continues to grow as scholars and scientists add to, refine, and enlarge it. To enlarge this corpus of knowledge, it is first necessary to know it. This knowledge base is antecedent to us, as the Idealists and Realists argue. It is there for us to learn and has an intrinsic value that makes it worth knowing. It, however, also has a use or instrumental value in that it can be applied to practices in many fields such as engineering, health care, social work, and teaching. It is important to keep the intrinsic and instrumental values in perspective. We must first learn a subject before we can apply it. We do not have to keep reinventing it but can use the inheritance that comes from the past. Change in education and society comes through the core of knowledge and not by ignoring or circumventing it.

The School

Preparation: the doctrine that schooling involves preparing, or getting a person ready, for the next high stage of education.

For the school as a multifunctional institution, see the chapters on Liberalism and Progressivism.

Essentialism defines the school as a society's educational agency whose primary role is to transmit the cultural heritage by instructing students in well-defined prescribed academic skills and subjects. Essentialists are wedded to two views of the school that Pragmatists and Progressives oppose: transmission and **preparation**. The school, as an agency of cultural transmission, passes essential skills and subjects on as a cultural inheritance from one generation to the next, thereby maintaining the cultural heritage in civilized society. It rejects the Liberal and Progressive orientation that the school as a multifunctional institution performs a variety of social, political, economic, and psychologically therapeutic roles. Essentialists oppose diverting the school's time, resources, and energy from its primary academic function. Essentialists see schooling as an upward movement through institutions beginning with preschool and kindergarten, moving upward through the elementary school's primary and intermediate grades, through the secondary education of the middle and high school, to the college and university. Each stage is to provide the skills, competencies, and academic subjects—the preparation needed for the next stage. Thus, educational institutions are linked, or articulated to, each other. Because schooling leads a student from one institution to the next higher one, it is important that the network of institutions, the educational ladder, be articulated in terms of the essential curricula. In such an arrangement, the higher institution sets many of the goals of the lower ones through its expectations and entry requirements.

Curriculum

Essentialists firmly endorse the subject-matter curriculum in which subjects, also referred to as academic or learned disciplines, are differentiated, departmentalized, and organized according to their own internal logic or chronology. They are suspicious of so-called innovative or process learning approaches such as Constructivism in which students collaborate to construct or create their own knowledge. They also oppose premature transdisciplinary or interdisciplinary programs. For them, it is necessary to learn the structure, content, and method of a particular subject before relating it to another subject. Interdisciplinary programs tend to be disorganized, unstructured, and confusing to students.

Essentialists argue that civilized people learn effectively and efficiently by using the knowledge that has been developed and organized by scientists, scholars, and other experts. There is no need to waste time and resources by "discovering" what is already known. There is no need to continually reinvent the wheel. Curriculum that ignores the past and is interdisciplinary or transdisciplinary—crossing subject-matter boundaries, as recommended by Experimentalists, Progressives, and Critical Theorists—results in superficiality: it may purport to be knowledge, yet blurs expertise. Based on the Essentialist principle that the school has a primary academic function to perform, the curriculum, too, is specific to instruction in what is termed the basic skills and subjects. The curriculum's skills and subjects need to be well defined in scope, have a sequence, be cumulative, and be designed to prepare students for the future. When subjects are related as in the history of science, it is necessary to be competent in both history and science.

For interdisciplinary programs, see the chapters on Pragmatism, Progressivism, and Critical Theory.

SCOPE. Essentialists are suspicious of education that knows no borders or boundaries. For them, reading and arithmetic are specific skills to be taught in a specific way at a definite time in a child's life. History as an academic subject is defined as a chronological description and interpretation of the human past. Essentialists are suspicious of interdisciplinary methods such as whole language learning, Constructivism, and broad area studies such as language arts and social studies. They believe that for something to be learned, it has to be taught. Children will not simply acquire knowledge of arithmetic, history, and geography as concomitant learnings as some Progressives (e.g., Kilpatrick) claimed.

Scope: organizing curriculum by boundaries that mark off one subject from another.

For concomitant learnings, see the chapter on Progressivism and Education.

SEQUENCE. Essentialists believe that instruction in particular skills and subjects is determined largely by the internal logic of that skill or subject. There is an order to be observed in teaching something. For example, the teaching of American history follows a definite chronological order such as (1) encounters between the Native Americans and Europeans; (2) European settlement; (3) the Revolutionary War and struggle for independence; (4) the early national period; (5) the westward-moving frontier; (6) the Civil War and Reconstruction; (7) industrialization and immigration; (8) the Progressive movement; (9) World War I; (10) the Great Depression; (11) World War II; (12) the Cold War; and (13) the new world order characterized by economic globalization and terrorist threats to American security. Sequence also means that instruction in a particular subject area is organized according to its order of complexity,

Sequence: instruction that is organized according to a skill's operations or a subject's logic, chronology, or structure; learning that proceeds in a series of related phases or steps.

abstraction, and difficulty. For example, mathematics instruction begins with basic arithmetical computation and operations such as adding, subtracting, multiplying, and dividing and moves to the more abstract algebra, then to geometry, and on to calculus and trigonometry. The principle of sequence means that skills and subjects are to be taught according to a definite procedure and not necessarily according to what may currently interest students.

Each subject has its own chronology or logic; it also has a method that is appropriate to it. For example, history uses the historical method. Essentialists are suspicious of the Experimentalist argument that the scientific method can be applied to all experiences. Although they favor critical thinking, they are suspicious of methods that claim that critical thinking is a process that can be separated from the content and context of thought. When a person thinks, she or he has to think about something. What students should think about in school is the subject they are studying.

Cumulative: curriculum and instruction in which each unit, or lesson, lays the foundation for the next unit or lesson.

CUMULATIVE. For Essentialists, the curriculum is a series of building blocks in which one level is **cumulative**, that is, it builds on the preceding level and supports the next level. The emphasis on the cumulative is especially important at the skill level. Skills such as reading, writing, and computation are generative; they generate habits and processes that prepare students for the next higher academic level but also transfer to a variety of situations in life. When related to preparation for the next higher level of education, literary and arithmetic skills are necessary for learning the content of subject-matter disciplines. Based on these foundations, students advance upward to other subjects that have a greater complexity and require higher order thinking. The end result is a cumulative effect in which the student attains a repertoire of skills and a body of knowledge that is needed for further education, for work, and for life.

Teaching and Learning

Reiterating Bagley on teacher education, prospective teachers need a general education in the liberal arts and sciences and a professional education in the historical and philosophical foundations of education, methods of instruction, and clinical classroom practices. For example, secondary school history teachers should have an academic major in history. Teaching methods would emphasize organizing a subject, such as chemistry or American history, for example, into teachable and learnable units based on the students' readiness and prior academic knowledge of the subject. Students might not be interested in the subject at first; however, the teaching of the subject does not depend on students' interest. Hopefully, through their efforts, students will become interested in the subject.

Essentialists such as Bestor (though not Bagley) tended to believe that content knowledge of a subject was generally sufficient to teach it. If a person knew the subject thoroughly, he or she would deduce how to teach it. For both teachers and students it is important to stay on task and to learn the skill or the subject. It is important not to be diverted into trivial and anti-intellectual sidetracks. Although Essentialists recognize that teachers and students have their own political and economic beliefs, they believe that instruction can objectively present contending points of view. Political, economic, and social issues can be explored where they are relevant. However, teachers should not use their classrooms to promote their favorite political, social, and economic ideologies and agendas. Schools should not be used as agencies of political indoctrination.

Essentialists do not believe that schools can solve society's problems and ills. When schools take on social, political, and economic issues that are outside of their academic function, they are bound to fail. While schools can teach about racism, poverty, war, and violence in their subject contexts, they, alone, do not have the power to solve these problems. What schools can do is to teach students the basic skills and subjects that will prepare them to deal with social, political, and economic problems in the future.

Essentialists are suspicious of so-called innovative or process learning approaches, such as Constructivism, in which students collaboratively construct or create their own knowledge. They also question so-called authentic assessment, in which students evaluate their own progress. Essentialists, in contrast, argue that civilized people learn effectively and efficiently by using the knowledge base developed and organized by scientists, scholars, and other experts. We need not waste time and resources by "discovering" what is already known. We need to understand what is known and apply it to situations and problems.

Competent teachers try to stimulate a student's interest, but curriculum content should be based on time-tested experience of the human race rather than what students are interested in at the moment. Students gain real freedom when they internalize the discipline of learning and stay with a task until they complete it. Emphasizing teacher-directed instruction, Bagley, for example, argued that children have the right to expect teachers, as trained professionals, to guide and direct their learning.[40] Similar to the Scientific Realists, Essentialists argue that students need to learn about the objective real world rather than misguidedly follow the Constructivist view that they should create their own version of reality.[41]

CONSTRUCTING YOUR OWN PHILOSOPHY OF EDUCATION

Now that you have read and discussed this chapter, reflect on Essentialism as a theory of education. Have you encountered Essentialism in your education, especially in learning skills and subjects? Have you had Essentialist teachers and professors who saw their role as primarily transmitting knowledge to students? Have you found Essentialist strategies in your teacher education program? Does Essentialism appeal to you as a teacher? Are there aspects that you reject? Why? Are there elements of Essentialism that you plan to incorporate into your philosophy?

Conclusion

During its various appearances and under such titles as "the three R's," the Essentialist platform, intellectual disciplines, basic education, the structure of disciplines, and the standards movement, Essentialists have been consistent in defining schools as primarily academic institutions. They have been equally consistent in defining the curriculum as basic skills and subjects that rest on a foundation in the liberal arts and sciences. It is important to recognize the core features of this reoccurring educational theory that has remained rather constant. It is equally important to recognize that Essentialists, in their educational constancy and commitment, see this approach to education as being the most certain path to human survival and civility. Although the social, economic, and political problems may change, the best response for schools, say Essentialists, is to reaffirm and rely on the tried, true, and tested curriculum of basic skills and subjects.

Questions for Reflection and Discussion

1. Have you found Essentialism in your clinical experiences? If so, describe the Essentialist practices that you observed.
2. Have you encountered discussions of standards in your teacher education courses and clinical experiences? Summarize and reflect on the standards movement in your own educational experiences.
3. Reflect on your own experience as an elementary and high school student. Do you recall an Essentialist or basic education orientation in these experiences?
4. Of the philosophies and ideologies examined in this book, which is most compatible and which is least compatible with Essentialism?

5. How much of your formal education has been based on the doctrine of preparation? Do you agree or disagree with the emphasis on preparation in education?
6. Do you think that the contemporary standards movement and the use of standardized tests resonate well with Essentialism? Why?
7. Essentialists often claim that teacher education programs are biased against their view of the purpose of the school and curriculum content and organization. Do you agree or disagree with this Essentialist contention? Why?

Topics for Inquiry and Research

1. In the classrooms and teachers observed in your clinical experience, do you find evidence of Essentialism? If so, describe these observations.
2. Make a list of the skills and subjects that you think are essential or necessary to a sound education. Does your list agree with the Essentialist position?
3. Debate the proposition: Genuine equality requires all students to enroll in the same curriculum.
4. Review several textbooks used in your teacher education program. Do they support or reject Essentialist educational principles?
5. If you have taken a course in educational methods, reflect on the course and conjecture how an Essentialist might react to it. Is one method emphasized in the course, or are there several?
6. Identify several innovative approaches to education that are emphasized in your teacher education program. Critique them from an Essentialist perspective.

Internet Resources

Consult the Council for Basic Education Web site at www.c-b-e.org and examine the council's educational philosophy.

For standards and accountability in the No Child Left Behind Act, consult the U.S. Department of Education at www.ed.gov/inits.html.

For the state Core Standards Initiative, access http://www.corestandards.org./

Suggestions for Further Reading

Bagley, William C. *Craftsmanship in Teaching*. BiblioLife, LLC, 2012.

___. *Education and Emergent Man: A Theory of Education with Particular Application to Public Education in the United States*. New York: Thomas Nelson, 1934.

Bestor, Arthur E., Jr. *Educational Wastelands: Retreat from Learning in Our Public Schools*. Urbana: University of Illinois Press, 1953.

___. *The Restoration of Learning: A Program for Redeeming the Unfulfilled Promise of American Education*. New York: Alfred A. Knopf, 1956. Reprint by Literary Licensing, LLC, 2012.

Bunzel, John H., ed. *Challenge to American Schools: The Case for Standards and Values*. New York: Oxford University Press, 1985.

Ellis, Brian. *Scientific Essentialism*. Cambridge, UK: University of Cambridge Press, 2001.

Gutek, Gerald L. *Basic Education: A Historical Perspective*. Bloomington, IN: Phi Delta Kappa Educational Foundation, 1981.

Hirsch, Edward D., Jr. *Cultural Literacy: What Every American Needs to Know*. Boston: Houghton Mifflin, 1987.

___. *The Knowledge Deficit: Closing the Shocking Education Gap for American Children*. New York: Houghton Mifflin Co., 2006.

___. *The Making of Americans: Democracy and Our Schools*. New Haven, CT: Yale University Press, 2009.

___. *The Schools We Need*. New York: Doubleday/Random House, 1996.

Kandel, Isaac L. *The Cult of Uncertainty*. New York: Macmillan, 1934.

___. *William Chandler Bagley: Stalwart Educator*. New York: Teachers College Press, 1961.

National Commission on Excellence in Education. *A Nation at Risk: The Imperative for Educational Reform*. Washington, DC: U.S. Government Printing Office, 1983.

National Governors Association Center for Best Practices and the Chief State School Officers. *Common Core State Standards*. Washington, DC: National Governors

Association Center for Best Practices and the Chief State School Officers, 2010.

Null, J. Wesley. *A Disciplined Progressive Educator: The Life and Career of William Chandler Bagley*. New York: Peter Lang, 2001.

___. *Peerless Educator: The Life and Work of Isaac Leon Kandel*. New York: Peter Lang, 2007.

___, and Diane Ravitch, eds. *Forgotten Heroes of American Education: The Great Tradition of Teaching Teachers*. Greenwich, CT: Information Age, 2006.

Oderberg, David S. *Real Essentialism*. New York: Routledge, 2007.

Ravitch, Diane. *The Death and Life of the Great American School System: How Testing and Choice Are Undermining Education*. New York: Basic Books, 2010.

___. *Left Back: A Century of Failed School Reform*. New York: Simon and Schuster, 2000.

___. *National Standards in American Education: A Citizen's Guide*. Washington, DC: Brookings Institute, 1995.

___. *The Troubled Crusade: American Education, 1945–1980*. New York: Basic Books, 1983.

___, and Chester E. Finn, Jr. *What Do Our 17-Year-Olds Know? A Report on the First National Assessment of History and Literature*. New York: Harper & Row, 1987.

___, and Joseph P. Viteritti. *Making Good Citizens: Education and Civil Society*. New Haven, CT: Yale University Press, 2001.

Ravitch, Michael, and Diane Ravitch, eds. *The English Reader: What Every Literate Person Needs To Know*. New York: Oxford University Press, 2006.

Rickover, H. G. *American Education—A National Failure*. New York: E. P. Dutton and Co., 1963.

___. *Education and Freedom*. New York: E. P. Dutton and Co., 1959.

___. *Swiss Schools and Ours: Why Theirs Are Better*. Boston: Atlantic-Little, Brown and Co., 1962.

Notes

1. Laurence Urdang, ed., *The Random House Dictionary of the English Language* (New York: Random House, 1968), 451–452.
2. Diane Ravitch, *Left Back: A Century of Failed School Reforms* (New York: Simon and Schuster, 2000), 293–294.
3. Clifton Fadiman, "The Case for Basic Education," in James D. Koerner, ed., *The Case for Basic Education* (Boston: Little, Brown, 1959), 5–6.
4. David S. Oderberg, *Real Essentialism* (New York: Routledge, 2007), 44–57.
5. J. Wesley Null, *A Disciplined Progressive Educator: The Life and Career of William Chandler Bagley* (New York: Peter Lang, 2003), xi.
6. For a biography of Kandel, see J. Wesley Null, *Peerless Educator: The Life and Work of Isaac Leon Kandel* (New York: Peter Lang, 2007).
7. William C. Bagley, "An Essentialist Platform for the Advancement of American Education," *Educational Administration and Supervision* (April 1938), 241–256.
8. Adolphe E. Meyer, *The Development of Education in the Twentieth Century* (Upper Saddle River, NJ: Prentice Hall, 1949), 149.
9. Bagley, "Essentialist Platform," 254.
10. Diane Ravitch, *Left Back,* 121.
11. William C. Bagley, "What Is the Crux of the Conflict Between the Progressives and Essentialists?" *Educational Administration and Supervision, 26* (1940), 508–511.
12. Ibid., 508–509.
13. See J. Wesley Null and Diane Ravitch, *Forgotten Heroes of American Education: The Great Tradition of Teaching Teachers* (Greenwich, CT: Information Age, 2006); and Diane Ravitch, *Left Back: A Century of Failed School Reforms* (New York: Simon and Schuster, 2000).
14. Clay Blair, Jr., *The Atomic Submarine and Admiral Rickover* (New York: Henry Holt and Co., 1954).
15. Hyman G. Rickover, *Education and Freedom* (New York: E. P. Dutton and Co., 1959), 131.
16. Hyman G. Rickover, *American Education—A National Failure* (New York: E. P. Dutton and Co., 1963).
17. Arthur E. Bestor, Jr., *Educational Wastelands: The Retreat from Learning in Our Public Schools* (Urbana: University of Illinois Press, 1953); and *The Restoration of Learning: A Program for Redeeming the Unfulfilled Promise of American Education* (New York: Alfred A. Knopf, 1955).
18. Bestor, *The Restoration of Learning,* 3–4.
19. Ibid., 7.
20. Ibid., 358.
21. Ibid., 364–365.
22. Ibid., 50–51.
23. Ibid.
24. My memories of Arthur E. Bestor, Jr., as a teacher were stimulated by Dr. J. Wesley Null, the biographer of William Bagley, who asked me in a conversation at a meeting of the Midwest History of Education, in October 2007, about my classes with Bestor at the University of Illinois.
25. National Commission on Excellence in Education, *A Nation at Risk: The Imperative for Educational Reform* (Washington, DC: U.S. Department of Education, 1983), 5.

26. Ibid., 18.
27. Ibid., 20.
28. Ibid., 22.
29. Ibid., 24.
30. Ibid., 27.
31. The College Board, *Academic Preparation for College: What Students Need to Know and Be Able to Do* (New York: The College Board, 1983), 7–11.
32. Ibid., 13.
33. No Child Left Behind (Washington, DC: U.S. Printing Office, 2001), 1.
34. Ibid., 8–9.
35. http://www.corestandards.org. (8/9/2012). Also, see National Governors Association Center for Best Practices and the Chief State School Officers, *Common Core State Standards* (Washington, DC: National Governors Association Center for Best Practices and the Chief State School Officers, 2010).
36. E. D. Hirsch, Jr., *Cultural Literacy: What Every American Needs to Know* (Boston: Houghton Mifflin, 1987).
37. Ravitch, *Left Back*, 15–18, 465–467.
38. Diane Ravitch, *The Death and Life of the Great American School System: How Testing and Choice Are Undermining Education* (New York: Basic Books, 2010.
39. J. Wesley Null, "Social Reconstruction with a Purpose: The Forgotten Tradition of William Bagley," in Karen Riley, ed., *Social Reconstruction: People, Politics, Perspectives* (Greenwich, CT: Information Age, 2006), 27–44.
40. Ibid.
41. Brian Ellis, *Scientific Essentialism* (Cambridge, U.K.: University of Cambridge Press, 2001), 37–40.

Perennialism and Education

Mortimer Adler (1902–2001), an advocate of the Great Books, who founded the Paideia approach to education.

14

CHAPTER PREVIEW

Perennialism, like Essentialism, has had a long and continuing presence in American education. It has appeared as the "Great Books curriculum" and as Paideia education. This chapter examines Perennialism's philosophical derivation and relationships to Realism, especially to Aristotle and Thomas Aquinas. It then discusses the ideas of its leading proponents, and its implications for education, schooling, curriculum, and teaching and learning.

We can turn to the dictionary to provide some clues about the meaning of Perennialism. Looking up its root, we find that **perennial** means "lasting for an indefinitely long time"; it also means "enduring, perpetual, continuing, recurrent, constant."[1] As an educational theory, **Perennialism** emphasizes an education that is enduring and lasting; a curriculum that is based on what is universal, eternal, and recurrent. Like a perennial plant, a perennial education lives through all the seasons of life. Our discussion of Perennialism in this chapter is organized into the following major topics:

- Perennialism's philosophical derivation from the Realism of Aristotle and Thomas Aquinas
- Robert Hutchins, Mortimer Adler, and Jacques Maritain as leading Perennialist theorists
- The relationships between Perennialism and other philosophies, ideologies, and theories of education
- Perennialism's implications for education, schools, curriculum, and teaching and learning

CONSTRUCTING YOUR OWN PHILOSOPHY OF EDUCATION

As you read and discuss this chapter, reflect on Perennialism and decide if it is relevant to you and your emerging philosophy of education. Have you encountered Perennialism in your own educational experiences? Did you have teachers and professors who emphasized reading the classics and the Great Books? Did they emphasize universal truth and values? See if Perennialism appeals to you as a theory of education.

PERENNIALISM: AN EDUCATIONAL THEORY DERIVED FROM ARISTOTELIAN REALISM

Perennialism, as a theory of education, is derived from Realism, especially from Aristotle and Thomas Aquinas. Perennialism asserts Aristotle's premises that truth is universal and eternal and that human beings, by their very nature, are rational in that they possess the intellectual power to reason. The

Perennial: refers to something that is constant, reappearing, recurrent, and enduring.

Perennialism: a theory that asserts that education is based on truth, knowledge, and values that are universal and eternal.

For the philosophies of Aristotle and Thomas Aquinas, see the chapter on Realism and Education.

same everywhere, truth is not determined by culture, place, or time. For example, 1 + 1 = 2 is true in every county and culture; a circle is the same everywhere. Human beings are endowed with the power of rationality, which is the defining, essential element in their human nature. The power of human rationality is perennial in that it reoccurs in each new generation. For the Perennialist, education should be based on the following universal characteristics of human nature:

- Our rationality defines us as human beings.
- People everywhere frame their thoughts in symbolic patterns and express them in language.
- People everywhere have used and continue to use ethical, aesthetic, religious, social, and political truths and values to direct their private and public lives.
- Our human intellect enables us to frame alternative propositions and to choose between them; our choice is informed when it is based on knowledge.

For the ideas of Plato, Aristotle, and Aquinas, see the chapters on Idealism and Realism.

Because human nature is universal, so is education. Foremost, education's aim is to cultivate our rational powers to grasp the truth and use it to guide our lives. Since the truth is universal and unchanging, a genuine education should also be universal and constant. The school's curriculum should emphasize the universal and recurrent themes of human life. It should contain cognitive materials designed to cultivate rationality; it should be highly logical and enable students to use the symbolic patterns of thought and communication. It should cultivate ethical principles and encourage moral, aesthetic, and religious criticism and appreciation. Perennialist education seeks to develop the intellectual and spiritual potentialities of the child to their fullest extent. Perennialist educational theory emphasizes the humanities as providing insights into the good, true, and beautiful. In these works, humankind has captured a glimpse of the eternal truths and values. Such insights, found in science, philosophy, literature, history, and art, persist as they are transmitted from generation to generation. Works such as those of Plato, Aristotle, and Aquinas, for example, possess a quality that makes them perennially appealing to people living at different times and in different places. Other ideas, which may be popular or current at a particular time but fail to meet the test of time fade quickly. For example, the instant celebrity, featured on the media, has but a fleeting moment of fame that quickly fades. It is not the stuff of true character. Perennialism is illustrated in the educational theories of Robert Hutchins and Mortimer Adler.

ROBERT M. HUTCHINS

Robert Maynard Hutchins (1899–1977) argued forcefully and consistently that education is properly devoted to cultivating human intellect. Most of Hutchins' life work was in higher education. A graduate of Yale University, he was a professor of law at Yale from 1927 to 1929. At age thirty, he became president of the University of Chicago and served until 1945, when he became the university's chancellor. In 1954, Hutchins was named head of the Fund for the Republic and was associated with the Fund's Center for the Study of Democratic Institutions, which was established to promote the principles of individual liberty in a democratic society.

Hutchins on Truth, Knowledge, Education, and Teaching

Hutchins' major books on education are *The Higher Learning in America* (1936), *Education for Freedom* (1943), *Conflict in Education in a Democratic Society* (1953), *University of Utopia* (1953), and *The Learning Society* (1968).[2] In these books, Hutchins clearly stated his educational principles. For him, the purpose of education is to draw out "the elements of our common human nature" which "are the same in any time or place." Therefore, "educating a man to live in any particular time or place, to adjust him to any particular environment, is . . . foreign to a true conception of education."[3]

Hutchins' purpose of education reiterated the Perennialist Aristotelian principles that the universe's truths and human nature are universal and timeless. He completely rejected ideologies and theories that claim that beliefs about "truth" depend on the cultural contexts in which they arise. After defining education, Hutchins proceeded to describe Perennialist teaching. He stated,

For a contextual view of truth and value, see the chapter on Social Reconstruction and Education.

> Education implies teaching. Teaching implies knowledge. Knowledge is truth. The truth is everywhere the same. Hence education should be everywhere the same. . . . the heart of any course of study designed for the whole people will be, if education is rightly understood, the same at any time, in any place, under any political, social, or economic conditions.[4]

For Hutchins, the teacher's role is clear, precise, and specific: There is truth, we have knowledge about it, and teachers are to teach the knowledge that is about the truth. Unlike the Existentialists, we do not choose the truths that we want. The truth is out there, as the Realists assert, ready to be known. This knowing, however, is not primarily by easy transmission as the Essentialists claim. It is reached through effort, through searching, discussion, and probing.

See the chapters on Existentialism and Essentialism.

After establishing that truth is universal and education is about the knowledge that leads us to the truth, Hutchins went on to describe an ideal education as "one that develops intellectual power." He stated:

> I arrive at this conclusion by a process of elimination. Educational institutions are the only institutions that can develop intellectual power. The ideal education is not an *ad hoc* education, not an education directed to immediate needs; it is not a specialized education, or a pre-professional education; it is not a utilitarian education. It is an education calculated to develop the mind.[5]

Confusion About Education's Purpose

Just as Socrates had to deal with the Sophists who had distorted and confused the nature of truth and the meaning of education, Hutchins felt he faced a similar challenge with the American society and public. Although he had clearly stated education's purpose, his message was not getting through to those who needed the education he had described. Like Socrates, Hutchins tried to correct the misconceptions that clouded the true meaning of education.

For Socrates and the Socratic Method, see the chapter on Idealism and Education.

Hutchins believed that a confused concept of democracy had generated the misconception that everyone should receive the same amount and degree of education. Although all people, by their nature, were rational, not all of them had the same motivation and ability for higher level thinking. In particular, higher education, he argued, should be reserved for students who have the interest in and ability for independent intellectual study.

Hutchins attacked the misconception of presentism in education that only what is happening here and now is worth studying. He attributed this misconception to a false notion of progress that had led to the rejection of the wisdom of the past; in turn, this erroneous view asserted that progress comes only from empiricism and materialism. A superficial empiricism had produced an anti-intellectualism that confused knowledge with collecting information and statistical data.

For the Progressive interpretation of Progress, see the chapter on Progressivism and Education.

Hutchins' interpretation of progress can be contrasted with how Progressives use the term. Drawing on the Enlightenment, Progressives believe that human intelligence needs to be liberated from the strictures of the past. They saw science as a means of this liberation. For Hutchins, however, the past, especially its great ideas, enlightened and liberated the mind. Hutchins' Aristotelian rationale came from pre-Enlightenment classical Greek philosophy. If he were surveying the contemporary educational landscape, Hutchins would admonish that the prolific information on the Internet and social media is not, in itself, knowledge. It is a mass of information that may or may not be accurate. Further, the various empirical studies, based on the collecting of statistical data, which drive curriculum and instruction, provide information but not necessarily knowledge.

Hutchins believed that overspecialization, especially premature specialization in education, was eroding the common core of ideas people needed for discourse in a civilized society. An overemphasis on specialization had pushed the liberal arts out of the general curriculum. Specialization had reached the point where a specialist could only communicate with another specialist in the same field. Without the integrating core of shared knowledge, specialists lack the shared ideas that make it possible to communicate experience. In secondary and higher education, highly departmentalized curricula reduced the needed common core, which for Hutchins, should be based on the ideas found in the Great Books of Western civilization.

Hutchins applied his critique of specialization to teacher education. He believed that the specialized courses in teacher education programs were making the field anti-intellectual and isolating teachers from the common body of knowledge that all people need. Like all people, teachers need a general education in the liberal arts and sciences. Teaching strategies can be found in the liberal arts disciplines of grammar, rhetoric, logic, and mathematics. These disciplines are potent instruments that prepare teachers to organize, express, and communicate knowledge.

Hutchins believed that American higher education was failing in its primary intellectual purpose. Rather than engaging in the search for truth, American universities were pushed and pulled away from their central intellectual mission. The constant competition for outside funding for grants, the pressure to have a winning football team, and the demands of special interests had taken universities off their intellectual path. Hutchins argued that universities should recapture their guiding purpose of discovering and teaching the truth.

The Curriculum: The Permanent Studies

Hutchins' ideas about curriculum and instruction were based on Perennialist principles that (1) people need a general education; (2) a general education includes the study and discussion of the great thinkers of Western civilization; and (3) the elements, the subjects, of a general education are permanent, that is, recurrent topics for each generation. Emphasizing these themes, Hutchins wrote:

> I have old-fashioned prejudices in favor of the three R's and the liberal arts, in favor of trying to understand the greatest works that the human race has produced. I believe that these are the permanent necessities, the intellectual tools that are needed to understand the ideas and ideals of our world. This does not exclude later specialization or later professional education; but I insist that without the intellectual techniques needed to understand ideas, and without at least an acquaintance with the major ideas that have animated mankind since the dawn of history, no man may call himself educated.[6]

For Hutchins, the curriculum, particularly at the secondary and higher education levels, should be composed of **permanent studies** that reflect the common elements of human nature and connect each generation to the best thoughts of humankind. He particularly recommended the study of the **Great Books**—classics contemporary in any age that embraced all areas of knowledge. He believed that four years spent reading and discussing the Great Books would cultivate standards of judgment and criticism and prepare students to think carefully and act intelligently. Hutchins and other Perennialist educators, such as Mortimer Adler, Alexander Meiklejohn (1872–1964), and Jacques Barzun (1907–2012), advocated the Great Books curriculum as a way to reemphasize the liberal arts and science tradition in American education, especially in colleges and universities.

Permanent Studies: the subjects that constitute a general education that is the same for all people across time.

Great Books: the classic books of Western civilization that should be read by all educated persons.

The Great Books are esteemed as the classics of Western civilization. As classics, they have perennial features that make them significant statements in their own time; however, because of their enduring themes, these books have relevance across generations. Their meaning is as compelling for contemporary readers as it was to their original readers. Representative Great Books from the classical Greek period are Homer's *Iliad* and *Odyssey*; Herodotus' *Histories*; Thucydides' *History of the Peloponnesian War*; Plato's *Dialogues*; Aristotle's *Works*; and Euclid's *Elements of Geometry*. From the Roman period, Cicero's *Orations*; Lucretius' *On the Nature of Things*; Vergil's *Aeneid*; Ovid's *Metamorphoses*; Plutarch's *Parallel Lives*; and Marcus Aurelius' *Meditations*. From the Medieval period, St. Augustine's *Confessions* and St. Thomas Aquinas' *Summa Theologica*. From the Renaissance, Dante's *Divine Comedy*; Machiavelli's *The Prince*; Erasmus' *The Praise of Folly*; More's *Utopia*; and Shakespeare's plays. From the Reformation, Luther's *Table Talk* and Calvin's *Institutes of the Christian Religion*. From the Enlightenment, Milton's *Paradise Lost*; Locke's *An Essay Concerning Human Understanding*; Newton's *Mathematical Principles of Natural Philosophy*; Rousseau's *Social Contract*; Smith's *The Wealth of Nations*; and Kant's philosophical works. From the nineteenth century, Malthus' *Essay on the Principle of Population*; Hegel's *Lectures on the Philosophy of History*; Austen's *Pride and Prejudice*; Tocqueville's *Democracy in America*; Mill's *On Liberty*; Darwin's *Origin of Species*; Marx's *Das Kapital*; Tolstoy's *War and Peace*; and James' *The Varieties of Religious Experience*. From the twentieth century, Freud's *The Interpretation of Dreams*; Dewey's *Democracy and Education*; and Russell's *Principia Mathematica*.

The emphasis in the Great Books curriculum is that students gain a direct encounter with the author of a Great Book by reading it as a primary source, not as a predigested extract in a textbook. The instructional strategy is primarily an open discussion and dialogue in which the teacher, in Socratic fashion, asks leading questions to which the students respond.

The Great Books curriculum has been controversial. Its proponents see it as leading students to the original foundational sources of Western thought. The books take the reader through the major periods of Western civilization, from ancient Greek to modern times. The Great Books are the significant works in literature, philosophy, history, politics, and science that shaped Western culture. Pragmatists, like Dewey, challenged the Great Books as a retreat from the problems of modern life to an intellectual refuge in the past. Postmodernists see the Great Books as enshrining a Western canon that glorified the dominance of white European males. For them, the Western orientation neglects Asian and African cultures.

For Pragmatism and Postmodernism, see the chapters on Pragmatism and Education and Postmodernism and Education.

In addition to the Great Books of Western civilization, Hutchins recommended the study of grammar, rhetoric, logic, and mathematics. Grammar, the analysis of language, contributes to the understanding and comprehension of the written word.

My Reflections on Philosophy of Education: A Reenactment of an Opera

I attended an educational event at the Brook Park public elementary school in La Grange Park, Illinois. The fifth-grade class was reenacting and performing an opera, *La Cenerentola, Cinderella,* by Gioachino Rossini (1858–1924), for a school-wide program to which the public was invited. My wife, Pat, and I had attended this program in the past and were especially interested this year since our granddaughter, Abby, was participating in the program. Each year the school staged an opera.

The district's music director worked with the students to select an opera and to study the composer's life and compositions. They would study the particular opera, its presentation, style, characters, and story. Then they would perform the opera, in an abbreviated form, for the students in the school and for the public. They performed the opera by lip-synching the pieces. Dressed in appropriate costumes, they acted out the gestures and movements involved in the performance.

When my wife and I arrived at the school, we were met by students who gave us our tickets and the program and by ushers who led us to our seats. The music director introduced the class and the opera. Then the performance began. The students had even arranged a screen on which translations of the Italian arias were displayed.

As I reflected on the performance, I tried to place it in philosophical as well as musical perspective. While there were aspects of the progressive project method, the students' operatic performance seemed to me to reflect Perennialism. The students were being introduced to opera, an important art form in Western culture. They were being introduced to the Western cultural heritage through the works of one of the great composers, Rossini, the creator of *Madame Butterfly, Tosca,* and *La Boheme*. Through opera, they were experiencing the interplay of person with music, settings, stories, acting, drama, and comedy. They were becoming participants in their cultural heritage.

Rhetoric provides the student with the rules of writing and speaking needed for intelligent expression; logic, the critical study of reasoning, enables a person to think and express himself or herself in an orderly and systematic fashion. Mathematics requires reasoning in its clearest and most precise form.

For their contrasting views of metaphysics, see the chapters on Idealism, Realism, Pragmatism, Existentialism, and Postmodernism.

In order to restore rationality in higher education, Hutchins advocated revitalizing of metaphysics. As the study of first principles, metaphysics pervaded the entire range of intellectual pursuits. Proceeding from the study of first principles to the most current concerns, higher education should examine fundamental human problems. Hutchins' argument that the underlying rationale of education should be rooted in metaphysics marked a return to Aristotelian and Thomist philosophy. He stood in stark opposition to philosophies such as Existentialism, Pragmatism, and Postmodernism that reject metaphysics.

MORTIMER ADLER

Mortimer J. Adler (1902–2001), an Aristotelian philosopher and educator, worked closely with Hutchins. Like Hutchins, he supported the idea of curriculum based on reading and discussing the Great Books of Western civilization. Adler founded and served as director of the Institute for Philosophical Research in 1952. He served on the board of editors of *Encyclopædia Britannica* since its inception in 1949 and succeeded

Hutchins as its chairperson in 1974. He developed the Paideia Proposal and Program in education.

The Paideia Proposal

Derived from the Greek, ***paideia***, referring to the "upbringing of children," signifies the general education all human beings need as intelligent and rational individuals. True to Perennialist principles, Adler's **Paideia proposal** argues that a genuinely equal educational opportunity should be available to all children. All students should be offered an education of the "same quantity," "the same number of years," and the "same quality."[7] Paideia educators oppose dividing students into tracks in which students are taught different subjects and have different educational experiences. Tracking causes inequalities in students' educational experiences.

Paideia: a Greek word meaning a person's complete formation or upbringing, including education.

Paideia Proposal: Mortimer Adler's design that all students should receive an education that develops their power to reason.

Affirming the Aristotelian principle of a common and universal human nature, Adler did not see equality of education as a leveling process that evened out the differences in individual capacities. Rather, education's ultimate goal is to ensure that "human beings become educated persons."[8] Construed in Aristotelian terms, schooling not only provides skill and knowledge but also cultivates the habits or dispositions for a satisfying and rewarding life.

Schooling in the Paideia Proposal

In Adler's Paideia program, the school, as an institution, is organized as a single rather than a multi-track system that provides the same curriculum to all students. The proposal of a single system raises significant social, political, economic, and educational issues.

Some advocates of multi-track schools claim that they are better able to deal with students' individual needs than single-track schools. Because of students' differing intellectual capacities, socio-economic backgrounds, and physiological-emotional needs, schools need to provide educational options that encompass a widely diverse student population. Other proponents of multi-track schools believe that students should be placed in homogeneous groups based on their academic abilities so that instruction cultivates their strengths and remediates their weaknesses. It is important that intellectually gifted students have subjects and instruction that challenge them academically. In contrast, Paideia proponents, like Perennialists in general, argue that all students deserve the same high-quality general education because of the their universal human nature.

Paideia schooling has three major common objectives for all students: (1) to provide the means of mental, moral, and spiritual growth and development; (2) to cultivate the civic knowledge and virtues needed for responsible citizenship; and (3) to provide the general skills that can transfer to a modern technological economy rather than specialized job training for a single occupation.

Both Hutchins and Adler wanted all people to receive a general education, based on the liberal arts and sciences, to cultivate their human nature and its undergirding rationality. Adler opposed the premature introduction of specialized vocational training before a student had received a general education. He also opposed streaming some students into vocational tracks that denied them a general education. Vocational specialization tends to weaken or reduce the time and resources devoted to general education. Specialized vocational training, at the expense of general education, limits a person to one economic undertaking that can quickly become obsolete due to the rapid pace of technological change. General competencies such as rational and logical thinking not only fulfill a person's human potential but also can transfer to a variety of situations in practical life.[9]

The Paideia Curriculum

Students in the Paideia program follow the same common curriculum for twelve years of elementary and secondary education. The exception is that they can elect their second languages. The curriculum is organized into three related learning modes, which have the goals of (1) developing and exercising learning and intellectual skills; (2) broadening the understanding of ideas and values; and (3) acquiring organized knowledge.[10]

For its emphasis on transferable skills, see the chapter on Essentialism and Education.

To develop learning and intellectual skills, Paideia teachers emphasize basic skills such as "reading, writing, speaking, listening, observing, measuring, estimating, and calculating."[11] Not taught in isolation, these skills are integrated into the entire curriculum. In its emphasis on basic skill learning, the Paideia program closely resembles Essentialism's accentuation of generative or transferable skills.

To broaden students' understanding, Paideia teachers emphasize the Perennialist theme—originated by Hutchins and reiterated by Mortimer Adler—that the reading and discussion of the Great Books or classics are vital in cultivating a truly educated person. In Adler's *The Paideia Proposal*, the scope of the great literature encompasses not only the enduring "historical, scientific, and philosophical" works but also the great works in film, drama, dance, and music.[12] Examples of primary source readings are Lavoisier's *Elements of Chemistry*, Sojourner Truth's *Ain't I a Woman*, Bacon's *Of Studies*, Lincoln's *Gettysburg Address*, and Hamlet's *Soliloquy*.[13]

Teaching and Learning in the Paideia School

Teachers in schools following the Paideia theory of education are expected to be liberally educated persons. In teaching the organized subjects that lead to the acquisition of knowledge, the method used is essentially didactic, or instructional, using well-organized narratives. To instruct students to master the essential foundational skills, the teacher uses coaching, which refers to organizing and correcting students to perform skills such as reading or listening correctly. In studying the great works of art and literature that enlarge human understanding, teachers and students enter into the Socratic mode, which uses probing questions and directed discussions.

MARITAIN'S INTEGRAL HUMANISM

Integral Humanism: Maritain's theory of Neo-Thomist religious Perennial education that emphasizes the cultivation of students' spirituality and rationality.

This section turns to a discussion of the educational ideas of Jacques Maritain (1882–1973), a leading interpreter of Thomist philosophy. Maritain developed **Integral Humanism**, a religiously oriented educational theory derived from the Theistic Realism of Thomas Aquinas that emphasizes the spirituality and personalism of the human being.[14] Like Hutchins and Adler, Maritain was influenced by Aristotle's Realism, which also shaped the thinking of Aquinas. A variety of religious, or faith-based, Perennialism, Maritain's Integral Humanism asserts that truth is universal and that human nature, in terms of its defining rationality, is the same regardless of time and place.[15]

Maritain, born in France in 1882, was educated at the University of Paris. He was born into a Protestant family but became a convert to Roman Catholicism in 1906. Dissatisfied with the skepticism among academic philosophers, Maritain was attracted to Thomism. He urged a reconciliation of faith and reason in philosophy, as exemplified in the works of Thomas Aquinas. Maritain wrote *Education at the Crossroads* (1943), *Man and the State* (1951), *On the Use of Philosophy* (1961), and *Integral Humanism* (1968).

The Perennial Purposes of Education

In *Education at the Crossroads*, Maritain identified the two major purposes of education as (1) assisting persons in cultivating their humanity and (2) introducing them to their cultural heritage. Maritain bases these purposes on his philosophical commitment to Aristotle and Aquinas. The concept of a universally shared humanity reflects Aristotle's dictum that the power to reason is the human's defining characteristic. The concept of the cultural heritage is based on a reverence for the inherited works in philosophy, theology, and the arts and sciences of the past that can illuminate the present and guide individuals to the future.

Misconceptions About Education

Just as Hutchins identified misconceptions that confused education, Maritain, too, identified errors that distort education's true purposes. The most pervasive negative influence came from Pragmatism and Naturalism. For Maritain, Pragmatism was a major error in education. He saw John Dewey's Experimentalism as a philosophy that had misled American educators. Pragmatists, like Dewey, had overemphasized means, the process of doing something, over ends or goals. Indeed, Dewey's concept of means as an "end-in-view" failed to distinguish sufficiently between means and ends. For Maritain, it was crucial that an end be thought of as a goal to be reached. Goals, no matter how interesting they may be, are not all of equal importance. Some are more important and should receive priority over others. In ranking goals, Maritain positioned the human being's spiritual salvation as the highest; then came the development of human rationality. Economic goals, though important, were ranked lower. In Maritain's scale, a goal had to be a worthy one. Then the means selected to accomplish that goal also needed to be worthy ones.

For Pragmatism and Experimentalism, see the chapter on Pragmatism and Education.

For Dewey on means, see the chapter on Pragmatism and Education.

In his critique of Dewey, Maritain asserted that the American Pragmatist's discussion of the relationships between means and ends was based on a mistaken concept of democracy. Although individuals are equal in a democracy, their goals are not equal. Dewey, in turn, would challenge Maritain's ultimate goals of spiritual salvation and universal rationality as so distant from ongoing experience that they could not direct the construction of the necessary means to achieve them. Further, these goals were so abstract that they were unverifiable; we could never know if we achieved them.

Pragmatism's obsession with means, for Maritain, had produced an aimless education without guiding principles. Too many teachers, especially Progressives, were so enamored with processes, procedures, and projects that their teaching was aimless. Going back to guiding principles, Maritain asserted that teaching's proper goal is to aid and guide students in realizing their fullest human potentialities. Genuine education rests on a conception of human nature based on the Judeo-Christian heritage. According to Maritain, education should guide individuals to shape themselves as human persons "armed with knowledge, strength of judgment, and moral virtues" while transmitting the "spiritual heritage" of their "nation and the civilization." Thus, it preserves "the century-old achievements of generations."[16]

Rousseau's Naturalism

Maritain identified Rousseau's naturalism as a misconception that affected many educators, especially American progressives. Rousseau's ideas about education, expressed in *Emile,* were based on Nature and the human being's natural instincts. A mixture of Enlightenment rationalism and romanticism, Rousseau's writings did not share Maritain's Thomist emphasis on the spiritual. Rousseau's stress on children's instincts, needs, curiosity, and stages of development appealed to child-centered educators, especially Progressives.

For Rousseau's naturalism, see the chapter on Progressivism and Education.

Maritain believed that Progressive teachers had exaggerated instincts and emotions in education. They had abandoned their responsibility as educated adults in guiding children. Instead, they were being led by children. By concentrating their efforts on educating the warm, good-hearted person, Progressives neglected the need to develop children's powers to reason. Maritain argued that the properly functioning person is governed by intellect rather than emotionalism.

Maritain on the Curriculum and the Teacher and Learner

As indicated earlier, Maritain's Perennialism derived from Aristotelian and Thomist Realist philosophy. His ideas about the curriculum reflected a Realist subject matter orientation. For Maritain, the teacher's role was what Thomas Aquinas called a vocation or a calling to service. For these reasons, Maritain presents a well-defined religious Perennialist approach to education.

Maritain's Curriculum

For the Essentialist emphasis on education as preparation, see the chapter on Essentialism and Education.

As a Perennialist, Maritain saw the curriculum organized into defined and structured bodies of knowledge. He believed the goals of education, like all goals, needed to be arranged in a hierarchy of importance. The overarching goals at the hierarchy's summit are cultivating students' intellectual powers and introducing them to the riches of their cultural heritage. Just as a hierarchy is arranged like a ladder, each rung, or grade level, in the school's ladder should provide the skills and knowledge needed to keep climbing upward. As they reach higher levels of their climb upward, students gain an ever-broadening perspective of their cultural landscape. Strongly imprinted in the Perennialist curriculum, and also in Essentialism, is the principle that education and schooling require students to prepare themselves for their future education and work.

For Bagley's emphasis on skill learning, see the chapter on Essentialism and Education.

PRIMARY EDUCATION. Education in the primary grades, like secondary and higher education, is based on Maritain's overall design of a subject-matter curriculum of the learned disciplines found in the liberal arts and sciences. Primary education is devoted to teaching and learning the skills of literacy, computation, listening, discussing, and researching that are needed for the successful study of the more systematic disciplines in the upper grades and secondary and higher education. In his emphasis on skill learning as preparation for higher studies, Maritain, a Perennialist, closely resembles Bagley, an Essentialist. Although Maritain rejected the emotional romanticism in Rousseau's naturalism, he emphasizes the importance of imagination in children's early education. Maritain agrees with Rousseau in rejecting the view that the "good" child acts like a miniature adult.

The child's world, says Maritain, is one of imagination. Primary teachers should begin their instruction within the child's own world of imagination. They should use stories and story-like narratives that begin with the imagined world and slowly lead children to explore the real world. The change from stories to narrative descriptions of geography, history, and science should be gradual so that children can move easily through the increasing complexity of these subjects. Although children's entry into education begins with and is carried through their imaginations, they need to be led to exercise their intellects in discovering the realities of the external world. Based on his Aristotelian and Thomist philosophy, Maritain subscribed to the Realist metaphysical claim that there is a world that exists independently of us. Children do not make or construct this reality; they discover it.

Secondary Education

After being prepared in the skills at the primary level, students, if adequately prepared, are ready for secondary education. Secondary education, designed to broaden students' intellectual perspectives, introduces adolescents to ideas and achievements of human civilization. The secondary school curriculum includes grammar, mathematics, literature, foreign languages, history, geography, and the natural and physical sciences.

Higher Education

Like Hutchins, Maritain was very interested in the undergraduate college curriculum. He divides the college curriculum into four years of study:

1. A year of mathematics and poetry, when students study these subjects as well as literature, logic, foreign languages, and the history of civilization
2. A year of natural science and fine arts, devoted to physics, mathematics, literature, poetry, and the history of science
3. A year of philosophy, which includes metaphysics, philosophy of nature, epistemology, psychology, physics and natural science, mathematics, literature, poetry, and fine arts
4. A year of ethical and political philosophy, which examines ethics, political and social philosophy, physics, natural science, mathematics, literature, poetry, fine arts, the history of civilization, and the history of science

Maritain, like his fellow Perennialists Hutchins and Adler, values the presence of the Great Books in the secondary and undergraduate curricula. These classics carry an authority, a timelessness not found in other books, despite their momentary popularity.

The Teacher

Maritain based his concept of the teacher on a semi-religious ideal that was shaped by Thomas Aquinas. The medieval scholastic educator Aquinas saw teaching as a vocation, a calling to serve humanity. Maritain's teacher not only epitomized the call to service but also was to be well educated in the liberal arts and science, cultivated in the fine arts, and a mature representative of the culture. The teacher possesses the knowledge that the students do not yet have but wish to acquire. Good teaching begins with what students already know and leads them to what they do not know.

For Aquinas on teaching as a vocation, see the chapter on Realism and Education.

Along with possessing knowledge grounded in the liberal arts and sciences, the good teacher has a repertoire of teaching strategies. Important in these strategies is knowing how to create a classroom climate that is genuinely educative. The classroom milieu should be orderly but open. Taking an Aristotelian middle road, it avoids the excesses of anarchy and despotism. Rejecting any kind of discipline, the anarchical classroom is characterized by a misguided permissiveness that appeases childish whims. Using fear of corporal punishment or psychological humiliation, the despotic classroom demands a standardized uniformity that punishes students' individuality, curiosity, spontaneity, and creativity. Good teachers, for Maritain, emphasize the importance of ideas in their teaching. They encourage students to enjoy the world of ideas and to use them creatively, especially as they convey and illuminate the culture in art, literature, music, philosophy, the fine arts, and religion.

The Student

Maritain saw the student in terms of his general Thomist conception of the human being. Though an immature human being, the student, as a person, is endowed by the Creator with an intellect that gives her or him the power to reason. Students, like all people, are in a personal relationship to God, and through grace, are called to divine life. Students need to open themselves to education which will teach them knowledge, judgment, and moral virtues. As social as well as intellectual beings, students need to learn to participate in social life and to contribute their service to the common good.[17]

The student, a rational and free being possessing a spiritual soul and a corporeal body, is endowed with an intellect that seeks to know. The teacher's task is to foster those fundamental dispositions that enable students to realize their human potentialities, which according to Maritain are (1) love of truth, goodness, and justice; (2) simplicity and openness to existence; (3) a sense of a job well done; and (4) a sense of cooperation.

NEO-PERENNIALISM

Neo-Perennialists such as Alan Bloom and Lynne Cheney, reasserting the traditional Perennialist themes of universal truth and values, reject relativism. They contend that general intellectual and ethical standards in education and society have been eroded by cultural and ethical relativism.

Allan Bloom

Allan Bloom (1930–1992), a professor at the University of Chicago, continued and revitalized the Perennialist tradition established by Hutchins, Adler, and Maritain. A student of philosophy and the classics, Bloom translated Plato's *Republic* (1968) and Rousseau's *Emile* (1979).[18] For Bloom, Western philosophy's roots reached back to ancient Greece. His theory of education, a revived form of Perennialism, gained national attention with the publication of *The Closing of the American Mind* in 1987.[19] Unusual for a philosophical work on education, the book was a best seller that attracted a wide readership outside of academia.

Taking a neo-Perennialist point of view that was shaped by his study of the classics, Bloom wrote a searching and stinging critique of American higher education that resembled Hutchins' *Higher Learning in America*. He charged that American universities were not only failing to educate their students but also miseducating them. Among the agents of miseducation were the professors in philosophy and the humanities who espoused philosophies such as Pragmatism, Language Analysis, and Postmodernism that denied objective truth and values. Engaged in endless analysis of terminology and repetitive deconstruction, these professors, while they preached openness, had closed their minds to older traditional standards and values. The end result was an unhealthy skepticism, a moral relativism, without standards. Although they claimed to be educated, many students, along with their professors, were ignorant of the great classics of Western thought and had turned the universities into rudderless ships, tossed in a sea in which anything goes. Bloom concluded that relativism in higher education had seriously weakened America's sense of intellectual and moral judgment.[20]

Lynne Cheney

Like Bloom, Lynne Cheney attacked trends toward cultural and ethical relativism in American education. She asserts that it is imperative that education transmit the models of excellence in history and literature that are based on truths that transcend time and circumstance. In particular, Cheney criticizes educators who allege that history and literature need to be interpreted through the lenses of socio-economic class, race, ethnicity, and gender. For her, universal truths and values transcend these particular lenses. Transcending class, race, and gender, they are relevant to all people, at all times.[21] It is necessary to protect these models of objective truth and value from those who would subvert and use them as ideological tools. Teaching and learning should be rooted in universal concepts of truth and justice.

PERENNIALISM'S PHILOSOPHICAL, IDEOLOGICAL, AND THEORETICAL RELATIONSHIPS

This section examines Perennialism's relationships with other philosophies, ideologies, and theories of education. Due to its origins in philosophical Realism, Perennialism is a highly metaphysical theory of education. Like the philosophies of Aristotle and Aquinas, Perennialism asserts the existence of an antecedent reality that human beings have not made, nor constructed. Importantly, human beings are endowed with intellectual power that enables them to know this reality. Perennialism is most compatible with philosophies, ideologies, and theories that have roots in metaphysics and least compatible with positions that are anti-metaphysical.

For metaphysics, see the chapters on Philosophy and Education; for their positions on metaphysics, see the chapters on Idealism, Realism, Pragmatism, Existentialism, and Postmodernism.

A Theory Derived from Realism

Throughout the chapter, it has been emphasized that Perennialism, as a theory, is derived from Realism, especially the philosophies of Aristotle and Thomas Aquinas. Perennialism borrows heavily from Realism's metaphysical principles of an antecedent objective reality and of humans as reasoning beings who can know this reality. Because reality is objective, truth about it is also objective; because reality is eternal, truths about it are eternal; and because it is universal, truth, too, is universal and does not depend on contexts and circumstances of time and place. Religious Perennialists such as Maritain, guided by Thomas Aquinas, see this reality as having spiritual and natural dimensions that human beings can approach through faith and reason.

For theories derived from philosophy, see the chapter on Theory and Education.

Essentialism: Similar but Different

Because of their similar positions on the role of the school and the skill and subject-matter organization of the curriculum, Perennialism and Essentialism are often linked. These two theories share many exterior features, but their different origins lead to different educational purposes. Perennialism and Essentialism agree that:

See the chapter on Essentialism and Education.

- The school's primary purpose is the academic development of students' intelligence and rationality.
- The curriculum should be composed of basic generative skills and academic subjects.
- Education should be based on a core in the liberal arts and sciences.
- Schooling prepares students for higher studies and economic, political, and social life.

While these similarities forge important connections between Perennialism and Essentialism, their differing origins lead to significant variations between the two theories. Perennialism as a theory, especially its metaphysical roots, is derived from Aristotelian Realism. Historically based, Essentialism is derived from an interpretation of history that asserts that skills and subjects have been and should remain the best educational practices.

Perennialism, true to its Aristotelian origins, asserts that truth and values are universal and timeless and that human beings are defined by their inherent rational nature. Essentialists look to history as a guide to what has worked in education. They claim that certain basic skills and subjects, as demonstrated by the past, are needed by each generation.

Both Perennialism and Essentialism agree that skills such as reading, writing, computing, listening, discussing, researching, and civility are necessary in future education and in life. They both assert that academic subjects, based on the liberal arts and sciences, provide the knowledge that cultivates rationality and that can be applied in life. Perennialists, however, emphasize the role of the classics—the great works in literature, music, and art—as a central focus of the curriculum.

Although they both see education as involving the transmission of the cultural heritage from one generation to the next, Perennialists and Essentialists hold somewhat different conceptions of transmission. For Essentialists, transmission is the rather direct instruction of students by skilled and knowledgeable teachers. It is important to be direct since getting to the point, teaching the skill or subject, is an efficient, effective, and verifiable way to learn. Perennialists, however, are not in a hurry. The cultivation of the intellect and the development of reasoning take a lifetime, of which schooling, though important, is but one phase. Using a Great Book, the teacher and students, really the readers, engage in searching dialogue and discussion to understand the author and to reach the book's meaning. The important goals are understanding and reflecting on the meaning of life and learning how to appreciate and participate in the heritage. While Essentialists and Perennialists agree on the importance of the liberal arts and sciences, they do so for different philosophical reasons. For Essentialists, the liberal arts and sciences have been developed over time, historically, as the best, or most civilized body of thought in Western civilization. For Perennialists, the liberal arts and sciences speak to human beings about universal and unchanging truths. For both Essentialism and Perennialism, the school's primary function is academic and intellectual, and curriculum should focus on basic skills and subjects.

Perennialism and Conservatism

See the chapter on Conservatism and Education.

Again, there are similarities but also differences between Perennialism and Conservatism. They agree that education should transmit the cultural heritage, that schools should be academic institutions, and that the curriculum should be organized into skills and subjects. Along with Essentialists, Perennialists would support the Conservative educational agenda of raising academic standards, reasserting discipline in the schools, and restoring public schools' intellectual quality.

Both Perennialists and Conservatives would agree that the works selected in the Great Books curriculum should represent the greatest thinkers in Western culture. However, they might disagree on which authors to include in the list. The Perennialist Great Books list includes those by Dewey and Marx, whose ideas most Conservatives oppose. They would also include Darwin's *On the Origin of Species,* a book many Christian Conservatives oppose. Further, the Perennialist emphasis on dialogue and interchange in discussing the Great Books does not guarantee prestructured outcomes. It is intended to lead to more questions rather than closed conclusions. Encouraged by well-educated teachers, students approach the great works of Western civilization with respect but also with questions that arise from their own search for identity, truth, and meaning.

Existentialism and Perennialism

See the chapter on Existentialism and Education.

The Existentialist attitude toward Perennialism is likely to be somewhat ambivalent. Existentialists would object to Hutchins' reasoning that truth is the same for everyone at every time and place; that knowledge is about truth; and since education is about knowledge, that it, too, is the same for everyone at all places and times. Hutchins' line of reasoning is too certain, too sure of itself. It eliminates the possibility for people to create their own perspectives on what they choose to believe.

Existentialists object to certain aspects of Perennialism, especially its metaphysical derivations that impose antecedent knowledge and prior definitions of human nature on students. If the human being, by nature and definition, is defined as an intellectual and reasoning being, where are the possibilities of choice and self-definition? Further, who defines the meanings of intelligence and rationality? Is there one meaning for all? Or are there multiple possibilities?

However, Existentialists would likely find the Great Books to be an interesting possibility in education. Some of these books present Existentialist themes in which their authors search for and create the meaning of their lives. Among the Great Books that tell about their authors searching for meaning in life are Henry David Thoreau's *Walden*, Herman Melville's *Moby-Dick*, James Joyce's *The Portrait of the Artist as a Young Man*, Jean-Paul Sartre's *Being and Nothingness*, and Franz Kafka's *The Trial*. Existentialists would also approve the Perennialist use of the Socratic method of engaging students in dialogues about the meanings found in the Great Books.

PERENNIALISM'S PHILOSOPHICAL, IDEOLOGICAL, AND THEORETICAL OPPONENTS

Resting on Realism's metaphysical premises, Perennialism is opposed by philosophies such as Pragmatism and Postmodernism that reject metaphysics. Affirming tradition and transmission in education, Perennialism is opposed by ideologies such as Marxism and theories such as Progressivism, Social Reconstructionism, and Critical Theory.

Pragmatist Objections

Pragmatists, especially Dewey, opposed Hutchins' and Maritain's arguments that truth and education are universal and timeless. Dewey dismissed Hutchins as marching backward to the Middle Ages rather than forward. Maritain's emphasis on eternal goals was so abstract and remote that it was useless in solving the problems of the present and in giving direction to the future. Rejecting metaphysics, Dewey objected to the Perennialist emphasis on antecedent knowledge, on the school as primarily an academic institution, and on the Great Books.

For Dewey's dismissal of universal truths, see the chapter on Pragmatism and Education.

Along with metaphysics, the crux of the educational difference between Perennialists and Pragmatists was epistemological, on how we know. For Perennialists, what we can know is out there, objective to us; because of our intellect, our reasoning powers, we can acquire knowledge. The best or most reliable knowledge is found in the liberal arts and sciences, as organized disciplines. Arguing against antecedent knowledge, Dewey said that our knowledge is based on our active and ongoing experience that results from our interactions with the environment. Just as we change and the environment changes, our ideas—what we know—need to be revised. Our knowledge claims are tentative, open-ended, and subject to revision in the light of more experience. Since humans interact with environments that are found in different places and at different times, experience is relative to these places and times. Our claims to truth need to be considered as culturally and temporarily relative, not timeless and universal as Hutchins claimed. While Dewey would not oppose reading and discussing the Great Books, he would consider them one of many paths to education.

Progressive Objections

For the Progressive emphasis on students' interests and needs, see the chapter on Progressivism and Education.

Progressives, especially those influenced by Dewey, would object to several features of Perennialism. They would find it a top-down theory of education in which the purposes of elementary and secondary schooling are set by colleges and universities. The idea that elementary education is to prepare students for secondary education, which in turn prepares them for higher education neglects students' interests, needs, and problems as the starting point of education. Further, the Great Books curriculum is too abstract and remote for children's and adolescents' experiences of the present.

Postmodernist Objections

Postmodern philosophers would raise strong objections to Perennialism's emphasis on metaphysically based universal and unchanging truth and values. They would see these Perennialist claims to universality as based on interesting but archaic classical thought. The philosophies of Aristotle and Aquinas, which the Perennialists exalt, are period pieces for the Postmodernists. Aristotle's distinctions between theoretical knowledge and applied practice justified the position of the Athenian leisure class of males who denied equality of women and maintained a slave economy and society. Aquinas' distinctions between soul and body and heaven and earth were used to justify the Roman Catholic Church's authority over medieval society and education. Aristotle's and Aquinas' works need to seen as statements justifying ruling elites that were raised to meta-narratives by Perennialists. Like any other texts, they can and need to be deconstructed to get to their real but limited meanings.

Postmodernists would raise serious objections to the Perennialist Great Books curriculum. The Great Books, no matter how interesting and engaging, are period pieces from another time and place. Hutchins, Adler, Maritain, and Bloom bestowed a privileged status to the Great Books. The Great Books, with very few exceptions, exalted the Western canon and ignored the contributions of Asians, Africans, and other non-Europeans to literature, art, music, and the humanities. Its privileging of the works of white Europeans and North Americans ignored multiculturalism.

Critical Theorist Objections

Critical Theorists would challenge Hutchins' claim that education, like truth and knowledge, is the same for all people regardless of time and place. These universalist principles have little or no meaning for teachers and students in economically deprived schools. They do not relate to the education of oppressed, repressed, and marginalized groups such as Latinos, African Americans, the working poor, women, and gays and lesbians. Either deliberately or unknowingly, Perennialists, claiming to possess universal truth, are reproducing the socio-economic class structure that empowers the powerful and marginalizes others. Rather than looking to the universe or to eternity for clues on education, schooling, and curriculum, teachers need to look where they are. They need to examine their particular school as an educational site. They need to connect their school and their teaching to the students, the families, and the communities that they serve.

Liberalism and Perennialism

While Perennialism is usually identified as a Conservative educational ideology because of its traditionalism, its major proponents, such as Hutchins, Adler, and Bloom, were not political conservatives. Ideologically, Liberals would not necessarily oppose the Great Books approach to education. For Liberals, the liberal arts and sciences and the Great Books have a place in education. However, they are not the only ways to educate people. Students need open-ended learning experiences that are experimental, creative, and process oriented.

Perennialists and Liberals are likely to disagree on the role of the school in society. For Perennialists, the school has the primary intellectual role of cultivating the rationality of students and introducing them to the great works of Western civilization. Liberals, in contrast, would see the school in more multifunctional terms; they would view its role as flexible and responsive to change rather than defined for all times. For Liberals, the functions of the school are responses to society's changing needs and issues. Wanting of make education more inclusive, Liberals might see the Great Books as a curriculum that is too narrowly focused on Western culture. It does not represent the inclusiveness needed in a multicultural global society.

For its multifunctional perspective on schools, see the chapter on Liberalism and Education.

PERENNIALISM EDUCATION, SCHOOLING, CURRICULUM, AND TEACHING AND LEARNING

This section examines Perennialism's implications for schooling, curriculum, and teaching and learning. These implications, like Perennialism itself, are heavily derived from Realism.

Education

The educational ideas of such leading Perennialists as Hutchins and Adler were shaped by their philosophical allegiance to Aristotle's Realism. Maritain's ideas were influenced by Aristotle and Thomas Aquinas. Perennialist educational purposes reflect the following Aristotelian principles:

- There is an objective reality that is governed by universal natural laws; education is to inform individuals about this reality and how its works.
- People, by their inherent human nature, are endowed with the power to reason; education is to develop and cultivate the individual's reasoning powers.
- The truth, like reality, is universal, timeless, and valid in all places at all times; since education is about truth, it, too, is the same everywhere.
- The liberal arts and sciences are based on what scholars and scientists have discovered about truth; education should be based on the knowledge contained in the liberal arts and sciences.
- Human beings are most rational when they act according to knowledge; education should cultivate choices that are based on knowledge.

The School

Perennialists believe that the school has a primary function in society: Its purpose is intellectual; it is to cultivate students' powers of reasoning. As an intellectual institution, the school is to introduce students to the Western cultural heritage so that they can share and participate in it.

Perennialists see elementary and secondary schools and colleges and universities as institutions governed by the same intellectual and cultural purposes. While their program is articulated to the students' readiness and stage of development, it is basically the same—to develop students' reasoning powers, intellectual outlook, knowledge, and participation in the cultural heritage. As with Essentialists, each level of education is to provide the skills, competencies, and knowledge that lead to the next higher stage.

Curriculum

Perennialists endorse a curriculum that consists of permanent studies—the cultural skills and knowledge that educated people have needed across time. The subject-matter curriculum derived from the learned disciplines—mathematics, history, literature, language, art, music, sciences—is based on the liberal arts and sciences. Students need to know the history, structures, and concepts of a particular subject. Once they have this disciplinary awareness, they can pursue interdisciplinary relationships among subjects. Ideally suited for interdisciplinary inquiry, the Great Books of Western civilization provide a means of relating knowledge areas to each other.

Teaching and Learning

The primary prerequisite for Perennialist teachers is that they be generally educated persons who have knowledge about and an understanding of the liberal arts and sciences. They need to be well versed in the great works of Western civilization. Ideally, they will have participated in discussions and dialogues about the Great Books. They are engaged with the life of the mind. This general education is necessary for good teaching.

With this grounding in the liberal arts and sciences, Perennialist teachers can explore ways to teach. Building a knowledge base comes first; then the various strategies, the methods of teaching, follow. The teacher needs skill in engaging students and introducing them to the great work and the ideas it contains. This introduction, however, is also a self-introduction by the student to the work that is being discussed and examined. The teacher needs skill in using the Socratic method, especially asking questions that lead students to broaden their intellectual horizons and their curiosity and appetite for more Great Books, music, and art. The teacher needs skill in teaching students how to understand, analyze, and appreciate a classic.

CONSTRUCTING YOUR OWN PHILOSOPHY OF EDUCATION

Now that you have read and discussed this chapter, reflect on Perennialism as you continue to construct your own philosophy of education. Do you agree or disagree with the Perennialist assertion that truth and values are universal and eternal? Do you agree or disagree that education is the same for all people, everywhere in the world? What is your opinion on the importance of reading and studying the Great Books? Does Perennialism appeal to you as a teacher? Are there aspects that you reject? Why? Do you plan to incorporate Perennialism or some elements of it in your philosophy of education?

Conclusion

Perennialism represents a clear illustration of how an educational theory is derived from a philosophy. Perennialism is of special interest as a theory that rests on a metaphysical foundation that asserts universal truth and the rationality that is embedded in human nature. The chapter illustrated how the ideas of Hutchins, Adler, and Maritain were shaped by the Realism of Aristotle and Aquinas. Although bound to the transmission of the Western cultural heritage, the Perennialist Great Books curriculum not only relates readers to the past but also provides opportunities for new interpretations of these classic works. Perennialism offers an alternative to more process-oriented approaches to education.

Questions for Reflection and Discussion

1. Have you encountered Perennialism in your own educational experiences? If so, describe and analyze these experiences.
2. Have you read one of the Great Books? What was the book and who is its author? Was the experience of reading a Great Book meaningful to you? Why?
3. Reflect on your own experience as an elementary and high school student. Do you recall an event, like the student-performed opera discussed in this chapter? Describe the event and its meaning for your education.
4. Of the philosophies, ideologies, and theories examined in this book, which is most compatible with Perennialism, and which is least compatible with it?
5. Do you think that there are books, music, and poetry that are necessary parts of a student's education? If you do, identify one of these necessary parts and explain your opinion.
6. Do you think that contemporary trends in society work against Perennialism as an educational theory?
7. Perennialists such as Hutchins believed that a subject's content was antecedent to and even more important than the method of teaching it. Do you agree or disagree?

Topics for Inquiry and Research

1. Select and read one of the Great Books. Do you think it is really a Great Book?
2. Design a school field trip to an art museum, based on Perennialist principles. What would you want the students to observe?
3. Suppose you are identifying a reading list for a high school course in American literature. List the books and write a brief statement of why they are included. Then imagine that Hutchins, Adler, or Maritain is reviewing your list. Would this Perennialist approve or disapprove of your list?
4. Access the Jacques Maritain Center at the University of Notre Dame at www.nd.edu/~maritain. Listen to the interview with Maritain.
5. Access the Great Books Foundation at www.greatbooks.org/. Identify the Great Books series appropriate to the grade or age level or the subject that you are teaching or preparing to teach.
6. Access the National Paideia Center at www.paideia.org/about-paideia/. Identify the Paideia curriculum appropriate to the grade or age level of the subject that you are teaching or preparing to teach.

Internet Resources

For a comprehensive collection of Maritain's works, books, papers, links, and an interview, access the Jacques Maritain Center at the University of Notre Dame at www.nd.edu/~maritain.

For the history, programs, series, and projects related to the Great Books, access the Great Books Foundation at www.greatbooks.org/.

For Paideia principles, instruction, and resources, access the National Paideia Center at www.paideia.org/about-paideia/.

Suggestions for Further Reading

Adler, Mortimer, J. *Paideia Problems and Possibilities: A Consideration of Questions Raised by the Paideia Proposal.* New York: Macmillan, 1983.

___. *The Paideia Program: An Educational Syllabus.* New York: Macmillan, 1984.

___. *The Paideia Proposal: An Educational Manifesto.* New York: Macmillan, 1982.

Bloom, Allan. *The Closing of the American Mind.* New York: Simon and Schuster, 1987.

Dzuback, Mary Ann. *Robert Hutchins: Portrait of an Educator.* Chicago: University of Chicago Press, 1981.

Hutchins, Robert M. *The Higher Learning in America.* New Haven: Yale University Press, 1961.

Maritain, Jacques. *Christianity and Democracy and the Rights of Man and Natural Law.* San Francisco: Ignatius Press, 2011.

___. *Natural Law: Reflections on Theory and Practice.* St. Augustine Press, 2001.

Mayer, Milton. *Robert Maynard Hutchins: A Memoir.* Berkeley and Los Angeles: University of California Press, 1993.

Notes

1. Laurence Urdang, ed., *The Random House Dictionary of the English Language* (New York: Random House, 1968), 986.
2. Biographies of Hutchins are Harry S. Ashmore, *Unseasonable Truths: The Life of Robert Maynard Hutchins* (Boston: Little, Brown, 1991); and Mary Ann Dzuback, *Robert M. Hutchins: Portrait of an Educator* (Chicago: University of Chicago Press, 1991).
3. Robert M. Hutchins, *The Higher Learning in America* (New Haven, CT: Yale University Press, 1962), 66–67.
4. Ibid.
5. Robert M. Hutchins, *A Conversation on Education* (Santa Barbara, CA: Center for the Study of Democratic Institutions, 1963), 1–2.
6. Ibid.
7. Mortimer J. Adler, *The Paideia Proposal: An Educational Manifesto* (New York: Macmillan Co., 1982), 4.
8. Ibid., 10.
9. Ibid., 10–17.
10. Ibid., 22–23.
11. Ibid., 26.
12. Ibid., 28–29.
13. http://www.paideia.org/.
14. For commentaries on Maritain and education, see the articles by Wade A. Carpenter, Gerald L. Gutek, Peter A. Lawler, Alice Ramos, and Madonna Murphy in Wade A. Carpenter, guest editor, *Educational Horizons, 83*(4), (Summer 2005).
15. In response to reviewers' recommendations, Perennialism is analyzed as a derived but distinctive theory of education as a separate chapter. This is a change from its placement in the chapter on on Realism in my *New Perspectives on Philosophy of* Education (Pearson, 2009).
16. Jacques Maritain, *Education at the Crossroads* (New Haven, CT: Yale University Press, 1960), 10.
17. Ibid., 62–67.
18. Allan Bloom, *The Republic of Plato* (translated with notes and an interpretive essay), 1968. (New York: Basic Books, 1991). Allan Bloom and Jean-Jacques Rousseau, *Emile* (translator) with introduction (New York: Basic Books, 1979).
19. Allan Bloom, *The Closing of the American Mind* (New York: Simon & Schuster, 1987).
20. Ibid.
21. For Lynne Cheney's ideas on education, see Lynne V. Cheney, *Humanities in America: A Report to the President, the Congress, and the American People* (Washington, DC: National Endowment for the Humanities, 1988); and Lynne Cheney, *Telling the Truth* (New York: Simon & Schuster, 1995).

Progressivism and Education

A statue commemorating Marietta Johnson (1864–1938), the progressive educator, who developed Organic Education, at the School of Organic Education at Fairhope, Alabama.

15

CHAPTER PREVIEW

Progressivism is a significant theory that promotes social and educational change and reform. It affirms the belief in "Progress," the possibility that human life and social institutions can be improved. We discuss Progressive education's origins in the Enlightenment, especially with the ideas of Jean-Jacques Rousseau, and then position Progressive education in the context of the Progressive movement in the American experience. After describing William H. Kilpatrick's project method as an expression of Progressive education, we identify and analyze Progressivism's implications for education, schooling, curriculum, and teaching and learning. The following topics are examined in the chapter:

- The origins of Progressivism in Rousseau's naturalism and in the Progressive movement in the American experience
- The Progressive education movement and internal divisions within Progressive education
- William H. Kilpatrick's project method
- Progressivism's philosophical, ideological, and theoretical relationships
- Progressivism's implications for education, schools, curriculum, and teaching and learning

As you read and discuss the chapter on Progressivism, reflect on your education. Did you encounter Progressivism in your school experiences? Did you have teachers and professors who used the project and activity methods? Did they emphasize educating the whole person—socially, intellectually, emotionally, and physically? Did they believe in learning by doing? See if there are aspects of Progressivism that appeal to you as a teacher.

ORIGINS OF PROGRESSIVISM

This section examines the origins of Progressivism and Progressive education. First, we examine the European origins of Progressive education by analyzing the ideas of Jean-Jacques Rousseau and then we consider how the Progressive movement shaped the context of American Progressive education.

Rousseau and Progressivism's European Origins

Progressive education's origins can be traced back to the **Enlightenment**, known as the Age of Reason. Enlightenment philosophers, especially the ***philosophes*** in France, challenged the theological doctrines of Christianity that viewed children, because of Adam and Eve's original sin, as born as either spiritually depraved or deprived. The *philosophes* challenged the idea that schooling was a

Enlightenment: the eighteenth-century Age of Reason that emphasized liberating human intelligence and using science to improve society.

Philosophes: French theorists of the eighteenth-century Enlightenment.

Naturalism: the theory that Nature is the source of clues about the patterns of human development and education.

remedy to exorcise children's instinctive inclinations to disorderliness, disobedience, and incivility.

Naturalism. Although they challenged the Christian theological doctrine of original sin, they continued to look to a Higher Power, an impersonal First Cause, which set the universe in operation. They generally subscribed to a Deist rather than a Theist view of the origin of life. For the Deists, the analogy of the Higher Power as a universal clock maker is often used. God, like a clock maker, made a universal clock, which ticks away time using its own internal mechanism. Once the universal clock begins ticking, it keeps on working on its own. The Power that started it no longer intervenes in its operations.

According to the Enlightenment theorists, God endowed human beings with the power to reason, but left it to them to work out their own destiny. In place of supernaturalism, the Enlightenment philosophers were most interested in nature and the universe's natural operations. They developed a naturalist concept of the universe's design that explained how the world worked. The Enlightenment theorists looked to and into nature to find how life should be lived. Education was important because, in the minds of the Enlightenment philosophers, it prepared people to live according to nature's principles.

The *philosophes*' concept of the scientific method was based on Isaac Newton's empiricism. In their tendency to search for natural laws, the *philosophes'* conception of *science* was not evolutionary and relativist as in modern science. Moving from Aristotle's deductive logic, the Enlightenment theorists were looking for specific empirical evidence and using induction to frame their generalizations about natural and social reality.

Importantly, the *philosophes* sought to liberate their thinking about science from the authorities of the past, especially from Greek and Roman classical philosophy and from the Church's theological doctrines. For them, the source of knowledge was Nature, itself. The book of Nature was always open, never closed. For them, the scientific method was an empirical, verifiable, and open way to observe natural phenomena. Through careful and consistent observation, it was possible to discern the laws or principles that made the universe work, such as the patterns of the revolution of the planets around the sun, the rotation of the earth, the growth of plants, and the circulation of the blood in the body. The idea that children learned by observing and reflecting on the natural and social environments in which they lived, rather than from books, became a consistent theme in child-centered American Progressive education. American Progressive educators would emphasize the role of the senses, the empirical, in learning. Children would learn most effectively and efficiently by using their senses in observing and experiencing the natural objects of their environment.

French *philosophes* such as Rousseau saw children as inherently good, not evil, at birth and as possessing instincts that needed to be followed so that they could grow and develop. The *philosophes'* strategy to improve the human situation was to use science to discover the natural laws, the general operating principles about how the universe functioned, and to use them to reform social, political, economic, and educational institutions. Embracing the ideal of **Progress**, the Enlightenment thinkers projected a better future if the human power to reason and to use science was liberated and used for reform. Freedom of thought meant that human beings needed to be liberated from arbitrary, authoritarian, and absolutist restrictions placed in their minds by the church and the state. From the Enlightenment theorists came four important principles that influenced the later Progressives: (1) children are naturally good, and

Progress: the concept, originating in the Enlightenment, that people can use their intelligence to create a better future. Also known as the Enlightenment Project.

their instincts and needs should guide education; (2) human growth and development is a natural process; (3) people can use their intelligence, especially the scientific method, to solve problems and reform society; and (4) humankind's future can be progressively better than its past.

Jean-Jacques Rousseau's Naturalism

Jean-Jacques Rousseau's (1712–1778) writings generated a major change in thinking about childhood and education that shaped child-centered Progressive education. Rousseau's ideas were an amalgamation of naturalism, romanticism, and science that, though not always coherent, offered a point of departure for later American Progressive educators. Rousseau's didactic novel ***Emile*** became a guidebook for many child-centered Progressives.[1]

Emile: Rousseau's educational novel about the education of a child in a natural environment that influenced Progressive education.

Rousseau's own childhood experiences shaped many of his ideas on education, which, in turn, he integrated into selected features of the Enlightenment's general ideology. The son of Suzanne Bernard and Isaac Rousseau, a watchmaker, Jean-Jacques was born in Geneva, Switzerland, the city where John Calvin once preached the doctrines of the Evangelical Protestant Reformation. Rousseau's mother died when he was nine days old. In reflecting on his own childhood, Rousseau claimed that he was overindulged by his highly emotional, impulsive aunt and his irresponsible, pleasure-loving father.[2] Rousseau recalled his father, his first tutor, read books to him that he did not understand and that filled his mind with vague mystical thoughts. In *Emile,* Rousseau warned against introducing books too early in the child's life. It is better for children to enjoy direct experiences of their immediate environment before reading about abstract concepts about which they know little or nothing. Rousseau's admonitions about the importance of direct experience and interaction with the environment and delaying reading became themes for American Progressive educators.

In 1739, when he was twenty-seven, Rousseau served as a tutor to the two sons of M. de Mably. He wrote about his experience as a tutor in his first treatise on education, the *Project of the Education of M. de Sainte-Marie.* In 1741, Rousseau went to Paris, the intellectual center of Europe's Enlightenment. In Paris, Rousseau entered into a relationship with Therese Levasseur, an illiterate maid. Rousseau and Levasseur had five children, all of whom Rousseau placed in orphanages shortly after their births. Readers of Rousseau's *Emile* find it ironic that Rousseau, an early proponent of child permissiveness, abandoned his own children.[3]

In 1749, Rousseau established himself as a *philosophe* with his award-winning essay, "Has the Progress of the Arts and Sciences Contributed More to the Corruption or Purification of Morals?"[4] Rousseau attacked the traditional view, still endorsed by Essentialists and Perennialists, that the arts and sciences, as the repository of Western wisdom, should be transmitted in schools. In contrast, Rousseau argued the arts and sciences tended to corrupt rather than liberate. His attack on the arts and sciences as the corpus of education differed from the view of Essentialists such as William C. Bagley and Arthur Bestor, Jr.

For their emphasis on the liberal arts and sciences, see the chapters on Essentialism and Perennialism.

Rousseau's major political work, *The Social Contract,* was published in 1762, the same year *Emile* appeared. In *The Social Contract,* Rousseau expressed his political philosophy on the origins of society, the state, and government.[5] Individuals came together to form an association when their need to survive was no longer met through their own independent action in the state of nature. In forming a society, the individual protected his natural rights by placing them with others' natural rights in what is called the "common good" or the "good of all." The "good of all" is determined by the "general will," a pervasive and all-embracing consensus. Although both Rousseau

For Locke, see the chapter on Liberalism and Education.

and John Locke argued that individuals formed political society to protect their natural rights (their inherent rights in the state of nature), their versions of the social contract differed. While Locke saw decisions made by majority rule, Rousseau gave the "general will" the paramount role. Locke's political ideas were was more influential on Liberal and Progressive theories than Rousseau's. However, the emphasis on creating consensus that some Progressives emphasized has elements of Rousseau's "general will."

On July 2, 1778, Rousseau died of uremia at Ermenonville, some thirty miles from Paris. He was buried on the Girardin estate. On October 11, 1794, his remains were transferred to the Pantheon in Paris.

Emile

Rousseau's *Emile,* or *On Education,* begins with "Everything is good as it comes from the hands of the Maker of the world but degenerates once it gets into the hands of man." For Rousseau, children are not born evil but rather are intrinsically good by their nature. It is an artificial miseducation that harms them. Children are not born as cheats, thieves, and liars but rather learn these vices from corruptive adults. Children's intrinsic natural goodness is spoiled by the corrupting influences of adults and their social institutions, including schools.

Amour de soi, or Self-esteem: values that arise from a person's natural and instinctive self-interests.

Amour propre, or Selfishness: the process by which a person learns to manipulate others for his or her own purposes.

For Rousseau, the educational challenge is to educate Emile in a natural environment where his naturally benevolent instincts can develop freely without being intruded on by the outside corruptive society. In an environment where he is free to develop, Emile can construct his self-identity through self-esteem, or ***amour de soi***. Rousseau contrasts *amour de soi* with ***amour propre***, or selfishness, by which a person learns to manipulate others for his or her own purposes.

Child-Centered Progressives: Progressive educators who base curriculum and instruction on children's interests and needs.

Child-centered Progressives, influenced by Rousseau, encourage children to follow their own instincts, needs, and interests and to design their own strategies for exploring their environment. This natural process is far better, they assert, than imposing adult standards and behaviors on them in schools. Socialization in traditional schools means curbing children's own inclinations so they can be taught to mimic adult-designed roles.

Rousseau's novel recounts how a tutor educates a well-to-do orphan, Emile, in a natural setting, a rural estate. This natural environment contrasts with conventional schools where the pre-established curriculum focuses on reading, writing, arithmetic, and subjects such as history, geography, and science, taught from reading books and memorizing and reciting their contents. Influenced by Rousseau, child-centered Progressives sought to replace the traditional school classroom with a more open, flexible, unhurried, and unscheduled environment.

ROUSSEAU'S STAGES OF DEVELOPMENT. In this natural environment, the tutor is determined to guide Emile to the experiences that are appropriate to his interests and readiness at a particular stage of development. Rousseau's concept of human beings proceeding through natural **stages of development** is especially important for Progressives. Rather than preparing children to learn the socio-economic roles for their adult life, Rousseau turned to nature, especially child nature, to identify the stages of development through which children pass as they move from infancy to adulthood. In the human life span, individuals are born, proceed through infancy and childhood, come to maturity, reach old age, and eventually die. There are appropriate experiences and activities for each developmental stage.

Stages of Development: the premise that human beings experience phases, or stages, of growth and development; education is to be appropriate to these stages.

Rousseau identifies infancy as the earliest stage of human life. He elongates infancy to extend from birth until the child is five years old. Diet, exercise, and freedom to explore the environment are important so Emile can grow into a physically healthy and mentally curious child. During infancy, the child, like an unspoiled primitive person, is close to the state of nature. The child's behavior is simple, unaffected, and natural. These simple and honest early behaviors are to be maintained and strengthened so Emile can grow into an adult with a natural disposition and attitude.[6]

Rousseau's elongated period of childhood is markedly different from the contemporary pushing and rushing of young children into academic activities as early as preschool and kindergarten. Echoing Rousseau, Progressive educators warned against the hurried and premature forcing of children into studies for which they are unready. Rousseau's second stage is boyhood, from age six through twelve. Becoming increasingly aware that some activities cause pleasure and others pain, Emile now begins to construct his own self-identity and to develop his earliest moral feelings. Rousseau develops two concepts of moral development: *amour de soi* and *amour propre.* Arising from a person's natural instinctive self-interests, *amour de soi* is the basis of healthy natural values. *Amour propre,* in contrast, is socially rather than naturally derived and causes the person to play roles and manipulate other people for self-aggrandizement.[7]

In arguing that values arise naturally rather than being forced on children, Rousseau warns against preaching to or lecturing children about what is right or wrong. It is more important that Emile learn that his actions have consequences than that an adult tells him what is good or bad and right and wrong. He will find out on his own that some actions bring either pleasure or pain. Again, Rousseau's ideas on moral education have influenced Progressive education. For example, Dewey saw genuine thinking and valuing taking place when the child begins to step back and reflect on the consequences of action. Other Progressives warned that talking about morality or taking a paper-and-pencil test about ethics are very different from actually living and acting as a moral and ethical person.

Rousseau warns against the "youthful sage," the highly verbal and seemingly precocious child who can glibly recite items of memorized information without really understanding them. Such children pattern their behavior to win praise from adults. They are learning to be artificial actors rather than naturally genuine persons.

Rousseau warns that books should not be introduced too early in a child's life. Children should not be pressured into reading. Emile will read when he is ready and wants to read. Emile, like a young scientist, uses his senses to observe the plants, animals, and objects in his environment and learns to estimate their size, shape, and dimensions.

Rousseau's second stage corresponds to the years during which many children attend elementary schools. Several of Rousseau's ideas shaped how Progressive teachers organize instruction. Rousseau's admonitions that children should engage in **sensory learning**, actively using their senses in direct explorations and observations of the environment, are an early version of Constructivism. Progressives, similar to Rousseau, believe children learn most effectively when they construct their own knowledge about reality. Still another Progressive strategy of extending the child's environment is the field trip—to arboretums, zoos, botanical gardens, museums, and other sites—where children learn through exploration and observation.

Sensory Learning: empirical learning based on using the senses.

Rousseau's third stage, from age twelve through fifteen, is when education focuses on learning about instrumental cause and effect relationships.[8] Continuing to explore his natural environment, Emile, still the young naturalist, asks the tutor questions about his observations, wanting to know what causes something to happen and how events relate to each other. Why is it light in the day and dark at night? Why do trees lose their leaves in the fall and sprout new ones in the spring? Why does water run downhill rather than uphill? It is important that the questions are asked by Emile and not the tutor. Emile makes his own maps to create his own guide to his surroundings. He learns to use his head and hands in performing a manual skill, such as carpentry. Emile, now wanting to read, spontaneously begins to read. His first book,

Robinson Crusoe, tells how Crusoe, marooned on a tropical island, learns to survive by living off the land. Emile learns about human relationships and how people come to depend on each other as he reads about the interactions between Crusoe and Friday, another person on the island.

Emile's next stage is the years between ages fifteen and eighteen.[9] Emile now has many questions about sex that the tutor answers directly, without embarrassment, coarseness, or mystery. Emile is also developing a social awareness about the needs of other people. In developing a sense of social justice, Emile builds on the early natural instincts of his childhood. Moral education, for Rousseau, does not come from preaching about avoiding what is evil or from speculating in an abstract sense about ethical dilemmas. It is acquired naturally through interactions with the environment, especially learning that one's actions will have consequences.

Rousseau's next stage, from eighteen to twenty, is the "age of humanity." Having enjoyed a natural childhood and adolescence, Emile now is ready to explore the broader world of culture, art, music, and literature. At age twenty, Emile is an adult. He meets and falls in love with his future bride, Sophie, who will be his wife and the mother of children raised in a natural family. Emile and Sophie's family will begin a new natural society. When the book ends, Emile promises his tutor that he will educate his children according to nature, just as he was educated.

Child-centered Progressives, inspired by Rousseau, view childhood as a very important phase of human growth and development. Their reading of *Emile* inspired them to have a strong commitment to permissiveness, which encourages children to follow their needs and interests as far as possible.

Rousseau made a very clear statement about the importance of education being appropriate to a child's stage of development and readiness. Readiness became a major theme in Progressive education. It warns against shortening childhood by pushing children into academic learning for which they are not developmentally ready.

THE PROGRESSIVE MOVEMENT AND PROGRESSIVE EDUCATION

In addition to European antecedents, especially Rousseau's educational ideas, Progressive education was part of a broad social and political movement in the United States from 1890 to 1920. Focused on reforming American society, its aims were social, political, economic, and educational. The Progressive movement continues to influence American society and education today.

Progressive Movement: a concerted effort, from 1890 to 1920, to reform government, society, the economy, and education in the United States.

Progressivism was rooted in the spirit of social reform that gripped the early twentieth-century **Progressive movement** in U.S. politics. As a sociopolitical movement, Progressivism held that human society could be improved by political, social, and economic reforms. Such U.S. political programs as Woodrow Wilson's "New Freedom," Theodore Roosevelt's "New Nationalism," and Robert LaFollette's "Wisconsin Idea," although varied in particulars, shared the common concern that the emerging corporate society needed to be regulated to function democratically for the benefit of all, not just some. Progressive political reformers represented the middle-class orientation to reform by gradual change through legislation and peaceful social innovation through education.

Francis Parker and Marietta Johnson: Originators of Progressive Education

To illustrate the development of Progressive education, we examine the ideas of two American theorists-practitioners: Francis Parker and Marietta Johnson. Both Parker and Johnson developed their theories of Progressive education as reactions against traditional school practices and from their own educational practices. Although they came from different backgrounds, they developed the core concepts, curriculum, and methods of Progressive teaching and learning.

Francis Parker

Called the father of Progressive education, Francis Parker (1837–1902), a former colonel in the Union army during the Civil War, gained notice among educators for reforming the schools of Quincy, Massachusetts. Parker constructed an eclectic theory of education that focused on children's direct experience and involvement with the concrete objects in the environment. Parker's focus on children made him a leading originator of child-centered Progressive education.

Parker's theory evolved as a reaction against traditional school practices such as drill and rote memorization that he believed impeded genuine learning. Instead of memorizing passages from textbooks, children began to read by learning simple words and sentences. Rather than memorizing sums and multiplication tables, children learned arithmetic by counting, grouping, and taking away and adding concrete objects. Instead of memorizing the names of continents, oceans, countries, capital cities, and rivers, children learned geography through field trips into the immediate environment.

In 1880, Parker became the principal of the Cook County Normal School in Chicago, Illinois, that prepared teachers for the city's schools. He advanced in his thinking from simply reacting against traditional practices to creating his own child-centered theory of education. Parker's curriculum was geared to fostering children's experiences rather than having them acquire antecedent bodies of knowledge.[10]

For the school as an academic institution, see the chapter on Essentialism and Education.

For Parker, the school was more than an academic institution, as Essentialists claimed. As a multifaceted and multifunctional social agency, it was a "complete community and embryonic democracy."[11] Parker wanted schools to be informal and relaxed places where children enjoyed learning.

Reacting against the formal textbooks, children, guided by their teachers, wrote their own small pamphlets to tell their own stories. As they read from the booklets they had written, they learned that language enabled them to share their ideas with others. Parker pioneered in developing the language arts as holistic learning.[12] Speaking, reading, writing, spelling, and grammar were taught as interrelated modes of expression and communication rather than as skills isolated from each other and drilled into children's minds as in traditional schools.

Intent on educating the "whole child" physically, emotionally, and intellectually, Parker encouraged children's aesthetic creativity and appreciation. Under Parker's guidance, art and music were central parts of the curriculum in which children sang, painted, drew, and sculpted to portray their insights and experiences.

For Parker, genuine education took place both in and out of the school in the child's own neighborhood, in museums and galleries, in parks, in woodlands, on the banks of ponds, and on the shores of Chicago's Lake Michigan. The school, the community, and the natural environment were interrelated educational spheres. The directed excursion, the educational field trip, was the ideal way to connect the child to the larger community and to nature. Parker's concepts of community schools, field trips, and integrated skills and subjects became important themes in later Progressive education.

Marietta Johnson

Organic Philosophy of Education: Marietta Johnson's version of child-centered Progressive education developed at the Organic School in Fairhope, Alabama.

Marietta Johnson (1864–1938), founded the **Organic Philosophy of Education**, which epitomized child-centered Progressive education. Johnson founded the Organic School at the Single Tax Community of Fairhope, Alabama. Fairhope was a planned community that was organized on the economic and social ideas of Henry George

(1834–1897). In his widely read book, *Progress and Poverty* (1879), George charged that an elite group controlled most of the land, the source of wealth. He proposed a single tax on land to correct the equal situation. Fairhope was established as a single tax corporation in which the community members owned the land and the products they made. Fairhope's citizens practiced the Progressive principle that people should have a strong sense of civic and social cooperation but also develop their individual interests. This sense of individualism within a cooperative community permeated Johnson's philosophy.[13]

Johnson moved from subject-based Essentialism to a child-centered Progressive orientation. Her organizing educational premise, similar to that of Rousseau, was that childhood needed to be lengthened rather than shortened.[14] Children's growth and development as human organisms should follow their own internal timetables rather than adults' scheduling. Possessing their own stages of readiness, children should not be pushed by teachers or parents to do things for which they unready. Teachers need to create a safe, friendly, informal, and engaging environment in which children learn at their own pace, according to their own interests. She wrote: "The aim of the school is to . . . know and meet the needs of the growing organism" and to "preserve the sincerity and unselfish-consciousness of . . . emotional life." The school should "provide for the finest, keenest intellectual activity, and minister to the all-round development of the nervous system. Ministering to growth, meeting the needs of the organism, is the sole function of the educational process—hence the term 'organic.'"[15]

Guided by her premise that the "main work of the child is to grow," Johnson attacked the traditional views that the purpose of education is to study predigested ideas in textbooks and to prepare children for future education and careers. Like Rousseau, she argued that book-based education often interfered with real thinking in which a person acted on a need, issue, or problem. For her, education is about the here and now and not something in the future such as preparing for more schooling, a career, or a profession.

As a child-centered Progressive, Johnson emphasized children's individual growth and development as well as their healthy socialization. Without being hurried or forced, social skills and sensibilities would develop when children were ready for them. Socialization was an ongoing process that developed as children played, learned, and worked together.

Johnson's activity-based curriculum included physical exercise, nature study, music, crafts, field geography, storytelling, dramatizations, and games. Creative activities such as dancing, drawing, singing, and weaving took center stage while reading and writing were delayed until the child was nine or ten years old.[16] Music and dancing were integral parts of the curriculum. There were unstructured nature field trips in which the teacher, without a preset lesson plan, was open to anything that captured the childrens' interests.

When the children were ready, the curriculum slowly began to merge activities into more systematic academic work. Nature study evolved into elementary science; stories about other people at other times evolved into literature, history, and geography. Arithmetic grew into practical and applied problem solving. Students presented adaptations of classical Greek plays, designing their own costumes and sets.

There were no proficiency or competency tests for promotion. Students simply moved forward. Just as she related schooling to children's developmental stages, Johnson centered high school on adolescence. Students at the Organic School studied the subjects in the standard high school curriculum—history, literature, foreign languages, mathematics, and sciences—but not in the conventional way. Using the organic method, they were free to follow their own interests, design their own projects, and make their own way through these subjects.

Johnson's school gained national attention when John Dewey visited Fairhope in 1913. In a highly favorable account in *Schools of Tomorrow*, Dewey praised Johnson's approach to education, saying the school demonstrates it "is possible for children . . . to progress bodily, mentally, and morally in school without . . . pressure, rewards, examinations, grades, or promotions, while they acquire sufficient control of the conventional tools of learning . . . ."[17] Johnson's Organic educational philosophy and her school also attracted a favorable response from child-centered Progressive educators.

Progressive Education as a Movement

Progressive educators redefined the concepts of childhood and adolescence in ways that contributed to the reforming of education and schools. Reacting against the prim and proper Victorian dictum that "children should be seen but not heard," Progressive educators wanted children to have more open, free, and liberating educational experiences than they had encountered. They viewed with disdain how the childhoods of working-class children in the cities and farm children in rural areas had been shortened by their families, who abruptly put them to work as soon as they could legally leave school. Like Rousseau, Progressive educators wanted to elongate the time of childhood and broaden children's experiences.

Progressive educators developed an American version of adolescence, the teenage years. Using the concept of stages of development, Progressives constructed an interval of growth that allowed time between childhood and entry into the adult workforce. They were informed by the educational psychologist G. Stanley Hall (1844–1929), who had researched and published his findings and opinions in *Adolescence* (1904). Hall identified adolescence as a crucial period of human development in which adolescents recapitulated the human race's progress from primitive to civilized life. Progressive educators sought to restructure the traditional academic high school into a new institution that reflected the new findings on adolescence.

For Dewey's Experimentalism, see the chapter on Pragmatism and Education.

For Dewey's Laboratory School, see the chapter on Pragmatism and Education.

Along with child and adolescent psychology, some Progressive educators eagerly used Pragmatism, especially John Dewey's Experimentalism. Dewey's Experimentalist philosophy exerted a powerful influence on Progressive education. Progressive educators were informed by Dewey's educational experiment at the University of Chicago Laboratory. Progressive educators eagerly accepted Dewey's proposition that a school should be like a laboratory where ideas about education could be tried and tested. Dewey's *The School and Society* (1900) and *The Child and the Curriculum* (1902) were widely read by Progressive educators. From Dewey, Progressives learned that the schools should be multifunctional community centers, where the curriculum originated from children's direct experiences and then extended into society's larger issues and concerns. Opposing the imposition of adult aims on education, Progressives were keen to accept Dewey's view that education's sole aim was human growth, an ever-broadening human experience.

PROGRESSIVE EDUCATION ASSOCIATION

Progressive Education Association: an organization of Progressive private and public educators established in 1919.

In 1919, Progressive private and public school educators and professors of education organized the **Progressive Education Association** (PEA), with John Dewey as the association's honorary president. The Association's journal, *Progressive Education*, disseminated articles about educational reforms and innovative programs across the country.[18] The PEA emphasized the following principles:

- Progressive education should encourage children's natural development and growth through activities that cultivate their initiative, creativity, and self-expression.

- Instruction should be guided by the child's own interest, stimulated by experience in the environment.
- Progressive teachers are to guide children's learning as directors of research activities, rather than as taskmasters.
- Student achievement should be measured in terms of mental, physical, moral, and social development.
- There should be greater cooperation among the teacher, the school, and the home and family in meeting children's needs for growth and development.
- The truly Progressive school should be a laboratory to test innovative practices.

Although they came in many varieties and had multiple goals, Progressives united in opposing traditional book-centered, teacher-dominated instruction. For them, the child should be the focus of classroom activity, with instruction arising from children's interests and needs rather than from externally imposed goals. Teachers in such situations should be directors of research and inquiry, who establish learning environments conducive to children's growth and development. Although Progressives agreed about opposing traditional school practices, they disagreed on the nature and degree of children's freedom. Dewey himself, in *Experience and Education*, challenged the notion of some child-centered Progressives whom he believed had exaggerated children's freedom as an educational absolute divorced from society.[19]

Progressive educators generally had a three-pronged agenda: (1) to remove the formalism, routine, and bureaucracy that devitalized learning in many schools; (2) to devise and implement innovative methods of instruction that focused on children's needs and interests; and (3) to professionalize teaching and school administration to make it more competent, efficient, and scientific. Progressive educators pioneered new methods of education such as "learning by doing," activity-based learning, group projects, and problem solving. Contemporary innovations such as Constructivism and process-based learning are latter-day versions of Progressive education.

Internal Divisions within Progressive Education

Although they were united in opposing traditional schooling, Progressive educators split into two factions: child-centered and Social Reconstructionist educators. Child-centered Progressives saw the child as education's vital focus. For them, the curriculum grew out of the individual child's interests and needs rather than being imposed as the prescribed, pre-established skills and subjects of the traditional curriculum. They believed that children, free from arbitrary rules, should be at liberty to pursue their own interests. Through their own self-initiated activity, children, guided by permissive and encouraging teachers, were to explore their environment and thereby enlarge their horizons of space and time.

Social Reconstructionists: Progressive educators who want schools used as agencies for deliberately directed social, political, and economic reform.

Like the child-centered Progressives, the **Social Reconstructionists** opposed traditional schooling's formalism, routines, and authoritarianism. Seeing education as a politically charged process, Reconstructionists wanted schools to be agencies for deliberately directed social, political, and economic reform.[20] Reconstructionists such as George Counts (1889–1974), Harold Rugg (1886–1960), and Theodore Brameld (1904–1987) sought to forge Progressive education into an ideological weapon to create a new society.[21]

For the Reconstructionist perspective, see the chapter on Social Reconstruction and Education.

The child-centered and Reconstructionist Progressives disagreed on the extent to which schools and teachers should deliberately attempt to direct social and political change. Some child-centered educators feared the Reconstructionist agenda was so ideological that it would lead to students' indoctrination. The Reconstructionists, in contrast, argued that Progressive educators, by not taking a stand on the major political and economic issues, were reinforcing the status quo. While these internal disagreements among Progressives gave the movement vitality, they also contained the seeds of conflicts.

Dewey's Critique of Progressive Education

Dewey's critique of Progressive education in *Experience and Education* (1938) makes his position on the movement clear. It also relates how educational theories are formed as reactions. Dewey warned that the controversy between traditional and Progressive educators had degenerated into an assertion of either/or positions. Although sympathetic to Progressivism and the honorary President of the PEA, Dewey believed that many Progressives were merely reacting against traditional school practices and had failed to formulate an educational philosophy capable of serving as a plan of pragmatic operations.

For another discussion of either/or positions, see Bagley's discussion of Progressive education in the chapter on Essentialism and Education.

Dewey's analysis of the traditional and the Progressive school highlights the contrasts between these two institutions. The traditional school, he said, is a formal institution that emphasizes a subject-matter curriculum composed of discretely organized disciplines, such as language, history, mathematics, and science. Traditionalists, such as Perennialists and Essentialists, hold that the source of wisdom is located in humanity's cultural heritage. Morals, standards, and conduct are derived from tradition and are not subject to the test of the scientific method. Esteeming the written word as the fount of wisdom, traditional teachers rely on the textbook as the source of knowledge and the recitation as the means of eliciting it from students. Traditionalists isolate the school from social controversies. Holding to their belief that learning is the transmission and mastery of bodies of knowledge inherited from the past, the Traditionalists ignore the learner's own needs and interests and neglect urgent social and political issues. Students are expected to be receptive to traditional wisdom, have habits and attitudes conducive to conformity, and be respectful of and obedient to authority.

For education and the cultural heritage, see the chapters on Essentialism and Perennialism.

Although Dewey shared the Progressive antagonism toward the traditional school, he feared that many Progressives were merely reacting against it. Too many Progressives had ignored the past and were concerned only with the present. In their opposition to the traditional school's passivity, some Progressives had come to emphasize any kind of activity, even purposeless activity. Many Progressives had become so antagonistic to education imposed by adults that they had begun to cater to childish whims, many of which were devoid of social and intellectual value.

After urging that Progressive educators avoid the polarization of an either/or educational position, Dewey outlined the philosophy that he believed was suited for the genuinely Progressive school. Progressive education needed a philosophy based on experience, the interaction of the person with the environment. Such an experiential philosophy was to have no set of external goals. Rather, the end product of education is growth—that ongoing experience that leads to the direction and control of subsequent experience. At this point in constructing a theory of Progressive education, Dewey is providing a philosophical foundation—Experimentalism. Truly Progressive education should not ignore the past but rather should use it to reconstruct experience in the present and to direct future experiences. For Dewey, education should be based on a continuum of ongoing experience that unites the past and the present and leads to the shaping of the future.

Dewey warned Progressive educators against becoming so absorbed in activity that they misunderstood the meaning of being active. Mere movement is without value. Activity should be directed to solving problems; it should be purposeful and should contain social and intellectual possibilities that contribute to the learner's growth.

The true Progressive educator is a teacher skilled in relating the learner's internal conditions of experience—that is, the student's needs, interests, purposes, capacities, and desires—with the objective conditions of experience—the environmental factors that are historical, physical, economic, and sociological.

Dewey asserted that Progressivism should be free from a naive romanticism of child nature such as that suggested by Rousseau. Although children's interests and needs are always at the beginning of learning, they are not its desired end. The child's instincts and impulses need to be refined and developed into reflective social intelligence. Some impulses contain possibilities for growth and development; other impulses have the opposite result in that their consequences impede growth. Impulse becomes reflective when the learner is able to estimate the consequences of acting on it. By developing an "end-in-view," the learner could conjecture the consequences that would result from action. Understanding the purpose of a particular act involves estimating the consequences that had occurred in similar situations in the past and forming a tentative judgment about the likely consequences of acting in the present. Thus, Progressive education should encourage the cultivation of purposeful, reflective patterns of inquiry in the learner.

Challenging Essentialism and Perennialism, Dewey warned educators against trying to "return to the intellectual methods and ideals that arose centuries before the scientific method was developed." Truly Progressive educators should systematically use the "scientific method as the pattern and ideal of intelligent exploration and exploitation of the potentialities inherent in experience."[22]

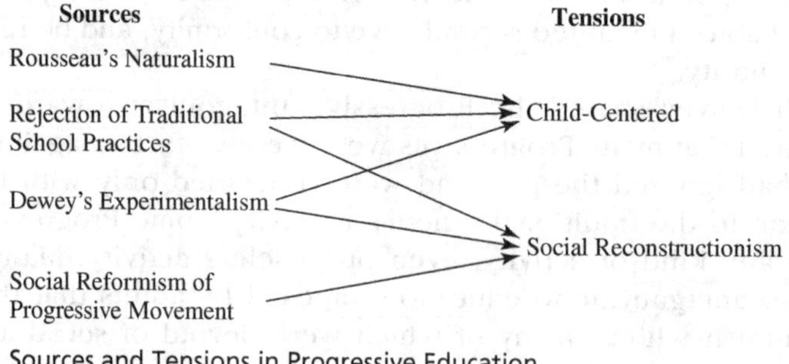

Sources and Tensions in Progressive Education

WILLIAM HEARD KILPATRICK AND THE PROJECT METHOD

As a teacher and school principal in rural Georgia, William Heard Kilpatrick (1871–1965) had devised his own version of Progressive education as a reaction against traditional school practices. Kilpatrick's efforts to construct his own philosophy of education illustrate how theory is constructed from practice. Kilpatrick believed that genuine learning came from children pursuing their own interests in a relaxed and informal school environment. Rather than sitting quietly at their desks as they wait for the teacher to call on them to recite a memorized lesson, students should be free to move about the classroom and collaboratively share their ideas. He replaced traditional report cards with monthly written progress reports.[23] He emphasized internal rather than external discipline.

Determined to make the study of education his career, Kilpatrick enrolled at Teachers College at Columbia University in New York City for his doctoral study.

There he encountered John Dewey and his Experimentalist philosophy. Kilpatrick was open to Dewey's emphasis on learning as problem solving according to the scientific method as well as his rejection of *a priori* absolutes that limited thinking. His study with Dewey, Kilpatrick said, "remade my philosophy of life and education." Dewey, in turn, praised Kilpatrick as his best student.[24]

In 1909, Kilpatrick joined the Teachers College faculty as a part-time lecturer in the history of education. In 1910, he received a full-time appointment and on January 11, 1911, successfully defended his doctoral dissertation on the Dutch schools of early New York. Until his retirement, Kilpatrick taught at Teachers College, earning the title of the "million dollar professor" because of the revenue his well-attended courses generated for the college.

As a professor of education at Teachers College, Kilpatrick became a noted interpreter of Dewey. His writings and lectures, which espoused themes associated with Experimentalist philosophy and Progressive education, attracted large and receptive audiences. A gifted lecturer, Kilpatrick clarified many of Dewey's more difficult theoretical concepts. He was not, however, merely an interpreter. He also advanced his own educational philosophy, which synthesized Progressivism and Experimentalism into the "purposeful act" or the "project method." Because he reached a large number of teachers in his classes, Kilpatrick had a great influence on American education.

The Project Method

Kilpatrick's "The Project Method: The Use of the Purposeful Act in the Educative Process" appeared in *The Teachers College Record* in July 1918.[25] Kilpatrick designed the **project method** to integrate Dewey's scientific method of problem solving, the "Complete Act of Thought," with Progressive educational practices. Today, the project method is used by teachers in schools throughout the world.

Project Method: widely used in instruction, students work in cooperative planning and activities to achieve an end, often a concrete result; doing something as a group to reach a goal.

Kilpatrick opposed traditional subject-matter-dominated and teacher-controlled school practices. He criticized the traditional school curriculum for its rationale that skills and subjects should be taught in the way adults conceived of them rather than as children actually experienced them. In traditional schools, teachers transmitted finished, prepackaged, secondhand subjects to students. Instead of learning by transmission, Kilpatrick argued that real learning occurs when, through exploration, children solve a problem or satisfy a curiosity in a way that explains their environment and adds to their experience.

Kilpatrick's project method rejected traditional education's reliance on a book-centered instruction. He asserted that books are not a substitute for learning through living. The most pernicious form of bookishness is the textbook's domination of conventional teaching. Too frequently, teachers rely exclusively on information in textbooks. This often leads to mechanically organized, secondhand experiences. The student who succeeds in the traditional school is frequently successful in memorizing but not always in understanding what was read. Because of its stress on memorization, conventional schooling had degenerated into devitalized mechanical routines in which teachers assign lessons from textbooks, drill their students on the assignments, hear recitations of memorized responses, and then evaluate them on their recall of the material. Such schooling, in Kilpatrick's view, stifled individual creativity, led to boredom, and lacked collaborative social purposes.

Following Dewey's lead in emphasizing education's social nature, Kilpatrick stressed the social significance of transforming classrooms into collaborative, democratic, learning communities. The project method incorporated several principles that Kilpatrick had developed as a teacher and teacher educator. Among them were "wholehearted purposeful activity," "primary responses," "associate responses," and "concomitant responses." To engage in wholehearted purposeful activity meant that students were motivated by their own interests, committed to do the work necessary to complete a project, and wanted to collaborate with their peers in mutually sharing the information and the skills needed in the process. A primary response was what students had to do to begin and complete a project. Associate responses were ideas, skills, and information generated by the primary response. For example, in setting up a balanced aquarium, the primary task, students might need to use library and research skills to read about fish and aquatic plants. Concomitant responses might be social, ethical, and political attitudes such as learning to cooperate with others—to share information and ideas, to take turns in using tools—and, more important, coming to understand that actions have consequences. Unlike the closed pre-structured curriculum, Kilpatrick's process was open ended in that the exact outcomes and responses could not be specified in advance.[26]

In contrast to the rote nature of traditional book-centered education, Kilpatrick designed his project method as a constructive Progressivism that exemplified Experimentalist methods. In the project method, students are to choose, plan, direct, and execute their work in activities, or projects, that stimulate purposeful efforts. As an Experimentalist method of problem solving, the project method enlists students, either individually or in groups, in defining problems that arise in their own experiences. Learning is task centered in that success comes from solving the problem and testing the solution by acting on it. Action from purposeful planning meets the pragmatic test of being judged by its consequences.

Kilpatrick recommended that the school curriculum be organized into four major classes of projects. First, the creative or "construction" project involves concretizing a theoretical plan. For example, the students might decide to write and then present a drama. They would write the script, assign the roles, design the set and props, and actually act out the play. Or the creative project might involve the design of a blueprint for a library. The test would come in the construction of the library from the plan devised by the students. Second, the appreciation or "enjoyment" project is designed to contribute to aesthetic experience. Reading a novel, watching a film, or listening to a symphony are examples of projects that lead to aesthetic appreciation. Third, the "problem" project is one in which students are involved in resolving an intellectual problem. Such problems as the resolution of racial discrimination, the improvement of the quality of the environment, or the organization of recreational facilities are social problems that call for disciplined intellectual inquiry. Finally, the "specific learning" project involves acquiring a skill or an area of knowledge. Learning to swim, dance, read, write, or use the computer are examples of specific skill acquisition.

Kilpatrick's project method should be interpreted both in terms of its suggested social consequences and its educational aims. To be sure, the project method has educational objectives, such as improvement in creative, constructive, appreciative, intellectual, and skill competencies. However, acquiring these competencies is only a part of Kilpatrick's plan. Kilpatrick believed, as did Dewey, that education as a social activity relates closely to human association and collaboration. In a free society, democratic discussion, debate, decision, and action depend on the willingness of individuals to use the methods of open and uncoerced inquiry. Kilpatrick believed that the project method lent itself to group work, in which students collaboratively pursue common problems and share in associative inquiry. Even more important than the acquisition of specific skills is the student's need to develop the attitudes that will allow them to participate in a democratic society.

My Reflections on Philosophy of Education: Experiencing the Project Method

Throughout the book, I have encouraged you to reflect on the philosophical implications of your own educational experiences. In writing this chapter section, I reflected on my own educational experiences to find examples of Progressive education. I thought back to my high school experience. I was attending Streator Township High School, in Streator, Illinois, a town of about 15,000 inhabitants. When I was a senior in high school, I was enrolled in a course in American Problems. My teacher, Miss Dorothy Bash, used the project method. The course examined issues in American society and government. Miss Bash, a Progressive teacher, related the topics in the course—the organization of the federal government, state and federal powers, and foreign policy—to current events. It was 1952—a presidential election year. The two major candidates were Dwight Eisenhower, the Republican nominee, and Adlai Stevenson, the Democratic nominee. It was inevitable in a class like Miss Bash's that we would discuss the election. However, we decided to do more than discuss; Miss Bash, using the project method, directly involved the class in the election campaign. The class designed a schoolwide project to "Get out the vote." We were going to make sure that the citizens in Streator exercised their right to vote.

Because I was very interested in politics, I had a leading role in the project. Most planning for the project was done by student committees. We decided that we would encourage a large voter turnout in the community with a contest. Local businesses were solicited by students and asked to contribute prizes that would be won by the elementary-age students who collected the greatest number of voters' tags. Many of the town's businesses joined in the project. High school students involved in the project would be stationed at the polls, the various voting places, and would give each voter a tag, indicating that they had voted. After the polls had closed, the elementary students who wished to would collect the tags, and those with the highest number of tags would receive the prizes. In this way, we got the community and the younger students involved in our project.

Miss Bash made sure that we had the approval of the high school administration to carry out the project. Students met with the principal, who reviewed and agreed to our proposal. Miss Bash said that we needed to inform the community about what we were planning to do, and I went with her to meet with the editor and publisher of the local newspaper. The editor, interested in our project, agreed to give it extensive coverage in the paper. At this point, the project was becoming a community-wide project.

Although we were all too young to vote, the students in the project decided to organize some events in the high school related to the national election. We arranged some presentations by students, who played the roles of the leading candidates. There was a school assembly in which the student playing General Eisenhower gave a campaign speech. I played the part of Governor Stevenson. We then conducted a mock election with all the high school students eligible to vote. At that time, voting was done with paper ballots and we used paper sample ballots. Students in the course on American Problems acted as election officials. The local election board allowed us to use the voting booths that would be used on Election Day. I don't know whether it was because of my speech but Stevenson carried the student vote. He would lose the actual election to General Eisenhower, however.

The project worked in many ways. The students in the American Problems course got to see how an election worked at the local level. The larger community became involved with the high school and its students in a community-wide project. For me, there were many of what Kilpatrick would call concomitant learnings. I learned how to work with other students on committees. I learned the process of discussion and of working out the inevitable issues and conflicts that arise in working with a group. I also made many friends that I would not normally have made.

The Progressive Teacher in the Project Method

Compared to instruction through transmission in traditional schools, Kilpatrick's Progressive teacher appears to play a secondary or supplemental role in the project method. However, the Progressive teacher's role is different rather than supplemental. The Progressive teacher needs to make the child her or his primary subject and to be knowledgeable about other kinds of subjects, information, and knowledge areas needed to accomplish a project's goals. The teacher needs to know the students as persons and must consider their family and ethnic backgrounds, prior experiences, and interests. The teacher is to guide but not control students' learning. The Progressive teacher exercises an important role in structuring the environment so that it is rich with opportunities for learning. The teacher is to guide students to new activities, new projects, new problems, and thus enlarge and broaden their social and cultural relationships.

The person whom Kilpatrick envisioned as a result of education based on purposeful collaboration is the democratic man or woman. Such a person would possess an experimental attitude and be willing to test inherited traditions, values, and beliefs. Through the project method, students would learn to use democratic methods of open discussion, carefully reasoned deliberation, decision making that respected both the rights of the majority and the minority, and action that resulted in peaceful social change.

Kilpatrick's model of the democratic citizen was much like that envisioned by middle-class Progressives in politics and in education. This person would use a democratic methodology and would expect opponents to use the same procedure. As a reconstructive person, this Progressively educated man or woman would believe that social institutions were creations of human intelligence and could be periodically renovated when the situation required it. The democratic citizen would be open to using the scientific method and would discard theological, metaphysical, political, and economic absolutes as dogmatic impediments that blocked human inquiry into the conditions of life. Above all, Kilpatrick wanted to educate individuals who shared a common framework of democratic values. Such men and women would be wholehearted and willing participants in the democratic community.

PROGRESSIVISM'S PHILOSOPHICAL AND IDEOLOGICAL RELATIONSHIPS

As a theory of education, Progressivism draws heavily from Rousseau's Naturalism and Dewey's Pragmatism. From Naturalists, Progressives appropriated the principle that children should be free to use their own needs and interests in their self-development. The child-centered Progressives' emphasis on children's needs and interests led them to conclude that the curriculum should develop from the child and that the most effective school environment is a permissive one in which children are free to explore and act on their interests. Progressives emphasize children's directly expressed needs and interests over the transmission of academic subject matter.

Progressives drew their educational rationale from Pragmatism, especially Dewey's Experimentalism. They reject the view that education is to exercise reason in knowing, or intellectually grasping antecedant knowledge. For Progressives, knowledge is a human construction that based on experience and not antecedent to it.

Although Progressives could agree that children should be liberated from repressive schooling, they disagreed on the extent to which education, as a social force, involved some degree of imposition. Believing that human intelligence is shaped by social interaction, Deweyan Progressives emphasize the group, social issues and problems, and the power of the scientific method in complete and reflective thought.

Progressivism rejects the more traditional philosophies of Idealism, Realism, and Thomism and their emphasis on antecedent reality, hierarchical categories, and subject matter curricula. Though they were reformers who wanted to promote social justice, many Progressives such as Dewey rejected Marxism as a dogmatic threat to freedom. Marx's preaching of inevitable class struggle and revolutionary warfare contrasted with the Liberal Progressive method of using democratic parliamentary processes to bring about reform. Taking a middle way between extremes, Progressives sought to educate individuals who, committed to democratic processes, would work to improve life. Progressivism is more compatible with Liberalism, in its modern social welfare form, than with other ideologies. Liberalism's concern for individual rights and freedom finds an educational corollary in Progressivism's emphasis on the individual child. The freedom to inquire and test ideas, exemplified by Liberal theorists such as John Stuart Mill, is also stressed by Progressives.

For their views on antecedent reality and knowledge and hierarchy in the curriculum, see the chapters on Idealism and Realism.

For its emphasis on individual rights, see the chapter on Liberalism and Education.

Both Liberals and Progressives favor change rather than maintaining tradition and the status quo. Conservatives, like Essentialists, see Progressive education as threatening cultural continuity, eroding the power of tradition as a stabilizing factor, and jeopardizing legitimate authority. Conservatives fear that Progressive permissiveness, like Liberal individualism, will weaken standards.

For the Conservative and Essentialist critique of Progressive education, see the chapters on Conservatism and Essentialism.

Progressives and Liberals are process, or procedure, oriented. They both emphasize representative institutions, due process of law, and gradual incremental reform rather than revolutionary change. Historically, Progressive social reformers have worked within the social and political system. Their efforts at reform were designed to improve the system by using representative institutions and processes to remedy its internal weaknesses. Progressive reformers, like Liberals in general, prefer open-ended reform, which has limited ends-in-view rather than preconceived ends.

Progressivism and Liberalism share many common themes: the Liberal commitment to reform through gradual processes of change; the following of shared procedures to adjudicate differences of opinion; open discussion and debate; and the freedom to express ideas are all viewed favorably by Progressives. Progressives, like Liberals, seek to be **consensus** builders. Democracy, for both Progressives and Liberals, requires the construction of a broad, general consensus or agreement on the procedures by which we govern ourselves, compromise our differences, and adjudicate our disputes. Education, especially through public schools, is seen as a consensus builder in which people learn the procedures, practice them, and are committed to using them.

Consensus: a broad, general, pervasive agreement in society on the role and functions of institutions and social, political, and educational processes.

Progressivism, as a theory of education, opposes many principles of Essentialism and Perennialism. Whereas Essentialists and Perennialists take an academic view of the school, Progressives see schools as multipurpose and flexible institutions—learning communities that serve a broad range of individual and social needs. Concerned with the education of the whole person, the school's aims are intellectual, psychological, moral, social, civic, and economic. Progressives warn against the Essentialist and Perennialist "four walls" philosophy of education that separates schools from their society and the community they serve.

For their view that the school has a primary academic function, see the chapters on Essentialism and Perennialism.

Based on education's multiple goals, Progressive curriculum and instruction reject Essentialism's traditional emphasis on predetermined discrete skills and subjects that are prior to children's experience. Rather, Progressives contend that the curriculum should come from children's interests and needs and their exploration of the environment. It presents occasions in which children encounter problem-solving situations, work out solutions, and construct their concepts of reality. Just as the goals of the Progressive school are multifunctional, the instructional repertoire of Progressive teachers needs to be highly versatile. Teachers, as Marietta Johnson stated, need psychologically informed insights into children's cognitive and emotional growth and development; they need to have a large range of skill and subject knowledge as a necessary background for teaching; and they need to be skilled in using group dynamics for cooperative learning.

Progressive educators are likely to object to the contemporary standards and common core curriculum movements. For them, relying on standardized tests to measure students' achievement and basing instruction on external standards is just misdirected traditional education in a contemporary guise. External standards, coming from legislators and learned academic societies, force children to do what adults determine they should do rather than what is appropriate to their own growth and interests. Genuine education arises out of a child's own stage of development and readiness; teachers should be free of external interference so they can create flexible guidelines for children's instruction based on child development and child and adolescent psychology. Externally imposed standards not only adversely affect students but also constrain teachers into teaching for the test rather than for the child.

Values or character education is an important point of conflict among Progressives, Essentialists, and Perennialists. While Progressives see values as arising in cultural contexts and changing within these contexts, Essentialists see values as stable and arising in humankind's historical experience. For Perennialists, values are universal and arise from an unchanging human nature. Progressives see values arising not from absolute and universal standards but as human reactions to a changing environment. Arising in the particular environmental situations in which they occur, the times and places in which people live, values are relative to these particular cultural situations. Valuing is the result of estimating and judging how behaviors contribute to human growth, development, culture, and satisfaction.

See the chapters on Postmodernism and Critical Theory.

Relating Progressivism to Postmodernism and Critical Theory reveals some interesting similarities but also differences. Progressivism is based on the concept of progress that originated in the Enlightenment. It accentuates the belief that humans can construct a better future by using their liberated intelligence and the scientific method. Postmodernists and Critical Theorists are hostile to the Enlightenment's privileged and powerful interpretation in Western history. For them, the Enlightenment project, including its doctrine of progress, is another historical metanarrative used to rationalize and justify domination by a ruling group. The objectivity claimed for the scientific method is but a mask for its use by powerful and domineering elites.

Still another point of contention is the Progressive tendency to use transactional reform in which parts of the school and parts of the curriculum are changed, generally by adding to it. Critical Theorists believe this limited and additive change preserves more of the status quo than it changes. Instead of transactional and piecemeal change, Critical Theorists, like Social Reconstructionists, want transformational change to radically reform schools and society.

Critical Theorists would agree with Progressives that the school should be closely related to the society. As an agency of community building, schools can use a local site-based strategy in constructing community-based democracy. Critical Theorists would commend the Progressive tendency to remove the departmentalized barriers among subjects and to use more integrated interdisciplinary processes in curriculum and instruction.

For its Progressive origins, see the chapter on Social Reconstruction and Education.

Critical Theorists would find much more compatibility with Social Reconstructionists, like Counts and Brameld, who argue that the school should create a new social order. Critical Theorists would agree with the Reconstructionists, who argued that following children's interests as the sole criterion of curriculum and instruction retreats into laissez-faire romanticism that reinforces the status quo rather than reforms society. Reconstructionist Progressives, like the Critical Theorists, want to use schools as agencies for social reform by emphasizing controversial issues that examine social, political, and economic problems and that seek to solve them.

PROGRESSIVISM'S IMPLICATIONS FOR EDUCATION, SCHOOLS, CURRICULUM, AND TEACHING AND LEARNING

As a theory of education, Progressivism was shaped by general ideas of educational reform such as Rousseau's naturalism; Pragmatism, especially John Dewey's Experimentalism; Liberal reformist ideology; and reactions against Victorian-era prescriptions and traditional school practices. Progressivism's implications for education can be considered in schools, curricula, and teaching and learning.

Education

Given the variety of Progressives, they more easily agreed on what they opposed than on what they proposed in education. Reactively agreeing that education was not the transmission of doctrines or dogma, Progressives saw education as requiring flexibility and openness to change. For child-centered Progressives, inspired by Rousseau and Johnson, education is highly subjective and personal. It provides the means by which children express themselves, free from Victorian-era constraints. For Dewey and the Pragmatically inclined Progressives, education means an openness to experience in which learners solve problems arising in their environment by using the scientific method. Progressives, influenced by Liberalism, see education as a way of informing people about what needs to be fixed to keep representative political, economic, and social institutions functioning properly and how life can be improved by reforming these institutions so that they function in the popular interests. For Liberal Progressives, an educated public could devise the strategies in which democratic government could regulate the economy, guarantee pure food and drugs, protect the environment, and end political corruption. Through these strategies, education is an instrument to bring about progress and improve life and society.

For Liberalism's relationships to Progressivism, see the chapter on Liberalism and Education.

Schools

The Progressive view of the school was both reactive against traditional schooling and proactive in envisioning a variety of new educational prototypes. The Progressive view of the school ranges from reforming existing schools to creating new ones. Historically, those who wanted to reform existing schools were educators who were already in the established system. They believed that they could reform school structures through incremental changes, deletions, and additions. For example, recitations of memorized materials could be deleted and field trips could be added. Progressives reactively sought to replace the more formal traditional skill and subject-focused and teacher-dominated school with learning spaces where teaching and learning were informal and child-centered. Others, like Dewey, saw the school in a new form as an educational laboratory to test new ideas about teaching and learning.

Naturalism, especially Rousseau's version, inspired the child-centered Progressives to view children as naturally good, or at least morally neutral, in their early years. Johnson, like Rousseau, contended that children's nurturing and education should be free of artificial restraints. She as well as Kilpatrick accentuated the educational efficacy of activities and excursions that connected the school and classroom to the natural environment and to the neighborhood and community.

Curriculum

The Progressives' concept of curriculum, like most of their beliefs, ranges from making small incremental alterations in the existing curriculum to constructing something completely new. Generally, Progressives rejected the Essentialist curriculum of separate skills and departmentalized subjects. Progressives believed that skills and subjects could be correlated with each other and taught in a more unified and integrated way. For example, reading, writing, spelling, and composition could be reorganized and integrated as language arts. In similar fashion, history, geography, civics, and government could be reorganized and taught in an integrated way as the social studies. In this move toward interdisciplinary fusion and integration, skills and subjects are still being taught, but in relationship to each other in a way that reflected both students' interests and society's needs. Progressives found the interdisciplinary integration of skills and subjects especially useful in problem solving. Problem solving required information and concepts from a variety of subjects, not just one.

For the learning as appropriation, see the chapter on Existentialism and Education.

Some Progressives wanted a completely new form of curriculum. Child-centered Progressives, inspired by Rousseau, argued that the curriculum should not be antecedent to the child and specified in advance. The curriculum should be an unfinished and ongoing act of construction that came from children's needs and interests. Similar to Existentialists, these Progressives saw the curriculum as something that the learners defined; it was not determined by teachers in advance of the learners' presence on the school scene. Dewey-inspired Progressives see the curriculum organized around children's interests and needs in relationship to humankind's past experience and current problems. They do not separate curriculum and methods but see them in a process-based interface. Using the scientific method to solve problems would arise in the present situation, take students into the past to gain its insights, and bring them from the present into a future that they could shape.

OPPOSITION TO EXTERNAL STANDARDS. Most Progressives would be opposed to standards externally imposed on teachers and students. For example, the child-centered Progressive Marietta Johnson condemned standards as "absolutely unnecessary." Johnson argued that external standards, such as those found in the contemporary standards movement, force children to do what adults determine they should do rather than what is appropriate to their own growth and interests. Because a genuine education arises out of a child's own stage of development and readiness, teachers can develop flexible guidelines for children's instruction based on child development and child and adolescent psychology but still reject external standards. Johnson argued that because "every individual is unique there can be no other reasonable standard of accomplishment." She charged that basing curriculum and instruction on what was examined on standardized tests geared education to a mythical average child who does not exist in reality. Rather than following expectations based on the achievement of the non-existent "average child," the teacher "should develop a keen and definite judgment of individual ability and endeavor to keep each pupil up to this standard."[27]

Kilpatrick joined Johnson in opposing externally imposed standards. Both the reliance on tests and the use of standards imposed external authorities on children jeopardize their following of their own interests to solve problems. Just as today there is a basic inconsistency between using portfolios in authentic assessment and giving standardized tests, there was an inconsistency in Kilpatrick's day between standardized testing and the project method. He fought against the domination of tests over education. Tests, he argued, assessed facts that could be easily looked up and ignored the genuine results of learning such as the ethical values of sharing, responsibility, and respect of others; in addition, tests neglected the aesthetic values of appreciating art and music. While tests could be used to diagnose readiness and prior learning, they were of little use in measuring genuine learning. Kilpatrick believed that the emphasis on testing and measuring was confining teachers and students in an educational straitjacket that gave them few options. An increasing emphasis on standardized testing was driving the curriculum and forcing teachers to teach for the test.

Teaching and Learning

Progressives agree that genuine teaching and learning are not transmitting existing subjects from teachers to learners. Neither are they having students memorize and recite what was transmitted to them by teachers and textbooks. For Progressives, inspired by Rousseau's naturalism, teaching means guiding learning by arranging a rich environment that excites children's curiosity and interests. It means refraining from intruding into children's learning by encouraging them without forcing them.

For Dewey-inspired Progressives, teaching and learning are process-based. Dewey's belief that education's sole purpose is growth for the sake of further growth corresponds to the Progressives' call for children's freedom to explore and learn from activities in the environment. His concept of experience as the interaction of the person with the environment corresponds with the Progressive emphasis on process, "learning by doing," projects, and activities. Dewey's Complete Act of Thought, or problem solving according to the scientific method, corresponds to the Progressive orientation that children learn best by reflecting on future actions and validating these actions in the consequences they produce. His emphasis on shared human experience, or associative living and learning, corresponds well with Kilpatrick's emphasis on collaborative group projects. For example, Kilpatrick's project method sees children and adolescents learning to be democratic members of society by sharing ideas, participating in mutual endeavors, and concretizing their ideas in completed projects. Conclusions, however, are not final but rather are constructions that can be revised through further research, experimentation, reinterpretation, and testing.

Constructivism

Progressivism would find the contemporary Constructivist approach to instruction to be highly compatible. Constructivism is a psychology of learning that sees children, through their interactions with the environment, constructing their own meanings of experience rather than appropriating those presented to them by others. Especially in early education, children in constructivist settings engage in exploring and defining their own environment. Through these interactions, they acquire a framework of meaningful ideas that is their own network for sorting out, cataloguing, and interpreting subsequent experiences. Progressives would find much to endorse in Constructivism, which approximates the Progressive theory (especially Dewey's version) of learning through problems that occur in environmental interactions.

CONSTRUCTING YOUR OWN PHILOSOPHY OF EDUCATION

Now that you have read about and discussed the chapter on Progressive education, reflect on how it might influence your philosophy of education. Do you believe that children learn from their experience and that project-based learning enhances that experience? Do you believe that children construct their ideas about reality from their interactions with the environment? Do you want your classroom to be a bridge to nature and society? Do you plan to use Progressivism, or some aspects of it, in constructing your philosophy of education?

Conclusion

Progressive education's influence is found in teacher education programs that emphasize such process-oriented learning strategies as "educating the whole child," "learning by doing," the project and activity methods, cooperative and collaborative learning, constructivism, portfolio use, and site-based management. Progressives contributed to reshaping the traditional elementary school curriculum from specifically defined skills and subjects into broad fields. For example, reading, writing, and spelling were reorganized into the integrated language arts; history and geography were restructured into the multidisciplinary social studies.

Progressivism continues to exert an ongoing influence on contemporary American education. It operates from an orientation that education is to help us learn to interact intelligently with our natural and social environments, as well as our national and global environments. It is to give us the intellectual tools to work out our social, political, economic, and cultural relationships in ways that are most satisfying for human growth and development. Indeed, our social knowledge and values are relational in that they are constructed through satisfying mutual interactions with our peers.

Questions for Reflection and Discussion

1. Do you think that most Americans believe in the concept of progress; that the future will be better than the past? If so, how does that belief shape their social, political, and educational expectations?
2. Do you agree or disagree with Conservative, Essentialist, and Perennialist critics of Progressive education who allege that it has weakened the academic quality of public education by inserting nonintellectual activities into the curriculum?
3. Reflect on Rousseau's ideas about stages of human development. Do you find an emphasis on stages of development in contemporary education?
4. If you have been involved in project-based learning as part of your own education or your teaching, reflect on Kilpatrick's rationale for the project method. Do you think he was right or wrong about the outcomes of project-based learning?
5. Do you agree with Progressives, who view the school as a multifunctional institution, or with the Essentialists, who see it as an academic institution?
6. Do you think that the ethical relativism associated with Progressive education is compatible with the current moral climate in the United States?

Topics for Inquiry and Research

1. Do you observe evidence of Progressivism in classroom situations that are part of your professional clinical experience?
2. Write a position paper in which you describe how Progressives might react to the standards movement and the use of standardized tests to measure student achievement.
3. Visit some kindergartens or preschool situations. Do you find evidence of what child-centered Progressives, such as Marietta Johnson, would call the premature, or too early, introduction of academic activities?
4. If you have been involved in assessments by portfolios and standardized testing, compare and contrast your reactions. How might Progressives react to your reflections?
5. In a group discussion, consider whether the contemporary situation is congenial or adversarial to Progressive principles of education.
6. View the video on Marietta Johnson's philosophy of Organic Education at http://www.fairhopeorganicschool.com/Home_Page.html. Identify and analyze this philosophy.
7. Access Steven Wolk, "Project-Based Learning: Pursuits with a Purpose" at http://www.ascd.org/publications/educational_leadership/nov94/vol52/num03/Project-Based_Learning@_Pursuits_with_a_Purpose.aspx. What are the educational purposes of the project method?

Internet Resources

For recent developments and an active voice for Progressive education, access the John Dewey Project on Progressive Education at the University of Vermont at www.uvm.edu/~dewey/.

For the project method, access http://www.stateuniversity.com.

For an overview of Progressive education, access www.uvm.edu/~dewey/articles/proged.html.

For a video about Organic Education, access the Marietta Johnson School of Organic Education at http://www.fairhopeorganicschool.com/Home_Page.html.

Suggestions for Further Reading

Beineke, John A. *And There Were Giants in the Land: The Life of William Heard Kilpatrick.* New York: Peter Lang, 1998.

Boyd, William, ed. *The Emile of Jean-Jacques Rousseau.* New York: Teachers College Press, Columbia University, 1966.

___. *The Minor Educational Writings of Jean-Jacques Rousseau.* New York: Teachers Press, 1962.

Carlson, Dennis. *Making Progress: Education and Culture in New Times.* New York: Teachers College Press, 1996.

Cranston, Maurice W. (1991). *Jean-Jacques: The Early Life and Work of Jean-Jacques Rousseau, 1712–1754.* Chicago: University of Chicago Press, 1991.

___. *The Noble Savage: Jean-Jacques Rousseau, 1754–1762.* Chicago: University of Chicago Press, 1991.

Cremin, Lawrence A. *The Transformation of the School: Progressivism in American Education, 1876–1957.* New York: Alfred A. Knopf, 1961.

Cullen, Daniel. *Freedom in Rousseau's Political Philosophy.* DeKalb: Northern Illinois University Press, 1993.

Dewey, John. *Experience and Education: The 60th Anniversary Edition.* West Lafayette, IN: Kappa Delta Pi, 1998.

Dewey, John, and Dewey, Evelyn. *Schools of Tomorrow.* New York: E. P. Dutton, 1915.

Engel, Brenda S., and Anne C. Martin, eds. *Holding Values: What We Mean By Progressive Education.* Portsmouth, NH: Heinemann, 2005.

Graham, Patricia A. *Progressive Education: From Arcady to Academe—A History of the Progressive Education Association, 1919–1955.* New York: Teachers College Press, 1967.

Hayes, William. *The Progressive Education Movement: Is It Still a Factor in Today's Schools?* Boulder, CO: Rowman & Littlefield, 2006.

Howlett, John. *Progressive Education.* Edinburgh, UK: Newwork Education Press, 2013.

Kliebard, Herbert M. *The Struggle for the American Curriculum, 1893–1958.* Boston: Routledge & Kegan Paul, 1986.

Melzer, Arthur M. *The Natural Goodness of Man: On the System of Rousseau's Thoughts.* Chicago: University of Chicago Press, 1990.

Necker, Albertine, and Adrienne de Saussure. *Progressive Education.* Ann Arbor, MI: University of Michigan Library, 2009.

Norris, Norman D. *The Promise and Failure of Progressive Education.* New York: Scarecrow Education, 2004.

Rousseau, Jean-Jacques. *Discourses on the Sciences and Arts: First Discourse and Polemics.* Hanover, NH: University Press of New England, 1992.

___. *Emile: or On Education.* Translated by Allan Bloom. New York: Basic Books, 1979.

Stallones, Jared R. *Conflict and Resolution: Progressive Education and the Question of Religion.* Information Age, 2010.

Stone, Marie Kirchner. *The Progressive Legacy: Chicago's Francis Parker School, 1901–2001.* New York: Peter Lang Publisher, 2001.

Tanner, Daniel. *Crusade for Democracy: Progressive Education at the Crossroads.* Albany: State University of New York Press, 1991.

Trachtenberg, Zev M. *Making Citizens: Rousseau's Political Theory of Culture.* London and New York: Routledge, 1992.

Weiss, Penny A. *Gendered Community: Rousseau, Sex, and Politics.* New York: New York University Press, 1993.

Zilversmit, Arthur. *Changing Schools: Progressive Education Theory and Practice, 1930–1960.* Chicago: University of Chicago Press, 1993.

Notes

1. Gerald L. Gutek, *A History of the Western Educational Experience* (Prospect Heights, IL: Waveland Press, 1995), 164–167.
2. William Boyd, ed., *The Minor Educational Writings of Jean Jacques Rousseau* (New York: Teachers College Press, Columbia University, 1962), 7–23.

3. William Kessen, "Rousseau's Children," *Daedalus* 107 (Summer 1978), 155–164.
4. Jean-Jacques Rousseau, *The First and Second Discourses,* ed. Roger D. Masters (New York: St. Martin's Press, 1964).
5. Jean-Jacques Rousseau and Maurice Cranston, *The Social Contract* (New York: Penguin Books, 1968).
6. Jean-Jacques Rousseau, *Emile: or On Education,* trans. Allan Bloom (New York: Basic Books, 1979), 37–74.
7. Ibid., 77–163.
8. Ibid., 165–208.
9. Ibid., 211–355.
10. Lawrence A. Cremin, *The Transformation of the School: Progressivism in American Education, 1876–1957* (New York: Alfred A. Knopf, 1962), 130.
11. Francis W. Parker, *Talks on Pedagogics* (New York: E. L. Kellogg, 1894), 450.
12. Cremin, *Transformation of the School,* 132–133.
13. Marietta Johnson, *Thirty Years with an Idea* (University of Alabama Press, 1974), 51.
14. Ibid., 20–21.
15. Ibid., 52.
16. Ibid., 52–55, 62–63, 86–95.
17. John and Evelyn Dewey, *Schools of Tomorrow* (New York: E. P. Dutton, 1915), 39–40.
18. The definitive history of the Progressive Education Association is: Patricia Albjerg Graham, *Progressive Education: From Arcady to Academe—A History of the Progressive Education Association, 1919–1955* (New York: Teachers College Press, Columbia University, 1967).
19. John Dewey, *Experience and Education: The 60th Anniversary Edition* (West Lafayette, IN: Kappa Delta Pi, 1998).
20. For the history of Social Reconstructionism, see Michael E. James, *Social Reconstructionism Through Education: The Philosophy, History, and Curricula of a Radical Ideal* (Norwood, NJ: Ablex, 1995).
21. George S. Counts, *Dare the School Build a New Social Order?* (New York: John Day, 1932), 17–18.
22. John Dewey, *Experience and Education,* 108.
23. John A. Beineke, *And There Were Giants in the Land: The Life of William Heard Kilpatrick* (New York: Peter Lang, 1998), 22–23.
24. Ibid., 59–61.
25. William H. Kilpatrick, "The Project Method: The Use of the Purposeful Act in the Educative Process," *Teachers College Record* (September 1918), np.
26. Beineke, *And There Were Giants in the Land,* 106–107.
27. Johnson, *Thirty Years with an Idea,* 106.

Social Reconstructionism and Education

George S. Counts (1889–1974), whose question, "Dare the school build a new social order," sparked Social Reconstructionism.

16

CHAPTER PREVIEW

This chapter discusses Social Reconstructionism, a theory of education that originated as a response to social and economic crises. It argues that educators cannot remain on the sidelines of social change but need to use schools and classrooms to respond to crises by creating a new, more just and equitable society. Reconstructionists urge teachers to engage as agents of directed change rather than to mirror and reproduce the status quo. Through an analysis of the ideas of George Counts, Harold Rugg, and Theodore Brameld, the chapter examines the origins, development, and influence of Social Reconstruction on education. George Counts inaugurated **Social Reconstructionism** with his book *Dare the School Build a New Social Order?*

Theodore Brameld then enlarged Social Reconstructionism's foundations by including educational anthropology as an agency of socioeducational interpretation, change, and reform. Harold Rugg designed a social studies curriculum in which teachers and students investigated and analyzed controversial social, economic, and political issues. Social Reconstructionism, also known as Reconstructionism, raised important issues for education, such as: Should schools and teachers attempt to bring about directed social change, or should they transmit existing "official" knowledge and values?

The chapter examines the following topics:

- Introducing Social Reconstructionism
- George Counts and Theodore Brameld as leading Reconstructionists
- Reconstructionist themes
- Reconstructionism's philosophical, ideological, and theoretical relationships
- Reconstructionism's implications for education, schools, curriculum and instruction

CONSTRUCTING YOUR OWN PHILOSOPHY OF EDUCATION

As you read and discuss this chapter, reflect on Social Reconstructionism as you proceed to construct your own philosophy of education. Have you encountered Social Reconstructionism in your own educational experiences? Did you have Reconstructionist teachers and professors who proposed that education should change society? Did they suggest a plan for bringing about social change?

Social Reconstructionism: an educational ideology or theory that argues that education and schools should be agencies to create a new, more equitable and democratic society.

Did you agree or disagree with them? Did your courses involve the examination of controversial issues? After you read the chapter, see if there are aspects of Social Reconstructionism that you plan to incorporate into your philosophy of education.

INTRODUCING SOCIAL RECONSTRUCTIONISM

Social Reconstructionism argues that education can and should be used to create a new, more democratic, more humane, and more equitable society. This process of educational reconstruction involves integrating selected cultural elements with new and emerging ones, such as bioengineering and the electronic dissemination of information by computers and other forms of technology to create a new social order.

It is not easy to position Social Reconstructionism as a philosophy, ideology, or theory because it connects with and overlaps these divisions. It has close philosophical ties to Pragmatism, and its leading proponents saw it as a philosophy. It also fits the pattern of being an ideology. For example, George S. Counts, like most ideologists, called for education that had an interpretation of the past, an analysis of the present from a particular point of view, and an action program for the future.[1]

Karen Riley, a historian of education, sees an examination of Social Reconstructionism as an intellectual and educational challenge of "understanding the American mind and what makes us tick."[2] Educational theorist William B. Stanley calls it "an influential school of thought in the current education reform dialogue."[3]

Contemporary Relevance

Wayne Urban, a distinguished historian of education, finds Social Reconstructionism relevant as a defense against current attacks on the concept of public education. Among these attacks are the contemporary movement for standardized testing that "threatens to rob the pedagogical process of any flexibility," and the efforts of fundamentalist religious groups to advocate home schooling as an alternative to what they perceive to be public schools' secular values.[4] William B. Stanley, a social studies educator and student of Reconstructionism, finds relevance in the Reconstructionist themes that:

- Social change outdistances the capacity of existing institutions, including schools, to make the needed adaptations.
- Social criticism is necessary in education.
- Futurist thinking—conjecturing how society might be improved—is a fruitful educational exercise.
- The groups who dominate society, politics, and education will use schools to reinforce and reproduce their control.[5]

GEORGE S. COUNTS AND THEODORE BRAMELD AS LEADING RECONSTRUCTIONISTS

Although there were and are many Social Reconstructionists, our analysis focuses on the theories of two originative educators: Counts, who inaugurated the movement, and Brameld, who broadened and developed Reconstructionist themes in education.

GEORGE S. COUNTS

When George S. Counts (1889–1974) asked the question "dare the school build a new social order?" he sparked the movement that developed into Social Reconstructionism. A pioneer in the social foundations of education, Counts used interdisciplinary lenses to examine education. He moved back and forth, crossing the boundaries of academic fields such as history, political science, economics, sociology, and comparative education to examine educational issues.[6] For most of his academic career, Counts was a professor of education at Columbia University's Teachers College, where from 1927 until 1955, he worked with other Progressives such as William H. Kilpatrick, Harold Rugg, and John Childs. These followers of John Dewey's Pragmatic Instrumentalist philosophy and self-styled "frontier thinkers" shaped early Social Reconstructionism during their frequent meetings. Of them, Counts, also a political activist, helped found the American Labor Party and then the Liberal Party in New York State.[7] Always supportive of organized labor, Counts was the American Federation of Teachers' president from 1939 to 1942.

Counts was a contextual thinker in that he placed education, especially schooling and teaching, within a context of time and place. This contextualism set him apart from the Perennialists who argued that education, as a universal process, transcended the particularities of specific contexts. As a scholar, Counts examined American education in its broad social, political, economic, and cultural contexts. His *Secondary Education and Industrialism* (1929) analyzed industrialization's impact on education, and *The American Road to Culture* (1930) examined the school's role in transmitting and shaping American culture.[8] The crucial years for the origins of Social Reconstructionism, however, coincided with the devastating economic crisis of the Great Depression of the 1930s. In 1932, Counts startled the members of the Progressive Education Association at their annual convention by asking, "Dare Progressive Education be Progressive?" He then broadened his challenge to the educators of the United States, asking, "Dare the School Build a New Social Order?"[9]

For universal themes in education, see the chapters on Idealism, Realism, and especially Perennialism.

We now explore the process that led Counts to ask his challenging question by examining the special mentoring relationship between Charles A. Beard and Counts. The Beard–Counts relationship illustrates the importance of mentoring in education, scholarship, and teaching. The distinguished historian, Beard, in providing Counts with suggestions and feedback, encouraged him to develop a frame of reference for his ideas. Today, mentoring is emphasized as an important process in teacher education and formation in which an experienced teacher guides and advises a novice teacher.

The Mentoring Relationship Between Charles Beard and Counts

Counts' theory of Social Reconstruction, especially the importance of placing education in its contexts, was shaped and refined by his association with Beard. When Counts seemed to be too radical and polemical in expressing his ideas, the more experienced senior scholar, Beard, would advise him to stop, wait a while, and reflect on them. Beard also encouraged Counts to take new directions in his research and writing.

Beard, who interpreted history from a progressive perspective, suggested that he and Counts develop a frame of reference for their vision of American education. Counts and Beard were colleagues who served on the American Historical Association's Commission on the Social Studies. A prominent contributor to the "new history," a Progressive interpretation of America's past, Beard emphasized the role of economics as a major force in shaping historical trends. He asserted that economic factors had shaped decisions at the Constitutional Convention at the country's founding.

Beard claimed that history and the social sciences, constructed and functioning in a context of time and place, could never be completely objective, or even neutral, but needed to be "organized around some central philosophy."[10] Instruction in the social sciences could not and should not be isolated from social issues but needed to respond to social change.[11] Beard's rejection of neutrality in education corresponded with Counts' emphasis on the importance of placing education in context. Beard made the case that teachers needed a frame of reference that recognized that American society (1) was in profound change; (2) was an industrial economy, based on science and technology; and (3) needed rational planning and intelligent cooperation in all its sectors. In addition, Beard argued that democracy requires informed public discussion, debate, and criticism.[12] Spurred by Beard and his frontier colleagues, Counts constructed a frame of reference that shaped Social Reconstructionism.

Frame of Reference: the strategy that educational policy and planning needs to be executed from a background of insights and findings from history, sociology, economics, political science, and psychology.

Counts' Frame of Reference

Counts prefaced his **frame of reference** on **contextual relativism**, that is, the importance that living in a particular place at a particular time has on culture and education. Like Beard, Counts stated that history was the story of people struggling to solve the real problems that affected their lives and future.

Contextual Relativism: the concept that cultural contexts, the particular places and times in which people live, are an important influence in shaping education and schooling.

THE IMPORTANCE OF CONTEXT. Arguing that education, like history, happened in a **context**, Counts wrote:

Context: the concept that education and schooling take place at a particular place and time.

> . . . education is always a function of time, place, and circumstance. In its basic philosophy, its social objectives, and its program of instruction, it inevitably reflects . . . the experiences, the conditions, and the hopes, fears, and aspirations of a particular people or cultural group at a particular point in history. . . . Education . . . is always relative, at least in its fundamental parts, to some concrete and evolving social situation.[13]

Counts' argument that education is always based on a context raises important philosophical issues. Critics, especially Idealists and Realists, argue that Counts' emphasis on specific contexts was so limited that it was embedded in ideology rather than philosophy. No longer general or transferable across contexts, it was limited to a specific place and time. These critics, as well as their educational allies, the Perennialists and Essentialists, argued further that Counts confused and blurred the distinctions and relationships between education and schooling. For them, education is a general and universal process found in all cultures and societies that transcends particular places; it is schooling that is particular to a given culture. For example, people worldwide speak a language; they are schooled by their context to use a particular language such as English, Chinese, or Russian. In rebuttal, Counts would reply that these philosophical generalities dodge the real issues of economics and politics that people face in their daily life that should be at the heart of the school program. For Counts, the concept of an educational context was large, often referring to the entire United States, but it was not, by its definition, universal. While particular school sites were important, they were part of a larger national setting, but not a universal one.

For their perspectives on education and schooling, see the chapters on Idealism, Realism, Essentialism, and Perennialism.

A PARTICULAR INTERPRETATION OF HISTORY. The first plank in Counts' frame of reference rests on a historical interpretation of the American past that relied on Beard's Progressive version of history. Counts interpreted American history in terms of two conflicting traditions: one based on Thomas Jefferson's popular democratic and egalitarian ideas and the other on Alexander Hamilton's elitism and special economic interests. Counts urged Americans, especially educators, to identify with the Jeffersonian tradition, which he believed provided the democratic and egalitarian heritage needed for the new social order.[14] Jeffersonian democracy and equality could be reasserted against the special economic interests, the big business corporations, and their

For the Progressive Movement in American history, see the chapter on Progressivism and Education.

conservative political allies. Although Counts selected Jefferson as the historical exemplar for his theory, he emphasized Jefferson's egalitarianism rather than his preference that the United States should remain an agrarian society of small landholding farmers. When he developed his theory that the new social order would be technological, Counts came close to the Hamiltonian model. However, he inserted Jeffersonian egalitarianism into this technological society.

Counts based his historical interpretation on a point of view deliberately committed to a particular version of social change. His critics charged him with **presentism**, the selective writing and teaching of history based on a political agenda in the present rather than an accurate understanding of the past.

Presentism: an argument that opposes a selective interpretation of history based on a contemporary political or economic agenda rather than a historical understanding of the past.

Rejecting a politically neutral or educationally objective position, Counts, like the contemporary Critical Theorists, urged teachers to commit themselves to social and economic as well as educational reforms. They should not be neutral on the major issues of the time but should take a stand for reform. Playing neutral yielded power to the dominant groups that controlled society.

For the Critical Theorist attack on educational neutrality, see the Chapter on Education and Critical Theory.

Cultural Crisis in an Industrial-Technological Society

After incorporating his version of the Jeffersonian democratic heritage into his frame of reference, Counts turned to the cultural crisis confronting Americans. At the time he developed his originative Social Reconstructionist ideas, the economic catastrophe of the Great Depression of the 1930s was the most obvious problem facing Americans. Counts, however, diagnosed it as a symptom rather than as the underlying cause of the great cultural crisis. The crisis, he reasoned, was caused by Americans' inability to reconstruct their institutions and values in terms of the emergent industrial-technological reality. The cultural crisis was aggravated by a **cultural lag** between the rate of material technological inventions and innovations and the society's ability to design the necessary institutions and processes to use technology for the public interest. In this part of his frame of reference, Counts relied on William F. Ogburn's cultural lag theory. According to Ogburn:

Cultural Lag: the belief that technological changes move at a faster rate than social change or social adaptation.

> The inventions occur first, and only later do the institutions of society change in conformity. Material culture and social institutions are not independent of each other, for civilization is highly articulated like a piece of machinery, so that a change in one part tends to effect changes in other parts—but only after a delay. Men with habits and society with patterns of action are slow to change to meet the new material conditions.[15]

There are many examples of cultural lag in contemporary society. Among them are global warming, containing the spread of nuclear weapons, the use of the Internet for humane purposes, the growing economic disparity between the wealthiest class and the rest of the population in the United States, and the widening gulf between the wealthy and poor nations of the world. We take one of these examples, global warming, to illustrate the problem of cultural lag. When Henry Ford (1863–1947) pioneered mass producing the Model T automobile, he began what would grow into a great industry. He made the automobile available at low cost to thousands of Americans. This material technological innovation had myriad, but often unexpected, consequences such as the construction of a network of highways, changes in traffic laws, the growth of the auto insurance industry, the development of motels, and the constantly growing demand for gasoline, which led to petroleum dependency.

The use of automobiles, powered by gasoline made from petroleum, a fossil fuel, in technologically developed countries such as the United States and in technologically growing countries such as China and India has resulted in massive emissions of carbon dioxide and other pollutants into the atmosphere, resulting in global warming. This has caused the melting of the polar ice caps and climate change that threatens the planet's health, the survival of species, and growing desertification. The lag occurs when countries, including the United States, are unwilling to develop alternatives for fueling automobiles and strategies for creating cleaner energy sources to check global warming.

This brief discussion of global warming illustrates the need for a frame of reference in approaching the problem. Developing strategies to deal with the crisis requires using information and insights from a number of disciplines: economics, engineering, chemistry, sociology, and political science.

For Counts, schools need to educate an informed citizenry, a knowledgeable public that is willing to take the challenge to close the lag, the cultural gap, between technological development and its use for the public good. In the example of global warming, schools need to include this issue as an important part of their curriculum. Students, guided by teachers, need to (1) analyze the meaning and causes of global warming; (2) develop alternatives to control, limit, and hopefully end the emissions of the by-products of fossil fuels that cause global warming; (3) work to build a constituency of informed people committed to solving the problem; and (4) actively work for the enactment of legislation to halt global warming at all levels—local, state, national, and international.

From Frame of Reference to Frame of Mind

Moving beyond developing strategies to narrow the cultural lag, Counts believed that schools, teachers, and students needed to develop a frame of mind that anticipates and plans for the future. It is necessary to develop bold strategies to harness technology as an instrument to improve society—to construct a new social order based on equality and justice. Counts argued that "The growth of science and technology has carried us into a new age where ignorance must be replaced by knowledge, competition by cooperation, trust in providence by careful planning, and private capitalism by some form of socialized economy."[16]

TECHNOLOGY IN THE CURRICULUM. Counts believed that students should study the meaning, processes, and functions of technology as part of the school curriculum. He defined technology as the application of science to material culture, especially industry. Relating technology to the scientific method, he saw technology's operations as functional, planned, dynamic, efficient, practical, purposeful, precise, and orderly.[17] He recommended infusing the study of technology throughout the curriculum to create the planning attitudes, the future-oriented frame of reference needed to reconstruct society. Technology, he reasoned, had the potential for improving the human condition, especially when integrated with the Jeffersonian democratic heritage.

Counts' argument that technology should be included in the curriculum can be illustrated by the contemporary emphasis on the use of computers and the dissemination of electronically stored and generated information in schools and in teacher education programs. Computer skills now are placed among basic skills such as reading, writing, and arithmetic. The impact of computers in society and schools illustrates their dynamic diffusion in the contemporary world. The diffusion of information on the Web makes it possible to access worldwide sources of information and to share messages anywhere. This dynamic aspect of electronic data transmission has changed teaching and learning, research and writing, the circulation of print information in books and newspapers, and the design and function of libraries. The Internet and social media were a factor in the demonstrations and revolution in the "Arab Spring" that toppled authoritarian regimes in Tunisia, Egypt, and Libya in 2011. While Counts would welcome the introduction of computer skills in the curriculum, he would likely question whether sufficient attention is being devoted to the long-term impact of electronic information on society, culture, economics, and politics.

Individualism versus Collectivism

Counts identified what he believed was a serious obstacle to reconstructing society—the embedded obsolete concept of individualism. He argued that the American ideal of the individual, part historical and part myth, conjured up an image in the American psyche of the solitary person who conquered life's obstacles alone.[18] The semiofficial pervasive tale of American individualism on the western frontier held such a strong grip on the collective American memory that it interfered with forming the cooperative attitude needed to reconstruct democracy in a technological world. Counts argued that vested economic and political interests used individualism as an ideological smoke screen to block needed reform, regulation, and reconstruction.

Counts called for a new concept, **democratic collectivism**, to replace the obstructive idea of individualism. Using collaborative group organization and action, the people, through representative processes, could seize the initiative and redirect the industrial-technological economy away from selfish special interests to meet common needs. Educators should join with other progressive forces in a great coalition to construct the new democracy. The school curriculum would be reconstructed to prepare the upcoming generation to understand the dynamics of technological change, to engage in social planning, and to build a new social order.

Democratic Collectivism: Counts' concept that the future American society should be a cooperative community that in the public interest incorporated Jeffersonian democracy and technology.

Counts' use of the term *democratic collectivism* was highly controversial. His conservative opponents labeled him a Communist or Socialist, and alleged that he was endorsing Soviet-style planning for the United States. Whereas the Conservative response was expected, democratic collectivism also generated a negative reaction from some Liberals and Progressives who saw it as advocating a closed rather than an experimental approach to social change.

For Communism and the former Soviet Union, see the chapter on Marxism and Education.

Again, Counts' call for collaborative group action can be placed in the contemporary American situation. The "Occupy Wall Street" mobilization and demonstrations in 2011 and 2012 represented a popular group action that Counts would likely have approved of, as least in some respects. The mobilization was a reaction against a deep economic recession, financial manipulation, and continuing unemployment. While Counts may have agreed with the issues identified by the protesters, he would have advised them that enthusiasm without a plan is insufficient and generally short lived. He likely would have told them to develop a frame of reference and a long-range plan.

A Social Reconstructionist Educational Strategy

Counts developed three key elements in his Reconstructionist frame of reference: (1) a Progressive interpretation of the American past that exalted the Jeffersonian democratic heritage; (2) a reduction of and perhaps eradication of the cultural lag by integrating the new elements of an industrial-technological economy and society with the democratic heritage; and (3) an educational and political action-oriented program to reconstruct American institutions.[19]

In particular, the school curriculum should (1) provide a "bottom-up" rather than a "top-down" social history about how ordinary people had created democratic institutions and processes; (2) examine the development of an industrial and technological economy and society; (3) identify and analyze the major contradictions and issues in America; and (4) develop the skills in making critical appraisals and intelligence choices to reconstruct society.[20]

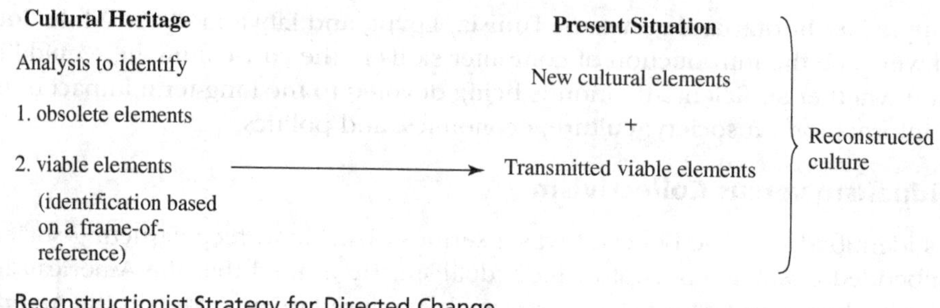

Reconstructionist Strategy for Directed Change

Although Counts was an originator of Social Reconstructionism, he turned to other educational interests. During the Cold War between the United States and the Soviet Union, especially in the late 1940s and 1950s, Counts, an expert in Soviet education, developed highly critical analyses of the Soviet system and Marxist-Leninist education.

THEODORE BRAMELD

Theodore Brameld (1904–1987) became the leading voice in articulating and reformulating Social Reconstructionism. In the post–World War II era, Brameld recognized that technological change, rapid communication, and transportation were creating an increasingly interdependent global society. He enlarged Counts' concept of context-based education to embrace a global community. Whereas Counts developed a historically based analysis of American society, Brameld took a more anthropological and human relationships perspective to education. He reconceptualized Reconstructionism to include a more future-oriented vision of a new world order that would improve the health care, economic conditions, and security of the great masses of people. The educational historian and biographer Craig Kridel portrays Brameld as a theorist who addressed and analyzed such major educational issues as "democracy in the schools," curriculum integration, "reconciling free inquiry with the inculcation of values," and encouraging "broader cultural and international awareness."[21]

Connecting Philosophy or Ideology of Education to Other Fields

For their interdisciplinary strategies, see the chapters on Postmodernism and Critical Theory.

Like the contemporary Postmodernists and Critical Theorists, Brameld moved across academic disciplines. Like Counts, Brameld continued to emphasize a frame of reference. Brameld's frame of reference was an interdisciplinary or transdisciplinary one that incorporated anthropology and human relations. Using this interdisciplinary approach, he constructed such new concepts as:

- **anthropological philosophy**, which integrated philosophy and anthropology
- **educology**, which studied education as distinct field of inquiry
- **anthropotherapy**, the directed course of human cultural evolution by the planned improvement of life that integrated cultural analysis with ethical and aesthetic values
- **culturology**, the examination of philosophy's significance in human culture.[22]

Role of Anthropology

Whereas Counts focused on the American context and had relied on a Progressive interpretation of history to construct his frame of reference, Brameld moved beyond particular contexts to construct a theory with global implications. Enlarging his vision to encompass a global society and culture, Brameld moved from particular national contexts such as the United States, Japan, and Puerto Rico, where he had lectured and taught, to a larger, more encompassing international theater of operations. Drawing on anthropology to analyze relationships between culture and education, Brameld stated that all cultures practice education, which he defined as the "entire range of practices by which a culture perpetuates and improves itself through acquainting each successive generation with its most important traditions, habits, and experiences."[23]

Brameld applied anthropologist Edward B. Tylor's definition of culture as the "whole complex—the knowledge, belief, art, morals, law, custom, and any other capabilities and habits—that human beings acquire as members of society" to his theory.[24] The verb *acquire*, by which each generation teaches its culture to the next in order to transmit it, is highly significant for education and schooling. Through the informal and formal educational process of **enculturation**, a culture transmits and modifies its institutions, beliefs, and values by passing it from one generation to the next.[25] Essential components of a culture that education needs to transmit, examine, and reconstruct are:

Enculturation: the informal and formal educational processes by which a culture maintains its institutions, beliefs, and values by transmitting across generations from adults to children.

- Order, the patterns of relationships in family, class, politics, economics, and religion
- Process, the dynamics by which individuals move in cultural institutions
- Goals, values that give direction and purpose to culture

Philosophical, Ideological, and Theoretical Reactions

At this point in the discussion, we can consider how some of Brameld's philosophical, ideological, and theoretical opponents might react to his anthropological version of Reconstructionism. Realists and Perennialists would agree with Brameld's contention that education is a global process, but they would go further and say that it is a universal one that is grounded in the metaphysical concept of human nature. Since Brameld does not base his philosophy on metaphysics, these critics would contend that he needed to find a substitute in anthropology. Conservatives and Essentialists would agree with Brameld's emphasis on education's role in transmitting human culture. However, they would ground their concept of transmission on the history of the human race. For them, Brameld's anthropological justification is merely a social science validation of what they asserted long ago, before Brameld was on the scene.

For the argument that education is a universal process, see the chapters on Realism and Education and Perennialism and Education.

For the Conservative and Essentialist view of education as cultural transmission, see the chapters on Conservatism and Education and Essentialism and Education.

CULTURAL CHANGE OR BLOWUPS. Brameld would counter his philosophical and ideological opponents by reminding them that education is about change and process. In particular, Reconstructionism is a theory in which education has the purpose of providing people with the knowledge and skills to create a more equitable and just world culture and society. The Realist and Perennialist version of universality is fixed and static, and is so abstract that it is removed from the changing situations of the human condition. He would contend that the Conservative and Essentialist approach to transmission is also fixed and static in that it emphasizes the transmission of the status quo but does not provide the knowledge and skills needed to change the unjust features of the existing economy and society.

Brameld reinforces the Reconstructionist emphasis on change by again relying on anthropology and introducing the concept of a "cultural blowup."[26] While Counts referred to the challenge of cultural crises, Brameld recast a crisis as a **cultural blowup**. Similar to Ogburn, in his "cultural lag" theory, Brameld saw human history proceeding through a series of major cultural events, or "blowups," that generate pervasive

Cultural Blowup: Brameld's concept of a major social crisis produced by the cumulative effects of a series of cultural changes and events.

social change. Education is to exercise a crucial reconstructive function in the process of social rebalancing or reconstruction. Social rebalancing, however, did not mean restoring the status quo that existed before the cultural blowup, as Conservatives argue. Echoing Counts' reconstructive theory, Brameld saw social reconstruction as a balancing or harmonizing of what remains viable in the old order with the new dynamic force or innovation that generated the cultural blowup.

If one surveys the sociocultural world landscape today, there are many forces or innovations at work that are generating cultural crises or blowups. Among them are chronic tensions in the Middle East, climate change, terrorism, genocide, and the impact of electronic information and opinion disseminated by computers and many other devices. The continuing economic recession that began in 2007 has had consequences not only in the United States and in Europe but worldwide. In the United States, there is the income gap between a small economic elite and the majority of the population. Brameld himself was concerned that the world community did not have a viable plan for harnessing and controlling the new dynamic of nuclear energy so that it would be used for peaceful purposes rather than for war and violence.

DEFENSIBLE PARTIALITY. *Viability* is a key term in the analysis of what is necessary in balancing or reconstructing a culture. Brameld linked viability with the concept of "defensible partiality." Viability does not mean neutrality for Brameld; rather, it means being partial to achieving particular goals that liberate human beings. What is viable does not stand out in objective relief on the cultural landscape. To be viable means that an institution or process, a belief or value, in a particular culture is sufficiently strong and meaningful to be sustained and to grow and develop. In reconstructing a society, a viable element in a culture provides a base or foundation on which other institutions and processes rest. For example, Counts identified the Jeffersonian democratic heritage as a viable element to link with the newer developing forces such as technology.

Defensible Partiality: Brameld's concept that educators do not need to be neutral on an issue; they can hold and support a particular position but must to be able to defend it in light of rigorous critical examination.

For their perspective on ideology and education, see the chapter on Critical Theory and Education.

For Brameld, determining what is viable in a culture requires a knowledge base in the social sciences, especially in anthropology, sociology, and human relations. While the educational policy maker can be informed by these social sciences, there is still the choice to be made, the choosing or determining of what and why something is viable. In making these choices, Brameld argued that the educator needs to exercise **defensible partiality**. Brameld anticipated Critical Theory when he argued that educational policymakers and teachers needed to identify and understand the ideologies that are operating in a particular situation, especially those that justify maintaining the status quo. They need to take a stand and be committed to (be partial to) what Brameld would call policies that will lead to a humane, just, and equitable democratic society. Defensible partiality involves ensuring that the preferred goals and means used to obtain them can be definitely and positively defended and sustained in light of rigorous critical examination and analysis by those who hold them.[27]

Defensible Partiality and Indoctrination

Brameld's argument for defensible partiality ran into criticism from educators, especially Conservatives and Essentialists, who saw it as a form of indoctrination. For them, partiality meant that the teacher was using the classroom to advance a particular social, cultural, political, or economic agenda. Rather, they contended that instruction should be impartial, unbiased, and objective. Brameld, like the contemporary Critical Theorists, would counter that all education and all teaching and learning always occur against and within an ideological backdrop or as Counts argued earlier a context. Brameld would argue that Conservatism, in particular, is partial to a version of the status quo that is Eurocentric, patriarchal, and pro-capitalist.

For arguments for objectivity, see the chapters on Liberalism and Essentialism.

Human Relations and Conflict Resolution

In addition to the rational scientific activities of human beings, Brameld considered the importance of the volitional and emotional aspects of human behavior, especially as they affect cooperative group activities. Found in all human behavior, irrationality causes ethnocentric and stereotypic thinking and conflicts at the personal, ethnic, racial, and religious levels. To deal with the irrational, it is important, he argues, to identify and analyze the nonrational forces that impede needed reconstruction.

Brameld believed that the important advances in human relations such as social psychology, counseling, and group and intercultural relations should be incorporated into the Reconstructionist educational strategy. Social Reconstruction needs to enlist the largest and broadest participation possible and should lead to a collaborative popular consensus. Simple voting at elections, although necessary, is not sufficient in building consensus. It is necessary that people reach a pervasive agreement, a consensus, on aims and ends. Educators, in particular, need to understand the dynamics of group relationships and the methods for bringing individuals into a comprehensive consensus. While a knowledge base is needed in arriving at consensus, it is not enough. Group interaction and collaborative engagement in society and in schools are often blocked by nonrational elements (stereotyping and prejudice) such as racism, classism, and sexism.

For their emphasis on consensus, see the chapters on Liberalism and Progressivism.

Human relations skills would be useful in resolving misunderstanding, tension, prejudice, hatred, and conflict. Teachers, he reasoned, need to use knowledge and strategies about human relationships when these tensions and conflicts among students interfere with learning. Brameld devised a strategy for conflict resolution and consensus building that involved the following:

1. When conflict occurs, the specific actors and causes of the conflict need to be identified, defined, and diagnosed. Who or what is causing the conflict? What is motivating those causing or involved in the conflict?
2. After the causes of the conflict are investigated, possible solutions need to be developed to resolve it. Several hypotheses, possible solutions, need to be constructed and considered before the most promising one is selected; it was important to conjecture likely consequences of acting on the particular hypothesis; any emerging hypothesis for resolving the conflict needed to be tentative and subject to further revision.
3. The selected hypothesis needed to be acted on and tested to determine whether it successfully resolved the conflict.[28]

While Brameld tended to think globally about conflict resolution and the building of consensus, there are many situations in which his theory of applying human relations skills is applicable in schools at the micro, or site, level. For example, human relations skills, such as those Brameld proposes, can be applied to conflict resolution in schools, especially those caused by racial, ethnic, and language stereotyping. These skills can also be applied to instances of gang violence and bullying, either in the classroom or on social media.

From Contextualism to Generalizations About One Human Global Community

Both Counts and Brameld shared a Pragmatist, Experimentalist, and Progressive educational orientation. Counts emphasized the importance of a particular context—a given time and place—on education. Brameld increasingly moved from particular

For their emphasis on a universal human nature, see the chapters on Idealism, Realism, and Perennialism.

contexts to the larger global community. Both Counts and Brameld rejected the more traditional philosophies such as Idealism and Realism, and Perennialism, which emphasized a universal human nature and universal education. While Counts later broadened his context from that of an American to the larger Western civilization, Brameld anticipated a global world society. In making this broad leap from contextualism to a worldview, Brameld began discussing human commonalities (what is the same about people worldwide) from a social science perspective, but avoided lapsing into a universalizing metaphysics. He believed he found a non-metaphysical explanation to the universalizing character of human culture in anthropology. The universalizing theme is that all people everywhere have developed some form of culture.

While he recognized the impact that cultural differences had on culture and education, Brameld sought to identify human commonalities that might be the basis of an international union of people. Brameld's efforts to find an overriding unity in the face of cultural diversity apply to multicultural and human rights education. For Brameld, the important question was: Although people are members of different cultural groups, do they share commonalities, especially on human rights and social justice? In answering the question, Brameld sought to build a broad consensus that embraced the contributions of different races, ethnic groups, and religions. In making the case for a global association of people, Brameld looked to the commonalities that different cultures shared, the common denominators that made for one human race living in a global community. Identifying common denominators that were functional, based on what people do, Brameld stated that people:

> . . . make love; they nourish themselves; they take care of their bodies; they play; they work; they learn; they worship; they create aesthetically; they make rules; they sorrow; they communicate; they govern; they shelter and clothe themselves; they protect one another; they count; they possess; they visit and trade; they cooperate and organize.[29]

Brameld proposed that a Reconstructionist philosophy should identify the common values that races, ethnic and language groups, religious denominations, and socio-economic classes share as well as the differences that separate them. Educators should attempt to establish, by discussion and consensus, the institutional patterns that empower people to satisfy their needs and to realize the values they share worldwide.[30]

Brameld's Reconstructive Design for American Education

Brameld argued that the "great imperative confronting American schools" is to "transform them into powerful institutions of cultural change toward the goal of a planet-wide democratic order." Education should devote itself to reconstructing the culture, which was in peril of collapsing if not revitalized.[31] For him, the needed reconstruction was no longer limited to the United States but required a far-reaching remaking of world culture. Like Counts, Brameld wanted technology to be used to alleviate poverty and to create economic security for people throughout the world. He identified the areas that needed to be examined in a broadened curriculum as:

- controversial political, social, economic, moral, scientific, and religious issues that were often closed in classroom discussions
- middle-class psychocultural beliefs and behavioral patterns in terms of their strengths and limitations
- technologically generated cultural and social change
- sexual relationships in their moral as well as biological aspects

- personal emotional and psychological problems
- the problems generated by nuclear energy, proliferation of nuclear weapons, and the implications of space exploration in the science curriculum[32]
- the global problems of population explosion, environmental degradation, and the disparity between the technologically developed and less technologically developed areas of the world[33]

A RECONSTRUCTIONIST SCHOOL AND CURRICULUM. To illustrate how Reconstructionism would function in a school setting, Brameld described it in a community college, with students ranging in age from seventeen to twenty. The curriculum would be organized around one central question: "What kind of world can we have and do we want?" The question would be pursued in a committed way by both students and teachers; however, there would be no attempt at indoctrination. The students' and teachers' beliefs and values would be clearly stated, according to Brameld's concept of defensible partiality, so that those who held them could articulate them to others and invite critical discussion and possible dissent. Students would examine the question from an interdisciplinary and multidisciplinary approach in its historical, political, economic, scientific, philosophical, and religious perspectives. A wide array of resources would be used from original research, journals and books, community experience, and expert authorities. Students and teachers would also approach the question from a discipline in the sciences and humanities.[34]

Brameld structured the curriculum over four years. The first year would be devoted studying the economic processes for producing, consuming, and distributing goods and services. In true Reconstructionist style, planning was emphasized and the focusing questions related to the equitable and environmentally safe use of energy, economic security, and full employment. The second year examined redesigning democratic political structures to safeguard majority rule and minority rights. The third year was devoted to the broad cultural sphere where students examined how human culture, especially health care, education, art, and religion, is affected by economic and political change and reconstruction. The fourth year is subdivided into examining the psychological sphere and the interrelations of the economic, political, cultural, and psychological dimensions of human experience.[35]

Reconstructionist Teaching

Brameld devised a school program, "Design for America," that was implemented as an experiment at Floodwood High School in Minnesota in 1944. The overriding goal of the project was to "build by cooperative thinking and exploration a blueprint of our future society."[36] The focusing questions that guided the project were (1) Is it important to construct a plan for America's future? and (2) Is it possible to state the plan's goals so precisely that they will clearly indicate what is needed for their implementation? Using collaborative learning and problem solving, the students recommended a national public works program; full employment; fair treatment of minorities, especially African Americans; and international and intercultural respect and social justice for all races and peoples.[37]

Brameld's Vision of Reconstructed Society

Brameld's Reconstructionism was future centered in that it pointed to a vision of a reconstructed America in a reconstructed world. Though originating with Dewey's Instrumentalism, Brameld's vision of a new world appeared to some to be utopian and too separated from the reality of the here and now. Brameld made no apologies

For the Conservative antagonism to utopianism, see the chapter on Conservatism and Education.

for being visionary, if not utopian. An expansive vision of the possibilities of humanity were needed to lead to a new and better future. The promised good life would encourage individuals to release and share their ideas and values with others. The future reconstructed society would be free of barriers that kept people apart, segregated, or confined to sexist, racist, and classist enclaves. In the new global world order, people of all nations would have unlimited freedom to meet each other through travel and open communication. Brameld's design for open travel and communication anticipated computer-based electronic messaging. He would have seen immense possibilities in social media as a way to reduce distances and bring people into global communication. A global democratic government would ensure that the earth's natural resources would not be monopolized by a wealthy minority but shared to benefit the majority of the world's people. Brameld would consider the economic disparity among the nations of the world and the people within a particular country to be one of major unresolved contradictions plaguing humankind. Education in the new world would have a large place for the arts and humanities as well as for the sciences.[38] Again, if Brameld were still with us, he would argue that the processes of globalization should not be resisted but reconstructed to benefit all.

RECONSTRUCTIONIST THEMES

Although the Reconstructionists saw themselves as philosophers of education, their ideas did not fit the traditional definition of philosophy. Even though Reconstructionism was a better fit with Pragmatism, there were differences between the two positions. Unlike the Idealists and Realists, the Reconstructionists, like the Pragmatists, did not base truth, knowledge, and values on a universal metaphysical foundation. The claims produced by metaphysical speculation, for them, could not be validated empirically. Their use of the scientific method, a core feature of Pragmatism, too, had to be reconstructed and related to the culture.

Counts anchored his originative theory of Social Reconstruction, which he called a "civilizational philosophy" of education, to the Jeffersonian tradition in American history, especially to Beard's Progressive interpretation. Brameld, too, anchored his theory to anthropology, calling it an "Anthropological Philosophy of Education."

Brameld, unlike Counts, had earned a doctorate in philosophy. While Counts was an educator who veered into philosophy, Brameld took the other route and was a philosopher who entered the field of education. To make Reconstructionism a philosophy, Brameld needed to stipulate his own definition of philosophy. He did so by redefining philosophy in terms of Reconstructionism rather than determining how Reconstructionism corresponded to the conventional definition of philosophy. Brameld defined philosophy not as metaphysics, epistemology, and axiology but rather as "the persistent effort of both ordinary and sophisticated people to make life as intelligible and meaningful as possible." It offered a means "to analyze and organize the premises" on which people conduct their "political, scientific, aesthetic, religious, and educational practices."[39] Anticipating Postmodernism and Critical Theory, Brameld used the term *operationalist* to describe Reconstructionist philosophy in that laws and morals were human constructions based on humankind's "ever changing transactions with nature and culture."[40]

In stipulating their own definitions of philosophy, the Reconstructionists met criticism. More traditional philosophers, especially those associated with Aristotle and Realism, alleged that the Reconstructionists were not genuine philosophers but were really politicians or ideologues posing as philosophers. For these critics, philosophy is the most general, hence most abstract, means of pursuing the truth. Accordingly, philosophy provides a highly general way to place history in a larger perspective.

Counts, however, reversed this order by making philosophy dependent on history. Brameld, they would assert, engaged in a similar reversal when he made philosophy dependent on anthropology. Even some of their Experimentalist conferees claimed that the Reconstructionists had imposed political ends on education, which should be an open-ended process of free inquiry.

Broadening the Meaning of Philosophy of Education

Just as they redefined philosophy, the Reconstructionists also reconstructed the meaning of philosophy of education and of education itself. Their very broad view of education went well beyond curriculum and instruction in schools. Philosophy of education, for the Reconstructionists, was to be interdisciplinary and to incorporate the most significant new research findings of the physical, biological, and social sciences as well as the innovative creations of the arts, literature, and architecture. Their multidisciplinary approach anticipated the Critical Theorist concept of "border crossings" across academic disciplines.

For their emphasis on interdisciplinary education, see the chapter on Critical Theory and Education.

The Reconstructionists' broad definition of education includes schooling but also encompasses a full range of informal and nonformal institutions and agencies such as the media, churches, clubs, museums, and galleries, and today would include the World Wide Web and the Internet. Reconstructionist philosophy of education is visionary and future oriented.[41]

Further, Reconstructionists see education in political, economic, and social terms, as well as cultural and pedagogical terms. Brameld, for example, argues that education should become the "copartner of politics—the politics of comprehending and implementing popular government on a worldwide scale." Thus, philosophy of education is concerned with constructing the foundations for such a partnership. For him, these foundations should be global and oriented to the public welfare. Internationally, they should encompass people and their institutions on a functional continuum from localities, states, nations, and regions to the world. They should be oriented to guaranteeing the general social and economic welfare of people—a welfare state of public service.[42] The public service state establishes and implements standards safeguarding human welfare in work, education, health care, and the environment.

Here, the Reconstructionists encountered the opposition of the Essentialists, such as William C. Bagley and Isaac Kandel, who argued that the Reconstructionists were placing impossible ideological demands on schools, that even if they were somehow agreed to, they could never be realistically implemented. If education included everything, they asked, what was special about schools? The Essentialists, countering the Reconstructionist argument, insisted that schools had the primary function of being places of academic learning that transmitted necessary skills and subjects that were based on the liberal arts and sciences and led students to their cultural heritage. The Reconstructionists would counter—the Essentialist argument, asking whose culture should the school transmit, that of the dominant class?

For Bagley's perspective on progressive education, see the chapter on Essentialism and Education.

Relating Ideology to Education

Although Counts called his Social Reconstructionism a "civilizational philosophy" of education, it closely resembles an ideology rather than a philosophy. Although concerned with moral and ethical considerations, Counts, unlike a philosopher, did not deal with broad metaphysical and epistemological issues. Rather, he developed a highly contextual ideology with its own version of the past and a program for deliberate social change. Counts was developing an educational ideology to be used as an instrument to mobilize the nation's Progressive and Liberal educators to join with like-minded allies in the struggle against vested special economic interests and the forces of Conservatism and reaction. Teachers were to be partisan, not neutral, and committed, not aloof, from the momentous issues facing the nation and, indeed, the world.

Contextualism and the Identification of Contemporary Issues

Social Reconstructionists emphasize the examination of the cultural, social, political, and economic contexts in which education and schooling occur. They tend to identify and examine the large national and international issues affecting schools and society. For Counts, the context was the United States; for Brameld, it was the international global economy and society. In their contextual analysis of schools, Reconstructionists locate socio-economic and political strains, inconsistencies, and tensions that can be defined and addressed as problems and issues. When educational problems are traced back sociologically, historically, economically, and politically to contexts in which they are situated, the analysis becomes multidisciplinary.[43] The contemporary issues that would attract the most attention from Reconstructionists are those that relate to social justice and equality. Reconstructionists, much like contemporary Critical Theorists, would seek to expose, examine, and end what they define as antidemocratic trends, such as hedonistic individualism and consumerism, profit-driven global economics, and disparities in the distribution of wealth.[44]

Cultural or Contextual Relativism

Cultural Relativism: the perspective that beliefs about knowledge and values arise in particular cultures, in specific times and values.

There were some differences in how the Reconstructionists approached the important issues related to beliefs and values. Counts, who related education closely to its contexts, was a cultural relativist. According to **cultural relativism**, beliefs and values are particular to and vary with different groups, living in specific places, at particular times in history. As the group's cultural situation changes, so do their belief and value systems. Beliefs and values are temporary and changing, not universal or eternal. Cultural relativism was easily translated into an educational principle—that education, too, especially when it was organized as schooling, expresses a particular culture's and society's beliefs and values during a particular period of history in a given geographical setting.

Brameld, unlike Counts, began as a cultural relativist but moved his interests to what he saw as a world or global society. If a society is global, then there are certain beliefs or values that likewise function globally or internationally. When Brameld made his leap to a global society, he was departing from a strictly culturally relative perspective. His problem became identifying such global values as universal human rights. As indicated earlier, he turned to anthropology for this identification.

For their emphasis on universal truths and values, see the chapters on Idealism and Education, Realism and Education, and Perennialism and Education.

Counts, Brameld, and the other Reconstructionists rejected the Idealist, Realist, and Perennialist view that just as truth was universal and eternal, so was education. They rejected the Platonic and Aristotelian philosophies in which education was a universal process, as Robert Hutchins and Mortimer Adler claimed, in which unchanging truths were the same at every time and place.

For cultural relativism, see the chapters on Pragmatism and Education, Postmodernism and Education, and Critical Theory and Education.

Cultural relativism is a major issue that sets Conservatism and Perennialism apart from Pragmatism, Reconstructionism, Postmodernism, and Critical Theory. The highly charged question is: Are people essentially the same or are they different? If they are the same, then they should have the same education; however, if they are different, then they need an education that reflects these differences.

The older and more traditional philosophies such as Plato's Idealism and Aristotle's Realism asserted that people, in all places at all times, shared a common

Contextual or Cultural Relativism versus Universal Truth and Values

Contextual or Cultural Relativism	Universal Truth and Values
1. Claims to truth and expressions of values are relative to contexts—particular places and times.	1. Truth and values are universal and are the same throughout the world.
2. Education and schooling reflect the cultural contexts in which they occur.	2. Education is the universal process of how people acquire learning; schooling is the particular process in which the culture is transmitted from adults to children.
3. Because values are relative to times and places, they are changing and reflect responses to environmental situations.	3. Values are eternal and universal and need to be transmitted deliberately by schools and teachers.
4. Human freedom is enhanced by providing people with the cultural and educational tools to reexamine, redefine, and reconstruct their values.	4. Human freedom is safeguarded by recognizing that people, by their human nature, have universal human rights.

nature that defined them as human beings. The Judeo-Christian religious heritage, too, asserts the reality of a universal human nature and a God-created and ordained world of universal and eternal truths and values. Educational theories based on this universality emphasize that truth is universal and timeless, and education should be based on this truth.

Pragmatists, such as John Dewey, challenged the doctrine of an unchanging human nature and emphasized that human beings live in, adapt to, and respond to a changing natural and social environment. Dewey and the Pragmatists looked to the process of the scientific method as the means by which human beings successfully interacted with ever-changing natural and social environments. Rather than looking to a universal human nature, Dewey and his Experimentalist and Progressive followers sought to find a process that could be applied to solving problems in an ever-changing environment. The Reconstructionists, emphasizing contexts, wanted an education that would aid people in solving the problems that arose in these changing and diverse social and cultural settings and situations.

For Dewey's view of change, see the chapter on Pragmatism and Education.

RECONSTRUCTIONISM'S IDEOLOGICAL AND PHILOSOPHICAL RELATIONSHIPS

Philosophically, Social Reconstructionism grew out of American Pragmatism, especially John Dewey's Instrumentalism. Although he associated with the Reconstructionists at Teachers College, Dewey did not identify specifically with Reconstructionism as an ideology or theory. However, the concept of the reconstruction of personal and social experience, which permeated Dewey's Instrumentalism, was a Reconstructionist theme. For Dewey, socially intelligent persons continually reconstructed their ideas and values as they used their previous experiences as instruments to solve new problems. Intelligent societies, like intelligent persons, also reconstructed their social, political, and economic experience when they faced problems. As individuals joined in communities and used open-ended experimental and democratic processes to solve their shared and mutual problems, they were on the way to creating the "great society," the great democratic community. Dewey's books *Individualism Old and New* (1929) and *Liberalism and Social Action* (1935) addressed issues raised

For the historical development of Liberalism, see the chapter on Liberalism and Education.

by Counts, Brameld, and other Reconstructionist educators.[45] Like Counts, Dewey called for a reconstruction of individualism and Liberalism that moved them from their laissez-faire origins to a more cooperative, associative, and revitalized process of thinking and acting. A revitalized and socially charged Liberalism could be an instrument in solving the problems of an increasingly corporate industrial and technological society.

The curriculum historian Gerald Podner identifies three significant ideas from Pragmatism, especially Dewey's Experimentalism, that shaped Reconstructionist theory: (1) the method of experimental science; (2) the concept of democracy; and (3) the concept of interdependence.[46] Reconstructionists believed that the scientific method needed to be applied to political decision making and, in turn, schools could cultivate the public use of the scientific method. Education could develop social intelligence as a democratic means of decision making. Reconstructionists endorsed Dewey's concept of democracy as an open-ended society, free from absolutes that restricted freedom of inquiry, but constructed a historically based frame of reference, as with Counts, and an anthropological one as in the case of Brameld. As a result, the use of the scientific method was ideologically referenced by Reconstructionists' more particular political and economic interpretations. They also emphasized that, like Dewey, American society was rapidly moving beyond individualism and voluntarism to a growingly interdependent society and economy.

Liberalism

Reconstructionists shared many Liberal principles, especially freedom of speech, press, and assembly; government through popularly elected legislative bodies; a fair and independent judiciary; public education; and academic freedom. They embraced the welfare-state version of Liberalism, especially the need for government-sponsored social security and health care programs.

There were significant differences, however, in how Liberals and Reconstructionists viewed social planning and directed social change. As incremental transactionists, Liberals responded to particular problems by designing and implementing specific solutions to them. Their concept of social and educational change was incremental—in small pieces or additions—rather than sweeping and transformative as was the case with the Reconstructionists. Further, Liberals were motivated to preserve and maintain the existing political, economic, and educational institutions by reforming or improving them rather than radically transforming them.

Progressivism

For Progressivism and the Progressive movement, see the chapter on Progressivism and Education.

The Progressive movement in education and the Progressive Education Association (PEA) were highly porous, large umbrella-like groupings that attracted like-minded people who had wide-ranging educational views. The movement was big and broad enough to include both the child-centered and the Social Reconstructionist educators. Child-centered Progressives believed that the curriculum should be based on children's interests and needs, which, if encouraged, would grow into personal and social intelligence. For the child-centered Progressives, Progressive schools would be indirect agencies of social change. The focus of education, for them, was the individual child. Free of coercion, the Progressive school would liberate children's creativity, which in turn would liberate society. However, the contours of the liberated society were not specified and were open-ended. The child-centered Progressives emphasized education that liberated children from unnecessary restraints on their curiosity and creativity. Although they may have thought that the Reconstructionist plans to create a new social order were well intentioned, child-centered Progressives felt that imposing an ideologically generated version of the future was another form of indoctrination that limited children's creativity and freedom by imposing a utopian project on them.

Like their child-centered confreres, Social Reconstructionism originated in Progressivism. The Reconstructionist admittedly had a socio-economic and political agenda. They would claim that they were returning Progressivism to its original goals of social, political, economic, and educational reform. For them, altruistic and well-meaning but also romantic child-centered Progressives had separated schooling from its social context. Now, the Reconstructionists were renewing the original Progressive agenda.

Social Reconstructionists saw the school as an agency to create deliberately a new democratic, cooperative, and egalitarian social order. The Reconstructionist school would follow an agenda and have a program designed to create this a new society. It was at this juncture that Progressive child-centered educators and Social Reconstructionist educators clashed.

Marxism

Marxism's influence on Reconstructionism is often debated. Counts, the catalyst for Reconstructionism, was a scholar in comparative and international education. He conducted on-site research in the Soviet Union, where the official ideology was Marxist-Leninism, in the late 1920s and early 1930s. Although he initially admired Soviet centralized planning in Stalin's first Five-Year Plan, he had grown disenchanted and become a decided anti-Communist by the late 1930s. Counts opposed international and American Communism throughout the rest of his career. Counts apparently heeded the advice of the historian Charles A. Beard, his friend and mentor, who advised him to base his educational theory on American rather than foreign sources. Counts, influenced by Beard, saw the economy as a largely conditioning but not necessarily determining cause of social and political change. Here Beard's and Counts' orientation departed from Marx's insistence that all history, politics, and society are economically determined and subject to the universal laws of dialectical materialism.[47] Referring to economic forces as a conditioning rather than a determining process, Counts stated: "It is contended here that man in history is neither wholly bound nor wholly free, that his life, though always conditioned, is never fated. . . . Within the bounds of the possible human preference operates."[48]

For Marxism and Communism, see the chapter on Marxism and Education.

Brameld had studied Marxism while a doctoral student at the University of Chicago, where he researched Lenin's writings for his dissertation, "The Role of Acquiescence in Leninism." Brameld's dissertation was revised and published as *A Philosophic Approach to Communism* (1933). Brameld would later find Marxism to be an inadequate dogmatic doctrine.

Postmodernism and Critical Theory

In many respects, Social Reconstruction theoretically anticipated Critical Theory. Both Social Reconstructionism and Critical Theory call for a rigorous critique of American society and education, argue against educational objectivity and neutrality, and are committed to a program of action to change society and schools.

For Critical Theory, see the following chapter.

There is a similarity between Counts' emphasis on the relativism of history and the Postmodernist emphasis on history as a construction of the record of the past by contending groups and classes. In his argument that history is contingent on those who interpret it and that their interpretation, in turn, reflects time, place, and circumstances, Counts argued that history is a construction. Critical Theorists would find Counts' and Brameld's contextual and multidisciplinary approaches to education congenial with their own call for border crossings between academic fields. Critical Theorists would commend the Reconstructionists' concern for the nation's unemployed and underrepresented masses and their argument that education should be a transformative force for popular change. Both Postmodernists and Critical Theorists would agree with Reconstructionists that education is never completely objective, unbiased, and neutral. They would commend the Reconstructionist call for teachers to be committed to an interpretation of history and to an analysis of social, economic, and political issues that would empower the dispossessed and downtrodden groups and classes.

Although there are important similarities between the Reconstructionists and the Critical Theorists, there are also distinct differences. Drawing from their Progressive origins, the Reconstructionists embraced the Enlightenment project's belief in progress, that the future, if intelligently guided, would be better than the past. For them, modernity, deriving from the Enlightenment, was a positive force to improve the human situation. They had faith in the power of science, social science, engineering, technology, and planning to promote social and economic progress.[49] How the Reconstructionists would react to Postmodernism, especially its rejection of the Enlightenment project, would be an interesting discussion.

The Reconstructionists were modernists, not antimodernists; they were in the Enlightenment tradition in that they believed in progress through the application of inquiry and science to society. They were not affected by a Luddite mentality of opposition to technology but saw technology instead as a force of liberation. For example, Reconstructionist educators would see global warming and the degradation of the environment as a major planetary issue. They likely would look to technology to find alternatives to the use of fossil fuels and not adopt a back-to-nature solution. In their attachment to the Enlightenment, progress, science, and modernity, the Reconstructionists differed from the Postmodernists and Critical Theorists who viewed the Enlightenment as the source of many of humankind's ills. Rather than being a necessarily liberating force, science, when bound up with progress and modernity, had become a source of power by which scientific elites, controlled and supported by dominant classes, controlled the oppressed. The whole Enlightenment rationale that ushered in the Age of Reason was an ideological smoke screen, an ideological pablum, fed to the uncritical masses to keep them waiting for the illusory promised land that was forever on the horizon but never in reach.

Postmodernists and Critical Theorists would find Counts overly impressed and overly committed to technology, which he saw as emanating from Enlightenment theory. Indeed, Counts had developed the concept of technology into what the Postmodernists would see as a meta-narrative. Arguing that technology was a transforming force that was working throughout the world, Counts was preaching the merits of modernity and modernization. It was not modernity that he feared, but rather that the engines of modernization would be appropriated and controlled by special interests. For Postmodernists, modernity itself is a historical construct that originated in and still sustains global oppressive power relationships, especially in the economically poorer countries of the world.

Reconstructionists and Critical Theorists also disagree on the degree of centralization and localism in social, political, and educational agencies. While Reconstructionists believed that only a centralized authority had the means needed to create a new social order. Critical Theorists emphasize the autonomy of the local site, especially the local community school. Brameld, however, provided a compromise when he called for a working synthesis that integrated centralized authority with decentralized administration.[50]

CONSERVATISM, ESSENTIALISM, AND PERENNIALISM. The Conservatives, Essentialists, and Perennialists would find much to condemn in Reconstructionism. They would condemn the Reconstructionist view of the school as an agency of deliberate social change as a serious attack on the school's primary purpose as an academic institution. To them, the school's primary mission is to transmit the cultural heritage as knowledge, organized into skills and subjects, from one generation to the next. Perennialists, in particular, would contend that the Reconstructionists used terminology carelessly, confusing the distinctions between education, in the general sense, and schooling, in the particular sense. Schooling might be contextual; education itself, however, is transcontextual and is a universal process of human growth and development. They would also contend that Brameld's use of anthropology to establish commonalities among people living in different societies and cultures was a feeble attempt to substitute social studies for Aristotle's metaphysical assertion of a universal human nature.

See the chapters on Conservatism, Essentialism, and Perennialism.

Essentialists would contend that Reconstructionists were foisting an ideology on the students and indoctrinating them in a particular version of history and the social studies. Further, their cultural relativism would lead to ethical relativism that would erode moral standards. For Diane Ravitch, Counts' ideological platform was another of the "failed reforms" of the Progressives and Reconstructionists that attempted to divert schools from their academic purposes.[51]

RECONSTRUCTIONISM'S EDUCATIONAL IMPLICATIONS

Using social analysis and criticism and concerned about the future of American and world culture, the Reconstructionists see the school as a transformative agent, an agency for bringing about deliberate social change. The school not only should dare to build a new social order but it is imperative that it does so. The school's curriculum should not be a mirror that reflects back the status quo, the officially approved beliefs and values of the dominant groups controlling the existing society. The image reflected back contains the injustices, inequalities—the unresolved issues and conflicts—of the status quo. It reflects the image of the powerful and how they think and what they value. No, the Reconstructionists argue, the school should do much more than reflect the existing society; it needs to change the society. The Reconstructionists believe that the school could and should take a leading role in building a new society.[52]

Reconstructionists challenge the Conservative and Essentialist idea that education and schooling should transmit the existing culture and society; for them, transmission is largely a process in which the school acts to preserve the status quo and its inequities. For Reconstructionists, the educational process is to reconstruct, reform, and renew the existing society.

Role of the Social Studies

Because of their emphasis on social, political, and economic analysis, a key Reconstructionist curriculum area is the **social studies**. The social studies, as a curriculum area, span both elementary and secondary schools. Unlike the older subjects of history, mathematics, and science, the social studies were developed in the twentieth century. Social studies represent a fusion and integration of knowledge, especially generalizations and methods, from history, geography, anthropology, sociology, economics, social psychology, and political science. This integrated study is especially amenable for the Reconstructionists, who in their theory building use an interdisciplinary approach from a range of subject-matter disciplines. The social studies, which are frequently reexamined and revised, meet the Reconstructionist demand that

Social Studies: a curriculum for social education that fuses and integrates generalizations and information from history, geography, anthropology, sociology, economics, and political science.

education and the curriculum not be set in stone as monuments to the past but instead experience constant reappraisal and reconstruction in the light of social, political, economic, and cultural change.

The social studies were shaped by historical and cultural relativists such as Charles Beard and George S. Counts, who believed that there were no universal laws of history but rather that historical trends were shaped or conditioned by the social, political, and—most important—economic forces and trends of a given time and place—a context. The past is written and interpreted in terms of the present's problems and the future's possibilities.[53]

Interdisciplinary social studies were opposed at the time of their origin and today face Conservative and Essentialist critics who see them as free floating and ill defined. These critics contend that the social studies are unsystematic and unstructured and to blame for American students' ineptitude in history and geography.

Harold Rugg and the Social Studies Controversy

The relationship of the social studies to Social Reconstructionism is nicely illustrated in the history of curriculum by the Rugg textbook controversy. Harold Rugg (1886–1960), a colleague of Counts at Teachers College, was a national leader in the social studies as well as a prominent Reconstructionist.[54]

Conceiving of the social studies as a multidisciplinary issues-focused area, Rugg wrote a social studies textbook series, titled *Man and His Changing Society,* that sold more than a million copies and enjoyed nationwide school adoptions in the 1920s and 1930s.[55] Rugg's texts were designed to involve students in critical thinking on controversial social, political, and economic issues. Most texts at the time reflected the prevailing attitudes and were used to cultivate patriotism and commitment to free enterprise capitalism; Rugg's texts, however, identified, examined, and criticized social and economic inequities and disparities in American society.[56] Rugg's issue-oriented books were deliberately intended to raise provocative, controversial questions such as, "Is the United States a land of opportunity for all our people?" The series' instructional guide advised teachers that the United States is not a land of opportunity for all and there were differences in living standards, income, and security between different socio-economic classes.[57] Rugg was challenging celebrationist school histories that pictured the country as a seamless community, united by American patriotism and enjoying political freedom and the competitive opportunities of an unbridled free market economy.

During the Depression years of the 1930s, Rugg joined other Reconstructionists such as George Counts in arguing that the schools should construct a new social order. Rugg's vision for America was that of a great society created by "large-scale social and economic planning" and by a reconstructed education that would "cultivate integrated and creative" persons.[58]

In the early 1940s, Rugg encountered staunch opposition from conservative business and political groups who launched a national investigation of his textbooks, claiming they were subversive to the American tradition and the free enterprise system. In 1941, for example, the American Legion distributed pamphlets, entitled *The Complete Rugg Philosophy*, that charged Rugg with undermining Americanism and seeking to indoctrinate students in socialism.[59] Under relentless attack, Rugg's books were withdrawn in many school districts and virtually disappeared from the schools.[60]

The episode regarding Rugg's textbooks signaled that the social studies would be a consistently controversial area. The social studies deal with citizenship education—the teaching and learning of civic knowledge and values. Social studies are often redefined and reorganized to incorporate developments in the parent social sciences on which they are based; they are also redesigned periodically to reflect contemporary social, political, and economic issues and trends. They come under attack from more traditional educators, especially Conservatives and Essentialists, who argue that history and geography provide a more stable and structured introduction to social knowledge about time and place.

The Rugg textbook episode remains highly instructive for teachers. There is always a risk in teaching controversial issues that deal with race, religion, ethnicity, language, class, feminism, and human sexuality. For example, sex education is controversial between those who argue that it should prescribe abstinence from sexual relationships outside of marriage and those who argue that it should inform students about methods of contraception. Even the issue of teaching about Darwin's theory of evolution of species remains highly contentious. The Social Reconstructionists urged teachers to risk being committed to a new vision of America and the world. What do you think?

Natural and Physical Sciences

Coming out of Pragmatism and Progressivism, the Social Reconstructionists saw science and the scientific method as an important instrument to be used in creating a new social order. Although they generally subscribed to Dewey's Experimentalism or Instrumentalism, they did not see the scientific method as a neutral process but saw it being used to reach defined goals such as social and economic equality. The social studies, or social sciences, most directly conveyed Reconstructionist themes in the curriculum, but the Reconstructionists also were proponents of science and the use of the scientific method. Indeed, they most likely viewed political science, anthropology, economics, sociology, and social psychology as evolving sciences. They generally aligned themselves with Dewey's emphasis on the scientific method and saw it as being encapsulated into solving social, political, economic, and educational problems. Some of their Pragmatist critics contended that their end of a reconstructed society involved slapping a preconceived nonscientific end on the process that closed rather than opened it. Nevertheless, Reconstructionists championed their version of the scientific method, as they conceived of it.

Counts, Rugg, and other Reconstructionists gave great importance to technology, which they saw as the application of science to industry and communications. They welcomed technology, and in their penchant for planning, developed a social engineering approach to educational policy making. For all of these reasons, science and technology are important areas in the curriculum.

Reconstructionist Philosophy of Science Education

An important issue is: Is science objective, neutral, and divorced from social, political, and economic issues? Does the scientist need to be a neutral observer who does not allow the intrusion of extraneous variables to jeopardize the experiment? As he dealt with the issue of teaching about religion, Brameld sought to answer the question by relating philosophy of science to philosophy in general and to the social sciences. Scientists, he argued, need to become conscious of the social and cultural consequences of their discoveries and inventions. What happens in the laboratory soon finds its way outside. For example, the splitting of the atom changed society and culture. The atomic bomb could end human life on earth. But then again, nuclear energy might be a new, less polluting way of running the engines of an increasingly technological society. The teaching of the natural and physical sciences—biology, botany, zoology, chemistry, and physics—needs to be reconstructed. Like the social studies, they should not be taught in departmentalized fashion, isolated from their interdisciplinary connections. The pervasive interconnections among science, the social sciences, the humanities, and the arts need to be made intrinsic to teaching and learning. The pressing issues are how science can improve health care, protect the environment, and improve the quality of all life—plant, animal, and human—on earth.

Religion in the Public Schools

In the twenty-first century, the issue of the role of religion in American society and education has again come to the surface. It is not the first time, however, that the role of religion, especially in government and education, has been debated in the United States. For some, the various Supreme Court decisions have legally mandated Jefferson's idea of the separation of church and state: Government should not support the establishment of religion, nor should it interfere with its free exercise. For others, especially some cultural conservatives and fundamentalist Christians, the U.S. Constitution does not specifically prohibit religious observances in public spaces, including schools. They also contend that the United States is founded on Christian principles.

Religion and its influence are historically significant in global and American history. How should this influence be examined in schools? The Supreme Court has stated that teachers can teach about religion but not teach a religion. What does it mean to teach about religion? Most Reconstructionists, because of their contextualism, were cultural relativists. They were also heirs of the Enlightenment scholars who interpreted events scientifically. They considered religious beliefs and practices private, definitely not public, matters.

Brameld, who spoke on issues that others feared to broach, addressed teaching about religion. He concluded that historically, human beings worldwide have had some kind of religious experience and that experience, like any other experience, should be studied in public schools. He carefully distinguished teaching about religious experience from teaching religion. The key word was *about*. Teaching religion meant instructing students in the doctrines and practices of a particular church or denomination. Brameld did not hesitate to discuss spirituality and spiritual values, which he believed needed to be included in any discussion of human values. For him, spiritual values, though they might be related to religion, were not necessarily confined to particular religions.

Brameld believed religion, as a dimension of human cultural experience, should be studied by using his principle of defensible partiality. Applying defensible partiality to the study of religious experience meant students should be exposed to a consideration of beliefs as they are expressed by the believers who held them. However, all beliefs, including religious ones, are subject to searching comparative analysis in which their adherents are compelled to defend them openly and publicly in the face of all possible evidence for and against their religious commitment.[61] The presentation and discussion of religious beliefs is to take place in an atmosphere of mutual respect.

The Indoctrination or Imposition Issue

The Reconstructionists urged schools, teachers, and students to go beyond the neutral or objective discussion of issues in which the teacher presents both sides of an issue and leaves it to students to make up their own minds. Conventionally, teachers might discuss controversial issues in their classrooms, but solutions were to be deferred until a later date, after the student had completed school and was an adult voter. Reconstructionists added, however, that the discussion of controversial issues should begin with a frame of reference and follow a method of discussion that led to a conclusion. The strategy of neutrality in teaching means that a frame of reference is absent and a conclusion is not reached. The Reconstructionists, like the Critical Theorists, contend that claims to objectivity and openness in teaching are not really neutral or objective. The absence of acting on a conclusion preserves the socio-economic and political status quo and leaves power in the control of dominant economically favored individuals and groups. Believing that claims of neutrality and objectivity are either phony or an attempt to step away from social responsibility and justice, the Reconstructionists call on teachers and students not only to examine issues but also to structure promising solutions and work for their implementation.

The Reconstructionist emphasis on commitment to agreed-on goals and strategies raises the issue of academic freedom. Should instruction be objective and neutral or should it be committed to a specific point of view? Reconstructionists, like the Critical Theorists, believed ideological neutrality was impossible since all education takes place in a context that is ideologically charged. Critics of the Reconstructionists, who included some child-centered Progressives and Pragmatists as well as the more traditional Essentialists and Perennialists, argued that the Reconstructionists, in pursuing their goal of creating a new social order, would indoctrinate students. They would use schools and teachers to impose their blueprint for the future society on students. Essentialists and Perennialists argue that the role of teachers is to transmit academic skills and subjects and not act as political activists in the classroom. Although many Reconstructionists came out of the Pragmatist philosophical tradition, some Pragmatists argue that the Reconstructionists are misusing the scientific method because the Reconstructionist new social order did not come from open-ended inquiry but involved adding their own antecedent plan to the process. The Reconstructionists, however, maintaining their position, replied that education, or schooling, always involves choosing some elements of human culture, some skills or subjects over others, and that this choice imposes a particular version of culture on children. Schooling, they contended, is never neutral but always committed to some ideological perspective.

Brameld, who argued for defensible partiality, claimed that the Reconstructionist position was not indoctrination. He argued that indoctrination is instruction that proceeds in only one direction—from the teacher to the student—to establish in the student's mind a firm acceptance of some doctrine without critical discussion and comparison to alternative doctrines.[62] He argued that the Reconstructionist teacher has to stand up to rigorous and open criticism and comparison and contrast to alternative positions.

Educational Leadership and Policy Making

Reconstructionism enlarges the social, political, and economic dimensions of school administration and teaching beyond pedagogy into educational policy making. Counts and others wanted to prepare a new kind of leader in education, an educational statesperson. This leader would go beyond curriculum construction and instruction and function in the larger, broader, and more politically and culturally charged context. This visionary statesperson would design the policies needed to reform and reconstruct educational institutions and processes to bring about deliberate social change.

My Reflections on Philosophy of Education: Envisioning a Reconstructionist Educational Scenario

In reviewing this chapter on Social Reconstructionism, I decided to engage in some educational visioning, conjecturing about when might happen in a course taught by a Reconstructionist teacher. The following scenario is drawn from my reflection on Social Reconstructionism.

The scenario for the illustration of Reconstructionist instruction takes place in a charter high school that emphasizes interdisciplinary teaching and learning. Ms. Martha Seward is teaching a social studies class. In a graduate course in philosophy of education that she is taking for her master's degree, she read the works of Harold Rugg and Theodore Brameld and decides to try their ideas in her class. Because she teaches at a magnet school geared to interdisciplinary teaching, she decides to introduce an issue-oriented approach.

Ms. Seward met her class of twenty sophomore students in early September and introduced the idea that they would be working on an issue in the social studies. Unlike the more laissez-faire Progressive teachers, Ms. Seward was more directive—she would introduce the approach but also encourage students to identify the particular problem.

Stage One: Identifying the Issue

In a large group discussion, Ms. Seward asked the students to think about the most important issues facing the United States and the world. She also told them that they would be asked to identify an issue that would be the class project for the entire semester. She asked them to watch the news on television and read newspapers; in class the next day they would identify the issues they had discovered in their reading and watching. She also encouraged them to talk to their parents, family members, and friends about these issues.

Over several classes, the students identified the issues. They came up with a whole range of issues: the war in Afghanistan, the tribal and religious conflict in Darfur in Sudan, the economic recession and the high rate of unemployment, the high cost of attending colleges and universities, terrorism, gun control, school violence, and global warming and climate change. Ms. Seward led the class discussion. The class decided that all the problems were important. Several students who had older brothers and sisters in the armed services in Afghanistan made the case that the war should be the topic. Others agreed, but contended that global warming was crucial. If the environment of the planet were in jeopardy, all life would also be in jeopardy. Ms. Seward did not have the students vote on the issue that they preferred. Rather, the students put forth their viewpoints and reached a consensus in which all agreed to pursue the topic. (Ms. Seward used Brameld's ideas about using human relations skills to arrive at agreement.)

Stage Two: Defining Terms and the Problem

Once the problem had been identified, Ms. Seward wrote the term *global warming* on the board. Now, she decided to see what the students would do with the term. She asked them to define *global warming.* Martin Swift, a student, volunteered, "It's obvious that it means that the temperature of the earth is getting higher and the climate is getting warmer." Mina Patel, whose grandparents had immigrated to the United States from India, volunteered, "When I visited India last year, the temperatures were much higher than in the United States and I had some problems adjusting to them." She asked, "Does global warming mean that the temperatures everywhere are getting higher, or is it something that is happening in specific countries?" Several students said they didn't know enough about the problem. Ms. Seward said that the class needed to define their terms and do some initial basic research on global warming. At this point, the class divided into teams to do preliminary research: Team A would do research in the library, trying to identify books and articles about global warming; Team B would access the Web and explore sites dealing with the topic. Anthony Cizek volunteered, "I'm taking Mr. Kleminski's class on the integrated natural sciences and he has discussed global warming. I'd like to invite him to visit our class and share some information with us." Ms. Seward agreed that would be a good idea. Students met in their research groups, shared their information, and prepared to report their findings to the class.

The students found out that global warming is a specific example of a more general term, *climate change*. Although there are natural causes for climate change, they found that much scientific evidence points to human factors, especially emissions from fossil fuels, that are contributing to it. The class stipulated a definition of global warming as the increase in the average temperature of the earth's atmosphere and oceans in recent decades, and in an open-ended way raised questions about its projected rise in the future. Mr. Kleminski, the science teacher, made a presentation in class. He had developed a PowerPoint program that included charts and graphs about patterns of global temperatures and carbon dioxide emissions in the atmosphere over the past one hundred years that showed a rise in the past decade. He said that many scientists, but not all of them, concluded that the increase in global temperatures since the mid-twentieth century is very likely caused by increases in "greenhouse gas emissions." At this point, Anthony Cizek raised his hand and asked Mr. Kleminski, "What are greenhouse gas emissions?" Mr. Kleminski replied, "They are caused by human beings who use fossil fuels such as oil, gas, and coal for energy; the emissions from these fuels rise in the earth's atmosphere and create a cover of pollutants that keep the temperatures close to the earth and over time caused them to rise." Mike Carbone, a student, asked, "What difference does global warming make to us; why should we worry about it?" Mr. Kleminski said that the increase in global temperatures is expected to produce changes such as glacial melting at the North and South Poles that will cause the oceans to rise and flood coastal areas and cities; it may cause serious weather changes, especially rainfall, that may spur the growth of deserts and reduce food production; it may lead to the extinction of certain species, such as polar bears and walruses, that cannot adapt to drastic climate change. The class thanked Mr. Kleminski, who as he was leaving turned to Ms. Seward and said, "Why don't we have a teachers' meeting on this subject?"

Interdisciplinary Cooperation

Later, Ms. Seward and Mr. Kleminski met over coffee in the teachers' lounge. Ms. Seward further explained that she was experimenting with Social Reconstruction in her social studies class and that her class had chosen to examine global warming as its problem. Mr. Kleminski said that his science class was also dealing with global warming as an issue in the sciences. At this point, they decided to work collaboratively on global warming. At certain times in the semester, they would bring their classes together to share findings and for discussion. They also decided to set up a student steering committee composed of members of both classes to plan and arrange interdisciplinary research and activity. The proposed cooperation was facilitated by the fact that a number of students were enrolled simultaneously in both courses.

Stage Three: Formulating the Problem

At the next class meetings, Ms. Seward decided to pull things together and refocus the issue on the social studies. She pointed out that the issue was a political, social, and economic one as well as a scientific one. Many countries, especially those in the United Nations and the European Union, had expressed concerns and many of them had signed the Kyoto Protocol, which was aimed at reducing greenhouse gas emissions. The United States, however, had not signed, mainly because of economic and political reasons. Further, she added that China and India were experiencing rapid industrialization and were likely to add more emissions to the atmosphere. In class discussions, the students, guided by their teacher, developed some focusing points. Chief among them was that although a great deal of scientific evidence supported the thesis of global warming, the issue included some further questions: (1) What would be the level of global warming in the future? (2) Were the arguments of those who discredited global warming valid? (3) Would there be changes around the world and especially in their own region in the Midwest? (4) Since the debate over what to do about global warming was more than a problem in science and the environment—it was also a political, social, and economic one—what position should the United States take on global warming? (5) What could they do as high school students?

Stage Four: Reporting Findings

Various student research committees reported their findings about global warming.

- Committee A: Climate and Temperature Effects of Carbon Emissions: The science students reported their findings that the major greenhouse gases are water vapor, causing between 36 and 70 percent of the greenhouse effect; carbon dioxide (CO_2), which causes 9–26 percent; methane (CH_4), which causes 4–9 percent; and ozone, which causes 3–7 percent. Concentrations of CO_2 and methane have increased by 31 percent and 149 percent, respectively, above preindustrial levels since 1750. These levels are considerably higher than at any time during the past 650,000 years. Emissions from fossil fuels have produced about three-quarters of the increase in CO_2 from human activity over the past 20 years.[63]

- Committee B: Planetary Changes Due to Global Warming: A rise in global temperatures may in turn cause such planetary changes as the melting of the polar ice caps, melting of glaciers, and the rise of sea levels. Changes in rainfall may cause flooding in some areas and drought in others. There may also be changes in the frequency and intensity of extreme weather events. Other effects may include changes in agricultural production, extinction of threatened species, and desertification.
- Committee C: Political and Economic Effects of Global Warming: Global warming has had a mixed impact on countries, business corporations, and individuals. Environmental groups, especially Green political parties and organizations, have organized demonstrations and protests to alert people to global warming. There has been some movement by business corporations, especially automobile manufacturers, toward increased energy efficiency. However, they also identified paid advertisements on television that urged people to contact their representatives to oppose more federal regulations on energy and to encourage support for a transcontinental pipeline that would move crude oil from Canada to refineries in the Gulf states. The world's primary international agreement on combating global warming is the Kyoto Protocol, designed to decrease greenhouse gas emissions. The Kyoto Protocol has been signed by 160 countries but not the United States, which is allegedly the world's largest source of emissions.

Stage Five: Structuring Possible Solutions

At this point, the class met to consider possible solutions. The point was raised that the large number of automobiles in the United States is an important factor in producing emissions. When a student asked about the number of cars owned by students' families, many responded that their family owned two vehicles and that they expected to drive and have their own car. A student volunteered that personal change was needed as well as that by government agencies. Tentatively, the students agreed to write letters to their U.S. senators and members of the House of Representatives in support of signing the Kyoto Protocol. They also concluded that more research was needed into the role of local and state business firms regarding their actions to curb emissions. The students agreed to continue working on the issue.

CONSTRUCTING YOUR OWN PHILOSOPHY OF EDUCATION

As you reflect on constructing your own philosophy of education, what themes or elements of Reconstructionism appeal to you as a teacher? Which appeal least? Why? Have you encountered Reconstructionism in your educational experiences? Have you had Reconstructionist teachers? Do you intend to teach from an ideological point of view? Do you plan to incorporate Social Reconstructionism or some elements of it in your philosophy of education?

Conclusion

Reconstructionism has continuing relevance for education. The school curriculum is based on the selection and emphasis of some skills and subjects over others. What is selected and rejected depends on the frame of reference of those who construct the curriculum. The Reconstructionists sought to construct a frame of reference that could be used to identify and distinguish the viable cultural elements from those that are obsolete in terms of contemporary issues. For them, the selective lenses of viability and obsolescence are relative to changing contexts. Curriculum construction involves locating and eliminating the forces that limit social justice and equality. The culture's viable elements need to be reconstructed in light of new elements and forces.

Summary Chart on Social Reconstructionism

Theory	Purpose of Education	Curriculum	Method	Philosophical and Ideological Relationships	Leading Theorists
Social Reconstructionism	To deliberately bring about social change and create a more equitable and democratic society.	Pressing social, political, and economic issues.	Applying group-centered discussion and problem solving on social, political, and economic issues.	Liberalism Marxism Critical Theory Progressivism Pragmatism	Counts Brameld Rugg

Questions for Reflection and Discussion

1. Assume you are a Reconstructionist teacher. How would you respond to a student who says, "I don't care about social, political, and economic issues. I'm more interested in music, sports, and hanging out with my friends. Anyway, I can't do anything about these issues."
2. Assume you are a Reconstructionist teacher. How would you respond to a student who says, "We hear a lot about social justice and multiculturalism in this class. Why?"
3. Have you ever reconstructed a belief or value? How did you do this?
4. What is the difference between subject-matter, disciplinary-based, and interdisciplinary curriculum and instruction? Have you encountered these approaches in your own education or in your teaching? What are the strengths and weaknesses of both approaches?
5. At a parent–teacher conference, a parent accuses you of indoctrinating students with your political beliefs and threatens to take her complaint to the board of education. How would you respond?
6. What is a frame of reference? Do you have a frame of reference? How does it impact your ideas about culture, society, politics, and the economy and your ideas about education, schools, curriculum, and instruction?

Projects for Reflection and Inquiry

1. Arrange a classroom debate on the question: "Dare the school build a new social order?"
2. Watch and listen to the news on television, radio, and the Internet for a week. List the issues reported and bring them to the class for further discussion. Especially consider why some issues are reported and others are not.
3. In class discussion, identify the major political, social, and economic problems facing the United States and the world. What might be a Reconstructionist response to these problems?
4. Access http://www.usip.org/guiding-principles-stabilization-and-reconstruction-the-web-version/social-well-being/social-reconst. Analyze the principles that are stated for reconstructing society in terms of the discussion presented in this chapter.
5. Access George S. Counts' "Dare Progressive Education Be Progressive?" at http://www.courses.wccnet.edu/~palay/. Do you agree or disagree with Counts' argument that Progressive educators should have a definite point of view regarding social change?
6. Reflect on recent trends in education such as standards, common core curriculum, process learning, technology in the classroom, Constructivism, collaborative learning, and authentic assessment. How might Reconstructionists react to these trends?
7. Reflect on Brameld's theory of defensible partiality and then arrange a classroom debate between advocates of evolution and Intelligent Design in which the participants argue from partiality.

Internet Resources

For principles of Social Reconstructionism, access "Social Reconstructionism" at the United States Institute of Peace at http://www.usip.org/guiding-principles-stabilization-and-reconstruction-the-web-version/social-well-being/social-reconst.

For Reconstructionism and curriculum, access www.oregonstate.edu/instruct/ed416/PP3.html.

For a discussion of Theodore Brameld, access www.newfoundations.com/GALLERY/Brameld.html.

Suggestions for Further Reading

Beard, Charles A. *A Charter for the Social Sciences in the Schools.* New York: Charles Scribner's Sons, 1932.

Bleazby, Jennifer. *Social Reconstruction Learning: Promoting Democracy Through Practical Philosophy in Schools.* New York: Routledge, 2012.

Brameld, Theodore. *Education for the Emerging Age: Newer Ends and Stronger Means.* New York: Harper and Row, 1965.

Counts, George S. *The American Road to Culture: A Social Interpretation of Education in the United States.* New York: John Day Co., 1930.

———. *Dare the School Build a New Social Order?* New York: John Day Co., 1932.

———. *The Social Foundations of Education.* New York: Charles Scribner's Sons, 1934.

Dennis, Lawrence J. *George S. Counts and Charles A. Beard: Collaborators for Change.* Albany: State University of New York Press, 1989.

———, and William E. Eaton. *George S. Counts: Educator for a New Age.* Carbondale: Southern Illinois University Press, 1980.

Evans, Ronald W. *The Social Studies Wars: What Should We Teach the Children.* New York: Teachers College Press, 2004.

———. *This Happened in America: Harold Rugg and the Censure of Social Studies.* Greenwich, CT: Information Age, 2007.

Gutek, Gerald L. *The Educational Theory of George S. Counts.* Columbus: Ohio State University Press, 1970.

———. *George S. Counts and American Civilization: The Educator as Social Theorist.* Macon, GA: Mercer University Press, 1984.

James, Michael E. *Social Reconstruction through Education: The Philosophy, History, and Curricula of a Radical Idea.* New York: Praeger, 1995.

Ravitch, Diane. *Left Back: A Century of Failed School Reforms.* New York: Simon & Schuster, 2000.

Riley, Karen, ed. *Social Reconstruction: People, Politics, Perspectives.* Greenwich, CT: Information Age, 2006.

Russell, Bertrand. *Principles of Social Reconstruction.* New York: Routledge, 1997.

Stanley, William B. *Curriculum for Utopia: Social Reconstructionism and Critical Pedagogy in the Postmodern Era.* Albany: SUNY Press, 1992.

Stone, Frank A. *Theodore Brameld's Educational Reconstructionism: An Intellectual Biography.* San Francisco: Caddo Gap Press, 2003.

Notes

1. When I wrote *New Perspectives on Philosophy and Education,* the predecessor of this edition, I thought carefully about whether or not to include a chapter on Reconstructionism. My own initial doctoral research and dissertation was about George S. Counts, an originator of Social Reconstructionism, but I wondered whether it was still relevant to contemporary American education. I knew it was especially relevant in the history of American education, but at first it seemed that Critical Theory had replaced Social Reconstructionism by appropriating many of its themes and issues. I have observed a considerable revival of interest in Social Reconstructionism stimulated by the work of Karen Riley and her colleagues and I decided that the book needed a chapter on Reconstructionism. The response from reviewers has been a strong endorsement of the chapter.
2. Karen L. Riley, ed., *Social Reconstruction: People, Politics, Perspectives* (Greenwich, CT: Information Age, 2006), xi.
3. William B. Stanley, "Education for Social Reconstruction in Critical Context," in Karen Riley, ed., *Social Reconstruction: People, Politics, Perspectives,* 89.
4. Wayne J. Urban, "Social Reconstructionism and Educational Policy: The Educational Policy Commission, 1936–1941," in Karen Riley, ed., *Social Reconstruction: People, Politics, Perspectives,* 162.
5. William B. Stanley, "Education for Social Reconstruction in Critical Context," 108.
6. George S. Counts, "A Humble Autobiography," in Robert J. Havighurst, ed., *Leaders in American Education: The Seventieth Yearbook of the National Society for the Study of Education* (Chicago: University of Chicago Press, 1971), 151–174. Also see Gerald L. Gutek, "George Sylvester Counts (1889–1974): A Biographical Memoir," in *Proceedings of the National Academy of Education,* 3 (Stanford, CA: National Academy of Education, 1976), 333–353.
7. Counts was chairman of the American Labor Party from 1942 to 1944, and a founder of the Liberal Party, serving as its chairman from 1954 to 1959 and as its candidate for U.S. Senator in New York in 1952.
8. George S. Counts, *The American Road to Culture: A Social Interpretation of Education in the United States* (New York: John Day Co., 1930).
9. George S. Counts, "Dare Progressive Education Be Progressive?" *Progressive Education* 9 (April 1932), 257–263; and Counts, *Dare the School Build a New Social Order?* (New York: John Day Co., 1932).
10. Charles A. Beard, *A Charter for the Social Sciences in the Schools* (New York: Charles Scribner's Sons, 1932), 34.
11. Ibid., 24.
12. Ibid., 34–51.

13. George S. Counts, *The Social Foundations of Education* (New York: Charles Scribner's Sons, 1934), 1.
14. Committee of the Progressive Education Association on Social and Economic Problems, *A Call to the Teachers of the Nation* (New York: John Day Co., 1933), 12.
15. William F. Ogburn, *Recent Social Trends in the United States* (New York: McGraw-Hill Book Co., 1933), 166.
16. Counts, *Dare the School Build a New Social Order?*, 48.
17. Counts, *The Social Foundations of Education*, 55.
18. George S. Counts, "Present-Day Reasons for Requiring a Longer Period of Pre-Service Preparation for Teachers," *National Education Association Proceedings, 73* (1935), 697.
19. George S. Counts, *The Prospects of American Democracy* (New York: John Day Co., 1938), 176–194.
20. Counts, *Social Foundations of Education*, 548–558.
21. Craig Kridel, "Theodore Brameld: Reconstructionism for Our Emerging Age," in Karen Riley, ed., *Social Reconstruction: People, Politics, Perspectives*, 70.
22. Ibid., 71.
23. Theodore Brameld, *Education for the Emerging Age: Newer Ends and Stronger Means* (New York: Harper and Row, 1965), 99.
24. Ibid., 114.
25. Ibid., 115.
26. Ibid., 112–113.
27. Kridel, "Theodore Brameld: Reconstructionism for Our Emerging Age," 76.
28. Brameld, *Education for the Emerging Age: Newer Ends and Stronger Means*, 132–133.
29. Ibid., 128.
30. Ibid., 139.
31. Ibid., 1.
32. Ibid., 12.
33. Ibid., 17.
34. Ibid., 34–35.
35. Ibid., 184–187.
36. Theodore Brameld, *Design for America: An Educational Exploration of the Future of Democracy for Senior High Schools and Junior Colleges* (New York: Hinds, Hayden, and Eldredge, 1945), 3.
37. Kridel, "Theodore Brameld: Reconstructionism for Our Emerging Age," 78.
38. Brameld, *Education for the Emerging Age: Newer Ends and Stronger Means*, 140–141.
39. Ibid., 21.
40. Ibid., 78.
41. Ibid., 76.
42. Ibid., 80, 85.
43. Urban, "Social Reconstructionism and Educational Policy: The Educational Policy Commission, 1936–1941," 153.
44. Stanley, "Education for Social Reconstruction in Critical Context," 94.
45. John Dewey, *Individualism Old and New* (1929). Reprint, New York: Capricorn, 1962; and Dewey, *Liberalism and Social Action* (1935). Reprint, New York: Capricorn, 1963.
46. Podner, "Social Reconstructionist Curriculum Impulses: Pragmatism, Collectivism and 'The American Problem,'" 242–243.
47. Dennis, *George S. Counts and Charles A. Beard: Collaborators for Change*, 2–4.
48. Counts, *The Prospects of American Democracy*, 76.
49. Podner, "Social Reconstructionist Curriculum Impulses: Pragmatism, Collectivism and 'The American Problem,'" 241.
50. Brameld, *Education for the Emerging Age: Newer Ends and Stronger Means*, 150.
51. Diane Ravitch, *Left Back: A Century of Failed School Reforms* (New York: Simon & Schuster, 2000), 465–66.
52. Podner, "Social Reconstructionist Curriculum Impulses: Pragmatism, Collectivism and 'The American Problem,'" 241–242.
53. Lawrence J. Dennis, *George S. Counts and Charles A. Beard: Collaborators for Change* (Albany: State University of New York Press, 1989), 19.
54. In the 1930s, Rugg wrote three major books on Reconstructionist themes: *Culture and Education in America* (1931), *The Great Technology* (1933), and *American Life and the School Curriculum* (1936). He later wrote *Now Is the Moment* (1943), *Foundations of American Education* (1947), *The Teacher of Teachers* (1952), *Social Foundations of Education*, with William Withers (1955), and *Imagination* (1963), which was published posthumously.
55. R. W. Evans, "Social Studies vs. the United States of America: Harold Rugg and Teaching for Social Justice," in Karen L. Riley, ed., *Social Reconstruction: People, Politics, Perspectives*, 46, 51.
56. Peter F. Carbone, Jr., *The Social and Educational Thought of Harold Rugg* (Durham, NC: Duke University Press, 1977), 24–25.
57. The quotation from Rugg and the paraphrasing from the teacher's guide is from Karen L. Riley, "The Triumph of Americanism: The American Legion vs. Harold Rugg," in Karen L. Riley, ed., *Social Reconstruction: People, Politics, Perspectives*, 115.
58. R. W. Evans, "Social Studies vs. the United States of America: Harold Rugg and Teaching for Social Justice," 52.
59. Riley, "The Triumph of Americanism: The American Legion vs. Harold Rugg," 111.
60. R. W. Evans, "Social Studies vs. the United States of America: Harold Rugg and Teaching for Social Justice," 46–47.
61. Brameld, *Education for the Emerging Age: Newer Ends and Stronger Means*, 167.
62. Ibid., 152–153.
63. "Earth's Annual Global Mean Energy Budget" (PDF). *Bulletin of the American Meteorological Society*, 78(2): 197–208, and "Water Vapour: Feedback or Forcing," *RealClimate* (6 Apr 2005).

Critical Theory and Education

A demonstrator protesting against large financial and business corporations as part of the "Occupy Wall Street" movement.

17

CHAPTER PREVIEW

Critical Theory is a complex of assumptions about society, education, and schooling that analyzes aims, institutions, organization, curriculum, and instruction in terms of power relationships. It seeks to raise consciousness and bring about transformative change in the society and in education. Critical Theory has been influenced by Marxism, Freire's Liberation pedagogy, Postmodernism, and multiculturalism. The word *critical* means to engage in a rigorous probing and analytical investigation of social and educational conditions, in schools and society, in order to expose exploitative power relationships such as domination and marginalization and bring about transformative change. The anticipated consequence of this analysis is to empower subordinant classes and groups to self-determine their own futures in an equitable society. Critical Theorists believe that many institutions, especially political, economic, and educational ones, maintain and reproduce inequitable and exploitative conditions that favor one group or class, the dominant one, over subordinate groups and classes. Self-determination is possible if people become conscious of and overthrow these exploitative forces.

CONSTRUCTING YOUR OWN PHILOSOPHY OF EDUCATION

As you read and discuss this chapter, reflect on your educational experiences. Have you encountered Critical Theory? Have you had teachers or professors who were Critical Theorists? What subjects or courses did they teach? How did you react to their teaching. Do you think that education should raise students' consciousness about social justice issues? Determine if Critical Theory appeals to you as a teacher. See if you plan to use all or some of Critical Theory in constructing your own philosophy of education.

The chapter examines the following major topics:

- Critical Theory's historical, philosophical, and ideological contexts
- Paulo Freire and Henry Giroux as leading contributors to Critical Theory
- Critical Theory as an educational theory
- Critical Theory's opposition to ideologies such as Conservatism and Liberalism
- Critical Theory's implications for schools, curriculum, and teaching and learning

PUTTING CRITICAL THEORY IN CONTEXT

For the emphasis on contexts, also see the chapter on Social Reconstructionism and Education.

Critical Theorists emphasize contexts—the places and times in which education occurs. Because of this emphasis, we examine the historical and philosophical context in which Critical Theory developed as an educational theory.

Historical Context

Critical Theory: a theory that analyzes control and power in institutions and schools and seeks to empower marginalized persons and groups in a capitalist society and economy.

Critical Theory, as a movement in education, originally gained impetus in the United States during the 1960s, a time of intense social change that was marked by the civil rights movement led by Dr. Martin Luther King, Jr., and by the antiwar movement in opposition to the war in Vietnam. The period saw the concerted effort by African, Hispanic, and Native Americans to organize for civil rights and to increase political, economic, and educational representation and opportunities. During the 1960s, the women's rights movement began a renewed effort to secure equal rights and equal employment opportunities and compensation for women. Environmentalist groups began the Green movement, campaigning against the degradation of the natural environment and for conservation of natural resources. Gays and lesbians, too, went public in their demands for recognition of their right to an alternative lifestyle and against discrimination in education and employment. The period was also a time of concerted protests, demonstrations, and teach-ins, often sparked by disaffected students and intellectuals, against the American corporate structure and its political allies.

Although some philosophers of education were taking a more radical and leftist stand, a new Conservatism was also growing in the United States and in some countries in Western Europe, especially the United Kingdom. In the 1980s, the election of Ronald Reagan as president of the United States marked the ascendancy of Neo-Conservatives to power and the apparent decline of Liberalism.

Neo-Conservative forces in the Republican Party, supported by the Moral Majority and Christian fundamentalists, succeeded in electing George H. Bush in 1988 and George W. Bush as president in 2000 and 2004. At the same time as the Neo-Conservative ascendancy in the United States, Margaret Thatcher led the Conservative Party to victory in the United Kingdom. By the end of the 1980s, the Soviet Union and its Communist satellites had collapsed in central and Eastern Europe and the Cold War ended after more than fifty years. With the Soviet Union's demise, state socialism or Communist Marxist-Leninism was discredited as an ideology. This posed a serious dilemma for Marxist theoreticians. Some Marxists had earlier declared their ideological independence from the Soviet version of Marxist-Leninism. They opposed the Soviet regime's oppressive policies in what were police states in the USSR and its eastern and central European satellites. Stating that Soviet Communism did not represent true Marxism and that it was a grossly distorted version of what Marx had said, Marxist intellectuals looked for ways to revitalize the ideology in the twenty-first century.

For Soviet Marxist-Leninism, see the chapter on Marxism and Education.

With Soviet Communism gone as a Cold War global adversary, the United States and other technologically developed countries embarked on a policy of globalization, often called Neo-Liberalism, that emphasized free market economics, the ending of trade barriers, reduced government regulation. Identified as Neo-Liberal, some aspects of globalization policy reiterated Classical Liberal economic doctrines of Adam Smith and David Ricardo.

For Classical Liberalism, see the chapter on Liberalism and Education.

In American education, the Neo-Conservative political ascendancy was marked by the resurgence of a new Essentialism, called *basic education*, the emergence of the standards movement, a greater association of schooling with economic training, mandated achievement testing, and the enactment of the No Child Left Behind Act.

Philosophical and Ideological Context

In educational philosophy and theory, the convergence of several trends paved the way for the emergence of Critical Theory as a force in the **foundations of education**. Modern, or Social Welfare, Liberals, who had dominated American politics since the 1930s, began to lose the support of some intellectuals, particularly some university professors and students, who accused them of abetting and contributing to the growth of the military-industrial complex and to economic globalization. As the influence of **Philosophical or Language Analysis** declined in philosophy of education, more radical theorists in the Foundations were drawn to the Frankfurt school and to the Liberation pedagogy ideas of Ivan Illich and Paulo Freire. Postmodernism also exerted a strong influence as educators encountered and adopted the ideas of prominent Postmodernist French philosophers Jacques Derrida and Michel Foucault. Critical Theorists, subscribing to Postmodernism and Liberation pedagogy, opposed the Neo-Conservative and Neo-Essentialist ascendancy in education.

Foundations of Education: the theoretical areas such as history, philosophy, sociology, and psychology of education that support and explain educational practices.

Philosophical or Language Analysis: a philosophy that was dominant in the 1950s and 1960s that emphasized analyzing language to establish its meaning.

MARXISM. A potent ideological force in Critical Theory, Marxism was discussed in an earlier chapter; the discussion here examines those aspects that relate to Critical Theory. Marxist concepts such as the economic base of society, class struggle for control of the means and modes of production, and alienation have influenced Critical Theorists. Critical Theorists have reduced the ideological rigidity of these concepts and employed them in a more flexible social and educational analysis. They use these concepts as tools to analyze society, education, and schools rather than as specific dialectical recipes for creating a revolutionary society. For example, Critical Theorists agree with Marx that those who control the economic base, the means and modes of production, also control social, political, and educational institutions in a particular society, especially a capitalist one. Seeing history as a determined inflexible process, Marx said that control of the economy would lead to an inevitable war between the capitalist exploiting class and the working class, the proletariat, with the inevitable victory going to the workers. Although Critical Theorists use the Marxist concept of class conflict, they have broadened it from economic classes to include other oppressed groups such as African, Latino, and Native Americans; women; the poor; and gays and lesbians. Critical Theorists, discounting the idea of an inevitable revolution, give a much greater role to education to raise consciousness about social, economic, and political injustices. Focusing on schools as social institutions, Critical Theorists contend that in contemporary America, educational institutions are controlled by powerful economic classes—the wealthy who are invested in the corporate economy. The educational needs of less-favored economic groups are subordinated to those of the rich and powerful. The struggle for control in schools centers on the curriculum as a contested area. By controlling the administration of schools and the organization of the curriculum, the upper socio-economic classes subordinate and **marginalize** the lower classes.

For Derrida and Foucault, see the chapter on Postmodernism and Education.

See the chapter on Marxism and Education.

Critical Theorists use the Marxist concept of **alienation**. In a capitalist society, the workers are exploited by the economic and financial elites who control the means and modes of production—the industries, businesses, banks, and corporations. The workers do not receive the benefits of their labor; instead, the value they create through work is expropriated, seized by the capitalists as profits. As a consequence, work in a capitalist society results in social and psychological alienation of workers from their labor and from the products, the commodities, they make. Critical Theorists have broadened Marx's concept of alienation to refer to the social and psychological states of people who have been marginalized, driven to the peripheries, of society—the homeless and those who live in poverty. In addition to the economically destitute,

Marginalize: to push or relegate an individual or a group to the margins of the school and the educational process.

Alienation: to feel separated from something; a sense of anger and frustration about losing something that has been unfairly taken by another.

others also have been alienated, or marginalized, in modern American society—African Americans, Hispanics, women, and gays and lesbians, for example. The struggle for Critical Theorists takes place in the immediate situation, the community and schools, the sites where actual education takes place. In this struggle, Critical Theorist educators seek to raise the consciousness of the alienated so that they can identify who and what is marginalizing them so that they can empower themselves to take their rightful place in an egalitarian society.[1]

THE FRANKFURT SCHOOL. The Frankfurt School—a group of social and cultural theorists that included Max Horkheimer (1895–1973), Theodor Adorno (1903–1969), and Herbert Marcuse (1898–1979) at the Institute of Social Research at the University of Frankfurt in Germany—also influenced Critical Theory.[2] The Frankfurt theorists developed several significant themes in Critical Theory analysis such as (1) ideology exerts a powerful impact on human consciousness; (2) more than academic skills and subjects, education is an agency of political, social, and economic socialization; and (3) broadly construed, education includes informal educational agencies, especially the media, as well as the more formal schools. Socialization, the acquiring of the beliefs and values of a culture, is not a neutral process but is always ideologically charged. There is not one culture, but several cultures in competition in a given society. In a capitalist society and economy, political and ideological socialization is intended to indoctrinate children in the officially mandated beliefs and values of the dominant class and to marginalize competing cultures, especially those of powerless people. The analysis of socialization, according to the Frankfurt School, requires a transdisciplinary method that examines the texts and representations used by the media and in schools and in politics and economics.[3]

The Frankfurt School theorists developed the idea of "culture studies" to examine the impact of technology and consumerism on the mass culture. The culture industries—the media, television, the Internet, intertainment, sports, and radio—exhibit features that are similar to industrial production: both are geared to produce mass tastes in a mass audience of consumers in a global market. The culture industries, with their approved story lines, tell of the stories of stellar individuals who have achieved economic riches. They act to legitimize existing capitalist societies and to socialize a mass audience by instilling a false consciousness into this world of global consumers.[4]

See the chapter on Postmodernism and Education.

POSTMODERNISM. Postmodernism is treated in another chapter; the discussion here emphasizes only those aspects that relate most directly to Critical Theory.

Critical Theory has been influenced by Postmodernism and shares its antipathy to metaphysics in the older Idealist and Realist philosophies. Like Postmodernism, it sees what is exalted as the great works of philosophers such as Plato, Aristotle, Aquinas, and Hegel to be meta-narratives used as rationales for the established way of thinking. Critical Theory, like Postmodernism, rejects the prominent role given to the eighteenth-century Enlightenment as a historical and scientific rationale for modernism. It is especially antagonistic to the Enlightenment's claims that reason, especially the scientific method, is an objective means of solving problems.

Critical Theory shares Postmodernism's focus on language, especially its use in constructing and deconstructing texts and canons. It finds language to be a construction that arises in specific contexts and not a reflection of a generalized reality. For both Critical Theorists and Postmodernists, the claims and interpretations of knowledge are never neutral or objective but are statements of power and ideology. They reject the compartmentalization of knowledge into areas with boundaries, claiming that the elites have constructed canons or texts that establish arbitrary definitions, illustrations, and cases that mark off one subject from another. By deconstructing the canon or text, it is possible to get to the motives and purposes of those who constructed them.

For Freire's Liberation Pedagogy, see the chapter on Ideology and Education.

LIBERATION PEDAGOGY AND DESCHOOLING. Critical Theory has also been influenced by deschooling and Liberation Pedagogy, especially the ideas of Ivan Illich (1926–2002) and Paulo Freire, two Latin American educators. Both of these educators, though concerned with education worldwide, developed many of their ideas by working with economically disadvantaged people in less technologically developed societies. Illich worked largely in Mexico and Freire in Brazil. Illich, in *Deschooling Society* (1971), argued that Westernized schooling is the instruction of neocolonialist exploitation and repression of the people in less technologically developed societies in Asia, Africa, and South America. Schooling had become a great "sales pitch" that imposed capitalist consumerist ideas on working-class and peasant children, conditioning them to want commodities they did not need. It also conditioned people to believe that all learning had to be in schools rather than in informal voluntary associations. Although Critical Theorists find much of Illich's analysis congenial to their ideological orientation, particularly their opposition to capitalist globalization, they do not call for the elimination of schools. Rather, they believe that it is possible to transform schools into agencies of human liberation. Illich's work, however, influenced Critical Theorists to think of the struggle to empower the dispossessed in global terms in which the marginalized groups in the United States are connected to the worldwide oppressed in less technologically developed societies.

Paulo Freire is an inspiration for many Critical Theorists. In *Pedagogy of the Oppressed* (1972), Freire called for an education to raise people's consciousness about the reality of their economic and social condition and encourage them to take the steps needed for their own **empowerment**. Since Freire is such an important voice for Critical Theorists, we discuss his Liberation Pedagogy in some detail and then turn to Giroux as a leader of the contemporary movement.

Empowerment: when an oppressed group becomes conscious of the conditions of their exploitation and takes power over their own lives.

PAULO FREIRE AND LIBERATION PEDAGOGY

For Freire's view of ideology, see the chapter on Ideology and Education.

Paulo Freire (1921–1997) developed Liberation Pedagogy while working in a literacy campaign among Brazil's impoverished peasants and workers in the late 1940s and early 1950s. Realizing that literacy means more than learning to read and write, Freire used it as a tool for **consciousness-raising**, for people to become aware of the conditions of their lives and work. Informed by their own consciousness, people, empowered by literacy, could identify and change the economic, social, and political conditions that caused their exploitation.[5]

Consciousness-Raising: a critical analysis that leads to recognition of the people and conditions that cause exploitation and the devising of strategies to end that exploitation.

At the time of Freire's literary campaign, Brazil's society and economy were unevenly developed between a small ruling elite and a large impoverished underclass. The peasants in its rural agricultural regions were very poor and exploited by landlords. Rio de Janeiro and São Paulo, Brazil's largest cities, with their avant-garde architectural centers, were ringed by sprawling urban slums with grossly inadequate sanitation, health care, educational, and social services. A powerful ruling elite of landlords and industrialists, backed by the military, controlled Brazil's government and economy.[6]

Freire, associated with the Catholic Action Movement, organized literacy circles to improve the situation of Brazil's impoverished classes. Freire's literacy teams taught the peasants to read by focusing their attention on the immediate social and economic conditions that shaped the contexts of their daily struggle to earn a living. Freire had learned that literacy had political as well as educational implications. Brazilian landowners and the military saw Freire's literacy campaign as a threat to their privileged positions. In 1964, a military coup, overturning a reformist government, seized control of Brazil and ruled for the next twenty-one years until 1985.[7] Freire was arrested, imprisoned, and then deported from Brazil. During his exile, Freire worked on literacy programs in Chile and was a visiting professor at Harvard University, where he was also a Fellow at the Center for the Study of Development and Social Change. While at Harvard, Freire wrote his well-known and influential *Pedagogy of the Oppressed*, which became an important text for Critical Theorists. He next served as an assistant secretary of education for the World Council of Churches. When military rule ended in Brazil, Freire returned to his home country, where he served on the faculty at the University of São Paulo and then as the minister of education for the City of São Paulo. He died at the age of seventy-five on May 2, 1997.

For their views on antecedent reality, see the chapters on Idealism and Realism.

Philosophically, Freire was influenced by Existentialism, which also found its way into Critical Theory. Similar to the Existentialists, Freire rejected the traditional positions of Idealism and Realism in which the human being is antecedently defined as a predetermined general category. In contrast, Freire sees individuals as incomplete presences in the world who can construct their own projects for making the world into a better place for humanity. Consciousness raising, in Existentialist terms, means that people, regardless of their socio-economic status, can become aware that they have the power to take the actions needed to complete themselves.[8]

See the chapter on Marxism and Education.

Ideologically, Freire was influenced by Marxism, but from his Existentialist perspective, rejected its historical determinism. He employs Marxist analysis when he urges that dispossessed and marginalized people raise their consciousness by examining the material conditions that have an impact on their lives.[9] These cultural, social, political, economic, and educational conditions, though historically derived, can be changed when people understand the conditions and the agents that repress them.

Religiously, Freire was a Roman Catholic who joined Catholic Action, an organization committed to improving the conditions of the poor and to promoting social reform. Thomas Aquinas, who shaped Maritain's ideas and probably some of Freire's, saw teaching as a vocation in which teachers led students to knowledge through their love of humankind. Freire also saw teaching as inspired by persons with teachable hearts, and maintained "Love is the basis of an education that seeks justice, equality, and genius."[10] Paradoxically, Freire was familiar with the spiritually oriented philosophy of such Catholic philosophers as Jacques Maritain as well as with Marx's dialectical materialism.[11]

Freire's Liberation Pedagogy

Key terms in Freire's educational theory are *liberation* and *pedagogy*. *Liberation* means freedom from the exploiting social, economic, political, and educational conditions that give a ruling group power over others, especially those who are impoverished materially and culturally. *Pedagogy,* a Greek word that means leading a person to knowledge, is an education that raises consciousness about the conditions of life and work and suggests strategies to improve them.

Raising consciousness is a major Freirean educational goal. It relates to the Portuguese word *conscientizacao,* which for Freire meant constructing a critical awareness of social, political, and economic conditions and contradictions under which people live and work. "Critical awareness" is an important concept in Critical Theory. More than intellectual knowledge, it is action oriented as it generates a desire within a person to act as an agent of change to replace oppression with freedom.

Similar to Marx, Freire sees history as a vital critical study in raising consciousness. Differing with Marx, Freire rejects the interpretation that history is determined by inexorable laws that make it beyond human control. Further, Freire, like the Social Reconstructionists, emphasizes the importance of concrete contexts in shaping our reality. Here, he disagrees with both Marx, a materialist, and Hegel, an Idealist, who see history as the working out of universal laws. Born in and living in concrete contexts, we have had a limited control over the persons and events that have shaped us. However, we have not had control over other persons who have controlled the events, primarily the economic and educational ones, that play a role in our lives. This lack of control is most pernicious when it is exercised by those who want to exploit us and minimalize us by telling us who we are rather than permitting us to define ourselves. These exploiters might be the landlord of a vast agricultural estate in Brazil, who exploits the peasants who work for him, or the more impersonal, but more powerful, multinational corporation that exploits workers by paying subsistence wages for work in unsafe conditions. Although others have been in control, this does not mean that we need to abandon our choices to them. Becoming conscious of our historical situation means that we no longer accept the status quo and see embedded institutions and practices as something to which we must adjust. We are not merely inheritors of history; rather, we have the power to make history. To begin, it is necessary to dispel the history that masks reality by justifying the status quo as a celebration of great achievements of the exploiting class. The critical study of history reveals that some groups or classes have seized control of natural resources and exploited them for their own aggrandizement without concern for the health of the planet or the welfare of its people. For Freire, our history is exactly that—it belongs to us as the authors of a narrative that is personal and social. If we are willing to empower ourselves and shoulder the responsibility that empowerment carries, we have the power to construct our own autobiographies—to tell our own life stories.

For their emphasis on contexts, see the chapter on Social Reconstruction and Education.

The Program of Action

Again, much like Counts, Rugg, Brameld, and the Reconstructionists, Freire sees all education, schooling, and teaching and learning as taking place in an ideologically charged situation. He distinguishes Liberation Pedagogy as a radicalizing ideology from extreme right- and left-wing political ideologies that misuse and distort history to build myths that create a sense of false consciousness. Freire argues that teachers who claim to be neutral are hiding behind a veil of objectivity that ignores human suffering, manipulation, and exploitation. Pretending to be neutral to avoid controversy actually allies teachers with the exploiters. Teachers need to recognize that what they do or fail to do in the classroom relates to issues of social justice. Freire urged critically minded teachers to make a stand that advances social justice.[12] Again, like Social Reconstructionism, Liberation Pedagogy is an educational theory whose purpose is to create a new, more open, social order.

For a discussion of ideology, see the chapters on Ideology and Education and Social Reconstructionism and Education.

Epistemology

Freire draws an intimate connection between thinking (being conscious) and practice (acting on our thoughts), or in his terminology, *praxis*. Having a critical consciousness means that we have seen through the ideological fog of false consciousness—the myths, theories, and rationales—the oppressors have constructed to confuse and indoctrinate dominated groups. These rationales, derived from the oppressor's ideology, serve to indoctrinate the oppressed into believing that their oppression is "right,"

For false consciousness, see the chapters on Postmodernism and Marxism.

"just," "the standard," or "the way it is supposed to be." To see this process at work in American history, one can go back in time and read school textbooks that described Andrew Carnegie and John D. Rockefeller as "captains of industry" who were giants of innovation that developed the American economy. Or you can find textbooks from the past that claimed that the slaves actually benefited from slavery and the slave owners were paternalistic and benevolent protectors of those they enslaved. Thinking critically means that one breaks through these rationales of oppression to see them for what they really are—the constructions used by exploiters to indoctrinate those whom they exploit. Critique, while necessary, is not enough for critical thinking. It requires an engagement in liberating dialogues that are alternatives to the status quo. In these dialogues, the oppressed get a voice to tell the truths that they have experienced. Through liberating dialogues, it is possible to construct a genuine consciousness of social reality.

Axiology

For Freire, the major conflict in values lies in choices to be made about the conditions that either humanize or dehumanize persons. A truly ethical person, motivated by social justice, becomes conscious of the conditions in which she or he lives and works, and deliberately seeks to change those that are unjust or pernicious to human freedom. The ethical person consciously accepts this responsibility to create a future filled with promises and possibilities.[13]

The most important issue in valuation is: Are values freely made and chosen by the person who embraces and is guided by them or are they prescriptions imposed on the oppressed by their oppressors? *Prescription* refers to the injunctions about what a person should do, whereas *proscription* is that which he or she should not do. We all know that traditional schooling, indeed most schooling, is replete with prescriptions and proscriptions. Freire opposes those prescriptions, that impose "one man's choice on another." In a class-based society, prescriptions about the sanctity of private property over human needs impose the dominant group's values on those who are powerless and marginalized. Prescriptions of oppression—imposed as the "right way" to act or as socially sanctioned behaviors—are often indoctrinated into the oppressed and reinforced by sanctions and threats or actual punishments.[14]

To create values freely, individuals, in true Existentialist fashion, need to know that their choices are theirs alone. They need to liberate themselves from automatically accepting the prescriptions and proscriptions that others, especially those with power, impose on them. Again, like an Existentialist, Freire tells people that they are "unfinished" agents, who can give themselves the power to bring themselves to self-definition.

Freirean Education

For Freire, schools, curriculum, and instruction reflect the contexts, the communities and sites, of which they are a part. Like all social, political, and economic systems, educational ones are conditioned and shaped by the ideology of those who control the economic structure. Schools, when controlled by the dominant groups, adjust or condition students to accept the official knowledge, the beliefs, of the power holders and to play the roles assigned them in the economic, political, and social relationships of the existing system. In contrast, when infused with Liberation Pedagogy, schools, curriculum, and teaching and learning can raise students' consciousness, encouraging them to reflect critically on social reality and empowering them to transform the conditions, the contexts, that shape their lives.

Education for consciousness raising involves exposing those actors, the administrators and teachers who, often because of their own ignorance, miseducate students. A leading cause of miseducation is imposing false consciousness, a Marxist concept, on students by transmitting an official version of history and beliefs, often masked as objective subject matter, on students. False consciousness comes from an uncritical belief in the rhetoric of those who hold power and control institutions. An education that defines a person's values in terms of wealth and power and sees schooling as a ticket to a place in the corporate system misses the mark of being truly humanizing.[15]

Freire attacks education that indoctrinates the young with false consciousness, which in schools comes in the transmission of alleged knowledge, really putting the words of the privileged class into the pages of textbooks and the mouths of teachers. Transmission relies on **teacher talk** in which a teacher plays the role of a "talking text" who describes and interprets reality for students. Teacher talk is backed by the classroom prescription that students should be attentive listeners who, fixing on each word spoken by the teacher, take it in and store it in their minds for recall on a test. Freire calls the teaching-listening-testing regimen **educational banking.**[16] Each bit of information is deposited in the student's mind, a mental bank, where it is stored and cashed in when needed, as in taking a test. The current standards movement that emphasizes standardized testing is an example of assessment based on the banking model of education. The elaborate testing mechanisms constructed to determine students' academic achievement in mastering externally imposed curricula is used to sort students into groups, reproducing the inequalities of the existing social and economic system.[17] The results of standardized tests can also be used to label schools as effective or ineffective and teachers as competent or incompetent. Critical theorists would ask who is doing the labeling and who is being labeled. Labeling is an instance of the exercise of power by one group over another.

Teacher Talk: the verbal or rhetorical transmission of information from teachers to students.

Educational Banking: storing deposits of information in the mind to be recalled for an examination.

Teaching as Committed Partiality

Freire completely rejects the proposition that teachers can and should be neutral or impartial on social, political, and economic issues.[18] He is especially critical of educators who claim to be ideologically unbiased and open minded in their teaching. For those who follow Liberation Pedagogy, claims to objectivity mean the teacher either is not conscious of the true conditions that affect education or he or she is engaged in a pretense that masks hidden ideological commitments.

For a very similar view on committed partiality, see the ideas of Theodore Brameld in the chapter on Education and Social Reconstructionism.

For Freire, genuine learning occurs when both teachers and students engage in a shared, ongoing dialogue that constructs rather than transmits knowledge. The construction of knowledge results when teachers and students share, reflect on, and critically evaluate their experiences.[19] According to Macedo, a close friend and interpreter of Freire, genuine teaching:

- recognizes that all social and educational situations are ideological.
- is ethically committed to fight racial, sexual, and class discrimination.
- requires a critical capacity, tempered by humility and reflection.[20]

For Freire, teaching is not transmitting information, nor is learning memorizing information to be retrieved in the future. Genuine teaching and learning require teachers and students to be mutually engaged in constructing knowledge through critical dialogue. Freirean-inspired teachers take a rigorous critical attitude in examining society, politics, and economics. Although tough minded in their analyses, they are motivated by love, respect, and humility for their students. This critical but loving attitude means that teachers need to challenge the status quo and what passes for the system's "best practices" as they confront the power structure both inside and outside of schools. Humility means that teachers need to recognize that as human beings they are limited in what they know and need to be open to learning from the community, especially its disempowered groups, and from students. Both participants in the educational dialogue—teacher and students—are re-forming themselves. Freire's concept of teaching and learning as mutual re-forming of the selves reflects his reliance on the Existentialist theme that the human condition is one of incompleteness in which we act to bring our lives, through our own actions, to wholeness.

Henry Giroux

Henry Giroux, a leading contemporary educational and cultural critic, is an important voice in Critical Theory. He sees education as a "principal feature of politics" by which individuals acquire "the capacities, knowledge, skills, and social relations" to see themselves as social and political agents.[21] Education includes schooling, yet it is much broader than the school and can take place on multiple sites. Education can be either an agency of social and political control or it can be a process of social and political transformation and liberation. Although schools are used by dominant classes to reproduce themselves and their control, they also can be liberated to become an alternative to reproducing domination. When liberated, they can be used as agencies to examine the institutions and processes of repression and to construct an alternative future. Giroux has constructed a broad cultural and educational theory that includes (1) a critical analysis of existing institutions; (2) resistance to the imposition of the dominant ideology; and (3) creation of a more egalitarian, democratic, and multicultural society and education.[22]

Giroux argues for education that is reflective and critical and that teachers, among others, act as public intellectuals. Like other Critical Theorists, Giroux works to expose the ways in which power pervades educational institutions to marginalize people, especially dispossessed groups. Like Freire, Giroux opposes the traditional view that instruction is the transmission of selected information from teachers to students. The transmission of official knowledge legitimizes an authoritarian view of knowledge in that it is prescribed by those who hold power as prepackaged content, safe methods of instruction, and controlled mechanisms of assessment.[23]

Giroux sees teachers as transformative intellectuals who are cultural workers and border crossers. As transformative intellectuals, teachers are much more than transmitters of the approved "official knowledge" that is prescribed in lists of standards and state mandates. Official knowledge is that which has been filtered and approved by power holders and the educational bureaucrats who serve them. Teachers need to devise strategies to bring "unofficial knowledge" into their classrooms. Especially in economically disadvantaged school attendance areas, the unofficial knowledge comes from the lives, the stories, of the members of the community and from the autobiographies of the students who live there. Teachers who follow the approved teachers' guides and manuals find themselves relegated as mouthpieces who speak the lines in a script that has been handed to them by those who are in charge. As transmitters, teachers are go-betweens, the transactive agents of those who hold power. To risk being transformative means that the teacher no longer serves to perpetuate the status quo but works to change the culture, politics, and economy of the local community in which she or he works and of the larger community of which it is a part.

Giroux's concept of the teacher as a cultural worker combines elements of the new cultural studies as well as earlier elements from Marxism, Existentialism, and Social Reconstructionism. As persons who use their efforts to transform society, teachers are workers. As transformative intellectuals, teachers are not only academicians but also dedicated individuals engaged in expending their efforts and energies on changing the schools, culture, and society. Teachers need to involve themselves with social and political movements and groups that work in oppositional public spheres outside of schools and in broader educational arenas. When they recognize themselves as cultural workers, teachers can proceed to break down the divisions between intellectual and manual labor that separate theory and practice in schools.[24]

Marx's concept of socially useful labor gave work a social instead of a profit-making purpose. The Social Reconstructionists urged teachers to join with other Progressive groups and organizations to build a new social order. Giroux and other Critical Theorists urge teachers, as public intellectuals, to join in social and political movements and groups that work in opposition to power holders both in schools and in other public spheres in the larger society.

In addition to enlarging the idea of the teacher as a cultural worker, Giroux broadened the concept of the culture. His idea of culture is shaped by the emerging field of cultural studies that examines the role of mass culture, especially the media, in creating a new dominant class hegemony. No longer seen as interpretations of the fine arts and literature, cultural studies examine how ideology and culture intersect and how culture is used to reproduce ideology. Dominant groups use mass cultural agencies—media, movies, television, and other forms of entertainment—to reproduce the dominant culture. These vehicles of mass culture meet and coincide with formal education, schooling, to shape the thought, especially the consumer needs, to support the economic control of the dominant culture. Giroux argues that culture must be analyzed within the social, political, economic, and educational systems through which it is reproduced.[25]

Giroux encourages teachers and students to be border crossers. A person who crosses a border is one who moves from the boundaries of a delimited territory, often those of a country, to another. The curriculum of secondary and higher education is territorialized; the academic provinces, the subjects, are marked by boundaries. Teaching and learning in traditional schools are to stay within departmentalized boundaries. The academic territory within the boundary has been mined, explained, described, and interpreted, or exploited, by the academic authorities, the experts in the field. For example, the expert authority about the past is the historian; about the natural and physical world, the scientist; about the political world, the political scientist; and so forth. These authorities construct an academically defined official knowledge that is found in the "definitive" texts that constitute the approved reading list. The division of the curriculum into academic fields or subjects leads to a departmentalization of the mind in which some areas belong exclusively to a particular field and related to other fields.

For a counter view on the need for subject departmentalization, see the chapters on Realism and Essentialism.

Giroux's advocacy of **border crossings** means that teachers and students should be free to cross subject boundaries and borders to find and use the information, the knowledge, and methods that they need. Giroux's concept of interdisciplinary and transdisciplinary border crossings is similar to Dewey's problem-solving method. Dewey argued that a genuine problem, as distinct from an academic one, is not restricted to one subject but requires interdisciplinary research in a variety of disciplines. For example, the problem of global warming crosses not only national boundaries but also subject-matter boundaries. Efforts to solve global warming deal with environmental studies, an interdisciplinary area that involves aspects of biology, botany, zoology, and other natural and physical sciences as well as political science, geography, and economics.

Border Crossings: Giroux's interdisciplinary strategy of moving across the boundaries that set off one subject from another in the traditional curriculum.

For Dewey's problem-solving method, see the chapter on Pragmatism and Education.

For Giroux, the issues that marginalize people today—racism, sexism, and classism—are not explained by a single academic subject but encompass many of them. As they investigate the cultural and social terrain in which they work, teachers will face complex issues that are not confined within disciplinary limits. They need to

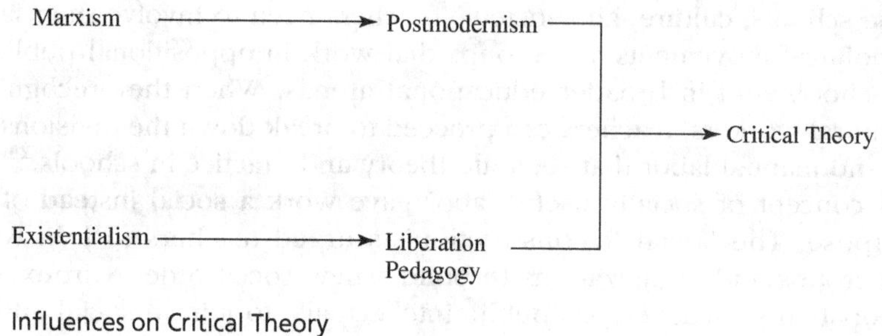

Influences on Critical Theory

understand that culture, society, race, class, language, and gender impact the students that they are teaching.

The educational process, like most other important areas, needs to be approached from interdisciplinary and transdisciplinary perspectives. Curriculum and instruction are complex processes and not a simple matter of teaching the basics as Conservatives and Essentialists contend. Complexity means that something is composed of interrelated parts or elements that make up a system. An educational system and the educational process cannot be explained one dimensionally from the viewpoint of a single subject matter or discipline. It needs to be approached from the multidisciplinary, interdisciplinary, even transdisciplinary perspective that Giroux's border crossing suggests. Education and schooling cannot be understood outside of the sociological, historical, philosophical, cultural, economic, political, and psychological contexts that shape it.[26]

CRITICAL THEORY AS A THEORY OF EDUCATION

This section examines Critical Theory as a theory of education. It identifies and comments on the constructs that guide Critical Theorists' social and educational analysis.

Social Control

Dominant Classes: those who hold power and use it to control, subordinate, and marginalize other groups and classes.

Dominant classes, particularly in a capitalist corporate society, control institutions, including schools. They use their social control to maintain, or reproduce, their favored position and to subordinate socially and economically disadvantaged classes. Schools are used by the dominant class to reproduce the status quo that ensures their dominance—often through the use of the official and hidden curricula.

An individual's socio-economic status, including educational expectations and opportunities, is largely conditioned by race, ethnicity, gender, and class. In the United States, the historically subordinated marginalized groups are the urban and rural poor; African, Hispanic, and Native Americans; women; and gays and lesbians. These groups are pushed to the periphery, to the margins, of society and schooling. The conditions of marginality in the larger society are reinforced by the school's organization and curriculum.[27] Their history is either neglected or added at the margins of the official history. It is possible, through a critical education, for subordinated classes and groups to become conscious of their exploitation, resist domination, overthrow the regimes of suppression, and empower themselves to determine their own future.

Institutions, including educational ones, are centers of contention, or conflict, between the dominant class and other less favored classes. Educational policy and practice, informed by Critical Theory, strives to empower marginalized groups to gain greater equity, fairness, and justice throughout the United States and in other countries as well.

The Critique

Much Critical Theory is a critique, a critical analysis, of existing society and institutions, including schools and colleges and universities. The critique is done at both the micro level, which examines the forces and conditions operating on site in particular schools, and at the broader macro level, which enlarges the immediate community context to examine the historical, social, political, and economic conditions in the larger society.[28] The Critical Theorist analysis is guided by such focusing questions as:

- Who really controls society and schools, and what are their motives?
- How are educational resources allocated, and who benefits from this allocation?
- Who makes the policies that govern schools, and who benefits from these policies?
- Who determines the goals and expectations of schools?
- Who establishes the curriculum, and does the curriculum relate to race, ethnicity, language, class, and gender?
- What power do teachers and students really have in schools and over the educational process?
- How is student academic achievement assessed and measured?

Critical Theorists begin to answer these questions on site—in the immediate context of a particular community and school. They begin their critique using **microanalysis**, by assembling and interpreting the demographic information, the case studies, and the life stories, the autobiographies of teachers and students. Often, schools in economically disadvantaged urban and declining rural areas are attended predominantly by the poor, by African, Hispanic, Native, and Appalachian Americans. The buildings are generally poorly maintained and the programs are underfinanced and lack adequate resources.

Microanalysis: an investigation of the forces operating internally in an institution such as a school.

Still using microanalysis, the Critical Theorists examine the conditions on site—in the school. They are likely to find that the typical inner-city urban school is enmeshed in a large web-like bureaucracy that operates in a hierarchical, top-down style. With orders coming down from the central office at the top, there is little opportunity for local community input and teacher participation in decision making. The official curriculum, too, is determined, prepackaged, and handed down from higher-level administrators, with little room for local initiatives that relate to the lived experiences of students in the school or people in the local community. Teachers within the school are isolated from each other, teaching in self-contained insulated classrooms. They have little or no power in setting goals or in making decisions about curriculum and instruction. Further, parents and others in the local community are kept at a distance, with little involvement or interaction with the school.

Then the critique is broadened from the school to the community, the neighborhood, where students live. The inner city or isolated rural community, like the school, is beleaguered by endemic social, economic, political, heath care, and educational problems. It is often physically and socially isolated from the hospitals, parks, playgrounds, soccer fields, grocery stores, museums, and art galleries—the health, recreational, and cultural resources of the larger society. There is a higher unemployment rate among adults in the community. The community is likely to be ineffectively organized to secure greater political representation. There is likely to be a high incidence of street gangs and drug and alcohol abuse.

Next, the immediate, microcritique of the local context is connected to the larger social, political, and economic macroanalysis. The immediate problems faced by local schools mirror those of the larger state, regional, national, and global contexts. The larger society is controlled by the economically affluent, who influence politicians and the media. The economically affluent—often living in gated residential areas in the large cities or comfortable wealthy suburbs—have isolated themselves from the problems in the inner cities and declining rural areas. Nevertheless, they control institutions, including schools, throughout the country.

Following a Neo-Marxist mode of analysis, Critical Theorists contend that the power of the affluent governing class comes from its control of the capitalist corporate economy. The members of the favored class use schools to maintain their power by educating their children in well-financed schools that prepare them for entry to prestigious colleges and universities and for positions of importance within the corporate and government structures. Invested in maintaining the status quo, they use their power and influence to reproduce the system that gives them control. Children of the less economically favored classes, indoctrinated in the approved official curriculum constructed by the powerful class, are conditioned to accept subordinate roles at the margins of the existing society.

For Critical Theorists, their critique of society and schools is not a mere academic exercise but is a necessary step in constructing a better future. Influenced by Freire's Liberation Pedagogy, they argue that the purpose of a genuine education is to raise the consciousness of dispossessed, marginalized individuals and groups. As they learn who and what are causing their subordination, members of marginalized groups will gain the knowledge needed to work out their own self-empowerment.

IDEOLOGICAL OPPOSITION TO NEO-LIBERALISM AND CONSERVATIVISM

For their views on education and schooling, see the chapters on Liberalism and Conservatism.

Seeing education and schooling as ideologically contested areas, Critical Theorists oppose countervailing ideologies such as Conservatism and Liberalism. Conservatism, which has been on the ascendancy in the late twentieth and early twenty-first centuries, is opposed as an ideology that argues for traditional academic and moral standards as a way to maintain the status quo. Freire, for example, saw Conservatism as an ideology that seeks to block or at least slow down the pace of social change by constructing an ideological interpretation of history and society that defends the ruling class's privileged position.

Critical Theorists see American Neo-Conservatism as an amalgamation of special interest groups and lobbies on the right, including corporate business interests and Christian religious fundamentalists who generally support conservative Republican candidates and have an ideological agenda for society and schools. Included in this agenda are:

- Restoring fundamental and traditional values in schools, school prayer, and the teaching of Creationism or Intelligent Design in the curriculum.
- Promoting sex education programs that encourage abstinence and do not include other forms of contraception.
- Enlisting efforts to keep the curriculum focused on basic skills and academic subjects by encouraging mandated standardized testing.
- Opposing curricular and instructional innovations such as process learning, Constructivism, and values clarification.
- Encouraging federal and state aid for private and religious schools and for vouchers enabling students to attend these schools.

Critical Theorists perceive that the Neo-Conservative agenda for schools is to maintain them as sites of marginalization and reproduction of the dominant power structure. To enact their own agenda, described earlier in the chapter, Critical Theorists oppose Conservative efforts to control schools.

A contested battleground between Critical Theorists and Neo-Conservatives is the cultural war over what should be included in and excluded from the curriculum. Conservatives, Essentialists, and Perennialists argue that all students should be required to study a cultural core based on the Western heritage. The Western cultural core consists of the great works of history, literature, and philosophy written by Europeans such as Plato, Aristotle, Augustine, Aquinas, Erasmus, Locke, and Rousseau. Critical Theorists resist the imposition of the Western cultural core as a kind of patriarchal Eurocentric educational imperialism that denies the importance of Asian, African, and South American literature. They argue for a core that is infused with multicultural and feminist history, philosophy, and literature that gives voice to hitherto marginalized and indigenous peoples who have traditionally been silenced in traditional education.[29]

For their support of a Western cultural core, see the chapters on Conservatism, Essentialism, and Perennialism.

Critical Theorists are also disenchanted with Liberalism. Although it promises equality of opportunity for minority members, Liberalism is transactional and piecemeal in its approach to educational change, usually adding something new to the curriculum and not really eliminating those areas that cause repression and marginalization in schools. Liberals are so focused on means rather than ends that they are educational tinkerers who keep adding new procedures and creating new bureaucracies that bog down administrators and teachers in a maze of paperwork instead of bringing about real transformative change. Liberals display a presumed benevolence toward subordinated groups but do not acknowledge that they, too, are enjoying a privileged position in gated communities and affluent suburbs. Rather than acting directly to end the repression of marginalized people, Liberals skirt the main issues and instead are content with piecemeal additive reforms that often secure their own position rather than improve the situation of those they pretend to help. Even the Liberal notion of welfare and assistance, benignly intended to aid the poor, can create dependency that locks the dependents into the system rather than liberating them from it.[30]

For Liberalism and transaction reform and change, see the chapter on Liberalism and Education.

An important difference between Critical Theory and Liberalism concerns the issues of a vital center and margins. Liberals see the creation of a vital center, marking a vast consensus on knowledge, values, and especially processes, as a desirable education goal. In contrast, Critical Theorists see consensus on what Liberals call a vital center as a subterfuge designed to construct a core of domination, but masked with benign characteristics. Critical Theorists are concerned with groups that have been relegated to the periphery, the margins, of society. They want education that does not blur and obscure differences in the name of consensus but that encourages multicultural differences.

Still another point of contention between Critical Theorists and Neo-Conservatives and Liberals is globalization. Critical Theorists refer to globalization as a form of Neo-Liberalism that is based on the Classical Liberal ideas of Adam Smith and David Ricardo and reiterated by contemporary economists such as Milton Friedman who argue for free trade, little government interference with international commerce, and deregulation. It needs to be pointed out that the market economy, associated historically with Classical Liberalism, has been appropriated by Neo-Conservatives. Modern Reform Liberals, though generally supporting globalization, argue that globalization is a modern and pervasive economic force, but that it should be regulated to protect the environment, eliminate child labor and the exploitation of workers, and provide higher wages and benefits. Critical Theorists question globalization as a new form of international capitalism that is causing economic exploitation and political repression worldwide.[31]

Critical Theory and Postmodernism are closely related contemporary movements in educational thought that, like Existentialism, reject metaphysically grounded

For its similarities with Critical Theory, see the chapter on Postmodernism and Education.

philosophical systems. Indeed, one of Postmodernism's major pursuits that is shared by Critical Theorists is to deconstruct oppressive texts, or canons.

Paulo Freire and some Critical Theorists emphasize that human beings are unfinished projects, not categories in a predefined system, who are free to choose who they will be and to write their own autobiographies. Existentialists and Critical Theorists would endorse the contemporary educational pursuit of encouraging students to write their own life stories as a means of developing their self-understanding. However, an important difference lies in how the Critical Theorists and the Existentialists see the individual. Critical Theorists view individuals as members of socio-economic classes and racial, ethnic, gender, and religious groups that largely define them. For them, education is a process that develops a person's consciousness about her or his group membership and how being in a dominated group marginalizes them. Existentialists take a different view of group membership. Certainly, they say, the groups of which we are members are "givens" of our social, political, and economic lives that shape us but that do not define us. Regardless of class, gender, race, or ethnicity, each person is free to define himself or herself by making significant life choices.

With this background into the constructs and strategies of Critical Theory, we turn our discussion to its educational implications.

CRITICAL THEORY'S IMPLICATIONS FOR SCHOOLS, CURRICULUM, AND TEACHERS

In this section, we consider Critical Theory's more direct implications for education. We consider how Critical Theorists conceive of the aims of education, the school, curriculum, and instruction.

Aims of Education

Critical Theorists believe that the aims of education are related to the larger and more inclusive social, cultural, political, and economic goals of social justice. As indicated, education should aim to raise the consciousness of those who are forced into lesser, marginal, and subordinate positions in society because of race, ethnicity, language, class, or gender. Such consciousness raising is necessary if people are to empower themselves.

Schools as They Are and as They Might Be

Critical Theory offers a two-dimensional appraisal of schools: as they now exist in a corporate capitalist society and how they might be in the future. Now and in the future, schools need to be interpreted as having historical origins and reflecting particular ideologies that support sociological, cultural, economic, and political interests. Schools are highly ideological and political sites in which conflicting groups struggle for power and control. Often relying on interpretations from revisionist history, Critical Theorists argue that schools have been controlled and used by the economically, politically, and socially dominant classes for purposes of social maintenance and control. To maintain the status quo that gives them a commanding position, the children of the dominant classes are provided with the kind of education that enables them to attend prestigious educational institutions that groom them for high-level careers in business, industry, and government. Children of socially and economically subordinated groups and classes are indoctrinated to accept the conditions that disempower them as being historically validated and economically, socially, and politically correct.

Schools are state-governed institutions that power-holding elites use to transmit official knowledge and values that confirm and support their socio-economic and political interests. States, through mandates and standards, establish the official curriculum that reflects the dominant ideology; teachers, as public employees, are required to transmit its approved content and values to students.[32]

Schools in a capitalist economy and society are expected to train the workforce to meet the demands of economic production and consumption. They sort students into tracks that prepare them to work in management, industry, technology, and service areas that are economically determined. Upper socio-economic class students are groomed for schools that prepare them to take their places in the dominant elite. Lower socio-economic class students, especially those from marginalized minorities, are trained as the workforce. Proponents of maintaining the status quo will use clichés about objectivity, neutrality as fairness, accountability, standards, merit, and saleable skills to mask the sorting processes actually taking place in schools.

While the powerful classes have dominated schools historically, Critical Theorists do not believe that this domination is inevitable. The schools of the future do not have to be like those of the past and the present. By challenging the dominant class and its ideological rationales, Critical Theorists hope to break the cycle of domination. It is possible to raise the consciousness of the exploited, to deconstruct the texts that support domination, to expose the conditions of oppression, and to organize to empower the dispossessed. Schools can become truly democratic public spheres in which young people learn to live the ethics of equality.

By recognizing and resisting the dominant ideology, schools can be sites for liberating students and society. To begin the process of creating an alternative future, it is important to understand schools not as ideologically neutral sites but as places of struggle and contestation between competing ideologies. Rather than accepting and transmitting the dominant ideology, teachers can guide students to construct their own social and political meanings. Teachers and students can explore their own backgrounds, write their own autobiographies, and advance their own liberation.[33]

Curriculum and Instruction

As with the other areas of education and schooling, Critical Theorists analyze curriculum as it now is and how it might be in the future. They see the curriculum as existing in two dimensions or layers: the overt formal **official curriculum** of skills and subjects and the **hidden curriculum** that unofficially permeates the school milieu, or environment. The prescribed curriculum of academic skills and subjects is the officially approved, state-mandated program that teachers are to transmit to students. The hidden curriculum refers to those values, behaviors, and attitudes that are conveyed and imposed on students through the school environment in a capitalist consumer-oriented society. Both the overt official and the hidden curriculum represent the knowledge claims and value preferences of the dominant group or class that controls the school system.

Official Curriculum: the state-mandated program that prescribes the subjects transmitted in schools and imposed on students.

Hidden Curriculum: the attitudes, behaviors, and values that students acquire from the school milieu or environment such as competing, cooperating, and valuing property that are concomitant and supportive of the official curriculum but not an overt part of it.

The dominant classes use the official curriculum to reinforce the status quo that maintains and reproduces their power, wealth, and status. They use it to transmit their particular beliefs and values as the legitimate version of knowledge for all students. For example, they have constructed an official version of history that portrays the American experience as a largely European-American series of triumphs in settling and industrializing the nation. The heroes in this version of history are typically white males of northern European ethnicity. African, Hispanic, and Native Americans are relegated to the margins of narratives about the American past. The portrayal of industrial capitalism is presented in favorable terms, with little discussion about the exploitation of workers or the pollution of the environment. The American role in foreign affairs is generally presented as altruistic and always on the side of what is right. Bilingual and multicultural education is viewed with suspicion as challenging the dominance of English as the official national language.

The favored method of instruction uses officially sanctioned textbooks to transmit information to students. The process of transmission, instead of critical thinking and analysis, usually reproduces the approved text—the officially constructed version of knowledge.

A key element in social control via the school is lodged in the hidden curriculum. It is called "hidden" because it does not appear in published state mandates or local school policies. Instead, it permeates the ideology and milieu of the public school. The early emphasis on "this is mine and that is yours" developed in early childhood education begins to build an attitude supportive of a capitalist consumer-driven mentality. In a class-biased society, prescriptions and proscriptions about the sanctity of private property impose the dominant group's values. The sexist attitude that males are better than females in mathematics and science courses builds a gender-specific attitude to ongoing education and careers.

Educational expectations based on race, gender, and ethnicity contribute to stereotyping and the prediction that some groups are bound to fail in school. Part of the ideology of dominant group interests is manifested in having low academic expectations for students from marginalized, especially minority, groups. The argument that certain groups lack either the native intelligence or the social motivation to succeed in school not only involves the transmitting of official knowledge but also requires managing, controlling, and disciplining students from educationally suspect groups. It is expected that students from marginalized classes and groups will dislike schooling, disrupt classrooms, score low on standardized tests, and eventually drop out of the system. When these things occur, the anticipation of low expectations is fulfilled.[34]

The way students are arranged, scheduled, and grouped in school organizations streams similar students together. Homogeneous grouping, though justified in terms of academic ability, actually perpetuates socio-economic stratification in schools and reproduces the classism, racism, and sexism of the larger society.

For Deconstruction, see the chapter on Postmodernism and Education.

For their perspectives on definitions and reality, see the chapters on Realism, Conservatism, Perennialism, and Essentialism.

Similar to Postmodernists, Critical Theorists use deconstruction in examining language, especially educational representations found in texts, curriculum, and instruction. Language is not a verbal reflection of reality but instead is a human construction that is contextual and changes as contexts change. If it is constructed, then it can also be deconstructed. Like all contextual elements, language is shifting and changeable, and its meaning depends on the contexts in which it is used. Definitions, too, are constructed and subject to revision. Critical Theorists challenge the Realist, Conservative, Perennialist, and Essentialist belief that a definition represents an unchanging reality such as truth, human nature, marriage, and family, for example.

Consider the social and educational implications of the question: What is a family? While Realists and others are likely to answer that a family is a man (a husband) and a woman (a wife) and their children, Critical Theorists are likely to answer by referring to extended, single-parent, same-sex, and other kinds of family arrangements. Consider the implication of these two kinds of definitions for society and schools.

Still another issue relating to language that has an impact on curriculum and instruction is whether there is a standard language or there are many variations in language. If there is a standard language such as Standard English, then there also is a correct grammar, syntax, and usage. If there are many variations in language, then each of these has its own grammar, syntax, and usage, which is appropriate to its speakers. Just as the meta-narratives purporting to stand for universal knowledge are deconstructed, so are the texts that support the traditional curriculum. The subjects, the areas that reinforce the beliefs of the dominant group, can be broken apart, analyzed, and deconstructed. Just as these fields were constructed by the dominant group, the disempowered also can deconstruct them. The purpose of this analysis is to raise the consciousness of both teachers and students about claims to legitimate knowledge.

After critiquing how the dominant class uses the curriculum to reproduce itself, Critical Theorists then turn to developing transformative strategies to create the schools they envision for the future. For them, knowledge and values that are truly legitimate in the curriculum arise in the local context, the immediate situation, the community in which students live, and in the school they attend. The curriculum would begin with the students' own life stories, their autobiographies, as they tell them to each other. In the multicultural society that the United States truly is, there would be many versions of the story of the American experience rather than an officially approved one. Members of each race, ethnic, and language group would give voice to their own stories. A convergence of life stories is likely to take place as similarities and differences are found. It is from these autobiographical beginnings that a historical mosaic of the United States as a multicultural society arises.

The students' community, the place in which the school is located, is a microcosm of the larger society. The place to begin the study of science, social studies, the career world, and the environment is the context in which students live. For Critical Theorists, the purpose of instruction through dialogue is to create rather than to transmit or digest knowledge. Students' autobiographies, images, reflections, and interactions create their own knowledge and values rather than having other-constructed versions imposed on them through the official curriculum.

Given the kind of far-ranging dialogue that Critical Theorists advocate, the boundaries that separate one subject from another are deliberately dissolved. They regard subject-matter boundaries to be academic constructions, defined by academic elites. The Critical Theorist approach to curriculum organization diametrically opposes the Aristotelian concept that the concepts found in a particular subject are naturally related. Rather than being subject specific as advocated by Essentialists and Perennialists, the curriculum is interdisciplinary and transdisciplinary. Critical Theorists also reject the concept of a hierarchy of knowledge that judges some subjects to be more important than others. Dialogue is not limited to specific locations in literature, science, and history; it uses all these disciplines and crosses, as Giroux argues, from one border to another, from one subject to another, depending on what needs to be said and what issue needs to be examined. The very crossing from one discipline to another leads to education that cuts across them all and becomes transdisciplinary.

For their emphasis on the subject-matter curriculum, see the chapters on Realism, Essentialism, and Perennialism.

Science in the Curriculum: Philosophical Considerations

Critical Theorists, like Postmodernists, are suspicious about the Enlightenment's lingering effects on Western culture and education. An important continuing effect of the Enlightenment is the belief in the efficacy of science as an objective and disinterested method of finding the truth. Although their definitions of the scientific method may differ, Scientific Realists, Experimentalists, and many Progressives all extol its use not only in the natural and physical sciences but also in the social sciences and in education. Critical Theorists argue that those who proclaim science's objectivity either misunderstand or ignore that science can be used as a political and

For their perspectives on science and the scientific method, see the chapters on Realism, Pragmatism, and Progressivism.

economic force to control and regulate people. The social, behavioral, and educational sciences, constructed in the nineteenth and twentieth centuries but originated during the Enlightenment—sociology, psychology, economics, political science, and anthropology—were used to manage and control the growing urban populations of an industrialized society. The creation of state-managed and controlled school systems, too, needs to be seen as an educational means of social control.

Critical Theorists dispute the power and objectivity of scientific predictability. Similar to Existentialists, Critical Theorists, especially those who take a Freirean perspective, see the world as so complex that scientific predictability is not possible in the social, political, and economic realms. Those who claim to be operating from an objective science with objective predictability either are deluded or are agents of the dominant power holders. Philosophically, Critical Theorists part company from the Marxists, who claim that change is caused by universal forces generated from the class conflict to control the means and modes of production. They also disagree with the Idealists, especially the Hegelians, who see history as the unfolding of the Universal Mind in an ordered and systematically functioning universe.

For their views on scientific objectivity and change, see the chapters on Idealism, Existentialism, Marxism, and Social Reconstructionism.

Critical Theorists also challenge the Realists, including the Scientific Realists, who contend that we discover reality. Like the Social Reconstructionists, the Critical Theorists assert that human beings construct their own meaning by living in concrete historical, social, political, and economic contexts and not outside of them.

Critical Theorists dispute the idea that education, even when it borrows from the behavioral and social sciences, can ever be scientific. Education, teaching, and learning are multidimensional and are located on school sites, which in turn are contexts. These community and school contexts are highly complex, dynamic, and so unstable that they resist neat scientific predictions or even statistical probability.[35]

Although Critical Theorists recognize the contributions of science in improving the quality of life, especially in working to eradicate certain diseases, and appreciate the informative power of the social sciences, they see science as another human construction that needs to be related to historical and social contexts. They are suspicious of those who, feigning objectivity, use science to sell commodities and regulate people. Critical Theorists raise questions about how science is used, especially to create new weapons of destruction or to promote economic globalization. They ask: How is science being used, and who does it profit?[36]

Constructing Values

For their value perspectives, see the chapters on Idealism, Realism, and Perennialism.

Unlike the Idealists, Realists, Thomists, and Perennialists, who see values arising from universal rational or spiritual principles, Critical Theorists see values—ethics and aesthetics—as resulting from informed public discourse and from putting equity and equality into practice. By constructing their own autobiographies, as Freire argued, individuals can enter into the discourse about what is right and wrong or beautiful or ugly. Values are not the products of imposition from those in power but are the results of the interface and sharing of people whose voices have an equal right to be heard.

Teachers should encourage students to voice their beliefs and concerns about their own values. From hearing different voices raised in open and shared discourse, they will come to understand that official standards and values are not truly theirs but have been imposed on them. Rather than one standard for all, there is a multiplicity of values. Critical Theorists emphasize a multicultural process of valuation that celebrates cultural differences. Genuine dialogue is inclusive of cultural differences; it does not erode them in a bland moral consensus, but celebrates them as expressions of diversity. Ethical discourse seeks to encourage students to find and use their voices, to articulate their beliefs and feelings, to value the opinions of others, and to become

My Reflections on Philosophy of Education: A Critical Theorist Review of a Movie

Critical Theorists contend that all students, but especially those who are marginalized by the dominant society, need to be given the opportunity to find and use their voice. The official curriculum, especially the approved version of history, denies them the use of their own voices, their experiences, and the opportunities to express their needs and expectations. Critical Theorists argue that students need to be offered the opportunity to engage in a variety of activities that allow them to speak for themselves and to their peers. One of these opportunities is to think about their lives and to write their own autobiographies.

A possibility for getting the autobiographical process started is to have students view the motion picture *Freedom Writers*, in which students in a high school English class actually write their own autobiographies. The movie is based on *The Freedom Writers Diary*, a compelling narrative of how Erin Gruwell, an English teacher at the Woodrow Wilson High School in Long Beach, California, used autobiographical writing as an educational method. Gruwell's students, categorized as "at risk," who were expected to drop out of school, kept diaries and then used their lived experiences to write their own autobiographies. They wrote about the conditions that they were experiencing in their own lived-in situations—street violence, gang warfare, drug abuse, and poverty. As they came to know themselves, they began to know each other. Their writing became a means of raising consciousness and self-empowerment. Contrary to the educational establishment's prediction, these students all completed high school.[37] After viewing the movie, students can discuss it. They can then read *The Freedom Writers Diary*. It might be possible that the students will want to begin writing their own autobiographies. These individual autobiographies might be shared and discussed and, more ambitiously, form the basis of a larger collective class autobiography.

Students can share their life stories to create a collaborative group autobiography that recounts experiences at home, in school, and in the community. They can further connect this group autobiography to the larger histories of their respective economic classes and racial, ethnic, and language groups. The United States' multicultural society provides many more versions of the American experience story than an officially approved one. Members of each racial, ethnic, and language group can tell their own story rather than having it told for them. After exploring their own identities, students can develop ways to recognize stereotyping and misrepresentation and to resist indoctrination both in and out of school. They can learn how to take control of their own lives and shape their own futures.[38]

aware of those people and situations that interfere with the free exchange of ideas and values and try to close the dialogue. Teachers are to guide the ethical discussion so that it gradually enlarges to see as injustice the silencing of those who are at the margins and to include them in the dialogue.

Empowering Teachers

As with education and schooling, Critical Theorists critique the contemporary situation of teachers in the United States and present an agenda for their empowerment. Historically, they find that elementary and secondary school teachers have had a severely limited role in determining their own professional life. Since the late nineteenth century, the majority of elementary school teachers have been women who were underpaid and oversupervised in contrast to males in the general workforce. Entry requirements for teaching are established by state authorities rather than by teacher professional organizations. The schools are governed by boards of education that typically represent the favored socio-economic classes. The administration of schools is controlled by educational bureaucrats. Critical Theorists would forcefully oppose the movement in some states to limit the rights of teachers, as public employees, to collective bargaining.

Along with the longstanding historical features that have disempowered teachers, several more contemporary trends add to their disadvantaged situation. School effectiveness, as determined by the Conservative Neo-Essentialist agenda, is defined in terms of students' performance on standardized academic achievement tests. Teachers and schools are judged by how well their students score on these tests mandated by state legislators and prepared by "experts" outside of the particular school. Thus, an external system has been imposed on teachers that orients instruction to success on the tests rather than to teachers' educational aims.

Critical Theorists see the contemporary standards movement as resting on a major misconception, a false ideology, in which students are members of one huge homogeneous group in which everyone has the same white, English-speaking, upper-middle-class socio-economic background.[39] This false ideology contributes to the idea that standardized tests can be administered to all students, without concern for their socio-economic class, or their racial, language, and ethnic background. It has the effect of attempting to homogenize a multicultural society.

For their views on organizing knowledge into lessons, see the chapters on Idealism, Realism, Pragmatism, Essentialism, Perennialism, and Progressivism.

Idealists, Realists, Essentialists, and Perennialists argue that teachers should prepare lessons based on their research into academic texts in history, science, mathematics, and literature. After researching these texts, teachers are then to construct lesson plans based on the information that they find in them. Teachers are to reorganize this information and transmit it to students. Experimentalists and Progressives challenge this traditional view of preparing lessons as a pre-packaged exercise that ignores students' real interests and needs and limits opportunities for creativity.

Critical Theorists accept but enlarge the Progressive concept that teacher research focuses on students but moves it from an individual analysis of students to a larger social, economic, and political one. Viewing students as socially constructed persons, teachers need to examine students in their lived-in situations.[40]

Critical Theorists urge teachers to begin their consciousness raising with the students in their classes and with an examination of the conditions in their neighborhood communities. Each student has her or his own life story to share; these life stories can form a collective autobiography that tells about what they are experiencing in school, in their homes, and in their neighborhood. These life stories can be connected with the larger histories of the economic classes and racial, ethnic, and language groups of which they are members. After exploring their own identities and meanings, students, guided by teachers, can work at developing ways to recognize stereotyping and misrepresentation and to resist indoctrination both in and out of school. They can learn how to take control of their own lives and shape their own futures. This kind of micro-level change can be the base from which larger reforms can take place. Endorsing consciousness raising by critical dialogue, Critical Theorists urge teachers to engage in a profound and far-reaching examination of the conditions in and out of schools that cause their disempowerment and the miseducation of their students. In addition to bureaucratically controlled schools, teachers need to be aware of the broader socio-economic and political factors that disempower the poor, racial and ethnic minorities, and women in the United States. Rather than simply reacting to change from above, teachers need to take on the role of transformative agents for real and significant social and educational change. They need to:

- find out who their true allies are in the struggle for school control.
- learn who their students are by helping them to work toward their own self-identity and self-empowerment.

- interact and work with the people in local communities for community improvement.
- join with like-minded teachers in collegial organizations that are controlled by teachers and work for real educational reform.
- engage in a larger critical dialogue about the political, social, economic, and educational issues that confront American society.

CONSTRUCTING YOUR OWN PHILOSOPHY OF EDUCATION

Now that you have read and discussed this chapter, reflect on how Critical Theory may or may not have informed your ideas about education and schooling. Have you encountered, either personally or by observation, instances in which some groups are dominant and others are marginalized in schools? Do you agree or disagree with the Critical Theorist perspective that education should raise students' consciousness about oppressive situations and conditions? As you construct your own philosophy of education, consider whether Critical Theory appeals to you as a teacher. Do you plan to use it or some aspects of it in constructing your own philosophy of education?

Conclusion

This chapter examined the philosophical and ideological influences of Marxism, Liberation Pedagogy, and Postmodernism on Critical Theory. The chapter discussed the Critical Theorist argument that political, economic, and educational institutions, including schools, in a capitalist economy, maintain and reproduce inequitable and exploitative conditions that favor one group or class, the dominant one, over subordinate groups and classes. It described strategies for liberating schools from the control of dominant groups and making them into agencies of human liberation. Informed by the educational ideas of Paulo Freire, Henry Giroux, and other theorists, Critical Theory seeks to raise consciousness and bring about transformative change in society and education. The social and educational agenda of Critical Theory is to empower marginalized groups to determine their own futures in an equitable society.

Questions for Reflection and Discussion

1. Reflect on the concept of marginality. Have you ever felt that you were at the margin rather than in the center of your school experiences? Identify groups that you believe are marginalized in existing school situations.
2. Identify the key knowledge areas and values that were considered important by teachers in your school experience. Do you believe that these knowledge areas and values were genuinely important to you as a person?
3. Critics of Critical Theory contend that it indoctrinates students in a particular political ideology rather than in an open-ended discussion of various political positions. Do you agree or disagree with these critics?
4. Do you agree or disagree with the Critical Theorist view that objectivity is not really possible in teaching?
5. Reflect on your education. Do you recall events or situations that raised your critical consciousness? If so, describe and analyze them.

Topics for Inquiry and Research

1. Do an analysis of your teacher education program from a Critical Theorist perspective. Do you find any evidence of class or gender bias?
2. In a dialogue with other students, reflect on how they learned to think about race, class, ethnicity, and gender.
3. Access "Critical Theory" at http://plato.stanford.edu/entries/critical-theory/ and define the concept of *multiperspectival* and relate it to education.
4. In a class discussion, identify what it means to have ideas based on false consciousness. During your

discussion, develop a list of the factors that contribute to false consciousness in American society.

5. In a class discussion, identify those who are empowered and disempowered in American society, in general, and in your educational context, your school or college, in particular.
6. Organize a dialogue that uses Critical Theory to examine what it means to be a teacher and a student.
7. Access the Freire Institute at http://www.freire.org. Examine Freire's life, ideas, and writings.

Internet Resources

For Critical Theory's perspectives on philosophy, ideology, and multiperspectival democracy and a bibliography and Web links, access "Critical Theory" at http://plato.stanford.edu/entries/critical-theory.

For a discussion of Critical Theory, access Douglas Kellner, "Toward a Critical Theory of Education," at http://.gseis.ucla.edu/faculty/Kellner/essays/towardcriticaltheoryofed.pdf.

For a discussion of Critical Theory that features Michael Apple, Paulo Freire, Henry Giroux, and Peter McLaren, access "Rage and Hope" at http://www.perfectfit.org/CT/index2.html.

For a discussion of Freire and Giroux, access http://www.freireproject.org/content/henry-giroux.

Suggestions for Further Reading

Doyle, Clar and Amarjit Singh. *Reading and Teaching Henry Giroux*. New York: Peter Lang, 2006.

Freire, Paulo. *Letters to Cristina. Reflections on My Life and Work*. London: Routledge, 1996.

___. *Pedagogy of Freedom: Ethics, Democracy, and Civic Courage*. Lanham, MD: Rowman and Littlefield, 1998.

___. *Pedagogy of Hope, Reliving Pedagogy of the Oppressed*. New York: Continuum, 1995.

___. *Pedagogy of the Oppressed*. Translated by Myra Bergman Ramos. New York: Continuum, 1984.

Gadotti, M. *Reading Paulo Freire: His Life and Work*. New York: SUNY Press, 1994.

Giroux, H. A. *Ideology, Culture, and the Process of Schooling*. Philadelphia, PA: Temple University Press, 1981.

___. *Teachers as Intellectuals: Toward a Critical Pedagogy of Learning*. Granby, MA: Bergin & Garvey, 1988.

Gore, J. M. *The Struggle for Pedagogies: Critical and Feminist Discourses as Regimes of Truth*. New York: Routledge, 1993.

Held, David. *Introduction to Critical Theory: Horkheimer to Habermas*. Berkeley: University of California Press, 1980.

Kinchloe, Joe L. *Critical Pedagogy Primer*: New York: Peter Lang, 2005.

Martusewicz, Rebecca A. and William M. Reynolds, eds. *Inside/Out: Contemporary Critical Perspectives in Education*. New York: St. Martin's Press, 1994.

McLaren, Peter and Peter Leonard. *Paulo Freire: A Critical Encounter*. New York and London: Routledge, 1993.

Morrow, Raymond A. and Carlos Alberto Torres. *Reading Freire and Habermas: Critical Pedagogy and Transformative Social Change*. New York: Teachers College Press, Columbia University, 2002.

Murphy, Mark and Ted Fleming, *Habermas, Critical Theory and Education*. New York: Routledge, 2012.

Zamudio, Margaret, Christopher Russell, Francisco Rios, and Jacquelyn Bridgeman. *Critical Race Theory Matters: Education and Ideology*. New York: Routledge, 2010.

Notes

1. Joe L. Kincheloe, *Critical Pedagogy Primer* (New York: Peter Lang, 2005), 51.
2. Ibid., 46.
3. Douglas Kellner, "Critical Theory," in Randall Curren, ed., *A Companion to the Philosophy of Education* (Malden, MA: Blackwell, 2006), 165.
4. Ibid., 166.
5. Richard Shaull, "Preface," in Paulo Freire, *Pedagogy of the Oppressed* (New York: Continuum, 1984), 9–11.
6. Philip L. Ralph, Robert E. Lerner, Standish Meacham, and Edward McNall Burns, *World Civilizations: Their History and Their Culture,* Vol. II, 8th ed. (New York: W. W. Norton, 1991), 785.
7. Ibid., 785.
8. Paulo Freire, *Pedagogy of Freedom, Ethics, Democracy and Civic Courage,* translated by Patrick Clarke (Lanham, MD: Rowman and Littlefield, 1998), 25–26, 54.
9. Donaldo Macedo, "Foreword," in Freire, *Pedagogy of Freedom: Ethics, Democracy, and Civic Courage,* xxiv.
10. Freire, quoted in Joe L. Kincheloe, *Critical Pedagogy Primer,* 3.

11. "People You Should Know: Freire," http://nlu.nl.edu/ace/Resources/Freire.html (August 11, 2003), 1.

12. Stanley Aronowitz, "Introduction," in Paulo Freire, *Pedagogy of Freedom: Ethics, Democracy, and Civic Courage,* 11.

13. Freire, *Pedagogy of Freedom, Ethics, Democracy and Civic Courage,* 25–26, 54.

14. Paulo Freire, *Pedagogy of the Oppressed,* trans. Myra Bergman Ramos (New York: Continuum, 1984), 31.

15. Aronowitz, "Introduction," 4.

16. Freire, *Pedagogy of the Oppressed,* 57–59.

17. Aronowitz, "Introduction," 4–5.

18. Freire, *Pedagogy of Freedom, Ethics, Democracy and Civic Courage,* 22.

19. Aronowitz, "Introduction," 8–9.

20. Macedo, "Foreword," xiii.

21. Clar Doyle and Amarjit Singh, *Reading and Teaching Henry Giroux* (New York: Peter Lang, 2006), 13.

22. Kellner, "Critical Theory," 171–172.

23. Doyle and Singh, *Reading and Teaching Henry Giroux,* 5.

24. Ibid., 26.

25. Kellner, "Critical Theory," 168–169.

26. Kincheloe, *Critical Pedagogy Primer,* 2, 16.

27. Angeline Martel and Linda Peterat, "Margins of Exclusion, Margins of Transformation: The Place of Women in Education," in Rebecca A. Martusewicz and William Reynold, eds., *Inside/Out: Contemporary Critical Perspectives in Education* (New York: St. Martin's Press, 1994), 151–154.

28. Rebecca A. Martusewicz and William Reynold, eds., *Inside/Out: Contemporary Critical Perspectives in Education,* v.

29. Kincheloe, *Critical Pedagogy Primer,* 26.

30. Macedo, "Foreword," xxviii.

31. Doyle and Singh, *Reading and Teaching Henry Giroux,* 7.

32. Ibid., 16–18.

33. Ibid., 18.

34. Kincheloe, *Critical Pedagogy Primer,* 7–8.

35. Ibid., 32.

36. Ibid., 30.

37. The Freedom Writers, with Erin Gruwell, *The Freedom Writers Diary: How a Teacher and 150 Teens Used Writing to Change Themselves and the World Around Them* (New York: Doubleday/Random House, 1999). The story of the Freedom Writers was portrayed in a motion picture in 2007. Also see: the Freedom Writers Foundation at www.freedomwritersfoundation.org.

38. Christine E. Sleeter and Peter L. McLaren, Eds., *Multicultural Education, Critical Pedagogy, and the Politics of Difference* (Albany: State University of New York Press, 1995).

39. Kincheloe, *Critical Pedagogy Primer,* p. 23.

40. Ibid., 19.

INDEX